THIRD EDITION

ADR Advocacy, Strategies, and Practices

for Intellectual Property and Technology Cases

Harrie Samaras and **Theo Cheng**
EDITORS

AMERICAN BAR ASSOCIATION
Intellectual Property Law Section

Cover design by Jill Tedhams/ABA Design

Printed in the United States of America.

29 28 27 26 25   5 4 3 2 1

Contents

CHAPTER 10

CHAPTER 11

CHAPTER 12

About the Contributors

Editors and Authors

Harrie Samaras (Chapters 1, 3, 6, 7, 9, 10) is a full-time neutral in her own practice where she focuses on arbitrating and mediating intellectual property (IP) and technology disputes involving U.S. and international parties. She is a Fellow of the College of Commercial Arbitrators and of the Chartered Institute of Arbitrators and a member of the Silicon Valley Arbitration & Mediation Center (SVAMC) Tech List and the Association of Commercial and Transactional ADR Professionals. Harrie is an American Arbitration Association (AAA) Master Mediator and she is certified by the International Mediation Institute. She serves as a neutral for alternative dispute resolution (ADR) organizations including the AAA and its international arm the International Centre for Dispute Resolution, International Institute for Conflict Prevention & Resolution (CPR), World Intellectual Property Organization, and the International Chamber of Commerce (ICC) International Court of Arbitration. She also serves as a neutral for the U.S. District Court for the Eastern District of Pennsylvania and the U.S. International Trade Commission.

Harrie has worked as an attorney in the private sector, focusing her practice on IP litigation at the trial and appellate levels, including representing clients in mediations and arbitrations. She has also worked in the corporate sector as the Director of Intellectual Property Litigation for a Fortune 500 telecommunications company, managing its IP litigation worldwide, and subsequently as Vice President Intellectual Property, Legal, managing all IP legal activities for a business unit of a pharmaceutical/drug delivery company. Early in her legal career Harrie served as a staff attorney at the U.S. Court of Appeals for the Federal Circuit and then as a law clerk for Chief Judge Helen Wilson Nies. Before that she worked as a patent examiner at the U.S. Patent and Trademark Office in the biomedical arts. Early in her professional career Harrie worked in research at the National Institute of Mental Health and at the John Hopkins University School of Medicine and Hospital.

Harrie received an LL.M. in patent and trade regulation law from the George Washington University Law School, a J.D. from the University of Baltimore School of Law, and an M.S. and B.S. from the University of Maryland in the life sciences and chemistry.

For many years Harrie has held leadership roles in professional organizations including the American Bar Association (ABA) (past Chair, Section of Dispute Resolution), the College of Commercial Arbitrators (past member, Board of Directors and Executive Committee), and the American Intellectual Property Law Association (past member, Board of Directors). Harrie is a frequent speaker at professional and bar organizations, ADR institutions, and academic institutions on the use of ADR in IP and technology disputes, and she is an ardent writer on the topic.

Theo Cheng (Chapters 1, 2, 5, 7, 11) is an independent, full-time arbitrator and mediator, focusing on commercial, IP, technology, entertainment, and employment disputes, both domestically in the United States and internationally. Theo has been appointed to the rosters of the AAA, the International Centre for Dispute Resolution, the CPR, Resolute Systems, the American Intellectual Property Law Association's List of Arbitrators and Mediators, and the SVAMC's List of the World's Leading Technology Neutrals. He is a AAA Master Mediator, a member of the National Academy of Distinguished Neutrals, and a Fellow of the College of Commercial Arbitrators.

Theo is also an Adjunct Professor at New York Law School where he teaches ADR-related courses and a Practitioner in Residence at the Intellectual Property (IP) Policy Institute at the University of Akron School of Law (previously at George Mason University Antonin Scalia Law School). He also co-founded and serves as the Chief Executive Officer of Sonata Academy, the premier, first-in-class institution of education and training for the ADR field, offering arbitration, mediation, and other related courses to both neutrals and advocates.

Before becoming a full-time neutral, Theo practiced for nearly 25 years as an IP and general commercial litigator covering all areas of IP. He honed his litigation skills at several prominent national law firms, where he counseled high net-worth individuals and small to middle-market business entities in a variety of industries (e.g., high-tech, telecommunications, entertainment, consumer products) and represented them in a broad array of business disputes. Some of his most well-known matters involved representing certified classes of songwriters and music publishers, in conjunction with motion picture studios and record labels, in industry-sponsored litigations against various internet, peer-to-peer file-sharing companies such as Napster and Grokster.

Theo received his A.B. *cum laude* in Chemistry and Physics from Harvard University and his J.D. from New York University School of Law, where he served as the editor in chief of the Moot Court Board. He began his legal career serving as a law clerk to the Honorable Julio M. Fuentes of the U.S. Court of Appeals for the Third Circuit and the Honorable Ronald

L. Buckwalter of the U.S. District Court for the Eastern District of Pennsylvania. Before law school, he completed a management training program at MetLife Insurance Company, eventually becoming a marketing consultant in its brokerage operations, where he held Chartered Life Underwriter and Chartered Financial Consultant designations and a Series 7 General Securities Representative registration.

Theo is a past President of the Justice Marie L. Garibaldi American Inn of Court for ADR (Garibaldi Inn), a past Chair of the New York State Bar Association (NYSBA) Dispute Resolution Section, and currently serves as the Vice President of the Copyright Society (he will serve as its President in 2026–2028). He received the 2024 Richard K. Jeydel Award from the Garibaldi Inn (demonstrated civility, professionalism, ethics, and excellence in and service to ADR) and the 2020 James B. Boskey ADR Practitioner of the Year Award from the New Jersey State Bar Association (NJSBA) Dispute Resolution Section. The *National Law Journal* named him a 2017 ADR Champion. In 2022–2024, Theo was voted a Top Arbitrator in the *New York Law Journal*'s Best of Reader Rankings Survey; in 2021, Theo was voted the Best Mediator/Arbitrator in the *New Jersey Law Journal*'s Best of Reader Rankings Survey. In 2007, the National Asian Pacific ABA named him one of the Best Lawyers Under 40.

Theo frequently writes and speaks on a wide variety of ADR issues. He writes a regular column called *Resolution Alley* in the *NYSBA Entertainment, Arts, and Sports Law Journal*, which addresses the use of ADR in those industries.

Contributing Authors

Cynthia Raposo (Chapter 3), former Senior Vice President, Legal of Under Armour, Inc., provides legal and consulting services to companies and law firms. Until her retirement from Under Armour in 2015, Cynthia was responsible for all litigation and IP matters globally, including early case assessment of IP disputes; counseling business executives on dispute resolution, litigation strategy, and management; and representing the company in mediations and arbitrations worldwide.

She began her legal career as a law clerk to the Hon. H. Chester Goudy at the Circuit Court for Anne Arundel County in Annapolis, Maryland. Thereafter, as a partner at a law firm in Rockville, Maryland, she litigated a variety of state and federal cases at the trial and appellate levels and practiced IP and business law. She also served as litigation counsel for MCI Communications, where she represented the company in numerous commercial litigations, mediations, and U.S. and international arbitrations, and managed the company's in-house commercial arbitration program.

Cynthia obtained a J.D. from the University of Baltimore School of Law, an M.A. from Brown University, and a B.A. from Emmanuel College. She has served on a number of nonprofit boards, including as Chair, Board of Directors of the Maryland Humanities Council and Co-Chair, Finance Committee, Board of Directors of the Sandy Spring Friends School. She currently serves on the Board of Directors of the Sandy Spring Museum.

Carol Ludington (Chapter 4) has been involved in dispute resolution for more than 40 years serving as a damages expert in U.S. litigation as well as U.S. and international arbitrations; as an arbitrator; and as a consultant. She is a Certified Public Accountant (CPA), Certified in Financial Forensics, and a Certified Licensing Professional Emeritus, with experience in hundreds of complex commercial and IP disputes involving a wide variety of industries and parties.

Carol has frequently served as a testifying expert, and as a consultant regarding early analysis of damages, creative dispute resolution processes and strategies, and other topics.

Carol is an Associate of the Chartered Institute of Arbitrators; on the AAA's Commercial Arbitration Panel; a qualified neutral under Rule 114 of the Minnesota General Rules of Practice; and has been involved with several domestic and international dispute resolution organizations. She has served as a sole arbitrator and as a member of three-member arbitral tribunals.

Prior to forming her firm Ludington, Ltd. more than 30 years ago, Carol was employed by two well-known international CPA firms. She is a frequent speaker and author on damages and ADR topics, including the use of early damages analysis as a dispute resolution tool, and she was a contributing editor for *The Sedona Conference Commentary on Patent Litigation Best Practices: Patent Mediation Chapter and Commentary on Monetary Remedies in Trade Secret Litigation.*

Merriann M. Panarella (Chapter 6) is a full-time independent arbitrator, mediator, and consultant whose practice includes U.S. and international complex contractual, IP, and technology disputes. Previously, she was a senior partner at WilmerHale where she litigated patent infringement and technology cases, and complex commercial, trade secret, and noncompete matters. Merriann counseled technology clients on ADR processes and represented clients in mediations, arbitrations, and mini-trials.

Merriann is a Fellow of the College of Commercial Arbitrators, and the Chartered Institute of Arbitrators where she has served as a tutor for their Accelerated Route to Fellowship in International Arbitration course from 2015 to 2022. She currently serves on the panels of many of the principal dispute resolution institutions including the AAA, CPR, World Intellectual

Property Organization, ICC International Court of Arbitration, American Health Lawyers Association, and Financial Industry Regulatory Authority. Since 2016, Merriann has been a member of the SVAMC Tech List.

Merriann is active in the ABA including in the Section of Dispute Resolution where she has played an active role in planning the Section's Arbitration Training Institute for multiple years and has been on the Institute's faculty. She is a founding member of the Boston International Arbitration Council and an active board member. Merriann is a frequent speaker and writer on dispute resolution topics including the use of ADR in technology and IP disputes.

Mark J. Abate (Chapter 8) is a partner at Pillsbury Winthrop Shaw Pittman LLP where he leads the firm's IP litigation practice in New York. He is widely recognized as one of the nation's leading IP lawyers, having been twice named by U.S. News-Best Lawyers as its New York City patent litigation "Lawyer of the Year" and having been repeatedly recognized in Chambers USA and IAM Patent Litigation 1000.

Mark concentrates his practice on trials and appeals of patent infringement cases, and has experience in matters involving a broad array of technologies and industries including electronics, computers/software, consumer products, material science, financial systems, electrical, and mechanical. He has successfully tried cases in the U.S. district courts and the U.S. International Trade Commission and has argued before the U.S. Court of Appeals for the Federal Circuit.

Mark received a B.S. in civil engineering from Rutgers University with highest honors and a J.D. from the George Washington University with high honors and Order of the Coif. Mark has served as the New York Intellectual Property Law Association (NYIPLA) President, the New Jersey Intellectual Property Law Association (NJIPLA) President, on the Federal Circuit Bar Association Board of Directors, on the Federal Circuit Historical Society Board of Trustees, on the New York University Engelberg Center on Innovation Law and Policy Advisory Board, on the U.S. Court of Federal Claims Advisory Council, and is an American Bar Foundation Fellow. Early in his career, Mark served as a law clerk to Chief Judge Howard T. Markey of the Federal Circuit.

Molly R. Grammel (Chapter 8) is an IP litigation partner at Goodwin Procter LLP. Molly litigates IP disputes, including infringement actions and licensing disputes, in arbitration and in federal district courts, state courts, and the U.S. International Trade Commission. Molly's legal experience also includes post-grant challenges at the Patent Trial and Appeal Board of the U.S. Patent and Trademark Office, appeals, licensing, counseling, due diligence, and advice concerning prosecution.

Molly has been repeatedly named in Benchmark Litigation's "40 & Under Hot List" and the Best Lawyers in America's "Ones to Watch" for her work in IP and patent litigation. Her expertise in cutting-edge technology IP spans a diverse set of industries, including biologic and biosimilar drugs, artificial intelligence, and machine learning. She has spoken and presented on various topics concerning artificial intelligence in the law, as well as IP considerations in the life sciences and medical device industries.

Molly received a B.A. in English literature *magna cum laude* from the University of California, Los Angeles in 2010 and a J.D. *magna cum laude* from the University of Pennsylvania Law School in 2013. She is a member of the Boston Bar Association and the IP Section of the Federal Bar Association. Early in her career, Molly served as a Special Assistant District Attorney in Middlesex County District Court, during which she first-chaired numerous criminal trials and evidentiary and non-evidentiary motion hearings.

Michael H. Diamant (Chapter 9) is of counsel at the Cleveland, Ohio, office of Taft Stettinius & Hollister LLP; previously, as a partner, he was a member of its Litigation and IP Practice Groups. For many years he litigated before juries and judges at all levels of state and federal courts in Ohio and around the country including the U.S. Supreme Court. Michael also represented clients before arbitration panels including in IP and technology disputes. He has served as an arbitrator and mediator for more than 35 years and he will continue that practice. Michael arbitrates and mediates for the AAA, its international arm the International Centre for Dispute Resolution, the CPR, and local federal and state courts. He is a Fellow of the College of Commercial Arbitrators and the Chartered Institute of Arbitrators, an appointee to the SVAMC, and a member of the SVAMC's Board of Directors and serves on its Executive Committee.

Michael focuses on engineering and technology disputes both in his litigation and ADR practice. He has tried cases, and decided them as an arbitrator, in a broad array of technologies that include computer software, medical devices, mechanical systems, chemistry, building design and construction, physics, and engineering.

He received a B.S. in engineering with high honors from Case Western Reserve University, and a J.D. *cum laude* from Harvard Law School. Michael is a frequent speaker locally and nationally on arbitration and mediation topics, and writes on similar topics.

Stephen P. Gilbert (Chapter 9) has been a full-time arbitrator and mediator since 2011. He is a Fellow of the College of Commercial Arbitrators, of the Chartered Institute of Arbitrators, and of the American College of e-Neutrals, as well as a member of the SVAMC Tech List, an AAA (commercial) Master

Mediator, and a Centre for Effective Dispute Resolution (CEDR) Accredited Mediator. Steve is on the panel of various ADR institutions, including the AAA and its international arm the International Centre for Dispute Resolution, CPR, World Intellectual Property Organization, New York City Bar Association, U.S. District Court for the Southern District of New York, and several foreign ADR institutions.

From 1988 to 2010, Steve was a partner in a major multinational law firm, the last three years as co-leader of its IP practice group. His legal experience includes trials, appeals, licensing, counseling, due diligence, and prosecution. Before working as a patent, trademark, and copyright attorney, he was a computer programmer, a chemical process engineer, and a consulting engineer (his undergraduate and graduate degrees are in chemical engineering). Steve has been a neutral in disputes throughout the chemical, biological, mechanical, and electrical space, as well as a neutral in non-IP commercial and business disputes.

Steve has presented and written on topics such as the use of ADR for resolving IP/Technology disputes, arbitration and mediation ethics, drafting arbitration clauses, IP, software, licensing, and awarding attorneys' fees.

Laura A. Kaster (Chapter 9) serves as a full-time neutral in the greater New York metropolitan area. She is an arbitrator and mediator for the AAA and its international arm the International Centre for Dispute Resolution, CPR, CEDR, Financial Industry Regulatory Authority, and the New Jersey and New York courts. Laura is a Fellow of the College of Commercial Arbitrators and the Chartered Institute of Arbitrators. She is on the Executive Committee of the National Association of Distinguished Neutrals' New Jersey Academy of Mediators and Arbitrators, and she is a member of the SVAMC Tech List. Laura is also a CEDR Accredited Mediator and certified by the International Mediation Institute. She is a member of the CEDR global panel of mediators and an AAA (commercial) Master Mediator.

In 2014, the NJSBA awarded Laura the Boskey Award recognizing her as the ADR Practitioner of the Year. In 2018, she received the Richard K. Jeydel Award for Excellence in ADR from the Garibaldi Inn. Laura is listed in Who's Who Legal, Mediation. She is a past President of the Garibaldi Inn, the only American Inn of Court devoted to ADR, a past Chair of the NJSBA Dispute Resolution Section, and an Adjunct Professor in ADR at Seton Hall Law School. Laura has published and spoken widely on issues involving arbitration and mediation. She is a co-editor in chief of *Dispute Resolution Lawyer*, the Journal of the NYSBA Dispute Resolution Section, and was as an editor for the *College of Commercial Arbitrator's Guide to Best Practices in Commercial Arbitration* (Fourth Edition).

Laura was chief litigation counsel for AT&T Corporation for almost ten years. Before holding that position, she was a partner at Jenner & Block where she worked for more than 20 years handling a wide variety of complex disputes. Early in her legal career, Laura was a law clerk to then-Chief Judge Frank M. Coffin on the First Circuit Court of Appeals.

Steven M. Levy (Chapter 10) is President of Accent Law Group, Inc. in Philadelphia, Pennsylvania. In his 35 years of practice, Steve's IP experience has been quite broad, but he has a particular focus on the enforcement of trademarks against domain names and social media user names and other online abuses. Steve has filed more than 600 domain name complaints under the Uniform Domain Name Dispute Resolution Policy (UDRP) and other domain name dispute arbitration policies. Although now largely retired from his law practice, he continues to serve as a panelist for the FORUM, the Czech Arbitration Court, the Canadian International Internet Dispute Resolution Centre, and the Asian Domain Name Dispute Resolution Centre, and has decided more than 400 cases under the UDRP and the .us and the .ca country code top-level domain (ccTLD) dispute policies.

His current activities also include public speaking on domain name disputes and other online abuse, as well as developing educational materials and policy recommendations to help support and improve the UDRP ecosystem. For many years Steve served on the Internet Committee of the International Trademark Association as well as on the Rights Protection Mechanisms Review Working Group at the Internet Corporation for Assigned Names and Numbers. Prior to creating the Accent Law Group, Steve led an eight-member IP practice team at the Home Depot that was responsible for the worldwide protection and management of the company's IP assets. He was also a Senior Associate at the New York City office of the Proskauer Rose law firm, in-house counsel at Sony Corporation in Tokyo, Japan, and a Junior Associate at the law firm Amster, Rothstein & Ebenstein. He received his J.D. degree in 1989 from Brooklyn Law School and his B.S. degree from the State University of New York at Buffalo in 1985. Steve is a member of the bar in Pennsylvania, New York, and the District of Columbia.

Gale R. ("Pete") Peterson (Chapter 12) is an arbitrator, mediator, and special master in IP litigation. He has served as a court-appointed special master overseeing claim construction and discovery in more than 70 cases for a variety of federal district courts across the United States. Pete has served as a mediator or arbitrator in more than 40 cases involving both domestic and international disputes, and as an expert in more than 30 cases. After serving as a patent examiner with the U.S. Patent and Trademark Office and as technical advisor to Chief Judge Howard T. Markey on what was then the U.S. Court of Customs and Patent Appeals (now the U.S. Court of Appeals for the Federal Circuit), Pete spent 38 years as a partner with Cox & Smith in San Antonio managing a broad litigation practice of IP and other commercial disputes, as well as licensing, prosecution, and service as a dispute resolution neutral. In 2014, he retired from Cox & Smith, and formed the Law Offices of Gale R. Peterson PLLC to focus on his practice as a neutral and litigation consultant.

Pete has served as Chair of the Texas State Bar IP Section, and in various leadership roles with the ABA as well as for local and national business and civic organizations, including the Society of International Business Fellows. He is a frequent writer and speaker on IP topics, especially Federal Circuit jurisprudence in patent cases, and he has authored more than 100 seminar papers, in addition to co-authoring an annual Federal Circuit Yearbook for Practicing Law Institute since 2003, two books—*Trade Secret Protection in an Information Age* (Nov. 1996) and *Understanding Biotechnology Law* (June 1993), and a number of book chapters.

Pete holds a B.S. in electrical engineering from the University of Nebraska, a J.D. *magna cum laude* from the University of Baltimore, and an LL.M. with highest honors from the George Washington University Law School. He has been listed in *The Best Lawyers in America* since 1991, *Texas Best Lawyers* since 2013, *Texas Super Lawyers* since 2003, and *Chambers USA America's Leading Business Lawyers*, 2003–2005.

Preface

In this Third Edition, we intend the book to continue to serve as a practical guide for attorneys (in-house or outside counsel), business persons whose work requires them to have knowledge and skills in using alternative dispute resolution (ADR), and neutrals (e.g., mediators and arbitrators) who resolve intellectual property (IP) and technology disputes. It presents strategies, skills, and practices that may be new, improving, or reaffirming. We hope that, in revising this book, we keep users of ADR informed about current practices for using ADR in IP/Technology disputes so that they may be more effective at what they do.

The concept for this book came from the simple reality that, as in-house and outside counsel, we recognized that no matter how large the client or significant the dispute for a client, there were limits to how much money, personnel, and time could be diverted from the business to deal with disputes. Furthermore, avoiding unnecessary risks (and public relations nightmares) required that disputes be resolved expeditiously and sometimes confidentially to avoid the escalation of a manageable dispute into a costly and uncertain situation. Thus, we discovered from our own experiences that attorneys representing clients in IP/Technology disputes and business personnel involved in such disputes must embrace the use of ADR as one of their core competencies. That is, they should have a working knowledge of ADR processes, and the requisite skills for using them to resolve disputes. These skills are best learned early in one's legal or business education and career and refined going forward. In the not too distant past, proficiency with ADR processes did not exist or was treated as not requiring any special education or training. That is not the case in today's reality. Indeed, debuting in a number of jurisdictions beginning in July 2026 and building on the successes of law school clinical education and ADR programs, the NextGen bar exam will test a broad range of foundational lawyering skills that will include coverage of negotiation and dispute resolution topics. Revising this book thus continues to satisfy a growing and recognized need for attorneys to develop such skills, particularly with regard to IP/Technology disputes.

To be clear, litigation continues to be an essential dispute resolution process. But what our experience as in-house counsel, outside counsel, and neutrals has taught us is that alternatives to litigation are equally essential to a business, particularly when strategically used. And, like a musician playing an instrument, to get the most out of an ADR process one must have respect for the process, understand how it works, learn to use it effectively, and practice, practice, practice.

Harrie Samaras and Theo Cheng

Acknowledgments

Our sincere gratitude to the authors, who shared our vision for the book and who committed themselves to developing chapters that reflected their wealth of knowledge and experience. They challenged and inspired us throughout the development of this Third Edition.

Thanks to Jeremy Greener and Josie Middione for their time and diligence with regards to the references and citations throughout the book. When they each began their work on this book, they were students at New York Law School. They have now both graduated and entered the legal profession.

Thanks to Philip Swain, who serves as a full-time arbitrator and mediator in IP/Technology cases, for his input and insights on various chapters of the book.

Thanks to the Circuit Mediators and staff from the Second, Sixth, Seventh, Ninth, and Federal Circuits for their invaluable assistance in helping us to broaden the scope of the chapter on appellate mediation.

Thanks to Steve Caltrider for writing the Foreword to this Third Edition of the book.

And for his guidance and support this third time around—thanks to Jeffrey Salyards, Executive Editor, Book Publishing, at the American Bar Association.

To my husband, Bryan, thank you for your patience with this third installment and your enduring support, encouragement, and love.

To my wife, Michelle, I am eternally grateful for your unwavering support and encouragement. Your constant love, kindness, and patience has allowed me to pursue all of my endeavors, including my work on this book. I also want to thank my co-editor and co-author, Harrie Samaras, for both giving me the opportunity to help make her book an invaluable resource and continuing success, as well as her sage editing and writing guidance.

Foreword

I met Harrie Samaras through the American Bar Association Section of Intellectual Property Law. Her expertise on a wide range of intellectual property (IP) matters was evident, as was her thoroughness, energy, and willingness to be bold and creative. Harrie has teamed up with Theo Cheng who shares and complements this expertise and approach. This depth of knowledge, thoroughness, and talent for finding creative solutions for intransigent parties makes them leading practitioners in alternative dispute resolution (ADR), particularly in IP/Technology cases.

Those same attributes are reflected in the Third Edition of *ADR Advocacy, Strategies, and Practices for Intellectual Property and Technology Cases*, authored and edited by Harrie, Theo, and their contributing authors who are well-steeped in IP/Technology disputes and the use of ADR. The book is an excellent blend of basic content for those new to ADR, unique insights for those experienced in ADR, and lessons learned from "Case History" or "Case in Point" anecdotes from real-life experience.

Having led an IP litigation practice group and served as general patent counsel of a Fortune 500 pharmaceutical company, I've participated in a multitude of arbitrations and mediations—candidly, with mixed success. I wish I would have read this book earlier in my career. It would have informed the deliberative process on whether to engage ADR, what ADR process or option would have worked best, and what strategies to deploy. I would have also been much better equipped to set expectations and communicate with the client. One of many "aha moments" as I read this book was that "[m]ediation *is not compromise*—it is negotiation."[1] The point reminded me that my past thinking that mediation was an exercise to convince the mediator who was "right" or an inevitable journey to the midpoint was simply wrong.

I appreciate the opportunity to review this book. I'm honored to do so and am a better lawyer for having done so. The book changed my myopic view of ADR as presenting two options—arbitration and mediation. These are important "tools" in the toolbox, but the variety of ADR options set out in the book should be top of mind for litigators, transactional lawyers, or any IP lawyer whose client seeks advice on a current or potential dispute. The

1. Chapter 6, Mediating IP/Technology Disputes: Design, Preparation, and Strategy.

book is a valuable resource for selecting the right option at the right time to achieve the right result for your client.

Thank you,
Steven P. Caltrider
Vice President and Chief IP Counsel,
Dana-Farber Cancer Institute
American Bar Association Section of Intellectual
Property Law, Immediate Past Chair

Introduction

Creating this Third Edition reaffirms an observation from the First Edition—alternative dispute resolution (ADR) has moved from a side course to the main course as a means for resolving many intellectual property (IP) and technology disputes. This Third Edition reimagines the use of ADR for resolving IP/Technology disputes of all sizes and of varying significance to businesses. The chapters are grouped together to reflect a practical approach for considering and using ADR in such disputes. The first group explores how others have used various forms of ADR to resolve IP/Technology disputes whether by way of pre-dispute resolution clauses or more "real-time" creative uses of ADR. A second group of chapters discusses early uses of tactical tools and approaches for resolving IP/Technology disputes, while a third group focuses on the practical use of mediation in various forums. The last group of chapters delves into adjudicatory options for resolving IP/Technology disputes.

In contrast to prior editions, this Third Edition of the book focuses in some areas and expands in others. For example, it coalesces three chapters on mediation from the first two editions that reflected various perspectives on mediation (i.e., magistrate judge, in-house counsel, mediator) into one chapter of practical guidance and tips for participating in IP/Technology mediations. This edition broadens its coverage of various topics (e.g., appellate mediation, domain name disputes, small copyright disputes) to provide additional insights and guidance from multiple appellate mediation programs, multiple administrators of Uniform Domain Name Dispute Resolution Policy (UDRP) cases, and a recently established tribunal for copyright cases.

As in the previous editions, the contributing authors, with decades of experience, education, and training, infuse each chapter with practical ideas for enhancing the use of ADR in resolving IP/Technology disputes. They are or were neutrals, clients, professors, consultants, litigation and transactional attorneys, and in-house counsel. Their approach focuses on how best to apply ADR processes in the simplest to the most complex IP/Technology cases routinely encountered. Each chapter opens another door on the use of ADR advocacy, strategies, and practices for IP/Technology cases.

Chapter 1 is newly co-authored by Theo Cheng and Harrie Samaras, who combine their litigation, in-house, arbitration, and mediation experience to discuss how success in using ADR in IP/Technology disputes depends on the willingness of, and careful planning and execution by, experienced

ADR counsel and their clients. In this new chapter, *Putting ADR to Work: Imagining Better Results for Resolving IP/Technology Disputes*, the authors use actual case studies to illustrate how thinking outside the box in using and combining ADR processes can have beneficial results in resolving IP/Technology disputes.

Chapter 2 is authored by Theo Cheng, who combines his litigation, transactional, arbitration, and mediation experience to demonstrate how those practice areas coalesce when drafting clear and effective pre-dispute ADR clauses. In this revised chapter, *Forward-Looking ADR Agreements: An Ounce of Prevention Is Worth Many Pounds of Cure*, the author addresses practical considerations for drafting ADR provisions in agreements (stand-alone or pre-dispute) relating to IP/Technology disputes.

Chapter 3 is co-authored by Cynthia Raposo and Harrie Samaras, who combine their litigation, corporate, and ADR experience to discuss how early case assessment can be used in IP/Technology disputes. In their revised chapter, *Early Case Assessment: A Strategic Tool for the Early Resolution and Management of Intellectual Property and Technology Disputes*, the authors examine the various facets of an early case assessment analysis for early or later settlement of IP/Technology disputes and for better managing litigation relating to such cases.

Chapter 4 is authored by Carol Ludington, who combines her forensic accounting, consulting, expert witness, and arbitration experience to discuss how an initial damages assessment (IDA) can be used in IP/Technology disputes. In her revised chapter, *Initial Damages Assessments: Focusing Early on Things That Count but Cannot Be Counted*, the author examines the use of IDA to gain an early, realistic view of damages, including an understanding of the key legal, business, and financial issues affecting recovery, for strategic decision-making.

Chapter 5 is authored by Theo Cheng, who combines his litigation, arbitration, and mediation experience to discuss strategic and novel uses of decision-making tools in resolving IP/Technology disputes. In this revised chapter, *Useful Tools to Persuade, Evaluate, and Communicate in ADR Proceedings*, the author describes various tools that attorneys, clients, and mediators can use to clarify issues, make the analysis of the case easier, improve advocacy, facilitate decisions, and render an ideal settlement agreement more likely.

Chapter 6 is newly co-authored by Merriann Panarella and Harrie Samaras, who combine their litigation and mediation experience as advocates and mediators to discuss useful mediation advocacy and strategies in IP/Technology disputes. In this new chapter, *Mediating IP/Technology Disputes: Design, Preparation, and Strategy*, the authors have synthesized important considerations regarding the successful design of, preparation for, and strategy relating to the mediation process in IP/Technology disputes by combining sage guidance from three previous chapters and perspectives (magistrate judge, in-house, mediator).

Chapter 7 is co-authored by Theo Cheng and Harrie Samaras, who combine their mediation experience in outlining effective advocacy practices for mediating cases at federal appellate courts. In this revised chapter, *The Skillful Appellate Mediation Advocate: Mediating Intellectual Property and Technology Cases in the Federal Appellate Courts*, the authors discuss practical aspects of appellate mediation, focusing on mediation programs in five federal circuits hearing IP/Technology cases, outlining relevant aspects and unique benefits of these programs, and providing insights into factors affecting why IP/Technology cases settle at the appellate level, as well as tips on how appellate advocates can and should make the most of these programs for their clients.

Chapter 8 is newly co-authored by Mark J. Abate and Molly R. Grammel, who combine their experience in IP litigation, Section 337 investigations before the U.S. International Trade Commission (ITC), and mediation in the ITC's mediation program to discuss the use of mediation in resolving IP disputes at the ITC. In their chapter, *Mediating Section 337 Disputes Regarding Infringing Imports at the International Trade Commission*, the authors discuss mediation in the ITC's mediation program and the unique features of a Section 337 investigation that provide various opportunities to mediate the underlying dispute and related matters.

Chapter 9 is co-authored by Michael H. Diamant, Stephen P. Gilbert, Laura A. Kaster, and Harrie Samaras, who combine their litigation and arbitration experience to discuss how counsel can effectively use the unique procedures and flexibility allowed by arbitration to provide an efficient and reliable means of adjudicating IP/Technology disputes. In their revised chapter, *Arbitrating IP/Technology Cases: Considerations for Businesspeople and Advocates*, the authors discuss particular aspects of arbitrating IP/Technology disputes that can influence the effectiveness of the arbitration process and result in a winning presentation.

Chapter 10 is co-authored by Steven M. Levy and Harrie Samaras, who combine their experience in trademark law and as panelists for various UDRP administering organizations to offer advocates ideas on how best to present their case in a UDRP proceeding. In this revised chapter, *UDRP Proceedings: How Advocates Can Put Their Best Foot Forward*, the authors discuss how advocates and clients can provide panels with the best and most complete evidence and arguments to address the key issues in UDRP proceedings.

Chapter 11 is newly authored by Theo Cheng, who combines his experience in litigating, arbitrating, and mediating copyright cases to discuss how small-value copyright cases can be efficiently and cost-effectively resolved. In this new chapter, *Resolving Small-Value Copyright Claims Through the Copyright Claims Board*, the author discusses the benefits of using the Copyright Claims Board and tips for advocates in representing clients before that tribunal.

Chapter 12 is authored by Gale R. ("Pete") Peterson, who combines his experience as a special master, arbitrator, and litigator in IP cases to discuss using special masters in such cases. In his revised chapter, *Mastering the Use of a Special Master in Intellectual Property Litigation*, the author describes the nuts and bolts of what practitioners need to know about effectively using special masters in IP cases.

***

The authors hope that, in reading this book, counsel, business executives, and neutrals learn and challenge themselves to apply new approaches, strategies, and practices when using alternatives to litigation in resolving IP and technology disputes.

PART I

Strategic Considerations for Using ADR in IP/Technology Disputes

CHAPTER 1

Putting ADR to Work: Imagining Better Results for Resolving IP/Technology Disputes

Theo Cheng and Harrie Samaras[1]

Necessity is the mother of invention.[2]

Introduction[3]

The proverbial expression—*necessity is the mother of invention*—reflects that when disputes needing attention arise, that need can lead to new and inspired approaches to resolution. Indeed, some of the most creative solutions for dispute resolution are developed in response to challenges that must be addressed.

The purpose of this chapter is to illustrate with real-life cases how parties faced with challenges in resolving intellectual property (IP)/Technology disputes have met those challenges by putting dispute resolution processes to work in inventive ways.

I. Perspective

Historically, IP/Technology owners looked to the courts to enforce their proprietary rights, including to obtain injunctive relief and damages for infringement, and to redress breaches of contract. However, the costs and delays of traditional litigation have been key factors driving IP and technology owners to litigation alternatives—alternative dispute resolution (ADR).

1. This chapter is a derivative work based upon Chapter 1 written by James F. Davis, Esq., from the First and Second Editions of this book. The authors thank Phil Swain, Esq. for his contributions to this chapter.

2. For a discussion of the proverb's origins, see *Necessity Is the Mother of Invention*, WIKIPEDIA, https://en.wikipedia.org/wiki/Necessity_is_the_mother_of_invention (last edited Apr. 7, 2024).

3. See Glossary for definition of frequently used terms.

Moreover, parties using ADR in IP/Technology disputes have discovered additional reasons for using it, including:

- Maintaining or salvaging valuable contractual relationships
- Addressing confidentiality concerns
- Selecting neutral decision makers and mediators having relevant expertise (e.g., industry, technology, legal)
- Concluding amicably and expeditiously contractual relationships that have ended or are no longer viable
- Resolving disputes on a "global" basis—related cases pending internationally or before different U.S. tribunals
- Addressing complex case scenarios
- Creating a fair and level playing field for international disputes

Despite the increase in the use of ADR over the years in IP/Technology cases by companies and outside counsel, some businesses have not ventured too far beyond negotiation for settling disputes. This may be because (1) they have legacy contracts that did not incorporate ADR provisions; (2) they have a history or mindset favoring litigation and being in a public (court) forum; (3) counsel[4] and business decision makers may lack information and experience with ADR processes, thus influencing the nonuse or sparing use of it; and (4) long-standing negative myths about ADR tarnish its usefulness. And for some who have tried ADR and had either a bad experience or one outside of their expectation, they may be reluctant to try or experiment with ADR again. Faced with these circumstances, credit must be given to in-house and outside counsel and neutrals who have taken professional risks and unpopular stances to persuade executives, clients, and opposing parties to use ADR, try it again, combine ADR processes, or try new ADR approaches. Similarly, the clients who have taken such risks should be equally recognized.

ADR is most effective if counsel and the parties are competent in knowing when and how to use it as a tool. *One size does not fit all.* The opportunities and limits of the ADR tools must be fundamentally understood as well as how they interrelate to one another and traditional litigation. Furthermore, contrary to the belief by some that ADR is a *stepchild* to litigation and requires less rigorous preparation and execution than litigation, this is not the case. The case histories in this chapter are a testament to that. Thus,

4. In July 2026, some candidates sitting to take the bar exam in the United States will be examined on the topics of negotiation and dispute resolution for the first time in the history of the exam. *See* Marilyn Wellington, *The Next Generation of the Bar Exam: Quarterly Update*, 91 Bar Exam'r 19 (2022), https://thebarexaminer.ncbex.org/article/fall-2022/next-generation-of-the-bar-exam-quarterly-update/. This modification to the bar exam could influence in the future the number of attorneys who have knowledge of ADR processes and put ADR to use for their clients.

another purpose of this chapter, and indeed the rest of this book, is to teach that ADR requires not only the traditional skills of advocacy, persuasiveness, and persistence, but also additional skills like creativity in legal and business problem-solving, which, after all, is what IP/Technology owners are looking for to resolve IP/Technology disputes.

II. ADR Options

There are a variety of ADR processes that can be used in IP/Technology cases. Set forth in the following sections is a typical continuum of ADR processes that is often viewed as a spectrum from least to most formal and from least to most costly. ADR processes may be used alone, in combination, modified, and even as an adjunct to litigation.[5] Set forth in the following sections are brief descriptions of some of the ADR processes that parties have used to resolve IP/Technology disputes, as exemplified in the case histories set forth in Section III of this chapter.

A. Mediation

Mediation in its simplest form "is a process that employs a neutral person—the mediator—to facilitate and guide negotiations between parties to a dispute in an effort to reach a mutually acceptable resolution."[6] It is voluntary, flexible, confidential, informal, and nonbinding (unless the parties reach a binding agreement). In IP/Technology disputes, it is not uncommon for the mediator to have experience in the kind of dispute involved.

---

5. *Hall Street Associates, LLC v. Mattel, Inc.*, 128 S. Ct. 1396 (2008), is an example of where an ADR process—arbitration—was conceived of during an active litigation to resolve one aspect of the case. As set forth in the background of that case, the Supreme Court recounted that "[a]fter a bench trial sustained respondent tenant's (Mattel) right to terminate its lease with petitioner landlord (Hall Street), the parties proposed to arbitrate Hall Street's claim for indemnification of the costs of cleaning up the lease site." *Id.* at 1398. "The District Court approved, and entered as an order, the parties' arbitration agreement, which, inter alia, required the court to vacate, modify, or correct any award if the arbitrator's conclusions of law were erroneous." *Id.* See other examples in this chapter at Section III (Case Histories No. 1, 11, 12) and the Case in Point in Chapter 6 at Section II.A.

6. *See* Bennett G. Picker & Conna A. Weiner, Commercial Mediation Practice Guide: A Practical Handbook for Lawyers and Their Business Clients 3 (3d ed. 2023).

B. Early Neutral Evaluation

Early neutral evaluation[7] (ENE) is a confidential process that encourages direct communication between disputants about possible claims and supporting evidence. At the evaluation session before the neutral evaluator (an informal setting), each party presents its claims or defenses and supporting evidence. In IP/Technology cases, the parties often seek a neutral with expertise in the applicable subject matter who would be able to evaluate effectively the issues in dispute. At an agreed-upon time after the evaluation session, the neutral evaluator will issue a written nonbinding report including an unbiased opinion of the issues presented. The report may enhance communications between the parties, result in settlement, encourage the parties to mediate (possibly with the neutral evaluator as the mediator), or narrow the issues in dispute that need to be resolved in other dispute resolution processes.

C. Neutral Fact-Finding

Neutral fact-finding is typically used in one of two ways: (1) a stand-alone process in which a neutral investigates and finds facts upon which the parties can attempt to negotiate a settlement; or (2) in litigation, a process in which the court may order fact-finding by an agreed-upon fact finder as part of the court's ultimate decision-making process. In IP/Technology cases, in both of the aforementioned situations, the fact finder is a person with training and experience in the subject matter of the dispute (e.g., an engineer, scientist, medical professional) and often also a lawyer. A neutral fact finder may be selected either by the disputing parties or by the court. Neutral fact-finding permits efficient crystallizing of fact issues, opportunity for prompt review, and hopefully a basis for final resolution of the dispute by settlement or expedited judicial consideration.

D. Standing Neutral

A standing neutral may be used for various purposes including to facilitate a contractual relationship between the contracting parties where a long-standing relationship is planned[8] or even to facilitate the cost- and time-efficient

---

7. *See* American Arbitration Association, Early Neutral Evaluation: Getting an Expert's Assessment, https://www.adr.org/sites/default/files/document_repository/Early_Neutral_Evaluation.pdf (last visited Mar. 23, 2025).

8. *See* Joe Basile, *How Standing Mediators Can Add Value in M&A Deals*, DISPUTE RESOLUTION MAG., Apr. 2024, at 24 (describing "a 'standing mediator' as a professional neutral whom parties to a long-term relationship engage on a 'clear day,' i.e. before any dispute arises"). The author points out that the value a standing mediator can bring to a mergers and acquisition (M&A) deal is premised on the fact that signing

resolution of focused disputes that may continually arise between competitors. See Case History #6 relating to use of a standing arbitrator. The neutral is a trusted and independent individual selected by parties early in their relationship and that person typically is continuously involved so real-time action on issues can occur using a process mutually agreed on by the parties.[9]

E. Mini-Trial[10]

Mini-trials are not actually trials but rather structured information exchanges attended by counsel, usually prospective witnesses (especially experts), and, most important, the businesspeople responsible for resolving the dispute—typically executives. Mini-trials usually run two to three days, during which the parties present truncated forms of their best cases in a nonbinding, confidential format with the hope that the businesspeople, who attend and witness the whole procedure, can thereafter resolve the dispute on a person-to-person basis, with or without the presiding neutral's assistance. Mini-trials have been characterized as *replacing the courtroom with the boardroom*, and some have been extraordinarily successful in resolving major corporate disputes.

The first mini-trial in 1977, in the patent dispute between Telecredit, Inc. and TRW, is described later in this chapter as a case study.[11] It remains the classic example of how to use the mini-trial.

---

such a deal "marks the commencement of a relationship that will extend over some period of time" rather than the culmination of negotiations. *Id.* at 26. Some of those ongoing negotiations in an M&A deal might relate to conditions to closing; purchase price adjustment; contingent consideration based, for example, on milestones; transition service agreements; and buyer equity. *Id.* at 26–27. Likewise, in the IP/Technology realm the signing of an agreement (e.g., involving co-development and marketing) is often just the beginning of an ongoing relationship where the value to both parties can best be achieved not only through performance of contractual responsibilities but also ongoing negotiations related to expected and unexpected circumstances.

9. *Id.* at 26 (describing the standing mediator's work as including "becom[ing] familiar with the terms of the parties' relationship, get[ting] to know the parties' representatives, and [being] available to work with the parties for the duration of their relationship both to prevent disputes from arising and to facilitate a resolution if a dispute does arise").

10. See Douglas A. Henderson, *Avoiding Litigation with the Mini-Trial: The Corporate Bottom Line as Dispute Resolution Technique*, 46 S.C. L. Rev. 237 (1995), https://scholarcommons.sc.edu/cgi/viewcontent.cgi?article=3331&context=sclr, for a historical review of the early use of mini-trials generally and in the patent dispute discussed in Case History #2 in this chapter. *See also* Michael C. Jensen, *"Mini-Trial" to Settle Lawsuit*, N.Y. Times (Aug. 8, 1978), https://www.nytimes.com/1978/08/08/archives/minitrial-to-settle-lawsuit-minitrial-to-settle-a-lawsuit.html.

11. James F. Davis, Esq., who originally authored Chapter 1 of this book, was the presiding neutral at the mini-trial involving Telecredit, Inc. and TRW. Jim's legal career included working as an arbitrator and mediator, chairing the IP practice group

F. Expert Determination[12]

Expert determination is a confidential, flexible procedure where the parties agree to submit a dispute between them to an expert who makes a determination on the matter referred. To be an effective process, the parties will look for a neutral having expertise relevant to their dispute. The expert's determination may be binding or nonbinding. Expert determination can be advantageous where it is necessary to determine issues of a technical, scientific, or related business nature. Examples of such matters include patent claim interpretation, inventorship, royalty determinations, valuing an IP asset, or the scope of a license.

G. Med-Arb and Arb-Med

Med-Arb is a hybrid, confidential two-stage process. It usually involves the parties agreeing to grant a mediator power to convert automatically to being an arbitrator, and to make a legally binding arbitration award, if the mediation fails to result in a settlement of the relevant dispute. The arbitration phase of the process will be legally binding, and the arbitrator's award will be enforceable like an award rendered in standard arbitration proceedings.

Arb-Med is also a hybrid, confidential two-stage process. Generally, the neutral first conducts an arbitration proceeding regarding all issues and, before releasing the binding award to the parties, the neutral conducts the mediation to settle the dispute. The parties and the neutral will have heard the presentation of each party's case before the mediation phase. This process can be extended to end in arbitration (Arb-Med-Arb) so that if the mediation is not successful the parties can agree to have the neutral unseal and issue his or her previously decided binding award, or alternatively, if the mediation resolves the dispute the parties can agree to have the neutral issue a consent award memorializing their settlement.

H. Arbitration

Arbitration, generally, is an adjudicatory dispute resolution process in which one or three arbitrators issue a decision in the form of an "award" after an adversarial hearing. It is a "rights"-based process, rather than the "interest"-based approach typically provided by mediation. Arbitration in IP/Technology disputes is typically pursued by party agreement, intended to be binding, and

---

at Howrey, Simon, Arnold, and White LLP, and serving as a trial judge with the former U.S. Court of Claims in Washington, D.C.

12. *See, e.g.*, *What Is Expert Determination?*, World Intell. Prop. Org., https://www.wipo.int/amc/en/expert-determination/what-is-exp.html (last visited Mar. 23, 2025).

often governed by the Federal Arbitration Act (FAA), which provides for court review with very limited grounds to amend or reverse an arbitration award.

Arbitrations in IP/Technology cases tend to run much like federal district court bench trials, but with more relaxed party-agreed time schedules, procedures, and evidentiary rules.[13] Arbitration in IP/Technology cases usually arises from contract clauses that require parties to arbitrate disputes. Most clauses specify an organization and its rules to govern the arbitration. Counsel who are experienced in arbitration along with an experienced arbitration panel sometimes choose to self-administer the arbitration proceeding.

Discovery or information exchange is limited, and most arbitrators place the responsibility on the parties to handle discovery informally with minimum involvement by the arbitration panel. Arbitrators, under the FAA, have some subpoena power and use it when necessary.

Arbitration awards can be brief and conclusive without explanation, but generally in IP/Technology cases the parties want sufficient fact-findings and reasons to explain the rationale for the award. Generally, experience has shown that arbitrations in IP/Technology cases are faster and less expensive than traditional litigation, which often involves full-blown discovery and both trial and appeal.

III. Case Histories—Seeing Is Believing

The following real-life case histories were chosen to show the kinds of disputes that can arise in IP/Technology cases. They are also illustrative of how imagining better results for resolving disputes is in the grasp of resourceful counsel, neutrals, and businesspersons who are knowledgeable about ADR and open to using it.

CASE HISTORY #1

Neutral fact-finding as an adjunct to litigation

A chemical company sued one of its former executives for theft of trade secrets after the executive had been discharged and started a competing company. The case was pending in state court before an experienced judge with no science experience or training, and it involved complex chemistry and a complex fact scenario.

Recognizing that the dispute (typical of trade secret disputes) involved two principal issues (what, if any, were the trade secrets, and were they unlawfully

13. See Chapter 9 for an in-depth discussion of the use of arbitration in IP/Technology disputes.

appropriated and used by the defendant), the court agreed with the parties to appoint a neutral fact finder to find facts on the two principal issues. In fact, the court appointed a neutral (a lawyer with a chemistry background) agreed on by the parties.

The court, with guidance from the parties, authorized the neutral to interview appropriate personnel of the defendant and the plaintiff (some of whom had already been deposed), as well as one party representative, in the presence of counsel, under an appropriate protective order. The neutral was further authorized to inspect the parties' manufacturing facilities, including books and records, and to make a confidential report to the court based on the interviews and the inspections.

The neutral performed the interviews and inspections but did not conduct the interviews under oath, and they were not transcribed. Counsel had the opportunity to ask questions during the interviews and inspections as they saw fit. The neutral provided a draft of the report to counsel for comments. Counsel made no material objection to the report, which the neutral sent to the court. The draft contained detailed findings on the chemical processes involved and what both parties were actually doing at their respective facilities. The draft also identified the alleged trade secrets.

The bottom line of the findings was that there were trade secrets, and the defendant had misappropriated and was using them. The court accepted the findings and asked the parties essentially, "Where do we go from here?" At that point, the defendant offered to stop using the trade secrets, to pay a modest sum for past damages, and to relinquish all shares of the plaintiff's stock that it owned. The plaintiff agreed to settle on those terms as long as the settlement provided that the neutral be required for six months to inspect defendant's plant, including books and records, for compliance with the settlement. Accordingly, the court retained control of the dispute and the neutral performed the inspections and prepared the reports for the court.

This case history is an example of ADR working at its best, hand in glove with traditional litigation. The parties, in conjunction with the court, tackled the heart of the dispute quickly and expertly with a knowledgeable fact finder. The parties minimized discovery costs and avoided the expense of party experts and lengthy proceedings.

CASE HISTORY #2

The mini-trial is born

Prior to 1977, there was no such thing as a *mini-trial* in the ADR lexicon. But frustration with a three-year-old patent infringement suit, moving at a snail's pace through the federal district court in Los Angeles, was about to change that.

The case started in 1974 when Telecredit, Inc., a company providing computerized check and credit-card authorization services, claimed that TRW had infringed several of its patents. Telecredit wanted an injunction and $6 million in damages. Discovery turned up more than 100,000 documents. After three years of discovery battles and $1 million in legal fees (substantial back then), no settlement was in sight.

Telecredit's patent license administrator and co-founder suggested binding arbitration. TRW refused. Thus, faced with a stalled lawsuit and management on both sides frustrated with no resolution, counsel created what was to become known as a *mini-trial.* The process entailed six weeks of expedited discovery, exchange of briefs, and then a two-day session attended by top management where each side would present a truncated form of its case on all issues. As the parties requested, the proceedings would be moderated by a neutral, experienced in patent litigation and preferably also with judicial experience, who would issue a nonbinding opinion with settlement recommendations and a prognostication of trial outcome if management was unable to work out a settlement after the mini-trial.

The mini-trial took place in a Los Angeles hotel in July 1977, attended by more than two dozen people. Among them were the chief executive officer (CEO) of Telecredit and the executive vice president of TRW. In the agreed-upon format, one side presented its case, followed by rebuttal, then reply, and finally questions from the executives. Then the other side put on its case. The cases were presented through the testimony of technical and legal experts and argument of counsel, with the neutral asking questions for clarification where appropriate.

The site for the mini-trial, a large banquet room at the hotel, was set up like a courtroom. The neutral sat in the middle at a bench-like table with the two corporate executives on either side of him. There were separate tables for counsel and a chair for witnesses and presenters and (as it was back then) blackboards or whiteboards were located around the room for displaying the many drawings, photographs, and the like.

The process went forward as agreed. When the mini-trial finished (in two days), the executives met alone with the neutral. At the executives' request, the neutral summarized the proceedings, stating that the central issue appeared to be the scope of the patent claims—whether the claims were entitled to a broad construction (as argued by the patentee) that would embrace the accused devices or whether they were entitled to a more limited scope in view of prior art not cited by the U.S. Patent and Trademark Office (the claims would be valid but not infringed).

Within half an hour, meeting without the neutral, the executives had the rough outline of a settlement (discussed with the neutral), which was finalized in a couple of weeks. The patents were to be submitted to the U.S. Patent and Trademark Office for reexamination in view of the new prior art, and if they were reissued with the broad claims, TRW would take a license at an agreed-to royalty rate. Both sides agreed that they had thereby avoided an extensive, costly trial several years down the road.

Fortune magazine published a feature article in 1979 touting the Telecredit/TRW mini-trial event as "A Businesslike Way to Resolve Legal Disputes" and quoting a top executive who agreed, stating, "I'm not a believer in letting lawyers solve business problems."[14]

---

14. Stephen D. Solomon, *A Businesslike Way to Resolve Legal Disputes*, FORTUNE, Feb. 26, 1979, at 80.

Over the years since 1977, the mini-trial approach has been tailored to fit other types of controversies where issues can be framed after a limited amount of discovery. As pointed out by the *Fortune* article, "This approach is not meant for cases that present novel questions of law, requiring a judge to establish new precedent; nor would it be likely to work in some of the largest cases where even trial-court opinions are merely preliminary to the real battleground, the appeals court."[15] The mini-trial has been used to resolve major dollar disputes (e.g., Westinghouse, many major electric utility companies, Shell Oil, Union Carbide, Borden, Texaco, Xerox, Gillette, American Can Co., Honeywell, and government agencies including the Department of Justice, the Army Corp of Engineers, and the National Aeronautics and Space Administration (NASA)).

CASE HISTORY #3

The mega-mediation/mini-trial

Background and overview

Occasionally, the opportunity arises to resolve a very large and complex multi-patent dispute by ADR, particularly mediation and/or mini-trial. So it was, with two of the largest U.S. manufacturers and sellers of information storage equipment, "Primo Co." and "Secundo Co." Each had extensive and impressive patent portfolios, of which they were justly proud, based on research and development and experience in the field. Both had increasing market shares and increasing competition in the marketplace leading to multiple patent litigations.

Senior management at both companies recognized that over time the companies would continue to have patent disputes between one another with the attendant costs, uncertainties, and disruption of employees' time. Senior management favored a paid-up royalty-bearing cross-license on all existing accused products. But there were problems with this approach: (1) each side believed its patents, on balance, were more valuable than the other side's; and (2) making market projections for sales of accused products during the unexpired life of the accused patents was a challenge. Thus, how could the parties determine the relative infringement value and who should pay whom?

Based on an earlier, unsuccessful mediation of the case in which the participants attempted to evaluate an extensive portion of the companies' patent portfolios, the parties, with the help of a new neutral, decided to take a different approach—a three-step hybrid mediation/mini-trial process, as follows:

- *Step one* was to identify only the infringed patents along with alleged infringing products and their past and projected future sales.

15. *Id.*

- *Step two* was to brief the infringement, validity, and damages/royalties issues and conduct a mini-trial before a neutral, each side to present its case as it saw fit. The mini-trial was scheduled for two days, with each side limited to five experts on liability issues.
- *Step three* was to have the neutral prepare an opinion/report for the parties' CEOs to consider, followed by a meeting of the CEOs along with the neutral. The report was to provide an analysis of validity, infringement, and damages/royalties on a patent-by-patent basis, with the probability of success on each issue, so that the CEOs could hopefully reach a settlement with a one-time payment. Critical to the process was an agreement that the CEO meeting must be within four months after the process started.

The process

The first hurdle in the process was to decide how many of the patents in controversy would be considered for the mini-trial, thus to avoid the overload problem that existed in the earlier mediation. The technology involved divided into three product areas. The parties wanted to choose five patents per side in each product area (15 patents) for analysis, thus 30 patents total. The neutral believed this was too many for the time allotted considering the technology and the factual/legal issues (implicating hundreds of products and hundreds of millions of dollars). Nevertheless, the neutral permitted the parties to brief 30 patents and corresponding accused products and to outline how they intended to present their cases at the mini-trial (e.g., witnesses, attorney argument).

After receiving the briefs, the neutral advised the parties that their submissions comprised "about 4,600 pages of briefs and documents including patent references, technical documents, expert statements, product information, [and] sales information," all of which was too much to handle in the agreed-upon time frame. After consultation with the parties, the neutral conducted the mini-trial with six (rather than 15) patents per side (a total of 12 patents) and one claim per patent. This worked well. The parties spent two full days to get through 12 patents, while expert testimony (including cross-examination) on validity and infringement took most of the time. Accounting, marketing, and royalty experts also presented on damages/royalties issues. The parties did not have the proceedings transcribed.

The neutral's opinion/report

The neutral's opinion/report, prepared specifically for the CEOs' consideration, comprised five sections (12 pages): Background, Evaluation Methodology, Royalty Rates, Analysis of Individual Patents, and Summary and Conclusions.

Because the audience for the report was high-level executive businessmen, the *Background* section provided succinct information regarding the technology and the legal claims in dispute.

The *Evaluation Methodology* section warrants a closer look because it was central to the CEOs reaching a confidence level sufficient to justify a large settlement based on limited sampling of information. The section began:

> The yardstick used to evaluate infringement, validity and enforceability was to apply the burdens of proof used by the courts, recognizing that the mediation environment is not a trial with witnesses, cross-examination under oath, etc., all of which are particularly important in patent cases because of complex law and technical issues. Proof of infringement requires a "preponderance of the evidence." Proof of invalidity and enforceability requires "clear and convincing evidence" because of the statutory presumption of validity accorded all patents. In each instance of evaluation, the neutral has indicated a "confidence level" to provide some guidance on the weight to be accorded his conclusions.

Further, because of the fact-intensive nature of the obviousness inquiry, and the "differences of opinion, especially expert opinion, thus normally requiring a trial," the neutral stated no opinion on the parties' obviousness arguments.

In sum, the neutral's liability evaluation addressed validity under 35 U.S.C. § 102 (e.g., prior disclosure or public use, on-sale bars) and also license issues (i.e., assertion that a patent was licensed to the other side). Infringement evaluation addressed both direct and doctrine of equivalents infringement.

The *Royalty Rate* section noted a wide spread of argued appropriate rates for different products. The neutral noted, "Neither party was forthcoming with licensing details of its own licenses for confidentiality reasons. Nor did they provide any information about industry practices (if there is any such information)." Accordingly, the neutral set royalty rate ranges as best he could from the parties' arguments, basically compromising between high and low positions of the parties.

The *Analysis of Individual Patents* section addressed each of the 12 patents under consideration, opining validity, enforceability, and infringement using the standards noted previously. The conclusion stated: "As was expected, the results of the evaluations are a mixed bag. Some of the patents are deemed valid and infringed, others not infringed or not valid, and it cuts both ways with the parties as set out in the summary and conclusions at the end of this report."

The *Summary and Conclusions* section reported as follows:

- Primo Co.: 5 patents valid and infringed; 1 patent not infringed; no patents invalid
- Secundo Co.: 3 patents valid and infringed; 2 patents not infringed; 1 patent invalidFinally, the neutral noted in the report:

> While only 12 of the 30 patents briefed by the parties and presented at the mini-trial are considered in detail here, the neutral has considered the parties' briefs on all 30 patents . . . and believes that based on the briefs and experience at the mini-trial, the results of further oral presentations would not materially change the relative position of the parties as set out above. The neutral believes this view is justified by the understanding that each party put its best

foot forward at the hearing with its strongest patents and nothing material would be gained by further proceedings.

The result

The CEOs met as scheduled, with the neutral attending at the beginning. The neutral set out a projected range of a proposed settlement in the eight- to nine-figure range. Thereafter, the CEOs met alone and settled the case in two hours. The results were never made known to the public or the neutral. The keys to the success of this mediation/mini-trial were twofold:

- Careful tailoring, preparing, and presenting of the issues at the mini-trial with active participation of the neutral
- A report to the CEOs in sufficient detail and with sufficient analysis to persuade them that the truncated snapshot of the respective parties' positions was sufficient upon which to base an overall resolution of their present and potential future conflicts under the asserted patents

Both sides agreed that the process saved them millions of dollars in prospective litigation expenses and expenditure of other corporate assets.

Furthermore, this case history illustrates that big-ticket patent disputes (in the hundreds of millions of dollars) can be resolved by ADR with careful preparation and proper defining of issues so that senior management can comfortably make rational decisions.

CASE HISTORY #4

If at first you don't succeed . . .

Background and overview

This case history illustrates two points: (1) mediation sometimes does not produce an immediate settlement (i.e., a settlement after one mediation session), but (2) with active participation of the mediator and the parties' willingness to seek and hear out the mediator's views, the parties may still settle their dispute.

In the early 2000s, "EuroComCo," a large European company, licensed "ProdCo," a major U.S. manufacturer, to use certain patented communications technology. ProdCo paid a one-time license fee of $9 million. The patents involved were to expire in 2012.

Several years later, a dispute arose regarding whether a new ProdCo product came within the license grant. ProdCo believed it did. EuroComCo disagreed and claimed a new license was required for the new technology. The new technology promised to be very popular worldwide but it was in its infancy, and the parties disputed its success in the future. EuroComCo, relying on early ProdCo market projections, believed that the new technology would be a big success in five or six years. ProdCo disagreed, believing that the early projections were not materializing.

The parties tried to settle on their own. EuroComCo offered $13 million. ProdCo rejected the offer, choosing to rely on its legal position that no further license was necessary. EuroComCo then demanded mediation as provided under the license.

Senior management of both companies attended the mediation, as well as in-house and outside counsel. In its pre-mediation statements, EuroComCo withdrew its earlier offer to settle for $13 million and presented an elaborate analysis of why, if the matter went to litigation, ProdCo would be held an infringer and liable for about $100 million.

ProdCo contended that even if it were held liable, the damages would be trivial because the new technology was just getting started and was having significant marketing problems with no predictable success.

Early in the mediation, the mediator met with each side privately. In response to the mediator's probing, EuroComCo said that its views from the time it offered to settle for $13 million had changed based on "learning much more about ProdCo and its new product from publicly available information on market projections, etc.," from which it concluded that its $13 million offer had been "woefully inadequate." The mediator expressed skepticism, noting it was difficult to believe that EuroComCo knew so little about ProdCo's public activities at the time of the $13 million offer. Furthermore, EuroComCo said it believed now that ProdCo's "back was to the wall" because it had invested substantial money in the new technology and needed the license to proceed forward.

In the private meeting with ProdCo, the mediator probed why ProdCo rejected the $13 million offer. ProdCo responded that its more recent review of the market justified a settlement of around $9 million at most, and it indicated a willingness to negotiate between $5 million and $9 million. At this point, the mediator persuaded ProdCo to make a $5 million offer, "to try to get things started."

EuroComCo predictably rejected the offer and countered with $33–$65 million. The mediator urged ProdCo to go up to $13 million to try to keep things going, believing that EuroComCo, on reflection, might return close to its initial offer of $13 million. ProdCo refused.

At the mediator's invitation, the parties met face-to-face to explain their positions and why each refused to move further in the negotiations. Neither side would budge, and things stalemated.

Mediator's efforts to break the stalemate

The mediator asked the parties if they would like to hear jointly the mediator's *reactions and suggestions* to the situation. The parties agreed. The following is a summary of what the mediator told the parties in joint session.

The matter should settle in the range of $14–$20 million. Here is why:

(1) ProdCo should conclude that a payment greater than $13 million, maybe as high as $18–$20 million, is justified. Despite dire

predictions of success, ProdCo seemed to believe that despite a slow start with the product, things would get better, though they never said so expressly to the mediator and certainly not to EuroComCo. It seemed to the mediator that the product, if successful, could result in the next five to ten years in hundreds of millions of dollars in revenue to ProdCo.

(2) EuroComCo should conclude that setting its sights on \$33–\$65 million is unrealistic in view of the history of the parties' dealings, in particular the initial license deal for \$9 million. The new technology is not sufficiently different in kind or importance from the previous license to expect such a large incremental increase. Between \$14 million and \$20 million appears to be fair and reasonable, particularly in light of the fact that EuroComCo was willing to settle for \$13 million just a few months earlier.

(3) Finally, the legal question as to whether the new technology is already licensed under the original license remains hotly contested, though to the mediator, EuroComCo is in the better place (i.e., the new technology is not licensed). In private meetings with the mediator, ProdCo had stuck adamantly to its view that no new license was needed, but the mediator said he suspected that their counsel was candidly advising the businesspeople of the substantial risks with that position.

The parties thanked the mediator and parted company.

All's well that ends well . . .

Three weeks later, the parties requested a second session with the mediator. That session lasted several hours and rehashed much of the earlier ground.

But, happily, it concluded in a settlement of \$25 million. While it was never clear what broke the ice here, presumably the mediator's efforts played some role in each side bending toward the middle.

A final observation about this mediation: The mediator's active role in setting out jointly to the parties his reactions and suggestions after stalemate raises an interesting point about the mediation of IP/Technology, and particularly patent, cases.

Experience teaches that counsel and participants are exceptionally well prepared and are not subject to much arm-twisting in reaching settlement. Those IP/Technology counsel who have a background in engineering and science tend to approach disputes with the exacting precision that only a scientist or engineer can understand (or tolerate). They also tend to be more concerned (than counsel without technical training) about having disputes resolved by judges unfamiliar with both relevant law and technology. And sometimes they are even more concerned about trying cases before jurors who usually have, at best, great difficulty deciding which set of scientists or engineers to believe.

Thus, in stalemate situations in mediations, the parties are understandably receptive to views of the mediator, especially ones with considerable real-life experience observing how these issues play out (e.g., litigators, arbitrators, judges), and in mediations attended by senior executives, they are especially looking for reality checks from someone experienced in the law and technology and not biased in either direction.

How much weight a mediator's thoughts are given in these circumstances is never really known for sure, but the parties often seek them, especially when they could make a difference.

CASE HISTORY #5

Arbitration, with a twist

Arbitrations do not usually offer opportunity for creative efforts to resolve the dispute short of a hearing and an award. But this is not always so. This case history illustrates a creative twist to resolve a dispute midway in the presentation of evidence in the arbitration hearing.

The dispute involved multinational parties and multiple foreign and U.S. patents covering medical products. It also involved issues of inventorship, patent ownership, and license rights. The arbitration was held under the International Chamber of Commerce Rules, administered from Paris. There were three arbitrators: a retired Canadian appeals court judge (the chairman) and two party-nominated arbitrators, one American and one British, both experienced patent litigators. Hearings were scheduled in Paris (two weeks), London (two weeks), and a wrap-up in the United States (one week).

After two weeks in Paris and on the eve of adjourning and moving to London, the parties advised the panel that they had agreed to stipulate to some of the London and U.S. testimony, which should shorten the hearings considerably. At that point, the panel considered whether further proceedings were necessary. Based on the evidence presented thus far and what appeared to be coming, the panel believed that if no materially contrary evidence was offered, the panel could promptly render a decision on each of the issues. The panel asked the parties if they would like to hear its views with the proviso that if any party believed that materially contrary evidence was coming, they should so advise the panel and the panel would withhold its views. Thus, it was up to the parties to agree unanimously with this procedure or it would not go forward.

The parties agreed on the proposed process with the understanding that no party would challenge any final award on grounds of having gone forward with this procedure. Thereafter, the panel chair told the parties which party(s) would prevail in an award on the present record, and why, and made it clear that this view could change with additional evidence.

The parties promptly settled, saving considerable time and money. Some arbitrators in the same or similar circumstances as presented in this case history might decide not to pursue a similar procedure for various legitimate reasons. That said, insofar as arbitration is a consensual process that also lends itself to time and cost efficiencies, this actual scenario suggests that in the appropriate circumstances thought should be given to exploring an adapted process for resolving the dispute as the panel and the parties did here.

CASE HISTORY #6

Standing neutral to the rescue for recurring disputes

Two large competitors in the telecommunications arena were in dispute on an ongoing basis about representations each made in weekly print ads for pricing competitive products/services—false advertising claims. Litigation would have been too costly and, more importantly, too slow for the business certainty of whether the weekly ads could run. Needing an expeditious and respected process to resolve the continuing disputes, the parties devised an expedited binding arbitration process overseen by a standing neutral comprising the following:

- Enlisting a standing neutral (arbitrator) who was familiar with the telecommunications field and the recurring disputed issues and who was respected by the parties
- Agreeing to an expedited process by which the parties received due process and the neutral could render an informed and timely award; this included a weekly expedited schedule for exchanging information (including the ads to be run) and concise briefing on the narrow, disputed issues
- Agreeing on a form award for the neutral to render his binding award
- Consistently following the expedited process
- Abiding (being bound) by the expeditiously rendered award

In IP/Technology disputes, there are various roles that a standing neutral (e.g., mediator or arbitrator) may serve. For example, one role is where parties have a project-dictated relationship (e.g., to develop a product) and they want to ensure if disputes arise related to the product development they are resolved quickly and fairly (i.e., by the decision of a respected, standing neutral) so that a valuable commercial relationship is not derailed. In these situations, standing neutrals can also play the role of "peacemaker" to remind disputants of the value of the relationship to their respective companies and to focus them on how to fix the problem rather than lay blame on the other party for it. Standing neutrals have also been used in a preventative role—their mere appointment. That is, when a dispute arises, parties may be more motivated to resolve their own disputes rather than resort to a standing neutral—call it pride, ego, or self-determination.

A standing neutral wearing a mediator's hat can help parties through a breakup. For example, in one case, two parties were engaged in a development contract that was valuable to both at the inception of the agreement, but because of changing circumstances, the contract became less valuable to one party. The breakup could have been expensive for both, attracted negative publicity, and engendered bad blood between the companies. The standing neutral helped the parties brainstorm ways to separate and in the end the party who wanted the separation decided to take a financial interest in the project so that in publicizing this, they provided positive publicity to the company continuing with the project, avoided negative publicity, and validated the work being done.

In this case scenario, two ardent competitors that were not strangers to litigation made a strategic choice in using the standing neutral process as a way to achieve the due process they needed under the circumstances, an expeditious binding legal decision, and, above all, the business certainty required to run their respective businesses.

CASE HISTORY #7

Nonbinding (advisory) arbitration meets mediation

In a patent infringement case ongoing in federal district court involving hundreds of millions in damages, the parties had been working with an experienced mediator for more than six months to settle it. It became apparent to the parties and the mediator that there were key fact issues relating to infringement and invalidity that the parties had significantly different perspectives on and that this was obstructing efforts to settle. A decision was made to pursue nonbinding input from each of three neutrals as an adjunct to the mediation process.

Three neutral arbitrators were engaged who had significant experience in litigating and deciding patent infringement cases. The parties agreed upon the materials that the neutrals would review to provide their nonbinding decisions, but they also permitted the arbitrators to request other materials if necessary. The parties also prepared form questionnaires (like special interrogatories) for each arbitrator to fill out to memorialize their nonbinding decisions on the fact issues that the parties had the most significant disagreement about. The arbitrators were prohibited from discussing with one another, the parties, or the mediator the materials or their thoughts about the disputed issues at any time during the proceeding. After the arbitrators were given time to study the materials, the parties held a one-day hearing (akin to a summary judgment hearing) before the arbitrators (the mediator was present) on the key issues they would decide. Then the arbitrators were given two weeks to provide their nonbinding decisions on the disputed issues set forth on the questionnaire forms and to send the completed form to the mediator. Thus, the parties ultimately received three questionnaires from each of the arbitrators reflecting their independent judgment on the disputed issues. The mediation continued for additional months with this input. The case ultimately settled.

Here, considering the magnitude of potential damages and the difference of opinion on key issues, the parties chose the nonbinding input of three experts having the requisite legal and technical expertise regarding the issues in dispute. Such input may have provided additional information as a reality check or risk assessment for the parties and the mediator. In the appropriate case where the parties in a mediation are getting sidetracked about a purely technical issue, they may decide to jointly engage a neutral technical expert or fact finder to obtain objective input on that issue to get beyond their rooted positions.

CASE HISTORY #8

Pre-dispute resolution agreement meets relationship building and conflict avoidance[16]

Litigation with competitors can be expensive, time-consuming, public, and not good for an industry. Indeed, sometimes even large companies with significant resources can get enough of litigation. After a particularly hard-fought patent and anti-trust litigation involving billions of dollars, Monsanto Company reached that realization. The company also recognized that collaborating with competitors could foster and accelerate research and development, insofar as innovation, an essential component to business opportunities and growth, is often beyond one company's resources. Thus, an idea was born to stem the tide of litigation with competitors by taking a relationship-based approach to dispute resolution and prevention in which businesspeople would take the lead in seeking business solutions to conflicts.

This relationship-based approach was intended to encompass all potential disputes between Monsanto and its competitors. It would be critical to have buy-in at the

16. In February 2016, the International Institute for Conflict Prevention & Resolution (CPR) honored Monsanto Company and Scott S. Partridge with its Inspiring Innovation Award for the innovation of the relationship-based approach to dispute resolution. A special thanks to Scott S. Partridge (Partridge LLC) for his time in providing the information set forth here. Mr. Partridge was formerly the General Counsel of Bayer US and before that the Vice President of Global Strategy for Monsanto Company.

most senior levels for the approach to be assimilated companywide. After crossing that bridge—a significant step, particularly for Monsanto and its first partner—both corporate heads signed on, and the companies constructed two important elements of their future relationship: a pre-dispute resolution clause and relationship teams. After Monsanto completed its first relationship-based partnership, it completed such arrangements with other competitors. The unique relationship-based dispute resolution and conflict-avoidance model that Scott Partridge designed and launched at Monsanto generally encompassed the following facets:

a. **Relationship agreement**. The senior executives from Monsanto and its competitors (e.g., CEOs/board chairs) and the business heads of the relationship teams (discussed further in this list) would sign an agreement of intent that was not otherwise binding—there were no teeth if the companies did not cooperate. The agreement, however, would commit the signatory companies to a number of forward-thinking principles to give them the latitude to compete in the marketplace yet also to build a productive, conciliatory relationship. Moreover, even if a dispute ended up in a public forum, the companies would commit to handling matters with discretion and civility.
b. **Relationship teams**. These teams are the means by which Monsanto and its competitors implemented their commitment to the relationship-based approach. Senior businesspeople or scientists would lead the teams, supported by others as needed (e.g., anti-trust counsel, finance, accounting, and regulatory personnel). And depending on the subject matter of the dispute, the relationship team could include an ad hoc member representing the involved business unit. The teams would focus on science, technology, and commercial opportunities, to provide for a productive discourse. No dispute would be too small or too big to address. The teams would meet on a regular basis (e.g., quarterly). Generally, they would start out meeting at a neutral location, although as the teams built trust with one another, they might meet at one or the other's facilities. At least initially, agendas would help to guide the discussion of issues as well as manage progress from meeting to meeting. An anti-trust attorney would routinely attend the meetings. Indeed, the companies might even include the Department of Justice in the loop to avoid any later repercussions.
c. **Pre-dispute resolution clause**. Guiding the relationship teams would be an escalated pre-dispute resolution clause that would be included in an agreement Monsanto and its competitors signed. The clause would be tailored to the companies' needs and cultural approaches, but generally it would take the form of an escalated dispute resolution process that began with negotiation in two stages: stage 1 involved negotiations between business owners (optional, business unit lawyers as advisors); stage 2 involved negotiations between the relationship team leaders of each company. If those stages were unsuccessful, then the dispute would

proceed to mediation, where both sets of negotiators participated. And when mediation was not successful, the dispute would proceed to arbitration. Monsanto's preferred arbitration process consisted of a single arbitrator chosen by a blind selection process, who would decide the disputed issues on the briefs after limited discovery. In IP cases, however, litigation was Monsanto's chosen method of adjudication if the other dispute resolution processes were not successful. That said, Monsanto built into the dispute resolution process a mechanism to keep the companies focused on settling rather than rushing to the courthouse—a strategy that can derail negotiation and mediation efforts. For example, if Monsanto and its competitor could not resolve a patent infringement dispute, they knew by agreement that whoever is the patent owner had the right to file first in federal court if settlement attempts were unsuccessful.

d. **Corporate integration of relationship teams**. Monsanto integrated the relationship team into their corporate structure, like other functioning groups within the company. It had a clear charter and authority known companywide, so when employees become aware of potential issues with one of Monsanto's relationship-based partners (e.g., patent infringement, licensing, contract, advertising, business competition), they knew to elevate the issues to the relationship team for investigation and resolution.

e. **Outgrowth of the relationship teams**. An outgrowth of the good will established through the relationship teams was that in between their scheduled meetings, the business heads would contact one another if, for example, they learned from employees of their respective companies about a possible intercompany issue. These could be addressed and often eradicated with a phone call. Furthermore, the teams provided an incubator for other collaborations, such as partnering on regulatory and legislative issues, collaborating on inventions, and even sharing manufacturing resources.

This relationship-based approach was originally created for use with multinational competitors, but Monsanto implemented it in areas such as customer relationships, complex litigation, and class actions—contexts where preexisting relationships are vastly different or nonexistent. With regard to customer relationships (e.g., seed companies, farmers), Monsanto used its sales and technical representatives as the eyes and ears of the company to identify concerns early about product performance. The early investigation of customer concerns coupled with a working relationship with the customer often dissipated concerns without having to use mediation. Monsanto also used its relationship-based approach to settle several cases related to the closing of chemical manufacturing sites. In addition to a history of contentious relationships among counsel, these cases presented no potential for a future business opportunity. Maintaining a dialogue with plaintiffs' counsel permitted Monsanto to establish trust in its commitment to finding a just resolution of all claims and ultimately resolving the cases.

Timing can be everything, and Monsanto found that two optimal times for approaching potential partners were right after a fight or before a conflict erupted. Needless to say, although reactions from competitors were mixed in the beginning, many relationships were forged, thus averting long, public, and expensive litigations. Finding solutions was not always easy or fast. In many cases Monsanto reached settlements when the usual threats of litigation and dislike for large companies were replaced with open discussion, cool heads, and principles of sound science or medicine. In sum, peace was achieved by corporate commitment and personal engagement, including a willingness to develop a relationship with the enemy.

CASE HISTORY #9

Adapted use of a step-up clause

An energy company experienced the malfunction of an expensive, key piece of equipment it used to provide energy to a neighboring state's electrical system serving significant numbers of customers. The malfunction created risk that the neighboring electrical system would not have enough capacity to serve its customers' energy supply needs during summer peak periods. In the agreement the energy company had with the equipment manufacturer, there was a step-up clause for resolving disputes requiring the parties to first attempt to resolve the dispute through consultation between the parties' responsible executives, then to mediate the dispute if not resolved, and finally to arbitrate the dispute if a nonbinding process did not achieve resolution. The parties realized that if they followed the step-up clause literally, even the mediation step alone would take too much time—customers could be without sufficient power supply for an unacceptable period of time. Instead of abandoning the clause altogether, however, the parties adapted it to the needs of the situation.

First, the parties used the mediation step to help them devise a plan to expeditiously get the malfunctioning equipment fixed and back into service, thereby ensuring customers had a sufficient energy supply. At the same time, they were also using the mediation step to define for determination by arbitration the liability and damages issues. Those issues included: Why did the equipment malfunction? Who was responsible for the equipment malfunctioning? Who was responsible for damages such as repair costs? Also, the parties developed a repair agreement to enable the time-sensitive repair work to proceed, along with a process to ensure payment risk was managed pending the outcome of the liability determination.

To help the arbitration panel determine the liability issues, the parties agreed to engage and share the costs for neutral experts having the requisite technical expertise, to work in conjunction with the repair work to test and evaluate the equipment that malfunctioned and had to be replaced, and to provide the panel with a report on issues including (1) background on the equipment's proper functioning; (2) what likely caused the malfunction; and (3) which party was likely responsible for the malfunction. The arbitration process was designed to resolve the liability and damages issues efficiently and in parallel with the repair and restoration of the critical equipment so that customers' energy supply needs continued to be met, and the parties could put the entire episode behind them and maintain a good working business relationship.

It cannot be overstated that the stakeholders involved in resolving the technical, business, and legal issues in a coordinated and focused way saw the benefits of employing ADR and they understood the risks of not finding a business solution expeditiously. It was critical to engage and manage the contributions of those stakeholders (e.g., business and technology representatives, outside counsel, litigators, transactional counsel) to, among other things, build trust between otherwise disputing parties, repair the equipment, interface with customers, negotiate and draft agreements so that the business could resume its services, and develop a focused arbitration process to address the legal and damages issues.

Once a specific dispute materializes under a contract with an ADR clause, the parties to the contract are free to modify that clause or, as the parties did here, to take a flexible approach to applying the clause to meet their current business needs and specific risks presented. The pivot that the parties made here to see beyond a traditional application of the step-up clause is a tribute to quick, practical, and dispassionate acting by the parties. Also, an understanding of the mediation and arbitration processes and how they could be best used was a must.

CASE HISTORY #10

Binding expert determination maintains a valuable collaboration

A pharmaceutical company and research university were working together to develop a medicinal product. A dispute arose regarding inventorship of the product as between the two parties. They had a good working relationship and wanted to get beyond the inventorship dispute to continue their valuable work together. In-house counsel for the parties structured a process for expediting that determination, keeping a flexible approach if the neutral they chose wanted some modifications. The parties agreed to (1) engage a neutral with the requisite technological expertise, legal background (i.e., knowledge of the law for determining inventorship), and experience in deciding disputes; (2) exchange a set of reliance documents by a date certain that supported their inventorship positions; (3) either hold an expedited arbitration-style hearing where the neutral could question a few relevant factual witnesses under oath regarding the development of the product or hold an informal session where the neutral could question the fact witnesses with both sides' in-house counsel present; (4) have the neutral render a binding short reasoned award; and (5) each contribute an equal share of a fixed sum of money to cover the entirety of the proceeding including preparation of the award.

The neutral whom the parties chose implemented their proposed process holding an expedited arbitration-style hearing, which was transcribed. She rendered the award within a month after receiving the hearing transcript and the parties continued their collaboration.

Self-determination was a driving force in the success of these parties, but also, their in-house counsel clearly understood the problems to be solved (legal and relationship aspects), they had a problem-solving (not positional) approach, and they understood how to use ADR strategically to resolve their dispute and maintain a valuable relationship.

CASE HISTORY #11

Focused arbitration takes a bite out of litigation costs to settle case

The owner of patents covering semiconductor manufacturing technology sued a semiconductor manufacturer for infringement of its patents. After more than a year of discovery, it became apparent that patent validity would not be an issue for trial, because the validity of the patents had been litigated in a previous case and their validity was upheld. The issues of patent infringement and damages were still vigorously contested. For time and cost efficiencies, the parties agreed to resolve these issues through an expedited binding arbitration process before an arbitrator with experience litigating patent infringement issues.

The arbitration hearing would be limited to evidence and arguments regarding the patent infringement issue (i.e., claim interpretation and infringement). In this regard, each party called only a few witnesses. To further focus the process, the parties agreed that after the selected arbitrator decided the question of infringement, depending on that outcome, the alleged infringer would pay either a high amount of damages, if the patent owner successfully proved infringement in the arbitration, or a low amount of damages if the alleged infringer proved noninfringement in the arbitration. The arbitrator had no discretion on whether there would be any payment of damages or the amount of damages defendant would pay.

An expedited hearing was held, after which the arbitrator issued a written reasoned award. Based upon the arbitrator's determination of infringement and the parties' prior agreement to predetermined high and low damages amounts, the defendant paid the higher agreed-to amount of damages. The parties then executed a settlement agreement based on the agreed outcome and dismissed the federal court case.

This case exemplifies how alternatives to litigation can be strategically combined with litigation to obtain an efficient outcome that the parties can trust. Through self-determination, the parties chose an arbitrator with the requisite experience and gravitas, extracted from the litigation the infringement and damages issues at the heart of their dispute, and tailored a focused and expedited arbitration process to provide business certainty.

CASE HISTORY #12

Can a presiding judge wear two resolution hats at the same time?

During a heavily contested patent infringement and trade secret misappropriation case pending in federal district court, it became clear to the parties that the largest amount of damages concerned the trade secret misappropriation claim. The defendant attempted to get the trade secret claim dismissed several times by various pre-trial motions (i.e., motion to dismiss, summary judgment), but each time the district judge denied the motions, holding there were contested issues of fact for the jury to decide. The parties were also far apart on the amount of damages, particularly on the damages for the trade secret misappropriation claim.

On the eve of trial, the district judge, who would be presiding over the jury trial, and who was very familiar with the facts and key legal issues, having decided the aforementioned pre-trial motions, proposed to the parties that he thought he could help them resolve the case through mediation. His suggested process was part mediator proposal and part nonbinding arbitrator. The parties agreed to engage the judge in this manner and they agreed to waive any objections related thereto. The parties and the judge tailored a process that would (1) allow the parties to "have their day in court"; (2) provide the judge with a brief summary judgment-style presentation on the contested issues; and (3) solicit from the judge a nonbinding settlement recommendation.

On the weekend before the jury trial was set to begin, the judge heard presentations from both sides on the contested patent infringement, trade secret, and damages issues in the case, with each party's principals in attendance. After the presentations, the judge sequestered himself, and the next day came back to the parties and principals with a detailed proposal to settle the case based upon his evaluation of the merits of the patent infringement and misappropriation claims, as well as the damages claims. The judge's proposal, which he delivered orally, was a compromise and it included a detailed plan for the payment of damages over time.

The principals of each party agreed that the judge's proposal was acceptable, so the case settled before the trial began based on that proposal.

This case exemplifies how parties can leverage the litigation process to obtain a settlement opportunity that embodies a fair alternative process, provides them with business certainty, removes the risk of significant financial exposure, and curtails further expense and time (including trial, appeal, and possible remand). Here, the parties had the benefit of full discovery and by way of multiple pre-trial motions the judge was already schooled in the legal issue presenting the most significant risk—trade secret misappropriation. Furthermore, the judge was someone who both parties respected in implementing the agreed-upon process and who had experience in other cases deciding similar issues.

How the parties proceeded here might not be a common choice for trial counsel or their clients and it might not be an opportunity presented often to parties and their counsel. But the parties grabbed a brass ring here in soliciting the judge's proposal (and a "reality check") at an opportune time. Perhaps, had the parties not agreed to the proposal "as is," they might have been incentivized to negotiate on their own or with the judge's help to reach a resolution, in any event.

Conclusion

Experience confirms that ADR works in resolving IP/Technology disputes practically and strategically. The case histories included here are just the tip of the iceberg. But, as espoused in this chapter, success is neither probable nor likely unless the parties and their counsel are willing and able to try ADR. Having counsel (in-house and outside) who are knowledgeable about, and experienced with, ADR processes is a significant benefit. Also, engaging an experienced neutral(s) whom the parties and counsel trust and respect is important. The neutral may help not only implement the ADR process, but also help plan it.

This chapter provides a taste for putting ADR to work to imagine better results for resolving IP/Technology disputes. The remainder of this book is intended to provide the means for doing so.

CHAPTER 2

Forward-Looking ADR Agreements: An Ounce of Prevention Is Worth Many Pounds of Cure

Theo Cheng[1]

The best preparation for good work tomorrow is to do good work today.

—Elbert Hubbard

Before anything else, preparation is the key to success.

—Alexander Graham Bell

Introduction[2]

For many intellectual property (IP) and technology disputes, alternative dispute resolution (ADR) often embodies less expensive, faster, and potentially more effective methods of resolution than court litigation. This is true for both U.S. and multinational, or cross-border, disputes. Moreover, unlike litigation, arbitration is widely enforceable across borders, and courts will often enforce the arbitration agreement even if the validity of the remainder of the contract is at issue. Another advantage of ADR is in crafting ad hoc rules, thereby creating a bespoke process that meets the parties' specific needs.

In drafting IP/Technology agreements, it is essential to consider a *forward-looking* ADR section comprising ADR provisions to address disputes before they arise. Also, in many other situations where the parties are

1. This chapter is a derivative work based upon Chapter 2 written by Frank L. Politano, Esq., from the Second Edition of this book. That chapter was a derivative work based upon Chapter 1 co-authored by David Hill, Esq., and Ronald Bleeker, Esq., from the First Edition of this book. For their assistance in preparing this chapter, the author gratefully acknowledges Adrienne R. Fields, Esq., founder of the Law Office of Adrienne Fields, and Lea Haber Kuck, Esq., retired partner at Skadden, Arps, Meagher & Flom LLP.

2. See Glossary for definition of frequently used terms.

not otherwise bound by contract, but where disputes over IP rights often arise (e.g., license, IP infringement, and false advertising disputes between competitors), it may make sense for the parties to have a standing, custom-crafted ADR agreement by which a dispute that may arise can be submitted to, for example, mediation and/or arbitration without resorting to court.

Where the parties to a transaction have the foresight to include a well-crafted ADR clause in their agreement, experience shows that the subsequent ADR process will normally work better and more efficiently than where this clause is absent or inadequate. Agreeing on the type(s) of ADR process(es) and key procedural elements is usually easier when the parties have not yet become adversaries. Although an ADR clause may not anticipate all of the issues that can arise in a dispute, its mere presence should afford the parties greater certainty as to how the resolution of a dispute will unfold and will reduce delay in getting the ADR started—a factor that can be critical once a dispute has erupted.

Surprisingly, many IP agreements do not address the issue of dispute resolution at all, or do so only in a cursory manner. Often this is because the parties do not want to delay the completion of the business deal by prolonging negotiations over how to handle a potential future dispute that, in the innocent enthusiasm of a new agreement, seems remote and improbable. Also, the important issues are often left for the last innings of the negotiation and, if held over until the end, are given short shrift. Consequently, ADR clauses are often inserted at the last minute before an agreement is executed, leading to their being referred to as "midnight clauses."

Some agreements simply refer the dispute to arbitration without providing important details, such as the arbitral authority or the rules that will control. In some cases, it is not clear whether the parties really mean arbitration or mediation. Another, but still deficient, variation is the agreement that specifies an arbitral authority (e.g., American Arbitration Association (AAA), World Intellectual Property Organization (WIPO), International Chamber of Commerce (ICC), JAMS), but omits key details, such as the location of the arbitration, the language to be used in the proceeding, the number of panelists, or the applicable substantive law. In such a situation, the clause is deficient only in the sense that the parties have lost control over being able to select those details by agreement (i.e., they are less likely to agree to new terms after the dispute arises).

Other agreements adopt a multistage process (such as a step or escalation clause) in which increasingly more senior executives of the parties engage in a series of good-faith talks to try to resolve the dispute. If these fail, the parties are either directed into a specific type of ADR process or are left to litigate if they wish. In corporations in which the senior executives have the motivation and determination to resolve disputes, this can be an effective strategy. But the multistage option may not be suitable for entities where corporate management are not committed to ADR or use the steps as a strategy to delay resolution. Likewise, some senior executives, especially those who have inherited an agreement, may be reluctant to settle IP/Technology disputes because they are unfamiliar with the history of the contractual relationship or are unwilling to take responsibility for the resolution.

A well-crafted ADR clause in an IP agreement should contain ample detail about the key elements of the ADR process to give the parties a good understanding of how it will work and to enable them to initiate the process promptly with minimum negotiation over procedural details. A number of ADR institutions helpfully offer model clauses and, of course, specify their own organization as the appropriate administering institution. Practitioners have developed their own model clauses from personal experience that can be used either with a specified administering institution or in an ad hoc (non-administered) process.

Alternatively, if the parties want to provide for ad hoc administration by an arbitration panel without developing their own rules and procedures, they may agree to use the rules of the United Nations Commission on International Trade Law (UNCITRAL)[3] or the non-administered rules of the International Institute for Conflict Prevention & Resolution (CPR).[4]

A cautionary note: The availability of model clauses or, worse, taking an ADR clause from another agreement, can be a dangerous temptation. The parties often consider ADR for future disputes very late in the negotiations and do not focus attention on important details. For these reasons, the parties may be tempted to avoid additional delay and negotiation by simply using an off-the shelf ADR clause. This chapter notes the importance of giving advance and careful thought to considering appropriate clauses for the agreement at hand, the parties to the agreement, and the anticipated nature of the disputes.

The following sections of this chapter identify some of the important factors to consider in drafting an ADR clause in an IP agreement—that is, before any dispute has arisen. The issues covered, however, are also

3. *See* UNCITRAL, UNCITRAL Arbitration Rules (2021), https://uncitral.un.org/sites/uncitral.un.org/files/media-documents/uncitral/en/21-07996_expedited-arbitration-e-ebook.pdf. UNCITRAL adopted the UNCITRAL rules in 1976. The General Assembly of the United Nations recommended the UNCITRAL rules for use in the settlement of international commercial disputes that same year. G.A. Res. 31/98 (Dec. 15, 1976).

4. CPR, CPR Procedures & Clauses for Non-Administered Arbitration Rules (2018) [hereinafter CPR Non-Administered Rules], https://drs.cpradr.org/rules/arbitration/non-administered/2018-cpr-non-administered-arbitration-rules (last visited Mar. 23, 2025).

relevant to the negotiation of arbitration agreements after a dispute has arisen and for the drafter in considering whether to use or modify a particular model clause.

Finally, it is desirable for the drafter of an ADR clause to have some understanding of the ADR process(es) selected and, ideally, some actual experience with them. Absent such experience, the drafter should at least consult someone with hands-on experience so that the details and choices of the ADR clause can be presented to the client in a real-world context.

I. Raising the ADR Issue in the Negotiation Process

At the outset, negotiators should consider this practical issue: when and how to raise the prospect of an ADR clause in the negotiation process. This is often the elephant in the room that no one wants to talk about.

Partly, this may result from the euphoria of striking a deal, when the parties do not want to dispel their good feelings by talking about unknown difficulties that may lie ahead. (It is like talking about a prenuptial agreement while planning a wedding—it seems to be in bad taste.) In addition, the ADR clause is not usually the provision that is uppermost in the minds of the business executives who are negotiating the deal. They are most concerned about issues such as (1) what they are getting (or giving) in the IP agreement (i.e., the scope of the license or permission, what IP and technology is and is not covered) and (2) what consideration they will have to pay or will receive. Once business-related points such as these have been negotiated to the parties' mutual satisfaction, interest in other clauses rapidly wanes, and there is impatience to get the agreement completed. Dispute resolution provisions are usually found near the end of the agreement, embedded among boilerplate provisions that are often of little concern to the business client. Engaging in a protracted dispute about one of these clauses, or attempting to draft a lengthy and elaborate ADR provision, at a late stage when the key provisions of the agreement have already been hammered out, is too often seen as lawyers holding up the deal.

If so, how does one raise the ADR issue in the negotiation process?

In answering this question, it may be useful to distinguish between domestic and international IP agreements. In international IP agreements, the use of ADR is a common way to resolve disputes. Indeed, in some countries (especially when dealing with companies that are effectively government entities), ADR may be required. For this reason, business executives who routinely negotiate international IP agreements will expect to see an ADR clause in the agreement and are familiar with the major provisions. Additionally, in the international context, arbitration is a common way to resolve disputes because it is generally easier to enforce an arbitration award internationally than a court judgment (except in the context where local law does not permit arbitration of IP/Technology disputes).[5]

In contrast, in domestic agreements between U.S. companies, there is much greater variation in practice. Some companies will routinely include an ADR clause, while others will not—they may be willing to engage in initial dispute resolution discussions between executives but, if those are unsuccessful, will reserve the right to pursue all other remedies (i.e., to bring suit). Many companies have signed a generalized pledge established by CPR[6] that says that they will "consider" ADR as a way of resolving disputes. In some cases, companies may actually have a policy against entering into arbitration (in favor of mediation), usually unwritten and often as the result of an unhappy prior experience. For these kinds of reasons, it is important to know the client's view of ADR (e.g., business, in-house counsel) before negotiating or drafting the IP agreement.

---

5. Many jurisdictions, including the United States, Canada, Australia, and the United Kingdom, permit parties to arbitrate all IP issues (including patent validity), whereas other countries, such as France and China, do not permit all IP issues to be arbitrated. *See* Joseph P. Zammit & Jamie Hu, *Arbitrating International Intellectual Property Disputes*, 64 Am. Arb. Ass'n Disp. Resol. J. 74, 74 (2010) ("When considering whether to provide for arbitration of IP disputes, one must consider not only whether such issues would be arbitrable under the laws at the seat of arbitration, but also under the laws of those jurisdictions where enforcement would likely be necessary.").

6. CPR describes its ADR Pledge as "a statement of policy aimed at encouraging greater use of flexible, creative and constructive approaches in resolving business-related disputes. It promotes systematic, early resolution and establishes a flexible framework for helping to resolve complex multi-party disputes." *Pre-Dispute ADR Processes*, CPR, https://www.cpradr.org/adr-101---pre-dispute-adr-processes (last visited Mar. 23, 2025). CPR's Corporate Policy Statement provides:

> We recognize that for many disputes there is a less expensive, more effective method of resolution than the traditional lawsuit. Alternative dispute resolution (ADR) procedures involve collaborative techniques which can often spare businesses the high costs of litigation.
>
> In recognition of the foregoing, we subscribe to the following statements of principle on behalf of our company and its domestic subsidiaries:
>
>> In the event of a business dispute between our company and another company which has made or will then make a similar statement, we are prepared to explore with that other party resolution of the dispute through negotiation or ADR techniques before pursuing full-scale litigation. If either party believes that the dispute is not suitable for ADR techniques, or if such techniques do not produce results satisfactory to the disputants, either party may proceed with litigation.

Corporate Policy Statement, CPR, https://www.cpradr.org/corporate-policy-statement (last visited Mar. 23, 2025).

If the client's position on ADR is unknown or undecided, it is important for counsel to raise the subject with the client early on, preferably before negotiations begin. In this discussion, one can present the different types of ADR that are available so that the client has a range of options to consider and to offer to the other side. (See Chapter 5 regarding tools to use for choosing ADR.) Some of the key points discussed, such as the location of the forum and timing, can easily be reviewed with the client in advance. Ideally, the drafter could prepare a sample ADR clause in writing that the client can review and have ready should the issue arise in the negotiations.

How is this issue raised with the other side? One effective way to accomplish this is to raise it early on in the initial term sheet or in the preliminary negotiation. Of course, this depends on many factors, including the personal relations between the parties and their counsel. However, it could be raised during a break in the negotiations or over lunch, merely to test the waters. Alternatively, one counsel could draft an ADR clause and give it to their opposing counsel to consider, perhaps with the statement that it is merely being offered to begin a dialogue. Who knows where such a dialogue may lead?

Finally, it may be quite beneficial for transactional counsel, at some point, to seek input from their litigation colleagues who, in representing clients in ADR processes set forth in a contract, have seen the consequences of these negotiations in practice (e.g., an arbitration clause that has practical limitations). Consulting with such colleagues when drafting and/or negotiating an ADR clause may help avoid pitfalls and problematic language that could prove to be detrimental to the parties years later.

Case in point: During the negotiations over a patent licensing agreement, the patentee's counsel raised the need for a possible dispute resolution mechanism early on in the discussions, rather than waiting until much closer to the time when the agreement would be executed. After a few rounds of comments and edits on that provision, the parties had nearly reached an agreement on the clause, but differed on a number of key points, including the nature and scope of the document and information exchange and whether depositions would be needed. As was the standard practice at her firm, the patentee's counsel sought the advice of her litigation colleague down the hall who had experience both mediating and arbitrating licensing disputes under a wide variety of different ADR clauses. Her colleague recommended several ways to streamline the process and minimize hurdles should a dispute arise, including advising on the benefits and drawbacks of undertaking an ad hoc versus an administered arbitration; which administering institution was the most appropriate and cost-effective for the anticipated disputes that might arise; the number of arbitrators that might be appropriate; and whether the arbitrators should be required to have any particular experience/training or technical knowledge. After consideration and further consultation, the colleague's recommendations made their way into the continued negotiations over the dispute resolution mechanism, which was ultimately finalized to both counterparties' satisfaction.

II. Selecting Rules and Procedures

Chapters 1 and 5 briefly discuss various ADR processes and tools commonly used to resolve IP/Technology disputes. Before endeavoring to draft an ADR provision, counsel will likely have discussed with their clients the kinds of ADR processes often used in IP agreements, as well as which are best suited to their client and to anticipated disputes under the agreement. Once the parties discuss and agree on which of those processes they want to use to resolve future disputes, they need to consider what rules and procedures might be most effective to govern the process(es). Broadly speaking, there are two approaches—ADR proceedings under ad hoc rules or under the rules of an established ADR-administering institution.[7]

A. Developing Ad Hoc Rules for an IP/Technology Dispute

An ad hoc ADR process is one that is not administered by an ADR institution. The parties determine all aspects of the process themselves, including the rules for conducting the process. The main advantage of developing rules from scratch is that the parties have the maximum flexibility to tailor a process to the type of controversy that is likely to arise from the agreement and that meets the parties' particular needs.[8] For example, if the dispute is likely to involve a particular technology, the clause can specify that one or more of the neutrals must have some background with that technology. Likewise, a party-designed process can define the precise scope of discovery that the parties want and the time limits for the process.

Ten essential provisions for an arbitration agreement are as follows:

1. The agreement to arbitrate
2. The disputes to be arbitrated
3. The governing rules
4. The institution, if any, that will administer the arbitration

---

7. It is possible to combine approaches in one escalation clause so that the parties will begin to resolve their dispute with ad hoc rules for discussions between executives, and if that stage does not resolve the dispute, then move on to mediation and/or arbitration under the rules of a specified ADR institution.

8. ADR institutions may have standard processes that the parties must adhere to without modification when using the rules of that institution. For example, under the ICC's rules, the parties and the arbitral panel must draw up a "terms of reference" as a preliminary matter in the arbitration process. This requirement adds time and cost to the proceeding. Panel selection is another area of institutional control where, if the parties have adopted administered rules that they have not modified, it is likely that they are limited to panelists on the institution's list and selection is by the institution's procedures.

5. The place (seat) of the arbitration[9]
6. In an international agreement, the language of the arbitration
7. The applicable (substantive) law, if not provided elsewhere in the agreement
8. The procedural law that will apply to the arbitration
9. The number of arbitrators and how they will be chosen
10. An agreement that judgment may be entered on the award

If parties want to avoid the risk of omitting something from their ad hoc rules, they can adopt, as part of those rules, the non-administered rules of an arbitration institution as a gap-filler for issues the parties did not address.[10]

Case in point: In a contractual dispute involving two biotechnology companies, the parties had set forth in their agreement an ad hoc arbitration process including identifying the arbitration seat; providing for limited document exchange, interrogatories, and depositions with efficient deadlines; providing for fact witness and expert disclosures and expert reports; describing the nature and deadlines for prehearing briefs and exhibits; describing hearing procedures for managing time and sequestering witnesses; and describing the form of the award. The panel worked with the parties to modify the ad hoc process somewhat to meet the parties' current needs. The AAA Commercial Rules filled in to address issues that the parties did not address in their agreement.

Ad hoc rules in IP/Technology agreements often reflect the parties' priorities and objectives. See the following examples of expedited binding arbitration under ad hoc rules.

Case in point: Two companies were parties to a license and development agreement containing an escalation clause with ad hoc procedures for good-faith negotiations of executives, followed by mediation and then arbitration. The arbitration procedures were geared to an efficient and pragmatic process, including (1) a one-month time frame to choose the arbitration panel; (2) a two-month time frame after choosing the

9. The seat of the arbitration is a significant choice in an arbitration proceeding and need not necessarily be limited to the location where the evidentiary hearings are actually held. There are other significant aspects to this choice that are covered later in this chapter. *See infra* Section IV.A.

10. For example: "The Parties and arbitral panel shall apply the arbitration rules of the United Nations Commission on International Trade Law that are then in effect for issues not addressed in these Arbitration Rules and Procedures or elsewhere in the Agreement."

panel to hold the evidentiary hearing; (3) a city identified to hold the hearing; (4) short times for exchanging reliance documents, propounding five document requests, and producing documents; (5) a ten-day time frame before the hearing for exchanging/submitting to the panel the exhibits, witness lists, a short pre-trial submission, and a proposed ruling/remedy without reasons on each issue to be resolved; (6) two hearing days (with details for ordering and streamlining the presentation of testimony and argument); (7) short post-hearing briefs filed a week after the hearing; (8) a two-week time frame for the arbitral panel to issue its award on the merits, which was the selection of one of the parties' proposed ruling/remedy of each of the disputed issues; (9) a short time frame for supplying submissions supporting attorneys' fees; and (10) a short time frame for issuance of the final award.

Case in point: In a non-administered arbitration of a multimillion-dollar dispute, a utility company and its counterparty agreed to a streamlined arbitration process that included prefiled written testimony and exhibits, a stipulation of undisputed material facts, and an opportunity for live cross-examination of witnesses on any genuine issues of material fact. The party-appointed panel managing the process embraced the approach, encouraged the parties' active collaboration and cooperation on scheduling and information exchange, and ultimately concluded the hearing in a single day, within nine months after the panel chair had been appointed. The parties reached a negotiated resolution before the panel issued an award.

Ad hoc rules can also play a useful role for certain recurring issues between the same parties (e.g., parties working together to develop a product or copyrightable work). More specifically, having customized ad hoc rules may provide a cost-effective, expeditious path to rendering multiple/ongoing determinations and the development of a body of decisions that act as a form of *stare decisis* to govern future disputes between, or ongoing conduct by, the parties.[11] In addition to development projects, in many industries where there is vigorous competition (e.g., over-the-counter drugs, car rental services, telecom services), conflicting advertising claims are often made. To minimize the cost and time of resolving such disputes confidentially, it is not uncommon for companies to customize a set of rules or procedures.

---

11. As mentioned in Chapter 1, parties to a contract or adverse to one another may use a "standing neutral" to help them resolve ongoing disputes. *See* Case History #6 in Section III of Chapter 1. Concomitant with the use of a standing neutral would be adopting ad hoc rules that the parties and the neutral implement to resolve any disputes that arise.

Some of the advantages of a predetermined customized set of ad hoc rules for arbitrating ongoing disputes between the same parties include:

- The use of a panelist that has developed familiarity with the industry, its customs and practices, and types of claims made
- The development of a specific body of law, or *stare decisis*, relating to typical disputes that can help quickly resolve ongoing disputes or enable the parties to avoid disputes
- A standardized set of temporal guidelines to enable disputes to be resolved quickly
- Streamlined submissions to keep costs low
- An efficient, cost-effective mechanism of reducing typical disputes to allow management to take risks it would not otherwise take with the certain knowledge that any disputes can be resolved quickly and at low cost

In IP/Technology disputes, mediation is often used as a dispute resolution process. It is not uncommon for parties to forgo adopting the mediation rules of an ADR organization or having an ADR organization administer the mediation. They often engage a mediator and then work with the mediator to tailor a process that works for them. That said, the parties will want to identify key terms (e.g., what kinds of disputes they agree to mediate in the future and the time frames for choosing a mediator and conducting the mediation) when drafting a pre-dispute resolution clause. Similarly, when disputing parties are not contractually bound but agree to pursue mediation before or even after filing a lawsuit, they often forgo adopting an ADR institution's mediation rules and having such an organization administer it. In both instances, the parties will choose the mediator on their own, the mediator administers the process (e.g., schedules calls and the mediation session(s), sends invoices, collects fees), and the mediator works with the parties to tailor a process by which the mediation will be conducted (e.g., making disclosures, setting date/time/location for the mediation session(s), determining date/kind of mediation submission(s), identifying participants, using joint sessions and caucuses, maintaining confidentiality). The mediator may set the agreed-upon ad hoc process in a letter agreement for the mediator and the parties to sign.

The downside to having custom rules for any ADR process(es) is that the parties must design the process from scratch and negotiate and articulate the rules and procedures in the IP agreement itself or in an addendum or side agreement. This can take vigilance and time to negotiate and draft.[12] If

12. The parties will want to keep both big-picture objectives in mind and essential details when drafting. For example, the parties may agree to arbitration, but neglect to mention that they want binding arbitration. "The overriding goal of the drafter of an

the anticipated future disputes are complex and involve sophisticated technology or unresolved issues of IP law, this drafting exercise may require careful consideration of how best to position the parties should a dispute arise. In simpler cases, parties can develop a straightforward plan to resolve a dispute with concise and well-defined rules.

Instead of developing rules, as mentioned earlier, parties wishing to pursue ADR processes such as mediation and arbitration on an ad hoc, non-administered basis may adopt in full the UNCITRAL or non-administered CPR rules mentioned previously and modify them to fit their particular needs.[13]

Informal meetings between increasingly senior levels of executives are often specified as a starting point for ad hoc proceedings. These are likely to be relatively informal proceedings, with little being specified in the ADR clause other than (1) the level (or else the title or sometimes even the name) of the executives involved; (2) the triggering event for the informal discussions; and (3) some time limits for various stages of the proceedings. For example:

> In the event of any claim, controversy, or dispute arising from or in connection with this Agreement, or with any amendments thereof, either Party may initiate a dispute resolution proceeding by giving written notice of its claim or position to the other Party. Within ten days of the date of such notice, the managers of the respective divisions of each Party that is involved in this Agreement will meet for not more than one day at a mutually convenient time and place to seek in good faith a resolution of the dispute. If the division managers do not resolve the dispute, then within a further ten days from their meeting, representatives of the senior management of each of the Parties will meet for not more than one day at a mutually convenient time and place to seek in good faith a resolution of this dispute.[14]

Another example of how parties can fashion ad hoc rules to meet their needs is specifying within the ad hoc rules the process for *neutral evaluation* or *expert determination*.[15] This is especially useful where one legal

arbitration clause should be to draft a provision that, if a dispute arises, will help the parties obtain an arbitration award without a detour through the court system." John M. Townsend, *Drafting Arbitration Clauses: Avoiding the 7 Deadly Sins*, 58 DISP. RESOL. J. AM. ARB. ASS'N 1, 1 (2003).

13. *See* Appendix to this chapter.

14. The parties may further provide in the ADR clause for mediation, a neutral evaluation, or arbitration if the senior managers do not resolve the dispute.

15. See Chapter 1 for a discussion of how such neutral evaluation and expert determination can be used in IP/Technology cases.

or factual issue is likely to be determinative (e.g., Is the product within the scope of the patent? Is the advertising false on its face? Does the product contain more than 50 percent of a certain compound? Who is the owner or inventor?). In this process, one or more neutrals are asked to give the parties their determination or opinion of the dispute or of some specified issue. If the parties adopt this approach, the ADR clause should provide whether the determination is binding or merely advisory. Other considerations for drafting the clause are:

- How the neutral gives the opinion (e.g., to both parties at the same time, to the parties separately)
- Whether the neutral merely gives an opinion or can engage with the parties to try to resolve the dispute; alternatively, the parties could provide that the neutral merely gives his or her views to the parties' executives, followed by some period of direct negotiation between the executives or mediation by another neutral
- What information (e.g., documents, speaking with fact witnesses, survey evidence) the neutral may consider in making a determination
- By what date the neutral should make a determination

Notwithstanding the foregoing, one of the main disadvantages of an ad hoc arbitration process is that there is no administering institution to appoint arbitrators if one party does not name one (in a party-appointed process) or the parties cannot agree on a chair. In such a case, the other party generally would need to seek court intervention.[16]

B. Mediating an IP/Technology Dispute Under Established Rules

Where parties feel the need to provide the governing rules, many of the established ADR institutions (e.g., WIPO, AAA) have model rules for mediation.[17]

---

16. But see CPR NON-ADMINISTERED RULES, *supra* note 4, Rule 6, by which the parties afford authority to CPR to intervene in a non-administered arbitration proceeding in the event that

> (i) a party has failed to appoint the arbitrator to be appointed by it; (ii) the parties have failed to appoint the arbitrator(s) to be appointed by them acting jointly; (iii) the party appointed arbitrators have failed to appoint the third arbitrator; (iv) the parties have provided that one or more arbitrators shall be appointed by CPR; or (v) the multi-party nature of the dispute calls for CPR to appoint all members of a three-member Tribunal pursuant to Rule 5.5.

17. *See, e.g.*, WIPO ARBITRATION AND MEDIATION CENTER, WIPO MEDIATION, ARBITRATION, EXPEDITED ARBITRATION, AND EXPERT DETERMINATION RULES AND CLAUSES (2020) [hereinafter WIPO RULES], https://www.wipo.int/edocs/pubdocs

The advantage of these rules is that they can easily be incorporated by reference into an ADR clause. The parties, however, need to be familiar with these rules before incorporating them into an agreement to ensure that they are acceptable, including that the parties will not be bound by unwanted procedures. Of course, the parties can also agree to supplement or modify these rules either at the time they are negotiating the contract or later, when either/both of the parties have invoked the mediation process (assuming, of course, they can agree to changes once a dispute has arisen).

WIPO, for example, has prepared a variety of model clauses for different forms of ADR that can be inserted into an IP agreement and provides assistance "in adapting the model clauses to the circumstances of [the parties'] contractual relationship."[18] What follows is the WIPO proposed contract clause for dispute resolution by means of mediation:

> Any dispute, controversy, or claim arising under, out of or relating to this contract and any subsequent amendments of this contract, including, without limitation, its formation, validity, binding effect, interpretation, performance, breach or termination, as well as non-contractual claims, shall be submitted to mediation in accordance with the WIPO Mediation Rules. The place of mediation shall be [specify place]. The language to be used in the mediation shall be [specify language].[19]

Mediation rules are often less detailed than arbitration rules, but they still prescribe time limits (e.g., for selecting the mediator, for holding the mediation) and other key elements of the mediation process. Typically, mediations employ only one mediator (although not always), and the ADR clause can even require that the mediator have a specific background (e.g., an IP attorney, a U.S. IP attorney, a U.S. IP attorney with a chemical background, or

---

/en/wipo_pub_446_2020.pdf; *see also* AAA, COMMERCIAL ARBITRATION RULES AND MEDIATION PROCEDURES (2022) [hereinafter AAA COMMERCIAL ARBITRATION RULES], https://www.adr.org/sites/default/files/Commercial-Rules_Web.pdf.

18. *Recommended WIPO Contract Clauses and Submission Agreements*, WIPO, https://www.wipo.int/amc/en/clauses/index.html (last visited Mar. 23, 2025). The model clauses are divided into two general categories: first, for contract clauses relating to *future* disputes; and second, for clauses suitable for submission agreements regarding an *existing* dispute, including a dispute pending before a national court. The first is relevant to this chapter. WIPO then divides that category into three main subcategories, each of which deals with a different type of ADR: mediation, arbitration, and expert determination. Finally, the subcategories are further divided to provide for expedited procedures or for combinations of types of dispute resolution, such as the use of expedited arbitration or mediation followed by either arbitration or expert determination. *See id.*

19. *Future Disputes: WIPO Mediation Clause*, WIPO, https://www.wipo.int/amc/en/clauses/mediation/ (last visited Mar. 23, 2025).

a U.S. IP attorney with a chemical background who is experienced in opinions/litigations). The more requirements that are added to an ADR clause in an effort to get a well-qualified mediator, the more condensed is the field of candidates who may be available and acceptable to the parties.

As mentioned previously with respect to ad hoc rules, parties may combine mediation with other forms of ADR to address issues that could enhance resolution. For example, some ADR institutions provide established rules for neutral evaluation or expert determination whereby the parties ask a neutral to give them his or her view of the dispute or of some determinative issue. The considerations discussed previously with regard to this process under Section II.A apply equally here. Parties may combine this process in a staged proceeding with mediation under established rules. For example, a sample clause for early neutral evaluations (ENEs) followed by arbitration administered by the AAA might be as follows:

> If a dispute arises out of or relates to this contract, or the breach thereof, and if the dispute cannot be settled through negotiation, the parties agree first to try in good faith to settle the dispute by Early Neutral Evaluation administered by the American Arbitration Association under its Early Neutral Evaluation Procedures before resorting to arbitration, litigation, or some other dispute resolution procedure.[20]

C. Arbitrating an IP/Technology Dispute Under Established Rules

Arbitration is the form of ADR that is most likely to contain a reference in the ADR clause to the formal rules of an established arbitral authority (e.g., AAA, WIPO, ICC, JAMS). As discussed earlier, the main drafting advantage of using established rules is that the clause can simply incorporate the rules by reference, thereby avoiding the need to burden the IP agreement with detailed provisions as to the various steps and elements of an ADR proceeding. Such rules may not address all possible issues, and there may be special factors, options, or variations that the parties may wish to address in the ADR clause. As in the mediation context, parties can also agree to supplement or modify their chosen rules either when they are negotiating the contract or when either or both of the parties have invoked the arbitration process.

Particularly in international IP agreements, specifying the rules of an established arbitral institution can alleviate concerns about perceived national or cultural biases. As discussed later in this chapter, some arbitral institutions

20. Sample taken from AAA, Early Neutral Evaluation: Getting an Expert's Assessment, https://www.adr.org/sites/default/files/document_repository/Early_Neutral_Evaluation.pdf (last visited Mar. 23, 2025).

are perceived, rightly or wrongly, as being more favorable to citizens of their home country or region, whereas others are considered more neutral.

If the parties include an arbitration provision to refer any dispute to a recognized arbitral institution without actually reading the relevant rules or without having experienced arbitrating under such rules, the parties may not appreciate the import of the rules on how they will resolve their dispute. For example, WIPO arbitration rules provide that, where a dispute is between parties of different nationalities, a single panelist should be a citizen from a neutral country, but that person may not be familiar with U.S. law.[21] In addition, arbitration proceedings under certain rules may have novel procedures (e.g., terms of reference under ICC rules) that add to the cost and time of the proceeding and may, therefore, not be optimal for a case where the amount at stake is low and time is short.

Many IP agreements adopt general commercial rules, such as the AAA Commercial Arbitration Rules. Some of the arbitration institutions (e.g., CPR[22] and AAA[23]) have specialized rules for patent cases. And several of those institutions, such as AAA and WIPO, offer alternative sets of rules in cases where the parties want an expedited procedure.[24] The main differences are that an expedited procedure will usually require only a single panelist, shorter time periods in which to prepare and file papers, and little

---

21. *See* WIPO RULES, *supra* note 17, art. 20(b).

22. In 1993, the CPR Technology Committee developed the Rules for Non-Administered Arbitration of Patent and Trade Secret Disputes, and, in 2005, CPR's International Commission on Patent Disputes revised them. *See* CPR, CPR PROCEDURES & CLAUSES: RULES FOR NON-ADMINISTERED ARBITRATION OF PATENT & TRADE SECRET DISPUTES (2005) [hereinafter CPR PATENT & TRADE SECRET ARBITRATION RULES], https://drs.cpradr.org/rules/arbitration/patent-trade-secret-arbitration-rules (last visited Mar. 23, 2025).

23. According to the Supplementary Rules:

> Unless the parties agree otherwise, these Supplementary Rules for the Resolution of Patent Disputes . . . , together with the Commercial Arbitration Rules and Mediation Procedures . . . shall apply to any dispute arising out of an agreement that provides for arbitration pursuant to any of the rules of the [AAA] where a party submits a patent dispute to arbitration and shall supplement any other applicable AAA rules.

AAA, RESOLUTION OF PATENT DISPUTES SUPPLEMENTARY RULES (2006) [hereinafter AAA PATENT SUPPLEMENTARY RULES], https://www.adr.org/sites/default/files/Resolution%20of%20Patent%20Disputes%20Supplementary%20Rules.pdf.

24. *See, e.g.*, WIPO ARBITRATION AND MEDIATION CENTER, WIPO EXPEDITED ARBITRATION RULES, SCHEDULE OF FEES, AND COSTS (2021) [hereinafter WIPO EXPEDITED ARBITRATION RULES], https://www.wipo.int/export/sites/www/amc/en/docs/expedited_arbitration_rules_and_fees_2024.pdf; AAA COMMERCIAL ARBITRATION RULES, *supra* note 17, at E-1 to E-10.

or no opportunity for discovery. This could be desirable in a case where the amount in question is small or the parties need a quick answer and they do not need discovery.

Arbitration clauses in IP agreements can range from the very short and simple to the lengthy and complex. Here is an example of a fairly simple arbitration clause referencing AAA's Patent Supplementary Rules:

> The Parties agree that any claim, controversy, or dispute arising from or relating to this Agreement, or to any amendments thereof, will be resolved by binding and final arbitration administered by the American Arbitration Association (AAA) under its *Resolution of Patent Disputes Supplementary Rules*. The arbitration will be conducted in English before a panel of three arbitrators appointed by the AAA. At least one of the arbitrators will be a U.S. lawyer who is experienced with U.S. patent litigation. The arbitration proceedings will be conducted in New York, New York. In determining its award, the arbitration panel will apply the internal, substantive laws of the State of New York without regard to any conflict of laws principles. A judgment based on the award of the arbitration panel may be sought by a Party in any court of competent jurisdiction, and the Parties hereby agree to personal jurisdiction in a court of competent jurisdiction in New York, New York, but solely for the purpose of entering and enforcing such judgment.

The following are other issues that could arise in the arbitration of IP/ Technology cases:

- Is there an overall time limit by which the arbitration must be concluded?
- Do the parties have to continue with performance during the pendency of the arbitration proceeding (e.g., royalty payments, transfers of technology)?
- Are there issues that the panel cannot consider (e.g., a panel could consider the scope of the agreement but not the validity of the licensed patents)?
- By incorporating a particular rule set, have the parties delegated arbitrability issues to the arbitrator?[25]

---

25. For example, the AAA Commercial Arbitration Rules provide that the parties have empowered the arbitrator to rule on arbitrability issues. *See* AAA COMMERCIAL ARBITRATION RULES, *supra* note 17, Rule R-7(a) ("The arbitrator shall have the power to rule on his or her own jurisdiction, including any objections with respect to the existence, scope, or validity of the arbitration agreement or to the arbitrability of any claim or counterclaim, without any need to refer such matters first to a court."). Most federal circuit and district courts and numerous state courts have held that, by

- Are the parties aware of any other pending arbitration proceeding that should be consolidated with the current one or any necessary parties who should be joined?[26]
- Should the clause cover in greater detail whether information exchange (discovery) is permitted? If so, what is the nature and extent of such discovery? Are there limits to discovery?
- Will the hearing include only written testimony or testimony by live witnesses?
- If the panel is required to provide a written award, what will be the scope of the reasoning (e.g., bare, reasoned, or findings of fact and conclusions of law)?[27]
- How are the costs of the arbitration divided between the parties?
- Is the prevailing party (however defined) entitled to its attorneys' fees from the non-prevailing party?

---

merely incorporating the AAA Commercial Arbitration Rules into an arbitration clause, the parties have clearly and unmistakably delegated that power to the arbitrator, consistent with the U.S. Supreme Court's holding in *First Options of Chicago, Inc. v. Kaplan*, 514 U.S. 938, 944 (1995). *See* TotalEnergies E&P USA, Inc. v. MP Gulf of Mex., LLC, 667 S.W.3d 694, 702–12 & nn.11–12 (Tex. 2023) (discussing and analyzing both federal and state court authorities, ultimately concluding that, "as a general rule, an agreement to arbitrate disputes in accordance with rules providing that the arbitrator 'shall have the power' to determine 'the arbitrability of any claim' incorporates those rules into the agreement and clearly and unmistakably demonstrates the parties' intent to delegate arbitrability issues to the arbitrator"). Notwithstanding this robust authority, the American Law Institute has taken the contrary view that mere incorporation is insufficient to operate as a proper delegation clause. *See* RESTATEMENT OF THE LAW, THE U.S. LAW OF INTERNATIONAL COMMERCIAL AND INVESTOR-STATE ARBITRATION § 5.1 (AM. L. INST. 2019).

26. Consolidation or joinder may be appropriate in situations involving multiple inventors, licensors, and distributors, and other linear relationships that may implicate several different arbitration agreements and/or non-signatories to such agreements. Administering institutions have promulgated rules addressing consolidation and joinder under certain circumstances. *See, e.g.*, AAA COMMERCIAL ARBITRATION RULES, *supra* note 17, R-8; CPR, CPR PROCEDURES & CLAUSES: ADMINISTERED ARBITRATION RULES Rules 3.12, 3.13 (2019), https://drs.cpradr.org/rules/arbitration/administered-arbitration-rules-2019 (last visited Mar. 23, 2025); JAMS, JAMS COMPREHENSIVE ARBITRATION RULES & PROCEDURES Rule 6(e) (2021), https://www.jamsadr.com/rules-comprehensive-arbitration/ (last visited Mar. 23, 2025).

27. In the international context, reasoned awards are generally required for enforcement purposes. Again, it would be prudent to consult in advance with local counsel in jurisdictions where enforcement might be required.

The parties can also construct a multistage procedure in which they establish in advance the rules for arbitration in the event that a prior mediation is unsuccessful. The following WIPO model clause exemplifies such a procedure:

> If, and to the extent that any dispute, controversy, or claim has not been settled pursuant to the mediation within 90 days of the commencement of the mediation, it shall, upon the filing of a Request for Arbitration by either party, be referred to and finally determined by arbitration in accordance with the WIPO Arbitration Rules. Alternatively, if before the expiration of the said period of 90 days, either party that fails to participate or to continue to participate in the mediation, the dispute, controversy, or claim shall, upon the filing of a Request for Arbitration by the other party, be referred to and finally determined by arbitration in accordance with the WIPO Arbitration Rules. The arbitral tribunal shall consist of a sole arbitrator. The place of the arbitration shall be New York, New York. The language to be used in the arbitral proceedings shall be English. The dispute, controversy, or claim referred to arbitration shall be decided in accordance with the internal, substantive laws of the State of New York without regard to any conflicts of law principles.[28]

Alternatively, rather than moving to arbitration, the parties may provide that a failure to achieve a resolution through mediation will be followed by an expert determination, which can be either binding or nonbinding. In yet another variation, the contract can contain a clause providing that the *initial* mechanism for dispute resolution will be an expert determination:

> Any dispute or difference between the parties arising under, out of or relating to [describe scope of the matter referred to expert determination] under this contract and any subsequent amendments of this contract shall be referred to expert determination in accordance with the WIPO Expert Determination Rules. The determination made by the expert shall [not] be binding upon the parties. The language to be used in the expert determination shall be English.[29]

Under WIPO rules, even where the parties designated the expert determination as binding, either party can nonetheless invoke a subsequent

28. *Future Disputes: WIPO Mediation Followed in the Absence of a Settlement, by [Expedited] Arbitration Clause*, WIPO, https://www.wipo.int/amc/en/clauses/med_arb/ (last visited Mar. 23, 2025).

29. *Future Disputes: WIPO Expert Determination, Binding Unless Followed by [Expedited] Arbitration Clause*, WIPO, https://www.wipo.int/amc/en/clauses/exp_det_arb/ (last visited Mar. 23, 2025).

arbitration if that party files a request for arbitration within a designated time period, as illustrated by the following clause:

> The determination made by the expert shall be binding upon the parties, unless within 30 days of the communication of the determination, the matter referred to expert determination is, upon the filing of a Request for Arbitration by either party, referred to and finally determined by arbitration in accordance with the WIPO Arbitration Rules. The arbitral authority shall consist of a sole arbitrator. The place of arbitration shall be London, England. The language to be used in the arbitral proceedings shall be English. The dispute or difference referred to arbitration shall be decided in accordance with the internal substantive laws of England and Wales with regard to any conflicts of law principles.[30]

III. Specifying an ADR Institution

Parties who want their ADR process(es) to be administered by an ADR institution, rather than handled ad hoc between the panel and the parties, need to choose the institution. There are many ADR institutions to choose from. A well-known administering institution for both domestic and international arbitrations favored by American companies is the AAA and its international division, the International Centre for Dispute Resolution (ICDR). There are several sets of AAA rules for different types of cases. Although the AAA Commercial Arbitration Rules are often cited and employed (alone) in IP cases, the AAA's Patent Supplementary Rules, which became effective on January 1, 2006, are particularly pertinent to patent and licensing disputes.[31]

In international IP agreements, based on experience, some foreign entities perceive the AAA as an American ADR institution. For this reason, a foreign party may seek to have the contract specify a more neutral authority. For many years, the most popular alternate choice was the ICC. Its rules tend

30. *Id.*

31. *See* AAA Patent Supplementary Rules, *supra* note 23, at 3. Note that these supplementary rules automatically apply unless otherwise agreed to by the parties. *See id.* Rule 1 ("Unless the parties agree otherwise, these Supplementary Rules for the Resolution of Patent Disputes ('Supplementary Rules'), together with the Commercial Arbitration Rules and Mediation Procedures ('Commercial Rules') shall apply to any dispute arising out of an agreement that provides for arbitration pursuant to any of the rules of the American Arbitration Association ('AAA') where a party submits a patent dispute to arbitration and shall supplement any other applicable AAA rules."). Thus, it is critical to understand what the parties have agreed to even if they are simply incorporating a particular set of rules.

to be fairly formal, with a great deal of emphasis on the terms of reference (i.e., the statement of the claims and issues in dispute and some particulars of the procedure). As with many rules, parties can use the ICC's rules to govern their arbitration proceeding in any city they choose for the hearing. However, the choice of forum for ICC arbitrations tends to be European cities, especially London, Paris, and Zurich.

For some time, arbitrations arising from disputes between Chinese government companies and Western companies were often held in Stockholm because that was acceptably neutral to Chinese entities. Today, however, Chinese companies often agree to other arbitral authorities, especially those that are relatively recent but well-established in East Asia. These include the China International Economic and Trade Arbitration Commission (CIETAC). Other regional ADR authorities have developed in commercial centers such as Tokyo, Cairo, and Singapore and may be of interest if both parties are located in that region. Each of these regional authorities has adopted its own set of rules.

Another administering institution that has emerged as a favorite in international agreements between Western and non-Western companies is WIPO, which is affiliated with the United Nations and based in Geneva. In 2009, WIPO published Mediation Rules and a set of Arbitration Rules (with separate rules for regular and expedited arbitrations), as well as a set of Rules for Expert Determinations, as mentioned earlier.

Institutional arbitration saves parties and their counsel the effort of drafting the arbitration rules and an arbitration clause, both of which are provided by the institution. Once the parties have selected an institution, they can incorporate that institution's clause into their contract *as is* or add other elements into the clause. Unless the parties have agreed to other rules, identifying the institution in the arbitration provision will inform the parties of the rules and procedures that will apply to their mediation or arbitration. For example, AAA's Commercial Mediation Procedures (M-1. Agreement of Parties) provide:

> Whenever, by stipulation or in their contract, the parties have provided for mediation or conciliation of existing or future disputes under the auspices of the American Arbitration Association or under these procedures, the parties and their representatives, unless agreed otherwise in writing, shall be deemed to have made these procedural guidelines, as amended and in effect as of the date of filing of a request for mediation, a part of their agreement and designate the AAA as the administrator of their mediation.[32]

32. AAA COMMERCIAL ARBITRATION RULES, *supra* note 17, M-1.

Likewise, AAA's Commercial Arbitration Rules (R-1. Agreement of Parties) provide:

> The parties shall be deemed to have made these rules a part of their arbitration agreement whenever they have provided for arbitration by the American Arbitration Association (hereinafter AAA) under its Commercial Arbitration Rules or for arbitration by the AAA of a domestic commercial dispute without specifying particular rules.[33]

Additionally, the benefits the parties receive from the institutional arbitration may include assistance from case managers (e.g., selection of arbitrators, scheduling, payment of costs/fees, conflict checking/disclosure issues) and access to lists of qualified arbitrators from many regions having various expertise.

IV. Customizing the ADR Clause

In addition to specifying the type of ADR process and (if appropriate) the administering institution whose rules will be used, there are a number of other features that should be considered for the ADR clause. The following is intended as a checklist, primarily for arbitration clauses. Some of the items may be more important to parties in a particular negotiation than others. Thus, they may wish to address them specifically in the arbitration clause. Others (such as the scope of any information exchange) could increase the length and complexity of the ADR clause, not to mention the ADR proceeding. If the length or the complexity of the clause becomes a critical negotiating issue with regard to particular aspects of the ADR process, it may be preferable to deal with such issues in a side agreement or as an addendum to the main agreement. Along with the issues in the following sections, parties may want to consider addressing in their arbitration clause (1) whether the parties must continue with performance during the period of the arbitration (e.g., royalty payments, transfers of technology); and (2) whether there are issues outside of the panel's jurisdiction (e.g., a panel could consider the scope of the agreement but not the validity of the licensed patents).

Some ADR institutions are trying to make drafting ADR clauses easier. The AAA has developed a ClauseBuilder® tool that is designed to assist users in developing custom ADR clauses. The tool provides a self-guided process that allows users to preview, save, review, and edit clauses.[34] Similarly, WIPO offers users a guided-choice "WIPO Clause Generator" that allows parties to

33. *Id.* R-1.

34. *See ClauseBuilder Tool*, AAA, https://www.clausebuilder.org (last visited Mar. 23, 2025).

develop ADR clauses and submission agreements[35] through steps that have the drafter (compiler) select whether the clause is for a current or future dispute; the type of ADR procedure(s) (e.g., mediation, arbitration, expedited arbitration, or appropriate combinations); and clause core (and additional) elements.[36]

A. Place (Seat) of the Arbitration

The clause should specify the seat (or place) of the arbitration. Parties not infrequently choose a place based on perceived geographic neutrality or the location of the chosen arbitral institution, or they provide that the arbitration will take place in the home city of the party that is not initiating the arbitration (intending to encourage the parties to settle their dispute so as to avoid the unpleasant prospect of conducting the arbitration in the other party's home court). Alternatively, parties may, in negotiations, trade away the choice of the seat for the choice of the governing law. These strategies can pose serious risks in international IP/Technology arbitrations unless the negotiators are familiar with the local laws regarding arbitration in both locations. As discussed in the following subsections, specifying the seat or place of the arbitration is an important consideration for several reasons.

1. Enforcement

The place of arbitration may affect the enforcement of the arbitration award. A forum country should be selected that is a signatory to an international convention, such as the New York or Panama Convention.[37] Enforceability

---

35. A submission agreement is a written agreement typically entered into after a dispute has arisen under which the parties agree to undertake an arbitration process to resolve their pending dispute. Such agreements in IP/Technology disputes can arise because, for example, the parties had not previously had a contractual relationship, or even if there is one, their contract did not provide for arbitration or for arbitration of the particular dispute at issue. Negotiating such an agreement may be challenging, in that the parties are already in a potentially contentious posture. But unlike the pre-dispute context, the parameters of the dispute would now be known, and the parties could theoretically focus on how best to use the flexibility inherent in arbitration to establish a cost-effective and expeditious process.

36. *See WIPO Clause Generator*, WIPO, https://amc.wipo.int/clause-generator/ (last visited Mar. 23, 2025).

37. The New York Convention is a treaty that requires courts of contracting states to give effect to private agreements to arbitrate and to recognize and enforce arbitral awards made in other contracting states. The Panama Convention generally accomplishes the same ends but is limited geographically to those contracting states who are members of the Organization of American States. The two conventions are codified, respectively, in Chapters 2 and 3 of Title 9 of the U.S. Code. *See* 9 U.S.C. §§ 201–208 (1990); 9 U.S.C. §§ 301–307 (1990).

of the award in other countries that are also signatories to those conventions is reasonably assured. Thus, consider whether an award rendered in the jurisdiction of the contemplated seat will be enforceable in the jurisdictions in which the opposing party has assets. Counsel should also always consult with local counsel in the jurisdiction(s) where any award is likely to need to be enforced, as they can advise of any unique requirements to ensure the award's enforceability or may even advise that the jurisdiction will not enforce an arbitration award in the particular context.

2. Arbitrator Selection

The place of arbitration may affect arbitrator selection by the designated institution. An institution empowered to select the sole panelist or the chair of a three-member panel (e.g., in accordance with the rules adopted) will likely look to panelists residing in the jurisdiction designated as the seat. This is because, if the parties hold the evidentiary hearing in the jurisdiction designated as the seat (they could agree to hold the hearing someplace else), it is less expensive and more convenient to appoint someone who will not incur significant travel expenses. Moreover, particularly in international cases, an arbitrator from the designated seat will likely be more familiar with the arbitration laws and procedures of the seat. Consider a party that wants a common-law panelist appointed, but does not specify that type of panelist in the arbitration clause. That party may have a better chance of having a common-law panelist appointed if the seat designated is a common-law jurisdiction rather than a civil-law jurisdiction.

3. Procedural Law

The place of the arbitration is an important factor when determining, for example, which laws (including procedural laws) will apply that may affect the arbitration proceedings as well as the rights of the parties in those proceedings. For example, proceedings ancillary to the arbitration that require court action (e.g., enforcement of the arbitration agreement or the arbitration award, discovery disputes, request for some form of relief) may be conducted in the courts of that location with the court applying local law. Thus, if the seat is Paris, then civil-law principles will govern. If, for example, the arbitration is being conducted through the ICC, the seat is in London, and a dispute arises as to the proper scope of the arbitration, the parties may end up litigating the matter in the High Court of England and Wales under common-law principles. Thus, research into the arbitral law of the seat, and the pro- or anti-arbitration attitude of the courts and laws there, is of substantial significance at the contracting stage.

4. Costs and Convenience

Although remote hearings are not exceptional, many parties prefer in-person hearings. If the parties are not geographically close to each other—as is often the case with parties to an international IP agreement—then the location of the arbitration evidentiary hearing can have a major effect on the parties' costs (e.g., airfare, hotels, a working venue) and convenience (e.g., easy access to the seat for parties, witnesses, and counsel). Each party will vie to locate the proceeding in or near its home court, but ultimately the parties, or possibly the administering institution, will select a practical compromise location. The parties should also consider the availability at the site for access to local counsel, interpreters, translators, and stenographers, as well as hearing rooms, telephone service, and internet access.

If the parties have chosen, for example, CIETAC as the administering institution, then it is likely that the arbitration will be in China. However, if the parties have chosen ICDR or ICC to administer the arbitration, that designation alone does not determine the place of the arbitration. Hearings often take place at the seat of the arbitration, but this is not always the case.

Thus, when thinking about what location to choose as the seat, consider how supportive of arbitration the national courts at the seat may be. If the seat is abroad, it is prudent to seek advice from local counsel regarding what the procedural laws are with regard to important issues the parties could be facing in the arbitration. Importantly, the parties should identify the name of both the city and the country.

Another aspect of cost and convenience to which parties and their counsel have become particularly attuned arising from the COVID-19 pandemic experience is the prevalence of using video teleconferencing platforms for everything from preliminary hearings and status conferences to the evidentiary hearings themselves. Using these platforms has brought about enormous savings in travel time and expenses; avoidance of logistical issues related to coordinating numerous calendars and schedules and accounting for unexpected travel delays; and removal of barriers to having additional participants attend who may otherwise have been precluded due to time or cost considerations.

B. Selecting the Arbitral Panel

One of the most valuable benefits for parties choosing arbitration to resolve their disputes is the opportunity to choose either their single panelist or a tri-partite panel. What follows are considerations to keep in mind for this important step while drafting an arbitration clause in a contract.

1. Background of Panelists

In disputes involving IP agreements, it is often important that the sole panelist or at least one panelist of a tri-partite panel be an attorney with the appropriate legal or technical expertise. This is particularly important if, for example, the case turns on a question of law in the IP field or on an issue of technology. In some cases, where there are multiple legal and technical issues, it may even be desirable to specify that one panelist have a particular practice background (e.g., IP litigation or licensing) and another have a particular technical background (e.g., polymer chemistry). The arbitration clause can specify any special requirements, but making the requirements too specific can make it difficult to find panelists generally, and particularly in a given country or geographic region. While an experienced IP attorney with the requisite technical background is often the best of both worlds, such a person is not always available due to constraints of time, geography, or conflicts.[38] Similarly, in international arbitrations, if there are concerns about national or cultural biases by the panel members, the arbitration clause could specify that they not come from the home country of either party. The downside of this requirement is that it may unduly limit the pool of potential panelists who are familiar with the law of a particular country, which is a problem if the arbitration is being decided under that country's law.

2. Number of Panelists

Should the parties provide for one or three panel members in their arbitration clause? The advantages of a single panelist are the ease of scheduling and lowered cost. Trying to coordinate the schedules of three busy panelists (especially in international arbitrations with potentially different time zones) can lead to greater delay in resolving the dispute. This is why expedited arbitration rules usually require the parties to use a single panelist.[39] Also, it is obviously less expensive for the parties to have a sole panelist. Nonetheless, many agreements provide for three-member panels.

Factors favoring the larger panel include the value of the contract and of any potential disputes, and the likelihood and nature of any disputes arising, including the technical complexity of any anticipated disputes. The best

38. In rare cases, a party may agree to waive its objection to a proposed panelist even though the candidate has disclosed a potential conflict. While this could be risky, it may be acceptable if the conflict is minor or tangential; if the pool of panelists with appropriate skills and experience is small; or if the candidate has such a high reputation for fair dealing that the adverse party believes that he or she would not be biased.

39. *See* WIPO Expedited Arbitration Rules, *supra* note 24, art. 14; AAA Commercial Arbitration Rules, *supra* note 17, at E-4.

rationale for a tri-partite panel may be that three arbitrators are more likely to take a balanced and reasonable view of a dispute. Put another way, some people subscribe to the notion that *three people are less likely to do something crazy than one person.* This can be a particularly important consideration given that there is no merits-based appeal of an arbitral award and the grounds for vacating one are very limited.

3. Selecting Panels

When parties adopt arbitration rules in their arbitration provision, the rules typically provide a process for choosing the panel. When drafting an arbitration provision, it is important for counsel and the contracting parties to read the rules to ensure that the predetermined process for selecting the panel is acceptable. When the parties choose to include their own selection process in an arbitration provision for tri-partite panels, a common procedure is to provide that each party will nominate one panelist, and then those two panelists will nominate the presiding panelist. A variation on this process is where each party picks one panelist, and the parties themselves must agree on the third panelist. The selection of this third person becomes crucial, as some believe or perceive that each of the panel members nominated by a party may favor their nominator's position. It is therefore important to provide that the panel members, and especially the third panel member, be neutral members acceptable to both sides and that any and all potential conflicts be disclosed.[40] The following is an example of a choice of arbitrator provision:

> Within ten days of filing of the Notice of Arbitration, each Party will provide the other Party with written notice of the identity of a person whom that Party wishes to nominate as an arbitrator, along with a resume or curriculum vitae for that person. Unless the other Party objects within five days of receipt of such notice, the designated individual will be deemed to be a member of the arbitral panel. Once both Parties have designated a mutually acceptable member of the arbitral panel, the two designated members will confer within five days to nominate a third member and notice of that person's identity will be given to the Parties. If neither Party objects within five days of receipt of such notice, then the third member will be deemed to be a member of the arbitral panel at that time and the panel will be duly constituted.

40. *See* AAA, The Code of Ethics for Arbitrators in Commercial Disputes (2004), https://www.adr.org/sites/default/files/document_repository/Commercial_Code_of_Ethics_for_Arbitrators_2010_10_14.pdf.

The foregoing implies that an objection raised by either party will bar a nominee from appointment. In practice, a party may withdraw its objection after further discussion. However, what if the objection is not withdrawn? Presumably, the process could keep going indefinitely, which may suit one party perfectly well. For this reason, some clauses provide that, if the parties cannot reach agreement on the members of the arbitral panel on their own within a certain specified time, then the chosen arbitral institution—or, if none is chosen, a third party—will appoint the third panelist.[41] Similarly, the parties may agree not to specify the number of panel members in advance and to decide in accordance with the size and complexity of the dispute if one arises. The disadvantage of this is that proceedings may be delayed if the parties disagree on the number of panelists once relations have broken down. If, however, institutional arbitration is used, the institution will decide the number of panelists.

Some of the issues to consider about panel selection in drafting an arbitration clause are:

- Should the parties designate a single panelist or a panel of three? Should the number vary depending on the specified dollar value or type of dispute?
- For tri-partite panels, should the selection process entail that each party select a panelist and the two party-appointed panelists select the chair or some other process? (This also may depend on the rules of the organization the parties select.)
- Should the parties specify that the panelist(s) be selected from a specialty roster or should the parties describe certain qualifications?
- If the matter is an international arbitration, should the panelists have different nationalities than the disputants? Should the chair be from a neutral nation? Is language proficiency critical?
- Should the entire panel comprise experts in a field? Consider whether the parties have a greater opportunity to educate a panel that has fewer preexisting views. In addition, overly detailed qualifications can sometimes drastically limit the pool of potential arbitrators and create difficulty in expeditiously selecting a panel.
- If the parties are focused on timing or management of the process, do they need to seek out a process specialist rather than a substantive specialist? Will able, managerial panelists better suit their needs?

---

41. *See, e.g.*, WIPO Rules, *supra* note 17, art. 17(b); AAA Commercial Arbitration Rules, *supra* note 17, R-11, R-12.

- If the parties have chosen to have a tri-partite panel, do they want to maximize the "wisdom of crowds" by having qualification, skill diversity, or other forms of diversity for the panel?[42]
- Do the parties want to include joint interviews for the selection process in the arbitration agreement?
- Have the parties ascertained the method of selection under the rules selected in case they cannot agree?[43]

C. Scope of Disputes Covered

The parties should explicitly state the matters that they want the arbitration agreement to cover. However, they should be aware that local law could restrict issues that may be subject to arbitration.[44] The arbitration clause should be broad enough to encompass all possible disputes and claims (e.g., damages and breach of contract) that the parties want covered. If the scope language raises questions about whether the disputed issues that arise are arbitrable, the parties are destined to spend unnecessary time and money trying to resolve such disputes if they cannot resolve them on their own. In this regard, it is not uncommon for parties to disagree about who has jurisdiction to decide the scope issues—a court or arbitration panel. This alone can result in the parties litigating this issue before a court and an arbitral panel. Once a court or the arbitral panel interprets the parties' scope language, the decision

---

42. *See generally* Scott Page, The Difference: How the Power of Diversity Creates Better Groups, Firms, Schools, and Societies (2007); James Surowiecki, The Wisdom of Crowds (2004).

43. CPR's model international administered arbitration clause highlights some of these issues:

> Any dispute arising out of or relating to this contract, including the breach, termination or validity thereof, shall be finally resolved by arbitration in accordance with the International Institute for Conflict Prevention and Resolution (CPR) Rules for Administered Arbitration of International Disputes by (a sole arbitrator) (three arbitrators, of whom each party shall designate one, with the third arbitrator to be appointed by CPR) (three arbitrators, of whom each party shall designate one, with the third arbitrator to be designated by the two party-appointed arbitrators) (three arbitrators to be appointed in accordance with the screened appointment procedure provided in Rule 5.4) (three arbitrators, none of whom shall be designated by either party). Judgment upon the award rendered by the arbitrator(s) may be entered by any court having jurisdiction thereof. The seat of the arbitration shall be (city, country). The language of the arbitration shall be (language).

See Model Clauses: International Administered Arbitration, CPR, https://drs.cpradr.org/model-clauses/international-model-clauses (last visited Mar. 23, 2025).

44. See *supra* note 5 regarding the arbitration of IP issues.

may leave the parties litigating some issues in court and pursuing others in arbitration. Thus, the parties must use clear and unambiguous language to demonstrate what disputes they agreed to arbitrate.

In the arbitration clause, the parties may choose to limit the types of issues that will be resolved. For example, in IP cases, the clause may limit the scope of issues to infringement and specifically exclude other issues, such as validity. Or parties may agree to arbitrate the commercial or contractual aspects of their agreement, but try to carve out IP/Technology disputes. Often these issues are inextricably intertwined and cannot be easily broken out. And, as mentioned with regard to unclear scope language, attempts to carve out arbitrable disputes from non-arbitrable disputes can lead to further litigation, additional costs, delays, and disappointment on the outcome.[45]

Case in point: An arbitration clause in a patent license attempted to exclude the issues of patent validity and scope of the license from arbitration. The licensor commenced an arbitration proceeding for unpaid royalties related to certain products. The licensee filed a separate declaratory judgment action in court to determine whether the products fell within the scope of the patent (infringement) and to challenge the patent. The parties litigated in federal district court and before the arbitral panel, which was to decide the issue of arbitrability and the interpretation of the arbitration clause. Time and money could have been avoided.

Although a jurisdictional issue can potentially be raised no matter how carefully the parties draft the language they use, there may be some circumstances where the parties make a jurisdictional demarcation that may be harder to dispute if a matter arises, such as in the following clause used in a neutral evaluation proceeding:

> In resolving the dispute that has been referred to it, the Neutral Panel may consider all issues relating to the infringement, validity, and enforceability of the Licensed Patents. However, the Neutral Panel may not consider or rule on any issues relating to damages (whether actual, consequential, or punitive) or on any claim based on the antitrust laws of the United States or any similar laws or regulations in any other jurisdiction.[46]

---

45. See the Case in Point in Section V.C.8 in Chapter 9 for an example of how the parties with the panel's help found a practical expedient to address this issue.

46. *See* Dist. No. 1 v. Liberty Mar. Corp., 70 F. Supp. 3d 327, 350 (D.D.C. 2014) (discussing generally the application of narrow arbitration clauses), *aff'd*, 815 F.3d 834 (D.C. Cir. 2016).

This issue of scope becomes even more critical in certain types of arbitration proceedings. For example, the rules of certain arbitral institutions (e.g., the ICC) emphasize the limiting effect of the parties' statement of the claims to be arbitrated. Under Rule 19 (New Claims) of the ICC Rules of Arbitration, the authority of the arbitration panel is limited to resolving only those claims or counterclaims that are set forth in the terms of reference, unless the panel allows otherwise.

D. Language of the Arbitration

Many arbitration clauses specify the language in which the arbitration will be conducted. This is significant in international IP agreements. As in designating the choice of law (discussed in Section IV.E), it can be a matter of national or cultural pride, particularly where a party is concerned about the fairness of the proceeding. In certain countries, the language of the arbitration may even be mandated when one party is the government or a government entity. Even without this, the choice of language has several practical implications for the arbitration proceeding itself. For example, if there will be live witness testimony, in what language will the witnesses be permitted to testify? Are interpreters necessary, and, if so, who will pay for them? If there are documents in another language, must they be translated? If so, who will do the translation and who will pay for it? And which version is the official version in the proceeding?

Many American companies simply assume that any arbitration will be conducted in English and therefore do not address this issue in their standard arbitration clauses. This can be a trap for the unwary—particularly when dealing with an international IP agreement. Depending upon the volume, complexity, and nature of important documents, their translation can have an effect on the schedule of the proceeding and its cost. Furthermore, the language of the proceeding may affect how witnesses come across and their credibility if their testimony must be interpreted. Can even an excellent interpreter present testimony as delivered (e.g., same intonation and credibility) by the witness in his or her own language? Can technical phrases or complex concepts be accurately interpreted?

The WIPO rules, like other rules, solve this problem by requiring the parties to be explicit about their choice of language. The sample WIPO rules put it very simply: "The language to be used in the arbitral proceedings shall be [specify language]." But does this selection make the chosen language the *official* language of the arbitration? To avoid doubt, consider a more detailed clause not only signifying the official language of the proceeding and of the arbitral award, but also addressing the issues of documents, witnesses, translations, interpretation, and costs, as discussed earlier.

E. Choice of Law in the Arbitration

The choice of the law that will apply (i.e., procedural or substantive law) can be a critical issue in the ultimate outcome of the arbitration. This is particularly true in an international IP arbitration, but may also be the case in a domestic arbitration. Thus, in drafting the choice-of-law clause, the parties should specify whether the clause covers only the substantive law to be applied to the dispute or also the procedural law.[47] Depending on the issues to be decided, there may be important substantive differences between the IP laws of different countries or states. As in the case of choice of language, the applicable law can be a sensitive issue of national or cultural pride in international cases. An American company that insists on choosing U.S. law is sometimes viewed as trying to bias the proceeding in its favor or even of implying that the law of the other country is somehow inferior. Sometimes this is put more delicately, as when a party states that it simply prefers to choose the legal system with which it is most familiar (e.g., a preference for a common-law versus a civil-law system). A few countries counter this by requiring that their own law will control in any arbitration proceeding.[48]

In international cases, a choice-of-law clause may influence—it may be a factor in—panel selection. An appointing authority may select an arbitrator familiar with that jurisdiction's laws (e.g., the specific laws or common law versus civil law) or someone who has the training that enables him or her to become familiar with those laws. If the choice of law is New York, a U.S.-trained attorney could presumably become familiar with New York laws (state/local) even if he or she is not licensed in New York.

One approach to resolving this dilemma is for parties to use the law of a neutral country. Since England is one of the few other common-law countries, international IP agreements between an American company and a non-Western company will often choose English law or the law of the United Kingdom. However, this may be deceiving insofar as there is a difference between the

---

47. Normally, unless the arbitration agreement provides otherwise, courts have ruled that a choice-of-law clause will be interpreted to apply only to the substantive law of the designated jurisdictions. *See* Jacada (Eur.), Ltd. v. Int'l Mktg. Strategies, Inc., 401 F.3d 701, 710–12 (6th Cir. 2005); Action Indus., Inc. v. U.S. Fid. & Guar. Co., 358 F.3d 337 (5th Cir. 2004); Sovak v. Chugai Pharm. Co., 280 F.3d 1266 (9th Cir. 2002). However, courts have construed language, such as where the "validity, interpretation, and enforcement" of the agreement is to be governed by the law of a particular jurisdiction, as referring both to the substantive and procedural law of that jurisdiction. *See* Cronus Invs., Inc. v. Concierge Servs., 35 Cal. 4th 376, 387 (Cal. 2005); Mount Diablo Med. Ctr. v. Health Net of Cal., Inc., 101 Cal. App. 4th 711 (Cal. Ct. App. 2002).

48. *See* Vitek Danilowicz, *The Choice of Applicable Law in International Arbitration*, 9 Hastings Int'l & Compar. L. Rev. 235, 243 (1986).

law of England and Wales (which operates as a unified system) and the law of Scotland, even though they are currently all parts of the United Kingdom. Other common choices include Swiss or German law, although these are civil-law countries whose jurisprudence differs significantly from a common-law system. In addition, Switzerland (like the United States) is a federal entity, with each canton having its own laws. Therefore, the appropriate reference in the arbitration clause should be to the laws of a specific canton, such as Zurich or Geneva. Germany is also a federal republic and has similar issues.

As with the choice of forum or seat, one variation in the choice-of-law clause (although less common than with choice of forum) is to require the party initiating the arbitration to use the other party's local law. Again, the purpose of this strategy when negotiating the arbitration clause is to incentivize the parties to reach an amicable settlement of their dispute rather than be subject to law that may be unfavorable to the party initiating the arbitration. However, despite how convenient this may seem as a solution, it should not be adopted without a true understanding of the other party's laws and how they may affect the arbitration proceeding, its substantive outcome, and enforcement of the decision.

Typically, the clause providing for arbitration within the IP agreement (e.g., license) will be governed by the substantive law specified within the larger agreement (here, the license).[49] Thus, if the parties arbitrate a dispute under the larger agreement, the arbitration panel will apply the substantive law set forth in that larger agreement, even though that law was not specifically mentioned in the arbitration clause. The parties may, however, specify a different law to be applied in the arbitration from the law governing the IP agreement. If they choose to do so, this should be clearly set forth, but, also, the effect of providing for a separate law to govern the arbitration from that used to interpret the larger agreement should be carefully considered.

In short, while parties to an IP agreement are entitled to choose, by contract, the law that they want to govern both the contract itself and any arbitration proceeding that may arise, there are real risks in agreeing to a foreign law without a good understanding of how it may impact an arbitration. For this reason, it would be prudent to seek advice from local counsel at the drafting stage.

F. Time Limits

When a dispute arises from an IP agreement, time is often of the essence. For example, consider a trade secret or know-how agreement where nondisclosure

49. This is not to be confused with the arbitration procedural law that would be applied, which generally arises from the seat of the arbitration.

or maintaining confidentiality is a key issue. If the licensor has reason to believe that the licensee is about to breach its confidentiality obligation (e.g., at a trade show or in a publication), then it wants to quickly obtain interim relief and a final determination. Similarly, consider an agreement that relates to the licensing of IP for a key product or component that is to be incorporated into a larger manufactured product or system, such as a car, a computer, or a refinery. If a dispute over IP or what the license covers precludes the licensee from supplying the product or component to its customer, then the completion of the larger produced good or system may be disrupted. Parties may go to court for interim relief or they may adopt interim rules from an arbitral institution. In the latter case, the institution appoints an *interim relief* panel to address such issues until a panel that will address the merits is appointed.[50]

If time is likely to be important in resolving future disputes, an ADR process(es) needs to be implemented that avoids delay. For example, in a staged ADR process, the series of escalating meetings between executives is often perceived as friendlier, but the meetings may not produce the expected resolution. In fact, they could delay the institution of such ADR processes as mediation and arbitration by several months (although, in an emergency, the parties can try to agree to remove some or all of the steps). Thus, it would be a prudent drafting practice to be specific about the time required for each stage before moving on to the next, accounting for the process of selecting the mediator or the panel and for dealing with any objections. A common drafting error is leaving those time periods vague and open-ended, thereby allowing one party to contend that, for example, the pending arbitration proceeding is not ripe because the parties have not satisfied the prerequisites to arbitrate.

Finally, when the parties adopt the rules of an established ADR institution, they may be faced with set time limits for the filing of papers, information exchange (if any), the time until any hearing, and the time for the panel to produce an award. If these time limits are not realistic, the parties can mutually agree to different time limits. And a party can, on its own, always request that the panel grant an extension of time if it can show good cause. Of course, some ADR institutions (such as WIPO) offer expedited rules, which are designed to produce a more rapid decision. Alternatively, the parties can modify the set of rules they adopt when negotiating the pre-dispute clause or later when the dispute arises.

In drafting time limits into an ADR clause, the parties should try to use realistic, not overly generous or overly ambitious, time limits that give busy people (including counsel, neutrals, and key executives) the latitude to perform the chosen ADR process(es) and their underlying responsibilities.

50. For further discussion, see Chapter 9, Section III.

Undue delay in resolving the dispute does not serve an important purpose of ADR, and it certainly does not respond to the exigencies that can arise in an IP/Technology dispute, as set forth in the beginning of this section. Similarly, an overambitious or unrealistic schedule can cause more disputes in attempting to fix it. In the case of arbitration, the parties should try to work with one another if time limits in an arbitration clause turn out to be unrealistic (it is likely that one or both parties will require an extension during the proceeding) or request that the panel work with the parties to modify or adjust the time limits. Setting realistic time limits in the ADR clause can be a way to keep disputes from dragging on, as legal proceedings tend to fill the time allotted.

Something that parties may consider including in any ADR clause to highlight the importance of time limits is a statement that any neutral must commit in advance to giving the matter his or her prompt attention and work within the preset schedule. In other words, the ability to commit the needed time becomes a qualification in selecting neutrals. When interviewing mediators and arbitrators, for example, it is not uncommon for parties to ask about their availability in view of the ADR clause and the parties' needs. So, for example, if an arbitration clause requires a decision within six months of initiating the arbitration, and the proposed panelist has two long hearings scheduled in that period with awards due, it may make sense to find another panelist.

To ensure that the ADR proceedings move at the pace the parties require, they should consider specifying in their ADR clause practical time limits for specific events, such as (1) the date by which the parties must select their mediator or arbitrator(s); (2) the date by which the parties must complete any information exchange; (3) a time frame for the mediation session or the evidentiary hearing; and (4) the date by which the arbitral panel must render its award (most arbitral institution rules provide this). Time limits also depend on what kind of award the parties have requested: a standard award, a reasoned award, or findings of fact and conclusions of law. Obviously, each requires a different amount of time to complete. If the parties have requested the panel to produce a reasoned award, then sufficient time should be allocated to complete it.

G. Information Exchange

One of the biggest differences between ADR proceedings and litigation lies in the approach to information exchange.[51] In the United States, this is the principal source of the expense and delay of litigation. In the case of mediations and

51. In addition to the ADR processes of mediation and arbitration that benefit from various degrees of information exchange, other forms of ADR rely upon a certain

ENE, which often occur in parallel with litigation, at least some discovery may have already occurred that can be used in the mediation or the parties may agree on their own, or with the help of the mediator, to some limited exchange as part of the process. Not surprisingly, there is considerable pressure (especially from U.S. counsel) to expand the concept of discovery into arbitration proceedings. Counsel from outside the United States (and civil-law countries, in particular) are, in contrast, less inclined to advocate for extensive information exchange. Historically, international arbitration had been characterized by a limited exchange of information under the tight control of the arbitral panel; however, even this is evolving to some degree.

In 1999, the International Bar Association (IBA) issued the IBA Rules on the Taking of Evidence in International Arbitration (the IBA Rules). In May 2010, the IBA Council adopted a revised version of these rules. The IBA Rules represent an effort to balance the broad, open-ended, U.S. style of discovery and the traditional international approach. The IBA Rules provide detailed procedures for prehearing document requests that are broader than typical international arbitral practices. This broadening is balanced by the further requirement that the requests be sufficiently detailed, narrow, and specific. The IBA Rules may apply by party agreement or "if the Arbitral Tribunal has determined" to apply them, barring a conflict with "any mandatory provision of law determined to be applicable to the case by the Parties or by the Arbitral Tribunal."[52] The parties and the arbitral panel may adopt the IBA Rules, in whole or in part, to govern their arbitration proceeding, and they may vary them or use them as guidelines in developing their own procedures.[53]

Except for certain specialized rules in patent cases, arbitration rules (both domestic and international) generally do not specifically provide for any sort of information exchange or even guarantee it; however, the parties can affirmatively provide for some exchange of information. How much and what kind of information is exchanged is case-specific, and to meet their particular situation, the parties may want to adopt rules or supplement existing rules that do provide for some information exchange in patent cases, such as CPR's Rules for Non-Administered Arbitration of Patent and Trade Secret Disputes or AAA's Supplementary Patent Rules.[54]

---

degree of information exchange, such as the mini-trial and neutral fact-finding. *See* Chapter 1, Section II and Case History #1 in Section III.

52. IBA, IBA Rules on the Taking of Evidence in International Arbitration art. 1 (2020), https://www.ibanet.org/MediaHandler?id=def0807b-9fec-43ef-b624-f2cb2af7cf7b (last visited Mar. 23, 2025).

53. *See id.* Foreword, at 6.

54. *See* CPR Patent & Trade Secret Arbitration Rules, *supra* note 22; AAA Patent Supplementary Rules, *supra* note 23.

Some of the issues to consider in drafting an arbitration provision addressing information exchange are:

- Should the parties provide for information exchange at all?
- If so, what is the permitted kind and scope of any exchange (e.g., will interrogatories, requests to admit, or depositions be permitted)?
- If so, what are the time limits to complete the information exchange? (This issue may be addressed in ad hoc procedures for arbitrating by providing an expedited timeline for arbitrating disputes related to IP agreements.)
- Will the parties merely be obligated to produce relevant documents? If so, what is considered relevant? What are the consequences for failing to produce a relevant document? Will the parties be able to submit reliance documents—that is, documents that the parties will rely upon during the proceeding?
- Will the parties be able to assert privileges or immunities (an issue that varies widely between countries)?
- Will e-discovery be allowed? If so, what will be the scope of such discovery?
- How will confidential information be treated?[55]
- If a witness is not available for the hearing, will a party be able to take the deposition of that witness and use the resulting testimony at the hearing?
- Will there be expert witnesses? If so, in what areas? How many? Who will pay for them? How will they be qualified?
- Will the expert submit a report in advance of the hearing? Will there be rebuttal reports?
- Will the expert testify in person at the hearing? Will the adverse party be able to cross-examine the expert?
- Can the panel call its own expert and will the parties get a chance to examine that expert before the hearing? At the hearing?

In response to criticisms that arbitration has become another form of litigation because of extensive discovery practice, various organizations became proactive and developed rules and procedures to curtail the costs of discovery (and other aspects of the process). For example, CPR published *CPR Protocol on Disclosure of Documents and Presentation of Witnesses in Commercial Arbitration*.[56] This protocol recognizes that clients and their

55. For further discussion, see Chapter 9, Section IV.

56. *See* CPR, CPR Protocol on Disclosure of Documents and Presentation of Witnesses in Commercial Arbitration (2021), https://drs.cpradr.org/rules/protocols-guidelines/protocol-on-disclosure-of-documents-presentation-of-witnesses-in-commercial-arbitration (last visited Mar. 23, 2025).

counsel may have different interests and expectations, so it offers *modes*, or choices, for the disclosure of documents and presentation of witnesses. The parties negotiating an arbitration provision may choose a mode that best suits them. Similarly, the ICDR developed guidelines for arbitrators concerning exchanges of information, which are now embodied, for the most part, in Article 24 of the ICDR International Dispute Resolution Procedures.[57] Placing carefully considered limitations on the nature and extent of the discovery and the use of expert witnesses may be an important consideration in forward-looking ADR agreements.

H. Award of Costs, Fees, and Damages

Many American companies mistakenly assume that, as in U.S. IP litigation, each party bears its own costs and expenses regardless of the outcome of the proceeding. It is not uncommon in arbitrations for the losing party to bear costs and fees, either because the rules so provide or because the panel is given the authority to award them. The governing law in some jurisdictions (e.g., the United Kingdom) actually requires cost-shifting regardless of the parties' agreement on that subject; this is yet another example of the importance of consulting with local counsel at the seat of the arbitration. Where the parties choose to develop their own ad hoc rules for an arbitration proceeding, they must consider whether they want to address this issue. In an international situation, where the expectations of the parties on this point may differ, it may be particularly important to make this clear in advance.

For example, parties to an ad hoc agreement may want the ADR clause to specify how the parties will bear the costs of the proceeding (e.g., costs or fees charged by the arbitral institution, and the fees of the panel, expert witnesses, stenographer, interpreter, translator). Many parties may assume that this will be evenly divided, but they need not be. For example, the clause may provide that costs will be automatically awarded to the prevailing party, or that the arbitral panel has the discretion to award them (although that may lead to further briefing and argument as to how one defines *prevailing*). Similar drafting issues relate to whether the loser pays the winner's legal fees or whether each party bears its own fees and expenses incurred in the arbitration.

An important issue with respect to damages is whether the arbitral panel can award punitive or consequential damages. The contract, the arbitral rules, or the choice of law may preclude such awards. Moreover, in some cases, the

57. *See* ICDR, International Dispute Resolution Procedures (Including Mediation and Arbitration Rules) (2021), https://www.adr.org/sites/default/files/ICDR_Rules_0.pdf.

parties may not want the panel to have the power to make such awards. If so, it may be important to specifically set this forth in the ADR clause.

Conclusion

It is strongly recommended that an IP agreement include an ADR clause to provide greater certainty from the outset as to how the parties will resolve any disputes that may eventually arise. Moreover, drafting the clause before the conflict arises should make it easier for the parties to agree on key elements of the ADR process because this is likely to be much more difficult after a dispute has arisen. And because the parties drafting and negotiating the IP agreement often lack familiarity with ADR issues and procedures, they would be well-advised to have those experienced in using ADR draft and review any ADR provisions.

Many IP agreements either fail to address ADR at all or contain a simple statement that the parties will arbitrate. Such clauses are inadequate because they fail to address many of the key procedural issues that are critical to any ADR process. At worst, such clauses can leave the ADR process in confusion; at best, the parties may find themselves in the hands of an ADR institution that is applying rules that are both unfamiliar and unanticipated.

This chapter provides a checklist of issues, considerations for what to include in an ADR clause, and some examples of ADR clauses and provisions. Obviously, it is impossible for an ADR clause to anticipate all of the fact situations that may arise, but parties can achieve greater predictability and reduce the time and expense involved by incorporating a carefully considered, well-crafted ADR clause in their IP agreements.

APPENDIX

Model Arbitration and Mediation Clauses

Model arbitration and mediation clauses for domestic and international disputes are set forth in this appendix. These model clauses may help counsel and parties begin to draft contract terms that meet their needs. While they offer a number of specific options, they are not exhaustive and do not include all possible provisions that may need to be considered, or may be desirable, in particular contracts. They should not be treated as the final product of the process of drafting an ADR clause.

I. Sample Clauses for Non-Administered (Ad Hoc) Arbitration

A. CPR[58]

1. Pre-Dispute

Any dispute arising out of or relating to this contract, including the breach, termination or validity thereof, shall be finally resolved by arbitration in accordance with the International Institute for Conflict Prevention & Resolution Rules for Non-Administered Arbitration by (a sole arbitrator) (three arbitrators, of whom each party shall appoint one) (three arbitrators, of whom each party shall designate one in accordance with the "screened" appointment procedure provided in Rule 5.4) (three arbitrators, none of whom shall be appointed by either party). The arbitration shall be governed by the Federal Arbitration Act, 9 U.S.C. § 1 et seq., and judgment upon the award rendered by the arbitrator(s) may be entered by any court having jurisdiction thereof. The place of the arbitration shall be (city, state).

58. *See Model Clauses: Non-Administered Arbitration*, CPR, https://drs.cpradr.org/model-clauses/arbitration-model-clauses/non-administered (last visited Mar. 23, 2025).

2. Existing Dispute

We, the undersigned parties, hereby agree to submit to arbitration in accordance with the International Institute for Conflict Prevention & Resolution Rules for Non-Administered Arbitration (the "Rules") the following dispute: [Describe briefly]

We further agree that the above dispute shall be submitted to (a sole arbitrator) (three arbitrators, of whom each party shall appoint one) (three arbitrators, of whom each party shall designate one in accordance with the "screened" appointment procedure provided in Rule 5.4) (three arbitrators, none of whom shall be appointed by either party). We further agree that we shall faithfully observe this agreement and the Rules and that we shall abide by and perform any award rendered by the arbitrator(s). The arbitration shall be governed by the Federal Arbitration Act, 9 U.S.C. § 1 et seq., and judgment upon the award may be entered by any court having jurisdiction thereof. The place of arbitration shall be (city, state).

3. Multi-Step

Negotiation Between Executives (A): The parties shall attempt in good faith to resolve any dispute arising out of or relating to this [Agreement] [Contract] promptly by negotiation between executives who have authority to settle the controversy and who are at a higher level of management than the persons with direct responsibility for administration of this contract. Any person shall give the other party written notice of any dispute not resolved in the normal course of business. Within [15] days after delivery of the notice, the receiving party shall submit to the other a written response. The notice and response shall include (a) a statement of that party's position and a summary of arguments supporting that position, and (b) the name and title of the executive who will represent that party and of any other person who will accompany the executive. Within [30] days after delivery of the initial notice, the executives of both parties shall meet at a mutually acceptable time and place, and thereafter as often as they reasonably deem necessary, to attempt to resolve the dispute. All reasonable requests for information made by one party to the other will be honored. All negotiations pursuant to this clause are confidential and shall be treated as compromise and settlement negotiations for purposes of applicable rules of evidence.

Mediation (B): If the dispute has not been resolved by negotiation as provided herein within [45] days after delivery of the initial notice of negotiation, [or if the parties failed to meet within [20] days,] the parties shall endeavor to settle the dispute by mediation under the International Institute for Conflict Prevention & Resolution (CPR) Mediation Procedure [currently in effect OR in effect on the date of this Agreement] [provided, however, that if one party fails to participate in the negotiation as provided herein, the other party can initiate mediation prior to the expiration of the [45] days]. Unless otherwise agreed, the parties will select a mediator from the CPR Panels of Distinguished Neutrals.

Arbitration (C): Any dispute arising out of or relating to this [Agreement] [Contract], including the breach, termination or validity thereof, which has not been resolved by mediation as provided herein [within [45] days after initiation of the mediation procedure] [within [30] days after appointment of a mediator], shall be finally resolved by arbitration in accordance with the International Institute for Conflict Prevention & Resolution Rules for Non-Administered Arbitration [currently in effect OR in effect on the date of this Agreement] by [a sole arbitrator] [three independent and impartial arbitrators, of whom each party shall designate one] [three arbitrators of whom each party shall appoint one in accordance with the "screened" appointment procedure provided in Rule 5.4] [three independent and impartial arbitrators, none of whom shall be appointed by either party]; [provided, however, that if one party fails to participate in either the negotiation or mediation as agreed herein, the other party can commence arbitration prior to the expiration of the time periods set forth above]. The arbitration shall be governed by the Federal Arbitration Act, 9 U.S.C. § 1 et seq., and judgment upon the award rendered by the arbitrator(s) may be entered by any court having jurisdiction thereof. The place of arbitration shall be (city, state).

B. UNCITRAL: Arbitration[59]

Any dispute, controversy or claim arising out of or relating to this contract, or the breach, termination or invalidity thereof, shall be settled by arbitration in accordance with the UNCITRAL Arbitration Rules.

[Note. Parties should consider adding:]

(a) The appointing authority shall be . . . [name of institution or person];

59. *See* UNCITRAL, *supra* note 4, at 30.

(b) The number of arbitrators shall be . . . [one or three];

(c) The place of arbitration shall be . . . [town and country]; and

(d) The language to be used in the arbitral proceedings shall be . . . .

C. IBA: Negotiation Followed by Mediation and/or Last Step of Arbitration[60]

1. *Negotiation as a First Step*

The parties shall endeavor to resolve amicably by negotiation all disputes arising out of or in connection with this agreement, including any question regarding its existence, validity or termination. Any such dispute which remains unresolved [30] days after either party requests in writing negotiation under this clause, or within such other period as the parties may agree in writing, shall be finally settled under the [designated set of arbitration rules] by [one or three] arbitrator[s] appointed in accordance with the said Rules. The place of arbitration shall be [city, country]. The language of arbitration shall be [. . .].

[All communications during the negotiation are confidential and shall be treated as made in the course of compromise and settlement negotiations for purposes of applicable rules of evidence and any additional confidentiality and professional secrecy protections provided by applicable law.]

2. *Mediation as a First Step*

The parties shall endeavor to resolve amicably by mediation under the [designated set of mediation rules] all disputes arising out of or in connection with this agreement, including any question regarding its existence, validity or termination. Any such dispute not settled pursuant to the said Rules within [45] days after appointment of the mediator, or within such other period as the parties may agree in writing, shall be finally settled under the [designated set of arbitration rules] by [one or three] arbitrator[s] appointed in accordance with the said Rules. The place of arbitration shall be [city, country]. The language of arbitration shall be [. . .].

---

60. *See* IBA, IBA Guidelines for Drafting International Arbitration Clauses 32–34 (2010), https://www.ibanet.org/MediaHandler?id=D94438EB-2ED5-4CEA-9722-7A0C9281F2F2 (last visited Mar. 23, 2025).

[All communications during the mediation are confidential and shall be treated as made in the course of compromise and settlement negotiations for purposes of applicable rules of evidence and any additional confidentiality and professional secrecy protections provided by applicable law.]

3. Multi-Step Negotiation, Mediation, and Arbitration

All disputes arising out of or in connection with this agreement, including any question regarding its existence, validity or termination ('Dispute'), shall be resolved in accordance with the procedures specified below, which shall be the sole and exclusive procedures for the resolution of any such Dispute.

(A) Negotiation

The parties shall endeavor to resolve any Dispute amicably by negotiation between executives who have authority to settle the Dispute [and who are at a higher level of management than the persons with direct responsibility for administration or performance of this agreement].

(B) Mediation

Any Dispute not resolved by negotiation in accordance with paragraph (A) within [30] days after either party requested in writing negotiation under paragraph (A), or within such other period as the parties may agree in writing, shall be settled amicably by mediation under the [designated set of mediation rules].

(C) Arbitration

Any Dispute not resolved by mediation in accordance with paragraph (B) within [45] days after appointment of the mediator, or within such other period as the parties may agree in writing, shall be finally settled under the [designated set of arbitration rules] by [one or three] arbitrator[s] appointed in accordance with the said Rules. The place of arbitration shall be [. . .]. The language of arbitration shall be [. . .].

[All communications during the negotiation and mediation pursuant to paragraphs (A) and (B) are confidential and shall be treated as made in the course of compromise and settlement negotiations for purposes of applicable rules of evidence and any additional confidentiality and professional secrecy protections provided by applicable law.]

II. Sample Clauses for Administered Arbitration

A. AAA (Domestic) Commercial Arbitration[61]

1. Step Up from Negotiation (Pre-Dispute)

In the event of any dispute, claim, question, or disagreement arising from or relating to this agreement or the breach thereof, the parties hereto shall use their best efforts to settle the dispute, claim, question, or disagreement. To this effect, they shall consult and negotiate with each other in good faith and, recognizing their mutual interests, attempt to reach a just and equitable solution satisfactory to both parties. If they do not reach such solution within a period of 60 days, then, upon notice by either party to the other, all disputes, claims, questions, or differences shall be finally settled by arbitration administered by the American Arbitration Association in accordance with the provisions of its Commercial Arbitration Rules.

2. Step Up from Mediation (Pre-Dispute)

If a dispute arises out of or relates to this contract, or the breach thereof, and if the dispute cannot be settled through negotiation, the parties agree first to try in good faith to settle the dispute by mediation administered by the American Arbitration Association under its Commercial Mediation Procedures before resorting to arbitration, litigation, or some other dispute resolution procedure.

3. Step Up from Mediation (Existing Dispute)

The parties hereby submit the following dispute to mediation administered by the American Arbitration Association under its Commercial Mediation Procedures [the clause may also provide for the qualifications of the mediator(s), the method for allocating fees and expenses, the locale of meetings, time limits, or any other item of concern to the parties].

4. Arbitration (Pre-Dispute)

Any controversy or claim arising out of or relating to this contract, or the breach thereof, shall be settled by arbitration administered by

61. *See* AAA, Drafting Dispute Resolution Clauses: A Practical Guide 10–12 (2013), https://www.adr.org/sites/default/files/document_repository/Drafting%20Dispute%20Resolution%20Clauses%20A%20Practical%20Guide.pdf.

the American Arbitration Association in accordance with its Commercial [or other] Arbitration Rules, and judgment on the award rendered by the arbitrator(s) may be entered in any court having jurisdiction thereof.

5. Arbitration (Existing Dispute)

We, the undersigned parties, hereby agree to submit to arbitration administered by the American Arbitration Association under its Commercial [or other] Arbitration Rules the following controversy: [describe briefly]. We further agree that a judgment of any court having jurisdiction may be entered upon the award.

6. Examples of Add-On Provisions[62]

a) Rules to Be Applied

This agreement shall be governed by and interpreted in accordance with the laws of the State of [specify]. The parties acknowledge that this agreement evidences a transaction involving interstate commerce. The United States Arbitration Act shall govern the interpretation, enforcement, and proceedings pursuant to the arbitration clause in this agreement.

or

Disputes under this clause shall be resolved by arbitration in accordance with Title 9 of the U.S. Code (United States Arbitration Act) and the Commercial Arbitration Rules of the American Arbitration Association.

or

This contract shall be governed by the laws of the state of [specify].

b) Language

The language(s) of the arbitration shall be [specify].

or

The arbitration shall be conducted in the language in which the contract was written.

---

62. *Id.* at 23–25.

c) Number of Arbitrators

The arbitrator selected by the claimant and the arbitrator selected by the respondent shall, within 10 days of their appointment, select a third neutral arbitrator. In the event that they are unable to do so, the parties or their attorneys may request the American Arbitration Association to appoint the third neutral arbitrator. Prior to the commencement of hearings, each of the arbitrators appointed shall provide an oath or undertaking of impartiality.

or

Within 14 days after the commencement of arbitration, each party shall select one person to act as arbitrator and the two selected shall select a third arbitrator within 10 days of their appointment. [The party-selected arbitrators will serve in a non-neutral capacity.] If the arbitrators selected by the parties are unable or fail to agree upon the third arbitrator, the third arbitrator shall be selected by the American Arbitration Association.

or

In the event that arbitration is necessary, [name of specific arbitrator] shall act as the arbitrator.

d) Place/Seat

The place of arbitration shall be [city], [state], or [country].

B. ICDR (International) Commercial Arbitration[63]

Any controversy or claim arising out of or relating to this contract, or the breach thereof, shall be determined by arbitration administered by the International Centre for Dispute Resolution in accordance with its International Arbitration Procedures.

The Parties should consider adding:

> *The number of arbitrators shall be (one or three);*
>
> *The place of arbitration shall be [city, (province or state), country];*
>
> *The language(s) of the arbitration shall be ___.*

---

63. *See* ICDR, Guide to Drafting International Dispute Resolution Clauses 2, https://www.icdr.org/sites/default/files/document_repository/ICDR_Guide_Drafting_Clauses.pdf (last visited Mar. 23, 2025).

C. WIPO (International) Arbitration[64]

1. Arbitration (Pre-Dispute)

Any dispute, controversy or claim arising under, out of or relating to this contract and any subsequent amendments of this contract, including, without limitation, its formation, validity, binding effect, interpretation, performance, breach or termination, as well as non-contractual claims, shall be referred to and finally determined by arbitration in accordance with the WIPO Arbitration Rules.

2. Arbitration (Existing Dispute)

We, the undersigned parties, hereby agree that the following dispute shall be referred to and finally determined by arbitration in accordance with the WIPO Arbitration Rules: [brief description of the dispute]

The arbitral tribunal shall consist of [a sole arbitrator] [three arbitrators]. The place of arbitration shall be [specify place]. The language to be used in the arbitral proceedings shall be [specify language]. The dispute shall be decided in accordance with the law of [specify jurisdiction].

3. Examples of Add-On Provisions[65]

a) Rules to Be Applied

The dispute, controversy or claim shall be decided in accordance with the law of [specify jurisdiction].

---

64. *See Arbitration*, WIPO, http://www.wipo.int/amc/en/clauses/arbitration/ (last visited Mar. 23, 2025). ADR may also be utilized in disputes involving voluntary licensing terms that are required by standards organizations (i.e., RAND (reasonable and non-discriminatory) and FRAND (fair, reasonable, and non-discriminatory)). *See generally* Margarita Kato, *Arbitration and Mediation: Resolving Patent Licensing Disputes in the World of Standardized Technology*, WIPO MAG. (Dec. 13, 2022), https://www.wipo.int/wipo_magazine/en/2022/04/article_0007.html. In that regard, WIPO makes available tailored model submission agreements that parties may use to refer a dispute concerning the adjudication of FRAND terms to WIPO (Expedited) Arbitration, as well as other resources and guidance in this arena. *See, e.g.*, *WIPO ADR for FRAND Disputes*, WIPO, https://www.wipo.int/amc/en/center/specific-sectors/ict/frand/ (last visited Mar. 23, 2025).

65. *See Arbitration*, WIPO, *supra* note 64.

b) Language

The language to be used in the arbitral proceedings shall be [specify language].

c) Number of Arbitrators

The arbitral tribunal shall consist of [a sole arbitrator] [three arbitrators].

Pursuant to Article 15(a) of the WIPO Arbitration Rules, the parties agree to the following procedure for the appointment of the arbitrator(s): [specify procedure].

d) Place/Seat

The place of arbitration shall be [specify place].

D. ICC (International) Arbitration[66]

All disputes arising out of or in connection with the present contract shall be finally settled under the Rules of Arbitration of the International Chamber of Commerce by one or more arbitrators appointed in accordance with the said Rules.

E. London Court of International Arbitration[67]

Any dispute arising out of or in connection with this contract, including any question regarding its existence, validity or termination, shall be referred to and finally resolved by arbitration under the LCIA Rules, which Rules are deemed to be incorporated by reference into this clause.

The parties should consider adding:

The number of arbitrators shall be [one/three].

The seat, or legal place, of arbitration shall be [city and/or country].

---

66. *See Standard ICC Arbitration Clauses*, ICC (Jan. 1, 2021), https://iccwbo.org/news-publications/arbitration-adr-rules-and-tools/standard-icc-arbitration-clauses-english-version/.

67. *See Recommended Clauses*, London Ct. Int'l Arb., https://www.lcia.org/dispute_resolution_services/lcia_recommended_clauses.aspx (last visited Mar. 23, 2025).

The language to be used in the arbitral proceedings shall be [ ].

The governing law of the contract shall be the substantive law of [ ].

III. Sample Clauses Promoting Diversity, Equity, and Inclusion

Addressing the dearth of women, people of color, and other underrepresented groups who are selected to act as arbitrators and mediators has long been a challenge.[68] There have, however, been marked improvements in recent years, one of which is the voluntary adoption of language in ADR clauses encouraging the selection of diverse arbitrators and/or mediators. The following are sample clauses incorporating that language.

A. CPR[69]

Any dispute arising out of or relating to this contract, including the breach, termination or validity thereof, shall be finally resolved by arbitration in accordance with the International Institute for Conflict Prevention and Resolution ("CPR") Rules for Administered Arbitration (the "Administered Rules" or "Rules") by (a sole arbitrator) (three arbitrators, of whom each party shall designate one, with the third arbitrator to be appointed by CPR) (three arbitrators, of whom each party shall designate one, with the third arbitrator to be designated by the two party-appointed arbitrators) (three arbitrators, of whom each party shall designate one in accordance with the screened appointment procedure provided in Rule 5.4) (three arbitrators, none of whom shall be designated by either party). The parties agree that however the arbitrators are designated or selected, at least one member of any tribunal of three arbitrators shall be a member of a diverse group, such as women, persons of color, members of the LGBTQ community, disabled persons, or as otherwise agreed to by the parties to this Agreement at any time prior to appointment of the tribunal. Where CPR is to nominate or select the arbitrators, CPR will convene the parties to discuss the selection. In the event the parties desire multiple qualifications, if CPR is unable to accommodate a qualification

68. *See generally* Theodore K. Cheng, *The Case for Bringing Diversity to the Selection of ADR Neutrals*, 9 NYSBA N.Y. Disp. Resol. Law. 18 (2016).

69. *See Diversity Commitment Clause*, CPR, https://drs.cpradr.org/model-clauses/arbitration-model-clauses/diversity-focus (last visited Mar. 23, 2025).

specified by the parties and diversity, CPR may use its discretion to nominate or appoint a diverse candidate or candidates to serve on the tribunal. [The arbitrator(s), and not the court, shall have primary responsibility to hear and determine challenges to the jurisdiction of the arbitrator(s). OR The court, and not the arbitrator(s), shall have primary responsibility to hear and determine challenges to the jurisdiction of the arbitrator(s).] The arbitration shall be governed by the Federal Arbitration Act, 9 U.S.C. §§ 1 et seq., and judgment upon the award rendered by the arbitrator(s) may be entered by any court having jurisdiction thereof. The place of the arbitration shall be (city, state).

B. JAMS[70]

The parties agree that, wherever practicable, they will seek to appoint a fair representation of diverse arbitrators (considering gender, ethnicity and sexual orientation), and will request administering institutions to include a fair representation of diverse candidates on their rosters and list of potential arbitrator appointees.

IV. Sample Clauses for Optional Appellate Review

There is generally no comprehensive merits-based review of an arbitration award as is typical in an appeal of a federal or state court judgment. Rather, subsequent review of an arbitration award is severely limited in scope[71] with one notable exception: where the parties elect to undertake an appellate review process.[72] Some arbitral authorities have promulgated optional appellate review procedures and rules. The following are sample clauses incorporating those provisions.

A. AAA-ICDR[73]

Notwithstanding any language to the contrary in the contract documents, the parties hereby agree: that the Underlying Award may

70. *See Alternative Dispute Resolution (ADR) Clauses*, JAMS, https://www.jamsadr.com/clauses/ (last visited Mar. 23, 2025).

71. *See, e.g.*, 9 U.S.C. § 10 (affording only limited grounds for vacatur of an arbitration award).

72. *See* Theodore K. Cheng, *Merits-Based Review of Arbitration Awards: A Potentially "Appealing" Option*, 22 NYSBA NYLitigator 21 (2017).

73. *See* AAA, Optional Appellate Arbitration Rules (2013), https://www.adr.org/sites/default/files/AAA-ICDR_Optional_Appellate_Arbitration_Rules.pdf.

be appealed pursuant to the AAA's Optional Appellate Arbitration Rules ("Appellate Rules"); that the Underlying Award rendered by the arbitrator(s) shall, at a minimum, be a reasoned award; and that the Underlying Award shall not be considered final until after the time for filing the notice of appeal pursuant to the Appellate Rules has expired. Appeals must be initiated within thirty (30) days of receipt of an Underlying Award, as defined by Rule A-3 of the Appellate Rules, by filing a Notice of Appeal with any AAA office. Following the appeal process the decision rendered by the appeal tribunal may be entered in any court having jurisdiction thereof.

B. CPR[74]

An appeal may be taken under the CPR Arbitration Appeal Procedure from any final award of an arbitral panel in any arbitration arising out of or related to this agreement that is conducted in accordance with the requirements of such Appeal Procedure. Unless otherwise agreed by the parties and the appeal tribunal, the appeal shall be conducted at the place of the original arbitration.

C. JAMS[75]

The Parties adopt and agree to implement the JAMS Optional Arbitration Appeal Procedure (as it exists on the effective date of this Agreement) with respect to any final award in an arbitration arising out of or related to this Agreement.

74. *See* CPR, CPR Arbitration Appeal Procedure and Commentary (2015), https://drs.cpradr.org/rules/arbitration/appellate-arbitration-procedure (last visited Mar. 23, 2025).

75. *See JAMS Optional Arbitration Appeal Procedure*, JAMS, https://www.jamsadr.com/appeal/ (last visited Mar. 23, 2025).

PART II

Tactical Thinking and Tools for Using ADR in IP/Technology Disputes

CHAPTER 3

Early Case Assessment: A Strategic Tool for the Early Resolution and Management of Intellectual Property and Technology Disputes

Cynthia Raposo and Harrie Samaras[1]

We should remember that good fortune often happens when opportunity meets with preparation.

—Thomas A. Edison

Introduction[2]

Picture an emergency room. The doctor in charge just learned that a fireworks display in a nearby park went awry, causing injuries to viewers. It already has been a busy July 4th weekend in the ER. She expects to treat scores of patients having injuries that span in severity from routine to life-threatening. The cases will range from those requiring little attention and treatment to those needing in-depth investigation and possibly expert consultation. Some patients will require immediate attention because the risk of waiting may exacerbate the problem, while others will remain stable awaiting care. With limited resources and time, the doctor in charge will need to triage, or sort, patients as they arrive to determine their relative needs and how best to treat them. A reliable method is needed to do this.

Readers of this book are probably not doctors working in an emergency room. They are most likely attorneys, businesspeople, or dispute resolution professionals who have seen their share of disputes. When a dispute first surfaces, it is not always apparent how much of a risk it poses to the business and how much attention will be necessary to resolve it. Some disputes demand immediate attention, although they may not ultimately present significant

1. Thanks to David Schramm, Senior Associate General Counsel, IP, at Bayer U.S. LLC, for his input to this chapter.

2. See Glossary for definition of frequently used terms.

risks to the business or require a long-term investment of time and resources. Other disputes may materialize in a less exigent form, but ultimately present significant risks requiring long-term attention and resources.

Insofar as time and resources can be scarce when they are needed most, triaging disputes, like triaging patients, can help manage risks for both the short and long term. This requires an assessment of each case as early as possible to obtain relevant information that can be used to determine which cases to handle first and how best to handle them. The process or protocol used to triage cases is called early case assessment (ECA).

For some, the purpose of this chapter is to introduce ECA; for others it will supplement preexisting knowledge and experience using ECA—a powerful tool for managing intellectual property (IP) and technology disputes. This chapter begins by defining ECA and its benefits. It then illustrates how to perform an ECA.

I. ECA

A. What Is ECA?

ECA is a dispute management process that facilitates informed decision-making at the early stages of a dispute. It is a systematic approach for investigating, collecting, and analyzing information not only about the dispute, but also about the business it impacts. Thus, an ECA is likely to uncover information about the following:

1. Legal claims implicated (e.g., infringement, inventorship, ownership, breach of contract)
2. Underlying motivation of the parties (e.g., competitors, residual animosity from a past encounter)
3. Business risks (e.g., enhanced damages, injunction against core product, reputational harm, trademark cancelation, invalidity of core patents)
4. Strengths and weaknesses of parties' legal positions
5. In-house stakeholders (e.g., technical, business, finance, risk managers)
6. Third-party stakeholders (e.g., insurance carrier, investors, business partners)
7. Relevant documents and things (e.g., licenses, assignments, impacted products, prior art, IP registrations, prosecution histories)
8. Custodians and location of relevant evidence
9. Governing corporate policies

10. Governing contractual provisions
11. Parties' interests and needs (e.g., plans for the IP, product, or service involved; strategic alliance with opponent; remove cloud before merger/acquisition)

The end result of the ECA process is a comprehensive and strategic analysis that decision makers can rely on at all stages of the dispute when evaluating options on how best to proceed. For purposes of this chapter, the written work product will be referred to as "the ECA Report." The ECA Report is a *living document* that can be revisited and updated much like a *litigation* or *risk assessment* memorandum that is updated on a regular basis as new events and circumstances unfold.

B. Why Use ECA?

In the short term, a company may believe that it is easier and less costly to approach litigation or arbitration or the threat of either more reactively, such as by investigating and researching the facts and law only when pressed, hoping the dispute settles before that time. A properly and timely conducted ECA, however, can be one of the most important investments that a company makes. ECA prevents surprises and affords predictability. Like the emergency room analogy, triaging disputes, like triaging patients, helps to determine early on how, when, and by what means to treat each dispute. Inherent in the ECA analysis is an evaluation of the risks involved, including their nature (e.g., monetary damages, injunctive relief, reputational harm, damage to a valuable business relationship), scope (e.g., potential back damages, impact on the company, business unit, and product line), and urgency. Armed with this assessment, a company will be in a much better position to evaluate its short- and long-term options for addressing the dispute. It gives clients control of the dispute and confidence in their decision-making. And, it provides clients with an opportunity to prepare for any likely damage impact.

ECA is also an effective mechanism for obtaining information that will help a company evaluate whether and how to settle (e.g., Are there compelling reasons to litigate this dispute? What is the monetary value of the case? Do the parties have complementary interests? Is there cross-licensing potential? Is it possible that one party is interested in selling the affected business or even the company to the other party?). Consequently, effective ECAs often result in better settlements.

ECA also avoids the drain on company resources that is associated with long-term litigation. This is particularly relevant in IP cases, which are notorious resource and money guzzlers. The care and feeding of a sizable IP case involves not only a large expenditure of funds for outside resources (e.g., outside counsel, testifying experts, document processing, trial graphics), but also imposes a distraction and drain on internal resources. Instead of focusing on new products or improvements, employees must spend precious time chasing down prior art or assisting lawyers with discovery, briefs, and testimony. When it comes to litigation costs, even the largest and healthiest companies have limited resources and budgets. By forcing a comprehensive examination of the risks early on, ECA, like triaging patients, helps companies focus their resources on the disputes that require the most attention.

Lastly, using the structure of the ECA Report as a basis for briefing decision makers about the dispute will produce far better results than an unstructured recitation of the dispute details. And, at the very least, if a dispute does not settle early, the ECA Report will help educate corporate personnel on some of the demands of litigation, help focus and manage the litigation, and facilitate outside counsel's preparation of an informed and realistic litigation budget.

As discussed later in this chapter, there are many factors that influence the scope and cost of an ECA. No matter what the cost, if an ECA is handled effectively, and the dispute is resolved early or is better managed in litigation, ECA efforts will pay for themselves.

II. A Framework for Performing ECA

When embarking on ECA for a particular dispute, the first step is to determine whether the company already has an established policy or practice that dictates whether ECA should be performed. Where such a practice or policy exists, it is worthwhile learning whether (1) it applies to all disputes or only certain categories and (2) the company intends for the process to be performed only early in the dispute or later as well, if it does not settle.

If the company requires ECA for a particular kind of dispute, it is next important to find out if the company prefers a particular ECA framework. Following the company's existing ECA framework is prudent for various reasons:

a. Why reinvent the wheel? Others have likely expended valuable time and resources developing a framework.
b. It may reflect the company's and legal department's policies (e.g., risk management), values, and preferences from prior good and bad experiences.
c. Corporate personnel outside the legal department may have bought into it and will cooperate more readily with the known process.

If, for some reason, a dispute requires adjustments to an accepted ECA framework, communication of such adjustments and sign-off for them may be necessary, or at least prudent, to obtain.

Where a company does not have an established ECA framework, developing one is not difficult, particularly with the resources that already exist. One of those is referenced here. Developed by the International Institute for Conflict Prevention & Resolution (CPR),[3] the Corporate Early Case Assessment Toolkit[4] consists of two main parts: (1) a detailed guide setting forth a comprehensive analytical model in a step-by-step process (Guide) and (2) an Executive Summary form (Short Form) for users more familiar with an ECA analysis. See the appendix to this chapter.

A. Steps to Consider for an ECA Analysis

The following flowchart depicts ten steps the CPR Guide suggests for performing an ECA. The chart can be adapted (e.g., add, subtract, substitute steps) for each new dispute. And it can be used as an organizational tool for designing the overall management of the project and determining the specific tasks, responsible personnel, and deadlines.

3. Established in 1977, CPR is an independent nonprofit organization that promotes the prevention and resolution of conflict to better enable the pursuit of purpose through the CPR and its subsidiary, CPR Dispute Resolution Services LLC.

4. *See* Corporate Early Case Assessment Commission, International Institute for Conflict Prevention and Resolution, Resources for Navigating Complex Business Disputes: Corporate Early Case Assessment Toolkit (2009), https://assets-002.noviams.com/novi-file-uploads/cpr/pdfs-and-documents/CPR_Early_Case_Assessment_Toolkit_2010-0827b5a4.pdf. In 2024, CPR published Corporate Early Case Assessment Toolkit for European Parties, which is available at https://www.cpradr.org/products/cpr-institute-corporate-early-case-assessment-toolkit-for-european-parties. The toolkit includes updates reflecting developments in the prevention and resolution of international disputes since 2011, and it contains a series of adjustments to reflect the European practice and approach to dispute prevention and dispute resolution.

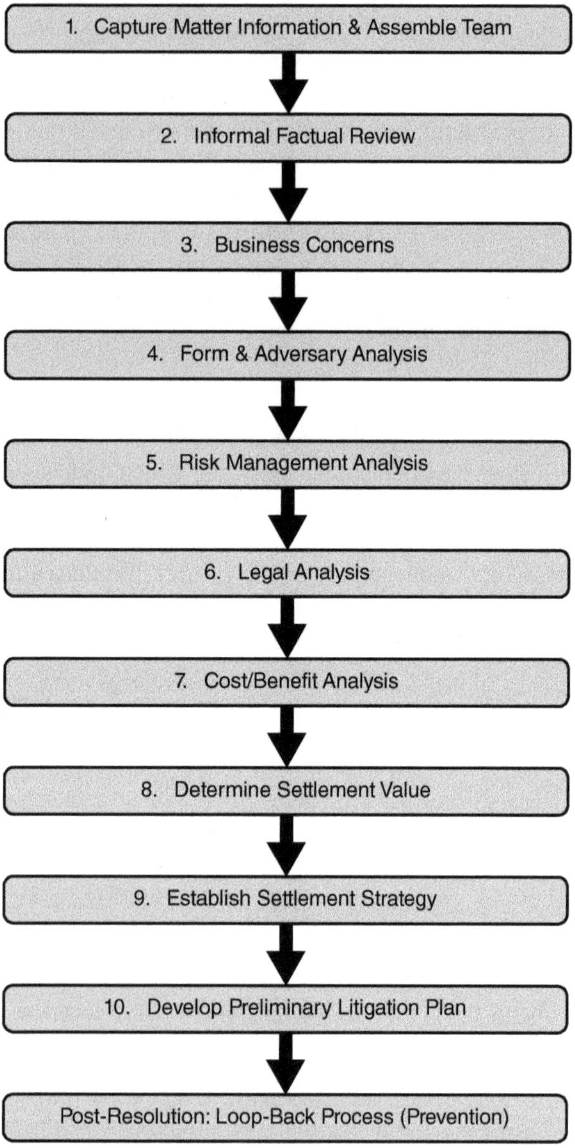

B. ECA Detailed Analysis

The detailed analysis or the Guide is a thorough and well-organized outline of issues pertinent to assessing a dispute for early or later resolution and for better managing a dispute that is not resolved early. For disputes that are complex (e.g., multiple patents, claims, IP assets, products, and parties) and where a lot is at stake for the company, investigating all of the issues in the analysis on an expedited basis can present a significant amount of work in a short time frame. For disputes that are smaller, the level of work required will be less. The benefits of addressing all the issues in the detailed analysis, regardless of the size or the complexity of the dispute, are the same—the company will have the valuable information it needs to make important decisions.

Absent the dictates of a company policy or procedure, the ECA Report does not have to embody any particular format. When deciding what format(s) to use, consider, for example, the audience and the format that would best capture their attention. A written report and possibly a slide presentation are options to brief corporate decision makers, memorialize key information, and even document the need for additional or missing information. In preparing the ECA Report, some narrative is helpful to present background, analyze data, and set forth conclusions.[5] Important information or recommendations, however, should never be lost in the text. Consider using a timeline, table, chart, or graph to present or emphasize key information or issues in a clear, logical, and effective way to capture the ECA team's attention for conducting further investigation and the corporate executives' attention for making important decisions. In addition, a bullet-point summary of conclusions (e.g., from tables or graphs), analyses, and recommendations is an effective style for business executives. Adding an executive summary as discussed in Section IV of this chapter may also be appropriate.

Because the ECA Report is intended to be a living document that can be updated, it is advisable to designate on the document *date prepared* as well as *date last updated*. Providing these dates on the document is a useful practice for indicating to corporate management whether the information, analyses, and recommendations are current. If a dispute is not resolved early, changing circumstances during the life of a dispute can affect the analyses and recommendations. Having a date on the document that predates the date any significant changes occurred signals that at least portions of the ECA and the document should be updated before decisions are made. Similarly, if a company has a policy or practice of employing ECA, and a dispute does not settle after the earliest assessment and recommendation, the policy may provide for periodic updates to the ECA. Thus, keeping track of when the last assessment occurred is important to ensure compliance with a corporate policy. In addition to noting relevant dates, the ECA Report should identify who prepared it and any revisions, should those individuals need to be consulted.

5. Consider the level of sophistication of the client regarding the scope of information to include. For example, for a start-up or small company that may be unaccustomed to litigation or arbitration, counsel may want to provide detailed background, including about the relevant adjudicative process, possible stages, and estimated time frames and costs based on publicly available information and their experience. For a company that is routinely in court (e.g., because of a company's size or the field involved), similar background information may be unnecessary and times and costs may be analyzed by way of past similar cases.

Insofar as the ECA Report may incorporate and embody information protected by the attorney-client privilege and the attorney work-product doctrine, appropriate measures should be taken to protect the ECA Report.

The Guide's steps are used as an outline here to illustrate how ECA can be used with IP/Technology disputes.

STEP 1—Capture Matter Information and Assemble Team

For this step, the Guide identifies the following tasks generally:

1. Identify counsel and the ECA team, the other disputant(s), and third parties.
2. Describe the matter (e.g., nature of the dispute, apparent amount in dispute, background and relationship of the parties, how the company learned of the matter, status of insurance and any related indemnity, and any applicable contracts or pre-dispute agreements).
3. Identify the stage of the dispute and any dispute resolution requirements.
4. If the dispute is in litigation, identify all that is known about the litigation.

The ECA team

Buildings are built on solid foundations, and an ECA analysis is no different. Because the ECA analysis is so important to decisions having risk management and strategic implications for a company, the ECA team is an important building block. The team must commit itself to see the process through in the necessary time frame, have the requisite knowledge and experience to handle the tasks, understand the importance of the ECA for corporate decisions, and competently perform each step. It is not low-level work. Thus, despite the ministerial nature of some of the tasks, if they are relegated to individuals who do not understand the importance of the information and the consequences of an incomplete or inaccurate collection of information, the analysis may suffer as well as the decisions based upon it.

There is no formula for determining how many people and who should be a part of an ECA team. A core team can be relatively small and very effective. Depending on the nature of the dispute (e.g., size, anticipated risks, complexity), an ECA team may consist of one in-house counsel assisted by a paralegal. Or, it may consist of an in-house counsel, business decision maker, and an outside counsel.

Case in point: In a trade secret misappropriation case, a small group handled all aspects of the ECA. Outside trial counsel collected key information (documents and witness statements) from the corporate personnel involved in the alleged misappropriation. Thereafter, trial and in-house counsel studied the information and developed a hearing-like slide presentation to present to and discuss with the head of the business unit that was charged with the misappropriation.

In a larger or more complex IP or technology dispute, the ECA team may need to be broadened to include the appropriate experts (e.g., a technical expert in patent or trade secret cases, a subject matter expert in copyright cases, a survey expert in trademark cases). It also may be prudent to include a damages expert and a corporate finance manager to perform, for example, risk analyses and damages calculations. And, as discussed in more detail later in this chapter, if insurance coverage is involved, then identifying contacts at the insurance company and within the client company (e.g., risk management) is important to obtain relevant information for the analysis.

If a company chooses to involve outside counsel in an ECA, it needs to assess whom to involve. For a routine dispute, the company may want to partner with one of the law firms it routinely engages to maximize the efficiencies and cost savings associated with engaging counsel already familiar with their business, products, policies, and the like. A related question is whether the outside counsel used to perform the ECA would be retained for the ongoing or future-filed litigation or arbitration. The outside counsel who has participated in the ECA is already well-versed with the risks, facts, and legal issues. Accordingly, continuing with them would avoid the cost of having to bring new counsel up to speed. However, for a bet-the-company, high-profile, or high-risk case, the company needs to consider whether ECA counsel not only excels in the knowledge and experience required to win the case, but also in their reputation (e.g., in relevant legal circles and with relevant tribunals). If ECA counsel is not retained for future litigation or arbitration, engaging another outside counsel will provide an additional objective view of the case for executives and decision makers.

The ECA process also must be well managed. The best-laid plans can get off the ground like a lead balloon. Managing the ECA process is like managing any other important or strategic project for a company. ECA has a beginning and an end, objectives, timetables and deliverables, and people involved in the process. Consequently, in choosing an effective manager, desirable attributes may include (1) credibility to interact effectively with an array of individuals at all levels of the company and even outside the company who have diverse personalities, dispositions, and stakes in the outcome; (2) an ability to work well under pressure; (3) good organizational skills; and (4) effective communication skills. Also, insofar as the ECA will likely involve the collection of confidential, even privileged, information, the manager should be experienced in implementing the best processes to maintain the confidentiality and privileged status of the information, including consulting with in-house and outside counsel regarding the same.

To be effective, ECA should be done early. It should be instituted and completed within a relatively short time once litigation is likely or merely foreseeable.[6] That said, it is important to allow sufficient time to obtain results that are reliable enough for counsel to advise their client about how best to proceed and for corporate decision makers to make informed decisions. A typical time frame quoted is 30 to 60 days, but longer times may be necessary depending upon a variety of factors, including the kind and amount of IP, contracts involved, and accused products; the urgency of the dispute; the number of forums involved (e.g., district court; International Trade Commission (ITC); U.S. Patent and Trademark Office (PTO); foreign tribunals); the number and location of key documents and individuals to interview; the types of legal issues and scope of remedies; and the budget.

Describe the matter

An effective ECA necessarily begins with a comprehensive identification of what the *matter* is about. The kind of information needed to accomplish this will vary from dispute to dispute. What follows provides the basics for a good start.

a. **The parties and their relationship**. Although identifying the parties in a dispute may seem like an easy task, this is not always the case in an IP/Technology dispute. There are many complexities to discern. Some parties are stand-alone companies with relatively simple histories, but many others are part of a more complex corporate structure formed from various mergers and acquisitions. Indeed, it is not uncommon for a sole inventor to start a company that is then acquired by a midsize company that is thereafter acquired by a large multinational company. Yet another complexity in identifying relevant parties is where one corporate entity (the holding company) owns the IP assets at issue and licenses them to another corporate entity (the parent company) that is making and selling products under the license from the holding company. Thus, carefully identifying the parties (and their predecessors) to the dispute is an important step. It may impact, for example, who can sue or be sued (i.e., the proper plaintiff(s) and defendant(s) in a lawsuit, where the case may be filed and maintained, which law firm could represent the company (conflict checks), and who could serve as a neutral (disclosures) if the parties pursue alternative dispute resolution (ADR).

   Furthermore, the other side should be carefully investigated to learn information relevant to costs and risks. What is the opponent's significance in the industry? How litigious are they? What kind of counsel may

6. Depending upon the circumstances, an early ECA may result in a decision to cure an alleged breach, cease making a product, and/or engage in early negotiation, mediation, or some other dispute resolution process.

they hire? This investigation could also avoid the debacle of suing a current business partner, vendor, or customer and injuring, if not destroying, the relationship. Having savvy and involved business managers join or be accessible to the ECA team will help avoid such a misstep.

Case in point: In a patent litigation, the plaintiff and the defendant were not strangers. A couple of years before, one party had considered purchasing the other party. During the due diligence phase, some mixed signals occurred when a third party tried to broker the deal. The purchase was never consummated. The patent litigation had not progressed very far when the parties decided to try mediation to settle the case. On the first day of the in-person mediation session, the parties got stuck on the number for back damages, which was significant. So, in the early evening, outside counsel sequestered themselves in a room (during the mediation session) to brainstorm about how the parties might continue their progress. One idea was to arrange for the principals from each side to talk alone, away from their respective teams. In formulating this, it became apparent to the outside counsel that there was a "history" between the parties from the abandoned deal a few years ago that was impeding progress. Counsel arranged for a breakfast the next mediation day where the two selected principals met, cleared the air on the prior dealings, and agreed on the centerpiece of the settlement for the patent litigation—how much should be paid. The case subsequently settled.

b. **Third parties**. In an IP/Technology dispute, identifying and obtaining cooperation from third parties can be a valuable asset to obtain early. For example, another company sued earlier by the same plaintiff may be willing (and able) to share information from its lawsuit that would be helpful in formulating defenses. Likewise, in patent disputes, third parties can be valuable sources of invalidating information, such as their prior uses and sales and other prior art. And in contractual disputes involving IP/Technology (e.g., licenses, assignments), third parties may have previously worked for the current disputants and have information regarding the disputed issues (e.g., contract interpretation, product or IP development).

c. **What is the nature of the dispute and how did the company learn of it**? The nature of the dispute could be characterized, for example, simply as a *copyright dispute* or a *breach of contract dispute*. But that characterization alone may not be meaningful. A more useful way of describing the dispute would be to include information such as (1) the forms of IP involved; (2) the products and services potentially affected; (3) in patent disputes, the number of patents and patent claims involved; (4) the potential legal or equitable claims for relief and defenses (IP and non-IP); (5) the agreements involved (e.g., licenses, research and development (R&D), marketing, distribution); (6) the possible kinds of monetary relief (e.g., damages for infringement, attorneys' fees, punitive damages, enhanced damages); (7) the amount at stake; (8) the impact of an injunction on the company; (9) the impact of the dispute (e.g., nuisance or bet-the-company); and (10) the urgency.

How the dispute arose may determine the best and most expeditious way to deal with it. For example, if a dispute arises after a trade show, scientific meeting, or the arrival of a cease-and-desist letter, then time is often on the accused party's side for responding. Depending on the scope of the dispute, the accused will likely have time to perform an ECA comfortably but diligently within a few months without risking an escalation of the dispute. This may also depend upon the nature of the communications between the parties and who is having those communications.

By contrast, if the dispute arises from the filing (no service) of a complaint, the circumstances compel a more time-sensitive response. Productive communications between representatives of the parties (counsel and businesspersons) may help to stave off service of the complaint and allow time for an ECA. Depending on the time pressures, the in-house legal team may be able to complete the ECA on its own. Where the dispute arises by way of written notice pursuant to a predispute clause, the ADR process(es), time frames, and rules or procedures set forth in the clause will impact how fast the ECA process must be conducted (assuming the parties have not varied the time frames by later agreement). A response also should comply with the governing ADR clause or process. For example, if there is an escalation clause that requires negotiation or mediation first, filing a lawsuit without first satisfying those conditions precedent may exacerbate the problem and cause jurisdictional issues later.

When the dispute is first uncovered with the filing of a temporary restraining order (TRO), preliminary injunction motion, or complaint, the circumstances are obviously more exigent, and time will play a more forceful role in when and how the ECA is performed and who performs it.

d. **Insurance and indemnities**. Identifying whether insurance coverage exists is necessary for compliance with Rule 26(a)(1)(A) of the Federal Rules of Civil Procedure. Notwithstanding Rule 26, knowing whether the client has insurance that covers the dispute and, if so, its scope and limitations, (e.g., advertising injury in trademark disputes) may be a key factor, for example, in determining settlement value.

Case in point: In a trademark infringement suit, there was a potential for coverage under the defendant's excess liability policy. The insurance company, upon notice of the suit, filed a declaratory judgment action seeking a ruling that there was no coverage. This resulted in a parallel suit where, in addition to retaining outside IP counsel to defend the trademark case, the defendant company had to retain expert insurance counsel to litigate the insurance claim. The effort was worthwhile because the defendant eventually reached a satisfactory settlement with the insurance company.

Case in point: In another trademark infringement suit, the defendant learned that its coverage did not apply to "equitable damages"—meaning that any judgment against it in the nature of unjust enrichment or to recoup profits gained by the defendant as a result of its alleged infringement would not be covered. Knowing this limitation early on helped the company evaluate risks, develop its defense strategy, and, eventually, settle the case within the policy limits before trial.

It is also important to locate and review all relevant agreements between the parties for indemnity provisions. Indemnities may exist in various kinds of agreements as well as in the battle of the forms related to the sale of goods. For example, a purchaser of goods accused of infringement may be able to demonstrate an indemnity for such a suit from the forms related to the sale of goods. Indemnities may vary in terms of which kinds of disputes, damages, and defense costs they cover. Notifying the indemnitor, like notifying an insurer, may spark a separate dispute that needs to be resolved in parallel with the original dispute. Where an indemnitee is a large customer of the indemnitor, the indemnitor may be less inclined to fight indemnification to maintain the relationship.

Case in point: An indemnitor sold a device to a large food manufacturer for displaying food in grocery stores. The indemnitee was sued for patent infringement for displaying its food using the device in a manner that allegedly infringed certain patents. In the contract for the sale of the devices (as well as in invoices that were sent and paid), indemnifications existed (covering damages and attorneys' fees), which the indemnitor honored to maintain a valuable relationship.

In addition to insurance companies, there may be others who have a vested interest in how and whether a dispute is settled. They may include investors and business partners with present and possibly future interests in a party. The extent of the influence they have regarding a particular dispute may be dictated by contractual obligations as well as business understandings.

e. **Dispute resolution requirements**. The early road to dispute resolution can take an unintended turn if relevant contracts, pre-dispute provisions, and even a prior settlement agreement between the parties, any one of which may set forth party agreements regarding future disputes, are not carefully reviewed. Such agreements may provide a host of terms and conditions that the parties must follow before they can pursue adjudication (e.g., arbitration or litigation). For example, there may be an escalation clause setting forth the dispute resolution mechanisms the parties chose, the forum for addressing interim relief, the rules governing any ADR proceeding, and timetables and limits on damages, all of which may affect the client's ultimate dispute resolution strategy.

If arbitration is a required step in a pre-dispute resolution clause (or it has commenced), alone or following a less expensive ADR process (e.g., negotiation, mediation), it would be useful to include in the ECA the following information:

- What the parties previously agreed to in the pre-dispute arbitration clause (if one exists), such as the ADR provider and the applicable rules, the seat of the arbitration, the number of arbitrators, and the arbitrator selection requirements
- Information a party currently has about a pending proceeding or can anticipate about a potential arbitration (e.g., pending deadlines, location of evidentiary hearing, scope of discovery, number and kind of claims and requested relief, format of the award), likelihood or existence of any threshold issues (e.g., jurisdictional challenges, joinder of parties), an estimate of the timing from the commencement of the arbitration to the issuance of an award, and the estimated monetary and nonmonetary costs (e.g., administrative fees, legal fees, arbitrator fees, expert witnesses, travel, disruption to the business, internal management costs, diversion of resources) and the factors affecting those costs

If a court action has been commenced and the ECA is being performed in response to it, the ECA should include all the information a party currently has about the case. See the discussion in Step 4 later in this chapter.

The stage of the dispute and related disputes

Knowing the stage of the dispute, like knowing the extent of a patient's injuries, may help determine who should be involved in trying to settle it and by what mechanism it may be settled. There is, however, no prescriptive wisdom to dispense. In the early stages, in-house counsel, business counterparts involved in the dispute (who can communicate dispassionately), or business counterparts who are a step removed from the fray are often effective in reaching an expeditious resolution. If the parties have chosen a summary jury trial or mini-trial (often followed by negotiation and possibly mediation), corporate executives typically participate. For high-stakes disputes that are mediated, and mediations involving small or midsized companies, corporate executives often attend as the decision makers. Even if the dispute proceeds to litigation, involving businesspersons or possibly executives who are familiar with one another can be very effective at the right time. This is certainly the case when parties pursue mediation in parallel with litigation later in the case and business decision makers are required to participate. The exigency and risks presented by the dispute also will influence whom to involve and how quickly. As to which settlement mechanism to employ, generally, experience shows that the earlier the stage of the dispute (particularly before litigation commences), the more ADR options there will be available to the parties (e.g., negotiation, mediation, early neutral or expert evaluation, mini-trial). Early-stage disputes are also more likely to settle regardless of the ADR mechanism where both parties have performed a diligent ECA.

Case in point: A trade secret misappropriation case involving a plaintiff and three defendants was pending in court for almost a year. One defendant was a corporate competitor of the plaintiff, another defendant was an individual who previously worked for the plaintiff and was now working for the defendant corporation, and the third was a licensee of the defendant corporation. The dispute was successfully resolved in mediation with the help of a key participant—the chief operating officer (COO) of the corporate defendant. Having the gravitas of the COO helped to engender trust in an emotionally charged situation, and it focused the parties on a business solution rather than their positions. His understanding of the underlying business risks, credibility with the mediator, relationship with the third-party licensee, reputation in the industry, and past history with the founders of the plaintiff were also key factors in finding a mutually acceptable business-based solution.

In IP disputes, in particular, it is not uncommon that other disputes between the parties exist (e.g., an ITC investigation, a district or state court case, a proceeding before the PTO, proceedings before foreign tribunals). Reviewing the status of these other cases may be useful for various reasons. For example, if settlement discussions are ongoing in one of these other matters, they could be used as a vehicle to settle the new matter—a global settlement. Likewise, starting settlement discussions in the new matter may be used to influence a settlement of all or some of the other matters. Also, information discovered or rulings issued in another matter may affect how or when the new matter should be pursued or provide leverage for settlement.

Identify everything known about the litigation

If the dispute is in litigation, collect all available information regarding the litigation, including the pleadings, the name of outside counsel, where the suit is filed, and who is the presiding judge. See Step 4.

STEP 2—Informal Factual Review

Multiple factors drive ECA, but facts always play a critical role. P.D. Villarreal, former Senior Vice President, Global Litigation, for GlaxoSmithKline, has stated: "Experience teaches us that if you conduct a very good early case assessment that looks at the facts and the law and the witnesses and the documents . . . when you complete your ECA, you will know 80 percent of all you will ever know about this case."[7] As Mr. Villarreal further reflected, this is not "perfect knowledge," but it is adequate and sufficient in many cases to make decisions about how to resolve them.[8]

For this step, the Guide identifies the following tasks generally:

1. **Conduct internal interviews**. This is to gather information from relevant legal and business personnel within the company and from client business contacts.
2. **Collect internal documents**. This includes hard copy and electronic.
3. **Identify witnesses and experts**. This includes identifying fact witnesses and their locations, evaluating the role of experts, providing a summary of the interviews with witnesses, and assessing witness capability and credibility.
4. **Make contacts with opposing counsel**. Obtain information from opposing counsel, including any agreements on informal discovery or information exchange.
5. **Collect information about similar issues**. This includes those handled by the company or occurring in the industry.
6. **Identify essential information needed**.

In this phase of the ECA, locate and assemble as much relevant factual information as possible outside of the formal discovery process (assuming the ECA is occurring before discovery or prior to litigation or arbitration). In-house and outside counsel should provide guidance about determining what information is privileged and confidential and how that information should be tracked, marked, and maintained. Furthermore, attention should be given to issuing a legal hold to the appropriate individuals so that potential evidence is preserved.

Potential sources of relevant information for an ECA (before discovery) include:

- Opponents (e.g., information disseminated at trade shows or scientific meetings, on websites, in press releases, and to investors;

7. *CPR's ECA Toolkit—A Great Contribution to Controlling Litigation Costs*, Metro. Corp. Couns., Nov. 2009, at 11 (an interview with P.D. Villarreal).
8. *Id.*

correspondence between clients and opponents or between their respective counsel)

- Publicly available information (e.g., internet and social media searches; government filings and issuances (PTO, Copyright Office, Securities and Exchange Commission, Food and Drug Administration); news-oriented publications and electronic platforms; trade and scientific articles; word of mouth)
- Clients' internal corporate documents and things (e.g., emails, lab notebooks and other development documents, brand development documents, drafts of copyrighted works, opinions of counsel, strategic planning documents, meeting minutes, test results, prototypes, financials, contracts)
- Clients' employees (e.g., R&D, marketing, business, advertising, finance, risk management, legal)
- Third parties (e.g., development documents from consultants (e.g., product design, software, musical composition, storyboards); potentially invalidating prior art (e.g., sales, product descriptions, printed publications, prior uses); expert opinions; insurance policies)

Identify potentially responsive and relevant documents by reviewing whatever information triggered the litigation or threat of litigation (e.g., court complaint, arbitration demand, cease-and-desist letter). Based on the scope of that information, create a plan to identify key employees (present and past) and other potential document custodians of relevant data as well as locations of relevant hard copy and electronic information (e.g., corporate offices and facilities, computers, legacy servers).

Be particularly thoughtful and thorough at this stage. Do not simply collect data—verify it. In the emergency room analogy, obtaining a patient's history and the facts surrounding the present injuries are important for determining how to treat the patient and what priority the patient should be given. Similarly, actions at this stage will significantly impact the later stages of the ECA analysis, and ultimately will inform the key decisions the client will have to make later. So, the phrase *garbage in, garbage out* applies.

A chronology of key facts is a vital tool for the ECA Report because it helps distinguish unexamined impressions about what happened from verifiable events. As facts and documents are discovered, use a timeline to memorialize and chronicle the information. Append important documents to the timeline as part of the ECA Report, and footnote or otherwise capture the sources of the facts on the timeline. Where possible, the timeline should include each side's version of the events and support (e.g., documents, witness statements) to highlight differences. A timeline also can be used to (1) organize and illustrate factual support for claims, counterclaims, and defenses; (2) illustrate weaknesses and strengths in the client's and opponent's cases; (3) jog memories for internal discussions; (4) elicit testimony later at depositions, a hearing, or a trial; and (5) present the results of the ECA analysis to decision makers.

An informal factual review may cover the following activities:

Conduct internal interviews

Consider beginning with high-level or more general interviews to get the *lay of the land*, such as the relevant personnel related to the contract, product, or services at issue; product history, design, and development; relevant market information; relevant corporate locations; individuals with relevant information; and the backstory of the dispute at hand. At this stage, the interviews may include current and former employees as well as consultants. With regard to former employees, counsel should investigate whether a former employee has a contractual obligation to cooperate in certain matters involving the company even after leaving the company. And regardless of any contractual obligation it is important to gauge whether the former employee would cooperate, if necessary, informally or formally (e.g., testify).

In the trade secret case in point mentioned earlier in this chapter, outside counsel interviewed the corporate personnel who actually worked with the third party to determine what access they had to the alleged trade secrets and how they developed their own process (e.g., how was the clean room set up to prove independent creation?). In IP/Technology disputes, individuals from various disciplines and at all corporate levels within the company may have relevant information (e.g., executives, sales, marketing, finance, technical, authors).

Collect internal documents

One objective of this task is to identify people likely to have documents relevant to the dispute ("custodians") and to collect the documents (hard copy and electronic) from them. Custodians may reside in various areas in a company (e.g., R&D, design, marketing, finance, legal, management). This step is not intended to be as extensive as formal discovery, yet the search for relevant documents should be as thorough as possible with the custodians and places selected.

Obtaining information from the client often requires some tenacity. As often happens, when the client is simply asked whether documents exist regarding a certain subject or fact, the response may be *no*. This is not necessarily because someone is intentionally withholding the information, but, rather, because people do not know, or they forget, what documents and information they have. Likewise, there often is a difference between facts communicated informally from memory or hearsay, and facts informed by, for example, documents and timelines.

Case in point: In a trade secret case, the head of a business unit claimed that his group had not misappropriated any trade secrets from a third party with whom the group had been collaborating. Moreover, he claimed that any information his group may have obtained from the third party was not worth much. He professed that any existing documents would support his understanding of the facts and, thus, refused to consider a settlement offer because he believed that the other side had overvalued its case. During an ECA, outside counsel directed informal document requests to the group of individuals who had worked with the third party. Emails from the business head's "right-hand guy" were among the documents collected. Those emails lauded the third party's proprietary process and valued it at an amount beyond what the third party was asking to settle the case. The business head was surprised to learn the actual facts, especially from documents authored by his "right-hand guy." The case settled.

One way to impress the importance of the information sought is to prepare informal requests for documents and interrogatories. These should be less formal than those served in accordance with the Federal Rules of Civil Procedure, but more formal than a simple list of queries for documents and information. Handing a formal list to the client will grab their attention and preview the type and scope of discovery they will have to address if litigation commences or continues. Focus the requests and interrogatories on *key* issues (e.g., possible claims, defenses, counterclaims) and provide them to individuals most likely to have the documents and information. Counsel should walk document custodians through the requests and encourage them to ask questions about the requests. This may result in a more thorough and meaningful search.

Another objective of this task is to collect information regarding the extent and whereabouts of relevant electronic documents (e.g., custodians, location, number, type, format, media) to assess the cost and effort of collecting, reviewing, storing, and processing such documents from the relevant location, and the possible role for a technical or e-discovery expert to help review and analyze the documents. Cast a wide net to ensure that all relevant electronic correspondence is collected (e.g., emails and texts with attachments), and efforts should be made to protect metadata. After reviewing the collected documents, counsel should attach key documents to the ECA Report, regardless of whether they strengthen or weaken the client's case.

Identify witnesses and create interview summaries or statements

Once witnesses are identified, interview them for information (e.g., facts they recall, documents and items in their possession or accessible to them) relevant to the dispute and memorialize this information in some form (e.g., interview summary or statement) so it is easy to reference in the ECA Report. These witnesses may be employees or consultants of the client or third parties (e.g., companies or individuals (including prior employees) with information to support a defense or counterclaim). In addition to interviewing the witnesses for facts, assess their capability to testify at a deposition and trial (e.g., calm demeanor, ability to think on their feet, credibility). While developing the factual landscape of the dispute, counsel should think about the role for experts (e.g., non-testifying and testifying, damages, survey, technical) as well as when and how the search for experts should begin. Sufficient time is often needed to find experts knowledgeable about the subject matter at issue and available to perform necessary tests, surveys, and analyses; to prepare expert reports; to provide testimony at hearings and trial; and possibly to conduct technical tutorials in patent and technology cases. Experts must also be effective in front of a jury, judge, or arbitrator. Addressing these issues early may avoid problems later no matter what resolution process the client pursues.

Contact opposing counsel

Opposing counsel can be a useful source of information for an ECA. If the disputants are parties to a contract with an ADR clause (e.g., a step-up clause), counsel should be in contact with one another to make arrangements to conduct the *first step* or first required dispute resolution process. These arrangements may include agreements on informal discovery or information exchange and document protection issues.

If an arbitration or court action has commenced, contacting opposing counsel may have short- and long-term benefits, such as extending impending deadlines and establishing a cooperative working relationship that may result in cost and time efficiencies for the parties and facilitate settlement discussions. Furthermore, an underutilized time and money saver is simply picking up the phone and asking opposing counsel what the dispute or lawsuit is about—beyond what is articulated in a court pleading or arbitration demand. What was the motivation for commencing the action or arbitration and what does the other party want and why? *No formal discovery is required* and the response can be illuminating.

Case in point: A software vendor sued his former customer for trademark infringement. In-house counsel asked the vendor's general counsel what the case was about—the alleged trademark infringement, the company's termination of the vendor's services years before, or something else. The general counsel replied that the company was strapped for cash and was looking for money. The case settled with the help of a mediator. In exchange for a cash payment, the vendor (trademark owner) assigned the trademark registration at issue to the former customer.

Review relevant company and industry historical information

Out of sight, out of mind. Investigate whether there is any valuable information lurking within the company or in plain view outside the company that may be relevant to assessing this dispute. With regard to the former, inquire whether the company has had disputes or claims similar to the present one (or if the current dispute is different in some way). If so, this information may be relevant to estimating the length of time to resolve such a dispute, who at the company might be knowledgeable about the prior disputes, attorneys' fees, the location of relevant documents (e.g., files and databases) and information, and the terms and conditions used previously in settling such cases (e.g., the royalty rate, terms and conditions of similar licenses). Relevant company history in the accused party's files may consist of a license, covenant not to sue, or an agreement (contract for the sale of the accused goods), including an indemnity. For example, in a trademark dispute, relevant company history in the trademark owner's files may consist of licenses for the same or similar marks; other documents relating to previous disputes involving the same mark (e.g., surveys); and evidence of national registrations, continuous use, common-law rights, fame, and advertising expenditures.

Furthermore, looking at client documents may uncover facts that could prevent or support the assertion of claims or defenses such as laches or estoppel. If the company has been involved in previous cases, it may be helpful to call on outside counsel who represented the company in those matters as their expertise may be useful for the current dispute.

Industry or public information that may be relevant includes orders or rulings regarding the same IP asset; license royalties in the field; prior art; the prosecution histories of the patent, trademark, or copyright at issue;[9] public information showing that the alleged trade secret may not be a trade secret; survey information regarding attorneys' fees for similar lawsuits; and information regarding damage awards and settlements in similar lawsuits.

Identify essential information needed

This task is an important reminder that after gathering all accessible information, the ECA team must identify any essential information that is missing (e.g., unknown or not available). The ECA Report should indicate, if possible, whether this information may be obtained (e.g., from the client,

9. Prosecution histories are often a treasure trove of information that can be used in one's favor and against one's adversary. Buried in them, for example, are admissions and statements that have been made to obtain the patent or registration, under oath, that can be used later against the party making them as support for a defense or counterclaim, or to contradict testimony.

informally from the opponent, with the help of a mediator, through formal targeted discovery). Consequently, when performing the factual review, it is important to keep track of the facts found because they often highlight those facts that are missing.

STEP 3—Business Concerns

For this step of the ECA analysis, counsel should identify not only the client's priority business concerns and interests but also those of its opponent. The purpose of identifying both is that counsel may find that the parties share common ground or complementary interests. This exercise is one that a mediator often requires the parties to perform in preparing for mediation. Identifying the parties' concerns and interests often leads to a collaborative dialogue between the parties either directly or facilitated by a mediator. Here are some of the concerns and interests the Guide generally outlines that merit consideration in an ECA:

1. Protecting sensitive data and information
2. Legal (e.g., need for precedent from a court, need for injunctive relief)
3. Economic (short and long term)
4. Timing
5. Relationships (e.g., protecting ongoing R&D or joint development efforts)
6. Publicity and reputation
7. Other concerns (e.g., need to enforce IP, core product at issue)

IP/Technology disputes present a range of concerns for a business, much like patients admitted into an emergency room. Assume, for example, that a company receives a cease-and-desist letter or a complaint alleging infringement of a product that demands both an injunction and damages. The level of impact on the business will depend on various factors. In some cases, the concern may not be great if, for example, the targeted product has not been a good seller and the company was considering discontinuing it before the lawsuit. Situations that may present more of a concern for a company include those where the IP or accused products are core to a company or business unit; the trademark at issue has given a company its identity for many years; and a copyrighted publication is one of the few revenue-generating assets for a company. In these situations, the potential loss of revenue, jobs, and market share resulting from an injunction and possibly modification of a core product could severely impact or cripple a business.

The following are examples of how companies may factor various business interests and concerns into their ECA analysis. Taken separately or in combination, they may militate in favor of an early settlement, possibly using an ADR process whereby the parties can address their concerns and satisfy important interests and needs. Alternatively, the identified interests and concerns may simply serve as an alert to the company of their existence, which the company may choose to address at a later appropriate time.

Protect confidential and sensitive information

An IP/Technology dispute typically involves sensitive[10] and confidential technical and business information, at least some of which the parties may need or want to exchange with the other party. The scope of that exchange will vary greatly depending upon the dispute resolution process the parties will encounter (ranging from negotiation to litigation) and the nature of the asserted claims, counterclaims, and defenses. Thus, two initial determinations to make with information collected from the ECA are (1) the nature and kinds of confidential and sensitive information uncovered; and (2) the potential scope of confidential and sensitive information that the parties ultimately may need to disclose or produce. The parties should also consider, depending upon the dispute resolution processes they may engage, whether the confidential and sensitive information identified in the ECA can be protected adequately according to typical means (e.g., confidentiality agreement, protective order, filing under seal). There may be information that a company does not want exposed to anyone outside the company under any circumstances (e.g., even under a confidentiality agreement or protective order, or by limiting disclosure to certain individuals), thus militating in favor of resolving the dispute early and by negotiation or mediation.

Legal concerns

Legal concerns may be on the mind of both parties. For example, parties to a patent infringement dispute over a pharmaceutical product may want to settle, but need to address antitrust concerns to avoid later problems. Such concerns may not be an impediment, but only a delay to settling. For example, if a company's primary interest is to set legal precedent for future cases, then that legal interest may influence how a company resolves a dispute. In such a situation, a company may decide that confidential processes such as negotiation, mediation, or arbitration are not acceptable.

10. The kind of sensitive information a party may uncover in an ECA may not be limited to business competitive information. For example, it may also constitute statements or decisions that corporate representatives made, which, in retrospect, could make the company look bad or culpable, or unfavorable surveys or test results.

Economic concerns

Some of the easily identifiable economic concerns parties face in an IP/Technology dispute are the extent of potential monetary harm (e.g., liability damages, costs, attorneys' fees, enhanced damages), the short- and long-term effects of any injunction on the business unit involved or the company as a whole, and the time and costs of fighting. Can the parties comfortably shoulder these? Do they want to? Additional economic concerns include the impact the dispute may have on customers and sales of the accused product(s), the stock price of the companies (assuming they are publicly traded), and, where the dispute involves a contractual relationship, future business between the parties. In some disputes, economic concerns and interests may influence when and how settlements are made. For example, an uncertain economy could drive an IP owner who needs money now to settle early and for less money to obtain the immediate infusion of cash. Similarly, an IP owner may settle early if they are concerned that waiting to collect on a larger verdict or award may become risky because of the economic condition of the accused. If the accused party also has economic concerns (e.g., pursuing expensive litigation) and would benefit from an early settlement, these overlapping concerns and interests would likely lead to an early settlement.

Timing

Timing is everything—even in IP/Technology disputes. Timing may catalyze an early settlement where, for example, (1) the parties are concerned about their revenue streams, reputation, and shareholder relations (assuming publicly traded companies) from a dispute made public; (2) the parties have too many other things going on (e.g., high-profile lawsuits or government investigations) and the new dispute puts an unwanted burden on monetary and personnel resources; (3) the accused company is not doing well financially and cannot afford to maintain the IP case or possibly pay significant damages; (4) the dispute is an unwanted cloud looming over a pending merger or acquisition; or (5) a party does not want the other party to obtain in discovery documents or testimony that could affect the party's culpability and the damages awarded (e.g., information showing enhanced damages because of when the alleged infringer learned of the patents, information showing laches because of when the IP owner learned of the infringing conduct, information establishing substantial damages because of how an internal document valued the alleged misappropriated technology). Similarly, where an accused product is no longer doing well in the marketplace or certain IP is no longer of value for a company (e.g., no longer *core* or where a patent has a short time to expiration), and a dispute commences with regard to such a product or IP asset, the timing of these circumstances may influence when settlement occurs.

Even when a dispute does not settle early, timing can play a role in catalyzing a settlement later in an IP/Technology case—for example, after the parties have had the opportunity to pursue discovery or they receive a particular ruling (e.g., claim construction, summary judgment).

Relationship between the parties

A preexisting relationship between parties does not portend whether they will be able to settle a dispute early, or even later. Sometimes disputes between parties in a relationship are so fueled by emotion and distrust and the relationship is so irreparably harmed that any settlement—early or later—is difficult to achieve. But where such a level of animosity or acrimony has not occurred, and the disputants have a current relationship (e.g., joint venture partners, co-developers, co-creators, licensor and licensee) that they want to salvage, an early settlement may be easier to achieve. Furthermore, it is not uncommon for competitors to find mutually beneficial terms to resolve their dispute. Peaceful solutions may occur for various reasons. They may be assisted by executives removed from the fray who have a relationship, or because the companies—competitors in one arena—work together in other arenas. And counsel can nurture settlement based upon, for example, the relationship they have with one another and their respective clients, and their approach to resolving their clients' disputes.

Publicity, reputation, and stock

When an IP/Technology dispute is played out in a public forum, there is messaging for the IP owner that they may need or benefit from. For example, a small company that has created new technology may find it necessary to confront in court a larger company that it alleges has misappropriated that technology to send a message to the world that it will protect its IP assets and it will not be bullied. Or a company that lost an employee to a competitor who breaches a confidentiality agreement may want to make an example out of the situation to dissuade others from doing the same and make clear that it protects its IP assets.

Conversely, however, there is the potential for adverse publicity, reputational harm, and other business risks from IP/Technology disputes. For example:

- Branding a company as a trademark bully, infringer, or trade secret thief may have effects in the marketplace with an explosion of hostile social media, frustrated customers, decreased revenues, and shareholder dissatisfaction.
- IP claims joined with related claims supported by the same facts, such as antitrust, tortious interference, and breach of contract, may paint additional unflattering images for one or both of the parties.

- Internal document review and interviews in an ECA may uncover documents and information that a company would just as soon not see produced in discovery or made public.
- If a company is the subject of a government investigation or in negotiations over a potential merger/acquisition, the timing of the publicity can create risks for a company.

The ECA Report should capture the fallout that has or might occur so that the parties can address or try to avoid financial harm and public relations issues.

Other considerations

a. **Importance of IP, product, and service**. How important is the IP asset to the IP owner and how important is the involved product or service to the alleged infringer? These are important questions because they require a dispassionate dialogue between counsel and business personnel so that the magnitude of the *fight* is proportional to the value of the IP and products at issue to the parties. Where each holds a high importance or interest to the parties, and the IP owner wants the accused product or service off the market, the chances of an early settlement may be unlikely. But where the IP owner would consider a license, this creates an opportunity for a possible settlement. Or, as mentioned earlier in this chapter (under Timing), if the IP owner recognizes that the value of the asset is limited (e.g., it is no longer core, the patent is expiring), this too creates options for an early settlement. Where a defendant or respondent has an interest in continuing to make or sell the product at issue, a license may be the answer if the IP owner is willing to grant one. Or, if its interests are only to continue making and selling for a set time (e.g., through an important selling season, or until another mark can be chosen and implemented), these short-term interests may be complementary with an IP owner's long-term interests.

b. **Human resource drain and distraction**. Corporate personnel may be polite when asked, but they typically do not have time to perform litigation support. Some companies consider the support of litigation or arbitration to be a cost of doing business, and they encourage and support it (an individual is not penalized for assisting even if he did not accomplish certain tasks in his "day job"). Other companies make individuals available to assist counsel but are not as supportive. IP/Technology litigation and arbitration, in particular, often require support and decisions from a variety of in-house personnel (e.g., attorneys, information technology, finance, business, marketing, scientists) and often at varying levels of authority (e.g., bench scientists, salespersons, business managers, corporate executives, chief IP counsel, general counsel, board of directors).

The requisite litigation support may be for many different tasks and decisions (e.g., responding to discovery; identifying and collecting documents; testifying at depositions, arbitration hearings, and at trial; assisting in designing around patent claims or choosing another mark; helping to develop litigation or settlement strategies; and participating in ADR processes). The time that any one person is required to spend on the life of a dispute can vary significantly. In some disputes, personnel key to the business of the company may be required to assist for long periods of time. Smaller companies are often hit harder than larger companies. Nonetheless, depending on the magnitude of the dispute and considering how lean companies of all sizes are run, the issue that must be considered is how equipped the company is to deal with the drain of human resources typically caused by IP/Technology disputes.

c. **Corporate culture**. Some companies prefer to settle disputes quickly, while others want to defend the company at all costs (or at least until it becomes cost prohibitive to do so).

d. **Global "peace."** It is often the case that parties in IP/Technology disputes have multiple disputes ongoing in various jurisdictions and forums (e.g., district courts, ITC, PTO, foreign tribunals), and that they have common concerns in continuing these battles and common interests in settling them soon, amicably, and in a coordinated way that makes sense for the business and strategies of both companies. Thus, where multiple disputes exist, parties can begin their settlement dialogue with a *bigger* pie to slice up, including a global settlement of multiple disputes.

As mentioned earlier, it is useful to identify the opponent's likely business concerns and interests to appreciate the full business reality so that possible options for resolving the dispute in a non-adversarial manner (e.g., negotiations and mediation) can emerge.

Case in point: Consider a patent infringement dispute over a product that had not been profitable in recent years but was about to have its biggest season of the year. Some of the defendant's concerns included an injunction stopping sales for the high season, paying *back damages* on a product that was not profitable, bad publicity before the high season resulting in a decrease in sales, and having to finance an expensive patent litigation. Some of the plaintiff's concerns included stopping an infringer to preserve and increase its own sales and market share and avoiding an expensive patent litigation (the sluggish economy had decreased sales and revenues). Considering the parties' concerns and interests, the following deal was struck: The plaintiff permitted the accused party to continue selling the accused product for one last season (i.e., plaintiff licensed this limited continued use). The plaintiff benefited from the royalty income and happy customers that would soon be theirs, and the defendant used its share of the revenue to offset the back damages it owed. As it happens, the defendant also had a patent covering the accused product and it was willing to assign its rights in that patent to the plaintiff (for future licensing and enforcement purposes). Thus, the accused company obtained value for an asset that would no longer be valuable to it, upon ceasing to sell the accused product, by using the value of the patent assignment to offset some portion of the back damages.

There is no prescribed means for identifying business concerns and interests for achieving a global peace. For a small company, talking with its chief executive officer (CEO) and chief financial officer (CFO) may suffice. When the dispute involves the business unit of a large company, talking with the unit's president or senior vice president, along with the general counsel or IP counsel, may suffice. In a larger company, consider consulting others outside of the business unit affected, particularly if any settlement may include a future business partnership or sale of goods that involves another part of the company. Strategic goals and objectives may be discovered as a result of the ECA that can be satisfied within the context of a global settlement (e.g., as described in the previous example, terminating an unprofitable product and obtaining value for patents that would no longer possess much value for the business unit).

The opponent's interests and future plans may be learned from consulting publicly available sources, talking with salespersons or scientists who attend professional or trade meetings where such information may circulate, and even from picking up the phone and having a conversation between counterparts (e.g., in-house counsel, outside counsel, businesspersons).

A wrinkle that can arise and must be anticipated is the consideration of the concerns and interests of people who may have the ultimate or a very influential say in settlement, or a key decision, but who are not involved in the day-to-day running of the business or litigation activities. In some circumstances, such stakeholders may include a group of investors or a contractual business partner, or even a board of directors. Depending on the significance of the dispute and the related IP or products and services, these individuals may need to be consulted if any global peace is to be reached.

STEP 4—Forum and Adversary Analysis

For this step, the Guide focuses generally on four separate analyses:

1. **Forum analysis**. If the dispute is in court, what is the judge's profile and track record and what is the potential jury pool? If the dispute is headed for mediation and possibly arbitration, what are the profiles of neutral candidates?

2. **Opposing counsel analysis**. What is the reputation and experience of opposing counsel, including in negotiations and at trial? What may be opposing counsel's possible incentives to settle early? How has opposing counsel handled similar claims for the same or other clients and what were the outcomes?
3. **Opposing party analysis**. Is there a continuing business relationship with the opposing party? What are the opponent's financial and legal resources? Does the opponent have any immediate needs that may support an early settlement approach? Are the opponent and client competitors?
4. **CPR Pledge**. Is the opponent a signatory to the pledge?

Forum analysis

The forum or forums that the parties are subject to can impact the time to resolution, the cost of resolution, and who decides the disputed issues. Thus, the time to resolve the dispute will vary depending upon whether the forum is, for example, a U.S. federal district court, the ITC, the PTO, a foreign tribunal, or an arbitration panel, and whether more than one forum is involved. So, too, will the nature and number of forums involved affect the cost to obtain a final resolution of the dispute, including appeals and possible remand. Also impacting time and cost are factors that may facilitate or impede resolution of the dispute (e.g., venue change, interlocutory appeal, preliminary injunction, governing arbitration rules, grant of dispositive motion, scope of discovery, jurisdictional challenges to the arbitration panel).

Investigating the forum would include examining not only the alacrity of the forum (e.g., *rocket docket* or ITC versus slower forum) but also (1) the volume of IP cases generally heard by the forum; (2) the number of similar cases that the assigned judge or administrative law judge (ALJ) or appointed arbitrator has heard (i.e., same IP area, similar technology or subject matter); (3) the governing rules and practices adopted by the forum, decision maker, and parties (e.g., use of patent rules); (4) whether the assigned judge, ALJ, or arbitrator issues rulings that are in or out of sync with the mainstream on legal issues important and pertinent to the dispute; and (5) the assigned judge's or ALJ's record on TROs, preliminary injunctions, summary judgment motions, discovery, and *Markman*[11] rulings, and managing the case. In some cases (e.g., courts, ITC), this kind of information can be obtained from publicly available sources, such as reported cases, litigation support services, court records, and local counsel. Local counsel also would be one of the best sources for identifying the potential jury pool. When selecting arbitrators, the parties may need to consult fellow advocates who have

11. *See* Markman v. Westview Instruments, Inc., 517 U.S. 370 (1996) and Glossary Definition.

knowledge of the arbitrator(s), other arbitrators who may have sat with the appointed arbitrator(s), and, if the appointed arbitrator(s) was a judge, his or her published opinions.

Parties in a contractual relationship may be contractually obligated to pursue particular dispute resolution process(es) in the event of a dispute. Thus, it is important to review the agreement with the following in mind:

- What process(es) have the parties chosen to resolve their dispute: negotiation, mediation, arbitration, or litigation?
- Who will administer any ADR process the parties have agreed to—an administering institution or the neutral they select (non-administered)?
- What rules will apply to the ADR proceeding(s)?
- Did the parties set forth qualifications for the neutral(s) who would be involved in the ADR process(es)?
- Did the parties stipulate to other conditions that may affect the forum analysis (e.g., situs or seat in an international dispute)?

Opposing counsel analysis

This analysis impacts internal and out-of-pocket costs of litigating or arbitrating the dispute. Are opposing counsel *scorched earth* litigators? Do they take a no-stone-unturned approach to discovery? Would they import litigation tactics into an arbitration? Similarly, how may their character or tactics influence settlement talks? Learning from the pleadings (assuming a filed court case or arbitration demand) or correspondence what law firm or specific attorney will be representing the opponent is a good start. If counsel does not know opposing counsel from direct experience or reputation, perhaps one of the best sources of information is attorneys who have dealt previously with them. In this regard, published opinions often identify attorneys who have served as opposing counsel or maybe even co-counsel ("reference attorneys").

Investigating opposing counsel representing a nonpracticing entity can often have its own built-in challenges. In such situations the client's business model often dictates counsel's approach to litigation and settlement. One approach for obtaining information useful to the ECA in this situation is simply to ask counsel directly what he or she is after. The answer may not be appealing, but it may clarify important information to factor into the ECA.

Opposing party analysis

If the opposing party is a company with whom the client has been doing, or was doing, business (e.g., license, exclusive distribution arrangement, joint venture partner, joint development), the client may have information regarding the opponent's financial ability to pursue or defend a case in court or arbitration as well as their corporate philosophy or propensity to fight or consider resolution through other means. Without such prior dealings, information about their litigiousness may be obtained from published court cases and reports and industry intelligence.

Often business relationships involving IP, technology, or products and services protected by IP (e.g., patented products, "trademarked goods," copyrighted publication, proprietary process) are strategically important to both companies because of the value each party invests in the relationship (money and employee time) and the value or profits anticipated from the resulting collaboration. The companies are likely to have publicized the relationship and the expected results to others (e.g., the public generally, shareholders, investors). Thus, the parties may have a lot to lose if they cannot resolve their dispute. In an ECA analysis, addressing a conflict between business partners should be handled thoughtfully and strategically. Furthermore, depending on the importance of the business relationship to the company (and maybe a particular executive), and the public relations implications, it may be necessary to obtain higher approval or to consult with others outside of the affected business unit for approval of case strategy and, possibly, involvement in resolving the dispute.

Case in point: A telecommunications company ("Company A") was poised to file a patent infringement suit in a U.S. federal district court against another company ("Company B") it alleged was infringing its patent. It occurred to Company A's in-house counsel that Company A might have a valuable industry relationship with Company B warranting a prudent strategy in pursuing the patent infringement lawsuit. Company A's in-house counsel talked with the relevant business executive within Company A to determine whether such a relationship existed and confirmed it did (i.e., the companies were working on the same side on federal legislation and other industry initiatives). Company A decided that it would file the complaint for patent infringement but would not serve it on Company B, and that an executive from Company A would contact his counterpart from Company B to let her know as a courtesy about the patent infringement dispute, how Company A was handling it in view of the industry relationship, and to encourage communications between the parties about the patent infringement lawsuit.

Accordingly, issues to consider in an opposing party analysis include:

- Must the relationship continue for strategic or economic reasons?
- Does the company require high-level approval for any reason, including if the potential damages could exceed a certain amount?
- Are the opponent's needs known and may they support an early resolution?

- What are both parties' best and worst alternatives if the dispute cannot be worked out?
- How did the dispute arise? Was there a change in personnel with either company that may have caused it?
- Who may be in the best position to mend fences within the companies or to amicably break up, if that is necessary?
- Is the opponent financially and legally fit to litigate the dispute if it cannot be resolved? Pay particular attention if the opponent is on the smaller side. Large companies tend to underestimate their opponent's financial and psychological fortitude (particularly if they are smaller) to fight if necessary. Investigate whether the opponent has litigation insurance, a war chest from similar litigations, committed investors, or third-party financing.

Signatory to the CPR pledge

Is the opponent a signatory of one of CPR's pledges? The pledges are a statement of policy aimed at encouraging greater use of flexible, creative, and constructive approaches for resolving business-related disputes early.[12] The pledges can open the door to communications about resolving the dispute early as well as constructive ways to do so. CPR's website lists the law firms and companies who have signed the pledges.

STEP 5—Risk Management Analysis

A risk management analysis may encompass various issues that a company routinely considers by practice or policy. The Guide focuses on collecting information related to two areas of risk management—electronic discovery and insurance—so the discussion here focuses on those issues. It is likely that at least part of the risk management analysis was performed earlier pursuant to Step 2, while collecting documents, identifying document custodians, and interviewing corporate personnel for overview and background information (e.g., head of information technology, general counsel), and pursuant to Step 1, while identifying possible insurance coverage. If that is the case, consider how to best capture this information in the ECA Report so that all information related to the risk management analysis is at least in one place.

E-discovery

How to manage the risks involved in electronic discovery (e-discovery) is beyond the scope of this book. That said, a company should take early steps to identify, preserve, maintain, and review all potentially relevant and discoverable

12. *See ADR Pledges*, CPR, https://www.cpradr.org/adr-pledges (last visited Mar. 23, 2025).

electronic data (Step 2 discusses the step of identifying e-discovery documents and communications). Preserving data typically entails identifying the client's e-discovery policies and procedures regarding preservation of electronically stored information, including (1) issuing legal hold notices and reminders for documents and emails and chronicling the recipients, dates sent, and length of hold; and (2) identifying document custodians of relevant hard copy and electronic documents. This usually requires suspending routine data disposal policies and practices within the company as well as contacting former employees and third parties under a party's control. Thought should be given to preserving documents on *legacy* databases (e.g., resulting from corporate mergers, use of new platforms), as well as currently used databases. Depending upon the forum (e.g., court, arbitration), governing rules and law, and the discretion of the judge or arbitrator, a party seeking documents maintained on a legacy database may obtain the right to have such documents produced. Thus, for the ECA analysis, consider appending a copy of the client's e-discovery policy and procedures to the ECA Report and memorialize how the policy has been followed for the dispute under investigation.

Insofar as e-discovery data in IP/Technology disputes may be collected from many sources and take many forms, consideration must be given to how to maintain the collected data so that it can be managed (e.g., searched, tracked, organized, retrieved, reviewed, and printed).

Insurance

Litigation involving IP can be expensive. In some instances, clients may choose to self-insure or assume the risks of incurring the costs of litigation. In others, a business may want to consider third-party funding,[13] or it may have insured some of the risk. There are various kinds of insurance policies available to companies that may cover, or are specifically designed to cover, IP litigation (e.g., costs, expenses, damages). And, a company may be able to mitigate some risk through indemnification, if such an option exists (see discussion in Step 1).

---

13. "Third-party funding" has been defined as follows:

> [Third-party funding], often referred to as litigation finance, is a financial arrangement in which a third party in a legal dispute provides funding to support the plaintiff's pursuit of a legal claim. In return, the third-party funder receives a portion of the proceeds if the case is successful. This funding model allows entities to bring lawsuits without shouldering the financial risks associated with litigation.

An Overview of How Third-Party Litigation Funders Are Being Addressed by Courts and Policymakers, Baker Botts (June 3, 2024), https://www.bakerbotts.com/thought-leadership/publications/2024/june/an-overview-of-how-third-party-litigation-funders-are-being-addressed-by-courts-and-policymakers.

Knowing whether the client has insurance to bring a claim or defend against one is an important starting point for the risk management portion of the ECA analysis. Other issues to confront are whether it even wants to make a claim for the IP dispute that is the subject of the ECA and whether the insurance company will, in fact, provide coverage for the claim. In the event the insurance company decides not to do so, and depending on the stage of the dispute, the client has other issues to consider, including whether to pursue the litigation without insurance, whether to settle the dispute and for what amount, and whether to pursue litigation against the insurance company.

The Guide provides the following questions to consider for addressing the issue of insurance in the ECA analysis:

- Is the claim insured or self-insured?
- If insured, has the carrier been notified? Has the carrier accepted coverage, disputed coverage, or issued a reservation of rights?
- If the carrier has not been notified, who is responsible for giving notice and when will notice be given?
- Who is responsible for locating all potentially applicable policies?
- Have all potentially applicable insurance policies been located?

Include the answers to the aforementioned questions in the ECA Report as well as the contact information for whomever the client contacted at the insurance company to obtain the answers, the dates of responses, any correspondence with the insurance company, and any other relevant documents (e.g., insurance policies, any opinions of counsel the insurance company requested).

STEP 6—Legal Analysis

This step includes an analysis of the claims (including counterclaims) and defenses that the parties may have already pled, or that they anticipate pleading in view of the facts marshaled; the strengths and weaknesses of those claims; estimated damages; the costs to achieve or defeat the claims and defenses; and additional information that may be necessary to refine the legal analysis of these issues. The Guide suggests generally the following to consider as part of the legal analysis: Ascertain and narrow scope of claims (including counterclaims) and defenses.

- Conduct risk assessment of each claim and defense.
- Estimate possible damages spectrum.
- Identify additional information necessary to evaluate damages.
- Determine whether a damages expert will be required.
- Estimate costs to completion.
- Estimate outside counsel fees.
- Estimate other litigation expenses and "hard" costs.
- Anticipate expenditure of internal resources and "soft" costs, including in-house lawyer time, business professional time, and witness time.

This analysis step in the Guide is positioned after the informal fact review for good reason. The more facts that can be marshaled from as many sources as possible—the client, third parties, the opposing party, publicly available information—the better the assessment of the strengths and weaknesses of contemplated claims, defenses, and forms of relief. Likewise, being fully armed with the facts will drive the investigation and analysis of the kinds of legal claims and defenses that may be asserted (e.g., state or federal, U.S. or international, PTO, ITC).[14] This step should also help eliminate claims and defenses that are not worth asserting now or later in litigation or arbitration, or raising in a mediation.

To conduct a reliable risk assessment of claims and defenses, it is important to research current relevant law. In the area of IP, the law is constantly changing and evolving. Do not assume that you generally *know the law* without researching the most current applicable law and studying it.[15] Perform the legal research and written analysis with the same effort and care used in writing an important brief. After all, decision makers are using the legal analysis for many purposes, including managing risks for the company (e.g., large damages, injunction) and avoiding a significant outlay of litigation costs. Furthermore, legal research may shed light on additional facts or documents to obtain. If the information is not available, note what is needed and the possible sources for it (e.g., from the opponent pursuant to a mediation, in discovery if litigation ensues). Insofar as ECA is intended to help manage a dispute if it does not settle early, the legal research also can be used later

14. For example, if an executive leaves a company and opens up his own business in competition with his prior employer, the facts may support legal claims and relief based on breach of contract, trade secret misappropriation, and business tort. And the same facts may support claims under both federal and state law providing different kinds of relief.

15. A risk assessment can be performed incorrectly if a client assumes it knows the law or relies on someone who does not know the relevant law.

Case in point: After a trade secret misappropriation case was filed against a large company by a small company, the head of the implicated business unit at the large company (Mr. X) consulted an in-house business attorney he regularly worked with and learned from him that the company allegedly had a full defense to the pending lawsuit. Another in-house counsel got involved who had deep experience in IP litigation, including trade secret misappropriation cases, and, after a condensed but thorough ECA including research into the relevant law, Mr. X was eventually convinced that the defense he learned of was unviable to the misappropriation claims, and that the company had a high risk of loss in the case that he would be responsible for. Mr. X settled the case.

in formulating discovery and deposition questions, for briefing, and possibly for settlement negotiations and mediation submissions.

An important aspect of risk assessment that routinely gets overlooked is "client-think."[16] These are unconscious influences (e.g., biases, unconscious barriers) that impair an attorney's ability to see critical facts, and to weigh appropriately those facts that attorneys see.[17] These biases coalesce in the lawyer-client relationship, magnifying the potential for misevaluation.[18] Client-think blinds attorneys to visible and knowable risk, resulting in an incorrect assessment of cases and their risk-adjusted value.[19] There are ways to improve risk assessments that include the following concepts:

- Once a team of lawyers is assigned to work on a case, choose one member of the team or someone not on the team to play the role of devil's advocate (i.e., assume the perspective of the adversary). This person will examine all the evidence in that light and bring damaging evidence or assessment directly to the lead lawyer and the client without gloss.
- Each team member should write down his or her views on each issue before performing a group risk analysis. Depending upon the firm or corporate culture, the team member can identify or note the view as his or hers. All views should be shared with the entire group and client.
- Conduct a moot court on important issues or important portions of the case.[20]

Consider compiling a list or chart of possible legal claims (assuming a case has not yet been filed), counterclaims, and defenses. Include in the chart relevant published cases setting forth the elements for each claim, and then list the supporting evidence to prove each element. Note any missing evidence that is needed to complete the chart.[21] This chart is useful for various

16. *See* Laura A. Kaster, *Improving Lawyer Judgment by Reducing the Impact of "Client-Think,"* Disp. Resol. J., Feb./Apr. 2012, at 1, http://appropriatedisputesolutions.com/site/wp-content/themes/twentytwelve/pdf/Kaster-4-11-12.pdf.

17. *See id.*

18. *See id.*

19. *See id.*

20. *See id.*

21. Counsel may find it useful to turn this chart or table of claims into a proof matrix, identifying for each element of every claim or defense (1) the witness who will testify about the claim or defense; (2) the document or other evidence counsel will introduce; and (3) possible hurdles or objections and responses. The proof matrix could also be used to begin strategizing discovery, the case theme, one's opening statement and closing argument, who will testify, what evidence to use at trial, the strengths and weaknesses of one's case, and whether certain motions should be pursued (e.g., preliminary injunction, summary judgment).

purposes, such as gauging the strengths and weaknesses of both sides of the case for internal discussions, discussing the case with opposing counsel (in-house or outside), preparing a mediation brief, and preparing pleadings (e.g., court, arbitration, ITC).

Another way for a party to deal with possible client bias is to obtain a third party's perspective by way of an abbreviated mock trial or hearing (see Section II of Chapter 5 for a discussion of the use of a mock arbitration panel). Mock trials should be undertaken after the early identification of key witnesses and documents. A mock trial can, among other things, provide an objective view of the strengths and weaknesses of an issue or case, the effectiveness of witnesses, and the persuasiveness of evidence and case themes. Counsel may also use the results of an early mock trial to develop or improve a discovery plan. Although the time and cost may not be appropriate for all cases, for bet-the-company cases, it may be worth the investment.

Another aspect of the legal analysis is estimating damages (including enhanced damages). For example, if a party can prove that a patent was infringed willfully, then damages may be enhanced up to three times. Similarly, if the trial court finds that claims or conduct during the litigation meets the standard of an "exceptional case" under 35 U.S.C. § 285, then reasonable attorneys' fees may be awarded to the prevailing party.

Case in point: A research engineer at Company A alerted the company's legal department of an issued patent by a competitor (Company B) that was in the field of a product that the engineer was developing for Company A. After review, the legal department advised that the product in development could have features 1, 2, and 3 without infringing the patent; but features 4 and 5 should be avoided, as a product with those features would likely infringe the competitor's patent. Because the engineer informed the legal department that features 4 and 5 were not being contemplated to include in the product, no invalidity investigation on the patent under consideration was performed. In fact, the legal department cited the competitor's patent in its own patent application for its product.

As it happened, after the research engineer passed the product from the research phase into the development and testing phases, features 4 and 5 were added without the research engineer or the legal department being consulted. The product was thereafter launched in the market and became the subject of a patent infringement lawsuit filed by the company's competitor. The competitor prevailed in the patent infringement suit and collected three times the amount of its damages because the court determined that the infringement had been willful (the company had knowledge of the patent, as evidenced by it being cited in the patent application, and had also received specific advice not to include the infringing features, which it nonetheless did). The court also felt that the company's behavior qualified the case as exceptional and additionally ordered it to pay all of the attorneys' fees of the competitor related to the litigation.

In estimating damages, parties need to consider the costs to obtain or avoid paying damages (or obtaining and defending against an injunction). A comparison of the two—estimated damages versus estimated costs to obtain damages and possibly other relief—may help a client consider its options—for example, pursue litigation, arbitration, licensing, or some other settlement structure.[22] Retaining a damages expert even at the earliest stages of a dispute can help formulate damages theories, estimate damages, collect and analyze relevant documents for the analysis, and determine what further information is needed. See Chapter 4 for a discussion of the use of initial or early damages assessments.

Who should be involved in the damages analysis will vary depending on the size and organization of the client. If the client is a small company, the team may consist simply of the outside counsel and the CEO. With a larger company, the team may expand to include outside counsel, in-house counsel, a senior business representative, and the CFO (or someone on staff). And, in some situations, it may be helpful to engage a damages expert to assist, depending on the amount at risk, the complexity of the issues, and the knowledge and expertise required to perform a reliable damages analysis. The number and kind of individuals to involve are not as important as ensuring that individuals with appropriate knowledge, expertise, and authority are part of the damages analysis.

As with the general facts needed to support a claim or defense, note in the ECA what facts may be missing to perform or refine the damages analysis. In addition to focusing on obtaining the missing facts in discovery, they may be available outside of discovery from the opponent pursuant to negotiations or mediation.

This step also includes estimating the damages spectrum. In an IP/Technology case, the damages may be easy to calculate or more involved. What follows are some of the issues to consider in estimating damages or a damages spectrum.

- Will damages constitute statutory damages?
- What is the expected interpretation and application of the applicable damages statute(s) and case law in relation to the infringing activity at issue?
- If a contract is at issue, what are the kinds of possible contract damages? What are the ranges of possible recovery based on various outcomes? Did the parties agree to exclude any types of damages or other recovery?

22. If settlement is a possibility, then a part of that calculus are the potential settlement values (e.g., potential damages awards being paid plus possible interest, minus various fees and expenses) based on net present value.

- What is the scope of infringement (e.g., the number and kinds of infringing goods, activities in the United States and abroad)?
- What are the possible applicable damages theories upon which recovery may be based?
- Are damages based upon reasonable royalties, lost profits, or a combination (how will lost profits be calculated)?
- What is the value of the IP asset?
- In patent cases, were the products marked with the patent number(s), if it was required?
- Are there laches and possibly estoppel issues?
- Are there any bases for increasing or enhancing damages and how likely is it that damages will be increased or enhanced?[23]

Turning to costs, a practical and realistic budget should be developed for each of the pending or anticipated cases (e.g., litigation, arbitration, ITC investigation, PTO proceeding). Each budget should focus on anticipated stages of the case as applicable to the kind of proceeding (e.g., prefiling, investigation and preparation of the pleadings (including removal and dismissal motions, motions to compel arbitration), discovery (fact and expert) and related motions, preliminary injunction motion, *Markman* determination, summary judgment motions, pretrial conferences, trial or evidentiary hearing, post-trial motions, and appeals). The costs may be hard (e.g., outside counsel, experts, document-processing vendors, trial or hearing graphics vendors, jury consultants, maintaining a war room, printing/duplicating costs, equipment rentals, lodging, food and travel, court reporters) and soft (e.g., the valuable time of in-house lawyers, corporate executives, and other corporate personnel (e.g., scientists, businesspeople, finance analysts, designers) needed to assist regularly throughout the case for depositions, trial, and ADR proceedings). The hard costs, in particular, should be estimated on a line-item basis for each stage of the case. Regarding experts, determine what kinds of experts may be required (e.g., to prepare pleadings, assist with discovery, assess damages, assist in a design-around, assess substantial similarity, develop and conduct a survey, or rebut survey evidence) and estimate how much their services may cost until the dispute is resolved.

Information useful for calculating costs may be based on actual costs in similar cases in which the client was involved, actual costs in similar cases handled by outside counsel, surveys such as the one conducted by

23. Given that patent cases, for example, may yield nine- and ten-figure damages awards and the potential for enhancing such awards by a factor of three, it is prudent to understand the incidence of enhanced damages and the variables affecting their occurrence, and to evaluate any risk that may exist.

the American Intellectual Property Law Association,[24] and estimates from experts based on similar cases and their assessment of the amount of work to be done in the case at hand. Vendors can also estimate potential fees based on similar cases and what is required for the current case. Some caveats to relying on costs from previous litigations are that the cost of goods and services goes up and they may be geographically determined (e.g., where the case is pending, where counsel are located). Thus, in comparing the costs for the outstanding dispute to similar cases, make sure that the cases are similar in meaningful ways that impact costs.

Outside counsel will be in the best position to provide the attorneys' fee portion of the costs in the form of a line-item budget for each anticipated stage of the case as well as estimates for litigation-related vendors and experts based on other similar cases and current rates. Regarding the discovery portion, in particular (the most expensive part of an IP/Technology case), the ECA should pinpoint the information needed and from whom (or where in the world) that information is likely to come (see e-discovery under Step 5). The client may use counsel's preparation of the budget to discuss alternative billing structures that could affect the cost-benefit analysis described in Step 7.

In-house counsel will be in the best position to provide an estimate on *soft time* possibly based on previous disputes involving the company. The soft time should identify with particularity (1) who at the company may need to serve as a witness for depositions, hearings, and at trial; (2) who would need to support the litigation on a regular basis; (3) the expected tasks involved in (1) and (2); (4) the estimated time needed to perform those tasks, including any required travel; and (5) the associated costs (e.g., transportation, lodging, food).

Lastly, it is not uncommon in IP/Technology cases for the scope of the parties' dispute to extend into different forums and countries (e.g., co-pending federal district court litigation and ITC investigation, co-pending federal district court litigation and PTO proceedings, co-pending U.S. court litigation and foreign litigation). Thus, the aforementioned analyses (i.e., legal, damages, risk assessment) and the estimated costs and fees will be impacted by the number and kind of forums that may be involved as a result of the parties' dispute and should be considered in the ECA.

---

24. The American Intellectual Property Law Association (AIPLA) publishes an economic survey it conducts every other year that examines the economic aspects of IP law practice, including the costs of IP litigation (e.g., between different subject matter areas, through discovery, through trial, and by major U.S. cities). *See The Report of the Economic Survey*, AIPLA, https://www.aipla.org/home/news-publications/economic-survey (last visited Mar. 23, 2025).

STEP 7—Cost-Benefit Analysis

This is the step in the ECA where all of the information gathered in the previous steps is translated into a meaningful cost-benefit analysis that serves as an ideal tool for communicating with business executives and decision makers. The Guide suggests that this step be conducted using a table that facilitates a comparison of the costs and benefits (e.g., percentage likelihood of success or loss, external legal costs, internal costs (high, medium, low), time to complete, advancement of business concerns) associated with each key disposition strategy (e.g., dispositive motion, negotiation, mediation, arbitration, discovery, experts, trial, appeal).

Disposition Strategies	Percentage Likelihood of Success	External Legal Costs	Internal Costs	Time to Complete	Whether Strategy Advances Key Business Concerns
Discovery					
Dispositive Motion					
Negotiate					
Mediate					
Arbitrate/Litigate					
Dual-Track Enforcement					

The table serves as a menu of available disposition options that may be selected or disregarded, depending on the desired goal and associated costs. For example, a negotiated settlement (with or without a mediator) may be selected over a dispositive motion because the probability of a successful outcome, the advancement of a priority business concern, or the protection of IP and products and services involved, is more likely to result from a negotiated or mediated compromise than from a legal ruling on the dispositive motion considering the cost of preparing such a motion and the time required to obtain the court's ruling.

Case in point: A company received a cease-and-desist letter from a nonpracticing entity alleging patent infringement. The number of accused products in the marketplace and in inventory was relatively low, but the company was considering plans to increase the product line that incorporated the allegedly infringing component and a design-around would have been costly. The company conducted an ECA and learned that there were significant grounds for invalidating the patent. The time and cost (outside counsel fees, uncertainty to business) to achieve this result, however, would be substantial because it could only be realized after winning a dispositive motion or at trial. Thus, the company decided to resolve the dispute quickly with a negotiated settlement that included a license for the remaining life of the patent at issue. The profit reaped from future sales more than made up for the cost of the settlement.

Assembling much of the information previously collected in a meaningful cost-benefit analysis facilitates a discussion with the client about certain basic issues, such as the client's goals for initiating, defending, or maintaining the dispute; how the client can best achieve those goals; what the dispute is worth to the client; and what the dispute will actually cost the client (over the life of the dispute, which could include an appeal and remand). Also, the cost-benefit analysis often provides much-needed objectivity (a reality check) and clarification around those issues (beyond, for example, the emotions generated after learning of, or being accused of, an infringement or misappropriation).

STEP 8—Determine Settlement Value

This step entails identifying what value the client is willing to ascribe to the dispute at a point in time. That value comprises both monetary and nonmonetary elements.

Chapter 5 discusses the use of decision tree analysis (DTA) for various purposes, including determining whether to settle and for what amount. Summarized here is a straightforward example of how to use DTA to determine a settlement range, which is a part of the calculus of determining the settlement value of a case. A party commencing an enforcement proceeding (i.e., plaintiff or claimant) will want to determine a range of settlement amounts—including the lowest—that they would accept. The accused party (i.e., defendant or respondent) will want to determine a range of settlement amounts—including the highest—that they would pay to settle the case.

In preparing a decision tree, identify key issues and the expected outcomes for those issues if they were adjudicated. For example, as the plaintiff in a patent infringement case, focus on outcomes related to issues such as a preliminary injunction motion; interpretation of a key patent claim term; summary judgment (e.g., invalidity); and infringement and willfulness (including enhanced damages). The probabilities of obtaining successful results for the identified issues are based on the information and analysis obtained from the ECA. Similarly, for identifying the range of possible damages, these prognostications are based on the work embodied in the ECA from the factual, legal, and damages analyses, possibly with input from one or more experts, as well as historical information on similar suits from the client and outside counsel. A DTA is a living analysis, which should be revised with new facts and legal information as well as new views of the same facts and legal information. For the following illustration, the issue of infringement liability is the focus.

1	2	3	4	5	6
Issue	Liability	Probability of Liability	Ranges of Possible Damages	Probability of Obtaining Damages in Each Range	Range of Values
Patent infringement	Yes	70%	$1M	50%	$350,000
			$2M	30%	$420,000
			$4M	20%	$560,000
	No	30%	No damages		

Column 1 shows the issue under analysis—patent infringement. Column 2 identifies two possible occurrences—the plaintiff proves infringement or does not. Column 3 assigns a probability to those two occurrences. For a successful outcome (proving infringement) a 70 percent probability is estimated, and for an unsuccessful outcome (failing to prove infringement) a 30 percent probability is estimated. Column 4 identifies estimates of three possible damages awards. Column 5 identifies estimated probabilities (50 percent, 30 percent, 20 percent) for obtaining those three possible awards, which are based on current information. The range of values in Column 6 was calculated by multiplying columns 3, 4, and 5 together (e.g., .70 × .50 × $1M) for each of the three damages estimates to obtain $350,000, $420,000, and $560,000.

Thus, in the aggregate, the plaintiff's possible damages ranges from a low of $350,000 to a high of $560,000, with an average of $443,333 ($350,000 + $420,000 + $560,000 = $1,330,000/3), based on the probabilities and estimated damages. Accordingly, the lowest amount that a plaintiff may accept before walking away from a settlement is $350,000. Discussed in the following list are other considerations for determining the settlement value of a case, but one important factor is the cost to obtain that amount (e.g., attorneys' fees and other litigation costs).

Settlement value is not determined solely on damages and costs. There are often other monetary and nonmonetary considerations to factor into the determination. The following list includes examples of other considerations that may affect a calculation of settlement value.

- **The impact of uncertainty on the business**. It may be in the best interest of the company, for example, to pay a higher settlement amount to resolve an infringement claim quickly to clear the path for a new and profitable product launch instead of deferring the launch until after the dispute is resolved or launching a new product under a cloud of uncertainty.
- **The distraction of company personnel from profit-generating activities that affect the bottom line**. As discussed earlier in this chapter, IP/Technology disputes often require significant time spent by valuable company personnel during the life of a dispute. Some key questions to ask are: What is the number and level of personnel who will be required to spend valuable time traveling, advising, reviewing documents, and providing testimony if litigation ensues? What is a realistic assessment of the time they will need to spend performing those tasks? What is the extent to which work on the litigation will impact revenue-producing work?
- **The cost to achieve the result or defend the case**. This includes the fees for outside counsel (trial and possibly appeal), experts, document-processing vendors, trial exhibit vendors, and payment of the other party's attorneys' fees (if ordered), including whether any portion of these costs is covered by an insurance policy or indemnity.
- **The time to obtain rulings or an arbitration award**. For example, considering the finite life of a patent, the time pressures of an upcoming product launch may militate against waiting for a decision. Similarly, considering confusion in the marketplace caused by a product bearing an infringing trademark, and resulting lost sales, waiting for a court decision may not be a prudent route if an early settlement can eliminate the problem.
- **The value of the product, service, or contract at issue**. Is the subject matter at issue worth the cost of the fight? Will future profits (from sales of the accused product or under the contract) recoup the amount paid to settle or litigate the matter?
- **The value of the IP**. Is the IP core to the company? How many years remain (e.g., patent, copyright)? What is the economic value of the IP?[25]

---

25. There are three main methods to determine the value of IP assets: market-based, cost-based, and income-based methods. The market-based method relies on market data and comparables. The cost-based method looks at the investments made in developing the IP asset. The income-based method determines the income potential

- **The opportunity for achieving a global settlement of multiple disputes between the parties.** The settlement of one dispute can be leveraged effectively to resolve other disputes between the parties or to establish a process for handling future disputes, such as executive escalation, mediation, or arbitration. This is particularly relevant to disputes between competitors that are likely to continue. Establishing a simple protocol for handling future disputes can prove to be very cost-effective.
- **Emotion and principle.** Some disputes are unavoidably cloaked with emotion. In these situations, rationale and economic analysis are not likely to yield their typical results. Other disputes may be based on a purposeful decision to litigate to judgment regardless of costs, perhaps to establish or clarify judicial precedent or to draw a line in the sand with competitors. In either situation, whether the driving force is emotion or principle, it is important to identify this early on so that it can be factored in accordingly.
- **Risk tolerance.** How risk adverse is the company generally or the managers involved with the product or contract at issue?

The Guide also suggests in this step considering nonmonetary solutions that may help resolve the dispute. In IP/Technology disputes, as in other disputes, there are many options that parties have used to settle disputes besides paying money to the patent owner and ceasing accused activities. These include licensing and cross-licensing of the IP in dispute or other IP the parties own or have licensed; assigning rights in IP; setting time to wind down use or sales of accused products; adding disclaimers; selling a business unit, company, or product line to an opponent; acknowledging the validity and enforceability of a patent or other IP right; agreeing on a design-around; purchasing products or services (either those at issue or others) from the opponent; issuing stock options; and contributing money to a third-party charity or association.

STEP 9—Establish Settlement Strategy

Step 9 of the Guide suggests generally taking the following information into consideration when establishing a settlement strategy:

1. Review the negotiation history and current demand or offer.
2. Assess settlement barriers to determine if mediation is warranted.
3. Determine the form of early resolution best suited to advance interests and business concerns.
4. Secure resolution authority.

---

and expected returns from the IP asset. This approach involves estimating the future cash flows associated with the settlement and discounting them to their present value.

Reviewing the parties' negotiation history and any outstanding proposals is a good place to start in establishing a settlement strategy. This avoids a discussion of issues that the parties may have already resolved, and it may narrow the scope of any further negotiations. Also, this review may lead to new ideas or approaches for resolving prior sticking points. And if the parties involve new decision makers or negotiators, their review of the settlement history may infuse the dispute with a new perspective, including new settlement options.

Sometimes there are aspects of prior settlement negotiations that, for whatever reason, did not resonate with a party or were rejected out of hand. What may change that perspective (in addition to a new decision maker or changed circumstances inside or outside a company) are the results of an ECA. Armed with the facts, law, and an objective assessment of the many pragmatic issues that an ECA forces clients to consider, reviewing the negotiation history of the parties and a current offer may lead to a new successful settlement strategy. For example, one of the parties may have previously suggested a means for resolving the dispute (such as mediation or arbitration of certain issues) that the other rejected but now seems worth pursuing considering the kind of issues in dispute, the drivers of the dispute, and the parties involved. Or, a settlement offer previously rebuffed is now looking much better after incriminating documents surfaced during the ECA.

If the parties have been unsuccessful in resolving their dispute on their own, they and their counsel should attempt to identify all possible settlement barriers to determine if some form of ADR (e.g., mediation) is worth trying. Such barriers may include unassisted negotiations that were unsuccessful; unrealistic expectations of case value or likelihood of success; emotional issues between parties or counsel; communication difficulties; and psychological (attribution biases, face-saving needs, reactive devaluation), process, cultural, and relationship or trust issues.

Chapters 5 and 6 discuss tools that can be used to determine, for example, whether mediation is best suited to advance the interests and business concerns of the parties. Dispute resolution options are plentiful for resolving IP/Technology disputes considering, for example, the issues in dispute, the drivers of the dispute, and the disposition of the parties and their counsel. Chapter 1 describes commonly used ADR processes that can be used alone or in combination to settle IP/Technology disputes. The case histories in Chapter 1 illustrate how commonly used ADR processes can be adapted creatively to meet the needs of the parties and their dispute.

The Guide also suggests securing "resolution authority" as part of the settlement strategy. An important aspect of that is determining not only what the authority is, but also from whom to secure it and how to obtain it. The following are some of the issues to consider:

- Will the authority be provided by one person, a group of people, or possibly various stakeholders (e.g., investors, a business partner, a parent company, an insurance company, indemnitor)?
- Will the authority depend upon the nature and amount of the settlement options?
- If briefing or preparation is required, how much time is needed to accomplish this and to obtain the required settlement authority?
- Is a process (formal or informal) involved in obtaining authority (e.g., internal resolution approval group)?

Factors impacting these considerations include the nature of the dispute, fiduciary obligations, contractual obligations, company policies, and business expectations. Regardless, settlement or resolution authority should be vetted and a definitive response secured as early as possible to avoid delay that may impede the resolution process.

Having clarified how to obtain settlement authority, determine what kind and amount of authority to request. It may include monetary and nonmonetary features and should be commensurate with the panoply of possible settlement options contemplated to settle the dispute, taking into consideration the work performed in Step 8 (determining the range of settlement values, monetary and nonmonetary factors affecting the value, and nonmonetary ideas for resolving the dispute). It is also important to consult with and obtain buy-in from in-house personnel who may be affected by any nonmonetary settlement, such as winding down a product line, adding a disclaimer, choosing another trademark, or agreeing to a design-around.

In preparing a settlement strategy, also consider revisiting the issues (and responses) covered in the ECA Report pursuant to Step 3, such as the parties' business interests and concerns. As pointed out in that discussion, identifying both parties' interests and concerns can lead to practical and creative business solutions that belong in a settlement strategy.

STEP 10—Develop Preliminary Litigation Plan

Hopefully, the settlement strategy developed in Step 9 will lead to a successful resolution that ends the dispute. If, despite their best efforts, the parties are unable to settle the dispute outside the courtroom or arbitration hearing, they need to have a plan in place to implement. This should include identifying future opportunities to reconsider settlement and establishing an initial budget and timeline for activities.

Base the plan on the research and analysis already conducted in Steps 1 through 6. For example, if litigation has not yet commenced, a plaintiff would rely on the results of the forum and adversary analysis conducted in Step 4 to select the most favorable jurisdiction in which to file suit. If being the first to file is important, the client may decide to instruct outside counsel to prepare a draft complaint so that it is ready to file suit as soon as settlement attempts fail. The legal analysis conducted in

Step 6 will be very useful for this task. Based on the facts and documents already assembled, and having noted along the way the information that is missing, strategic discovery requests to the opponent and third parties to fill in the gaps should be ready to propound. In preparing the litigation plan, revisit the ECA to determine whether any portions of it need to be updated. For example, there may have been intervening changes in the law, changed corporate priorities, or information learned from failed negotiations that will inform the litigation strategy.

During the course of the ECA, a theme may have emerged that is consistent with the facts and that best describes the events from the company's perspective. This theme will resonate through pleadings, motions, discovery, and trial. In preparing the litigation plan, consider returning to the witnesses interviewed earlier to enlist their help in whatever roles they will play and inform them about the theme of the case.

There are many events in the course of a case that present an opportunity for the parties to reconsider settlement, for example: after entry of a preliminary injunction or a *Markman* or summary judgment ruling; after some or all of discovery concludes; after certain individuals are noticed for deposition; after the deposition of certain individuals; and after the costs of the litigation begin to mount. Identify the likely pressure points applicable in a particular case in the litigation plan and pursue an appropriate settlement strategy when the time is right. Also, be alert to any changes in the business and management of the client or opponent that may cause the parties to revisit settlement (e.g., merger/acquisition, new CEO or head of relevant business unit, changes in demand for accused product). Work with the client to establish a time-line of activities from which to prepare a budget for the litigation, and update both on a regular basis. As mentioned earlier, the results of an ECA assist in effectively managing the litigation and the costs.

III. Post-Resolution: Loop-Back Process ("Prevention")

The flowchart depicted earlier in this chapter and the Guide suggest as the final step a *post-resolution: loop-back process*. That is, after the dispute is resolved, the company should use the circumstances of the dispute to effectuate remedial measures that may be taken to avoid a similar dispute, prosecute or defend a case more effectively, and amend business practices (e.g., revisions to contracts, policies or procedures, enhanced training programs). This is an important risk management step that can be illustrated in the following case studies.

Case in point: An employee at XYZ Company purchased a copyrighted publication (copyright notice on each page) and shared it with a consultant who showed interest in obtaining a copy. The XYZ employee obliged by photocopying the publication for the consultant, and he even made ten extra copies to pass around at the XYZ Company. The consultant subsequently learned that there was a supplement to the copied publication and called the publisher to purchase one. The publisher asked the consultant for his name and learned that he was not on a master list of purchasers. From this communication, the publisher also learned that XYZ Company had provided the free, unauthorized copy to the consultant. The publisher sent XYZ Company a cease-and-desist letter requesting destruction of the unauthorized copies and enhanced damages for willful copyright infringement. The case settled after in-house counsel performed an ECA, the unauthorized copies were collected and destroyed, and the business unit paid statutory damages for the copying. In the aftermath, in-house counsel set in motion policies to avoid the problem in the future and discussed these with the business unit involved.

Case in point: A company was sued for putting its trademark on the equipment of a competitor for a print ad. After settlement, the company set up a process whereby all print ads underwent legal review.

Case in point: After a trademark infringement suit, a company developed a training module for all new employees on the basics of trademark law, including the importance of respecting other companies' IP rights and having all product names and slogans cleared by the company's legal department before use.

Payment of damages and the embarrassment of the situation certainly may suffice to prevent a recurrence, but adding an extra step to determine what further measures could be instituted on a companywide basis to avoid similar infractions can prove to be a good risk management step for the future.

IV. ECA Executive Summary

The Short Form (see Appendix A to the Guide) highlights the key results of the ECA. Use this form as an executive summary to focus on the important results of the analysis to include with the ECA Report, or use the Short Form as a shorthand checklist. Here is what the Short Form covers:

a. **Dispute information**. This includes claimant, type of claims, amount of claim, business unit affected, and current status.

b. **Assessment of issues and outcomes including the rationale**. The assessment should contain a discussion of the goals and objectives of all the parties to the dispute.

c. **Identification of interests**. This should be made for each of the parties and include possible joint interests.
d. **Assessment of settlement value**. Identify the range of monetary settlement that would be a good result as well as any nonmonetary solutions for possibly settling the case.
e. **Proposed resolution strategy and rationale**. Identify these using a DTA or by summary: resolution phases, time frames, preliminary litigation management plan, and budget and costs (e.g., counsel, forum fees, liability estimates) for a selected period as well as any special circumstances affecting strategy.

Conclusion

After performing triage, some patients have been sent home, some have been admitted to the hospital, and others are in surgery. Not all outcomes are yet known, but the magnitude and scope of the problems have been assessed and disaster has been averted. The ER staff is tired, but they effectively used the resources they were allocated to the highest priorities.

Like triage, ECA provides a means of taking control over an unplanned event (i.e., a cease-and-desist letter, lawsuit, arbitration demand) and for making an informed decision about the best way to handle it. The ECA Report integrates and organizes into a logical framework key information and analyses that corporate executives can rely on when making important decisions related to the dispute. ECA will help predict and manage any potential loss or damage to the business and the time and cost of future litigation. It will serve as an important guide when deciding whether to settle or to seek resolution through ADR.

The quality and reliability of an ECA depends on the depth and extent of the fact-gathering and analysis conducted in completing each of the ten steps. As with triage in the ER, apply the appropriate resources quickly to ensure that all key facts are timely uncovered and assessed. To ensure that an ECA is a reliable and effective tool, keep the following four tips in mind:

1. Develop a game plan that is tailor-made to the dispute and execute it efficiently and effectively with an accomplished team.
2. Strive to obtain the best available information (facts and law).
3. Strategically analyze the information with the appropriate stakeholders and advisors.
4. Choose the most effective means for implementing a settlement strategy that contains something of benefit or gain for all parties involved.

APPENDIX

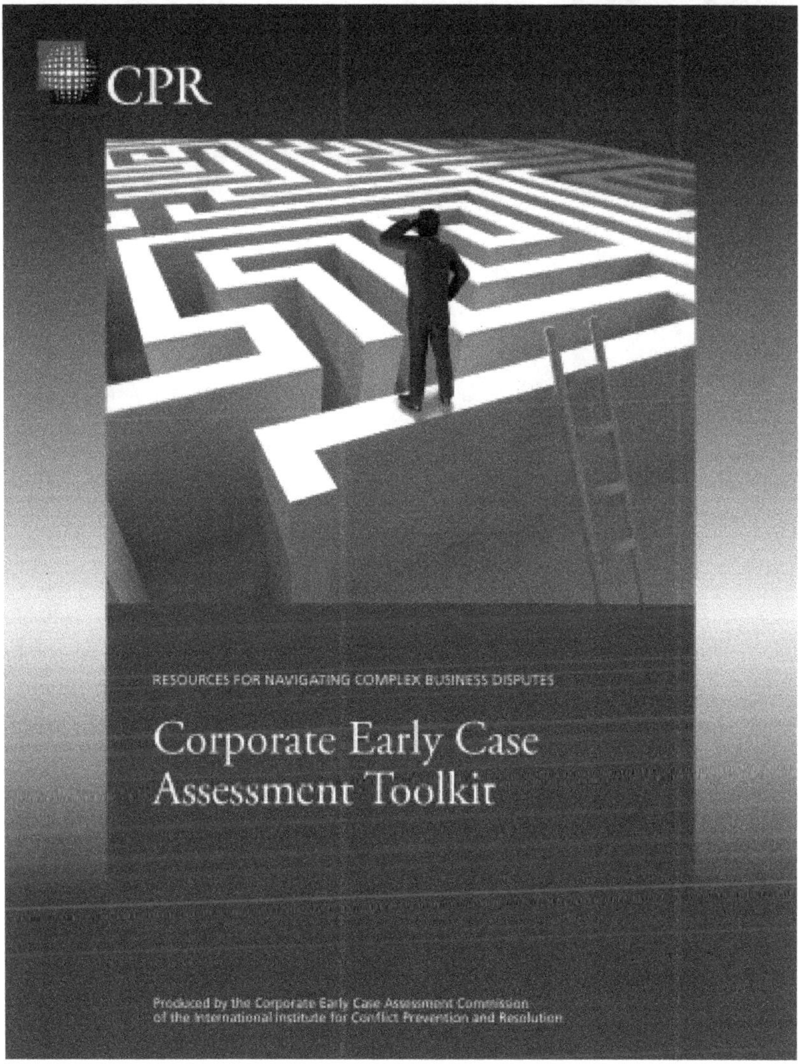
CPR
RESOURCES FOR NAVIGATING COMPLEX BUSINESS DISPUTES
Corporate Early Case Assessment Toolkit
Produced by the Corporate Early Case Assessment Commission
of the International Institute for Conflict Prevention and Resolution

CPR

International Institute for Conflict Prevention & Resolution

575 Lexington Avenue, 21st Floor
New York, NY 10022
+1.212.949.6490
www.cpradr.org

CPR assembled a commission of leading corporate counsel, attorneys and academics to collaborate in the production of an Early Case Assessment tool which could be used across a broad spectrum of commercial disputes. The organization gratefully acknowledges the individuals who contributed their expertise and insights to this project.

Lawrence N. Chanen
Senior Vice President &
Associate General Counsel
JPMorgan Chase

Dan S. Dunham
Senior Corporate Counsel
Pfizer, Inc.

Anurag Gulati
Assistant General Counsel
General Mills, Inc.

J. Andrew Heaton
Associate General Counsel
Ernst & Young LLP

Paula A. Johnson
Senior Counsel
ConocoPhillips

Janet S. Kloenhamer
President, Discontinued Operations
Fireman's Fund Insurance Co.

Patrick Lamb
Valorem Law Group

Prof. John Lande
Director, Program in Dispute Resolution
University of Missouri School of Law

Melanie Lewis
Director, Solutions Program
Coca-Cola Enterprises, Inc.

Duncan R. MacKay
Assistant General Counsel,
Dispute Resolution
Northeast Utilities

Deborah Masucci
Vice President & Director of
Dispute Resolution
American International Group Inc.

Julie S. Mazza
Senior Counsel
Citigroup Inc.

Barbara McCormick
Assistant General Counsel
Johnson & Johnson

Richard N. Papper
Vice President &
Senior Litigation Counsel
Bank of New York Mellon

Roland Schroeder
Senior Counsel, Litigation &
Legal Policy
General Electric Company

Beth Trent
Legal Director
Schering-Plough Corporation

Patricia Caycedo-Smith
Associate General Counsel, Litigation
Duke Energy Corporation

Nancy L. Vanderlip
Vice President & General Counsel
Electronic Components
ITT Corporation

Jennifer Boyens Victor
The Victor Law Firm

Thomas R. Woodrow
Holland & Knight LLP

CPR Staff:

Kathy Bryan
President & CEO

Cathy Cronin-Harris
Senior Consultant

Thomas L. Aldrich
Senior Consultant

Titles and affiliations reflect participants' positions at the time of drafting (2009). The views expressed in these ECA Guidelines do not reflect the views of the participating CPR Members' companies.

Fundamentals of Early Case Assessment

CPR Definition: Early Case Assessment

CPR's Early Case Assessment Toolkit (ECA) outlines a simple conflict management process designed to facilitate more informed and expedited decision-making at the early stages of a dispute. The process calls for a team working together in a specified time frame to gather the key facts of the dispute, identify the key business concerns, assess the various risks and costs the dispute poses for the company, and make an informed choice or recommendation on how to handle the dispute.

While one of the possible recommendations could be to settle or resolve the dispute, CPR wishes to emphasize that these Guidelines are not about settlement, although that could be one possible outcome of Early Case Assessment. Instead, these Guidelines focus on evaluating the dispute so that an appropriate strategy can be formulated, whether that is settlement, full-bore litigation, or something in between, with an eye toward reducing or eliminating disputes as soon and as inexpensively as possible.

Benefits of Using Early Case Assessment

In today's highly litigious business climate there are numerous business and legal trends supporting the use of Early Case Assessment. These trends include an increasing volume of claims and litigation, the increasing complexity and protraction of claims, and the resulting higher legal fees and settlements. In this climate, many legal departments have worked to develop new definitions of "value" and "win" by treating disputes as a business process, and protracted litigation as a defect to be remedied. One effective tool for controlling disputes and reducing or eliminating litigation is the ECA process.

CPR

There are numerous potential benefits of implementing an Early Case Assessment program, including:

- Enhanced, early case analysis
- Enhanced, early risk identification and analysis
- Enhanced, early evaluation of potential end-game solutions
- Enhanced ability to gauge business needs and solutions, and improved client relations
- A reduction in legal costs and expenses
- A reduction in settlement and resolution costs
- A reduction in the "claim-through-resolution" cycle time

Setting the Stage for Successful Early Case Assessment

The growing adoption of Early Case Assessment programs arises from the mandate of in-house legal departments to better and more effectively manage litigation, in terms of outcome and cost, and to do so with better calculation of the business interests and objectives implicated by that litigation.

In addition, in-house legal departments have at their disposal more and better tools for gathering necessary data to assess litigation risks and solutions, measure progress, communicate lessons learned, and track successful strategies and solutions. Early identification of risks, business prerogatives, likely outcomes, and potential alternative resolutions should be a part of every Early Case Assessment program.

Using CPR's ECA Toolkit

CPR's ECA Guidelines provide a structured approach for conducting early evaluation of a dispute. It is intended to be a flexible tool that may be adjusted by in-house counsel to meet the particular needs of their business. It can be applied in whole or part depending on dispute circumstances to conduct early, rapid and consistent analysis of a dispute to find the most effective resolution path geared toward limiting corporate expenditures, serving business concerns and utilizing the most appropriate conflict resolution process.

2 | Fundamentals of Early Case Assessment

Many companies employ a computerized matter management system for purposes of tracking litigation, claims, government investigations, and related legal matters. The ECA is not intended to take the place of a matter management system; however, one may usefully become a component of the other. Therefore, corporate users are encouraged to tailor these guidelines and tools to their particular needs and requirements.

CPR's ECA Toolkit comprises:

- A detailed, step-by-step guide for users who are less familiar with the concept of ECA and seek a comprehensive analytical model.
- A short Executive Summary form for sophisticated users who are familiar with the elements of the ECA process. See Appendix A.

For more assistance with your ECA process, contact info@cpradr.org. To download materials in an electronic format, please visit CPR's website at www.cpradr.org.

About CPR

The International Institute for Conflict Prevention and Resolution (CPR) is an independent, nonprofit think tank that promotes innovation in commercial dispute prevention and resolution. By harnessing the expertise of leading minds in ADR and benchmarking best practices, it is the resource of choice for multinational corporations with billions of dollars at risk. CPR is also a trusted and respected destination for lawyers seeking superior arbitrators and mediators and cutting-edge ADR tools and training. Our elite membership includes General Counsel from global corporations, attorneys from the top law firms in the world, sitting and retired judges, highly-experienced neutrals and ADR practitioners, and leading academics.

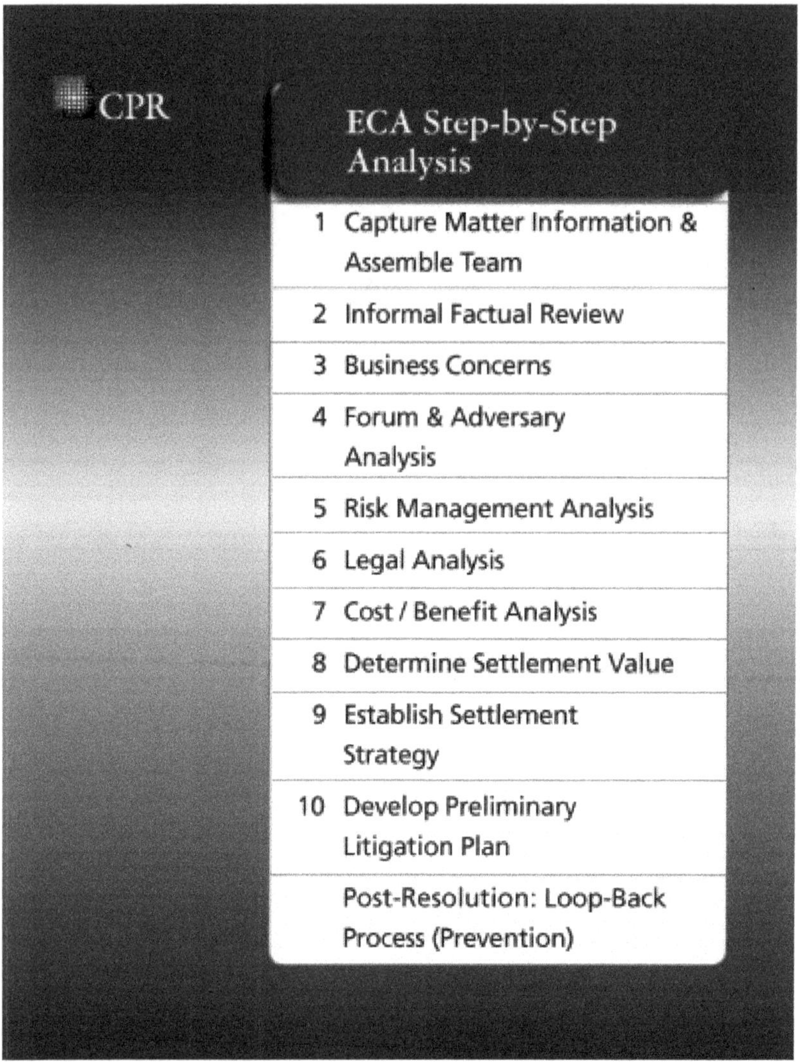
CPR
ECA Step-by-Step Analysis
1 Capture Matter Information & Assemble Team
2 Informal Factual Review
3 Business Concerns
4 Forum & Adversary Analysis
5 Risk Management Analysis
6 Legal Analysis
7 Cost / Benefit Analysis
8 Determine Settlement Value
9 Establish Settlement Strategy
10 Develop Preliminary Litigation Plan
Post-Resolution: Loop-Back Process (Prevention)

STEP 1
Capture Matter Information & Assemble Team

1 Capture Matter Information & Assemble Team
2 Informal Factual Review
3 Business Concerns
4 Forum & Adversary Analysis
5 Risk Management Analysis
6 Legal Analysis
7 Cost / Benefit Analysis
8 Determine Settlement Value
9 Establish Settlement Strategy
10 Develop Preliminary Litigation Plan
Post-Resolution: Loop-Back Process (Prevention)

Describe the Matter

- Parties: Claimant/Plaintiff; Respondent/Defendant; Third Parties
- Nature of dispute
- Apparent amount at risk
- Background and relationships of parties
- How company learned of matter
- Status of insurance and any related indemnity agreements
- Identification of other applicable contracts, pre-dispute agreements, and agreements regarding how disputes may be handled

Identify the Stage of Development and Contractual Requirements

Note: Do not duplicate matter management system which may contain some of this data.

- Status of negotiations
- Review relevant dispute resolution provisions of contract
  - Negotiation
  - Two-tiered negotiation in company
  - Mediation
  - Arbitration
  - Other

ECA Step-by-Step Analysis | 5

CPR

- If arbitration will commence, identify
  - ADR provider
  - Applicable arbitration rules
  - Arbitrators
  - Commencement date
  - Causes of action
  - Damages/remedies

- If litigation filed, attach the complaint and identify:
  - Court/Location
  - Judge
  - Docket no.
  - Date filed *(By whom)*
  - Cause(s) of action
  - Damages/other remedies sought *(Claim for Injunctive/Prelim. Relief)*
  - Court-ordered mediation required/completed
  - Dispositive motions filed (*When/Outcome?*)
  - Filing deadlines approaching
  - Jury trial matter

Note: May be omitted if the Complaint is attached or if the matter is a repeating matter, such as a class action or mass tort.

Identify Counsel and Team for Company, Other Party and Third Parties

- Inside counsel
- Outside counsel
- Business unit/person(s) involved/affected
- Insurance representatives

Assign Duties and Time Frame to Complete ECA Process

The key benefit of a systematic ECA review is to assemble the information and focus the team on the issues that may be most relevant to settlement before the astronomical costs of discovery and motion practice begin. How early can it be done? Depending on the complexity of the case, the lawyers who use these methods regularly believe that the review should be completed within the first 30-90 days.

The purpose of the ECA is not to conduct an exhaustive legal and factual analysis, but to collect essential information, understand the basic strengths and weakness of the legal positions and use that information to conduct an early cost/benefit analysis. The ECA redefines what the essential information is in order to value the case quickly and as effectively as possible.

With an ECA policy in place, it is even better if all the parties can agree to stay discovery and the filings in the case until the ECA is complete. In pattern cases, or situations where both sides are willing to have further discussions before discovery, an agreement to postpone discovery may be more likely.

STEP 2
Informal Factual Review

- 1 Capture Matter Information & Assemble Team
- 2 | Informal Factual Review
- 3 Business Concerns
- 4 Forum & Adversary Analysis
- 5 Risk Management Analysis
- 6 Legal Analysis
- 7 Cost / Benefit Analysis
- 8 Determine Settlement Value
- 9 Establish Settlement Strategy
- 10 Develop Preliminary Litigation Plan
- Post-Resolution: Loop-Back Process (Prevention)

Conduct Internal Interviews

- Information gathered from discussions with company, law firm, and other lawyers with knowledge of the matter
- Information gathered from client business contacts with knowledge of the matter

Collect Internal Documents

- Hard copy documents
- Electronic documents, including number, type, format, media, cost of storage and production, and possible role for e-discovery expert

Identify Witnesses and Experts

- Identify the fact witnesses and their location
- Evaluate role of experts, if any
- Provide a summary of the interviews with witnesses
- Assess witness capability and credibility

Contacts with Opposing Counsel

- Information garnered
- Agreements on informal discovery or information exchange

Review Relevant Company and Industry Historical Information

- History of similar claims in the company (if any)
- Average number of days to resolution of such claims
- Special circumstances differentiating this case from other similar cases
- In-house, law firm, and other lawyers with relevant experience on similar matters
- Business client contacts with knowledge of similar matters
- Relevant company files and/or databases
- Similar matters in the industry/industry concerns/history
- Damages awards and settlements
- Length of litigation process and procedural issues
- Other relevant public data/records or information that might be available

Identify Essential Information Needed

- If key information is currently unavailable that is essential in selecting resolution strategy, describe informal routes to acquire that information

CPR

STEP 3
Business Concerns

1 Capture Matter Information & Assemble Team
2 Informal Factual Review
3 Business Concerns
4 Forum & Adversary Analysis
5 Risk Management Analysis
6 Legal Analysis
7 Cost / Benefit Analysis
8 Determine Settlement Value
9 Establish Settlement Strategy
10 Develop Preliminary Litigation Plan
Post-Resolution: Loop-Back Process (Prevention)

Identify Client's Priority Business Concerns and Interests

- Protecting sensitive data
- Legal *(E.g., Need new precedent; need TRO or PI; etc.)*
- Economic: short term, long term
- Timing
- Relationships (including confidentiality)
- Publicity and reputation
- Psychological *(E.g., understand occurrences; receive apology; be heard by authority figures; vindicate action; clear name; change policies for others in similar situation; etc.)*
- Other special/unique/sensitive concerns affecting disposition strategy:
  - Corporate survival/treasury at risk
  - Business relationship at stake
  - Reputation/public relations/stock price
  - Repetitive claim/floodgates issue/class action
  - New product under scrutiny
  - New or existing legal precedent
  - Technical issue, e.g. intellectual property
  - Location of proceedings: forum, venue, jury issues
  - Industry concerns; possible co-defendants
  - Possible criminal liability; corporate governance; compliance; government oversight; RICO
  - International matter, FCPA, or foreign political concerns
  - High level executive testimony required

10 | ECA Step-by-Step Analysis

Assess Opponent's Likely Priority Business Concerns and Interests

- Protecting sensitive data
- Legal *(E.g., Precedent; PI; etc.)*
- Economic: short term, long term
- Timing
- Relationships (including confidentiality)
- Reputation
- Psychological *(E.g., understand occurrences; receive apology; be heard by authority figures; vindicate action; clear name; change policies for others in similar situation; etc.)*
- Other

Define Successful Resolution from a Business Perspective

NOTE: Identification of mutual concerns and interests may lead to dialogue with opponent and possible Early Case Resolution through collaborative negotiation.

A good ECA process should evaluate the business interests of both parties in the resolution of the dispute. Interest-based questions, which typically give rise to opportunities to find common ground, are often not explored until actual settlement discussions were underway. Lawyers using the usual adversarial practices often fail to uncover elements of the dispute that might be relevant to settlement but may be unrelated to the legal claims in front of them. For example, considerations which focus on the relationship of the parties and business strategy and goals should be analyze and reviewed.

CPR

STEP 4
Forum & Adversary Analysis

Forum Analysis

- Judge's profile *(including circuit or state court rulings out of sync with majority on relevant issues)*
- Potential jury pool
- Mediator's profile
- Arbitrator's profile

Opposing Counsel Analysis

- Reputation or experience of opposing counsel:
  - Negotiation reputation
  - Trial reputation
- Counsel's incentives to settle early
- Similar claims litigated against the opposing lawyer? What was outcome and what approach was used by opponent?

Opposing Party Analysis

- Any continuing business relationship with adversary *(Anything over $_________ requires business or other higher level approval of case strategy)*
- Specify financial and legal resources of the adversary
- Immediate needs of adversary that might support use of an early settlement process *(E.g., financial crisis; etc.)*
- Signatory to CPR Pledge©?

STEP 5
Risk Management Analysis

Legal Hold Notice Issuance, Date and List of Recipients

- Documents
- E-mails
- Length of hold; renewal reminders
- Expansion of document custodians

Insurance

- Is the claim insured or self-insured?
- If insured, has the carrier been notified? Has the carrier accepted coverage, disputed coverage or issued a reservation of rights?
- If the carrier has not been notified, who is responsible for giving notice and when will notice be given?
- Have all potentially applicable policies been located?
- Who is responsible for locating all potentially applicable policies?

1 Capture Matter Information & Assemble Team
2 Informal Factual Review
3 Business Concerns
4 Forum & Adversary Analysis
5 | Risk Management Analysis
6 Legal Analysis
7 Cost / Benefit Analysis
8 Determine Settlement Value
9 Establish Settlement Strategy
10 Develop Preliminary Litigation Plan
Post-Resolution: Loop-Back Process (Prevention)

STEP 6
Legal Analysis

1 Capture Matter Information & Assemble Team
2 Informal Factual Review
3 Business Concerns
4 Forum & Adversary Analysis
5 Risk Management Analysis
6 | Legal Analysis
7 Cost / Benefit Analysis
8 Determine Settlement Value
9 Establish Settlement Strategy
10 Develop Preliminary Litigation Plan
Post-Resolution: Loop-Back Process (Prevention)

Ascertain and Narrow Scope of Claims and Defenses

Conduct Risk Assessment of Each Claim and Defense

Estimate Possible Damages Spectrum

Identify Additional Information Necessary to Evaluate Damages

Determine Whether and Type of Damages Experts that will be Required

Estimate Costs to Completion

- Outside counsel fees
- Other litigation expenses and "hard" costs
- Anticipated expenditure of internal resources and "soft" costs, including
  - In-house lawyer time
  - Business professional time
  - Witness time

14 | ECA Step-by-Step Analysis

STEP 7
Cost/Benefit Analysis

DISPOSITION STRATEGY AS APPLICABLE	Percentage Likelihood of Success/Loss	External Legal Costs	Internal Costs High (H); Medium (M); Low (L)	Time to Complete	Does Strategy Advance Priority Business Concerns or Not?
Dispositive Motion					
Negotiate (without any mediator)					
Mediate (with a mediator)					
Arbitrate					
Discovery or E-Discovery & E-Discovery Vendor Use, if any					
Experts					
Trial					
Other: Dual Track; Appeal; etc.					
TOTALS					

CPR

STEP 8
Determine Settlement Value

1 Capture Matter Information & Assemble Team
2 Informal Factual Review
3 Business Concerns
4 Forum & Adversary Analysis
5 Risk Management Analysis
6 Legal Analysis
7 Cost / Benefit Analysis
8 | Determine Settle Value
9 Establish Settlement Strategy
10 Develop Preliminary Litigation Plan
Post-Resolution: Loop-Back Process (Prevention)

Identify the range of monetary settlement that would be a good result and identify any non-monetary solutions with the potential to resolve the dispute. Consider attaching a decision-tree or similar analysis. A detailed overview of Decision-Trees can be found here.

16 | ECA Step-by-Step Analysis

STEP 9
Establish Settlement Strategy

Review Negotiation History and Current Demand/Offer

Assess Settlement Barriers to Determine if Mediation is Warranted

- The following common settlement barriers can be effectively addressed via mediation:
  - Unassisted negotiations have already failed
  - Communication difficulties and past history foreclose dialogue
  - Emotional barriers to settlement exist between parties or counsel
  - Psychological barriers exist such as partisan perceptions, attribution biases, face-saving needs, reactive devaluation, etc.
  - Process barriers exist such as no settlement event, lack of settlement authority, positional bargaining limitations, etc.
  - Cultural barriers to effective dialogue exist
  - Merit barriers exist such as unrealistic expectations, insufficient key information to settle, etc.
- The following more difficult settlement barriers often foreclose settlement. However, even these barriers have been overcome in mediation:
  - Fundamental corporate or other principle at stake that cannot be settled
  - Need for new precedent is critical
  - Managerial responsibility at center of matter including corporate finance or reorganization cannot be settled
  - Public message needed including defending claims that may open the floodgates to similar claims

CPR

- Public vindication sought
- Extreme power disparities between parties foreclose ability to bargain
- Absence of resources that can be used for trade-offs in negotiation

Determine Form of Early Resolution Best Suited to Advance Interests and Business Concerns

The final step is to use the information and analysis gathered through the process to evaluate whether the matter can be settled through one of many ADR techniques, which can include any of the following, alone or in combination:

- Negotiation by:
  - management
  - in-house counsel
  - outside litigation or settlement counsel
  - collaboratively trained lawyer(s)
  - other third-party skilled or technical facilitator
- Early Neutral Evaluation
- Early Discovery Exchange
- Competitive Mock Trial
- Shared Focus Study
- Mediation
  - Court conducted mediation
  - Private mediation
    - General or technically trained mediator
- Summary Jury Trial
- Arbitration
  - Non-binding
  - Binding for all or some of the claims

Alternatively, the case could simply be kept on a litigation track heading toward a court trial on the merits.

Secure Resolution Authority

STEP 10
Develop Preliminary Litigation Plan

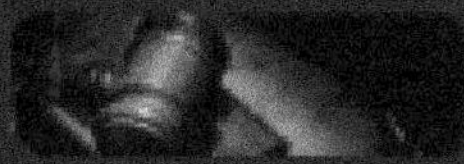

Plan Adjudication Route if Settlement Path is Not Successful

Identify Future Opportunities to Reconsider Settlement

Establish Initial Budget and Timeline of Activities

1 Capture Matter Information & Assemble Team
2 Informal Factual Review
3 Business Concerns
4 Forum & Adversary Analysis
5 Risk Management Analysis
6 Legal Analysis
7 Cost / Benefit Analysis
8 Determine Settlement Value
9 Establish Settlement Strategy
10 | Develop Preliminary Litigation Plan
Post-Resolution: Loop-Back Process (Prevention)

POST-RESOLUTION Loop-Back Process (Prevention)

1. Capture Matter Information & Assemble Team
2. Informal Factual Review
3. Business Concerns
4. Forum & Adversary Analysis
5. Risk Management Analysis
6. Legal Analysis
7. Cost / Benefit Analysis
8. Determine Settlement Value
9. Establish Settlement Strategy
10. Develop Preliminary Litigation Plan

Post-Production: Loop-Back Process (Prevention)

Once a dispute is resolved, the collaborative team may well benefit by engaging in a "lessons learned" exercise, not only to capture the valuable insights gained from any dispute for application to another, but also to identify appropriate business practice corrections, which may include contract or policy or procedure revisions, enhanced training programs or revised business processes to prevent recurrence.

Appendix A:
Executive Summary

Date prepared: ______________________ Date last updated: ______________________

Matter/Dispute

Claimant

Type of Claim

Amount of Claim

Business Unit(s) Affected

Current Status: ☐ *Court* ☐ *Arbitration* ☐ *Mediation* ☐ *Unassisted Negotiation*

☐ *Other (specify):* ____

Assessment of Issues and Outcomes including Rationale

(Include goals and objectives for all parties to the dispute)

Identification of Interests: Ours/Theirs/Joint

Assessment of Settlement Value

(Identify the range of monetary settlement that would be a good result and identify any non-monetary solutions with the potential to resolve the dispute)

Proposed Resolution Strategy and Rationale including Special Circumstances Affecting Strategy

Use decision tree analysis or summarize:

- Resolution phases
- Time frames
- Preliminary litigation management plan
- Budget/costs including counsel fees, forum fees, and liability estimates
  (Total budget for short matters; 12 month budget with "ballpark" totals for prolonged matters)

(Optional: Attach Decision Tree Analysis, if appropriate)

CHAPTER 4

Initial Damages Assessments: Focusing Early on Things That Count but Cannot Be Counted

Carol Ludington

Not everything that can be counted counts, and not everything that counts can be counted.

—Albert Einstein

Introduction[1]

Imagine an intellectual property (IP) case that has been hotly contested for more than a year, with significant time and money already spent on liability issues. A mediation session is scheduled to try to resolve the dispute. Both parties are well prepared to discuss their liability positions and to assess their risks related to liability. Regarding damages, however, the IP owner vaguely argues that its damages are "huge," while the accused infringer responds in kind, arguing that damages are minimal. Because the parties have not performed a damages analysis, they cannot clearly articulate their damages positions, assess the probabilities of recovery, or formulate a negotiation strategy. No mediated resolution is reached, and this opportunity to resolve the dispute is lost. As the case progresses, each party discovers that its original damages position was unsupportable.

Had the parties performed an initial damages assessment (IDA) before the mediation session, they could have gained a realistic view of damages, including an understanding of the key legal, business, and financial issues affecting recovery. Furthermore, they would have been able to clearly articulate their damages position and its support to the mediator and their opponent, and determined for themselves what would be a fair amount to pay or receive. The parties may have settled the case the day of the in-person mediation session (or even before it), or at least determined what additional information they needed to structure a settlement or, in the event that settlement did not occur, to complete their damages analysis and arguments.

1. See Glossary for definition of frequently used terms.

I. What Is an IDA?

In general terms, an IDA is an analysis that provides an overview of damages. Analogizing to the well-known Pareto Principle (otherwise known as the 80/20 rule), 80 percent of the information necessary to evaluate a case is often made available in the first 20 percent of the time allotted, and the remaining 80 percent of the allotted time (and expense) will often yield only 20 percent of the information needed to evaluate a case.[2] An IDA applies this 80/20 concept, providing significant value for relatively small cost.[3]

As depicted in the chart below, the goals of an IDA are to address key damages considerations that may affect recovery; estimate realistic damages magnitudes;[4] inform decision-making regarding settlement and dispute strategies; enable focused, efficient discovery; and improve quality. An IDA is not intended to provide a precise quantification of damages.

The analysis typically relies on information collected from a party, such as information from the party's own business and finance personnel, publicly available sources (e.g., websites and market reports), and possibly the parties' exchange of information (e.g., pursuant to informal negotiations, a mediation, or formal discovery). Thus, when conducted with the help of an experienced damages expert, preferably before formal discovery, an IDA does not have to be expensive or require extensive amounts of documents.[5]

---

2. *See* SEDONA CONFERENCE, COMMENTARY ON PATENT LITIGATION BEST PRACTICES: PATENT MEDIATION CHAPTER sec. III.B (April 2017 ed.), https://thesedonaconference.org/sites/default/files/publications/Sedona%2520WG10%2520Patent%2520Lit%2520Best%2520Practices-Mediation%2520Ch.%2520%2528Apr.%2520217%2520ed%2529_04-06-17.pdf. Put another way, the 80/20 principle asserts that a minority of causes, inputs, or effort usually leads to a majority of the results, outputs, or rewards. *See* RICHARD KOCH, THE 80/20 PRINCIPLE: ACHIEVE MORE WITH LESS (4th ed. 2022).

3. An IDA is not intended to be a completed damages analysis or to provide all of the information that will likely be needed to complete an expert report. If a dispute does not settle after an IDA is completed, additional discovery, documentation, and analysis will likely be necessary to complete the damages analysis. In this event, the IDA provides a framework to streamline discovery and analysis and to allow strategic, informed decisions regarding dispute management.

4. Damages magnitudes can be thought of as orders of magnitude akin to $10,000, $10 million, or $1 billion.

5. An IDA should not be relegated to a damages expert's staff or to inexperienced counsel. The knowledge and insight of an experienced expert and the involvement of senior counsel having in-depth knowledge of both the liability and damages aspects of a dispute are optimal for performing the IDA efficiently without excessive research and time. Accordingly, to ensure that proper resources are spent on an IDA, and to maximize the benefits, consideration should be given to specifying the individual(s) who will perform the IDA.

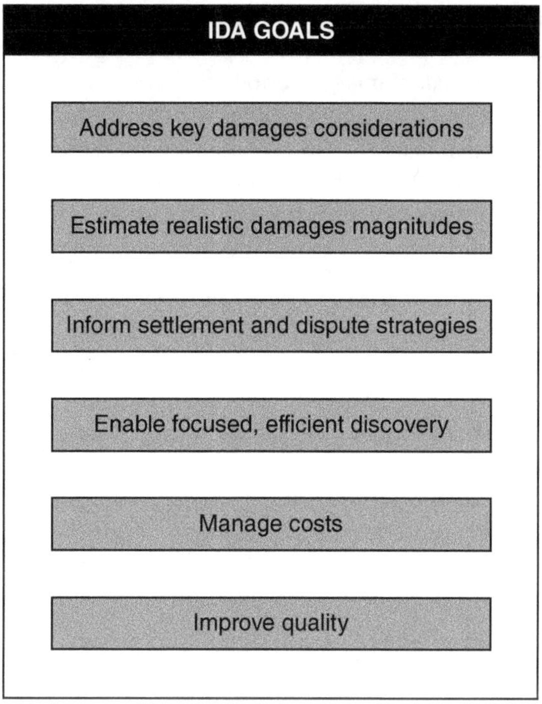

Most of this chapter contemplates an IDA performed by one party in confidence with a damages expert, but, as discussed at the end of this chapter, a neutral or jointly retained damages expert can also perform the IDA on behalf of both parties.

The information learned from an IDA provides many benefits. For example, it can facilitate strategic and informed decisions regarding litigation and settlement; focus the collection of documents and other information related to damages; streamline the damages analysis; reduce costs (e.g., by avoiding unnecessary boilerplate discovery); avoid unpleasant surprises (e.g., spending more to litigate a dispute than the amount of a realistic recovery); often lead to early dispute resolution; and improve the quality of the available damages information and analysis.

Each goal of an IDA is discussed in the following sections.

A. Address Key Damages Considerations

One or more key considerations in the analysis of IP damages frequently result in widely disparate damages claims by the parties in a dispute, the exclusion of damages claims, and the adjustment or reversal of damages awards. These key considerations include:

- Which damages measures are applicable (e.g., whether the requirements to establish a particular measure of damages can be met)
- The appropriate damages period
- The importance of the technology at issue to the marketplace
- Whether damages should be based on the entire market value of covered products or whether apportionment is appropriate
- Whether acceptable alternatives or design-around options exist
- Whether the terms of particular agreements are relevant[6]

These are examples of things that "*count but cannot be counted*."

Some of these questions may be answered during the IDA, but others may require focused discovery (e.g., to obtain relevant agreements that could have an impact on damages or data and information to support apportionment) and/or the development of information (e.g., research and analysis by a damages expert or development of information regarding design-arounds or available alternatives). If the need for discovery or information to address these considerations is not identified early, opportunities to obtain the information may be missed, the quality of the damages analysis may suffer, and outcomes may not be optimized. Instead, identifying the need for this information through an IDA increases the likelihood of obtaining important information and improves the quality of the damages claim.

B. Estimate Realistic Damages Magnitudes

Understanding the potential damages magnitudes permits a party to make informed decisions about whether to pursue litigation, how much to spend litigating the dispute, and appropriate settlement choices.[7] For example, a dispute in which the magnitude of realistic damages is in the tens of millions of dollars warrants spending more time and money pursuing the dispute than one in which the magnitude of realistic damages is less than $100,000. In the absence of an early, realistic assessment of the amount of potential damages, parties sometimes spend more money litigating IP disputes than the amount of realistic damages, only to face an unpleasant surprise later when this economic imbalance is realized. Identifying a realistic damages magnitude through an IDA helps eliminate this surprise factor and helps manage expectations.

---

6. IP damages considerations, which are informed by statute, case law, and practice, continue to evolve. Accordingly, this is not intended to be an exhaustive list of considerations.

7. Other remedies, such as an injunction, may also be considered. Those are outside the scope of this chapter.

Too often, the size of the emotions driving a dispute do not reflect a realistic damages amount. Emotions are often large in IP disputes and, too often, litigation proceeds based on a presumption that damages are also large. An IDA assists a party in addressing damages without the emotion and assists in making informed decisions regarding overall case strategies and discovery so that efforts are proportional to the realistic amount in controversy.[8]

In an IDA, potential damages magnitudes are estimated taking into consideration the relevant actual or estimated sales and profitability, relevant damages measures, relevant damages period, key factors (such as those outlined in *Panduit*[9] and *Georgia-Pacific*[10] for a patent case), and other available information. The specific methodology, considerations, assumptions, and judgments that may be appropriate to identify these magnitudes differ from one case to another and can be informed by a damages expert working with litigation counsel.

For an IDA, it is not necessary to identify specific amounts, and it may be appropriate to identify a range of damages determined by virtue of possible rulings on a particular key issue (e.g., in an IP case, these issues may include the appropriate damages period, applicability of entire market value or apportionment, or admissibility or relevance of certain agreements), with one amount if a key issue is assumed to be resolved in one way and a different amount if that issue is resolved in another way.[11]

---

8. Pursuant to the Federal Rules of Civil Procedure:

> Unless otherwise limited by court order, the scope of discovery is as follows: Parties may obtain discovery regarding any nonprivileged matter that is relevant to any party's claim or defense and *proportional* to the needs of the case, considering the *importance of the issues* at stake in the action, *the amount in controversy*, the parties' relative access to relevant information, the parties' resources, the *importance of the discovery* in resolving the issues, and *whether the burden or expense of proposed discovery outweighs its likely benefit.*

FED. R. CIV. P. 26(b)(1), Duty to Disclose; General Provisions Governing Discovery (emphasis added). An IDA can help address these considerations.

9. Panduit Corp. v. Stahlin Bros. Fibre Works, Inc., 575 F.2d 1152, 1156 (6th Cir. 1978).

10. Georgia-Pacific Corp. v. U.S. Plywood Corp., 318 F. Supp. 1116, 1119–20 (S.D.N.Y. 1970), *modified and aff'd*, 446 F.2d 295 (2d Cir. 1971).

11. For example, damages based on the entire market value of a product can be many times greater than if damages are based instead on amounts apportioned to only a particular feature. Similarly, the magnitude of realistic damages may be significantly lower if there is a viable design-around alternative that can be established, versus if there is no such option.

C. Inform Settlement and Dispute Strategies

With information from an IDA, parties can make informed decisions regarding settlement strategies, such as:

- What constitutes a reasonable settlement amount
- Whether to delay settlement discussions to pursue focused discovery or to request information informally from the other party
- Whether to forgo recovery of damages on some issues because the magnitude of possible damages does not justify derailing an otherwise solid settlement on other issues

Information from an IDA may also be used to plan case strategies (e.g., narrowing legal claims to focus on those having the most significant damages) and allocate and manage resources (e.g., time, costs, personnel, discovery, and analysis) to those issues that matter most.

The importance of considering damages early and as an integral part of trial advocacy and strategy can be demonstrated by the approach students took in an international moot arbitration competition. The moot problem involved a case with two breach of contract issues. The first issue involved interesting and challenging legal topics, but relatively small potential damages. The second issue involved less intriguing legal topics, but significant damages. Many of the competition participants invested much more time and energy in the intriguing liability topics of the first issue, while shortchanging the more valuable (but less legally intriguing) second issue. Insofar as this was a moot arbitration competition and the participants were judged on presentation of the liability aspects of the case, this is understandable.

In real life, however, focusing on the relative magnitude of damages related to each of the issues would likely shift the allocation of time and energies to a more appropriate balance between the issues. In an actual dispute, each party would obviously prefer to win on both issues. However, if they could win on only one issue, each party would typically prefer to win on the issue involving the biggest amount of damages. Applying a cost-benefit analysis to the moot problem, the parties would have likely preferred that the first issue be resolved or eliminated quickly rather than spend more resources than they were likely to recover (unless perhaps an answer to the liability issue was important for other business reasons). Performing an IDA facilitates this cost-benefit analysis.

D. Enable Focused, Efficient Discovery

An erroneous perception persists that damages-related costs can be avoided if attention to damages is deferred until late in the litigation process. Actually, parties typically incur costs related to damages early in the case even if little attention is being paid yet to damages issues. For example, early document requests routinely include a number of boilerplate requests related to damages, inviting responses that are often equally boilerplate; thus, responsive documents often reflect quantity over quality. Furthermore, the producing party spends considerable time gathering and producing responsive documents, and the receiving party spends considerable time handling and reviewing those documents. Subsequent requests for supplementation often occur, as well as time-consuming and expensive discovery motions. This unproductive routine is then repeated until the parties eventually focus on the critical damages issues and tailor requests and disclosures accordingly. This approach is expensive and inefficient.

Most disputes over damages in IP cases do not result solely from the numbers or arithmetic (*things that can be counted*). Instead, the biggest disparity between the parties' damages positions often stems from a difference of opinion regarding *things that count but cannot be counted.* To effectively address these issues, the parties may benefit from input or evidence from technical fact witnesses or experts. For example, technical witnesses may assist in explaining how the IP at issue benefits customers (i.e., why customers do or do not care about the IP at issue) and in identifying acceptable alternatives or design-around options. If written discovery, depositions of technical witnesses, or technical expert reports are completed before the parties turn their attention to damages issues, the opportunity to obtain relevant damages information from these sources may be missed and the damages analysis may suffer. Similarly, third-party discovery may provide information regarding existing license agreements and market considerations. If the need for this information is not identified until late in the process, there may not be sufficient time to complete such discovery. Instead, with information obtained in the IDA process, a plan can be developed that focuses on obtaining discovery to effectively address the issues that are likely to have the most significant impact on damages issues, and that is proportionate to the likely value of the dispute. At the same time, decisions can be made to limit discovery and costs related to topics that are not likely to have a significant impact on the recovery of damages.

E. Manage Costs

Too often an IDA is not done due to a misperception that performing an IDA will increase costs. To the contrary, an IDA can provide critical information to facilitate effective cost management. Without an IDA, time and costs are often spent on unnecessary or irrelevant discovery, and dispute resolution strategies are often driven by emotion rather than information. Instead, an IDA can better inform dispute management decisions and reduce discovery costs by focusing the discovery on what matters most. For example, an IDA can help identify topics that are likely to have significant impact on damages. With that information, discovery can focus efforts on these important topics. Conversely, an IDA may identify damages approaches that are not viable or that are unlikely to result in significant damages. With this information, informed decisions can be made to minimize discovery efforts on these less fruitful topics. In this way, discovery efforts and costs can be directed to those areas with the most potential value.

F. Improve Quality

It is possible to participate in a mediation session, conduct discovery, and prepare a damages analysis without the information and analysis that an IDA affords. Performing an IDA, however, is more likely to improve both decision-making and the end results.

II. The IDA Process

The process for performing an IDA is intentionally flexible so that it can be tailored to fit the needs of a particular case. It can typically be completed within one to three weeks, assuming the availability of counsel, the damages expert, and relevant interviewees.

An IDA should be done as early in a dispute as practical. For example, it can be done as part of an early case assessment (ECA), as discussed in Chapter 3, as part of pre-litigation due diligence, or soon after a case is initiated. Here are some examples of how an IDA has been used:

Case in point: Shortly after litigation commenced, an IDA was performed for a defendant in an IP dispute. An experienced damages expert acting as a consultant conducted the IDA. Through interviews with outside counsel and the company's controller and vice president of marketing, the expert gathered information, including the legal issues in dispute; the IP at issue; estimated sales figures; profitability data; a description of the market; and the competitive positions of the parties. Within two weeks, the expert verbally communicated the findings and analysis, including a range of potential damages amounts, key issues, and the strengths and weaknesses of potential damages approaches to outside counsel and party representatives. With this information, the potential defendant realized it had more significant financial exposure than it had previously thought and determined that a business arrangement with the plaintiff was more attractive than incurring the time and cost of litigation and possibly paying significant damages. A business solution was negotiated with the potential plaintiff, and the litigation was quickly ended.

Case in point: Prior to commencing litigation, an IDA was performed for a potential plaintiff using a similar methodology to that described in the previous case. Through the IDA, the potential plaintiff realized that the damages claim it envisioned was not viable. Instead, as part of the IDA, a different damages approach was developed, along with a list of key data and evidence that would be useful to develop and support the new damages claim. The plaintiff was able to make an informed decision to commence litigation based in part on the information learned from the IDA, and to articulate a viable damages approach from the outset. Shortly after the litigation commenced, the plaintiff propounded focused discovery based on information identified during the IDA, thus increasing the likelihood of receiving the "right" information the first time and avoiding costly, prolonged discovery disputes. (In the event that the defendant did not timely produce the requested information, the plaintiff planned to file a motion to compel production of this key information, with the enhanced ability to clearly articulate its relevance and importance gained from the IDA.) The resulting discovery improved the quality of the evidence and analysis to support the damages claim, and, throughout the dispute process, the knowledge gained from the IDA allowed the plaintiff to make informed strategic decisions regarding case management and settlement.

The following list summarizes the IDA process. The simplicity of the process leverages the expertise of a damages expert to maximize value.

- *Interview outside counsel* to understand the legal issues (e.g., patent infringement, misappropriation of trade secrets, laches), the IP/technology at issue, and the background facts (e.g., the relevant products, how long the products have been sold, relevant dates, defenses).
- *Interview party representatives* to obtain relevant information regarding the market and financial information (e.g., competition, customers, product features, agreements).
- *Obtain actual or estimated sales and profitability information* to assist in quantifying estimates. If the parties have already exchanged basic sales and profitability data related to the accused products before the IDA is performed (e.g., in negotiations, mediations, or early discovery), this data may be provided to the damages expert for the IDA.[12] Alternatively, if the IDA is performed before this data exchange occurs, the damages expert may obtain actual data from the party retaining the expert and rely on estimates of the magnitude of the opposing party's sales and profitability from the retaining party's representatives and publicly available sources. Because the IDA is focused on magnitudes rather than specific amounts,

12. Subject to any protective order or confidentiality requirements in place.

these estimates may be adequate.[13] If the parties are involved in or headed toward some dispute resolution process, such as negotiation or mediation, they may reduce unnecessary and expensive discovery efforts by agreeing to exchange voluntarily the information or with the help of the mediator or the court. Cooperation between the parties to reach agreement regarding the scope and format for the needed information helps ensure that the information produced coincides with the information desired, and minimizes the need for repeated rounds of requests, objections, and production.[14] Although the parties may desire additional data at a later date if they cannot settle the case, this initial data production often provides much of the information needed for the IDA.

- *Obtain additional information* if needed (e.g., information regarding competitors and products) from publicly available sources (e.g., websites, press releases).
- *Consider the information obtained and develop an IDA* to identify and address key damages considerations, estimate realistic damages magnitudes, inform settlement and dispute strategies, and enable focused, efficient discovery, as discussed earlier in this chapter.
- *Provide IDA feedback to outside counsel and/or party representatives* to permit them to understand the likely damages measures, key damages issues, suggestions for how to address these issues, estimates of damages magnitudes, and how to formulate a discovery plan, as well as to identify next steps. This feedback is typically provided orally, allowing for the fluid exchange of information, addressing questions as they arise, and avoiding the cost of preparing a written report.

Furthermore, as with the ECA process, an IDA will likely involve the collection of confidential, even privileged, information; thus, all involved should be mindful of maintaining the confidentiality of the information.

---

13. In some situations, it may not be possible to obtain estimates of accused sales or other financial information at the time the IDA is performed. Although this may hinder the identification of damages magnitudes, the IDA can still provide valuable information, such as identifying key damages issues, developing a discovery plan, and considering dispute resolution and process alternatives.

14. Information voluntarily exchanged may include, for example, sales revenue, sales volumes, manufacturing costs, and profitability data related to the products at issue. Additional details or data may also be relevant, and care should be taken to identify the information desired with sufficient specificity, possibly by exchanging a spreadsheet with column and row headings that the producing party can populate with the applicable data.

III. Other IDA Applications

This chapter has primarily discussed an IDA performed by one party in confidence with a damages expert, which is consistent with current U.S. dispute practices. Although not commonly done, the parties may cooperatively utilize an IDA.[15] For example, a joint IDA can be performed by a jointly appointed expert serving as a neutral (e.g., damages special master, damages advisor, expert determiner, arbitrator, or mediator)[16] who communicates the results to both parties, identifies areas of agreement,[17] or provides early resolution of one or more damages issues. The damages neutral's work may be

15. Although the IDA uses discussed in this section are not currently used often in U.S. disputes, they are discussed here to encourage creative and cooperative dispute strategies and processes.

16. The use of damages neutrals is discussed in various international alternative dispute resolution rules and model clauses. *See* World Intellectual Property Organization Arbitration and Mediation Center, WIPO Mediation, Arbitration, Expedited Arbitration, and Expert Determination Rules and Clauses (2020), https://www.wipo.int/edocs/pubdocs/en/wipo_pub_446_2020.pdf; Sedona Conference, *supra* note 1; see also Fed. R. Civ. P. 53, Masters (emphasis added), which identifies damages as an area for which a special master may be appropriate, as follows:

> (a) Appointment.
>
> > (1) *Scope.* Unless a statute provides otherwise, a court may appoint a master only to:
> >
> > > (A) perform duties consented to by the parties;
> > >
> > > (B) hold trial proceedings and make or recommend findings of fact on issues to be decided without a jury if appointment is warranted by:
> > >
> > > > (i) some exceptional condition; or
> > > >
> > > > (ii) *the need to perform an accounting or resolve a difficult computation of damages*; or
> > >
> > > (C) address pretrial and post-trial matters that cannot be effectively and timely addressed by an available district judge or magistrate judge of the district.

Using a special master for IP damages is also discussed in Chapter 12.

17. For example, each party can confidentially submit a list of possible areas of agreement to the damages neutral; the neutral can compare the lists and then compile a list of those areas that overlap. In this way, parties can suggest areas of agreement confidentially without "tipping their hand" to the opposing party. In another variation, the neutral may provide a list of suggested agreement areas based on experience and knowledge of the case as a starting point, and then assist the parties in reaching a stipulation.

binding or nonbinding, depending on the selected role of the damages neutral and the agreement of the parties.[18]

The benefits of using a damages neutral are maximized by involving the neutral as early in a dispute as possible. If the parties have not already agreed to using a damages neutral, appointment of a damages neutral should be addressed at the initial scheduling conference or as soon as practicable. If the parties agree to mediate a dispute prior to the court's scheduling conference, appointment of a damages neutral should be considered sufficiently in advance of the mediation to perform or facilitate an IDA and to facilitate the mediation.[19]

A joint IDA can also be used to

- provide substantive damages disclosures;
- bring clarity to an issue that is a sticking point for settlement purposes;
- facilitate settlement by identifying key damages considerations and a realistic damages magnitude;
- resolve an issue (if the parties agree to make the findings of the IDA binding); and
- narrow the issues in dispute.

A joint IDA can further be used to facilitate discovery, as described in the following sections.

A. Early Damages Disclosures

The parties may voluntarily, or with the help of the court in a pending case, exchange initial damages contentions, such as identifying claimed damages measures (e.g., lost profits, price erosion, unjust enrichment, reasonable royalties); information about the accused products; a description of the market; sales volume, revenue, cost, and profits data for relevant products; relevant licenses or other agreements; and preliminary computations or estimates of damages.[20] Not only will such disclosure crystalize each party's position,

---

18. Although appointing a damages special master, a damages advisor, or an expert determiner does result in some cost to the parties, these costs can be offset by savings that result from early resolution and streamlined discovery, and the parties, court, or tribunal may be provided with better information with which to efficiently manage each case.

19. A damages neutral should be experienced in financial, accounting, marketing, and damages issues (i.e., a damages expert).

20. For a discussion and sample of initial damages contentions, see SEDONA CONFERENCE, COMMENTARY ON CASE MANAGEMENT OF PATENT DAMAGES AND REMEDIES ISSUES: PROPOSED MODEL LOCAL RULE FOR DAMAGES CONTENTIONS (June

it will also help to address proportionality, help to tailor discovery to the information that matters most, and inform settlement and litigation strategies. Without a clear, early understanding of each other's damages positions and key damages considerations, the parties' early damages contentions may lack sufficient information or specificity, or may differ dramatically from the parties' ultimate damages positions. A joint IDA enables informed substantive initial damages contentions.

B. Narrowing and Resolving Key Damages Issues

Although the parties' damages positions typically differ from each other, these differences often primarily relate to a limited number of issues, while there are many facts, assumptions, and opinions about which the parties and the party-retained experts do not differ. Unfortunately, in current practice, these areas of agreement are typically not clearly articulated. Thus, the experts prepare lengthy written reports covering every aspect of their analyses, including those areas about which the experts do not disagree. Similarly, trial evidence and testimony often covers much of this same ground, consuming trial time with uncontested topics. Pretrial stipulations may alleviate some of this at trial, but those stipulations typically do not occur early enough in the litigation process to prevent unnecessary redundancy in expert reports. Instead, using a joint IDA, the parties may be able to reach resolution of some topics, facilitated by a damages neutral, thus avoiding unnecessary discovery, time, and costs, and focusing efforts on topics that matter most.

Similarly, if each party performs its own IDA, another way of reaching agreements on narrowing and resolving key damages issues is for the experts to communicate directly with each other to work out any agreement (i.e., an expert conference). Although this is not typically done in the current U.S. IP

2017 ed.), https://thesedonaconference.org/sites/default/files/publications/Sedona%2520WG9%2520Damages%2520Contentions%2520Proposed%2520Model%2520Local%2520Rule.pdf; U.S. District Court Northern District of California, Patent Local Rules (Oct. 19, 2023), https://www.cand.uscourts.gov/rules/patent-local-rules/. Early damages disclosures are also contemplated in the International Institute for Conflict Prevention & Resolution (CPR) Protocol on Determination of Damages in Arbitration, which prescribes that arbitrators address, in or about their initial conference with the parties, the subject of damages, having the parties articulate their theories of compensation and their defenses, including mitigation of damages. *See* CPR International Committee on Arbitration, CPR Protocol on Determination of Damages in Arbitration (2010), https://static.cpradr.org/docs/CPR-Protocol-on-Determination-of-Damages-in-Arbitration-fnl.pdf.

litigation culture and practice, the effectiveness of this approach has been demonstrated in England[21] and in international arbitration.[22]

Conclusion

Not everything that can be counted counts, and not everything that counts can be counted. Heeding these sage words from Albert Einstein, an IDA focuses on those things that count but cannot be counted, provides an efficient and effective tool for strategic decision-making that facilitates traditional dispute resolution, and enables creative dispute resolution processes tailored to fit each case.

---

21. This is addressed in the English Rules of Civil Procedure, 1998 S.I. 3132/17, art. 35.12 (U.K.), which states as follows:

> (1) The court may, at any stage, direct a discussion between experts for the purpose of requiring the experts to—
>
> (a) identify and discuss the expert issues in the proceedings; and
>
> (b) where possible, reach an agreed opinion on those issues.
>
> (2) The court may specify the issues which the experts must discuss.
>
> (3) The court may direct that following a discussion between the experts they must prepare a statement for the court setting out those issues on which—
>
> (a) they agree; and
>
> (b) they disagree, with a summary of their reasons for disagreeing.
>
> (4) The content of the discussion between the experts shall not be referred to at the trial unless the parties agree.
>
> (5) Where experts reach agreement on an issue during their discussions, the agreement shall not bind the parties unless the parties expressly agree to be bound by the agreement.

In at least one application of this process, counterpart experts meet to discuss the issues to see if it is possible to reach agreement and therefore narrow the issues. The meetings are normally deemed work product. At the end of the process the experts produce a joint statement that, when agreed and signed, is no longer work product.

22. International Bar Association (IBA) rules provide:

> The Arbitral Tribunal in its discretion may order that any Party-Appointed Experts who will submit or who have submitted Expert Reports on the same or related issues meet and confer on such issues. At such meeting, the Party-Appointed Experts shall attempt to reach agreement on the issues within the scope of their Expert Reports, and they shall record in writing any such issues on which they reach agreement, and any remaining areas of disagreement and the reasons therefore.

IBA, IBA Rules on the Taking of Evidence in International Arbitration art. 5 (2020), https://www.ibanet.org/MediaHandler?id=def0807b-9fec-43ef-b624-f2cb2af7cf7b.

CHAPTER 5

Useful Tools to Persuade, Evaluate, and Communicate in ADR Proceedings

Theo Cheng[1]

We shall neither fail nor falter; we shall not weaken or tire . . . .
Give us the tools, and we will finish the job.

—Winston Churchill

Introduction[2]

This chapter will address four categories of tools: (1) screening tools, (2) reality testing with a mock panel, (3) decision tree analysis (DTA), and (4) visual aids. These categories of tools are applicable to a wide range of disputes, including the most complex intellectual property (IP)/Technology problem. They clarify issues, make the analysis of the case easier, improve advocacy, facilitate decisions, and render an ideal settlement agreement more likely.

I. Screening Tools

Parties can use one or a combination of many different alternative dispute resolution (ADR) processes to help them resolve a dispute. Among the most prevalent processes are mediation and arbitration. Most ADR processes are invoked because the parties have a contractual obligation to use a particular process (or a series of processes) to resolve any disputes that arise under their contract. Without such a contractual obligation, if the parties nonetheless desire to pursue ADR, the question arises: Which process? Counsel may answer these questions using screening tools that help determine whether to litigate or use ADR, which ADR process would be most effective, and who should conduct the process.

1. This chapter is a derivative work of Chapter 7 from the First Edition and Chapter 13 from the Second Edition of this book authored by Kevin R. Casey, a retired partner in the law firm of Stradley, Ronon, Stevens & Young, LLP.

2. See Glossary for definition of frequently used terms.

A. Overview

A voluntary decision to engage in ADR occurs in about 40 percent to 65 percent of cases.[3] Successful ADR relies on an early, inexpensive, and straightforward determination of whether a dispute is suitable for resolution through ADR. Suitability screening tools pose questions designed to help determine the likelihood of resolving a dispute through ADR, and to evaluate objectively relevant factors that tend to show the likelihood of success or failure of using ADR. Screening tools permit counsel to evaluate disputes at a very early stage.

Two useful screening tools developed by the International Institute for Conflict Prevention & Resolution (CPR) are the *CPR Mediation Screen Questions Worksheet* (the Mediation Screen) and the *Questions Regarding Choice of Arbitration or Litigation* (the Arbitration Screen).[4] Although one answer to a suitability screen question may tend to support the use of a particular ADR process (e.g., mediation or arbitration), and another answer may suggest that the process is not likely to resolve the dispute, the suitability screen is intended to be *predictive* rather than determinative. That is, determining the suitability of a dispute for resolution by an ADR process is a matter of judgment. It cannot be resolved by a mere numerical comparison of the factors favoring and disfavoring use of ADR. In addition, answers to some questions may carry more weight than others in a particular case, while those questions carrying less weight in one case may be critical factors in another case. Regardless, including perhaps less important factors on the suitability screen is worthwhile so that it acts as a checklist of factors to consider in most, if not all, cases. Counsel should also consider how the views of opposing counsel (and not just the opposing party) will affect suitability for resolution by ADR; ADR requires agreement by both parties to the process.

Because suitability screens are qualitative rather than quantitative tools, no numerical outcome ensures that a case is better for ADR than litigation, or that a case is better resolved by a particular ADR process. These decisions remain a matter of judgment for counsel and their clients. Although the decision of whether to use ADR is still more art than science, suitability screens help to make this decision more objective, thereby increasing participants' confidence in the decision to try ADR. Moreover, the *process* of using a

3. *See, e.g.*, David B. Lipsky & Ronald L. Seeber, Cornell University, The Appropriate Resolution of Corporate Disputes: A Report on the Growing Use of ADR by U.S. Corporations (1998), http://digitalcommons.ilr.cornell.edu/icrpubs/4; *see also* Jeanne M. Brett et al., *The Effectiveness of Mediation: An Independent Analysis of Cases Handled by Four Major Service Providers*, 12 Negot. J. 259 (1996).

4. *See* Chapter 6, Section I.A.

screen to evaluate a dispute can be more important than the actual results of the screen. Screening tools stimulate analytical thinking and decision-making; they are not intended as a definitive measure of which disputes should be referred to an ADR proceeding rather than litigated. Screening tools also stimulate conversation (i.e., communication) between counsel and client and between in-house decision makers.

B. ADR and, if So, Which Type of ADR?

Figure 5.1 summarizes most of the well-known ADR procedures:

Figure 5.1: Well-Known ADR Procedures

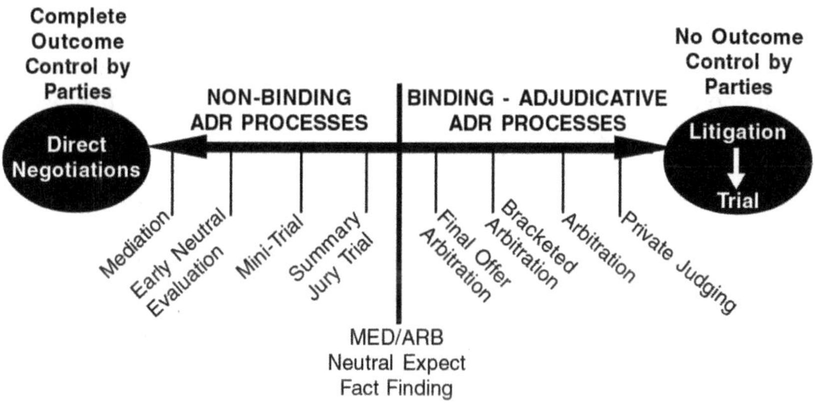

Insofar as mediation and arbitration are the most prevalent ADR procedures, the discussion here focuses on the use of the Mediation Screen and the Arbitration Screen found in Appendix A to this chapter.

1. Mediation Screen

The Mediation Screen asks a series of questions grouped into three factors: (1) the parties' goals for managing the dispute; (2) the suitability of the dispute for a problem-solving process; and (3) the potential benefits of mediation for the dispute in question. The answers to these questions do not dictate an answer; rather, they assist parties and practitioners in understanding what they want to achieve from the process and whether the dispute is potentially compatible with mediation. At the end of the day, the parties and their counsel, with the Mediation Screen answers in hand, must use their best judgment about whether to proceed with mediation, another ADR process, or litigation.

a) Factor 1: The Parties' Goals for Managing the Dispute

At the outset of any IP/Technology dispute, it is important to understand the parties' business objectives in either pursuing or defending against pending or threatened claims. The Mediation Screen suggests three categories of goals to consider—overarching, legal, and pragmatic.

Overarching goals. These include whether it is important for the parties to maintain a relationship with the opposing party in the future, control over the outcome of the dispute, and control over the adversarial process by which the dispute is decided. Mediation can provide parties with the opportunity to achieve each of these objectives in a manner that arbitration or litigation cannot. In the IP/Technology context, if the dispute is between a licensor and licensee, joint developers, or a supplier and distributor, then mediation provides an opportunity for the parties to work through issues in a cooperative fashion and preserve important business relationships, or even begin a relationship. A mediated settlement also allows the parties to have greater control over the outcome and broader territorial reaches than would be possible with a court judgment. If the IP/Technology dispute has ramifications in global markets or multiple forums, a mediated solution could provide resolution between the parties in multiple jurisdictions.

Legal objectives. These include whether a dispositive motion will conclude the matter, if injunctive relief or legal precedent is necessary, and whether formal discovery is imperative. While parties may decline to mediate if they believe they have a strong summary judgment motion, a decision denying the motion may change the parties' outlook. And if a party seeks a pronouncement of legal precedent, then the privacy of the mediation process and the lack of any ruling would not meet such a need. If a party wants, or thinks that they need, formal (and full) discovery, mediation may not be suitable until that has occurred. But formal (and full) discovery is very expensive and often not necessary for settlement.

Pragmatic objectives. These include the estimated monetary cost of pursuing litigation relative to what either party could realistically expect to recover by a decision in their favor, as well as the importance of a speedy resolution, the need for confidentiality, and a party's often mistaken belief that it will potentially *hit the jackpot* by going to court or arbitration.[5] If the parties desire a relatively low-cost, expeditious, and confidential proceeding, mediation will meet those objectives. For example, parties may use mediation when a company has an opportunity to be acquired but pending patent litigation is an unknown liability. Or an expeditious resolution of a

5. Although performing an early case assessment (as discussed in Chapter 3), including an early damages assessment (as discussed in Chapter 4), can help a party face the pragmatic realities of litigation, a mediator can bring an often-needed reality check to a party that is discounting the various costs, overplaying the benefits, and overlooking the risks.

trademark dispute may be necessary when the mark and ad campaign have just been, or are about to be, launched.

b) Factor 2: The Suitability of the Dispute for a Problem-Solving Process

The Mediation Screen also provides questions designed to have the parties confront whether the mediation process suits them and their situation—for example, their capacity for problem-solving, the quality of their relationship, and the practical realities.

Capacity. Parties may not have the capacity or motivation to pursue a problem-solving process. Rather, there may be fundamental principles at stake, the need for vindication, or the conviction of prevailing in court that is the motivating factor.[6]

Relationship. The climate and trust between the parties and their counsel may shed light on whether mediation can be a worthwhile process. Experience repeatedly shows that the better the relationship, at least between counsel, the more productive the mediation sessions can be.

Practical realities. Creative solutions that are a hallmark of the mediation process may be stifled by the circumstances of a particular case. Do the parties have the necessary resources to negotiate worthwhile trade-offs? Can a trademark owner entice an accused infringer to stop using one mark and begin using another expeditiously? Are there patents of interest to trade? Can a trademark be restricted to certain lines of business? Do terms in pre-existing licenses prevent agreed-upon terms?

c) Factor 3: The General Benefits of Mediation

Mediation is not for every dispute or for every party or counsel. Mediation has potential advantages, but they must be in line with what a party and its counsel want or need, or think they want or need. Such benefits include:

- Assistancc in clarifying issues
- Assistance in controlling anger or other negative emotions
- The opportunity to tell their story and be heard by the other side
- A *reality check* from a knowledgeable intermediary on the parties' positions or expectations
- A confidential setting in which to explore one another's interests and needs
- Assistance in exploring creative solutions
- An intermediary who can make, and help the parties make, offers and counteroffers more acceptable

6. For example, if a large corporation's key objective is to financially cripple an emerging competitor by an expensive and lengthy patent litigation, and if the small corporation wants to show its tenacity to its opponent and others like it, mediation is not likely to satisfy either party's key objectives.

If the parties both believe that, on balance, these benefits may aid in a resolution, then mediation is likely to be worth pursuing. And if the parties pursue mediation, but the case does not settle, any preparation and case assessment done for mediation is not wasted effort. As discussed in Chapter 3, such endeavors remain useful throughout the settlement process, as they help focus any additional discovery and educate decision makers on realistic probabilities of litigation success and the avenues available for resolution.

Mediation is not always feasible, available, or ideal. When a dispute cannot be resolved through mediation, other forms of ADR such as arbitration may be more suitable—or even litigation instead of ADR. If the parties elect arbitration or litigation, they should nevertheless keep in mind that their answers to the questions presented in the Mediation Screen may change as arbitration or litigation progresses. Thus, parties should consider revisiting the Mediation Screen at various stages to determine if the dispute has become more amenable to mediation after the arbitration or litigation procedure has begun to unfold.

2. Arbitration Screen

If the parties decide not to proceed through mediation, the Arbitration Screen assists users in determining whether the dispute may lend itself better to arbitration or litigation based on the goals of the parties and the attendant circumstances of the dispute. As with the Mediation Screen, the answers to the questions about arbitration and litigation do not dictate a particular procedure. Instead, the answers provide information to assist the parties in making their decision. Table 5.1 illustrates some of the criteria that may prompt parties and counsel to select an IP/Technology case for arbitration rather than litigation.

Table 5.1: Sample Criteria for Selecting an IP/Technology Case for Arbitration

A. Characteristics of IP/Technology Disputes That Render Arbitration Suitable	Yes	No
1. Parties want to avoid costly, time-consuming discovery.		
2. Complex technical issues make resolution by a judge or jury difficult and unpredictable.		
3. Highly confidential proprietary data is involved, or sensitive public relations issues exist, or the IP owner wants to retain valid enforcement rights against the world (as opposed to just the other party).		
4. The parties are comparable in size and resources.		

5. There is a continuing business relationship between the parties or the industry is fairly closed so that all know one another.		
6. Settlement remains a possibility.		
7. Time is of the essence.		
8. One of the parties is a foreign corporation.		
B. Characteristics of IP/Technology Disputes That Render Arbitration Unsuitable		
9. One of the parties wants to send a message.		
10. A party needs (or wants) liberal discovery.		
11. A party adopts an uncompromising position (e.g., refuses to agree on selection of a suitable arbitrator).		
12. A party embraces the risks inherent in litigation.		
13. The parties have not already been involved in IP litigation.		
14. The parties want to create legal precedent.		

An important factor in the quality of the mediation or arbitration process is the quality of the neutral (i.e., the mediator facilitating or the arbitrator(s) deciding) whom the parties select. Generally, selecting a mediator or arbitrator is a decision that should be made on a case-by-case basis, not a one-size-fits-all approach. IP/Technology disputes present particular considerations for the mediator or arbitrator that are not normally associated with other types of cases. For example, IP/Technology disputes may involve complex technology, esoteric IP law concepts, highly technical or nuanced IP practices, and multiple forms of IP. Therefore, even an experienced mediator or arbitrator of commercial disputes without an IP or technology background may not be the best choice for a particular case. For a comprehensive discussion of selecting mediators and arbitrators for IP/Technology disputes, see Chapter 6, Section III (mediators) and Chapter 9, Section II (arbitrators).

II. Do We Have a Good Case or What? Ways for Getting a Dose of Reality

Counsel may believe that they have the greatest case, but without an effective presentation before the arbitration panel, they may not attain the desired results. Particularly when the stakes are high, obtaining objective feedback may sharpen the presentation of evidence and arbitration hearing strategy. There are various ways to do this. For example, a mock panel may be convened from a party's law firm, a party's in-house legal department, and/or external arbitrators.

A. Why a Mock Panel?

A mock arbitration panel can perform multiple functions. It can serve as critic, fact finder, consultant, or all of these.[7] As a critic, the mock panel can provide valuable feedback—for example, about how to improve presentations, briefs, and demonstratives. As a fact finder, the mock panel can opine about key issues and provide its supporting reasoning. Once the panel has reached its decision, it can provide the hearing team with feedback regarding a variety of issues possibly affecting the outcome of the case (e.g., case theme, educating the panel about technology issues, witness presentations).

Objective feedback from a mock panel can counter *group think*—the feeling that the team working on a case has that its case is great and its client will win. Going outside one's comfort group to hear objective feedback can be enlightening and help improve the chances of actually winning.

B. Considerations When Using a Mock Panel

Consider the following in developing a plan for conducting a mock arbitration:

- **Focus on aspects of the case that would most benefit from objective feedback**. For those aspects that are particularly complex or nuanced (e.g., technical, regulatory, or damages issues), the mock panel can provide guidance on ways to present the evidence most clearly and persuasively. Similarly, it can make recommendations for improving perceived case weaknesses—accentuating the positive evidence and neutralizing or de-emphasizing the negative factors.
- **Set and work within a budget**. Even when much is at stake and the value of a mock arbitration is apparent, clients do not want to be surprised by its cost. Prioritize the objectives for using a mock arbitration panel and then discuss options with the client for satisfying those needs. Stick to an established budget. A fee arrangement with the panelists who will participate in the mock proceeding may also help to keep on budget.

---

7. The discussion in this chapter relates to a mock panel used by a party to an arbitration to gain information that might influence strategies or decisions related to their case. See Chapter 1, Section III, Case History #7, for an example of how a mock arbitration panel may be jointly used by parties in a mediation to obtain expert feedback on hotly contested issues.

- **Choose a model that fits a client's needs and budget.**[8] A mock panel may consist of a sole panelist. This limits costs but it also limits perspectives. Three-member panels are not uncommon in complex technology cases, particularly where important issues are at stake. Tri-partite mock panels may be conducted in one of two ways. One way is to provide a group decision following a private deliberation and/or feedback on particular aspects of a case. Counsel have the advantage of learning from three panelists the factors that went into each one's thinking on the decided issues and obtaining feedback on presentation and witness credibility. In comparison to the one-panelist model, parties gain three times the feedback, but with three times the cost. Another way is to engage panelists who do not deliberate to obtain a joint decision. The advantages are that a party obtains multiple separate decisions as opposed to one decision from three panel members where they possibly negotiated or compromised their individual views for a consensus; and they save some time (and cost) by eliminating joint deliberations.
- **Reflect the actual panel.** When engaging a mock arbitration panel, consider the characteristics and background of the panel members who will ultimately decide the case (e.g., their technical, subject matter, and industry background and experience). There is no guarantee that this will be a good predictor of the rulings from the actual panel; however, experienced panelists mirroring the actual panel are more likely to provide relevant and helpful feedback.[9]
- **Maximize time with the mock panel.** Assuming that the entire case is not presented formally to the mock arbitration panel, consider summarizing the entire case strategy to the panel so that it can provide feedback on influential issues, such as what legal theories to emphasize; what graphics to present; what evidence to use and how best to present it; how to allocate limited hearing time; and how experts may be most useful. The feedback and guidance may suggest that certain evidence be eliminated, altered, or added for a more effective and efficient presentation.
- **Scoring points.** Even for a panel with some background and experience related to the technical issues in the case, at the actual evidentiary hearing, parties will need to provide sufficient background

---

8. *See* Amy Rothstein, *Mock Arbitrations: A New Kind of "Jury" Research*, N.Y.L.J. (Sept. 10, 2009), https://www.law.com/newyorklawjournal/almID/1202433679158/.

9. *See* Edna Sussman, *Improving Your Arbitration Presentation with a Mock Arbitration: Two Case Studies*, 5 NYSBA N.Y. Disp. Resol. Law. 15 (2012).

and context for the novel technical evidence that fact and expert witnesses will present (e.g., particular laboratory or clinical tests, analyses, test results, critical measurements, scientific or regulatory standards). A mock panel can advise on whether background technology and the related legal arguments have been presented clearly and effectively. Other feedback may include how best to present a witness testifying by video or using witness statements.

- **Consider including a mock opposing counsel.** Consider using someone who is not already familiar with the case (i.e., not someone on the arbitration team). Although including a mock opposing counsel will increase the cost of the exercise, the mock panel will be in a better position to assess how strong each side is on the key disputed issues and perhaps help to strengthen a weak argument or presentation. It is critical, however, that counsel present both sides of the dispute as effectively as possible to obtain relevant feedback.

III. DTA

IP/Technology attorneys often handle complex cases (e.g., multiple claims, parties, venues, forms of IP). They must help clients decide whether to litigate or settle, and whether to try ADR. Then, once a decision is made among those options, a myriad of decisions follow. For litigation, those decisions may include whether to challenge jurisdiction; bring a summary judgment motion; or take a particular deposition. For mediation, those decisions may include who will mediate; what is the likelihood of success on various claims; how much may a party have to pay; how much will it cost to achieve the desired results; and what *cards* will be disclosed? DTA is a means to both evaluate the options available for each decision and to facilitate communication between counsel and client.

What follows is a basic explanation of the mechanics of DTA—what it is and how it is used. This is followed by a discussion regarding its advantages and, specifically, its application by mediators. DTA, however, is not a panacea or *cure all* for all cases; therefore, the limitations of DTA are also set forth.

A. DTA Mechanics

Figure 1 (see Appendix B to this chapter) is as an example of DTA. A young man is at a fair. In front of him is a booth with a large jar having 200 marbles: 50 each of blue, red, green, and yellow. The game is free to play, and the person wins $40,000 if he draws a blue, red, or green marble. Unfortunately, if he draws a yellow marble, he must pay $100,000. Should he play?

The choice is to play or not. If not, the player gets nothing (but loses nothing). That option must be compared to the *expected value* of what will happen if he plays. Suppose he plays. There is a 75 percent probability, P, that he will draw a blue, red, or green marble and win $40,000. The expected value of this possibility is 0.75 x $40,000, or $30,000. There is a 25 percent probability, however, that he will draw a yellow marble and have to pay $100,000. The expected value of this unfortunate possibility is negative $25,000 (calculated as 0.25 x $100,000 and given a negative value because he must pay). Adding the two expected values gives an overall expected value of plus $5,000 ($30,000 minus $25,000)—so he should play because the positive expected value trumps the alternative *no play* choice of zero. The expected value, $5,000, will never itself be realized. The expected value can be viewed as the average of all outcomes if he played many times. Moreover, a risk-averse person (or a smart one who does not have $100,000 to lose) may choose not to play despite the likely reward.

To apply the power of DTA in the IP/Technology context, consider the choice of bringing a patent infringement case as the plaintiff or accepting a $500,000 settlement offer. How should counsel advise a client? The first step is to construct a dependency or influence diagram like that of Figure 2 (see Appendix B). This takes some time and requires significant thought, but it is critically important. Once counsel constructs the diagram (a table may work as well for some cases), they should discuss it with members of their litigation team and the client. It is worthwhile to include as many likely issues (called variables in mathematics) as possible. If counsel is performing a DTA in conjunction with an early case assessment (see Chapter 3),[10] they have probably identified many of the issues needed for the diagram. The issues will interact, and those interactions should be identified by cross-arrows (e.g., the answer to the question *Will the court find patent infringement?* depends on the answer to the question *Will the court give a favorable patent claim interpretation?*).

10. The EDR Institute, a nonprofit organization founded in 2016, has, in fact, promulgated procedures and protocols that combine early dispute resolution principles with the use of DTA and offers training to in-house counsel, outside attorneys, and neutrals. For more information, see https://www.edrinstitute.org/ (last visited Mar. 23, 2025).

Consider sub-issues, like materiality and intent for the issue of unenforceability. The process of critically thinking about the issues and how they relate will help analyze the case, including its complexity, the potential costs, the type and extent of discovery needed, and the case strengths and weaknesses. Thus, preparing the diagram facilitates communications between counsel and their clients about what issues may need to be addressed.

Counsel can create the tree of Figure 3 (see Appendix B) by hand, using paper, pencil, and a calculator; using electronic tools, such as an Excel spreadsheet; or via available DTA software, some of which are available for free on the internet.[11] The square at the left represents the decision: litigate or settle for $500,000. The tree grows to the right by adding circular branch points representing key uncertain events that will occur and affect the outcome. Project the likelihood of success for each event, based upon best estimates regarding the strengths and weaknesses of the case (e.g., slam dunk issue = 0.9; likely to occur or *good chance* = 0.7; even chance = 0.5; not likely to occur = 0.3; very poor chance = 0.1), and multiply the probabilities for each branch of the tree. Whether counsel work by longhand or use software, by performing this calculation, they will have a series of probabilities, one for each tree branch.

The next step is to provide the expected award at the end of each tree branch (i.e., if all of the possible outcomes that define a branch occur). Each expected award will be based on experience and judgment (taking into account such applicable factors as units sold, margins, existing license royalty rates), likely in combination with expert advice. Referring to Figure 3, focus on the top line of possible outcomes (which is the plaintiff-patent owner's *best case*). This line represents the culmination of the plaintiff succeeding in proving (1) literal infringement; (2) the patent is enforceable (or not unenforceable); (3) that at least one key claim is valid (or not invalid); (4) the defendant's equitable defenses of laches and estoppel are unavailing; (5) that no limitations on damages (e.g., 35 U.S.C. §§ 286, 287) apply; (6) lost profits; and (7) the defendant's infringement was willful. If all of these events occur in favor of the plaintiff, then estimate an award of $6 million. Next, estimate the award (or possible outcome) for each of the various tree branches by applying a damages analysis.

The calculator or computer does the rest. The probability of each individual outcome is simply the product of all intermediate probabilities. Returning to the top line of Figure 3, the probability that the plaintiff will succeed in proving (1) literal infringement is estimated at 30 percent; (2) the patent is enforceable is estimated at 90 percent; (3) at least one key claim is valid is estimated at 80 percent; (4) the defendant's equitable defenses of laches and

11. *See, e.g.*, SilverDecisions, https://silverdecisions.pl/ (last visited Mar. 23, 2025).

estoppel are unavailing is estimated at 90 percent; (5) no limitations on damages apply is estimated at 90 percent; (6) lost profits is estimated at 30 percent; and (7) the defendant's infringement was willful is estimated at 20 percent. The probability of all of these events happening, as the plaintiff would like, is the multiplication product of the probability of each event happening, or 0.3 × 0.9 × 0.8 × 0.9 × 0.9 × 0.3 × 0.2 = 0.01 (or about 1 percent). The expected value of this particular award (or outcome) is the probability that the outcome will occur (0.01) times the amount of the award ($6,000,000), or $60,000.

After calculating the expected values for each branch, as summarized in Table 5.2, counsel can add each of the branch expected values to calculate the overall expected value of the litigation option. See Figure 4 (in Appendix B). The overall expected value is theoretically about $764,225 (recall from our marble example that the overall expected value is best viewed as an average litigation outcome were the case to be tried multiple times). Compare $764,225 versus the $500,000 settlement option . . . and consider filing suit.

Table 5.2

Branch No.	Outcome (Award)	Probability of Award	Expected Value
1 (Top)	$6,000,000	1% (0.01)	$60,000
2	$2,000,000	4.2% (0.042)	$84,000
3	$3,000,000	2.4% (0.024)	$72,000
4	$1,000,000	9.8% (0.098)	$98,000
5	$0	1.9% (0.019)	$0
6	$0	2.2% (0.022)	$0
7	$0	5.4% (0.054)	$0
8	$0	3% (0.030)	$0
9	$6,000,000	1.5% (0.015)	$90,000
10	$2,000,000	5.9% (0.059)	$118,000
11	$3,000,000	3.4% (0.034)	$102,000
12	$1,000,000	13.7% (0.137)	$137,000
13	$0	2.7% (0.027)	$0
14	$0	3% (0.030)	$0
15	$0	7.6% (0.076)	$0
16	$0	4.2% (0.042)	$0
17	$0	28% (0.280)	$0
Totals	(within rounding errors)	**100%**	**$764,225**

There are other considerations that may militate against filing suit, of course, despite the logical conclusion provided by the DTA. Such considerations include public relations issues and the distraction of litigation to the business and its employees.

Parties can generate much useful information from the tree. Focus on only two of the many items of information with reference to Figures 5 and 6 in Appendix B. Figure 5 is a bar chart that shows the probability distribution of the various outcomes. The plaintiff can expect to recover nothing almost 60 percent of the time, yet it has a 2.5 percent chance of recovering $6,000,000. If the plaintiff brought the same suit 100 or 1,000 times, an *average* recovery of about $764,225 may be expected. The bar chart also indicates the cumulative probability that the plaintiff can expect to recover at least a certain amount: the plaintiff has nearly a 20 percent (i.e., 18 percent) chance of recovering at least $2,000,000.

This same information about the cumulative probability of a particular amount of award can be gleaned from the DTA of Figure 4 (in Appendix B) itself, or from Table 5.2. Start from the top-most award on the right-hand side of the tree and progress to the bottom. There is a 1 percent probability of a $6,000,000 award, a 4.2 percent probability of a $2,000,000 award, a 2.4 percent probability of a $3,000,000 award, a 1.5 percent probability of a $6,000,000 award, a 5.9 percent probability of a $2,000,000 award, and a 3.4 percent probability of a $3,000,000 award. Adding these probabilities (0.01 + 0.042 + 0.024 + 0.015 + 0.059 + 0.034) achieves a total probability of about 0.18 that the award will be at least $2,000,000 (i.e., $2,000,000 or more).

Finally, Figure 6 (in Appendix B) is a *sensitivity* chart. Consider four issues, or variables (e.g., enforceability, willfulness, literal infringement, infringement under the doctrine of equivalents), and change the probability of success for each. By graphing the ultimate expected value of the litigation for each probability value, the impact of the variable on the outcome can be seen. That is, one can tell how significant or influential a particular issue is to (or on) the overall outcome of the litigation. This helps to identify *critical* issues and may advise counsel to spend more time to develop information about those issues to better evaluate the likelihood of success for those issues.

B. DTA Advantages

DTA offers many advantages, particularly in the context of settlement negotiations and mediations.[12] A quick search of the internet reveals empirical

12. *See* CPR, Report of the CPR Patent Mediation Task Force: Effective Practices Protocol 9–10 (2012), https://www.mandw.com/PUBLICATIONS/CPR-Patent_Mediation_Task_Force(2014).pdf.

evidence of the growth of DTA in general and its use in mediation in particular. The inquiry—Decision Tree Analysis—using the Google search engine triggered about 217,000,000 results in 0.89 seconds on June 23, 2025. The search inquiry—Decision Tree Analysis—and—Mediation—triggered about 5,120,000 results. A similar search nearly ten years ago yielded far fewer results. Indeed, 15 years ago, three full chapters of the American Arbitration Association's *Handbook on Mediation* (2d ed. 2010) addressed DTA. Mediators have found that they can use DTA to help parties achieve settlement through the mediation process.[13]

Anecdotal evidence of the successful use of DT to facilitate mediation has also been surfacing and continues to escalate. Even more than a decade ago, a leading proponent of DTA, Marc B. Victor, Esq., President of Litigation Risk Analysis, Inc., described his experiences using DTA as follows:

> I have been asked to present decision trees as an advocate in mediation, and it certainly helps show the mediator that my client and I have a reasoned basis for our settlement position. I have also been retained by mediators on several occasions in large cases to help the mediation process by getting the parties to agree on the appropriate decision trees, discuss arguments, and assess probabilities and verdict ranges. These cases have typically involved hundreds of millions of dollars, and by way of example include the $1.1 billion class action settlement of the Microsoft antitrust claims in California a few years ago.[14]

DTA at its best is the product of a team effort. Clients increasingly demand an early case assessment of the risks and costs of potential litigation and early development of a case management strategy. See Chapters 3 and 4. DTA helps to plan and manage the processes of litigation, settlement, and ADR. Having produced or at least reviewed a DTA together, counsel and their client are on the same page and understand the risks, benefits, and likelihood of uncertain outcomes. And they can revisit and revise the DTA as they obtain more information or circumstances change (e.g., during discovery, winning a partial summary judgment motion).

Here are four key advantages to encourage the use of DTA (as advocate, corporate decision maker, or mediator) in settlement negotiations and mediations:

---

13. *See, e.g.*, Marc B. Victor, *Resolving a Dispute by Getting a Neutral to Provide Probability Assessments*, 31 ALTS. TO HIGH COST LITIG. 36 (2013).

14. *John DeGroote, Advanced Decision Tree Analysis in Litigation: An Interview with Marc Victor, Part 1*, SETTLEMENT PERSPS. *(July 3, 2009)*, http://www.settlementperspectives.com/2009/07/advanced-decision-tree-analysis-in-litigation-an-interview-with-marc-victor-part-i/.

1. Advantage 1: Focus and Expand

First, DTA can help the mediator and parties both focus (i.e., narrow issues) and expand (i.e., bring outside interests to bear) the negotiations. DTA accomplishes this by giving the parties a way to identify the complexity in a case (i.e., the various issues and possible outcomes) and to address that complexity by confirming (in numbers) intuitive determinations, or by causing counsel to question or challenge those determinations (e.g., how strong is the case on infringement?). Insofar as DTA uses diagrams and charts, it also engages the visual part of the brain and can illustrate issues for both sides of a dispute. If the parties can agree that a decision tree is an accurate analysis of the case, the potential settlement amount of the case becomes clearer. Attorney Patrick Hofer gives an example of the benefits of a decision tree in negotiation:

> I have successfully used decision trees to settle dozens of cases . . . . I have used them to convince opponents of the reasonableness of my client's deal—from in-house counsel at a large multi-national conglomerate, who viewed themselves as God's gift to the law, to the owner of a dry-cleaner who didn't have a high school diploma. In every case I settled using a decision tree, the deal stuck and did not come unglued or get retreaded, because both sides saw the value in the deal they made. Decision trees are amazingly effective, efficient and powerful tools to get parties to settle their differences.[15]

Consider focusing and expanding in the context of a trademark infringement dispute. Two of the issues that typically arise in such a case are (1) establishing that a protectable trademark exists and (2) proving that consumers are likely to confuse the accused mark with the trademark owner's mark. The mediator may work with the parties in caucus to produce decision trees that translate their predictions into probability estimates for these issues. This allows the mediator to compare the parties' decision trees to determine how far apart the parties are on their prediction (the probabilities) of the aforementioned issues. Assume that the mediator compares the trees and notes that the parties are relatively (1) close in their respective assessments of the plaintiff's ability to establish trademark rights, but (2) far apart in their respective assessments of the plaintiff's ability to prove likelihood of confusion. The mediator can use the results of this comparison to focus the negotiations on the issue most clearly in dispute—establishing a likelihood of confusion.

---

15. John DeGroote, *Decision Trees in Mediation: A Few Examples*, SETTLEMENT PERSPS. (Apr. 22, 2010), http://www.settlementperspectives.com/2010/04/decision-trees-in-mediation-a-few-examples/.

The mediator can also use the DTA to focus on fact disputes. For example, the question of likelihood of confusion requires a court to consider (when relevant) and weigh up to 13 different factors (e.g., how related are the parties' respective marks, how similar are the parties' respective goods or services, whether the parties' customers are sophisticated, whether the parties sell through similar trade channels). Sensitivity analysis can help the parties and the mediator identify, and then shift their focus and attention on, those factual disputes that have the greatest impact on the settlement value of the case. Thus, for example, whether the parties' customers are sophisticated may have little to no impact on the predicted ultimate finding of likelihood of confusion in a particular case. The mediator can, therefore, focus the parties on other factors in the analysis that they believe will have the greatest impact on the ultimate finding of a likelihood of confusion.

DTA can also help the mediator expand the discussion. A DTA can be used to have the parties consider issues that are outside the scope of the dispute but are possibly related. In the trademark example, the parties may be trying to resolve a dispute that, if not settled, will be tried before the International Trade Commission. They may also have a related, but separate, opposition proceeding that is ongoing before the Trademark Trial and Appeal Board of the U.S. Patent and Trademark Office. The parties can use DTA to determine a reasonable settlement value for these multiple disputes that exist between them. The parties can expand the tree (or create separate trees) to account for the options and uncertainties associated with the collateral disputes and then use an aggregate model to determine an appropriate *package* or total settlement value.

2. Advantage 2: Enhance Communication

The second potential advantage of using DTA in a mediation is that it facilitates and enhances communication between the parties and with the mediator, as well as between counsel and their clients. DTA accomplishes this by helping advocates and mediators transform an abstract, emotional debate about the general merits of a case into a concrete, objective discussion about the strengths and weaknesses of (and, thus, the probabilities and costs associated with) specific events. Thus, DTA avoids communication lapses inherent in such comments as "we're likely to win," "there is a good chance," "there is a definite probability," and "in all likelihood."

Suppose a team is analyzing whether to pursue a copyright infringement claim. All may agree that the judge will *probably* rule in their favor but team members may have a different understanding of what *probably* means. One may believe that the chance the judge will rule favorably is 55 percent, while another may believe it is 90 percent. Both members used the same word to describe the chance of success, but the DTA shows that they, in fact, have very different ideas of the strength of the case. A DTA quantifies words into concrete probabilities and, more importantly, challenges counsel to ensure that they have the support for that 90 percent. Accountants, engineers, executives, and scientists—all are often more comfortable with concrete probabilities and dollar values than with subjective terms like *probably*. And, although clients may like to hear the subjective terms, they ultimately want a clear assessment of who will win and why. Therefore, it is not surprising that DTA is a valuable tool used by the business world, in the public health arena, and by many other professions. Indeed, mediator Rebecca Bowman uses DTA to appeal to quantitative-focused people:

> Engineers and many accountants generally prefer finite things. It can be extremely powerful to have a clean, concrete decision tree to evaluate risk. Quantitative sorts find it very comfortable to wrap their heads around a 60% probability of an outcome of X dollars. Fold in a time prediction and they can fold in a time-value-of-money factor. If you can show the parties a way to reduce the mushy, often gut-feel outcome predictions to something concrete that they can evaluate, it has been my experience that they are much more likely to march directly to a resolution.[16]

The process of creating a decision tree necessarily requires the parties and the mediator to share information and assumptions. This process can facilitate settlement by minimizing what mediators call *information imbalances* that often exist between parties.

Case in point: The mediator developed a joint DTA during a group discussion (with the parties' permission) from two decision trees that the mediator had asked the parties to prepare before the mediation. As the individual trees showed, the parties disagreed greatly about the likelihood that the plaintiff could prove infringement at trial. A focused discussion ensued that resulted in (1) the exchange of useful information supporting each party's analysis and (2) an agreed-upon assessment of the likelihood of proving infringement, which helped resolve the overall dispute.

Even if the parties cannot agree on the data that is included in the decision tree, DTA can prove a helpful tool. DTA focuses attention on what further information would be helpful to the analysis (e.g., more facts or legal research on damages or invalidity, or input from an expert). Most important,

16. *Id.*

the process of creating the tree and going through it as a team may be more helpful than the outcome. As Marjorie Corman Aaron has stated:

> A decision tree approach requires candid discussion between lawyer and client about the likelihood of each branch on the tree, each twist in the litigation path. That discussion is always worth having. Even if the decision tree is used for nothing more than adding clarity in the conversation of trial alternatives and the client's comfort with attendant levels of risk, the tree has added value.[17]

Opposing counsel may realize that the settlement amount they had in mind is outside the realm of possibility after viewing the decision tree. Two authors explained how useful DTA was in their settlement negotiations:

> [Opposing counsel] accepted our decision tree structure—although not our estimates of probabilities and verdicts!—as an accurate analysis of the case. We encouraged them to choose their own values for certain probabilities and values. We then demonstrated that even under their most optimistic scenario, the expected value was much higher than their initial settlement offer.[18]

Typically, mediators require each party to be represented during the mediation by someone with full settlement authority. Sometimes, however, a party attends the mediation without that person on its team and tentatively agrees to a mediated settlement. In that case, the party may have to explain to the person having authority (who was not present at the mediation) why the mediated settlement makes sense in order to obtain final approval. Even in a case where someone with full settlement authority attended the mediation, that person may have to explain the settlement to others back at the company. DTA can be a helpful tool explaining the reasons for entering into an agreement.

3. Advantage 3: Separate the People from the Problem

A third advantage of DTA is in helping the mediator separate the people, who may be emotionally involved and not entirely objective, from the problem in need of resolution. By providing an objective and logical evaluation tool that helps to transform the dispute into a business problem (e.g., time to trial, cost of settling versus cost of trial and appeal, distractions to the

17. *See* The Handbook of Dispute Resolution (Michael L. Moffitt & Robert C. Bordone eds., 1st ed. 2005).

18. Ron Friedmann & David Post, *Software Makes Decision Analysis Easy*, Legal Tech. Newsl. (Dec. 1990), https://prismlegal.com/litigation_risk_analysis/.

business during litigation), the mediator can use DTA to move beyond emotional issues and *separate the people from the problem.*

During the mediation, using DTA can help to provide clients with another perspective or additional information beyond that of counsel, who may lose objectivity (especially after living with the case for a while).

Case in point: In a mediation, an attorney had opined to his business client that the company had no exposure to a patent infringement charge. The presence of that attorney at the mediation session caused the client to become wedded to the position of no exposure, thereby devaluing alternative outcomes and ultimately precluding settlement. DTA may have provided an objective way to highlight the benefit of those alternatives and help the client see the dispute from a different perspective. The party, unfortunately, was not open-minded to using DTA.

Also, counsel may exaggerate the merits of the client's case to create the appearance that there is no zone of potential agreement in an effort to shift the bargaining range in their client's favor (or to avoid letting the range shift in the adverse party's favor). The mediator needs a tool to identify and curtail such exaggeration or posturing. By encouraging parties to work together on a joint solution, a mediator can use DTA to minimize posturing and other behavior that interferes with a resolution. Some posturing will necessarily take place as the details of the tree are developed, but it is likely to be more focused and less obstructive than grandstanding about the value of the case.

Finally, mediation sometimes fails when one party declares, "It's a matter of principle." There are times when an issue of law, precedent, public policy, or pride is at stake, and parties will resist settlement because the confidentiality of mediation does not allow this interest to be vindicated publicly. The mediator can use DTA to highlight and challenge the party's implicit valuation of the declared principle by calculating the expected cost of adherence to the principle.

4. Advantage 4: Break Psychological Barriers

A fourth strength of DTA is that it gives the mediator another tool to address the various psychological barriers to a mediated settlement. Several of those barriers are discussed here along with how DTA can help a mediator address them.

The psychological principle of *reactive devaluation* is the tendency of the recipient of an offer to conclude "it can't be good enough for us if they're willing to offer it." Reactive devaluation occurs when one party suggests a solution to another party, either directly or through the mediator (i.e., the mediator advises Party A that Party B suggests a particular solution). Even if the suggested solution is objectively good for the recipient, the recipient may reject it because the suggestion came from an adversary. This reactive devaluation principle can prevent ratification of workable solutions. DTA can temper reactive devaluation by creating acceptable settlement figures through the application of a rational framework.

Another psychological principle that may not be novel to mediation, but is at play, is *risk aversion*. This principle explains a party's willingness to forgo a chance to win a large gain in order to be guaranteed a smaller one—or, as in the marble example, to forgo a gain in order to avoid a loss. Returning to the marble example, recall that a party playing the game had a significant (75 percent) chance of winning $40,000 and could *expect* to win $5,000, and, therefore, objectively should play, but risked losing $100,000. An objective person would play the game; a risk-averse person will not. Thus, DTA can illuminate differences in risk preferences in a constructive way. The mediator (and the parties) can use the decision tree to test each party's risk preferences. Such preferences may be critical when the decision between playing the marble game or not is replaced with the decision between settling for a certain amount or not (with subsequent litigation).

A mediator can use DTA to adjust one party's or both parties' expectations by providing a rational basis for a settlement that initially may seem unsatisfactory. The mediator can use a decision tree privately with one party to test portions of the party's case assessment. The mediator can also use a decision tree in a joint session to enhance cooperation by the parties in arriving at a mutually agreeable basis for settlement. In that context, the parties must work together through the process of creating a tree. Finally, whether private or joint, the use of the scientific valuation method offered by DTA, especially when implemented on a computer, adds an air of legitimacy that can facilitate settlement.

As should be evident by now, the mediator who wants to use DTA to facilitate the mediation procedure may have to address several issues. Parties and lawyers who are uncomfortable with math or with computers may resist the use of the tool because it is unfamiliar. Parties may fear that the use of DTA deprives them of control over the mediation procedure, vesting that control instead in a *black box*. Similarly, lawyers may be reluctant to use DTA for fear that the parties' expectations will later become anchored around an as-yet-unknown figure. The mediator can deal with some of these issues by emphasizing that DTA is merely a tool to help identify and sort out the issues in the case, and that nobody commits to anything by merely engaging in the analysis.

DTA can be a useful tool in a mediation that facilitates the negotiation process. A mediator who brings a laptop, ready to develop a decision tree with the parties in both joint and private sessions, can add flexibility and legitimacy to the procedure. A reasonable guess is that DTA will become more and more prevalent in mediating disputes, especially in complex IP/Technology disputes involving parties who are relatively comfortable with numbers and computers.

C. DTA Limitations

DTA is a tool to help make informed decisions; it cannot be expected to give the (nonexistent) one and only correct answer. Therefore, the tool should not be oversold. Common criticisms about DTA include daunting mathematics, unreliable inputs, and nonobjective assessments.

Although some will find the math daunting, the team can easily include someone comfortable with the tool and available software. To avoid the "garbage in, garbage out" predicament, do not rely on uninformed inputs.[19] But the very process of selecting issues, crystal-balling possible outcomes, and assigning probabilities to uncertain events is itself a useful exercise. And careful thought (including detailed lists of reasons supporting the particular input or information from an early case assessment) turns the garbage into useful input. *Quality ingredients in, quality product out.*

Finally, keep nonobjective assessments and intangibles in mind. Nonobjective assessments include biases, inexperience, recency, and primacy. There is a lot of psychology here. Intangibles include the value (or cost) of injunctive relief, precedential ramifications, the effect on stock price, and distraction to managers and researchers. Although it is possible to value such intangibles, one approach is to simply list the intangibles without including them in the tree and take them into account as options are evaluated.

One criticism of DTA is *not* its lack of power or inability to take into account all objective factors. The analysis can be made as inclusive and complete as desired to encompass fully all available information. For example, an augmented option analysis offers a tool that integrates factors such as interim cost and elapsed time for possible options with conventional DTA. Augmented option analysis also aggregates the probabilities of all possible ultimate outcomes to provide a more complete picture of the risk-reward possibilities associated with any option.[20]

---

19. *See* Richard Lane White & Brian Henthorn, *How to Use Risk Analysis to Calculate Settlement Value*, LAW360 (Feb. 19, 2014), http://www.law360.com/articles/511092/how-to-use-risk-analysis-to-calculate-settlement-value.

20. *See* Paul Prestia & Harrie Samaras, *Beyond Decision Trees: Determining Aggregate Probabilities of Time, Cost, and Outcomes*, 28 ALTS. TO HIGH COST LITIG. 4 (2010).

There are four possible reasons, summarized in Table 5.3, to explain why DTA is inapplicable to a particular situation.

Table 5.3

Reason No.	Reason	Counter
1	The case is so simple or involves so small a dollar amount that it does not warrant DTA.	Even simple cases or those with small dollar amounts at stake warrant simple or small DTA—perhaps just using a napkin and pencil over dinner.
2	Settlement will be achieved regardless.	If settlement is likely, use DTA to evaluate the settlement amount.
3	The IP owner may not want to sue its own customer, so what is the benefit of using DTA?	To help select an appropriate ADR option.
4	Precedent-setting litigation is required.	Use DTA to help plan litigation strategy and the necessary resources.

Parties can use DTA when a dispute first arises, during settlement negotiations (particularly to evaluate the merits of a settlement offer), at the outset of litigation or an ADR proceeding, and even continuously during the proceeding to reevaluate options based on updated information as uncertainties resolve themselves. DTA is a dynamic tool that can and should be updated often as new information arrives and uncertainties are resolved.

Thus far, the use of DTA has focused on how parties (including in-house business representatives), their counsel (in-house counsel and outside law firms), and opposing parties and their counsel can adopt this tool.

IV. Selective Use of Charts, Exhibits, and Other Visual Aids

Visual aids are commonly used and helpful tools for conveying information in an efficient and easily understood way. Counsel know, understand, and use these tools in non-ADR contexts. For example, they frequently use visual aids in courtrooms to facilitate fact-finding, especially in complex IP/Technology disputes. Visual aids such as photographs, videos, models, exhibits, presentation slides, computer simulations, charts, and graphs provide a wealth of information in an easily understood form. Similarly, counsel need to sell points in arbitrations just as in litigation. And in mediation, they need to convince the other side of the merits of their positions and respond when the mediator tries to test the reality of those positions.

Like in litigation, in ADR processes, counsel may use multiple and different types of visual aids to illustrate different aspects of the dispute and communicate a story to the viewer—whether the viewer is an arbitrator, a mediator, or an adversary—in a way that will provide a greater impact than a simple narrative. For example, photographs or videos may illustrate how an accused device infringes, how a competitor's website is substantially similar to a party's copyrighted website, or how trademarks are confusingly similar. Films and animations may show particular aspects of technology not otherwise apparent to the naked eye. Models or exhibits provide a hands-on demonstration of the internal working of a machine or system to better understand infringement issues. Models and exhibits are particularly useful where it is not practical to use or explore the full-size or actual machine or system.

Computerized visual aids such as slide presentations, timelines, computer simulations, and printed visual aids (e.g., document excerpts, charts, graphs) distill complex information to a simpler form. For example, visual aids help compare data or refine raw data. Graphical representations of refined data can be used, for example, to show trends, to demonstrate economic harm, or to illustrate how damages or assets should be apportioned. A party's chief financial officer can undoubtedly present numerical figures showing damages much more convincingly by way of charts than verbally.

Pie charts are especially useful tools to help convey information, and they may be even more useful in the context of ADR than in other contexts. Pie charts simply render information visual, which facilitates communication—especially to those who understand visual information better than information conveyed orally. One use of pie charts is to enhance settlement negotiation and mediation procedures involving multiparty suits. Pie charts allow for expression of emotion, establishment of priorities, and communication among the parties.[21] The interest in multiparty IP/Technology suits expanded in the age of patent infringement suits brought against entire industries by nonmanufacturing entities.[22] Successful resolution of a multi-

---

21. *See* Robert Creo, *A Pie Chart Tool to Resolve Multiparty, Multi-Issue Conflicts*, 18 Alts. to High Cost Litig. 5 (2000).

22. *See* Brian M. Buroker & Maya M. Eckstein, Hunton & Williams LLP, Multiple Defendant Patent Infringement Cases: Complexities, Complications, and Advantages, https://www.hunton.com/media/publication/3157_Multiple_Defendant_Paper_AIPLA.pdf (last visited Mar. 23, 2025).

party dispute often requires a determination of relative fault and commensurate damages amounts. Pie charts can facilitate such a determination.

For example, suppose that there are three defendants. All admit liability or have been adjudged liable, but differ in assessing their share of damages. Suppose further that one of the defendants, Manufacturer, is directly liable for manufacturing a widget protected by the asserted patent. The other two defendants—Induce A and Induce B—are liable for inducing (or contributing to) Manufacturer's direct infringement. Assume that the plaintiff patent owner is seeking $5 million in lost profits. Finally, suppose the defendants agree that the plaintiff would likely settle for $3 million. The only contention among the defendants is apportionment of damages.

Each defendant can use a pie chart to delineate and communicate its perspective on liability in confidence to the mediator so that she or he can ultimately present the composite offers from the defendants to the plaintiff. The following set of ground rules provides a process for accomplishing that:

1. No defendant to the dispute knows of any other defendant's contribution to the total settlement amount. Each defendant provides to the mediator in private the portion of the pie it is willing to pay as damages. The mediator takes this information and designates on the pie these relative portions and presents them to all of the defendants before presenting it to the plaintiff.
2. This process allows all the defendants to acknowledge their liability without worrying about low-balling from the other defendants after making their offer.
3. Only if the plaintiff accepts the settlement offer will the defendants know the contributions of everyone involved.

Next, following the previous guidelines, each defendant draws a pie chart and divides the pie into slices that represent its view of liability based on a percentage for each party bearing responsibility. These pie charts are then given to the mediator confidentially. Using the earlier simple example, Manufacturer, Induce A, and Induce B may submit the following respective charts:

Figure 5.1: Manufacturer, Induce A, and Induce B

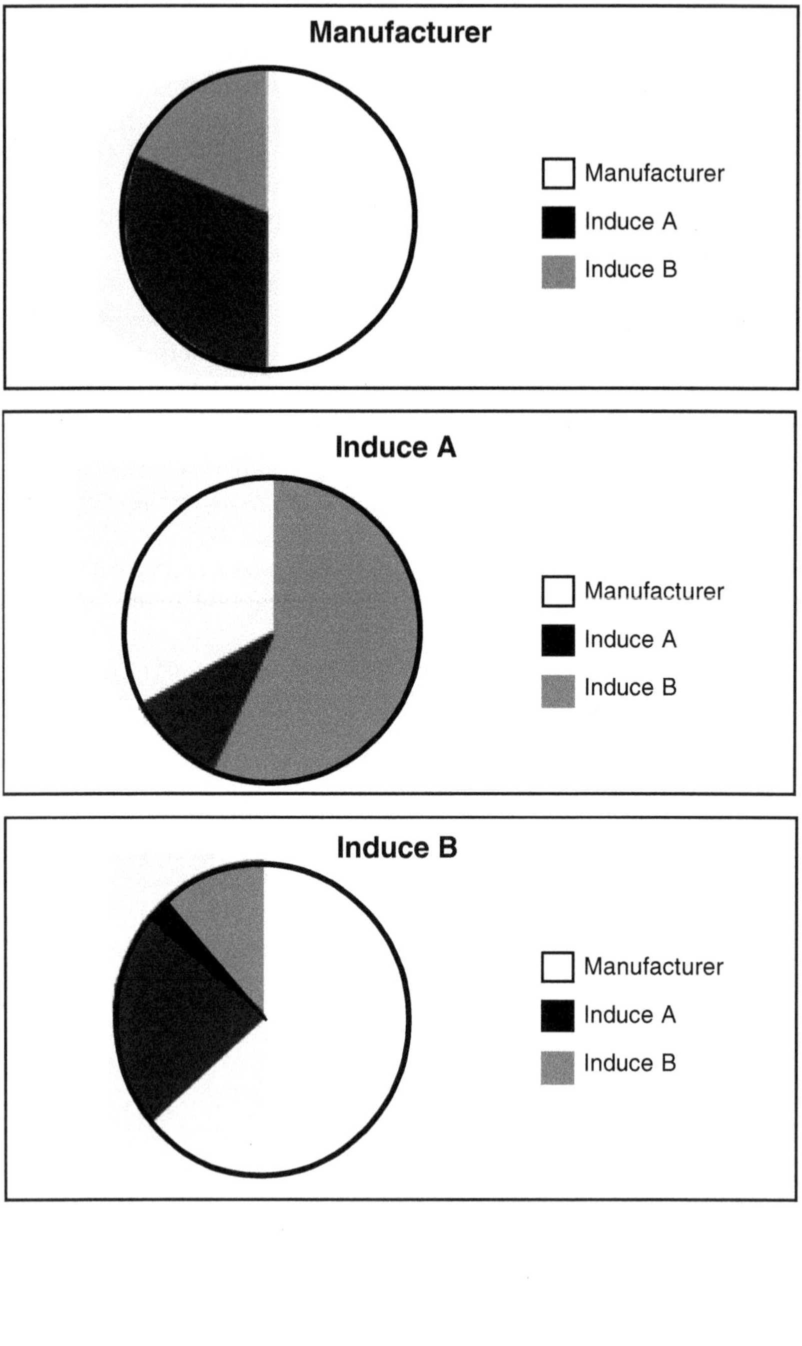

These charts show that there is a consensus that Manufacturer should bear the most responsibility. Averaging the three inputs, Manufacturer is 58 percent responsible, Induce A is 22 percent responsible, and Induce B is 20 percent responsible. After determining the consensus of responsibility, the mediator performs privately the first round of caucuses with the individual defendants so that they can discuss confidentially the pie charts they had submitted to the mediator.

Assume that, in the first round of those caucuses, the following contributions to the pie were proposed: Manufacturer = $600,000, Induce A = $200,000, and Induce B = $75,000. Therefore, the total amount of the pie proposed is $875,000. This is lower than the amount the plaintiff will likely accept so another round of caucuses must take place. Assume the following enhanced contributions to the pie: Manufacturer = $1.2 million, Induce A = $400,000, and Induce B = $200,000. The total amount of the pie is $1.8 million. This is still lower than the $3 million that the plaintiff is expected to demand, and, therefore, the plaintiff could be expected to reject an offer of that amount. The plaintiff is unaware of the defendants' use of the pie chart tool; the mediator only presents to the plaintiff the defendants' collective offer of $1.8 million (although the defendants now know what each would pay).

The mediator should, at this point, advise the defendants what contributions would meet their consensus for responsibility and achieve a settlement. In this case, Manufacturer would need to contribute at least $1.74 million (0.58 x $3 million), Induce A $660,000 (0.22 x $3 million), and Induce B $600,000 (0.20 x $3 million). Assume the following amounts were then authorized: Manufacturer = $1.6 Million, Induce A = $600,000, and Induce B = $600,000. This results in a pie of $2.8 million. These amounts are close to the consensus of responsibility and to the total amount likely to be accepted by the plaintiff, perhaps achieving satisfactory resolution of the dispute. The mediator would present to the plaintiff the defendants' collective offer of $2.8 million with the hope of resolution (and using whatever other techniques the mediator deems warranted). Iterations of the process can be performed as necessary.

Conclusion

The foregoing four categories of tools—screening tools, mock arbitration panels, DTA, and visual aids—are designed to make the analysis of an IP/Technology dispute easier, lead to a more equitable and mutually beneficial resolution of the dispute, and streamline the entire dispute resolution process. Each of the individual tools within these four categories is relatively easy to learn and implement. Each tool can greatly enhance the ADR experience for everyone involved in resolving an IP/Technology dispute.

APPENDIX A

CPR Mediation Screen and Arbitration Screen

CPR ADR Suitability Guide

CPR MEDIATION SCREEN QUESTIONS WORKSHEET

■ BENCHMARK QUESTION

Before you begin, in order to provide a benchmark against which to compare your analysis, indicate here whether your instinct, unaided by analysis, tells you that settlement of this dispute:

___ a) Is not foreseeable at any stage.

___ b) Is highly likely, even if only on the courthouse steps.

■ FACTOR ONE: The Parties' Goals for Managing the Dispute

– A. Overarching Goals –

1. **How important to the parties is maintaining a relationship with each other?**

___ a) One or both sides cares only about the substantive outcome; the impact on the relationship with the other side is irrelevant.

___ b) Although the substantive outcome is important, both sides would benefit to some degree from preserving or enhancing their relationship.

___ c) Preservation or even improvement of the relationship is of considerable importance to both sides.

2. **How important to the parties is maintaining control over the *outcome* of the dispute?**

___ a) Both sides prefer to have a judge [or arbitrator] decide the outcome.

___ b) Maintaining control over the outcome is moderately important to at least one of the parties.

___ c) Controlling the outcome is important to both parties.

3. **How important to the parties is maintaining control over the *process* by which the dispute is resolved?**

___ a) Neither side cares at all about maintaining control over the process used to resolve the dispute.

___ b) Maintaining control over the process is moderately important to at least one of the parties.

___ c) Controlling the process is an important desire of both sides.

– B. Legal Goals –

4. **What is the likelihood that this case can be disposed of by a prompt, dispositive motion?**

___ a) Very likely.
___ b) A possibility.
___ c) Very unlikely.

5. **Is injunctive relief, a legal precedent from a court or other relief only available from a adjudicative body needed by a party?**

___ a) Very likely.
___ b) A possibility.
___ c) Very unlikely.

6. **How certain is the need to engage in formal discovery?**

___ a) Totally certain; only formal and extensive discovery is likely to surface crucial information.

___ b) Uncertain; it may be possible to acquire the relevant information in other ways.

___ c) Unnecessary; both sides would be better served by avoiding burdensome or intrusive formal discovery.

7. **Do the parties only seek a neutral evaluation on the extent of damages or other specific issue?**

___ a) Very likely.
___ b) A possibility.
___ c) Very unlikely.

The CPR Institute is a nonprofit initiative of 500 general counsel of major corporations, leading law firms and prominent legal academics whose mission is to install alternative dispute resolution (ADR) into the mainstream of legal practice.

– C. Pragmatic Goals (Costs and Risks) –

8. What are the estimated monetary costs of pursuing litigation [arbitration] relative to what either side can realistically expect to recover by a decision in its favor?

___ a) Small, relative to the potential gain.

___ b) The monetary costs are by no means negligible, but may be worth expending.

___ c) High, given what is at stake.

9. How important is a speedy resolution of the dispute?

___ a) Either unimportant to both parties or one party is best served by delaying resolution.

___ b) Moderately important to both sides.

___ c) Very important to both sides.

10. Is there a need for privacy in the resolution process?

___ a) No, this is not a need of either side.

___ b) Yes, this is a likely need, but only for one side.

___ c) Yes, this is a likely need of both sides.

11. How likely is it that a party will gain a financial bonanza by going to court [or arbitration]?

___ a) Very likely.

___ b) The possibility is there, but with low probability.

___ c) Virtually nonexistent.

■ FACTOR TWO: The Suitability of the Dispute for a Problem Solving Process

– A. The Parties' Capacity for Problem Solving –

12. To what extent are matters of fundamental principle at stake?

___ a) Clearly at stake for at least one of the parties.

___ b) Hard to judge with accuracy.

___ c) Not a factor for either side.

13. How important to the parties is the securing of public vindication?

___ a) An important objective for at least one side.

___ b) Moderately important or hard to judge.

___ c) Of no interest to either side.

14. How certain are the parties that they will prevail in court [or in arbitration]?

___ a) At least one side is confident it will prevail.

___ b) Hard to judge with accuracy.

___ c) Neither side is certain it will prevail.

15. How receptive is the leadership on each side to the general idea of mediation?

___ a) Unsupportive or uninterested.

___ b) Moderately receptive but with little or no experience with mediation.

___ c) Very receptive.

– B. The Quality of the Parties' Relationship –

16. What is the emotional climate between the parties?

___ a) One of deep-seated hostility, contempt, and distrust.

___ b) Moderately antagonistic and distrustful.

___ c) Relatively objective.

17. What is the relative "power" of the parties as to their financial resources and business sophistication?

___ a) So disparate that one side may gain advantage over the other outside the civil justice system.

___ b) There is a moderate disparity in power.

___ c) Substantially comparable.

18. How compatible are the styles of opposing counsel (as distinct from the parties themselves)?

___ a) It would be hard to imagine more contrasting legal styles and frameworks for dealing with conflict.

___ b) Moderate differences exist.

___ c) The attorneys' styles and frameworks for dealing with conflict are highly compatible.

CPR ADR Suitability Guide

– C. Practical Realities –

19. Do the parties have the necessary resources to negotiate worthwhile trade-offs or to create new options?

___ a) A major problem is the lack of resources of any kind.
___ b) Resources exist, but are not abundant.
___ c) Reasonably good resources are available.

20. Is this a dispute that involves critical areas of managerial responsibility (e.g., matters of corporate finance or corporate reorganization)?

___ a) Yes, and in very significant ways.
___ b) Perhaps.
___ c) No.

21. What is the stance towards mediation of the jurisdiction in which the dispute is pending?

___ a) The court has little or no interest in mediation and/or has taken no steps to encourage mediation.
___ b) Ambivalent, unclear, or modest.
___ c) Very positive and encouraging and/or mediation is required for this kind of dispute.

■ FACTOR THREE: The Potential Benefits of Mediation for the Dispute in Question

Would mediation benefit the parties by:

22. helping them clarify the issues in dispute?

___ a) No.
___ b) Perhaps.
___ c) Yes.

23. helping them to channel or control anger or other negative emotions?

___ a) No.
___ b) Perhaps.
___ c) Yes.

24. giving one or both parties an opportunity to tell their stories and to be fully heard by the other side?

___ a) No.
___ b) Perhaps.
___ c) Yes.

25. providing an opportunity for an apology?

___ a) No, an apology would not be relevant or helpful.
___ b) Perhaps.
___ c) Yes, an apology would be very useful.

26. providing them with a "reality check" from a knowledgeable intermediary on their positions or expectations?

___ a) No.
___ b) Perhaps.
___ c) Yes.

27. providing a confidential setting in which to explore each other's interests and needs?

___ a) No.
___ b) Perhaps.
___ c) Yes.

28. helping them to explore the possibility for trade-offs or creative solutions?

___ a) No.
___ b) Perhaps.
___ c) Yes.

29. helping to educate the decision-makers on either side?

___ a) No.
___ b) Perhaps.
___ c) Yes.

30. providing an intermediary who could make offers and counteroffers more acceptable by presenting them as his or her own ideas?

___ a) No.
___ b) Perhaps.
___ c) Yes.

31. providing an intermediary who can reframe proposals?

___ a) No.
___ b) Perhaps.
___ c) Yes.

CPR ADR Suitability Guide

QUESTIONS REGARDING CHOICE OF ARBITRATION OR LITIGATION

The following series of questions may assist in deciding between arbitration or litigation. An (a) response below indicates a case characteristic suggestive of arbitration; a (b) response indicates a case characteristic suggestive of litigation.

1. **Does a party seek to secure a decision in a public setting?**

   __ a) no
   __ b) yes

2. **Does a party want to prevent the specter of a massive or unpredictable jury award?**

   __ a) yes
   __ b) no

3. **Is establishment of precedent or articulation of public policy an important goal for either party?**

   __ a) no
   __ b) yes

4. **Is a vital corporate interest or "bet the company" case involved that requires the full panoply of procedural protections afforded by a court, including full appellate rights?**

   __ a) no
   __ b) yes

5. **Is there a need for continuing court supervision of the case or parties?**

   __ a) no
   __ b) yes

6. **Is the ability to have some degree of control over case scheduling issues an important objective for either party?**

   __ a) yes
   __ b) no

7. **Does either party (or both) seek to retain unabridged appellate rights?**

   __ a) no
   __ b) yes

8. **Is the selection of the decision-maker an important objective for either party?**

   __ a) yes
   __ b) no

9. **Does the case require an understanding of complex or technical factual issues?**

   __ a) yes
   __ b) no

10. **Is the ability to conduct full discovery an important objective for either party?**

   __ a) no
   __ b) yes

Interpreting Questionnaire Results

a) ______

b) ______

A response pattern in which (a) responses are significantly more frequent than (b) responses suggests a dispute that is an excellent candidate for arbitration. If the results are more evenly divided, the weight to be given to responses to particular questions must be assessed on an individual basis. For further guidance, see Commercial Arbitration at Its Best: Successful Strategies for Business Users (T.J. Stipanowich & P.H. Kaskell, Editors, CPR/ABA, 2001).

APPENDIX B

DTA Applications

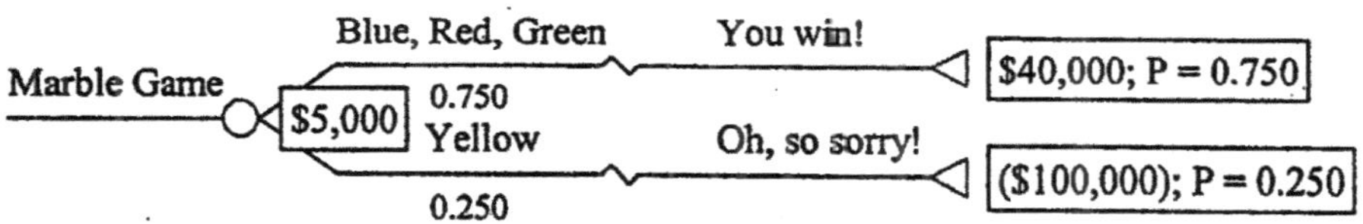

You are at a fair. In front of you is a booth with a large jar having 200 marbles: 50 each of blue, red, green, and yellow. The game is free to play, and you win $40,000 if you draw a blue, red, or green marble. Unfortunately, if you draw a yellow marble, you must pay $100,000.

Would you play?

$40,000 x 0.75 = $30,000

-$100,000 x 0.25 = -$25,000

$30,000 -$25,000 = $5,000

CONCLUSION: Yes, because the Expected Value is positive, but there is significant risk.

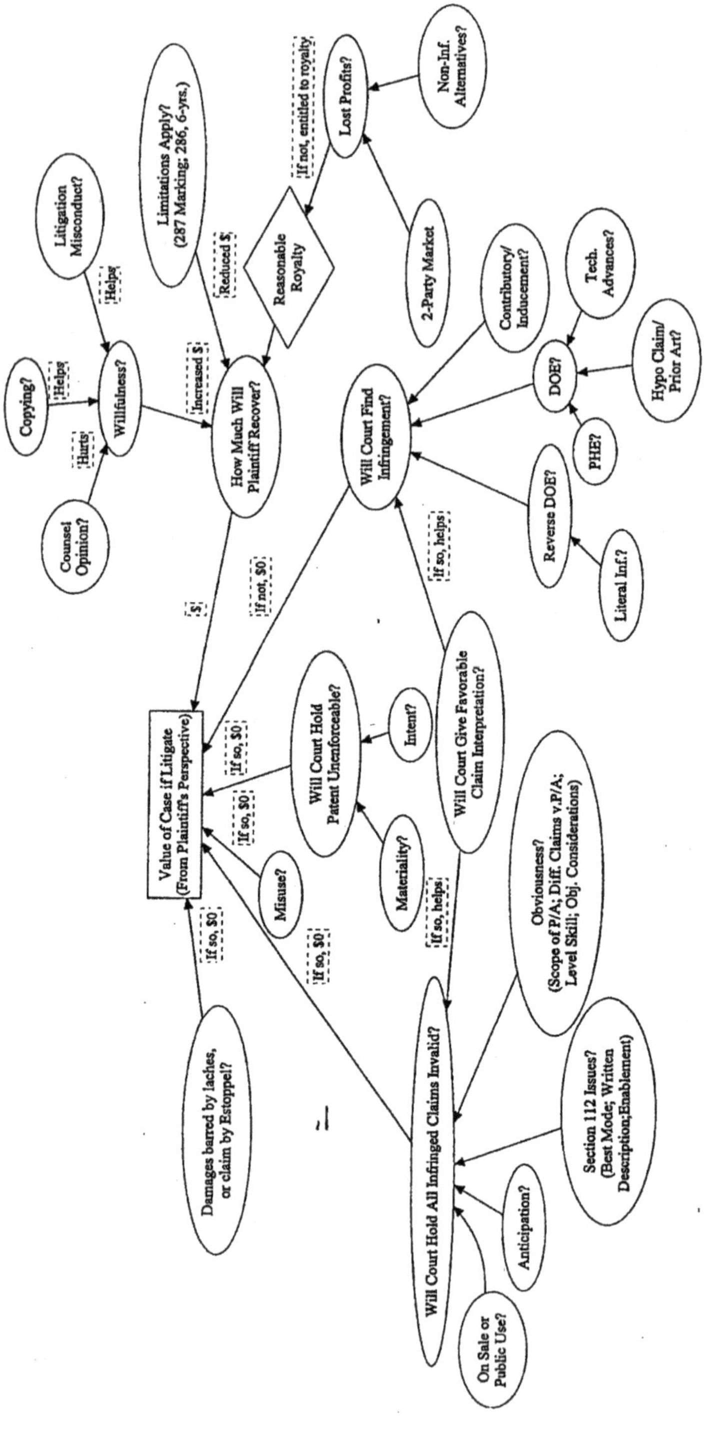
Copying?
Helps
Hurts
Counsel Opinion?
Willfulness?
Litigation Misconduct?
Helps
Increased $
Limitations Apply? (287 Marking; 286, 6-yrs.)
Reduced $
How Much Will Plaintiff Recover?
Reasonable Royalty
If not, entitled to royalty
Lost Profits?
Non-Inf. Alternatives?
2-Party Market
Will Court Find Infringement?
Contributory/ Inducement?
Tech. Advances?
DOE?
Hypo Claim/ Prior Art?
PHE?
Reverse DOE?
Literal Inf.?
If so, helps
$
If not, $0
Value of Case if Litigate (From Plaintiff's Perspective)
If so, $0
Will Court Hold Patent Unenforceable?
Intent?
If so, $0
Materiality?
Misuse?
Will Court Give Favorable Claim Interpretation?
If so, helps
Obviousness? (Scope of P/A; Diff. Claims v.P/A; Level Skill; Obj. Considerations)
If so, $0
If so, $0
Damages barred by laches, or claim by Estoppel?
Will Court Hold All Infringed Claims Invalid?
Section 112 Issues? (Best Mode; Written Description;Enablement)
Anticipation?
On Sale or Public Use?

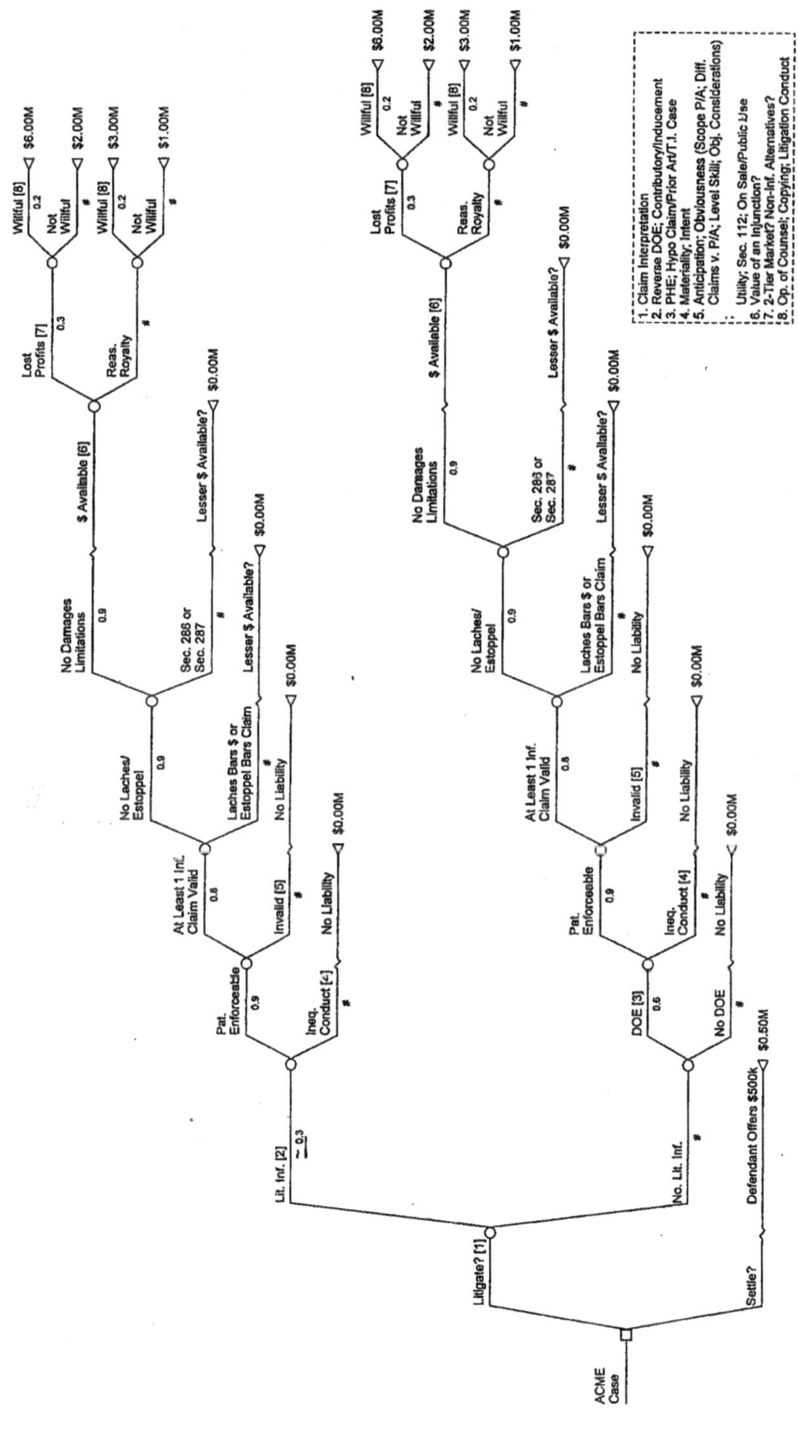
ACME Case
Litigate? [1]
Settle?
Defendant Offers $500k
$0.50M
Lit. Inf. [2]
~ 0.3
No. Lit. Inf.
#
Pat. Enforceable
0.9
Ineq. Conduct [4]
#
No Liability
$0.00M
At Least 1 Inf. Claim Valid
0.8
Invalid [5]
#
No Liability
$0.00M
No Laches/ Estoppel
0.9
Laches Bars $ or Estoppel Bars Claim
#
Lesser $ Available?
$0.00M
No Damages Limitations
0.9
Sec. 286 or Sec. 287
#
Lesser $ Available?
$0.00M
$ Available [6]
Lost Profits [7]
0.3
Reas. Royalty
#
Willful [8]
0.2
Not Willful
#
$6.00M
$2.00M
Willful [8]
0.2
Not Willful
#
$3.00M
$1.00M
DOE [3]
0.6
No DOE
#
No Liability
$0.00M
Pat. Enforceable
0.9
Ineq. Conduct [4]
#
No Liability
$0.00M
At Least 1 Inf. Claim Valid
0.8
Invalid [5]
#
No Liability
$0.00M
No Laches/ Estoppel
0.9
Laches Bars $ or Estoppel Bars Claim
#
Lesser $ Available?
$0.00M
No Damages Limitations
0.9
Sec. 286 or Sec. 287
#
Lesser $ Available?
$0.00M
$ Available [6]
Lost Profits [7]
0.3
Reas. Royalty
#
Willful [8]
0.2
Not Willful
#
$6.00M
$2.00M
Willful [8]
0.2
Not Willful
#
$3.00M
$1.00M
1. Claim Interpretation
2. Reverse DOE; Contributory/Inducement
3. PHE; Hypo Claim/Prior Art/T.I. Case
4. Materiality; Intent
5. Anticipation; Obviousness (Scope P/A; Diff. Claims v. P/A; Level Skill; Obj. Considerations)
Utility; Sec. 112; On Sale/Public Use
6. Value of an Injunction?
7. 2-Tier Market? Non-Inf. Alternatives?
8. Op. of Counsel; Copying; Litigation Conduct

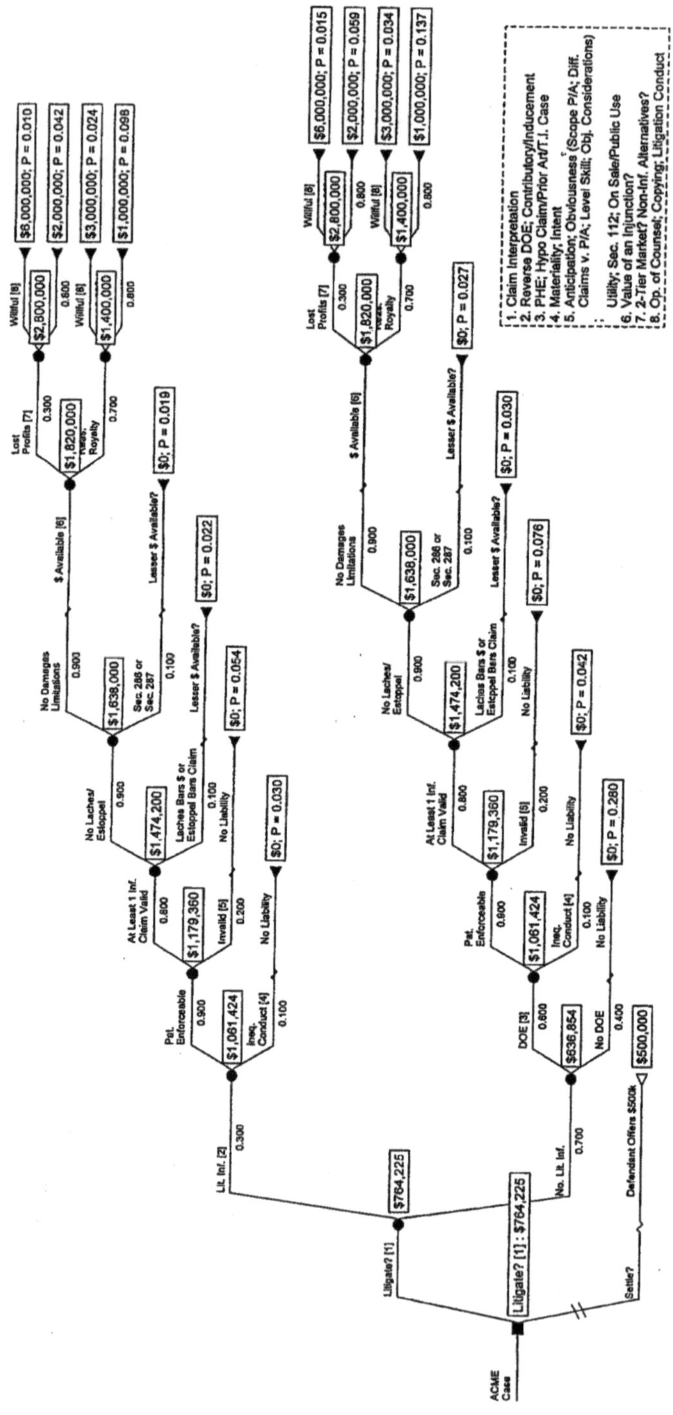

ACME Case
Litigate? [1] : $764,225
Litigate? [1]
$764,225
Settle?
Defendant Offers $500k
$500,000
Lit. Inf. [2]
0.300
Pat. Enforceable
0.900
$1,061,424
Ineq. Conduct [4]
0.100
No Liability
$0; P = 0.030
At Least 1 Inf. Claim Valid
0.800
$1,179,360
Invalid [5]
0.200
No Liability
$0; P = 0.054
No Laches/ Estoppel
0.900
$1,474,200
Laches Bars $ or Estoppel Bars Claim
0.100
Lesser $ Available?
$0; P = 0.022
No Damages Limitations
0.900
$1,638,000
Sec. 286 or Sec. 287
0.100
$ Available [6]
Lesser $ Available?
$0; P = 0.019
Lost Profits [7]
0.300
$1,820,000
Reas. Royalty
0.700
Willful [8]
$2,800,000
0.800
Willful [8]
$1,400,000
0.800
$6,000,000; P = 0.010
$2,000,000; P = 0.042
$3,000,000; P = 0.024
$1,000,000; P = 0.098
No. Lit. Inf.
0.700
DOE [3]
0.600
$636,854
No DOE
0.400
$0; P = 0.280
Pat. Enforceable
0.900
$1,061,424
Ineq. Conduct [4]
0.100
No Liability
$0; P = 0.042
At Least 1 Inf. Claim Valid
0.800
$1,179,360
Invalid [5]
0.200
No Liability
$0; P = 0.076
No Laches/ Estoppel
0.900
$1,474,200
Laches Bars $ or Estoppel Bars Claim
0.100
Lesser $ Available?
$0; P = 0.030
No Damages Limitations
0.900
$1,638,000
Sec. 286 or Sec. 287
0.100
$ Available [6]
Lesser $ Available?
$0; P = 0.027
Lost Profits [7]
0.300
$1,820,000
Reas. Royalty
0.700
Willful [8]
$2,800,000
0.800
Willful [8]
$1,400,000
0.800
$6,000,000; P = 0.015
$2,000,000; P = 0.059
$3,000,000; P = 0.034
$1,000,000; P = 0.137
1. Claim Interpretation
2. Reverse DOE; Contributory/Inducement
3. PHE; Hypo Claim/Prior Art/T.I. Case
4. Materiality; Intent
5. Anticipation; Obviousness (Scope P/A; Diff. Claims v. P/A; Level Skill; Obj. Considerations)
Utility; Sec. 112; On Sale/Public Use
6. Value of an Injunction?
7. 2-Tier Market? Non-Inf. Alternatives?
8. Op. of Counsel; Copying; Litigation Conduct

Probability Distribution
of Plaintiff's Expected Litigation Damages Awards

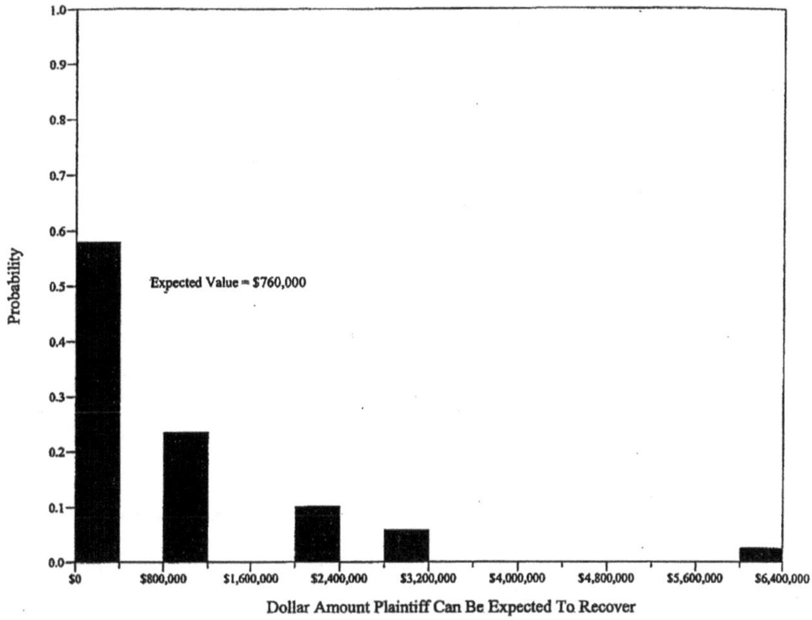

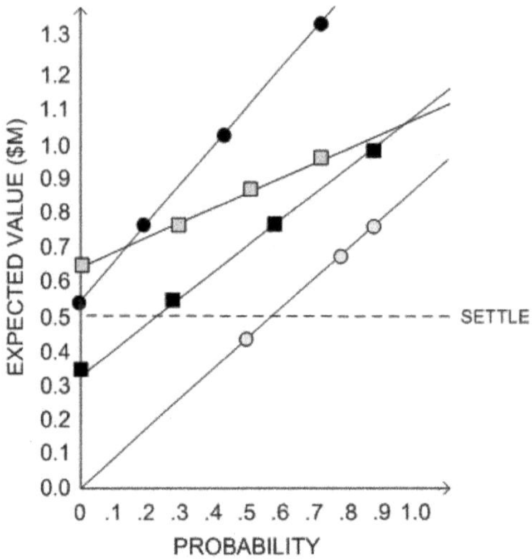

UNCERTAINTY = ENFORCEABILITY
○

Probability	EV of Litigation
0.9	0.76M
0.8	0.68M
0.5	0.42M

UNCERTAINTY = WILLFULNESS
●

Probability	EV of Litigation
0.0	0.55M
0.2	0.76M
0.5	1.09M
0.7	1.31M

UNCERTAINTY = LITERAL INF.
□

Probability	EV of Litigation
0.0	0.64M
0.3	0.76M
0.5	0.85M
0.7	0.93M

UNCERTAINTY = DOC. OF EQUIV.
■

Probability	EV of Litigation
0.0	0.32M
0.3	0.54M
0.6	0.76M
0.9	0.99M

PART III

Mediating IP/Technology Cases in Varying Venues

CHAPTER 6

Mediating IP/Technology Disputes: Design, Preparation, and Strategy

Merriann Panarella and Harrie Samaras[1]

We cannot solve our problems with the same thinking we used when we created them.

—Albert Einstein

Introduction[2]

Einstein's admonition suggests that the adversarial mindset (I win, you lose) leading to a dispute will not resolve the dispute. Mediation is a non-adversarial process that relies upon a different way of thinking to resolve disputes from the way disputes typically are created. As many disputants who have resolved intellectual property (IP) and technology disputes using mediation can attest, mediation is a problem-solving process worth using and mastering.

Mediation is a good match for the complexity of IP/Technology disputes because it has many advantages to leverage for resolving such disputes.[3] In

1. This chapter is a compilation of content and a derivative work from Chapters 5, 6, and 7 of the prior (Second) edition of this book, previously authored by Chief Magistrate Judge Mary Pat Thynge (retired, March 31, 2023, formerly of the U.S. District Court for the District of Delaware)—Chapter 5; Kevin Rhodes (Executive Vice President and Chief Legal Affairs Officer at 3M Company)—Chapter 6; and Merriann Panarella and Harrie Samaras—Chapter 7.

2. See Glossary for definition of frequently used terms.

3. As reflected by Judge Thynge:

> Patent cases are by far the most complex and technical civil matters to manage (particularly in addressing and controlling e-discovery), try, and decide. They often demand substantial time to analyze numerous briefs and mountains of exhibits spawned by *Markman* hearings, summary judgment motions, and post-trial motions, in addition to fostering lengthy opinions.

Mary Pat Thynge, *Mediation: One Judge's Perspective (or Infusing Sanity into Intellectual Property Litigation)*, *in* ADR Advocacy, Strategies, and Practices for contrast to adversarial (non-negotiated) dispute resolution processes, such as litigation or arbitration, mediation offers the opportunity for markedly greater control, creativity, and flexibility, both in the process and in the range of potential outcomes.[4] And, in comparison with non-facilitated negotiations, mediation offers the ability to leverage the presence of a neutral expert to help manage or buffer the interpersonal dynamics that can make it difficult for disputants to find common ground.

The aforementioned advantages of mediating are not automatic. Taking Einstein's guidance to heart, attorneys and their clients must understand the thinking behind the mediation process and embrace it for each dispute they mediate. They should eschew using mediation as another forum of litigation, and counsel should prepare their party representatives accordingly.

This chapter is not designed to teach all that is necessary to know about mediation or mediation advocacy; it assumes a basic knowledge. Rather, the chapter focuses on those aspects of mediating IP/Technology disputes (pre-filed and pending court cases) that can influence how parties adapt and manage the mediation process to achieve an effective and successful process. Chapters 7 and 8, respectively, cover the unique aspects of mediating IP/Technology cases at select U.S. courts of appeals and the U.S. International Trade Commission (ITC).

I. To Mediate or Not to Mediate . . . That Is the Question

Is mediation suitable for the dispute at hand?[5] To answer that question, each party should consider factors that are relevant to them and the particular dispute (see Section A in this part). Even parties who have a history of resolving

---

INTELLECTUAL PROPERTY AND TECHNOLOGY CASES 171, 174 (Harrie Samaras ed., 2d ed. 2017) (footnote omitted).

4. The parties are not limited to damages and/or an injunction and they can settle disputes in multiple jurisdictions and forums, which typically is the case in IP/Technology disputes.

5. It is not uncommon for parties to "inherit" the mediation process because it is incorporated in a dispute resolution provision in a contract that is the subject of a dispute. Even in that situation, the parties need not pursue mediation if they analyze the extant dispute and surrounding circumstances and conclude that mediation would not be productive. Thus, the parties to a contract having a mediation provision could nonetheless agree to override the mediation provision (i.e., amend the contract) and proceed to another dispute resolution process such as arbitration or litigation. Even if that is their decision, they could later agree to mediate their dispute in parallel with arbitration or litigation if they pursue such an adjudicative process.

prior disputes should acknowledge that each dispute is unique and requires a thoughtful consideration of how best to resolve the existing dispute. First, it is important to reflect on what mediation is and is not.

Mediation is a nonbinding (unless a settlement is reached), non-adjudicative negotiation process in which a neutral (mediator) helps the litigants resolve a dispute themselves. The mediator does not resolve the case. Moreover, mediation of any IP/Technology matter is the negotiation of a business dispute, where commercial objectives, interests, and needs are the primary concerns of both sides.

IP/Technology disputes potentially bring emotional baggage to the bargaining table for numerous reasons: the perception that a property right has been stolen or violated; the relationship of the disputants (e.g., competitors, former or current business associates or partners); or the personal characteristics of the affected individuals and the risks to them and the business from the dispute. Mediation injects objectivity into the controversy, helping the parties to evaluate settlement options impartially and exercise their judgment in forging a resolution.

The focus is not on who is right and who is wrong. Mediation *is not compromise*—it is negotiation.[6] The process is directed to those business factors that help fashion a resolution.[7] As Judge Thynge has noted, mediation "requires on the part of the mediator, counsel, and the business representatives the three Ps: preparation, patience, and persistence."[8] Settlement *need* not, and frequently *will* not, occur during the first mediation session.[9] Rather, it results from the preparation that the parties invest before the mediation

---

6. To understand mediation, a quote from the book *Primal Fear* is most apropos:

> If you go in thinking compromise, you assume you're going to give up something. If you go in thinking negotiation, you decide what you want and what you don't give a damn about. That way, you get what you want and give up what doesn't matter. Cuts through the [B.S.].

WILLIAM DIEHL, PRIMAL FEAR 23 (1993).

7. As expressed by the Rolling Stones, each side does not always get what they want, but they usually get what they need.

8. Thynge, *supra* note 3, at 177. A fourth "P"—avoid pessimism—is also frequently needed. *Id.* n.23.

9. The term "mediation" is often used to refer to the in-person mediation meeting involving the mediator, counsel, and the party representatives. In this chapter, that meeting will be referred to as the "mediation session" and it will be assumed that it is the first in-person meeting between the parties, their counsel, and the mediator. The general term "Mediation" (or "mediation process") should be understood more broadly, as defined in the Glossary of this book.

session and the work counsel, representatives, and the mediator invest during and, often, after the mediation session.

Mediation returns to the parties what litigation takes away—control. It allows the parties to control the decision-making process. Unlike litigation and trial, it requires their direct, intimate involvement and judgment, and thereby provides them the means to tailor a result, whether through a settlement agreement, license, or other business arrangement, which addresses their individual needs. It gives parties resolution opportunities beyond the limited constraints of a particular case, allowing a global, rather than piecemeal, approach to finality. Mediation can mend business relationships, allow parties to begin new business relationships, and cushion the blow for those that are ending. And, mediation maintains privacy within the confines of the law and mandatory reporting obligations.

It is worth emphasizing what mediation is not. Mediation is not the opportunity to convince a neutral to force the opposition to capitulate. It is not intended to focus solely on legal issues or theories. Nor should it operate as a dress rehearsal for a *Markman* hearing[10] or oral argument on case-dispositive motions. Mediation is one process available as an alternative to continued litigation, eventual trial, inevitable appeal, possible remand, and frustrating retrial.

A. Is Mediation "Right" for These Parties and This Dispute?

The International Institute for Conflict Prevention & Resolution (CPR) developed Mediation Screen Questions (the Screen) to help determine whether a dispute is suitable for mediation.[11] The Screen relies on three overarching factors:

1. The parties' *goals* for managing the dispute
2. The *suitability* of the dispute for mediation
3. The general *benefits* of mediation

The Screen is organized with short questions and multiple-choice answers under each of the aforementioned factors. The answers to the questions suggest that a particular dispute is, or is not, likely amenable to resolution using mediation.[12] Using the Screen to evaluate a dispute can be more

10. *See* Markman v. Westview Instruments, Inc., 517 U.S. 370 (1996). *See* Glossary for a definition of "*Markman* hearing."

11. *See* Chapter 5, Appendix A (CPR Mediation Screen and Arbitration Screen).

12. As discussed more fully in Chapter 5, although one answer to a question may tend to support use of mediation and another answer may suggest that mediation is not likely to resolve the dispute, the Screen is intended to be predictive rather than a definitive measure.

important than the actual results because the process of addressing each question stimulates strategic thinking, decision-making, and communication between an attorney and his or her client and, possibly, with the other side. That is, analyzing each factor in relation to the parties and their particular dispute may result in a foundational change in the mindset of the parties and their counsel moving them away from an adversarial mindset and towards a negotiation mindset. Chapter 5 discusses the relevance of each of the three factors in IP/Technology disputes and is instructive in applying the Screen as a tool to determine whether mediation is "right" for the involved parties and their dispute. As discussed below, parties can equally apply the Screen to Abbreviated New Drug Application (ANDA) cases, which some consider difficult to mediate, to assess whether mediation might be a viable dispute resolution option.

1. A Word About ANDA[13] Cases . . .

One mantra often heard is "this case can never be settled," or "this is not a case for mediation." Such beliefs are often expressed in ANDA cases, particularly with the first filer. Even defendants who are not the first filer will assume that mediation is not a worthwhile exercise. Although these matters have their challenges, as this chapter discusses, external, nonlegal factors play a major role in whether a matter will likely settle, and those same factors influence *all* cases and, yet, many cases settle. With regard to the unique variables that may influence whether settlement in an ANDA matter is likely,[14] rather than automatically reject mediation of an ANDA case, counsel should explore the significant factors that influence *both* sides' positions to discern whether commonality exists from which potential settlement may occur. The following examples exemplify that.

---

13. ANDA litigation often involves high-stakes disputes with major brand companies seeking to block the entry of generic manufacturers offering a low-cost alternative to the branded drug.

14. Such variables may include the life remaining on the patent at issue (a longer life in excess of five years, the more difficult to settle); the importance of the drug in the brand company's portfolio and its success in the marketplace; the bioequivalence of the generic company's medication; the true strengths of the legal arguments; validity issues; whether the drug covered by the patent involves a unique or complex composition; the likelihood of the generic company's success in the U.S. Food and Drug Administration (FDA) process; whether the brand company intends to capitalize on its own generic product; and the existence of other medications in the brand company's arsenal of interest to the generic company.

Case in point: In an ANDA matter involving a major-brand company and a large generic drug manufacturer, the parties initially expressed hesitation regarding mediation. Despite the parties' reservations, mediation was scheduled, primarily based on a read of counsels' responses to the mediator's questions and an interpretation of what was expressed (and not said) during the initial and subsequent teleconference with the parties. The parties were very familiar with each other, and each side knew and identified the representatives they preferred and felt were needed to have a productive mediation.

In a later teleconference, certain of those identified representatives were required to participate. During that teleconference, the mediator suggested that a pre-mediation discussion among those principals would help identify the business topics and concerns each side felt were crucial to a resolution. The extent of that discussion was left in the representatives' capable hands. Because of that pre-mediation meeting, the mediation was more focused on business matters, and both sides had detailed outlines that concentrated on not only the important business issues, but also solutions addressing each concern.

Although settlement on the drug product at issue did not occur at the mediation session, the pre-mediation conference and mediation identified other areas where the companies' interests overlapped, resulting in an agreement for the generic company to become an exclusive authorized generic for other drugs. That agreement changed their relationship and eventually segued into settlement of the litigation. The value both sides received from the authorized generic agreement on other drugs allowed them to modify their positions on the more challenging issues in the litigation, such as the entry date into the market prior to expiry of the patent at issue.

Case in point: In a multi-defendant ANDA matter involving two first filers, after a couple of separate teleconferences with plaintiff and each defendant, it was apparent that neither first filer was ready to mediate. However, the other generics expressed interest in settlement. It is preferable, if possible, to mediate initially with the first filer before mediating with the non-first filers because, when the settlement parameters are resolved with the first filer, subsequent settlements with the remaining generics often occur quickly. Rather than losing a potential opportunity with the non-first filer generic, a separate mediation was scheduled between plaintiff and each of those defendants. Over a two-month period, the four non-first filers settled under similar terms, including launch date, market protection terms, accelerated launch date, and other common provisions in ANDA settlements. During the following six to eight months, the brand's outside and in-house counsel and the mediator had continued separate discussions with the first filers, including four mediation sessions, which led to settlement, with one becoming an authorized generic for the plaintiff and the other entering a manufacturing/supply arrangement with the brand. All settlements occurred before a claim construction opinion was rendered. Both persistence and a divide-and-conquer approach assisted in the mediation process.

Although the discussion in this section focuses on encouraging an analysis about whether mediation might be "right" for the parties and their dispute, it is important to note that the mediation process can be beneficial to parties even if a mediated settlement is not reached after a first try. With the right mindset and effort put in, there are numerous benefits derived from participating in the process, such as clarifying or narrowing issues to be determined in a later arbitration or litigation, focusing discovery, obtaining information informally that may change a party's strategy, and learning perspectives and business interests that may result in a later settlement.

B. A Candid Discussion About the "Costs" of Litigation

At the outset, parties will often express their commitment to fight to the end to prove or defend their case—but at what cost? Although effective mediation involves a commitment of time and expense by the parties, their counsel, and the mediator (i.e., preparation, mediation time, travel), the potential return more than compensates for that by reducing time-consuming, distracting, and expensive litigation. The costs associated with pursuing litigation, especially in the IP/Technology area, are often significant.

In addition to quantifiable or direct costs (e.g., outside counsel, experts, document and trial exhibit vendors, trademark surveys, and prior-art investigations), reaching a mediated settlement saves time for the business—an incalculable (indirect) but invaluable asset of mediation often overlooked. In this regard, IP/Technology cases usually require substantial time from all levels of employees including business executives (e.g., chief executive officer (CEO), chief financial officer (CFO)), other businesspeople, technical and information technology (IT) personnel, and in-house counsel. Such cases also demand the attention of an army of the party's employees to comply with the essentials of litigation:

- Responding to multiple waves of discovery including collecting, collating, and answering questions about documents and background information
- Providing technical support
- Supplying current and historical information about relevant markets, industries, and standards
- Developing infringement positions or invalidity defenses (claim by claim)
- Providing deposition and trial testimony
- Locating third parties and experts
- Providing tutorials to counsel and experts

These demands slash productivity, interrupt commercial profit-making activities, and decrease revenue. Furthermore, should the case proceed to trial, the time of at least a party representative will be dedicated to that proceeding.

Even when parties settle later in a case, mediation can eliminate future trial-related obligations and attendant significant costs, including summary judgment and other motions, the pretrial conference and trial preparation (e.g., preparing jury instructions, developing trial graphics and/or animations, working with experts and fact witnesses), drafting post-trial or judgment as a matter of law (JMOL) motions and briefs, and the exposure to appeal and remand.[15] Furthermore, as addressed in Chapter 3, other indirect costs abound in IP/Technology cases like the uncertainty of the outcome of a dispute to a business, its vendors and customers and its IP, as well as the risks of losing the case, public relations or reputational issues, and damage to important relationships. A mediated resolution can address a myriad of issues that a jury or judge verdict cannot address in a cost- and time-efficient manner. So how do the parties get to the mediation table?

II. Getting to the Mediation Table

A Chinese proverb says: "The hardest step is over the threshold." What follows are practical ideas and strategies for making it easier to step over the threshold into the mediation process.

A. Timing and Strategies—Sooner or Later?

The best time to mediate varies from case to case. Counsel owe it to their clients (and themselves) to challenge the notion frequently espoused that parties cannot successfully mediate a resolution early in a case. Earlier mediation provides opportunities that usually are lost or unavailable with later mediation. Mediation may be used to streamline discovery and to determine what information is needed to settle. Early mediation can enable the mediator to facilitate and oversee an earlier exchange of information on relevant issues. When a litigation is pending, early mediation allows sufficient time within case management order deadlines to let the process percolate without the distractions of briefing and trial preparation. It permits enough time for business representatives to incorporate the process into their busy

15. The median time to trial for a patent case is about 2.6 years, according to PwC's 2018 Patent Litigation Study (https://www.pwc.com/us/en/forensic-services/publications/assets/2018-pwc-patent-litigation-study.pdf); *see also Table C-5, Median Time Intervals from Filing to Disposition of Civil Cases Terminated, by District and Method of Disposition, During the 12-Month Period Ending June 30, 2023*, U.S. Dist. Cts., https://www.uscourts.gov/statistics/table/c-5/statistical-tables-federal-judiciary/2023/06/30 (last visited Mar. 23, 2025) (indicating that the median time in months to resolve civil district court cases is 33.1 months).

schedules, minimizing conflicts with other commitments that detract from their involvement. That allows for multiple sessions and continued negotiations between sessions. Also, early mediation helps define issues blocking resolution and determine whether those issues may be carved out and handled through another form of alternative dispute resolution (ADR), such as arbitration, or are best left for trial.

Case in point: In one patent matter dealing with microprocessors, after two mediation sessions, one remaining issue prevented a final settlement—whether certain activities by the defendant were permitted under the plaintiff's contract with a third party involving the patented technology. During the first session, the parties and their counsel, with the help of the mediator, agreed to provide information focused on that issue, as well as limited discovery on other liability concerns and damages. That exchange occurred between the two sessions. As a result of further negotiations during the second session, a total settlement amount was reached covering an entire family of patents and all issues in the case, including the contract matter.

Under the final settlement agreement, a percentage of that figure was earmarked to the contract issue, so only that dispute (not the amount of damages) would be tried to the district judge, who would determine whether the defendant's conduct was protected under the contract. If the defendant's conduct was not covered by the third-party contract, the earmarked percentage would be paid to the plaintiff; otherwise, that amount would not be paid. The outcome of the trial was binding on the parties, with no right of appeal.

Thus, through the effective use of focused discovery exchanged during the mediation process, the parties settled the entire matter, with final resolution of the payment amount determined by a two-day bench trial on the contract issue rather than a ten day jury trial on all issues. This example also shows the benefit of thinking outside the box—how invaluable imagination and creativity are in crafting a settlement and a resolution process.

Cases often settle when the parties know enough about a dispute to intelligently agree to resolve it. But the notion that it is impossible for parties to intelligently and effectively negotiate a settlement of litigation until after discovery has been completed (and the parties have incurred substantial costs) has been discredited by the many cases that settle early. Mediation, before discovery is in full swing, can yield just as valid and final a resolution as mediation on the eve of trial. To feel comfortable that an early mediation in a case has the potential to be worthwhile, counsel should be prepared to address three common concerns:

1. Is there sufficient information to negotiate effectively?
2. Will proposing early mediation send a message of weakness to the opponent?

3. In the case of a prospective plaintiff before litigation has commenced, can a party propose early dispute resolution without triggering a declaratory judgment action?

Each is addressed here.

B. Bridging the Information Gap

A common concern expressed by counsel against early mediation is lack of information about the other side's case, and the resulting effect on advising their clients. Most counsel prefer to wait until discovery is closed or summary judgment motions are decided before mediating. They often complain that mediation serves as a means for *free discovery* by the opposition. Most information disclosed during mediation, however, is discoverable in any event. Thus, counsel should consider and weigh whether there is any advantage to waiting to disclose particular information through discovery versus enhancing the possibility of settlement by revealing such information during mediation. In certain cases, a late mediation, after the close of discovery or shortly before trial, may benefit from more information. One downside of late mediation, including the monetary and nonmonetary costs expended, is that significant funds (and emotion) have been invested in the litigation, and the position of the parties may be immovably entrenched.

As discussed in Chapter 3, in many cases, plaintiffs who perform diligent pre-suit investigations know much of what they needed to know to evaluate the case before filing the complaint. Likewise, defendants who moved quickly to perform their early case assessment soon after learning of the other side's claims, know much of what they needed to know within 60 to 90 days of receiving the complaint, if not before. See also Chapter 4.

Granted, there may be some significant gaps in knowledge that make it impossible to ascertain a position on settlement without at least some additional information. Sometimes that information is available from publicly available sources. Other times, a party may seek it from their opponent. For example, a patentee contemplating a paid-up license for the future and a lump-sum payment to compensate for past sales of infringing products may need information only the defendant can provide about its sales volumes, the identity of other products that arguably fall within the scope of the asserted claims, and where those products are manufactured and sold. A defendant accused of trade secret misappropriation will likely need more detailed information than would be found in the complaint about the nature of the alleged trade secrets so that it can consider erecting acceptable barriers between what it already knew and intends to continue using, and what it may agree to forgo using for some future period.

Before hurtling headlong into full discovery, consider identifying a discrete set of information targeted to what is absolutely necessary to fill any gaps and negotiate (alone or with the mediator's assistance) to exchange that information informally. Three options the parties could pursue are (1) prioritize their responses to certain discovery requests (if discovery has already been served); (2) respond to informal letter discovery that does not preclude formal discovery on the same topics if the mediation fails; or (3) exchange information through the mediator. If concerns linger about the reliability of informal responses, counsel may gain additional comfort by including representations and warranties in the settlement agreement regarding the accuracy and completeness of the information provided or by establishing a process for the mediator or a third party to verify the information. As this information almost certainly would be discoverable outside of mediation, there is really no prejudice from the early disclosure if mediation fails, and much to be gained by a negotiated resolution if mediation is successful.

Case in point: In an IP case, during the initial teleconference to discuss a mediation date, the defendant advised that mediation would not be beneficial since prior discussion between counsel indicated the parties had significantly different settlement figures in mind. The defendant also did not want to proceed with mediation due to the expense of having counsel and the parties travel from California. In response to an inquiry about prior settlement offers, counsel related that the plaintiff "was around 75 while defendant was at 12." Further questioning revealed that both the demand and offer were five-figure amounts and not seven. In light of the minimal settlement range and the substantial expenses likely to be incurred in litigation, an early mediation was scheduled requiring pre-mediation statements to focus on damages and approaches to settlement. The mediator encouraged the parties to exchange limited economic information, such as past sales and net profits, before the submission of their mediation statements. Because the relevant patent had expired, only past damages were at issue. At the time, videoconferencing was not prevalent so the mediation session was held telephonically rather than in person. The matter settled during the first session.

C. Managing the Message

Some counsel and their clients worry that proposing early mediation (or other dispute resolution processes) will communicate weakness or lack of confidence in their case. While it is impossible to control what the other side thinks, there are ways for either party's counsel to raise the subject of early dispute resolution while minimizing the wrong impression. For example, many companies have internal policies or operating procedures that include exploring early settlement of disputes, which parties can use to break the ice.

If counsel can truthfully tell an opponent that they or their party has a policy or practice of proactively approaching an opponent to discuss early resolution in virtually every case, the decision to do so in this particular case does not suggest weakness but simply a business-savvy willingness to explore the alternatives.

If, however, neither company subscribes to such internal policies, parties may want to reference CPR's Corporate Policy Statement on Alternatives to Litigation, which was developed in the 1980s specifically to overcome the concern that a party's suggestion of ADR would be seen as a sign of weakness.[16] Thousands of companies and law firms have signed "The Corporate Pledge," which compels the signatories to explore with adversaries resolution of disputes through ADR before filing suit. As the names of the signatories are available on CPR's website, counsel can see whether the opposing party or opposing counsel's firm is a signatory as a prelude to raising the subject of mediation.[17] Approaching one's opponent with a policy or philosophy of early dispute resolution discussions, coupled with hiring an attorney known for his or her willingness and ability to try cases if a matter cannot be resolved on favorable terms, may strike just the right chord. If opposing counsel does not want to mediate now, the seed has been planted for future discussions.

Another way to pursue mediation with an opponent without suggesting an intent to roll over is through in-house counsel or a business executive or manager who has a professional relationship with a counterpart in the opponent's organization. That relationship can often be leveraged to raise the issue of settlement.[18] Moreover, simply picking up the phone to learn what a recently received cease and desist letter or a recently filed lawsuit is really about often cuts out time-consuming and expensive letter writing and litigation, and brings key business issues to the forefront. A series of conversations can yield more practical information than months of discovery and serve as a springboard to how best to resolve the actual issues between the parties. What follows are some possible questions to get the conversation started.

---

16. *See* CPR, Report of the CPR Patent Mediation Task Force: Effective Practices Protocol 7 (2012) [hereinafter CPR Report], https://www.mandw.com/PUBLICATIONS/CPR-Patent_Mediation_Task_Force(2014).pdf.

17. *See Pledges, Corporate Policy Statement and Law Firm Policy Statement on Alternatives to Litigation*, CPR, https://www.cpradr.org/adr-pledges (last visited Mar. 23, 2025).

18. In IP/Technology cases, personnel between corporations may know one another or have a relationship from active participation in legal, industry, or trade organizations and associations, from prior work experience at the same company, from a prior dispute or business relationship, and from a current ongoing relationship between the companies.

Possible Questions	Purpose
We were just served with a complaint, can you explain what's this about?	Parties file lawsuits based on IP rights or contracts for a variety of reasons that are not always reflected in the complaint.
What are you looking for?	Explore whether the parties are willing to give or do something expeditiously to resolve a dispute.
We would like to obtain from you [information, documents] to prepare for the mediation. What do you need from us?	This overture intends to communicate that we're taking the mediation seriously and a reasonable exchange of information will better prepare both of us for settlement discussions. It also communicates fairness and parity—that we're not asking from you what we're not willing to provide in the mediation.
Can we get a confidentiality agreement in place and talk about how we might resolve this short of going to court?	This may remove an obstacle quickly and demonstrate a party's interest in having a candid conversation.
Can we demonstrate to you that our product doesn't do what you think it does?	Such a demonstration may begin a productive dialogue related to a design-around or provide a reality check, which ultimately is likely to be provided in the course of any litigation.

Party representatives enlisted to talk to their counterparts about mediation should be knowledgeable regarding the mediation process and its potential benefits, should understand the implications of the dispute for the business involved, and should be creative problem solvers. An idea for a negotiated business relationship that may be of real interest to the other side can also provide a credible platform for discussion that does not sound like concession.

If the parties in dispute have a contractual relationship, counsel should review the relevant contracts between the parties to see whether they contain a dispute resolution provision that would require mediation before a party may file a notice of arbitration or a complaint in court.

D. Avoiding the Preemptive Strike

Because early mediation can so often be both productive and cost-effective, many companies incorporate mediation into the dispute resolution provisions of licenses and other IP-related agreements. Such provisions typically provide for notice, business-to-business discussion, and then mediation, with an adversarial adjudication, such as arbitration or litigation, as a last resort only if those efforts fail.[19]

If the dispute has arisen between parties who do not have such an agreement in place, however, proposing pre-litigation settlement discussions could present some delicate issues. In *MedImmune, Inc. v. Genentech, Inc.*, the U.S. Supreme Court made clear that a rights owner cannot protect itself from the risk of a declaratory judgment action simply by communicating its willingness to offer a license to the allegedly infringing party.[20] Instead, the Court held, a declaratory judgment plaintiff only needs to prove that "the facts alleged, under all the circumstances, show that there is a substantial controversy between the parties having adverse legal interests, of sufficient immediacy and reality to warrant the issuance of a declaratory judgment."[21] As a result, a party who proposes mediation before filing suit may wake up the next morning to find that its overture has been rewarded not by an expression of reciprocal interest, but by the filing of a declaratory judgment action in the other party's favorite forum.

Although there are no perfect answers to this dilemma, there are some strategies that may help the rights owner who wishes to propose pre-litigation mediation while minimizing the risk of losing its choice of forum if the negotiations fail.

1. Pocket Filing

One such strategy, probably the least risky, is to file the complaint but not serve it, instead sending the alleged infringer a copy of the complaint along with a letter offering to defer service while the parties attempt to resolve the matter. The parties will then have time to attempt resolution under an appropriate confidentiality agreement before the plaintiff would be required to effectuate service of the complaint. (The plaintiff should reserve the right

---

19. Some parties include in an ADR provision an exception allowing the rights owner to seek immediate judicial relief if needed to avoid immediate irreparable harm, and mandatory, exclusive jurisdiction and venue clauses so that the parties are not thinking more about racing to their respective hometown courthouses than they are about giving the ADR process a chance to work.

20. *See* 549 U.S. 118, 127 (2007).

21. *Id.* A detailed discussion of how to navigate the post-*MedImmune* world of declaratory judgment jurisdiction is beyond the scope of this chapter. For a practical analysis of some of the cases interpreting *MedImmune* and possible strategies for patentees and alleged infringers, see, e.g., Dugal S. Sickert et al., *Navigating the Declaratory Judgment Minefield to a Patent License*, ACC Docket, Sept. 2009, at 54.

to declare impasse and serve the complaint more quickly if negotiations do not prove productive.)[22] The advantage of this approach is that it largely, if not entirely, eliminates the risk of a successful declaratory judgment action in another venue. Yet, the act of filing the lawsuit—shooting first—may be viewed by the other side as aggressive and inconsistent with the espoused desire to negotiate, thus undermining mediation. In addition, the defendant may still attempt a declaratory judgment action in another jurisdiction, serve it immediately, and argue that the second-filed action should proceed. Generally, however, the court in the second action will simply transfer the case to the jurisdiction of the first-filed case.[23]

2. Standstill Agreement

Another strategy for proposing pre-litigation settlement discussions is for a party to communicate very generally with the alleged infringer about its desire to discuss certain IP in which it believes the alleged infringer may be interested, but not to identify the accused products. Such a communication would be accompanied or followed by a proposed standstill agreement providing, among other things, that neither party would file suit during the term of the agreement, that any discussions would be treated as confidential settlement discussions, and, ideally, that the discussions and information exchanged would not be admissible to establish jurisdiction for a declaratory judgment action.

Either party would be permitted to terminate the agreement, but the confidentiality obligations would survive termination, and, ideally, there would be a defined period following termination during which the rights owner would have the sole option of filing suit if it chooses. The advantage of this approach is that, from the beginning, the message is more consistent with the proposal to mediate. At the same time, proposing such an agreement may carry a higher risk of being deemed, under all the circumstances, sufficient to trigger declaratory judgment jurisdiction, particularly if the surrounding facts, litigation history, and areas of overlap between the parties make it relatively easy to identify the rights and products at issue and to anticipate that litigation will result if the negotiations are not successful.[24]

---

22. Under Federal Rule of Civil Procedure 4(m), the deadline for service of the complaint is generally 90 days after the complaint is filed, absent a showing of good cause by the plaintiff.

23. *See, e.g.*, Elecs. for Imaging, Inc. v. Coyle, 394 F.3d 1341 (Fed. Cir. 2005).

24. This is not to say that declaratory judgment jurisdiction would inexorably attach if a patentee sent a more traditional letter identifying its patent rights and inviting the other party to take a license. As Sickert et al. point out, the declaratory

Notably, sending cease and desist letters, without taking the precaution of filing first or even entering into a standstill/confidentiality agreement, is a much more common practice in trademark, copyright, and even trade secret cases (particularly those that involve enforcement of employee noncompete agreements), than in patent cases, perhaps because such disputes are typically more easily and quickly resolved. Moreover, the perceived advantage of certain district courts over others seems to be greater in patent cases, thus increasing the likelihood of a preemptive strike to secure the venue of choice. That being said, courts have held that the relaxed declaratory judgment standard articulated in *MedImmune* is not limited to patent cases.[25] Thus, as with patent cases, if the rights owner is not willing to take the risk of a declaratory judgment action in an unfriendly forum, it should take steps to mitigate that risk before engaging with the alleged infringer.

Although Chapter 3 espouses the virtues of early case assessment and mediation, each case has its own chemistry and rhythm. That one case may be ripe for mediation in the early stages does not mean that every case is. Events and developments in the life of the case or of the parties themselves can set the stage for new or renewed negotiations at virtually any point during the lifespan of a case.

E. Court Involvement

Various jurisdictions have adopted local ADR rules or programs in recognition that full, formal litigation can impose large economic burdens on the parties and can significantly delay resolution of disputes. For example, the U.S. District Court for the Northern District of California has Local ADR Rules that state, "Sometimes an alternative dispute resolution procedure can improve the quality of justice by improving the parties' clarity of understanding of their case, their access to evidence, and their satisfaction with the process and result."[26] In the U.S. District Court for the Southern District of Florida, the court refers every civil case, with limited exceptions, to mediation and maintains a list of certified mediators.[27] And, with regard

---

judgment jurisdiction bar for any given court "is still a moving target." Sickert et al., *supra* note 21, at 60 and accompanying notes.

25. *See* D.P. Harvey et al., *Shoot First and Ask Questions Later? The Impact of* MedImmune v. Genentech *on Declaratory Judgment Actions in Trademark Disputes*, TRADEMARK REP., Sept.–Oct. 2010, at 1147.

26. N.D. CAL. ADR LOC. R. 1-2(a), http://www.cand.uscourts.gov/localrules/ADR (last visited Mar. 23, 2025) (providing local rules for ADR).

27. *See* S.D. FLA. ADR LOC. R. 16.2(d), https://www.flsd.uscourts.gov/sites/flsd/files/23-11-01%202023%20Local%20Rules%20effective%20120123%20-%20REDLINE.pdf.

to trademark cases specifically, since 1997, the U.S. District Court for the Northern District of Illinois has maintained a mediation program for all Lanham Act[28] cases.[29] Pursuant to this Lanham Act Program, the parties are required to file a joint statement indicating whether they wish to participate in the voluntary program.[30] Parties who decline to do so must provide a statement summarizing the reasons for that decision.[31] So counsel should explore the local rules in the jurisdiction in which the case will be filed or the matter is pending to determine that jurisdiction's approach to dispute resolution generally and mediation in particular.

Even if the applicable procedural rules do not make mediation mandatory, counsel can use the suggested settlement conference to begin a discussion with one another about mediation, including when and how they could implement the process. Federal Rule of Civil Procedure 16(c)(2)(I) specifically addresses dispute resolution as a pretrial conference topic.[32] ADR, usually in the form of mediation, is initially discussed with the district judge assigned to the case during the Rule 16 scheduling conference; however, an attorney and their client should seriously confer and address ADR with the opposition beforehand. Also, Rule 16(c)(2)(L) refers to exploring the use of procedures other than litigation to resolve the dispute. This includes urging the litigants to employ adjudicatory techniques outside the courthouse.

Counsel may also consider using the court as a means to broach the topic of mediation with their opponent. In many federal district courts, magistrate judges serve as mediators and spend significant time in settlement conferences. Often, magistrate judges are amenable to suggesting mediation if approached by one of the parties. Also, as discussed in detail in Chapters 7 and 8, both federal circuit courts of appeal and the ITC have active mediation programs that the parties can use for pursuing mediation in those forums.

---

28. *See* Lanham Act, 15 U.S.C. §§ 1051–1141 (2016).

29. *See* N.D. Ill. ADR Loc. R. 16.3, https://www.ilnd.uscourts.gov/_assets/_documents/_rules/LRRULES.pdf.

30. *See id.*

31. *See id.*

32. Rule 16(c)(2)(I) states:

> (2) Matters for Consideration. At any pretrial conference, the court may consider and take appropriate action on the following matters: . . .
>
> > (I) settling the case and using special procedures to assist in resolving the dispute when authorized by statute or local rule[.]

F. Litigation Events

It has long been acknowledged that events in the life of a lawsuit (or the life of an ITC investigation or U.S. Patent and Trademark Office (PTO) proceeding) may affect a party's perception of its likelihood of final success on the merits or its exposure to a significant damages award. Such events may influence parties to settle, including by mediation. Early in the case, settlement negotiations may be attractive when the court issues—or declines to issue—a temporary restraining order or a preliminary injunction affecting a product or asset that is core to a party's business.[33] Even an early procedural motion such as an attack on personal jurisdiction or venue can alter the parties' respective assessments of the likely outcome, as well as the timing and cost of the case (e.g., a different judge, a court with different rules, a rocket docket), and, therefore, their attitude toward settlement.

The onset of even routine discovery in an IP/Technology case may also cause one or both parties to reevaluate their interest in settlement. Experienced litigants in such cases already know the tremendous cost of discovery, both financially and from internal distraction and disruption, while others may not fully appreciate those costs until invoices from outside law firms and vendors start rolling in, and they are faced with intrusion into their confidential information and the burden on their employees of addressing copious discovery requests.

In patent infringement cases, litigation events that could be propitious times to pursue mediation include after the claim construction hearing,[34] after the court issues its claim construction determination, after the court rules on dispositive motions, and after expert reports are exchanged. The timing for *Markman* proceedings varies, however, and, in many jurisdictions, it occurs only after substantial discovery. At the same time, it is not unheard of for a court to entertain an early summary judgment motion, grant limited discovery for responding to the motion, and issue an order without great delay. Thus, if the parties agree that claim construction will be key to their settlement evaluation, they may want to ask the court to enter a case management order that sets the *Markman* hearing at an earlier stage after focused discovery.

Another catalyst for settlement is the appellate hurdle. The time and expense of pursuing an appeal (after briefing, argument, or a decision that

33. Likewise, the appealability of injunctions under 28 U.S.C. § 1292, Rules 62 and 65 of the Federal Rules of Civil Procedure, and Rule 8 of the Federal Rules of Appellate Procedure may encourage settlement discussions.

34. While early mediation is recommended, the CPR Report also states, "The optimal time to mediate is when both parties are somewhat unsure about their respective litigation positions." CPR Report, *supra* note 16, at 14.

could include a remand) could motivate the parties to discuss settlement before an appeal is pursued or while one is pending (see Chapter 7).

G. Party Events

Events occurring within a business may also precipitate a new or renewed interest in settlement.[35] Changes in management, for example from mergers and acquisitions to new hires, are routine in companies and can bring new perspectives to old disputes. Take, for instance, where an employee leaves a company and begins competing with the former company allegedly using misappropriated trade secrets. When the managers who had been directly involved with the employee and emotionally invested in the circumstances of the defection to a competitor move on to other responsibilities, new management may be able to view the dispute with a more conciliatory approach. Similarly, a change in management may determine that an unprofitable accused product line is not worth continuing, thus supporting a business-interest based approach to resolving costly patent infringement litigation. In considering ways to resolve IP disputes, new management may have different ideas from their predecessor regarding product lines and strategic initiatives, which raise as issues whether the business would be better served by exclusivity or by licensing the IP-in-suit, or by pursuing the possibility of an acquisition, cross-license, joint development agreement, or other strategic business partnership with the disputant. And, as is the case, companies often merge or acquire other companies and it is not uncommon for new leadership or former leadership with new business objectives to decide that settlement discussions would be timely and productive.

The bottom line is that, as the case proceeds, it behooves counsel and their clients alike to be alert to all of the developments that may affect the business objectives of the party and the decision drivers for the opponent, and to assess whether mediated settlement discussions should be pursued.

Assuming the parties have agreed to pursue mediation, they next have to select the mediator.

35. There may be others who influence or determine whether a settlement materializes. For example, investors who risk money to capitalize a business and its assets may have a lot to say about how those assets are used or treated (e.g., licenses, assigned). Settlements have been quashed or delayed to address investor expectations and return on investment.

III. Practical Considerations for Selecting a Mediator

As neutrals, mediators are loyal to the mediation process and, through interactions with the parties, serve them jointly as well as each party separately. Mediators serve many functions. For example, they:

- Help to ease tension
- Ensure a fair process
- Encourage parties to develop settlement options
- Provide feedback regarding proposals
- Perform reality checks
- Prevent (or address) obstacles to settlement

In selecting and working with the mediator, counsel should remember that a mediator does not adjudicate the subject matter of the dispute, but instead guides the course of negotiations. Thus, the negotiation traits of the mediator are important to determine how the mediator may effectively motivate either side to settle. Consider how the mediator may persuasively express the strengths of either side's position to the other side, or educate each side on the major weaknesses of their case.

It is difficult to overstate the importance of selecting the right mediator in IP/Technology disputes. To the extent counsel can agree on attributes and qualifications, so much the better. Keeping the mediator's functions in mind enables the parties to better choose their mediator.

The parties should take the process of selecting a mediator as seriously as they would the process of selecting outside counsel. Even the most motivated and otherwise prepared parties can find themselves walking disappointedly out of a mediation session if the mediator mishandles the interaction between them. The rockier the relationship between the parties, the more complex the business context, or the more tentative the motivation for resolution, the more critical is the parties' choice of the mediator. Moreover, selecting the mediator may be the first opportunity the parties will have to show they are capable of reaching agreement.

Even among the most qualified, well-trained, effective mediators, not everyone will be right for every case. Finding the right mediator, like finding the right attorney, requires research and due diligence. The parties can compile a list of possible candidates by reviewing, for example, websites, directories, and rosters of qualified neutrals,[36] but there is no substitute for

---

36. Many of the well-known administering ADR institutions have specialty panels (i.e., technology and/or IP) from which parties can select candidates. There are other organizations, such as the Silicon Valley Arbitration & Mediation Center (SVAMC) and the International Mediation Institute (IMI), that are not administering organizations but they set standards and some vet individuals to qualify for their list (e.g., the SVAMC's "Tech List" of specialized technology-knowledgeable neutrals). Many of

doing homework, including interviewing the mediator and talking with both outside and in-house counsel who have worked with that mediator to resolve complex IP/Technology disputes. In-house and outside counsel can and should share the responsibility for researching the candidates. Indeed, in-house counsel will often have greater success getting candid and meaningful feedback from other in-house counsel. In vetting the candidates, their reputation and references are important, but look for more than conclusory recommendations (e.g., "Joe is a great guy. He really banged heads."). When choosing a mediator, counsel should consider to whom the other side (and the party representatives) would listen.

Set forth in the following sections are some considerations for interviewing and selecting mediators.[37]

A. Threshold Issues

In compiling a list of possible mediators, the following are issues to address at the outset with the mediator candidates.

- **Conflicts**. To assist the mediator candidate in performing a conflicts check and making any necessary written disclosures, counsel should consider carefully what information they provide to the mediator, such as the names (and name changes) of the parties and related entities;[38] all counsel involved on a case, not just those involved in the mediation; the key people involved in the dispute; the IP (e.g., patent, trademark and copyright registration numbers, products at issue); and any other information that could give rise to a conflict.
- **Fees and costs**. Request the mediator's fee structure, including the rate (daily or hourly), charge for preparation time, the cancellation

the neutrals appearing on those lists appear on the rosters of well-known ADR institutions. Once candidates are identified, the parties have various options for investigating their background and experience. They may obtain online information about a candidate's education, experience, credentials, publications, and presentations from, for example, the candidate's website, the website of certain arbitral institutions (e.g., *Search Neutral Directory*, JAMS, https://www.jamsadr.com/neutrals/search (last visited Mar. 23, 2025); *Find a CPR Neutral*, CPR, https://drs.cpradr.org/neutrals/find-a-neutral (last visited Mar. 23, 2025)), and professional and honorary associations of which the candidate is a member.

37. Section I.B of Chapter 5 discusses tools to find and investigate qualified and experienced mediators for IP/Technology disputes. These include sample criteria lists and CPR's "Due Diligence Evaluation Tool for Selecting Arbitrators and Mediators" (i.e., a grouped listing of questions, which can be used when talking with attorneys who have used the services of the mediator under consideration).

38. With large corporations involving numerous subsidiaries and related entities, the list could consist of multiple pages. Party representatives will know who in the company to contact for the list (e.g., the tax or corporate departments).

policy (if any), travel or administration fees, and any other billing policies. Generally, the parties share equally the mediator's costs, but in certain circumstances creative arrangements (e.g., one party pays for the first day of the mediation session and the opposing party pays for a possible second day) may be a strategy to bring a reluctant party to the table.

- **Availability and time constraints**. In many cases, parties are under time constraints to complete at least one mediation session. Thus, they should ensure that the mediator candidates are available to conduct the mediation within the required time period. An associated time-related consideration is whether the mediator is someone who is willing to stick with the parties during the course of the day (as long as necessary) and into the next day if the parties are willing.

B. Criteria for Selection

If the parties are in a contractual relationship and contractually bound to pursue mediation, then they should consult the relevant agreement(s) to learn if there are any selection criteria for the mediator upon which they previously agreed. If no such criteria exist because there is no agreement (the parties are not in a contractual relationship) or the contract does not set forth such criteria, then the parties should try to work together to identify mutually acceptable selection criteria. If the parties are working with an ADR administering organization (e.g., American Arbitration Association (AAA), JAMS, CPR) then their case manager will help them compile a list of mediators that meet the parties' criteria or the most important criteria of each party (if the parties cannot agree on criteria). What follows are common, useful criteria to consider when compiling one's own list and discussing mediator candidates with opposing counsel.

1. Balancing Process Skills with Expertise

A gateway question in choosing a mediator in IP/Technology disputes is often whether it is more important to choose a mediator with strong mediation process skills or with technical and/or subject matter expertise. In one survey, counsel were asked, "What personal qualities, skills or techniques did [the named mediator] demonstrate that helped move the parties toward settlement?" The top three answers were (1) empathy and approachability; (2) high integrity demonstrated by neutrality, trustworthiness, and protection of confidences; and (3) knowledge about the relevant contract or the law.[39]

---

39. Stephan B. Goldberg & Margaret L. Shaw, *The Secrets of Successful (and Unsuccessful) Mediators*, JAMS DISP. RESOL. ALERT, Winter 2008, at 1, https://kipdf

In the report of a task force studying the use of mediation for resolving patent disputes,[40] participants listed the following attributes as important (in no particular order) when selecting a mediator, that the mediator:

- Be fully informed about the background of the dispute: key facts/ legal issues, the parties, business issues[41]
- Be patient, optimistic, persistent, neutral, a good listener, an excellent communicator, committed to parties during and after the mediation session, willing to tailor the mediation process, and have strong people skills
- Explore the nuances of the case, allow the parties to fully express the strengths and weaknesses of their respective positions, and challenge the parties concerning unrealistic positions and expectations
- Work diligently with the parties and propose creative solutions to their business problems
- Avoid simply conveying settlement demands and responses back and forth trying to force the parties to meet somewhere in the middle[42]

There was a general consensus among task force participants that *successful* mediators in patent cases should have strong mediation skills, experience mediating patent cases, and a thorough understanding of patent law and patent litigation.[43] The CPR's Report of the CPR Patent Mediation Task Force: Effective Practices Protocol (CPR Report) reflected that a mediator who lacks strong mediation skills, notwithstanding a thorough knowledge of patent law, is unlikely to be successful because he or she will not likely have the skills necessary to help the parties reach consensus.[44] And the CPR Report noted that, because parties often rely on the mediator to conduct reality testing and to provide a reasoned explanation as to why they should alter their proposals, a mediator with strong mediation skills but little or no

.com/the-secrets-of-successful-and-unsuccessful-mediators_5ac4f7a41723ddb9b6b185e2.html.

40. *See* CPR Report, *supra* note 16, at 10–11.

41. Experience shows that, in IP/Technology mediations, even if the mediator has the requisite subject matter background, if he or she is not prepared or fully informed about the background of the dispute at issue, or lacks an understanding of the relevant field or the importance of the dispute to the business, the party representative may not have respect for the mediator and be disillusioned by the process.

42. Furthermore, although IP/Technology disputes are business disputes, misappropriation, infringement, and breach of contract issues can engender significant trust and emotional issues that are best dealt with by a mediator who is known to have the disposition and skills to deal with such issues.

43. *See* CPR Report, *supra* note 16, at 11.

44. *See id.*

patent experience will be at a disadvantage in discussing with the parties the strengths and challenges of their respective positions.[45] For example, a trademark or copyright specialist who can talk knowledgeably with the parties about the scope of a likely injunction if the plaintiff prevails at trial may be the most effective mediator. Or a patent mediation may be most effectively handled by a patent attorney who understands the implications of a pending PTO inter partes proceeding.

Similarly, to be effective, a mediator ordinarily will not need to have a Ph.D. in polymer chemistry or be an expert in the optical properties of multilayer films. In fact, in some cases, the parties may want a mediator who is not a technical expert and can give them some insight into how well or how poorly a jury is likely to understand their case. Then again, in cases where the parties differ greatly in their assessment of the likelihood of success on a complex technical issue, a mediator who has some familiarity with the technology may be able to provide a needed reality check for the parties.

Furthermore, the CPR Report indicated that "[s]pecific experience with the technology disclosed in the patent is not essential unless the dispute turns entirely on technical issues or the parties have requested an evaluative mediation."[46]

Some counsel have go-to mediators that they count on to exhibit certain attributes and a particular mediation style (see discussion in the following section) that fit the needs of particular cases (e.g., more reality testing or evaluation, more hand-holding, or more imposing). Of course, counsel must take into account factors such as timing, mediator availability, cost, opposing counsel preferences, and their client's preferences in choosing a mediator who is best suited for the mediation.

2. Personal Style

What is the style of the mediator candidates and, in particular, how do they deal with difficult personalities? If there are strong personalities on one or both sides, the parties will want to select a mediator who can be firm and control the process, but not incite a power struggle. Ask the candidates for examples of how they have dealt with personality issues in past cases. Or tell them something about the challenges anticipated and ask them how they may approach getting past those obstacles and building trust. Avoid having a mediation session run aground because the mediator was not effective in keeping the decision makers on task and engaged in a positive way.

45. *See id.*
46. *Id.* at 12.

3. Experience with Complex Cases

In IP/Technology cases, complexities impacting the resolution of such cases may include the existence of multiple parties involved in the dispute, cultural differences between the parties,[47] involvement of an insurance carrier, and related proceedings pending in various jurisdictions in the United States and internationally. Learn what experience candidates have in resolving complex business cases with sophisticated business solutions (i.e., solutions that involve elements other than just the exchange of money for a release of liability, or a simple license agreement). If possible, ask the mediator candidates or their references to give the parties examples of such resolutions they have previously mediated and describe how their approach or creative problem-solving contributed to those outcomes. How articulate is a mediator candidate in describing such resolutions and what does it say about how articulate that person would be in carrying a complex business proposal to the other side in a mediation? On a related subject, inquire of the references whether the mediator candidates can be relied upon to keep straight what they are not supposed to communicate to the other side. Much of what a party says to a mediator in the privacy of a breakout session is for background only and never intended to be relayed to the party in the next room. Good mediators have developed effective techniques for segregating what they are permitted to pass along from what they are not.

4. Mediator Work Ethic

The best mediators bring a strong work ethic before, during, and after the mediation session. They prepare carefully, often including pre-mediation interviews with counsel and careful review of the parties' written statements. Before walking into the mediation session, they have thought about the approach or approaches that will likely fit the particular case and party dynamic. They bring a calm but determined energy to the mediation process that does not cut off (or cut out) promptly at 5:00 p.m. and does not fade

---

47. There are various cultural issues that might arise in IP/Technology mediations, such as the need for an interpreter; a party's comfort level with how a mediation is conducted and by whom; and whether a U.S.-based party whose parent company is located in another country requires certain approval procedures of the settlement that are culturally driven. Counsel and the mediator need to be attuned to potential cultural issues and discuss the same before the mediation session to avoid any misinterpretations or miscommunications, or create any trust issues. *See generally* John Barkai, *What's a Cross-Cultural Mediator to Do? A Low-Context Solution for a High-Context Problem*, 10 Cardozo J. Conflict Resol. 43 (2008); Theodore K. Cheng, *Developing Skills to Address Cultural Issues in Arbitration and Mediation*, 72 Disp. Resol. J. 1 (2017).

when the parties get cranky or lose their momentum. They are also willing to invest time and energy in the aftermath, because many cases that do not settle at the mediation session can still be resolved afterward if the mediator is willing to follow up with the parties and keep the parties focused.

To obtain an accurate perspective of a mediator candidate's work ethic, the parties should explore this with the mediator's references. Be attuned to whether a mediator seems to value getting a deal done above all else. A bad deal is not better than no deal at all. Listen, for example, for whether the reference describes a mediator candidate as someone who will knock heads together. That is not necessarily an endorsement. Find out, for example, whether a mediator tries to put pressure on a party into accepting a deal that just does not meet the party's needs or is so motivated to get a deal done that the mediator ignores or masks important issues or facts to reach a desired endpoint within a particular time frame. In the spirit of "learn from the mistakes of others because you won't live long enough to make them all yourself," here is a situation to avoid.

Case in point: The plaintiff had told the mediator repeatedly and unequivocally that it would not pay the defendant anything on its counterclaims. The mediator relayed settlement proposals back and forth between the two sides, but never told the plaintiff's team that the defendant was continuing to demand a payment to settle its counterclaims. In fact, the mediator told the plaintiff that money was "off the table." To make matters worse, the mediator did not tell the plaintiff when the key decision maker for the defendant left to catch a plane in the middle of the afternoon. The mediator no doubt thought—probably correctly—that, if the plaintiff had all the facts, it would have declared impasse and ended the mediation session. Thus, he opted to hide the information from the plaintiff on the theory that, if he could keep the discussion going, there was hope it would all come together in the end. It did not. The moment of truth came when the plaintiff made a best and final offer late in the evening and learned for the first time that (1) the defendant was still seeking money for its counterclaims and (2) the defendant's team did not have the authority to make a deal even if it had wanted to.

Needless to say, the plaintiff walked out and the case was litigated for the better part of a year before either party was willing to risk another experience with mediation.

5. Mediation Training and Experience

Have the mediator candidates taken mediation training, and, if so, what was the nature of that training? Many self-described mediators are retired judges or attorneys who have not had extensive mediation training. Mediation is a skill that can only be developed through training, study, and experience in mediation. Even a litigator who has settled dozens of cases is not automatically equipped to be a mediator. Likewise, even a retired judge universally respected for effectiveness on the bench is not necessarily going to be an effective mediator. In fact, the opposite may be true if the judge continues to think of herself as someone who will decide the case on the merits, rather than facilitate the negotiations. At the same time, a former judge, especially one who is also a trained mediator, may be just the right choice to help an unrealistic party understand the challenges of its case in front of a judge and jury.

When a sitting judge serves as the mediator, the *power of the robe* no doubt strongly influences cooperation with the process, including the exchange of pre-mediation information and ensuring that the appropriate party representatives participate. Private mediators have an enforcement arsenal as well—prestige and deference. Since the parties have selected the private mediator, that person enters the process with inherent respect. Unlike court-assisted mediation, the parties usually have mutually decided that a resolution is desired, mediation is the preferred format, and the chosen mediator is with whom they want to mediate.

6. Mediation Style and Process

Many commercial mediators generally, and those mediating IP/Technology disputes in particular, use a hybrid approach, beginning with a purely facilitative style[48] and later working into a more evaluative style or preferring *reality testing* (e.g., asking probing questions to have the parties consider the weaknesses of their case and the strengths of the other party's case, sharing thoughts on the risks of the particular litigation, explaining how a third-party adjudicator might view and weigh the evidence) if the parties get stuck in their positions on an issue.

An evaluative approach can be used in IP/Technology cases. Experience shows, however, that a critical downside with a purely evaluative mediation, or at least one commencing the mediation in this style, is once the mediator has opined on the likely outcome of a matter, the mediator loses the trust and rapport of the party who has received critical feedback on the merits of an issue(s). Where there are multiple issues to opine on, and the mediator's

48. A mediator who uses a facilitative style tries to discern the parties' interests that underlie their stated legal positions and to assist the parties in analyzing options to resolve the dispute, including ways to create value as opposed to simply dividing up the preexisting pie. Insofar as the facilitative approach is used in some form in a variety of settings, including noncommercial disputes, some have questioned the effectiveness of that approach in IP/Technology cases where counsel want a mediator to employ an evaluative approach from the beginning, "bang heads," or tell the other side they are wrong.

evaluation may be negative for both parties, then both are often jaundiced for the rest of the mediation. Thereafter, the parties may stand firmer in their positions, thus elevating emotions, decreasing flexibility, and lowering the chances of a successful mediation. If parties want an evaluative mediation and the mediator agrees, the parties should think carefully about why they need such a process and how it should be carried out to gain the most benefit and avoid the downsides. The party representatives should be fully apprised of the process and why counsel believe it will be effective.

Case in point: Two parties were dissolving a long-term successful relationship relating to the marketing and distribution of a pharmaceutical product. Three amicable negotiation sessions involving individuals representing each party who had known one another during the course of the business relationship occurred but were unsuccessful. The main sticking point involved the interpretation of a key provision (and two other minor provisions) regarding the winding down of the relationship. Counsel requested a mediation that would begin with a full-fledged evaluation of the key disputed issue and then proceed with a facilitative process because the success of the business dissolution hinged on the interpretation of the wind-down provisions, mainly the key provision.

The aforementioned process was agreed upon by counsel, the parties, and the mediator and memorialized in a mediation agreement that all signed. The mediator was sent documents to interpret all the provisions at issue. After studying the materials, the mediator made the requisite determinations on each issue and prepared reasons for each that would be orally delivered at the mediation.

Both parties had senior management present at the mediation. The mediation began with a joint session where the mediator reiterated the process the parties and counsel requested, and asked if the parties had any questions or concerns about the process as well as any last-minute objections. Hearing none, the mediator began in caucus with the party who had the most to lose on the key provision.[49] The mediator provided a full interpretation (relevant facts and law, and a careful analysis) of the key provision to the CEO of that party and other senior business executives who had traveled from Europe. The CEO and senior executives listened intently to the evaluation and expressed appreciation for it then, and later, when the parties settled. Part of the preparation for this evaluative process, however, was having outside counsel prepared to hear an evaluation in real time that went counter to their position.

As suggested, this evaluative mediation was a carefully planned and executed process, agreed upon by all of the stakeholders, and aimed at providing the decision makers with thoughtful information and analysis that they could use to get beyond the impediment of the parties' differing interpretations of the key contractual provision.

49. The mediator addressed the other two provisions in caucus with the other side.

How important is judicial experience in the mediation context? Like so many other factors, it depends on the dispute, the parties, and the former jurist. Not all judges are alike; they have distinctive styles and skill sets that must be taken into consideration. Depending on the parties, a former judge may add a layer of credibility to the process and make otherwise reluctant parties more comfortable with it. A former jurist is also well suited to provide an evaluative perspective that can assist the parties in weighing the strengths and weaknesses of their cases. Some former judges favor an evaluative style and often counsel will assume that is the style the judge will use in the mediation. If counsel have used the former judge before, the assumption is likely correct. If it is a former judge that they have not used before, counsel should inquire about the judge's style when they contact him or her. There are retired judges who *do not want* to conduct settlement conferences; they want to conduct a facilitative mediation.

Mediation style and process go hand in glove. Thus, when selecting a mediator, counsel should have discussed the kind of process they want so that, when they are investigating mediator candidates, they can inquire about whether the mediator is willing to work with them on the process contemplated. Some questions to ask mediator candidates may include:

- What is your approach or philosophy toward the mediation process? Do you adhere to a particular process and why?[50] Or, do you have a number of tools in your toolkit that can be used as appropriate for different situations?
- How flexible are you to modify a "typical" process? Ask for actual examples of that flexibility and creativity. Let the candidate know what the parties have in mind for the process.
- Based on information that I can share with you about the dispute, what suggestions do you have for conducting the mediation, including dealing with [describe party issues or novel circumstances]? Invite the candidate to describe how they have dealt with similar challenges in the past.

Mediators often are helpful in facilitating the exchange of information between the parties before and during the mediation session. If the parties have the information they need, it is a helpful step in the direction of settlement and can curtail the need for spending time and money to obtain it in

50. Mediators have varying approaches to the mediation session; for example, some mediators keep the parties together in a joint session the entire time, while some do so only as long as possible, and others do not use joint sessions at all, or on an as-needed basis. Likewise, some mediators provide counsel and their party representatives the opportunity to give opening statements, while others hold an introductory joint session to review mediation basics and ground rules, and then they go right into private caucuses.

discovery. Counsel should inquire whether the mediator candidates are willing to facilitate the exchange of information and how they have been able to do this in other cases.

In sum, whether counsel ultimately consider a mediator *good* or *bad* often begins with (see Appendix):

- Identifying what the parties need from a mediator for a particular case (e.g., credentials, style, skills)
- Compiling a list of mediators who may satisfy those needs and interviewing them to determine if they, in fact, do
- Communicating to mediator candidates what the parties are looking for (e.g., "We want someone to bang heads." "We do not want a touchy-feely mediator." "We want a settlement conference approach.") so that the candidate understands the expectations of the parties
- Obtaining references from the candidates and contacting the references to confirm further that the mediator is likely to meet the required needs
- Selecting a mediator that best fits the parties' most important identified needs

IV. Commencing the Mediation Process—The Planning Conference

Once the parties have chosen a mediator, counsel and the mediator should meet on a call or videoconference to plan a mediation process that is tailored to help the parties resolve their dispute. Insofar as mediation is a flexible process, the original plan may ultimately vary somewhat to meet the parties' needs. Mediators typically initiate the joint planning call or videoconference,[51] but if the mediator does not do so, counsel should request one. Similarly, if the mediator does not send to counsel a list of items to be addressed during the planning conference or a draft mediation agreement with such items set forth, counsel should request one from the mediator. The

51. Joint teleconferences or videoconferences after the joint planning call may be used to confirm that the necessary information counsel agreed to exchange is being exchanged; revisit the mechanics of the mediation (e.g., use of presentations, content for mediation statements, or the date when a particular defendant will mediate in the case of multiple defendants); confirm the attendance of business participants; and address any other issues that may affect the mediation process. Ex parte conferences may be used to discuss concerns about proposed mediation participants, the planned process, and the mediation statements. Both the initial planning conference and subsequent conferences are part of the mediation processes intended to produce an organized and productive mediation session.

topics typically covered in a pre-mediation joint planning conference are set forth and discussed briefly in the following sections.[52]

A. The Nature of the Dispute and Relevant Background

The parties should provide to the mediator a general overview of the case (not an oral argument) including the legal and factual issues in dispute and the procedural posture of the dispute (e.g., status of discovery). This information often helps the mediator understand the dispute to be mediated (e.g., court deadline for the mediation, need for information exchange, the kind and content of mediation statements—in view of court submissions, complexity of the dispute). The mediator may also want to know the scope of the issues to be mediated and the history between the parties. This information may inform the mediator about whether (1) there are other issues or disputes between the parties that they want mediated; (2) there is progress to build upon from prior settlement discussions; and (3) past impediments to resolution can be addressed in the mediation. Furthermore, counsel should inform the mediator about the status of any pending litigation or other proceedings (e.g., ITC, PTO, foreign tribunals) involving the parties and the subject matter of the present dispute, especially if the parties want to settle all the disputes between them (i.e., a "global settlement").

B. Information Exchange

It is not uncommon in IP/Technology cases for the parties to seek certain information for the mediation, commonly financial or information related to calculating damages. The amount and kind of information may depend upon factors including the legal claims and the extent of discovery that has occurred in a pending case. Before the planning conference, the parties should try to work out any information exchange issues. If that does not occur, then counsel should raise the need for information at the conference. The mediator may be able to facilitate the information exchange. Even if one or both parties are not willing to exchange the requested information before the mediation session, the mediator may encourage them to bring such information to the mediation session, because they may be more willing to share it later in the process when its relevance and need for finalizing a settlement is apparent or critical.

52. Other issues that may be discussed at the initial conference are the mediator's fees and payment arrangements, any agreement that the parties will need to sign, particularly in ad hoc mediations (e.g., covering fees and payment, confidentiality, the agreed-upon process, general expectations), and any special needs that the parties have.

C. Mediation Style and Process

As mentioned earlier, counsel should revisit with the mediator the kind of mediation style (e.g., facilitative, evaluative, or a combination) they want as well as the general process for the mediation session and obtain confirmation that the mediator is comfortable with both. Counsel and the mediator should also discuss at the conference whether there will be an opening joint session and the nature of it. As discussed in Section VII.A, in some cases, the level of acrimony between the parties suggests that any form of a joint session is not advisable. In other cases, a joint session may constitute a meet and greet with the mediator making some opening remarks or it may include opening statements by counsel or the party representatives. It is often the case in IP/Technology mediations that any joint session is followed by the mediator visiting the party representatives and their counsel in their respective conference rooms or in caucus. It is also not uncommon for there to be some sort of joint session during the mediation session (e.g., party representatives meet alone or with the mediator; all the participants meet; a representative from one side joins the mediator to meet with the other side) for a particular purpose. The mediator may raise with counsel at the planning conference the option of such a later joint session during the course of the mediation session and the possible benefits of one to garner feedback (positive or negative) and so that the party representatives can be prepared should the mediator suggest a joint session during the mediation session.

Case in point: In one successful mediation, one of the parties came to the session with the view that the lawyers in the case (their own as well as their opponent's) had been, and would continue to be, obstacles to settlement. The mediator, having learned of this deep-seated concern during ex parte pre-mediation conversations with the principals, decided to hold extensive face-to-face discussions between the lead business representatives with no counsel present. The attorneys got involved during the separate caucuses to make sure the necessary legal terms were included in the negotiations and, later, to hammer out final language, but otherwise were not a part of negotiating the principal terms at all.

D. The Timing and Date for the Mediation Session

The mediator and counsel need to determine how many days to set aside for the mediation session and schedule mutually agreeable dates for it. With regard to the length of the mediation session, while many can be concluded within a day, it is often advisable to have the parties and the mediator reserve two days. There are several advantages to scheduling the extra day. For example, first, it ensures that none of the principals will expect to catch a late afternoon flight the first day, which means the mediation session can continue into the evening if necessary. Second, it allows some breathing room if progress is being made late in the first day but one or both parties need to gather additional information or consult with additional stakeholders not attending the mediation session, or the mediation participants conclude that the negotiations would be more productive after a good night's rest. Even if counsel agree to set aside only one day for the mediation session, they should plan to stay as long as is feasible on that day.[53] Counsel should try to avoid surprising the other side with an arbitrary time limit for departure from the mediation session. More than one mediation session has come to a screeching halt when a necessary participant suddenly announced that he had to be on a 4:00 p.m. flight, leaving the other side feeling frustrated, disrespected, and wary of any future overtures. Counsel should approach the scheduling (e.g., timing, length of time, availability of counsel and decision makers) with as much flexibility as possible to set a conciliatory tone.

E. In-Person Locations

If there is no preexisting agreement that dictates the location of the in-person mediation session, the parties will need to agree on a location. Like the choice of mediator and a date for the mediation session, this is another opportunity for them to build a track record of cooperation that may be helpful when the actual negotiations begin. That does not mean, however, that one party needs to go wherever the other side—or the mediator—wants. The parties' time is very valuable, and it would not be prudent to communicate to one party that its convenience is secondary to that of the opposing party.

Generally, unless there is an acknowledged difference in bargaining position, or one party has concluded that a small compromise at this stage will pave the way for larger compromises by its opponent later, it makes sense to suggest a neutral location in a city that is relatively easy for both parties and the mediator to reach. Other venues for the mediation session include at one of the counsels' offices, at the mediator's office, at a local bar association, or, if the mediation is conducted under the auspices of an ADR organization, at those offices. If the parties are remote and the mediation

53. If parties are traveling from out of town, scheduling an extra day provides the ability to continue the negotiation if the parties are close, or to permit party representatives to have breakfast or talk together *fresh* after a day of negotiations. It is not an uncommon situation that, until the mediation session, neither party has spoken to the other directly, or at least the party representatives who attend have not spoken directly. The party representatives often realize the value of connecting with their counterpart at the mediation session, and the extra time permits that.

session occurs at a locale in between them, conference centers or hotel facilities are possible venues.

F. Videoconferencing

During the pandemic, counsel and parties had few options for conducting mediation sessions other than on a videoconferencing platform. The significant increase in the use of such platforms at that time uncovered shortcomings that platform providers quickly improved, such as those related to security, privacy, breakout rooms, and sharing documents. Since the pandemic, remote mediations generally, including IP/Technology cases, have become a popular way to conduct mediations, evidencing the acceptance and benefits they have to offer (e.g., having preferred decision makers present who might otherwise not be able to travel at the optimum time for the mediation, having a mediator with subject matter or mediation experience conduct the mediation who the parties might not have otherwise selected for geographic and cost reasons). Even when a mediation session is being conducted in person, videoconferencing may also be used when, for example, technical or financial explanations from in-house personnel are needed to clarify issues on the spot.

G. Facilities

Regardless of the location for the mediation session, counsel need to take responsibility for the adequacy of the facilities. Ideally, three rooms should be reserved—one for each of the parties and one for joint sessions (and for the mediator to use when he or she is not meeting with either party). If there are more than two parties and their settlement positions are not necessarily aligned, additional rooms may be needed. If rooms are at a premium, the joint session room may double as one party's separate meeting room. There are several disadvantages to that arrangement, however. First, it deprives the mediator of a separate space. Second, there may be several interparty sessions during the day that would require one party to visit the party that has set up shop in the joint session room, forcing the resident party to scramble to put confidential materials away or cover up white board notes or the like before the meeting. In addition, some parties may get hung up on the perceived symbolism of meeting in one camp or the other rather than on neutral ground. Whoever is arranging the facilities should know about the size and location of the available rooms so that they can assure that the facilities meet the parties' needs and concerns (e.g., some parties do not want their caucus rooms to be adjoining).

The parties will also need to think about how they will arrange for food and beverages over the course of the mediation session. This includes not only the logistics—ordering out versus going out to eat—but also whether and how to take advantage of meals as an opportunity to "break bread" together. Particularly if the mediation session is being held on one party's home turf or at least in a city where the party knows the territory, offering to bring in lunch for everyone, or hosting everyone for dinner the evening before or breakfast the morning of the mediation session, can send a positive message that costs very little, and may yield big returns by helping to break the ice and build some trust between the parties.

Case in point: In one case in which the parties held deep-seated suspicions of each other that threatened to derail any chance of a negotiated resolution, the mediator hosted a breakfast where only the decision makers were present and all discussion of the case itself was forbidden. The attendees discussed their children, travels, hobbies, and favorite books, and in the course of the discussion learned of several mutual interests. The case was still enormously difficult to settle, but the temperature and blood pressure of the participants was significantly lower when the mediation session began after breakfast, and each party was at least able to concede at the outset that it was not the devil in the other room.

Finally, do not forget about equipment. A whiteboard or flip chart in each room is very helpful to talk through points in an offer or counteroffer. If counsel intend to make a presentation to the mediator and/or the other side at the opening session or at any point during the day, and they want to use visual aids in that presentation, check ahead of time to make sure the necessary audiovisual equipment will be available. If the mediation session is held at the mediator's offices, do not assume he will have a computer projector or screen. Counsel may have to bring their own, or bring printouts of the presentation for the parties and the mediator. Also check on high-speed internet availability because access to online resources and email is often required.

H. Party Representatives and Settlement Authority

One of the most key issues to ascertain at the planning conference or shortly thereafter is whether the necessary decision makers from each side will be attending. Having the appropriate people at the mediation session is critical to a successful outcome. That includes ensuring that the party representatives in attendance have full settlement authority.[54] Furthermore, the

54. Full settlement authority typically does not mean simply sending persons allowed to accept or offer a minimum or maximum dollar amount. Rather, the party representatives should be individuals who can make independent decisions and have the knowledge necessary to generate and consider creative solutions.

identities of any non-parties with an interest in or influence on the outcome of the litigation or settlement (e.g., investors, litigation funders, ratifiers, indemnifiers) should be disclosed. In such situations, counsel should be prepared to discuss the need for their involvement in the mediation process. For example, if a parent company, board of directors, investor, or influencer will need to approve a settlement, the attending party representative should have sufficient authority such that those other sources of authority or influence are likely to approve the settlement negotiated at the mediation session. Similarly, the opposing party should know sufficiently before the mediation session that a final approval or review from others outside the mediation session is necessary even if a resolution is reached at the session.

If a business arrangement is even a possibility to settle the dispute, it should be identified and explored very early in preparing for the mediation session, as it would likely involve a new set of stakeholders and very possibly a separate negotiation within a party's own company to resolve how income, liability, and control in connection with the deal would be allocated among the stakeholders.

Case in point: Mediation in a patent case was scheduled after the parties completed their initial exchange of documents. Because of their mutually exclusive beliefs regarding liability, neither side was hopeful that mediation was worthwhile, and both were very hesitant to mediate at that time. During caucuses with each side, the defendant, a smaller, privately held company, disclosed that it was interested in merging with a larger business, while the plaintiff wanted to expand into areas where the defendant had expertise. This information led to exploratory discussions between the principals during the first mediation session and further meetings thereafter. Those negotiations achieved settlement by the defendant merging with the plaintiff and becoming one of its business units, with the defendant's CEO as head of that unit. The parties would have forfeited this opportunity and incurred unnecessary expense if they had mediated later. Moreover, the trust required to negotiate such an arrangement would have eroded if the parties had continued to litigate. This example likewise demonstrates the importance of having the appropriate decision makers in attendance at the mediation session, and it shows that focusing on money alone may be a myopic approach to settlement.

Also, the parties will want to know if principals of the same or similar perceived level within their respective companies will attend. This can often be an issue when the two parties are of very different sizes. If one of the parties is a small company whose decision maker in attendance will be the company owner, but the other party is a large corporation whose ranking decision maker is the mid-level manager for an involved product line, the small company may be less impressed by the fact that the manager has the necessary authority than by the perception that the big corporation on the other side is not taking the mediation, or it, as seriously as it should. In large companies, an executive manager may not have the time or the in-depth knowledge of the dispute to be willing or able to add value to the mediation process. If counsel believe, for example, that the party representative for the other side will not be effective for any reason (e.g., is not likely to have full settlement authority, personality issues), raise the issue with the mediator on an ex parte call as soon as possible before the mediation session.

I. Written Statements

The mediator and counsel should jointly decide whether pre-mediation statements are required, what their length and format should be, and whether the statements will be sent to the mediator alone (ex parte) or exchanged with the opposing party, or both (ex parte and exchanged). More on the content of pre-mediation statements is discussed later in Section VI.

J. Confidentiality

Counsel should clarify with the mediator, opposing counsel, and their respective teams the confidentiality terms pertaining to the mediation, which generally preclude any use, discussion, or disclosure, to the court (in a pending case) or otherwise of anything said in connection with the mediation. Confidentiality terms may be included in the mediator's mediation agreement (when the parties have engaged the mediator on an ad hoc basis), in a standstill and confidentiality agreement, as part of the rules of an ADR provider (when the parties have used their services to engage a mediator and adopted their rules), in an ADR provision (if the parties are in a contractual relationship), or a tribunal's rules (e.g., court, ITC) when the parties have instituted the mediation under the rules of a tribunal. If there is a protective order in the case, parties sometimes ask the mediator to sign whatever declaration is required by the protective order if there is any chance confidential or highly confidential information will be communicated to the mediator.

V. Preparing for Success

Ben Franklin is credited with saying, "By failing to prepare you are preparing to fail." All too often counsel approach the mediation process as one meriting little preparation. Considering that mediation can be, and often is, a case-dispositive event, responsible counsel ought to use the same care in preparing for a mediation session that they would in preparing for a major hearing.

Unpreparedness can seriously hamper a party's ability to negotiate, including (1) assessing the merits of proposals; (2) making informed proposals; (3) analyzing the best and worst alternatives to a negotiated agreement (i.e., best alternative to a negotiated agreement (BATNA), worst alternative to a negotiated agreement (WATNA)); (4) assessing the parties' business needs and interests; and (5) generating creative solutions—each important to the mediation process. Preparing for a mediation session is different than preparing for trial.

In mediation, the goal is not to have a winner and a loser but two winners—parties who have had important needs and interests shared and met. Although counsel and the party representatives will certainly inform the mediator about the strengths of their case and the weaknesses of their opponent's case, they will equally need to consider the opposite realities.

Proper preparation initially involves counsel preparing himself or herself before involving the party representatives in the preparation. Both aspects of that preparation may involve a number of hours over a period of several weeks before the mediation session, homework between preparation sessions by the party representatives and counsel, and even an opportunity for role-playing so that party representatives attending the mediation session can become comfortable with a facilitated negotiation. Given the stakes, counsel should undertake preparation with a thoughtful plan.

Moreover, preparedness demonstrates to the opposing party, its counsel, and the mediator a party's level of commitment to resolving the dispute and the likely trial preparation that will ensue if the matter is not resolved. Lack of preparation is often evident to the other side (and the mediator). Experience shows that, if an unprepared party loses its audience (i.e., opposing party and its counsel) as a result, it may be difficult or even impossible to regain it.

Summarized here are items to consider in preparing for the mediation session starting with counsel preparation followed by preparing the party representatives.

A. Counsel Preparation

To prepare party representatives for the mediation session, it is critical for counsel to prepare themselves so that preparation of party representatives is effective. Consider the following nonexclusive checklist of topics counsel should consider in preparing themselves.

1. Review Relevant Procedures

Mediation in IP/Technology cases often occurs because a pre-dispute resolution clause in a contract between the parties provides for it. The parties may have expressly included in the clause process steps (e.g., time for choosing the mediator and holding the mediation) and/or adopted mediation rules from an ADR institution. The mediation clause may also be a condition precedent for arbitration, which may affect the timing of the mediation. If the mediation is conducted under the auspices of a court, it is likely to have mediation procedures in place that counsel should review.[55] If there is no contractual relationship between the parties or if the parties have a contractual relationship but there is no mediation provision in the contract, the parties may develop ad hoc procedures or adopt rules that set forth procedures for the mediation process.

2. Identify Sources of Relevant Information

Identify relevant business and technical employees (other than party representatives attending the mediation session) as additional sources of information to prepare for the mediation session. These individuals may be able to provide information about the opponent and counsel representing the party. For example, in contrast to the party representatives attending the mediation, they may have more intimate knowledge about day-to-day operations and strategic planning for the affected business, including the future direction of the business and plans for the involved IP and products at issue. In patent matters, for example, business and technical employees can provide invaluable assistance in fashioning a design-around or providing information concerning the phasing out of an accused product or process. Similarly, in a trademark dispute, those individuals can develop proposed designs and provide guidance regarding the phaseout period and the costs related to new advertising and promotion.

3. Gather Key Facts and Perform Relevant Analyses

A consensus published in the CPR Report indicated that full discovery is not necessary for a successful mediation. "If the parties have sufficient information (from initial discovery or the cooperative exchange of information) to evaluate each other's cases, if counsel know and respect one another, and if the parties are motivated to settle, mediation can be effective."[56] Thus, in

---

55. For example, the U.S. District Court for the Eastern District of Texas has a Court Annexed Mediation Plan. *See Court Annexed Mediation Plan*, E.D. Tex., https://txed.uscourts.gov/?q=court-annexed-mediation-plan (last visited Mar. 23, 2025); *see also* Standing Order Governing All Matters Referred to a Magistrate Judge for Alternative Dispute Resolution/Mediation (D. Del. Jan. 20, 2016), https://www.ded.uscourts.gov/sites/ded/files/chambers/StandingOrderforADR-Mediation%20%281%29_0.pdf; *Procedures for Voluntary Mediation Program for Lanham Act Cases*, N.D. Ill., https://www.ilnd.uscourts.gov/ViewRuleDetails.aspx?nbMuy18vodc= (last visited Mar. 23, 2025) (establishing mediation program for all cases filed under the Lanham Act).

56. CPR Report, *supra* note 16, at 13.

preparing for mediation, counsel should think strategically about what they need and why.

The information parties need will differ from case to case depending upon the kind and size of the case, what is at stake, what the parties have learned through discovery, what information is publicly available,[57] and what information the parties have gathered on their own.[58]

Where the parties are seeking information from one another to prepare for a mediation session and are concerned about disclosing it, they need to consider that, if litigation ensues or continues, they will likely have to produce it.[59] A party can enlist the assistance of the court, in a pending matter, to compel focused discovery for purposes of the mediation (particularly when the court has mandated that the parties mediate). Depending on the case (e.g., the relationship of the parties including counsel), there are various ways for parties to obtain information for a mediation session, including:

- Having in-house or outside counsel call their counterpart directly to request the necessary information while showing receptiveness to provide information requested of them
- Seeking the assistance of the mediator to broker an exchange of the relevant information
- Providing information (e.g., financial data) in summary form, with the agreement that any settlement agreement would include a representation as to its accuracy
- Providing the information only to outside counsel or a key person attending the mediation
- Bringing the information to the mediation session even if a party is not willing to provide it before the session; when parties acknowledge that progress may be impeded when information is lacking, they often reevaluate the prudence of withholding the information[60]

---

57. Some parties may refuse initially to provide certain information, unaware of the fact that all or some of the information is publicly available. If the requesting party has done a thorough investigation and found at least part of the information it is seeking, it can use what it has found to approach the party and/or the mediator to obtain the additional information sought.

58. See Chapter 3, Section II.B, Step 2—Informal Factual Review, discussing some of the publicly available sources of information in IP/Technology cases.

59. In mediating cases involving nonpracticing entities (NPEs), a party will sometimes turn information over early to the NPE to debunk information the NPE has that may be driving the lawsuit against that party (e.g., if sales are lower than assumed). In other cases, parties flatly refuse to provide information to NPEs in conjunction with a mediation, preferring the discovery process of litigation to any voluntary exchange.

60. In some circumstances the parties may have some concerns about exchanging information in the context of a mediation. Those concerns may be addressed in

Chapter 3, which discusses early case assessment in IP/Technology cases, instructs counsel and parties on how to prepare for mediation in both early- and late-stage disputes, including what facts to collect and analyses to perform. Furthermore, Chapter 4 discusses how parties can perform an early damages assessment to, among other things, prepare for mediation.

Another category of "facts" to address is any history between the parties, including prior business relationships, dealings, contracts, and how they might have been negotiated and who were involved in the negotiations. Similarly, explore any disputes related to those past relationships and, if any, how they were settled and by whom. In addition, learn whether there were any prior disputes between the parties regarding the current subject matter before you were retained and, if so, who was involved and what prevented settlement. This historical information may help you guide your party representatives regarding who should be (or should not be) the party representatives at the mediation session, understand what kind of negotiator the opponent is, and appreciate prior impediments to settlement.

4. Bring a List of Material Terms and a Draft Settlement Agreement

If the parties reach an agreement at the mediation session, they often sign a term sheet, followed shortly by executing formal settlement documents. Even when signing a term sheet, the parties will want to ensure that they have addressed all of the material terms and resolved whatever issues were in dispute. Counsel should consider drafting a set of stand-alone issues or terms before the mediation and sharing them with the mediator and possibly the other side to ensure that all issues are addressed. Alternatively, drafting a settlement agreement incorporating possible terms and conditions for the particular dispute is another way to provide a list.[61] Having the draft settlement agreement at your disposal expedites settlement if the parties are ready to sign it. The following list is intended to provide a general sample of the kinds of terms that may be implicated in settling IP/Technology disputes:

- Scope of any license
- Payment amount(s) and payment terms (e.g., up-front or in installments with or without interest, running royalty percentage, royalty base, any milestones, minimum payments or caps)

---

a mediation agreement (common in ad hoc mediations) signed by the parties or their counsel and the mediator or in a confidentiality agreement signed by the parties.

61. If a license, assignment, or other agreement is possible, counsel should draft and bring it to the mediation.

- Future business relationship terms, IP included (e.g., in a patent matter, whether an entire portfolio or family, continuation-in-part and divisional applications are included)
- Taxes (who pays and whether the settlement is net of foreign taxes)
- Transfer of ownership, control issues, and assignability
- Admissions (e.g., infringement, validity, or enforceability)
- Any most-favored-nation (MFN) clause
- Scope of any release
- ADR (how future disputes will be handled)
- Confidentiality (with or without teeth, any press release allowed, and contents of a press release)
- Marking (in a patent case)

5. Learn Relevant Party Business Interests

A party's interests in settling a case often change over time. That may result from changes in circumstances arising from within or outside the company. Moreover, determining relevant business interests related to the outstanding dispute can be challenging when party representatives are busy and focused on their daily responsibilities (e.g., meetings, traveling, working in different time zones). Also, it is often the case that party representatives may want or need to consult with others at their company before confirming what important interests are at stake in the dispute. These individuals may include personnel from all corporate strata and areas (e.g., finance, business, product development) as well as interested parties (e.g., investors). Accordingly, as part of their preparation for the mediation session, counsel should not only explore business interests with their party representatives but, also, prioritize those interests with party feedback. This exercise is core to formulating negotiation strategies and should be updated during the course of the dispute. Times to discuss interests and priorities may include at least preparing the mediation statement(s) and preparing the party representative for the mediation session.

To learn a party's relevant interests, be prepared to ask questions including:

- What business interests and objectives are at stake in the dispute that are important to the company generally and/or the involved business unit[62]—and how should the interests be prioritized?

62. It is not uncommon in IP/Technology cases for the parties to be involved in multiple disputes (ongoing or threatened) regarding the same products, technologies, trademarks, or patent family in the United States and overseas before various tribunals. Thus, counsel must determine their clients' objectives in resolving these matters. One of the first things counsel needs to discuss with their party representatives is whether their goal is a global settlement or solely the resolution of the case that

- How relevant is the IP and technology to those objectives?
- How might success or failure in the case affect those objectives?
- Does the party have any hidden or private agendas, and, if so, what are they and how might they affect settlement?
- How does the party perceive the future of the relevant industry and their part in it?

The opposing party's objectives are equally important. Analyzing the dynamics of the process from the opposing side's point of view may provide insight into any commonality between the parties upon which to build a settlement. It may also stimulate out-of-the-box options for settlement.

Case in point: In a trademark dispute, the plaintiff was a wheelchair-bound veteran and CEO of his small software company. He had personally designed the entity's mark. He intended to develop sufficient income from the business to help disabled veterans. In the five years the company existed using the mark before the purported infringing logo/name was introduced, it had operated at a loss and was barely functioning on a shoestring budget. The defendant was a medium-sized software company and competed in a similar market to the plaintiff. The similarities between the plaintiff's mark and the accused logo/name were obvious. The plaintiff felt that the defendant's infringement caused confusion, lost profits, and significant damages even though his business never experienced a profit or any substantial sales before the infringement. Further, the geography of the plaintiff's business was limited, while the defendant sold its products throughout the United States and in certain foreign countries. The plaintiff, however, had developed a unique software line in which the defendant had considered expanding.

During mediation, the mediator explained the plaintiff's interest in disabled veterans to the opposition. The defendant's CEO's deceased brother had been a disabled veteran. The parties settled by the defendant agreeing to buy the plaintiff's software products and assisting plaintiff financially in developing new product lines for the defendant, as well as purchasing the mark, with credit to the plaintiff noted on the defendant's literature and website. In addition, a percentage of profits the defendant earned from the plaintiff's software line was contributed to agreed-upon veterans' charities. By recognizing what was important to the plaintiff and not just concentrating on standard settlement approaches, the defendant garnered a positive commercial result and expanded its software services. Plaintiff salvaged a floundering business, developed a profitable business arrangement, and satisfied his charitable interest.

---

resulted in the mediation. If the former, it will be essential not only to gather all of the necessary information related to those other disputes and to consult with essential decision makers, but also to alert the other side that your client wants to pursue a global settlement so that they are also fully prepared to negotiate those issues (or communicate that they do not agree to that increased scope).

6. Know the Limits of What Information You Can Share with Your Party Representatives

As counsel prepares to spend time with their party representatives discussing, for example, the strengths and weaknesses of their opponent's case, how to motivate their opponent to settle, and financial terms, it is easy to forget that some of the best information a counsel has may be subject to a protective order and cannot be shared with the party representative. Review the boundaries of the other side's confidential information. If counsel anticipates that it will be difficult to have a meaningful dialogue with its party representative about settlement without sharing some key confidential facts with that person, consider asking the other side for a limited, reciprocal exception to the protective order that would allow each party to share specified information with key members of their respective teams for the purpose of evaluating the case and preparing for the mediation session.

B. Selecting the Party Representatives—The Negotiation Team

Section C addresses preparing the party representatives, but first, you need to select who that will include. As with any business negotiation, a party's chances of a successful mediation outcome will depend in large part on having the right people involved—individuals who have the necessary interest, knowledge, skill set, mindset, disposition, and authority, and who will take the time to prepare.[63] Determining who they are, however, may be difficult. Mediators require the attendance of decision maker(s) from each of the parties who have full authority to act on behalf of the parties, including the authority to negotiate a resolution of the matter and to respond to developments during the mediation process. In deciding who has the requisite characteristics, counsel often must rely on party input. Therefore, the party needs to be educated and have a full understanding about the mediation process. If the right people are not present, mediation can be defeated before it begins or become an exercise in frustration. That said, figuring out whom to avoid is often as important as whom to include.

With this in mind, where there have been previous productive negotiations between the parties, consider whether the individuals who participated

63. With pressure in companies to focus efforts on the bottom line, involvement in litigation is typically not viewed as a career-enhancing opportunity. The right players, however, can be persuaded (if counsel take the time to explain to them and their superiors) that their active participation will contribute to the bottom line if the mediation leads to a resolution that serves the company's business objectives and ends or avoids costly litigation.

in those discussions might be proper mediation participants. Where certain individuals have developed a good working rapport, those same individuals should be considered as participants in the mediation. Conversely, if personality clashes or personal animosity have developed during prior negotiations or dealings, it is advisable to have other individuals attend the mediation.

Counsel should also determine if the decision-making process is a group effort, and, if so, which members of the team are essential.[64] As discussed later in this chapter, select party representatives based on an individual's ability to make a meaningful contribution to the process, and not just on an individual's title. Consider whether certain information sources, such as key employees (e.g., IT staff, engineers, business managers) or interested parties (e.g., investors, board members, other party counsel), with direct knowledge of the underlying facts and issues, should be present or available for consultation during the mediation session.

Case in point: In a patent mediation, the defendant brought its mediating attorney to the mediation, in addition to in-house counsel, trial counsel, and a managing business representative. The mediating attorney was not a patent litigator or a prosecution counsel, but had been employed by the defendant in other matters to assist in negotiations. He was thoroughly familiar with the defendant's business and the industry involved. Once his function and involvement were explained to the plaintiff's counsel and representatives (unruffling feathers and allaying protective order concerns), the mediation proceeded.

At the end of the first session, the parties were $25 million apart on a paid-up license, with the plaintiff advising that further compromise would not occur absent substantial movement by the defendant. Periodic teleconferences occurred thereafter between the mediating counsel and the mediator discussing approaches to break the apparent stalemate. Those approaches were subsequently explored with the plaintiff's representatives and its counsel in separate, private teleconferences. Through this process, the settlement range was narrowed, and, in another mediation session, the matter settled. The matter resolved in part because of the insight and knowledge that the mediating attorney brought to the process and his relationship with the defendant.

---

64. It is essential that each member of the mediation team understands his or her role, including speaking roles and key messages in face-to-face discussions with the other side and the mediator. Most important, the team should talk through and resolve ahead of time any fundamental differences in opinions, for example, about business objectives, evaluation of the case, willingness to go to trial, and openness to alternative business arrangements. Indeed, when selecting who should attend the mediation session, keep in mind the old adage "less is more." It is very difficult to coordinate effectively a "team" of more than four or five people. And if consensus is not possible on all issues, at least make sure the team understands the importance of not airing that split in front of the mediator or the other side.

As exemplified in the case in point, the key advisor was the mediating attorney, whose prior experience with the party was invaluable.

Certain participants may be less helpful to the negotiation, but, at the same time, necessary for the mediation. The company's in-house legal department may be overly interested in defending its contracts and the IP it procured and, thus, ideally, should not be the sole party representative at the mediation session. Furthermore, in-house counsel may be more focused on a purely legal approach, such as taking a license, and they may fail to explore other more creative business solutions. Businesspeople with knowledge of past and present relationships are helpful in broadening and crafting solutions for settlement.

With this background in mind, consider the usefulness of possible participants.

1. The Business Lead

First and foremost, the team must include someone with full authority to negotiate a resolution and who will commit to attending the mediation session as planned (in-person or remote).[65] The absentee decision maker who has not "lived" the process with the other participants often simply second-guesses the offers and counteroffers and undermines the hard work done by the parties who participated in real time. Furthermore, a party's choice of business lead conveys to an opponent that the party takes them and the process seriously and the person is there to get the case settled.

The business lead must be someone who can see the big picture and should be in a position to consider and, ideally, agree to creative business solutions. That said, even if the business lead indicates that a creative solution is of interest, such as one company acquiring some or all of the assets of the other or the parties entering into a joint development agreement, it is understood that such resolutions would require due diligence and multiple levels of approval by both parties. The business lead needs to be patient, relatively free of emotional baggage related to the dispute, a good listener, and articulate, including being prepared to speak compellingly on the importance of the dispute to the company.

Occasionally, the person whose title suggests he or she ought to be the business lead (and whom, therefore, the other side expects will attend the mediation session) will not be the best person for the mediation. Consider then having another individual with the necessary knowledge, temperament, and negotiating skills on the team. The "titled" business lead can still play

65. In the case of remote mediations where all of the participants are present in the same space and at the same time, having the decision maker(s) present for the entirety of the mediation session has similar value to having them in person for the entirety at an in-person mediation session.

an important role by attending, in so doing assuring the other side and the mediator that he or she has the necessary authority (both real and apparent) and the company is serious about resolving the matter.

2. Additional Business Team Members

In addition to the business lead, a party may need other members of the business team, for example, the head of research and development (R&D), the marketing manager, or the finance manager, at the mediation session, or at least have them involved in the preparation and easily reachable throughout the mediation. For example:

- If the mediation involves an alleged misappropriation of a party's trade secrets, the head of R&D can discuss the acceptable metes and bounds of an agreement by the defendant to cease and desist.
- The head of R&D may also be a key team member in a patent dispute mediation if design-arounds are in play or where settlement could include a joint development agreement.
- The marketing manager in a trademark dispute can discuss how quickly the company could realistically transition to a new mark.
- The finance manager can provide historical information about sales and profits. That person can also help analyze the comparative return on investment of a prospective settlement versus continuing litigation in view of available information or educated assumptions about, for example, price erosion, declining market share, litigation costs, likelihood of success, anticipated royalty payments, the cost of converting to a new design or trademark, timing of payments, currency translation issues, and how any receipts or payouts would be treated from a tax and accounting perspective.

3. The Lead Outside Trial Counsel

Lead trial counsel who knows the case well, is confident in the merits, and has the trial experience to be effective with a jury is a good choice to lead the mediation team, especially if substantive opening statements are planned. At the same time, this person should be someone who has demonstrated competence, skills, and experience in mediation, and who respects the mediation process and the role of the corporate decision makers in it. Lead trial counsel must understand that mediation is not something he or she needs to win—*it is the party's show.*[66]

---

66. Indeed, there are lead trial counsel who know themselves too well and choose not to attend mediations because they are aware that their litigation prowess and

4. In-House IP and Business Counsel and Technical Experts

In-house IP and business counsel are individuals who understand the business and the business objectives, as well as the technology at issue. They are trusted by the business lead and they know the ins and outs of negotiating and drafting licensing, coexistence, or other IP/Technology agreements. However, they may also be vested in defending their work product. In-house IP counsel may have a hard time being objective and may dismiss potential flaws with regard to the issued or registered IP and prosecution history. Inventors often have an emotional investment in the patent—it is, after all, their creation. Excluding inventors from mediation entirely, however, is unlikely, especially when they are employed by the plaintiff. Similarly, the owner who designed or built the business on a trademark is emotionally attached to that mark and will look for extensive protection of it. Such individuals bring unique challenges to a mediation but can be helpful (i.e., "on call") when considering settlement options.

5. Outside Experts

Almost uniformly, experience indicates that bringing experts—particularly damages experts—to a mediation session is generally not helpful. It paints the process with an adversarial brush and telescopes a *trial win* starting point for negotiations. Thus, experts are generally not encouraged to be involved in the mediation process. Alternatively, providing a summary of the expert's reasoning as part of the analysis in the mediation statement may be productive.

Case in point: In a patent infringement mediation involving an eye medication, the perfect storm occurred. The plaintiff's representatives at the mediation session were the inventor, the patent prosecuting attorney (who was also trial counsel), local counsel, and the consultant for damages. With these particular participants, no progress occurred during the first session, and all the participants found the experience frustrating. The inventor and the patent prosecuting attorney were defensive about the validity of the patent at issue; trial counsel was adamant about winning; and the damages consultant was fueling the damages fire. Glaringly absent was any business focus on getting a deal done. The matter ultimately settled, but only after the plaintiff's business representatives became directly involved and negotiated with their counterparts on the defense side during a second session.

---

approach do not fit in a mediation process. Insofar as many parties opt not to have an opening statement made by lead trial counsel or not to have an opening statement at all, the absence of lead trial counsel is not a downside. In the absence of lead trial counsel, the party representative can be well served with another person on the trial team who is an adept mediation advocate, such as the "client minder" who may oversee all of the party's matters for the law firm or in-house counsel who knows the case well.

C. Preparing the Party Representatives

No responsible attorney would show up with her party representatives for an important evidentiary hearing without proper preparation. Yet many otherwise responsible and litigation-savvy counsel devote little time to preparing their client (the decision maker) for the mediation process, even though such preparation is critical to a successful resolution of their dispute. Indeed, one of the first missteps that counsel and their representatives make is that they collapse the mediation process into the mediation session instead of optimizing the joint and ex parte conferences and communications that occur before the mediation session. Preparation of party representatives is essential to engage them in the process, to avoid frustration, to meet their expectations, and to the successful resolution of the dispute. There is no need for party representatives to be needlessly frustrated and disappointed, for example, if they expect one type of ADR process and receive another, or if they expect something out of the process or the mediator and receive something different.

> **Case in point**: About 30 minutes after the mediation of a patent infringement case was scheduled to begin, an attorney for one of the parties came hurriedly into the mediator's offices. The party representative had been waiting at the venue for at least 45 minutes without his attorney. The party had never participated in a mediation session. The other side and its attorney were also made to wait by the other attorney's lateness. The late-arriving attorney made no apologies to anyone and asked the mediator if he could meet alone with his party representative because he had not yet met with him regarding the mediation. To ensure that the party received some preparation for the mediation, the mediator began in caucus first with the other side. That short amount of time was not sufficient to adequately prepare the party representative, but it was better than nothing. The case nonetheless settled at the end of a long day.

> **Case in point**: A large multinational company was in a dispute with a much smaller consulting company over a contract that received a significant amount of press. Representing the large company at the mediation were three outside counsel, the in-house counsel who worked on the contract, in-house litigation counsel, and the party representative, a Ph.D. involved in the performance of the contract. The in-house litigation counsel dominated the discussions in joint sessions and caucuses and overshadowed the party representative. When the mediator insisted that the representative answer some questions related to the contract and the business, the representative sheepishly admitted that he did not know why he was there, nor was he prepared for any form of negotiations.

Mediation is a process that, by its very nature, takes time. Parties often want to tell their side of the story, explain their case strengths, and feel that they have been heard. Forming and evaluating proposals and counter-proposals and dealing with stumbling blocks when the parties' trust and confidence in each other is strained are all part of the process. A well-prepared party representative is in a much better frame of mind and negotiation position than one who is ill-prepared or not prepared at all.

In IP/Technology cases, party representatives, whether representing large or small companies, often hold a significant position in the company. Notwithstanding how busy they are and how inaccessible they can be, if counsel make clear that mediation is a process that can dispose of a dispute relatively quickly and inexpensively, and meet important business interests, experience has shown that party representatives will gladly make the time to meet with counsel and to prepare as required. Here are some ideas for preparing party representatives for participating at the mediation session.

1. Explain What Mediation Is (and Is Not) and What to Expect

It is not uncommon for well-educated individuals to confuse mediation and arbitration. Counsel need to ensure that party representatives understand that the mediation process is a facilitated negotiation and is distinct from arbitration and litigation. The representatives should understand that the mediator is not an arbitrator or a judge, and a mediation does not result in a decision. And, although it is important to help the mediator understand the strengths and weaknesses of the parties' cases, the objective is not to convince the mediator that one side is right and the other side is wrong.

Case in point: In a contract dispute, the mediator asked an attorney for one of the parties before the in-person mediation session if the party representative participating at the session (a senior vice president) had experience with the mediation process. In this regard, the mediator offered several times to talk with the representative so that he would be comfortable at the mediation session with the agreed-upon mediation process. The attorney assured the mediator that the representative had a lot of experience with mediation. After the initial joint session (during which counsel made opening statements) and a few caucuses later, the representative was becoming impatient. He told the mediator that prior mediations went much faster and did not take all day. The mediator asked the representative to describe those prior experiences and it turned out that the experience the representative had was with arbitration, not mediation. In preparation for the mediation, this was not uncovered by his attorney. That confusion was cleared up at the mediation, but not the avoidable frustration.

A word to the wise without offending a party's representative: learn whether the party representative has, in fact, had prior experience with the mediation process, understand generally the circumstances of that prior experience and the representative's perspectives of the mediation process, and discuss what differences may occur in the upcoming mediation session.

Counsel should review the agreed-upon plan for the mediation session that they discussed with their respective parties and the mediator during the planning conference (e.g., joint sessions, if so, when, caucusing). For example, if the parties had agreed to commence a mediation session with a joint session and some form of opening statements, counsel should point out that the joint session presents a prime opportunity for the parties to observe both the demeanor and style of the opposing party and its counsel. Counsel should prepare their party representatives to listen dispassionately while the opposing side is speaking and to refrain from interrupting. Attentive listening and thoughtful observation may lead to increased understanding of the opposing party's approach to the issues in dispute and provide useful information, even if the matter cannot be resolved. The party representatives should also be prepared for caucus sessions with the mediator. Counsel should highlight the importance of caucuses in a mediation session and the opportunity they present for the party representatives to ensure that the mediator understands their interests and priorities, to listen and respond to questions raised by the mediator, and to address points raised by the opposing party.

Party representatives should understand that the mediator will be focusing on them to discern their business interests, formulate proposals, and engage in reality testing. They should be aware that the mediator engages in reality testing with both parties, and that a discussion of the opposing party's positions or business interests does not indicate that the mediator is biased toward that party, as the mediator will be engaging in the same process with the opposing side. Counsel should also discuss with their party representatives the possibility that the mediator may suggest meeting with the principals alone at some point during the process if the mediator thinks such a meeting will increase the likelihood of reaching an agreement.

2. Address the Tempo and Possible Outcomes of the Mediation Session

The tempo of the mediation session may surprise and aggravate a party who is unfamiliar with the mediation process. The pace can seem excruciatingly slow, as one party waits while the mediator caucuses with the other. As with any strategic negotiation, the parties will need time to make tangible progress. Each member of the team should be prepared to spend all day, into the evening, or even the following day, if necessary. The parties should not expect to make that 4:30 p.m. flight home, and each one should demand a commitment from the other that they will not leave until the session has run its course.

Before and at the close of the mediation session, the party representatives should understand that outcomes include (1) signing a term sheet that fully or partially resolves the matter; (2) signing final settlement documents;

(3) continuing negotiations (possibly after overcoming a stumbling block);[67] or (4) acknowledging that an impasse has been reached and continue with another dispute resolution process, such as arbitration. Indeed, even if an impasse is reached, the mediation process can provide tangible benefits to the parties, such as clarifying or narrowing issues to be determined in a later arbitration or litigation, focusing discovery, obtaining information informally that may change a party's strategy, and learning perspectives and business interests that may result in a later settlement.

3. Review the Key Facts

Counsel should review with their party representatives any key facts and documents to ensure that all relevant facts are known and there are no discrepancies. During the course of the mediation session, a party may need to dispel certain factual misconceptions or address incorrect expectations that are impeding settlement. Counsel will also want to confirm that the information he or she gathered is sufficient for making informed proposals and decisions or learn if there is necessary information lacking that is in the hands of others at the company or third parties who need to be contacted before, or made available during, the mediation session.

4. Update Party Representatives on Litigation Status, Costs, Damages Exposure, and Return on Investment

Counsel is in the best position to ensure that their party representatives are current on the latest litigation activities. This often includes sharing the results of an internal document review and interviews with key witnesses, a high-level summary of what has been learned in discovery, the highlights of witness deposition testimony, and any important rulings that may affect either side's case assessment. With this review, counsel can address any necessary adjustments to an objective assessment of the case and desired changes in strategy.

A well-prepared party representative should also have an update on costs incurred and the likely costs ahead. Costs include not only the anticipated fees and expenses (vendor expenses such as costs for e-discovery, experts, and

---

67. The parties could hit a stumbling block simply because they are tired, they need time to think away from the mediation environment, or they need more information. The information may be readily available so that they can schedule a defined break for a specific purpose. If the parties are stuck on their positions regarding a particular issue, they could decide to employ a joint expert to provide a nonbinding evaluation or they may pursue a ruling from the PTO or court that will serve as a reality check.

jury research) but also the intangible costs (party time and distraction during discovery, disruption of customer relationships, and potential intrusion into proprietary information). IP/Technology litigation cost information is available from several sources including past experience in similar cases and the American Intellectual Property Law Association's (AIPLA's) biennial Report of the Economic Survey,[68] which lists the typical costs for IP litigation.

Counsel should analyze with their party representatives the return on litigation investment, taking into account the costs and risks of a case at various points along its lifespan, as well as the value that would be derived if the case proceeds to trial and the parties achieve the verdict/award/order they believe is most likely. Depending on the type of case, that analysis may require information and expertise from a variety of people within the business, including the finance manager, marketing manager, and R&D director, as well as outside experts if the parties have engaged them. Also, party representatives need to consider whether the case may have value beyond the potential award, such as sending a message to other plaintiffs or other potential infringers that the party will not simply roll over in the face of a tough opponent or significant litigation expense.

An attorney representing a defendant (or counterclaim defendant) should also brief their client on their assessment of likely and possible exposure to an award of damages. If a party does not already know, find out who within the business needs to be aware of those projected costs and potential liabilities and make sure they are included in internal preparation meetings.

5. Assess and Discuss the Emotional Hooks on Both Sides

While the underlying disputes in an IP/Technology case may be business and IP/Technology-driven, the obstacles to resolution are often underlying emotional or relationship issues between the parties. There may be, for example, a history of competition between the companies, animosity between the principals, a sense of betrayal about the move of the plaintiff's key employee to work for the defendant, anger that litigation was filed before settlement was attempted, or a past history of failed transactions. Counsel should be aware of these lurking challenges and prepare for the best way to defuse emotions that impede a resolution.

Possible approaches to managing emotional issues include addressing them in an initial joint session in opening comments, at a shared meal or drinks before the session begins (e.g., the evening before), or in a candid description in the ex parte statement to the mediator requesting the mediator's

68. *See Report of the Economic Survey*, AIPLA, https://www.aipla.org/home/news-publications/economic-survey (last visited Mar. 23, 2025).

assistance. Each party should also look at what role emotions play in their view of the case and whether the team members are able to channel those emotions constructively during the process. If a party's business decision maker is volatile or tends to rise to the bait, consider limiting their speaking role, looking for an alternative representative for the mediation session, or pairing them with someone who can temper the emotional representative. Negative emotions that are not properly channeled can undermine a party's interests at the mediation session. They may not only erupt at inappropriate times, but may also disrupt a party's ability to evaluate objectively the risks and merits of the case, possible alternative resolutions, and the other party's proposals.

Case in point: The parties in a mediation had previously settled a patent infringement lawsuit, in which, among other things, the defendant had agreed to stop making the accused product. Thereafter, the former plaintiff learned that the defendant was selling the enjoined product, which was made and shipped into the United States from the defendant's manufacturer in Mexico. On their own, the parties tried to work together to recall the product and quantify the damages but, even though progress was made, mistrust ensued and derailed a resolution. In an ex parte call before the mediation session with the defendant's outside counsel, the counsel admitted to the mediator that the defendant had "f---ed up." He explained that the defendant (a U.S.-based company) had not communicated clearly to its Mexican manufacturer that the accused product should not be made any longer or shipped. The parties agreed to an initial joint session to begin the mediation session that could include remarks from outside counsel and in-house counsel. Although the defendant's outside counsel's remarks were conciliatory throughout, beginning with a sincere apology and an admission that the defendant had "f---ed up," the plaintiff never accepted the apology nor believed the defendant's explanation, and the plaintiff's prior mistrust dominated the negotiations. That said, the case nonetheless settled.

6. Determine the Parties' Business Interests

As mentioned earlier in Section V.C, preparing the party representatives for the mediation session provides counsel with another opportunity (e.g., in addition to the mediation statement) to examine directly with the representatives the key interests at stake in the dispute for the party and, if known, its opponent. The goal at this time—closer to the mediation session—is to obtain updated information from the party in the event that changes within or outside the company have affected a party's prior articulated interests and objectives related to the outstanding dispute.

Because business interests and needs are often the focus in resolving an IP/Technology dispute—to achieve a business outcome that is typically not possible in a court of law[69]—each party must understand its own business goals and, to the extent possible, those of its opponent. Accordingly, when formulating a negotiation strategy before (see Section V.C.8) and implementing it at the mediation session, the offeror should include terms that satisfy not only *its* business objectives but also those of the opponent so that proposals will be seriously considered. In that way, the parties may create a better working relationship and generate better solutions. In updating party objectives, counsel should at least revisit the questions they had used earlier with their party representatives (see inquiries set forth in Section V.A.5) and add other lines of inquiry to dig deep into the key interests at stake in the dispute and the parties' priorities.

Depending upon who the chosen party representatives are, in revisiting party interests for a small company, it may be sufficient for counsel simply to talk with the company's CEO (who may be the party representative).[70] If, however, the dispute involves the business unit of a large company, talking with corporate personnel closely involved with the product, IP, and technology at issue may include the unit's president or senior vice president, relevant scientists, finance managers, and the general counsel or IP counsel. Counsel may obtain relevant current interests about an opponent from those same individuals, as well as information gleaned from recent trade shows, financial and securities filings, presentations at professional or trade association meetings, websites, press releases, and common and prospective customers.

7. Determine Realistic BATNAs and WATNAs[71]

Determining a party's key business interests related to the dispute is important in preparing the party representatives for the mediation session because those decisions will be used in determining realistic BATNAs and WATNAs. That

69. Many mediated settlements are form-fit to the parties' particular needs and circumstances. Such circumstances may include impending mergers or acquisitions, global settlements involving the same IP and products ongoing in various forums, one party acquiring all or part of the other party's business, or the winding down by one party of selling the product of another. Parties may contemplate long-term relationships (e.g., licenses, joint development) or short-term relationships (e.g., licenses long enough to design around a patent, find another trademark, or sell a patented product for one more season before ceasing further sales). Parties may even license or cross-license IP or assign rights completely away.

70. Small companies, in particular, may also have to consider the business interests of others such as investors and a company's board of directors.

71. The parties should assess and discuss their opponent's BATNA and WATNA as well as their own. Parties can obtain the information upon which to base this analysis from a variety of sources including those mentioned previously to investigate an opponent's business interests. Also, a careful read of an opponent's correspondence

is, in preparing the party representatives, counsel must have them consider what success—or failure—will look like if they cannot resolve the matter on acceptable terms. In this regard, the mediator will expect the party representatives to articulate their BATNA and WATNA.[72] One way to think of a party's BATNA is to consider what other options a party has when the deal on the table is not sufficiently favorable to it. A strong, realistic BATNA can provide leverage that permits the party to make the deal happen to its advantage or provide it with a reason to walk away from the mediation session.

Determining a party's BATNA and WATNA also involves looking at the likelihood of success in the litigation and what remedies or adverse consequences would be forthcoming. It might also involve exploring self-help measures (e.g., a design-around (in a patent case) or choosing another trademark (in a trademark dispute)) or any other outcome that a party can derive without the cooperation of the other side. It is important to factor in the odds of those successful outcomes, and the costs associated with achieving them.

Case in point: In the mediation of a patent infringement case, the defendant's representative insisted that his best alternative to the deal on the table was to eliminate certain functions on the accused device, thereby avoiding infringement. The mediator asked the representative the following questions: (1) where would those features be removed (outside or in the United States)—the accused device was made outside the United States; (2) what were the costs of modifying the devices; (3) would the costs to remove the alleged infringing functions increase the price of the device to customers; (4) would the time to modify the devices slow the fulfillment of sales; (5) could the elimination of the features be accomplished without affecting the value of the rest of the device; and (6) would the demand for the device without the patented features be affected and, if so, to what extent. The defendant's representative rethought the feasibility of the alternative. The case ultimately settled.

A realistic and well-defined BATNA comes from planning, preparation, and flexibility. A party may enter the talks with a preconceived idea of the best alternatives available to both parties but must not be wedded to them. Circumstances can change due to new information shared by the parties during the mediation session, information learned by the proposals

---

and litigation filings related to the dispute may also provide insight about an opponent's BATNA and WATNA.

72. Like a party's BATNA, understanding a party's WATNA is one way for a party to assess options and make more informed decisions at the bargaining table. For example, in a patent infringement dispute, a potential finding of invalidity of a currently licensed patent is likely to be a WATNA that a patent owner must take seriously while considering proposals from an opponent.

exchanged at the session, market and political changes, new legislation or court decisions, or internal changes affecting the parties. Such changes can affect the strength of either party's BATNA during the mediation process. When developing BATNAs (before or during the mediation), a party should:

- Consider both its negotiation positions and business interests, and then brainstorm all of the available options that could satisfy its positions and interests.
- Narrow the options to those that are the most promising alternatives and develop them into practical options, and then determine the same from the opponent's perspective.
- Consider the costs (both short- and long-term) of doing the proposed deal versus pursuing the BATNA, if cost is a consideration.[73]
- Evaluate which options, if any, are the most feasible or realistic—something that should be tested lest it give a party a false sense of security.[74]
- Determine which option(s) will be best for a party considering its current state of affairs.

It is not uncommon for a party to devalue a deal in favor of an unrealistic and ill-defined alternative. Counsel, the mediator, or someone other than the party representative (present or not present at the mediation session) should test the reality of such an alternative to lend the proper perspective.

8. Develop a Negotiation Strategy with Party Representatives

Counsel should help their party representatives develop a negotiation strategy for attaining their business goals at the mediation session. As an initial matter, counsel should review with their party representatives the party's negotiation history and any outstanding proposals relating to the dispute. This could avoid a discussion of issues that the parties may have already resolved. Furthermore, particularly if the party representatives were not involved in prior settlement

73. Counsel have an important role to play in making sure their party representatives are being realistic and not merely theoretical in identifying their BATNA and WATNA. For example, as illustrated in the preceding case in point, a design-around may look good on paper but it may take time and resources to engineer or commercialize, and the commercial success of the design-around may be far from clear. And, of course, the plaintiff (or a third party) may have infringement arguments against that new design as well. Likewise, a favorable verdict on infringement may not necessarily mean an injunction will be forthcoming.

74. For example, a trial on a trade secret case may win the battle but lose the war if it results in further exposure of a party's highly sensitive information.

discussions, reviewing the settlement history may bring a new perspective and elicit settlement options not previously considered.

Counsel should generate with their party representatives a range of acceptable negotiated outcomes (possible offers and counteroffers) making sure that, before the mediation session, party representatives obtain the necessary authority to agree to those outcomes. The range should prioritize the possible outcomes and be organized in the form of a settlement matrix that sets out not only what the party deems necessary, but also identifies items that are relatively unimportant to a party that may be of value to the other side (and therefore can serve as bargaining chips). This will help party representatives focus on priorities so that, during the negotiation, they do not inadvertently bargain away something of value to keep something that is expendable.

Furthermore, counsel and party representatives may want to subject their possible offers and counteroffers to reality testing before the mediation session by in-house or outside counsel who are not close to the dispute.[75] Doing so will afford the party representatives feedback about their BATNA and WATNA and whether their range of damages and other terms are reasonable. Often a decision tree analysis helps party representatives gain perspective about the complexity and interrelationship of the issues, the length and cost of litigation or arbitration, and the estimated probability of winning or losing. (See Chapter 5.)

Developing a negotiation strategy also entails counsel working with their party representatives to:

- Determine if relevant information that was not previously disclosed to the opposing party might need to be disclosed to support a proposal and, if so, how such disclosure will be carried out to allay any concerns a party representative may have.
- Determine whether there are any obstacles to potential agreement terms. For example, if a possible settlement may involve periodic reporting to the other side, find out whether the relevant data systems are set up to record and report that information. Or, if a possible settlement may involve a license agreement, determine whether there are any contractual commitments to other parties that may conflict with the prospective deal, such as an existing exclusive supplier relationship or an MFN clause.

---

75. Too often, plaintiffs come to a mediation session increasing their demands from what was last offered in prior settlement negotiations. Rarely is there a change in the facts, law, or circumstances to justify this, and presenting it to the other side often inflames emotions and douses a willingness to be flexible. Likewise, demanding attorney's fees and/or treble damages seldom engenders good faith and flexibility. It is the rare occasion when one party does not want something from the party in the other room. Thus, reconsider a negotiation strategy that is inflexible and fails to take into account an opponent's important needs and interests.

- Determine whether the parties should secure any necessary legal counsel about issues that may arise in connection with possible proposals, including antitrust or unfair competition issues.

VI. Preparing Effective Mediation Statements

Mediation statements are common in IP/Technology mediations and can be prepared for the mediator's eyes only, exchanged with the opposing party, or both.[76] Counsel should prepare such statements with the same focus and attention to detail as they would for any key briefing. The written statements are not only a vehicle to convey information to the other side and/or the mediator, but also an opportunity to establish credibility with the mediator.

Often, where a case is pending in court, parties assume that the mediator can be educated by reviewing court filings (e.g., *Markman* briefs, summary judgment motions, invalidity contentions, expert reports). Such filings may provide helpful background information on the disputed legal and factual issues including the IP and contracts at issue. They will not, however, assist the mediator in understanding key factors that often impact the success of a mediation, including the parties' business interests and needs, the parties' BATNAs and WATNAs, personal and business factors that could impede settlement, and the parties' thoughts on settlement proposals. Mediation statements should specifically and strategically address issues pertaining to the dispute being mediated. To accomplish this objective, the party representatives' involvement in preparing the mediation statement is essential.

A. Exchanged Statements

Whether the parties exchange statements will depend upon the circumstances of each case.[77] Exchanged statements provide the mediator with a common source of information that he or she may refer to in joint sessions and caucuses,

---

76. The statements are usually due at least seven days before the mediation session. If the mediator plans on holding ex parte calls with each side (before the mediation), he or she typically likes to have the statements before those calls.

77. Such circumstances include whether the parties want to prepare exchanged statements and/or the mediator believes that he or she will be in a better position to help the parties having them; the expense of preparing them considering what is at stake; the time that the parties have to participate in a mediation session (e.g., a court may order the parties to mediate in a short time period); or the status of the dispute (e.g., whether the dispute or filed case is in its early stages and the parties have not had an opportunity to conduct discovery or understand the opposing party's legal and factual positions). It is possible that information, perspectives, or proposals not previously shared could make a constructive difference in the other party's preparation.

and they address the dispute with a focus on the mediation. When the parties and the mediator agree to exchange statements, the mediator will likely request that they address certain topics, including the following:

- The business of the parties generally and as it relates to the dispute
- The relevant background of the dispute—who, what, where, when, and how
- Who will attend the mediation session for each of the parties—the party representatives who will have full settlement authority
- Issues that need resolution—these may or may not be limited to the legal issues expressed in written communications (e.g., a cease and desist letter or settlement correspondence) or in pleadings and briefs filed in an ongoing litigation;[78] comparing the list of issues from both parties will help frame the agenda for the mediation session and help in preparing for the mediation session
- Legal and factual points on key issues—especially in early-stage disputes; counsel will want to set forth provable facts and legal arguments on their strongest liability positions and the relief they are seeking, including key cases and perhaps a few limited documents that support their factual contentions
- A summary of settlement discussions—while a nuanced account of the history of settlement discussions would be more appropriate in the ex parte statement, an exchange of views gives the parties the opportunity to compare notes and ensure that they are on the same page before commencing the mediation; areas of overlap need to be noted, and the parties' perceptions of what occurred may uncover miscommunications that need to be corrected
- A sincerely stated commitment to work toward a resolution at the mediation session

B. Ex Parte Statements

The advantage of an ex parte statement is that it allows the parties to reveal only to the mediator candid considerations and factors that may help her understand the case and personal dynamics, as well as the challenges and opportunities for resolution, without sharing them with the other side.

Particularly when a litigation is pending (e.g., pleadings are filed, some discovery may have been exchanged), counsel are normally familiar with

78. For example, the parties may want a global settlement of all outstanding issues between them. Or, in a trade secret case involving covenants not to compete, one party may insist upon a non-disparagement clause and/or a clause designating the settlement agreement as confidential.

the facts and legal arguments of their case before preparing their mediation statements. Inordinate emphasis on legal arguments in the ex parte mediation statement is counterproductive. It tarnishes the process with a rights-based approach. The other side usually feels just as passionate about its legal arguments. Since mediation of an IP/Technology matter is a negotiation of a business dispute, settlement rarely rises or falls on the strength of legal arguments. Thus, when the mediator asks the parties to address certain questions that are not directed to the merits of the dispute, such questions should be answered thoughtfully and candidly *with the party representative's assistance*. This exercise not only helps the party representative understand that mediation is different from litigation, but it may also provide counsel with the opportunity to learn something from the party representatives that they would not have but for working with them on responding to the questions.

Counsel should not hide the ball from the mediator. If there is information of particular importance—a *slam dunk* winning argument, a desired business arrangement, or significant business or legal strategies that should not be disclosed to the other side—that information should nevertheless be conveyed in the mediation statement. During the mediation session, counsel and their party representatives may authorize the mediator to disclose such information to *seal the deal* or explain to the other side why a seemingly intractable position is being taken. That time may not come, but without knowledge of such critical information at the outset, the mediator cannot properly guide, analyze, assess, or suggest settlement approaches.

The following are the types of questions that parties may be asked to address in ex parte statements.

1. Underlying Story or Perspective

Is there a *backstory* of the dispute from the party representative's perspective? Are there relationship, emotional, or trust issues that might play a role?

Case in point: Consider the human element in a trade secret misappropriation dispute involving a large company that was accused by a smaller company of misappropriation. The smaller company's president had invented a life-saving device for individuals with a particular medical condition from which his sister had died. The alleged misappropriation and the effect it had on the smaller company in terms of its ability to help others was personal to the president. After progress was made on the framework of a deal, the principals sat down alone with the mediator so that the president of the smaller company could express to the other executive the importance of his company to him, his family, and others, as well as the emotional toll the dispute was having. The case settled after the emotional issue had been addressed.

2. Parties' Interests and Needs

While both parties want to win the arbitration or litigation and, thus, take the position that their legal arguments will prevail, what do they actually need or want—what are their interests—as a potential acceptable outcome from the mediation? As mentioned earlier in this chapter, the perceived interests and needs of the opposing party should also be addressed, as they will provide a deeper understanding of the dispute, potential options, and the ability to formulate proposals that are more likely to be considered and accepted by the other side. For example, a plaintiff may explain that their opponent (defendant) is only one of a number of suspected trademark infringers, and, therefore, the resolution of this case will have ripple effects on its credibility in enforcing marks against other parties. Or, an attorney may want to let the mediator know that the party he is representing has MFN clauses in other licenses that limit its flexibility with regard to the royalty rate it can accept. An attorney should also be prepared to articulate why a resolution on unacceptable terms could be worse than losing the case after trial.

3. Prior Settlement Efforts

Address confidential perceptions or observations about the individuals involved in the dispute, cultural issues, and trust concerns. Explain the reasons for rejecting prior offers or demands and assess why negotiations have been unsuccessful.

4. Obstacles to Settlement

Counsels' perspectives on why the matter has not yet been resolved may assist the mediator in developing strategies to avoid or address obstacles. Such obstacles may include relationship issues, the choice of party representatives for the mediation, company politics, misinformation, misperceptions, strongly held beliefs, getting stuck on unrealistic expectations, and lack of trust. On occasion, there may be interests or issues directly or indirectly involved in the matter that may frustrate settlement.

Case in point: Consider a pending patent infringement case involving two companies based in different countries. Two years before the mediation (and the litigation), the defendant company (prior purchaser) was interested in purchasing the plaintiff. A third-party broker arranged for representatives of the purchaser to travel to the United States to meet at the plaintiff's offices. The broker orchestrated the visit, including not permitting the founder and president of the plaintiff from meeting the purchaser's party representatives. This bothered the principals of both corporations, but nothing was said or done at the time. The purchase was not consummated. Two years later, those same representatives are present at a mediation session regarding the patent dispute. Picking up some nuanced discussion by both parties in their ex parte statements and in caucuses, the parties' counsel discovered the unresolved issue and suggested that the principals have breakfast to discuss what occurred two years ago. They did. Any misunderstandings were cleared and the case ultimately settled.

5. BATNA and WATNA

These analyses will not only help the parties prepare for the negotiations at the mediation session, but will also help the mediator perform a reality check with the parties. See the discussion at Section V.C.7.

6. Settlement Options and Terms

As discussed earlier, in IP/Technology cases, there are often options for settlement in addition to the payment of money. Consider *half-of-the-loaf* approaches as well, such as elimination of peripheral issues by a final or interim partial settlement, a stipulation to end or stay part of the case, or an agreement to informally set aside certain issues pending resolution of the main claims. Counsel should brainstorm creative settlement scenarios with their party representatives before the mediation session to ensure that they will have full settlement authority to offer such options and to ensure that creative scenarios are legally viable (e.g., in pharmaceutical disputes—no antitrust issues).

Be ready to present the key terms of a proposal at the outset. Nothing can unravel apparent progress in a mediation session faster than if a party springs new terms on the other side late in the session. A party should include in its ex parte statement a bullet point list of its key settlement terms and include a firm offer. This will avoid wasting time at the outset of the session determining what an opening offer or (if offers were exchanged leading up to the mediation session) the next offer should be.

7. Case Strengths and Weaknesses

Although each case is unique and is influenced by dynamics among the parties and counsel, within parties, within the industry involved, and, to some extent, due to the nature and stage of the litigation, *rarely does a party have no weaknesses.* A party should not avoid discussing the weaknesses in its case and the strengths of its opponent's case. A party can set forth the arguments it believes the other side will be emphasizing in its statement or at the mediation session, and then discuss its response. That will show the mediator that he can count on the party to be realistic and straightforward in its approach. Credibility with the mediator is important, just as it is with the judge or jury. Cultivating an objective view of one's case can provide the necessary realistic perspective in developing a negotiation strategy in preparing for the mediation session. It may also foreshadow the reality testing the party may hear from the mediator.

Also, when discussing the weaknesses of an opponent's case, consider preparing a list of the opponent's principal contentions/defenses in order of importance, along with a rebuttal for each, to educate the mediator on the main issues separating the parties and to provide the mediator with ammunition when he speaks with the opposition.

8. A Final Thought Worth Repeating . . .

Parties should prepare the ex parte statement with the same seriousness they would exercise for any other key briefing. Do not throw the statement together at the last minute or guess at the answers to the mediator's questions. Do not relegate it to a junior person on the litigation team. Mediation is a team sport with the party representatives at the helm. Thus, they should be involved in preparing the mediation statements.

C. Pre-Mediation Session Conferences

After the initial joint planning call involving counsel and the mediator, the mediator may have ex parte calls or videoconferences to resolve ancillary issues involving, for example, logistics, information exchange, or party representative issues. In IP/Technology cases, it is often the case that the mediator may want to speak ex parte with counsel at least, and their party representatives, after reviewing the written statements. Such a pre-mediation session ex parte conference has a variety of important purposes, including:

- Ensuring an efficient exchange or explanation of background information (e.g., technology, key dates, key players, prior settlement negotiations) with the mediator
- Answering questions that the party representatives may have regarding the mediation process and the mediation session
- Building trust and rapport between the mediator and counsel and their party representatives
- Providing the opportunity for counsel and party representatives to vent
- Providing the opportunity for counsel and party representatives to address any unanswered or sensitive questions the mediator might have

The time spent on discussing the listed issues serves as a "warm up" for the mediation session. That way, when counsel, the party representatives, and the mediator convene at the mediation session, they can continue, rather than just begin, the negotiations. Indeed, on occasion, the pre-mediation session conferences may also include an exchange of settlement terms before the mediation session occurs. Some mediators may schedule pre-mediation session conferences at the time of the initial planning conference with counsel, while others may wait until a later time. The ex parte pre-mediation session conference has become an accepted and valuable part of the mediation process.

VII. The Mediation Session

The mediation session, which may be held in-person, remotely, or in some combined fashion (also known as a hybrid format), is where the heavy lifting of the negotiations begins. How the session will be conducted, generally, would have been discussed and agreed upon by the parties, counsel, and the mediator before the mediation session occurs, often at the initial joint planning conference (see Section IV). That said, a mediator may focus more on shuttle diplomacy in one case, but encourage more face-to-face interaction in another. Also, because mediation, as a conciliatory process, is at heart a negotiation, party representatives are more involved in it then they are in the adjudicative processes of litigation or arbitration. This means that the party representatives play a greater direct role in all aspects of the process—identifying and refining the interests; preparing and creating the negotiating strategy; preparing pre-mediation statements; and participating in all phases of the mediation. Furthermore, mediation permits party representatives to communicate with each other through channels other than their counsel, yet with their counsel present and watching out for their legal interests. This can be especially important in overcoming barriers to settlement where, for example, counsel is screening relevant information from the party representatives or pursuing aggressive litigation tactics that put off the opponent, or where one or both of the principals feel their opponent has discounted their worth, interests, or concerns.

Creativity is essential in mediation. Do not look solely to the mediator for creative thinking. In the mediation statement and during the mediation session, it is expected that the parties and their counsel will make suggestions on how to constructively address issues and how to proceed with the negotiations. Further, mediation is not merely the back-and-forth exercise of demand, offer, counter, and so on. IP/Technology cases frequently require more imaginative negotiations. If counsel and their parties have not discussed creative ideas earlier in preparation for the mediation session, using the private caucuses to develop and express more unique approaches to resolution is well worth their time.

What follows is an overview of the key aspects of a mediation session.

A. Joint Sessions

At the initial joint planning conference, the mediator and counsel should discuss whether to hold an initial joint session at the mediation session and the nature of it. Generally, a joint session is where each side (counsel and party representatives) and the mediator occupy the same room (in-person or remotely) for a period of time. In contrast, caucuses involve the mediator and one side meeting separately. Mediators have different approaches to format, but even if the parties have opted not to make opening remarks, many mediators will start the mediation session with a joint session, the agenda for which will vary with the mediator and the case circumstances. Some mediation sessions begin with a joint session that embodies both general and case-specific communications. The general communications typically made by the mediator may include introductions;[79] expectations for the day(s); confidentiality protocols; reconfirming a commitment to the mediation process; explaining the roles of thc mcdiator, counsel, and the party representatives;[80] confirming the issues or scope of the mediation (e.g., global settlement, disputes to resolve); and housekeeping issues (e.g., meals).[81] The case-specific communications may be presented in the form of *opening statements* delivered by counsel and/or the party representatives; questions and answers to

79. It is not uncommon in IP/Technology cases that party representatives at the mediation session have never before met one another either over the phone or in person (e.g., competitors, companies based in different countries, corporate turnover—the person who negotiated the agreement at issue is no longer at the company, the designated party representatives are not the ones involved directly in the dispute at issue). Thus, the opportunity for the representatives to meet can be a significant ice-breaker if not the key to settlement.

80. Some trial counsel are comfortable and prepared to serve in the various roles required during the mediation session—as presenter, advocate, counselor, and conciliator. Others choose not to participate because, admittedly, they cannot dial back their trial persona. Party representatives should understand that advocacy in a mediation session requires negotiation skills more than courtroom skills.

81. There are some cases where a mediator may suggest that the parties eat lunch together to keep a conversation going, albeit *light* talk. This in itself is a form of joint session. Such an opportunity alone or in combination with a more substantive joint session may open the door to furthering conciliatory talks, breakfast, or drinks between party representatives after the formal mediation session.

learn facts, clear up misunderstandings, and explore common interests; or negotiations.[82]

It is also possible for a mediation session to begin in separate caucuses without a joint session. This may occur, for example, where there is a level of acrimony between the parties or counsel that is sufficiently palpable such that meeting together in the same room would jeopardize the continuation of the mediation session.

During the mediation session, joint sessions are not limited to the initial joint session. A joint session may be productive after the parties have begun caucusing because, upon reflection, they want to clarify something that was said in the initial joint session or that was conveyed by the mediator to them in a caucus, or inquire about information that was obtained in discovery, exchanged pursuant to the mediation process, or found in publicly available sources. For example, in an IP/Technology case, a party representative having financial information may join the mediator (with or without his counsel) in the caucus room of the other side to explain financial or technical information that the party representative is willing to share. Or, with the agreement of both parties, a party representative from each side and the mediator may meet in a joint session to discuss a particular issue that may be a sticking point or that helps to close the deal. The strategic choice of when and why to use a joint session, and with whom, can have a significant impact on the negotiations. The mediator does not have a monopoly on making such suggestions; counsel and the parties should take an active role recommending to the mediator that a joint session may be helpful, identify its purpose, and suggest who should participate.

Case in point: In a dispute over the breach of a technology-related contract involving a defendant's performance of services, the mediation began with a joint session where counsel exchanged their views of the case. The plaintiff's outside counsel was convinced, from talking only to employees of the party he was representing who were not at the mediation session (discovery had not yet occurred), that the services had been performed in a way that caused the breach. Believing that the plaintiff might be relying on misinformation in maintaining its negotiation posture, the mediator convinced the plaintiff's counsel and the party representative to join her in a joint session with the defendant's outside counsel and party representative—a corporate vice president having a long history with the company and extensive knowledge about the services rendered. The plaintiff's counsel asked the vice president every question he

82. Some commercial mediators try keeping the parties communicating and negotiating in an initial joint session as long as possible. This is not a common approach in IP/Technology cases. Mediators who use this approach will typically communicate that to counsel during the interview process.

had asked his own party representative, plus others, to test his understanding and veracity. Face-to-face the vice president answered every question clearly, completely, and genuinely. The plaintiff's counsel returned to a private caucus with his party representative, and then informed the mediator that the plaintiff was dropping one claim and reducing its request for damages on the other. The case settled that day.

Case in point: In a case ostensibly involving patent and licensing issues, but encumbered by feelings of distrust and anger from a long-term relationship that was crumbling, one party refused to provide the other with certain financial information before the mediation. The mediator persuaded the producing party to bring the information to the mediation session, which it did in summary form. As progress was slowly occurring, it was clear that the financial information was important to the negotiations. The producing party would not part with the summary sheet but agreed that the CFO and the party's long-standing business attorney (other party representatives were present but stayed in their caucus room) would present the information to the other side in the presence of the mediator and answer any questions. The discussion went far to inform and build trust through the subgroup of participants.

Case in point: In an international patent infringement matter involving active cases in two separate jurisdictions, counsel were conflicted on whether to begin the in-person mediation session with a joint session that would include opening statements. One counsel had some questions about the other side's counterclaims that she wanted addressed in a joint session, not just between counsel. The parties worked with the mediator all morning and through lunch in caucuses, making progress. The parties agreed to convene in a short joint session after lunch so that questions about the counterclaims could be explained. Having made progress in the morning (and counsel got along well), the joint session yielded a good discussion with candid answers, and the proponent of the counterclaims did not press them in the negotiations that followed.

1. A Word About "Opening Statements" . . .

Opening statements during the initial joint session are used less frequently than they may have been in the past.[83] There are pros and cons that can

83. The CPR Report (*supra* note 16, at 17) indicates that, in patent cases, the decision whether to have opening statements turns on "the character of the parties, the nature of the dispute and the mediator's and counsels' assessment of their usefulness

be different for each case in starting a mediation session with an opening statement. Even the most educated and sophisticated mediation participants (counsel and party representatives alike) can become incensed by what they hear, spending much of the time in the subsequent caucus reacting to the rhetoric rather than taking it in stride. Counsel must make a strategic choice as to whether the use of an opening statement will promote settlement given the facts of the matter and the personalities of the parties.

Some of the reasons to consider having an opening statement include the following:

- It is a unique opportunity for counsel to address opposing parties directly without the filter of their lawyer—to hear and see weaknesses in their own case and strengths in their opponent's case. For representatives who can absorb the content, it may provide a modicum of reality testing that could cause them to rethink their risk and damages analyses, along with their BATNA and WATNA, and ultimately close the deal. If a party uses visual aids in an opening statement to underscore or illustrate points, consider allowing the other side and the mediator to take copies for reference during caucuses.
- It gives the opposing party a preview of the effectiveness of opposing counsel's presence, advocacy skills, persuasiveness, and ability of lead trial counsel—for example, his command of the facts and the technology, and his ability to communicate his party's position on the complex technical issues in the case in a manner that is understandable and persuasive to a lay audience. Thus, by the end of the remarks, the parties will know how convincing counsel will be before a jury or judge.
- It provides each party with the opportunity to hear directly from the other. The impact of having one party representative talking directly to another in a candid yet conciliatory manner can provide information and perspective that is often *never achieved through discovery*. The exchange can clear the air, change the mood, and open the door to further direct negotiations.
- When mediation occurs very early in the case and when the parties have exchanged relatively little information through discovery, opening statements can be helpful to focus on risks and obtain key information that would be expensive and time-consuming to obtain.

---

in the case." That said, the CPR Report noted a trend away from using opening statements in patent disputes. *See also* BENNETT G. PICKER & CONNA A. WEINER, COMMERCIAL MEDIATION PRACTICE GUIDE: A PRACTICAL HANDBOOK FOR LAWYERS AND THEIR BUSINESS CLIENTS § 7.2, Opening Statement (3d ed. 2023).

- It can defuse misimpressions plaguing the parties that may be driving an emotional reaction to settlement. In most cases, even IP/Technology cases, there is an emotional component—perhaps a perception by one party that the other has not listened to its concerns, has not competed fairly, or has not respected its business or IP. This is especially common when the litigation is between companies of very different sizes, leaving the smaller company feeling bullied or discounted. Opening comments by the smaller company's business representative can help vent those feelings and allow the parties to set the emotional baggage aside and focus on problem-solving. Opening comments by the larger company's business representative could send a message of respect and good faith while still explaining what its objectives are and why the case is important to it.
- It can help build trust at least for purposes of settling the case.
- One party can assure the other party in an opening statement that it is prepared to work hard to settle the case.
- It permits the mediator to refer in a caucus to the information exchanged during the joint session for reality testing or probing the interests and needs of the parties.

Some of the reasons to consider forgoing an opening statement include the following:

- Forgoing can save time, particularly if the parties are familiar with each other's case from briefings and/or rulings on key issues by a court (e.g., preliminary injunction, *Markman* proceedings, summary judgment, appeal).
- Parties can avoid an uncomfortable or potentially inflammatory situation if there is strong animosity or distrust between them.
- It may get the mediation session off on the wrong note where the litigation has been proceeding for a while and the parties are well aware of each other's positions. Or, in a case where emotions are running high on one or both sides, even the most carefully framed opening statement could inflame rather than inform.
- Forgoing can avoid delaying or derailing the parties' adoption of a problem-solving mindset. The inclination is to want to react or respond to the merits of what was said (as in a court setting) rather than considering the information for what it is worth for a party's own risk analysis and otherwise focus on the negotiations.
- Parties can avoid setting a negative tone by counsel presentations that include "performing" or grandstanding—especially in the presence of their party representatives.

When venturing into the waters of the opening statement, here are some considerations to keep in mind:

- **The environment**. Even in large conference rooms, the type of presentation or persona that is effective in a courtroom will seem overdone for the environment (e.g., no judge, jury, or courtroom).
- **The process**. Mediation is not an adversarial process like litigation or arbitration. Thus, an adversarial stance in making remarks may send the message that a party is not there for a negotiation. The speaker's tone, forcefulness, posture, and facial expressions should be practiced before the mediation session to see what message they may send. Will it persuade the other side to rethink a position? Compromise? Keep an open mind? The party representatives must feel that their story has been told. Most essential is for counsel to clearly and objectively communicate their party's position to the mediator and the other side, and not engage in or invite debate.
- **Who will make the opening statement**? The party representative may be in the best position to tell a compelling story and explain facts that have not yet surfaced. Or a hybrid approach could involve the party representative telling the story, followed by their counsel summarizing the legal positions. If a party representative speaks, prepare that person for any ensuing questions. In deciding whether, and to what extent, the party representatives should actively participate, their temperament, personality, and ability to maintain control and civility should be weighed. Some degree of righteousness is expected and acceptable, but the party representatives should not preach to the other side.
- **Active listening**. The receiving party should actively listen and ask nonjudgmental questions that demonstrate an understanding of the other side's position as well as interests. Listen for business opportunities that might present themselves, as well as ways the parties may jointly work together to create value.

B. Caucusing

As mentioned earlier in this chapter, caucuses are private meetings during the mediation session apart from the other side. A caucus may be considered a meeting between counsel and the party representatives alone or with the mediator. These private sessions are where much of the heavy lifting gets done. They have an array of purposes, including the ones set forth in the following table.

Information Exchange	Probing	Proposal Work
Voicing concerns, emotions, frustrations, etc. . .	Performing reality testing (e.g., BATNA/WATNA, risk analysis)	Brainstorming and discussing options for proposals
Discussing mediation session strategy	Exploring case strengths and weaknesses for each party	Receiving coaching from the mediator for understanding opposing party's proposals and developing counterproposals
Educating the mediator about practical and sensitive issues (e.g., company changes, interparty dynamics, business interests)	Investigating key interests and settlement options	Discussing whether additional information, time, and/or the input of others is needed to consider or make a proposal

Counsel should expect, and party representatives should be forewarned and prepared, to actively participate in the caucus discussions. As mentioned earlier (Section VI.B.7), when preparing the ex parte statement, a party should consider preparing a list of the opponent's strongest allegations *against* them in order of importance, along with a rebuttal for each, so that the mediator has ammunition when caucusing with the other side. Similarly, during the caucuses, a party should provide an outline of its strongest arguments against what the opponent raises at the mediation session so that the mediator can use that as a reality check in the caucus with the other side. That said, although the cathartic need for counsel and their party representatives to express their position during these caucuses is recognized, solely focusing on the strengths of their own legal arguments does not foster settlement.

During the course of the day, mediators typically hold numerous rounds of caucuses. Not only should counsel have an overall strategy for the mediation session, but also a specific strategy or purpose for each caucus considering the ongoing and evolving nature of the negotiations. Following are some considerations for caucuses.

1. Focus on the Party

The mediation session is the parties' negotiation that the mediator is facilitating and that counsel is supporting. As previously recommended, counsel should ensure that their party representatives (who are often in upper management in IP/Technology cases) are prepared to negotiate and make decisions. They may, however, also need to be prepared to tell their side of the story, answer questions from the mediator (e.g., regarding business interests, the IP and technology at issue, the product, the market), ask questions of the mediator, digest information and consider proposals from the other side, and vent. Counsel should permit and encourage the communications to flow primarily between the mediator and the party representatives. The trust that develops between them can have a significant effect on the success of the mediation. Counsel should play a supportive role both before and during the mediation session.

2. Have a Plan

Counsel and their party representatives should have a clear sense of what they want to accomplish in the caucuses with the mediator. To do that, consider the following:

- What materials should a party bring to a mediation session to educate, illustrate, support, or corroborate for the mediator and an opponent the key points of its case, settlement proposals, and business interests?
- Is further discussion of legal or factual issues with the mediator necessary beyond what is presented in the statements or pre-mediation session calls?
- In preparing the mediator for reality testing with the other side, will disclosing a technical specification in a trade secrets matter, or survey results in a trademark dispute, further establish the party representative's credibility or strength on a particular issue?
- Is the party representative prepared for the probing or reality testing that a mediator will undoubtedly perform?
- When should additional or new information be shared with the opponent to have the most positive effect on the negotiations?
- Does the mediator need to be educated regarding business interests unrelated to the IP/Technology dispute but possibly a factor in when and how the deal gets done (e.g., a proposed sale of the business division involved)?
- What information do counsel want from their opponent?
- How might a proposal be received by the opposing party?
- Does the mediator understand what the parties need to settle the matter?

As discussed earlier, the party representatives and their counsel should have thought through how the negotiations are likely to progress—opening offer and anticipated subsequent moves. They will then be better prepared to explain those moves to the mediator so that she can, in turn, explain them to the other side in a way that demonstrates a rational, well-supported approach. While the parties will have time during the session to analyze and determine their response to counterproposals, it is best if they do not have to start from scratch to prepare each new offer. Even the most patient opponent will become restless if every time it makes an offer it takes the other side two hours of discussion to formulate a response.

In preparing, parties should also have considered identifying their client's bottom line (i.e., the least a party would be willing to accept, or the most it would be willing to give, to resolve the case based on a current analysis), as well as the point at which a party would walk (i.e., close the discussions for the time being). Note that these two positions are not necessarily the same. If one party is not evincing a willingness to move toward a settlement that would be acceptable to the other party, it probably does not want to put its best and final offer on the table only to have the other party reject it, and then claim it is the new floor or ceiling for subsequent negotiations.

In addition, there may be significant case events on the horizon that could materially alter a party's view of its case and increase the likelihood that it could do even better than the current bottom line. Thus, the team will want to talk ahead of time about what signals or positioning from the other side would lead it to conclude that this particular session has run its course. This could include, for example, much smaller incremental moves from one side than the other, or the other side's continued insistence on a term that was already unequivocally rejected. That said, a party should not feel locked into a specific series of moves.

3. Anticipate Questions and Reality Testing from the Mediator

Mediator questions and reality testing are tools the mediator uses to obtain information, influence strategic and objective thinking, and challenge the parties' positions and perspectives. In preparing for the mediation, counsel should have discussed with their party representatives the strengths and weaknesses of their case and possible risks, and performed a cost-benefit analysis. As the mediator shares information from the opposing party, counsel should anticipate the mediator asking how the additional information affects its analyses and the current settlement proposal. The parties should know their (and their opponent's) BATNAs and WATNAs to provide perspective in evaluating the proposals the mediator presents.

The mediator may also be interested in a party's reaction to the latest proposal presented, particularly what the party likes and does not like about it and why. In conveying proposals to the other side, the mediator may ask how the other side will receive each proposal (e.g., does it meet any of the other side's important interests?). The mediator may explore with the parties how value can be created to increase the pie (e.g., cross-licenses, future collaboration) and whether there are any nonmonetary options for settlement.

4. Make the Most of Caucus Downtime

While the mediator is caucusing with the opposing party, the other side should use that time to prepare for the next caucus, review new information, decide whether there is any additional information needed and contact others for it, and keep interested parties informed (e.g., investors, board members, overseas parent company). And if the mediation session shows signs of success, counsel should begin drafting a term sheet with the agreed-upon terms or fill in the draft settlement agreement counsel has brought. Counsel and their party representatives should also be developing the next proposal with supporting reasons that the mediator can communicate to the other side, even where numbers are the focus. Where possible, the reasons should evidence that one party heard the other party's key interests and needs and provided for them in the proposal.

5. Use the Mediator Strategically

The mediator is in a unique position, having information regarding each of the party's interests and business goals and having observed the dynamics of the parties. Counsel should use the mediator to gain insight into how the opposing party will react to a settlement proposal and why. If reactive devaluation[84] is in play, ask the mediator to offer a proposal to the other side as one that is coming from him or her. The mediator is in the best position to cushion information that may be provocative to the opposing party. Use the mediator to brainstorm potential solutions. In addition to the mediator's experience with a myriad of IP/Technology settlements, he or she is in a position to know what might work for the opposing party.

The mediator needs the parties' help to convey one party's position effectively to the other side, particularly if it appears that the other side's party representatives do not fully appreciate the strengths of their opponent's case or the weaknesses of their case. In addition, a party should determine whether there are additional facts the mediator should know in confidence. This can include time constraints, alternative proposals, and negotiating frameworks, as well as any insights a party has about what may motivate the other party to settle.

84. "Reactive devaluation" refers to the fact that the very offer of a proposal or concession, particularly if the offer comes from an adversary, may diminish its apparent value or attractiveness in the eyes of the recipient.

A good mediator will provide candid feedback about proposed moves, potentially steering a party away from unseen hazards that could thwart settlement. Each side needs to be open to that input. The participants on each side should establish a relationship of trust with the mediator and use the mediator not only as its spokesperson to the other side, but also as a negotiation coach, an agent of reality, and, ultimately, a resource in the face of apparent impasse. For example, mediators can help create settlement packages containing creative ideas for resolution; evaluate the case for all parties; assess the real gap between the parties' numbers; do a mediator's proposal; or suggest a different process such as binding arbitration for the remaining issues in dispute.

C. Dealing with Slowdowns in Progress

Because mediation is a process, if settlement is not reached during the mediation session, mediation has not failed. Thereafter, communication among counsel, the party representatives, and the mediator often continues via email, letters, telephone, and videoconference to continue the progress. Indeed, when evaluating potential mediators, parties should consider a mediator's willingness to be engaged with the parties after the mediation session.

Progress in mediation generally, and in a mediation session in particular, can take time, and it often involves ups and downs along the way. Parties can become tired and frustrated with the process and the participants during a mediation session when efforts seem unappreciated and progress seems slow. The slowdown may be just that, or it could be that the parties have reached an obstacle that may or may not be surmounted—what some call an impasse.

One of the best ways to avoid obstacles is to anticipate what could cause them and discuss these with the mediator and party representatives before the mediation session. For example, if the lack of information could stall negotiations, try to obtain that information in advance, find a third-party source for it that can be tapped during the mediation session, or have ready options that may be presented to the other side and the mediator for obtaining the information expeditiously, even if the parties need to take a short break to obtain it (e.g., it may be helpful for the parties to further investigate and consult with experts or technical people). Under the protective umbrella of mediation, the technical people from both sides can meet and exchange agreed-upon information.

Case in point: In a patent dispute involving a process to make microprocessors, the parties were stuck on whether the silicon disk was dry after the cleaning operation, a significant claim element. Neither would accept the other's analysis of the defendant's process. At the close of the first mediation session, with the mediator's assistance, the parties agreed to an independent laboratory to perform the defendant's process and negotiated the steps and parameters of that cleaning operation to be provided to the laboratory. The associated costs were equally shared. In addition, since this review was being done under the auspices of mediation (and, thus, confidential), and the findings would be provided only to the mediator, the parties confirmed that the results would not be discoverable, and the laboratory personnel could not be deposed or used as experts or consultants in the case. In a subsequent mediation session, after the testing was completed and the findings were available, the parties left it to the mediator's discretion whether to use that information in further negotiations. She did and the matter settled during the subsequent session.

Similarly, if the success of the mediation depends on having a certain person present, consider trying to schedule it around that person's availability and communicate candidly to opposing counsel that not all potential participants are fungible. Having the wrong party representative participate may be avoided by careful advance planning. Lack of preparation (counsel and/or party representatives) will impact the success of the mediation from the start, make the session a painful process for the party representatives, and cause the other side to lose faith and engagement.

There are a number of other tools that mediators have at their disposal to reignite progress (e.g., linked moves, range bargaining, mediator's proposal). Counsel, too, may want to consider the following ideas to avert a slowdown or stumbling block.

- **Be creative**. Although an exchange of money may be an essential term of the deal, the parties are not tied to exchanging currency if a new collaboration or discount on products purchased, for example, may provide a future monetary gain, which becomes part of an overall agreement.
- **Mix it up**. Change often helps the parties take a fresh approach. This technique includes assessing the interaction of the players and having different players meet. If the parties seem amenable, consider having just the decision makers meet without counsel or the mediator. If a technical collaboration may be part of an agreement, consider having the technical people speak with each other to see whether there are fruitful areas and let the others take a break. Counsel may also suggest changing the subject being discussed to a less controversial one. A change in venue or taking a break could provide a respite and allow the parties to consider progress made and reassess their options.
- **Take a recess**. If the parties fail to reach agreement at the mediation session, a recess may enable them to reconsider their options, review their litigation budget, and come to peace with the need to make more

concessions than they thought would be necessary. Counsel may ask the mediator to arrange a status call in a few days, to schedule another session, to continue the mediation caucus sessions by telephone, and to assist the parties in keeping the door to settlement open.

D. Memorializing the Agreement

When the parties' hard work results in an agreement, it is important to memorialize it before the session ends. As discussed earlier in this chapter, the parties should come to the mediation session, *at a minimum*, with an outline or list addressing the key settlement terms relevant to their dispute. The relevant provisions of settlement do not require a detailed document with every "t" crossed and "i" dotted. Often, the parties sign an informal agreement (e.g., term sheet), setting forth in bullet format the essential terms and conditions to which they have agreed.[85] Thereafter, counsel will prepare whatever formal documents are required, such as a settlement agreement, license, and voluntary dismissal. In some cases, however, parties are able to execute the formal documents at the mediation session. Thus, counsel should come to the mediation session with drafts of formal settlement documents loaded onto a laptop computer so they are easy to modify. In fact, even if the parties do not reach the point of signing formal documents at the session, having the drafts helps the parties and their counsel identify the essential terms of a deal, address whether there are any nonstandard settlement terms that need consideration, and determine what form the settlement documents should take.[86] When parties have not taken the time before the mediation session to try to identify all the material terms they need to discuss during the session, and terms are raised later when formal documents are being drafted, some parties may see this with a jaundiced eye—for example, as

85. Counsel should consider whether this informal document will operate as a binding contract if the definitive agreement cannot be finalized.

86. The parties' internal advance discussion and preparation of their settlement terms and conditions must include not only their desired business and financial terms, but also required legal and procedural terms, such as venue provisions, confidentiality, and a process for handling future disputes. Prepare to articulate why each of those terms is important, and discuss ahead of time which ones to yield in return for concessions on other terms. Furthermore, if there is any possibility of a meeting between the business representatives without counsel present, counsel must prepare its respective representatives about the legal terms deemed necessary to any acceptable final agreement (e.g., admissions of the validity of the IP). They should also be well educated about acceptable and unacceptable terms from an antitrust perspective and what they should do if the other party proposes terms that could constitute an illegal restraint of trade.

one side trying to get out of the deal or trying to get something more. This could reopen the negotiations, which could detain or derail settlement.

When the parties have a term sheet in hand and they contemplate drafting formal documents after the mediation session, some mediators will discuss next steps with the party representatives and their counsel, such as:

- What documents need to be drafted?
- Who will draft the documents?
- When will counsel exchange drafts?
- When will the parties execute final documents?
- If there is a pending litigation or arbitration, when will that be dismissed?

If the mediator does not raise these issues, counsel should. The parties appreciate knowing that the business certainty they sought by pursuing mediation will soon be realized. In the event that disputes arise during drafting that may require possible further discussions, counsel should consider enlisting the help of the mediator to resolve them.

In the exuberance of settling the dispute and after a long day in the mediation session, counsel should be careful in drafting the term sheet. Here are some tips worth considering:

- Articulate all of the agreement's material terms (e.g., confirming them with the issues set forth in exchanged mediation statements and at the initial joint session, and in the drafted settlement documents that counsel brought).
- Use clear and definite language in memorializing the terms regarding what is agreed to or what is required. Counsel should review the language from a judge's perspective to determine whether the terms are clear enough to enforce.
- Consider including some form of ADR clause if a dispute should arise in the future.
- Sign and date the term sheet.[87] If the parties are relying on a term sheet, they should also state that the parties intend the term sheet to be binding and enforceable (if, in fact, that is what they intend), or state that the settlement is effective only upon the execution of subsequent formal documents. The parties may want to describe specifically any subsequent settlement documents that they will need to execute.

87. Particularly in remote mediations, some counsel will request that the mediator circulate by email (which has a date) to all of the parties the terms as agreed upon at the mediation session with a statement to the effect that these are the terms that the parties have agreed upon.

When drafting the final agreement(s) following the mediation, avoid *nit-picking* over peripheral concerns or issues. Many a settlement is delayed (or lost) when the final agreement is *over-lawyered.* Rather than allowing drafting disagreements to cause the death knell of the settlement, re-involve the mediator before dissension becomes insurmountable.

Regardless of the nature of the dispute or the forum for negotiation, the chances for the long-term success of the agreement—true peace in the valley—are best if both parties are clear about what they believe the agreement means. An agreement that is premised on the unrealistic hope of one or both parties—that they have slipped something in unnoticed by the other party, that they can extract themselves from a tight spot for the moment but raise the very same issues a year from now, that a court will interpret a term to mean something other than what they know the other party believes it to mean, or that an obligation left deliberately vague will never be invoked—is likely only to defer the dispute to another day when the parties will be even angrier and trust will be virtually nonexistent. All are best served if the agreement is a true meeting of the minds, and not simply an expedient but illusory and short-lived ceasefire. Opt for transparency about what is meant by the terms and language proposed so that there are no *gotchas* by either side after the deal is signed.

Finally, remember that, even if a deal does not result after one mediation session, a well-conducted mediation will lead to a clearer understanding of each party's case, the obstacles to agreement, and whether an agreement can ever be reached. It can also build trust and open channels of communication between the parties so that the possibilities for resolution can be explored further when both parties are ready. *One must begin to end.*

Conclusion

Mediation can be a powerful process for resolving IP/Technology disputes. The courtroom is a forum where counsel live: it is not home to business-people. For them, the adage about litigation generally applies: "As a litigant, I should dread a lawsuit beyond almost anything short of sickness and death."[88] But mediation is not a spectator sport for counsel, party representatives, or the mediator. To harness the power of mediation, counsel and their party representatives should be knowledgeable about the mediation process, committed to seeing the process through, prepared for negotiations, armed with the information they need to evaluate their case, predisposed with a

88. *See* Learned Hand, *The Deficiencies of Trials to Reach the Heart of the Matter, in* 3 LECTURES ON LEGAL TOPICS 89, 105 (1926), *quoted in* FRED R. SHAPIRO, THE OXFORD DICTIONARY OF AMERICAN LEGAL QUOTATIONS 304 (1993).

problem-solving mindset, and patient. So, too, the chosen mediator should be skilled and experienced in the process, committed to seeing the process through, prepared to guide the parties through their negotiations, willing to help the parties exchange information they need to evaluate their case, a problem solver, patient, and appropriately selected to provide the parties with the process and style they want.

APPENDIX

Possible Criteria for Selecting an IP/Technology Mediator

Criteria
1. Conflicts—impartiality/neutrality
2. Availability to serve
3. Scheduling constraints
4. Mediation experience (e.g., years, number of mediations, similarity of cases, success rate)
5. Mediation training (e.g., institution, number of hours, nature of training)
6. IP/technical and subject matter experience
7. Relevant non-mediation experience (e.g., years in practice, IP field, litigation, transactions, technical, IP prosecution, industry)
8. Process style: (1) facilitative, evaluative, transformative; (2) joint/separate caucuses; (3) parties and/or counsel participate in joint and separate sessions; (4) reality testing; (5) pre-mediation submissions; (6) parties participate in designing process; and (7) facilitate some information exchange
9. Personal style (e.g., personality, demeanor, discretion, communication and interpersonal skills)
10. Cost/fee structure
11. Professional reputation (e.g., generally, in IP/technology, as a mediator)
12. Membership/leadership in professional organizations
13. Relevant published materials and presentations
14. References

CHAPTER 7

The Skillful Appellate Mediation Advocate: Mediating IP/Technology Cases in the Federal Appellate Courts

Theo Cheng and Harrie Samaras[1]

I was never ruined but twice: once when I lost a lawsuit, once when I won one.

—M. de Voltaire

Introduction[2]

In 1974, the U.S. Court of Appeals for the Second Circuit established the country's first federal appellate mediation program. It currently comprises two full-time circuit (staff) mediators and a Pro Bono Appellate Mediator Panel with approximately 15 volunteer mediators. Only the Federal Circuit also utilizes outside, volunteer mediators.[3] All of the other circuit appellate mediation programs handle those mediations entirely in-house through a staff of circuit mediators. For example, the Seventh Circuit, like the Second, employs two full-time circuit mediators, while the Sixth Circuit employs four and the Ninth Circuit employs eight.

When the Federal Circuit implemented a voluntary pilot mediation program in October 2005, it was the last of the 13 federal appellate courts to delve into appellate mediation. With exclusive jurisdiction over patent

1. This chapter is a derivative work based upon Chapter 8 in the First and Second Editions of this book co-authored by Wendy Levenson Dean, Esq., Harrie Samaras, Esq., Dina Leytes, Esq., and J. William Frank and Harrie Samaras, respectively. For his assistance in preparing this chapter, the authors gratefully acknowledge Phillip Swain, Esq., retired partner at Foley Hoag LLP. The opinions expressed in this chapter are those of the authors and are not meant to represent the opinions of any of the federal appellate courts.

2. See Glossary for definition of frequently used terms.

3. The Federal Circuit's mediation program currently comprises approximately ten volunteer mediators administered by one court employee in the court's Office of General Counsel.

appeals,[4] the Federal Circuit's adoption of such a program occurred in the face of significant controversy. Initially, the court had concerns that complex patent cases could not settle, and that it would be hard to encourage participation by the government in cases in which it was a party. However, the success of other federal appellate mediation programs, among other reasons, encouraged the Federal Circuit to initiate a pilot voluntary mediation program. Since 2006, the mediation program has been a mandatory and permanent part of the court's day-to-day practice, currently administered by the Circuit Executive, through the Office of the General Counsel.

Today, all of the 13 federal circuit courts of appeals except the Eighth Circuit have an appellate mediation program under Federal Rule of Appellate Procedure 33.[5] Tens of thousands of cases have been mediated in the various federal appellate court programs, all of which have adapted their respective programs to suit the needs of the regional bench and bar and, as a result, have generated valuable information for the mediators, practitioners, and parties. The purpose of this chapter is to share some of that information so that parties can make the most of these programs and lawyers can become more skillful appellate mediation advocates in the process.

This chapter discusses mediation at the appellate stage, referring in particular to the Second, Sixth, Seventh, Ninth, and Federal Circuits. These circuit courts were chosen because their established mediation programs typically hear a larger volume of intellectual property (IP)/Technology appeals involving, for example, claims of patent infringement, trade secret misappropriation, copyright infringement (e.g., software), and contractual disputes involving technology (e.g., licenses, distribution agreements, manufacturing agreements). The chapter outlines relevant aspects and unique benefits of the mediation programs in those courts, and provides feedback about what the courts expect from participants. The chapter also provides insights into the factors affecting why IP/Technology cases may settle at the appellate level, as well as tips on how appellate advocates can and should make the most of the programs for their clients.

---

4. *See* 28 U.S.C. § 1295(a).

5. Federal Rule of Appellate Procedure 33 provides:

> The court may direct the attorneys—and, when appropriate, the parties—to participate in one or more conferences to address any matter that may aid in disposing of the proceedings, including simplifying the issues and discussing settlement. A judge or other person designated by the court may preside over the conference, which may be conducted in person or by telephone. Before a settlement conference, the attorneys must consult with their clients and obtain as much authority as feasible to settle the case. The court may, as a result of the conference, enter an order controlling the course of the proceedings or implementing any settlement agreement.

I. The Benefits of Mediation at the Appellate Stage

A. Appellate Mediation: Why It Is Worth the Parties' Time

By the time one or both parties take an appeal, there has already been at least one *winner* and one *loser.* Furthermore, appeals are relatively cheap compared to trial practice, which can run into the hundreds of thousands, if not millions, of dollars, as compared to litigation at the trial level. So why mediate now? Well, as experienced appellate practitioners know, things can drastically change on appeal. A randomly selected panel of three judges—particularly in a court like the Federal Circuit that is known for a high reversal rate in certain areas of the law—will offer parties very few options—affirmance, reversal, and remand, in whole or in part. Often a *win* at the appellate level is a remand—a chance to return to the trial court for more motion practice, another jury trial, and/or post-trial motion practice followed by yet another appeal. In other words, the parties get the *chance* to spend more money and dedicate more hours to additional litigation instead of their respective businesses. Thus, an appeal may not be the end of a dispute. To the contrary, it may be yet another beginning.

Mediation is a form of *alternative* dispute resolution (ADR)—a process that allows for creative problem-solving, real savings in time and money, and an overall win-win result for the parties. If mediation is to be successful, however, it is important to avoid prejudging whether mediation will be successful or beneficial on appeal—regardless of your prior experiences (good or bad) with mediation. Prejudging could deprive parties of a necessary opportunity to gain valuable benefits that are unavailable from the appellate court or the district court on remand, or that are available to the parties only if they fail to prevail. This chapter sets forth considerations that may influence parties to think twice about *not* wanting to try mediation in the court's program.

Case in point: In a trade secrets case over a medical device technology, the defendant filed a summary judgment motion and won. The plaintiff appealed. The case was mediated in the appellate court's mediation program. It settled on appeal with the plaintiff acquiring the defendant, subject to the district court's vacatur of its summary judgment ruling, which the parties were successful in obtaining.

Case in point: An Abbreviated New Drug Application (ANDA) case involved a large branded pharmaceutical company and a smaller generic pharmaceutical company that were the subject of patent litigation for four years in federal district court. During the course of the litigation, the district court ordered the parties twice to try to settle the case with a magistrate judge's help. The parties, however, did not settle. The case proceeded to trial and ended with a judgment of noninfringement. The branded company appealed. The case was mediated in the Federal Circuit's mediation program and settled with the contingency that the district court would agree to vacate its noninfringement ruling. The district court did so. At the end of the mediation session, the parties signed a term sheet and consulted with antitrust counsel before finalizing the settlement.

Sometimes, mediation at the appellate stage presents just the right opportunity to settle a case. With prior wins and losses on all sides, parties may feel open to pursuing mediation on appeal. Ultimately, they have little, if anything, to lose. And, even though a court can require the parties to mediate, it can never compel any party to settle.

In addition to timing, the effect of the mediation process on the parties can bear fruit that does not typically result from the adversarial litigation process. With many cases resolved on summary judgment and potentially high reversal rates on particular issues (e.g., claim construction at the Federal Circuit), parties have merit-based reasons for commencing an appeal. Both sides may have high hopes for success regardless of whether they are the appellant or the appellee on one or more issues. Furthermore, parties appeal for emotional and face-saving reasons. The reality, however, is that parties on appeal have been litigating for quite some time—usually years—and have spent a lot of money and corporate resources along the way. They have understandably become entrenched in their positions, particularly if one party emerged as the victor following a trial, an injunction, or a ruling on summary judgment. Litigation is about taking positions and, on appeal, having a three-judge panel vindicate those positions through adjudication. By contrast, mediation at the appellate stage, like mediation generally, is not about vindicating the parties' positions by a decision maker. Rather, it is about facilitating a resolution by the parties that puts them in a decision-making role so that they can resolve their own dispute in a manner that makes business and/or emotional sense for them.

The result of a mediation may not always seem fair, if such a thing can be judged objectively. However, there are no guarantees of a fair result from the court. It is all about perception. Mediation can offer peace and certainty, and return the parties to a life without litigation (e.g., uncertainty, time, costs, distractions, possible reputational harm). Mediation can offer a business solution that meets important interests, unlike the limited remedies a court typically orders.

Introducing parties to the mediation process does not immediately convert them or their counsel to the conciliatory nature of mediation. It is not always easy to put the brakes on litigation momentum or to quickly and easily change parties' perspectives. The federal appellate courts' mediation programs are proactive, in that trained mediators explore with counsel, usually early in the life of the appeal, whether their appeals are amenable to mediation. It is not uncommon for the possibilities of fruitful mediation to be apparent to the mediator, but not necessarily yet to the parties.

Furthermore, the mediation style used is not strictly facilitating. The mediators do far more than simply carry numbers back and forth between caucus rooms. They typically challenge assumptions that the parties and their counsel may have and possibly provide evaluative feedback about the strengths and weaknesses of the case and the appeal, if requested. If nothing else, counsel may leave the mediation session able to write a better, more focused brief or to give a sharper appellate argument after an unsuccessful mediation session.

Beyond the previous general discussion, several specific factors militate towards mediating appeals.

B. Managing Relative Costs

The cost of pursuing mediation in a court program has not emerged as a factor dissuading parties from pursuing mediation. Indeed, it is a significant benefit to the parties that the programs waive any mediator fees. Furthermore, where the court permits mediators to travel to a location that is most convenient to the parties (sometime, even outside the United States), the overall cost of the mediation can be minimized. In any event, even if the parties are expected under the program's rules to reimburse the mediator's out-of-pocket costs, those costs pale in comparison to the hundreds of thousands or millions of dollars spent on the case through trial. And although the parties will still incur certain costs associated with preparing for and participating in the mediation session (e.g., possible travel and lodging, attorneys' fees for preparing the mediation submission and participating in the mediation session), the opportunity for achieving *global peace* between the parties is worth the investment. That global peace may include the resolution of related litigation or administrative proceedings regarding the IP or products in dispute (e.g., international proceedings, a concurrent U.S. International Trade Commission (ITC) investigation or district court proceedings, U.S. Patent and Trademark Office (PTO) proceedings), for which the meter is running, plus the cost of the appeal and any potential remand and follow-on appeals.

The litigation landscape for parties is dynamic. An IP case that was important at one time may not, over time, have the same significance to a party's business as it once did. It is not uncommon for parties to express that there is, or may be, on the horizon, other more pressing cases that overshadow the one on appeal. Even for healthy companies with the biggest profits, there is internal competition over limited money and resources. Companies are always rebalancing whether a lawsuit is worth the costs and risks—risks that change from pretrial, to trial, to appeal and sometimes beyond (e.g., remand, PTO proceedings). Unless one or both of the parties needs to resolve the case in court, for example, to make a statement to the industry, the appellate stage may just be the right time to broker a settlement.

C. Preserving, Enhancing, and Developing Business Relationships

It may also be that money alone is not the best or only resolution of an appeal. Perhaps the products or services at issue are not core to the business any longer or may not be the profit makers they once were. Perhaps a patent is nearing the end of its life, or the competitive landscape has changed since the case's inception. Maybe corporate leadership wants a graceful way to end a long-running dispute that is draining time and resources.

A mediated resolution may incorporate innovative solutions to aged disputes that curtail losses and result in a win-win, or, at the very least, result in face-saving solutions for all involved. Some examples of solutions that the parties themselves may discover and create, when given the chance, with experienced and prepared mediators and advocates include cross-licensing, royalty rate negotiations, mergers, acquisitions, distributorship deals, authorized generic deals, geographic limitations, payments-in-kind, resolution of related disputes in other jurisdictions, or virtually any other business solution (as opposed to the limits of judicial remedies). These are all options that "expand the pie" from a winner-takes-all mentality, thereby lowering the risk for all involved. By negotiating a win-win solution, parties who may have a history of cross-licensing or cooperation, or may have other joint business ventures, can continue to cooperate productively without upsetting the balance of their relationship. Additionally, where parties create their own settlement that best meets their interests, they are more likely to honor the agreement, resulting in a durable, lasting peace.

Case in point: A trademark opposition appeal from the Trademark Trial and Appeal Board (TTAB) involved a U.S. and a non-U.S. company that had related disputes and proceedings pending, including infringement actions, in a number of other countries. The companies had been in business together before becoming embroiled in a dispute. After the dispute arose and they were unable to settle it, the companies terminated their relationship. As a result of this past history, there was a significant lack of trust between the companies. They wanted a global settlement that would establish who could use the marks at issue and settle all the pending proceedings. As a result of the mediation, there was an agreement that provided for one company phasing out the use of the contested marks and assigning certain other marks to the other party, along with a dismissal of all the related proceedings. The mediated agreement provided a fresh start to the parties and gave them the opportunity to craft an agreement that made sense for their businesses, and that the parties would be motivated to abide by in the future.

D. Avoiding Unpredictable Results and Seizing upon Certainty

There are simply no guarantees should the appeal proceed. Sometimes, even an affirmance by a circuit court does not end the dispute as there may be related cases in the United States or elsewhere that will continue. Many appeals lead to a remand that result in more cost and uncertainty. The subsequent judgments by the trial court and possible appeals may lead to defeat or a mixed result for the party that initially *won* at trial. A remand often represents money spent by both sides with no guarantee of ultimate victory. Earlier wins may ultimately mean nothing except lost time and money. Think of the patentee who won an infringement ruling only to lose the patent on a future validity challenge in the same case. Even though parties think they are in control, relinquishing their business dispute to a third party to resolve—a judge, a panel of judges, a jury—will result in uncertainty to the businesses and often unpredictable results. Although judges and juries will do their best to find the facts and apply the law, they do not know the parties' businesses, and it is not their job to resolve disputes and determine remedies based upon what is in the best interests of both parties.

Mediation can offer a custom-tailored approach to unique problems, yielding timely, creative, and collaborative results. Despite the finality of the judgment being appealed, each party has a significant risk that it will lose on appeal. The statistics on reversals and remands at the appellate level somberly demonstrate some of the risks on appeal for the prevailing party. This uncertainty militates in favor of trying a process that decreases uncertainty and puts control of the outcome in the parties' hands.

Furthermore, the unpredictability of results on appeal, and with litigation in general, creates uncertainty for a business, such as impeding implementation of a specific strategic business plan. Perhaps a party involved in an appeal is poised to sell the company or the business unit whose products or IP is involved in the appeal. The lawsuit may be a deal-breaker or serious impediment to closing the deal; it may simply devalue the sale price. Resolving the litigation quickly and with certainty, facilitated by a mediator who will maintain the party's confidential motivations, may remove a critical and expensive risk or loss for the party.

In mediation, the parties are in control and have the opportunity to develop a business solution that may be a much better outcome than what the court can and will provide, with added benefits, such as confidentiality, timeliness, and certainty. Each party's first priority is its business, which is not normally litigation.

E. Maintaining Privacy and Ensuring Confidentiality

Court programs typically provide for maximum confidentiality at all stages of the mediation process.[6] The program rules, policies, and procedures enable parties to protect trade secrets and other proprietary information, and to speak freely with an eye towards resolution. There are no written transcripts, recordings, or opinions,[7] and the settlement terms may be kept secret within federal reporting requirements. A failure to adhere to these court rules, policies, and procedures—especially those involving confidentiality—may be deemed sanctionable conduct.[8]

---

6. *See, e.g.*, 2D CIR. LOC. R. 33.1(e) ("Information shared during a CAMP [Civil Appeals Mediation Program] proceeding is confidential and is not included in court files or disclosed to the judges of this court except to the extent disclosed by an order entered as a result of a CAMP proceeding. The attorneys and other participants are prohibited from disclosing what is said in a CAMP proceeding to anyone other than clients, principals or co-counsel, and then, only upon receiving due assurance that the recipient will honor confidentiality."); 6TH CIR. R. 33(b)(4)(D) ("Communications in mediation conferences or in connection with the mediation process are confidential. They may not be disclosed or otherwise used by any mediation participant, except as agreed in advance by all participants."); CIRCUIT MEDIATION OFFICE, U.S. COURT OF APPEALS FOR THE SEVENTH CIRCUIT, FREQUENTLY ASKED QUESTIONS 2 (2024) [hereinafter 7TH CIR. FAQs], https://www.ca7.uscourts.gov/assets/pdf/CMO_FAQs .pdf ("The Court requires all participants to keep what is said in these mediations strictly confidential. Oral and written communications that take place in the course of Rule 33 mediations may not be disclosed to anyone other than the litigants, their counsel, and the mediator."); 9TH CIR. R. 33-1(c) (setting forth detailed "rules to achieve strict confidentiality of the mediation process"); U.S. COURT OF APPEALS FOR THE FEDERAL CIRCUIT, APPELLATE MEDIATION PROGRAM GUIDELINES ¶ 5 (2013) [hereinafter FED. CIR. APPELLATE MEDIATION PROGRAM GUIDELINES], https://www .cafc.uscourts.gov/wp-content/uploads/Mediation/MediationGuidelines.pdf.

7. *See, e.g.*, *Mediation (CAMP) FAQ*, 2D CIR., https://www.ca2.uscourts.gov /staff_attorneys/mediation_faq.html (last visited Mar. 23, 2025) (Q-34) ("CAMP does not permit recordings of any mediation, including by CAMP, and there are no transcripts of any mediations to maximize confidentiality protections."); 7TH CIR. FAQs, *supra* note 5, at 2 ("Rule 33 mediations are official proceedings of the Court but are off-the-record and relatively informal.").

8. *See, e.g.*, 2D CIR. LOC. R. 33.1(g) ("The court may, after affording notice and an opportunity to be heard, impose sanctions on an attorney or party who does not

Thus, a mediated resolution can shield the participant's terms from the eyes of the public and generally remains unknown to the court. Confidentiality is threefold in an appellate court's mediation program. First, there is a high and thick wall between what happens in the mediation program and the judges of the court. A court may, in rare circumstances, know that an appeal was mediated.[9] Absent bad-faith (perhaps sanctionable) behavior in mediation (including the failure to cooperate with the mediator or other court staff), however, the court will never know anything about the substance of the mediation, such as the positions taken by the parties, the issues raised, and other matters confidential to the mediation. Second, nothing seen, done, or said in the context of the mediation can be used as a basis for future action against the other side, unless that information or material is otherwise independently discovered during the course of the litigation. Finally, as noted earlier in this chapter, the mediators maintain strictly to themselves any confidences that the parties share with them outside of joint sessions in private calls, correspondence, and caucuses.

Some volunteer mediators may also employ an agreement that is similar to the one they use in their private mediation practices. In these agreements, the mediator and the parties typically agree to maintain as confidential the information shared as part of the mediation process. And, insofar as many volunteer mediators review documents provided by the parties as part of their preparation for the mediation, the parties may request that the mediator sign and be bound by any relevant protective order entered by the court in the action.

---

participate in good faith in the CAMP program."); 6th Cir. R. 33(c) (setting forth instances where sanctions can be imposed for noncompliance with the mediation program rules); Fed. Cir. Appellate Mediation Program Guidelines, *supra* note 5, ¶ 9 ("Any party, counsel or outside mediator who fails to materially comply with any of the provisions of this document . . . may be subject to appropriate sanction by the court."). For example, in the Sixth Circuit, under 6th Cir. Rule 33(c)(3):

> If an attorney or party fails to comply with a provision of this rule or a mediation order, the court may take any or all of the following actions: (A) Remove the case from mediation; (B) Assess reasonable expenses caused by the failure, including attorney's fees; (C) Assess all or a portion of the appellate costs; (D) Dismiss the appeal; and (E) Impose further sanctions as the court deems appropriate.

9. The fact that a case is being mediated is not itself confidential. *See, e.g.*, Fed. Cir. Appellate Mediation Program Guidelines, *supra* note 5, ¶ 5.

F. Achieving an Efficient Resolution: Timeliness

The appellate process is generally slower than a mediated resolution. In appeals, parties must allow time for the varying pace and workload of different authoring judges, as well as time for concurrences, dissents, rehearing briefing and consideration, remand, and the possibility of an en banc hearing.

In contrast, after a case is referred to a mediator, the mediation session generally takes place soon after the appeal has been docketed and most certainly before any appellate briefing commences. Some court programs issue a scheduling order setting the day and time for the mediation session, at which the designated lead appellate lawyer and a party representative are expected to attend (see Section II.A). But there are variations in practice amongst the programs, so it is always a best practice to consult the local court program rules, policies, and procedures, as well as the court's website, for additional guidance. Confidential mediation statements may also sometimes be submitted by the parties depending on the local court rules (see Section II.B). Some mediators also schedule a preliminary phone call with the parties to set up a schedule for the mediation and to review other preliminary matters, like the mediation agreement, as well as the content and format of the confidential mediation statements and other submissions to the mediator.

Because it is often challenging to schedule a mediation date, once a date has been set, the parties should not expect continuances of the mediation absent good cause, such as an unexpected conflict involving necessary counsel or parties. Time frames for completion of a mediation can also vary. Some are completed on the same day of the mediation session with a binding term sheet in place and a voluntary dismissal or remand following closely behind. Others take far more time, many months in some cases. For instance, if a settlement involves one party acquiring the other party, a due diligence period will ensue that can lengthen the estimated completion time. Conversely, a simple forward-running royalty agreement and/or lump-sum payment may be completed in mere days. If progress has been made at the mediation session, but no agreement is reached, the mediator will often agree to continue to work with the parties to determine if a settlement is possible. Appellate briefing schedules may also possibly be modified to accommodate the additional time required to consummate a resolution (see Section II.A).

Case in point: An initial face-to-face mediation session lasted two full days. After the second day, the parties agreed on several key points, but they remained relatively far apart on other issues. Before the parties left the mediation session, they agreed to continue the discussions by email and telephone with the mediator's assistance. A complete settlement agreement was finally reached after almost five additional months of communication among the parties. During that time, the mediator had numerous ex parte phone calls with each party during which the parties and the mediator discussed the best ways to move forward to a settlement. As part of this process, the parties and the mediator exchanged proposals by email and draft agreements. Sometimes, the emails were between one party and the mediator, and, other times, there was a direct exchange of information between the parties. Although additional face-to-face sessions were discussed as part of the process, in the end, these were not needed. The mediator also communicated the parties' progress to the court's appellate mediation program, which was authorized under the applicable court rules to extend the parties' appellate briefing schedule.

Mediation is a process, not an event, that can take time to complete. And the time to resolve the dispute is often largely in the parties' control. Counsel and the parties should be prepared to devote sufficient time and resources to the mediation to determine if it has a chance of settling and, if not, why not.

G. Achieving a Global Resolution of Multiple Litigations/Multiple Parties

It is not uncommon for appeals, especially those involving issues relating to patents, trade secrets, copyrights (e.g., software), and technology licenses, to involve corresponding proceedings in the United States and abroad over the same IP and products or for the parties to have other disputes involving unrelated issues. The mediation process provides an open forum for parties to resolve related and unrelated disputes, even with parties not currently before the court. Except for out-of-pocket expenses and perhaps reimbursing the expenses of a volunteer mediator (if provided for under the program), as mentioned earlier, the parties incur virtually no cost for participating in an appellate court's mediation process, and the communications in the mediation are protected. The mediator strives to resolve all disputes between the parties, leaving a lasting peace between them.

Case in point: In a patent infringement case, the district court dismissed several parties from the case for lack of personal jurisdiction. The patentees obtained a final judgment as to the dismissed parties pursuant to Federal Rule of Civil Procedure 54(b) and filed a notice of appeal to the Federal Circuit. The volunteer mediator invited the remaining parties—none of them a party to the appeal—to participate in the mediation to resolve the entire district court case on the merits. The entire case settled.

II. What Advocates Need to Know About the Mediation Process

A. The Mandatory Nature of the Process

Generally, under the rules of most federal appellate court mediation programs, only cases in which the parties are represented by counsel (counseled cases) are eligible for the mediation program. With the exception of habeas corpus, sentencing, and mandamus appeals, nearly all other types of civil appeals are generally eligible for mediation.[10]

An appeal may enter a court's mediation program through three possible routes: (1) the court staff selects the case; (2) the parties (singly or jointly) request mediation through the program; or (3) a merits panel (to which a case has been assigned) refers the case to the program (on its own initiative or in response to an application). For example, in the Second Circuit, the program "screens all eligible appeals for mediation suitability" based upon factors such as the "information provided by the parties on Form C [the Civil Appeal Pre-Argument Statement], the underlying record (including decisions, prior mediations, briefing, etc.), the relief sought on appeal, the relationship between the parties, the length of time the parties have been litigating, the clarity of appellate issues, and appellate jurisdiction."[11] If the program determines that the appeal is suitable for mediation, it will issue an order scheduling a mediation session, generally before the filing of any appellate briefs.[12] That order will typically indicate the date and time of the mediation; the format (i.e., whether it will be conducted in person, over a videoconferencing platform like Zoom, or by telephone); and who is required to attend (e.g., lead appellate counsel, clients, insurance representatives).[13]

10. *See, e.g.*, 2D CIR. LOC. R. 33.1(a) ("The Civil Appeals Mediation Program (CAMP) applies to all civil cases except proceedings in which at least one party appears pro se, matters initially placed on the court's Non-Argument Calendar, petitions for writs of mandamus or prohibition, and habeas corpus cases and proceedings under 28 U.S.C. § 2255."); 7th Cir. FAQs, *supra* note 5, at 1 ("With the exception of habeas corpus, sentencing, mandamus and pro se appeals, all types of civil appeals are eligible for mediation."); *The Mediation Process*, 9TH CIR., https://www.ca9.uscourts.gov/mediation/the-mediation-process/ (last visited Mar. 23, 2025) ("Almost all civil cases in which the parties are represented by counsel are eligible for the Mediation Program."); FED. CIR. APPELLATE MEDIATION PROGRAM GUIDELINES, *supra* note 5, ¶ 2 ("All cases in which the parties are represented by counsel are eligible for the program.").

11. *Mediation (CAMP) FAQ*, *supra* note 6, Q-5.

12. *See id.* Q-6.

13. *See, e.g.*, *id.* Q-9, Q-12, Q-16; 6TH CIR. R. 33(b)(2); 7TH CIR. FAQS, *supra* note 5, at 1.

Similarly, in the Sixth Circuit, the program conducts an initial review "to determine whether mediation would be appropriate. If so, a mediation conference is scheduled."[14] Other programs may also solicit the input of counsel in advance on an ex parte basis regarding the suitability of the appeal for mediation, which may have an impact on whether a mediation is actually scheduled.[15] This is an opportunity for counsel to discuss objectively the appeal without fear that anything will be reported back to the court or the opponent, or otherwise used against the party. Additionally, one or more of the parties to the appeal may contact the program and confidentially request to schedule a mediation session.[16] If the request is not being made by all parties to the appeal, a staff mediator will reach out to the other counsel, taking into consideration if the request to mediate can be disclosed, and gauge whether there is any interest in participating in a mediation process. If the response is uniformly positive, it is more than likely that a mediation will be scheduled.

Instead of using the free services of a circuit (staff) mediator or a volunteer mediator (if the program maintains such a panel), the parties may also utilize the services of a private mediator at their own expense. The program

14. 6TH CIR. R. 33(b)(1). Factors considered by the Sixth Circuit's program include the nature of the underlying suit, whether counsel are involved, the documents filed in the district court, the relative level of case activity, the status of the appeal, whether the matter has been mediated previously, any agreed-upon briefing schedules, and any other unique circumstances that may impact the best use of the program's resources. In the Federal Circuit, screening by the court staff for mediation happens with the filing of the docketing statement, which is due within 14 days after the case is docketed (or within 30 days if the case involves the United States or a federal agency). *See* FED. CIR. R. 47.6.

15. *See, e.g.*, FED. CIR. APPELLATE MEDIATION PROGRAM GUIDELINES, *supra* note 5, ¶ 3 ("The Circuit Executive, through the Office of General Counsel, contacts principal counsel in cases selected for mediation to determine whether the case is a good candidate for mediation and seeks the opinion of counsel regarding participation in the program. If at the outset it appears to the designated court officials that mediation will not be fruitful, then court mediation efforts cease."). In the Ninth Circuit, the appellant is required to file a Mediation Questionnaire within seven days of the docketing of an appeal or a petition for review, after which the program usually schedules a mandatory telephonic settlement assessment conference with counsel, at which, among other things, the participants are provided "an opportunity to exchange information about the case, discuss options for mediation, and to ultimately decide whether the parties want to engage in settlement work. . . . At the conclusion of the call, counsel and the Circuit Mediator will decide whether further discussions would be fruitful." *The Mediation Process*, *supra* note 9.

16. *See, e.g.*, *Mediation (CAMP) FAQ*, *supra* note 6, Q-8; 6TH CIR. R. 33(b)(1); 7TH CIR. FAQS, *supra* note 5, at 1; *The Mediation Process*, *supra* note 9; FED. CIR. APPELLATE MEDIATION PROGRAM GUIDELINES, *supra* note 5, ¶ 3.

would then coordinate with the mediator to monitor the progress of the parties' exploration of a resolution.[17]

In the end, all of the courts' programs expect a mediation session to go forward when they are noticed, with at least the lead appellate counsel for each party attending, if not also the clients and any insurance representatives.[18] In that sense, these programs are mandatory in nature (i.e., the parties are required to participate in the mediation process, but they are not required to settle, thereby preserving that aspect of the parties' self-determination).[19]

---

17. *See, e.g.*, *Mediation (CAMP) FAQ*, *supra* note 6, Q-25 ("Parties are always free to have their matter mediated privately. However, it is often helpful to do so in procedural coordination with the CAMP office."); *Mediation—Frequently Asked Questions*, 9TH CIR., https://www.ca9.uscourts.gov/mediation/frequently-asked-questions/ (last visited Mar. 23, 2025) (Q17) ("If parties wish to hire a private mediator, the Circuit Mediator will continue to assist with case management issues."). In the Federal Circuit, district court magistrate judges are also accepted as volunteer mediators for any cases that originated in their court.

18. *See, e.g.*, *Mediation (CAMP) FAQ*, *supra* note 6, Q-7 ("Under Local Rule 33.3, the Court has the authority to direct counsel and parties to participate in a mediation conference.") & Q-16 ("The Court's order will instruct who the required attendees are—i.e., Counsel must attend with clients (and, if relevant, insurance representatives), unless otherwise provided by CAMP. Under Local Rule 33.1, CAMP is authorized to require clients to attend mediation."); 6TH CIR. R. 33(b)(4)(C) ("Lead counsel and any other attorney with primary authority on behalf of each party must participate in the conference. Co-counsel or other attorneys whose participation would be beneficial are welcome to participate as well. . . . Clients' attendance in the initial conference is not mandatory but is welcome. . . . The mediator may direct that clients participate in subsequent conferences."); 7TH CIR. FAQS, *supra* note 5, at 1 ("When a Rule 33 mediation is scheduled, participation is mandatory. . . . Clients and insurance representatives are required to attend Rule 33 mediations whenever the mediator so directs. If clients or insurance representatives are not directed to attend the initial mediation session, they must be available—with full settlement authority—to be consulted by phone for the duration of the mediation session. . . . It is essential that each party be represented at the mediation by an attorney who not only is conversant with the case but is the attorney on whose advice the party relies. If more than one attorney meets these criteria, any of them may represent the client in the mediation."); 9TH CIR. R. 33-1(b) ("A judge or circuit mediator may require the attendance of parties, and counsel at a conference or conferences to explore settlement related issues."); FED. CIR. APPELLATE MEDIATION PROGRAM GUIDELINES, *supra* note 5, ¶ 6 ("The court requires that the principal attorney for each party attend all sessions and that at the initial session a party representative with actual settlement authority also attend.").

19. *See, e.g.*, *Mediation (CAMP) FAQ*, *supra* note 6, Q-7 ("Under Local Rule 33.3, the Court has the authority to direct counsel and parties to participate in a mediation conference. Nonetheless, any result reached in mediation is entered only upon consent of the parties."); 7TH CIR. FAQS, *supra* note 5, at 1 ("Whether to settle is for the parties and their counsel to decide. However, counsel and parties are required to participate with the utmost diligence and good faith.").

There may be situations where client participation may not advance the process (e.g., highly emotional circumstances, difficult client persona), in which case, so long as counsel have full settlement authority (see Section II.C), the mediator may excuse the client from attending. However, in the typical case, client participation tends to be beneficial and advantageous, and, thus, their participation is expected.

The programs may also permit adjournments and rescheduling of the mediation session, but usually only upon consent of all the parties or upon a showing of good cause.[20] Moreover, some programs will modify the appellate briefing schedule to take into consideration the parties' continued exploration of a resolution.[21] In lower dollar-value cases, the parties generally want to avoid the expense of briefing; in some of the large verdict cases, the parties may agree to mediate after briefing to allow a full vetting of issues before the mediation. Counsel may be required to send the program periodic status reports or updates as necessary and appropriate. Of course, in cases where a merits panel has referred the appeal to mediation, there needs to be coordination between the panel and the mediator in order to establish appropriate time frames in which the appeal may remain in the mediation process relative to the appeals process as a whole.

Ultimately, mediation is, and is meant to be, a flexible process. The mediator is not bound by a defined formula or approach to mediating a case, and the mediator conducts the mediation as he or she deems appropriate. The mediation session ceases when the mediator, in consultation with the participants, concludes that further efforts will not be fruitful that day. The purpose of mediation is to settle the appeal. This may include a global settlement of matters not currently before the court, including any international matters.

---

20. *See, e.g.*, *Mediation (CAMP) FAQ*, *supra* note 6, Q-21 ("A timely adjournment request should be made in writing by email to camp_support@ca2.uscourts.gov, and copied to opposing counsel. If the request is on consent, counsel should provide at least three agreeable alternate dates. Last minute requests will only be granted in case of an emergency.").

21. *See, e.g.*, 7TH CIR. FAQs, *supra* note 5, at 2 ("Briefing is usually deferred until after the initial mediation session. If further modification of the briefing schedule would be conducive to settlement, an order to that effect may later be entered."); FED CIR. APPELLATE MEDIATION PROGRAM GUIDELINES, *supra* note 5, ¶ 7 ("While cases in mediation remain subject to the normal scheduling for briefs and oral argument by the Clerk of Court, counsel may file a motion for an extension of time. If the mediator believes that multiple mediation sessions are required, that the filing of a brief or the scheduling of oral argument will interfere with good faith settlement efforts, and that additional extensions of time are needed, then motions for additional extensions may be filed."). *But see Mediation (CAMP) FAQ*, *supra* note 6, Q-23 ("[T]he briefing schedule required under Local Rule 31.2 is not extended or otherwise adjusted because of a scheduled mediation.").

B. Preparing the Confidential Mediation Statement

Many, but not all, programs solicit the submission of a short, confidential mediation statement from each party before the mediation session. Some programs make this submission completely optional and some actually encourage their submission, while others make it a requirement.[22] These statements help prepare counsel and the parties for the mediation, and they help the parties prepare the mediator.

The mediation statements are not a public document (i.e., they are not filed with the clerk's office), and they are not shared with opposing parties or the court. In the statement, the parties should focus, for example, on issues versus positions, creative settlement ideas, and candid assessments of risks. More specifically, the mediator may request that each party provide the following information:

- Identify who will attend the mediation session and confirm that they will have full settlement authority.
- Cite to any other cases (pending or decided) in any tribunal involving the same parties, including any related cases in the same court as the instant appeal (attaching copies).
- Identify any other cases or proceedings (e.g., PTO, ITC, district court, international tribunals) involving the same IP.
- Identify any controlling or particularly relevant authority.
- Describe any insurance coverage, including whether the carrier must approve any settlement agreement.
- Identify any jurisdictional issues raised by any party.
- Describe any and all prior settlement discussions between the parties, including offers made and reasons for rejection.
- Identify the strongest and weakest issues for all involved parties.
- Discuss any positions that cannot be compromised.
- Identify the essential terms of any settlement currently acceptable.

---

22. *See, e.g.*, *Mediation (CAMP) FAQ*, *supra* note 6, Q-28 ("The mediation statement is not required but is strongly encouraged."); 6TH CIR. R. 33(b)(3) ("Counsel must submit the Confidential Mediation Background Information Form as directed in the mediation conference notice."); 7TH CIR. FAQs, *supra* note 5, at 2 ("Pre-mediation submissions are not required, but counsel are free to contact the mediator in advance, by phone or in writing, if they wish."); *Mediation—Frequently Asked Questions*, *supra* note 16, Q12 ("A mediation statement is not required for the initial Assessment Conference. If the case progresses further in the mediation process, the Circuit Mediator may request that counsel submit mediation statements."). In the Federal Circuit, a mediation statement is not explicitly required; rather, the mediators themselves determine what information or materials are needed and/or required for each mediation and conduct the mediation as they deem appropriate.

- Identify any additional information needed before agreeing to any settlement.
- Identify any interests or issues not directly involved in this case that may frustrate or further settlement.
- Estimate the cost of the appeal and the further costs that will be incurred if the case is remanded to the district court for further proceedings, including future appeals to the same court and the costs of related litigation between the parties. Also state the amount of legal fees and costs expended in this litigation to-date and indicate if there is a contingent fee arrangement in place between any prior or current counsel.
- Explain the standard of appellate review on each issue involved in the appeal.

Although IP/Technology disputes are just as resolvable as other disputes, they nonetheless have some unique attributes, and a confidential mediation statement may be a suitable vehicle to convey some of those aspects to the mediator. For example, the participants—the top decision makers, line businesspersons, in-house lawyers, and sometimes the appellate advocates themselves—will bring with them an enormous amount of specialized subject matter expertise (e.g., industry, business, technical, legal) regarding the IP and/or the technologies at issue into the mediation session. That may counsel for making wise use of both pre-mediation communications and the initial joint session to ascertain the real issues driving the dispute and to ensure that everyone is on the same page about the issues that need resolving.[23] A technology tutorial for the mediator's benefit may also make some sense.

Additionally, as discussed earlier in this chapter (see Section I.E), IP/Technology disputes raise a host of issues relating to the protection of confidential and proprietary information—perhaps more so than in the average commercial dispute. Documents and information will more than likely have been disclosed and used under a protective order that provided for their filing under seal, thereby limiting a mediator's access to those materials absent consent from the parties. Although broad mediation confidentiality provisions may suffice to overcome any disclosure and access objections, the parties may desire additional assurances and/or measures during the mediation process.

Moreover, injunctive and other equitable relief is oftentimes an aspect of the district court proceedings in IP/Technology disputes that is the subject of the appeal. Finding appropriate modifications and avenues for compliance with the relief ordered by the trial court may be a particularly sensitive and delicate issue between the parties. For example, on an appeal from a ruling

23. In the Federal Circuit, the assigned volunteer mediators determine the content of the mediation statements needed and required for each mediation.

on an injunction, a party may indicate that it is a direct competitor with the other party, and the patent owner will never license it (i.e., it wants the party out of the market).

Other challenging situations arising in an IP/Technology mediation include instances where (1) a nonpracticing entity (NPE) has sued a large practicing entity that sees itself as a target for such entities and feels that it must take a "stand" against this one to reduce future similar litigation; (2) a sole inventor sues a larger business entity because the inventor feels the invention was stolen and he or she was mistreated or taken advantage of; (3) international companies are involved in disputes with differing cultural expectations; (4) parties who have had a long, ongoing relationship find themselves in a dispute; (5) even arranging for all the parties to be in one place, especially where there are multiple parties and the parties are geographically dispersed, becomes a logistical and housekeeping challenge; (6) a small company whose IP has been misappropriated by a larger company needs to show the industry that it cannot be taken advantage of; and (7) a company whose IP has been infringed or misappropriated wants the world to know that it will enforce its IP rights.

Finally, the kinds of resolutions achieved in IP/Technology disputes tend to be more complex and have longer-term consequences than in an average dispute. This might counsel for setting aside multiple sessions in advance; allowing sufficient time and opportunity to conduct due diligence activities; investigating and exploring the possibility for a global resolution of multiple, concurrent disputes in different jurisdictions and forums; and accounting for ample time to draft appropriate settlement documents.

The foregoing attributes can and should be highlighted in any mediation statement so that the mediator is apprised from the very beginning of the possible challenges that might arise in facilitating a resolution. Note that the mediators, in their discretion, may request that the parties exchange their mediation statements, prepare joint statements or exhibits of information common to both parties, and otherwise change the format of any mediation briefing. Often, mediators will conduct a private conference with each party to review the statements before the face-to-face mediation session. The mediator will use this conference to go over questions he or she may have about the statement and begin gauging each party's willingness to settle the dispute.

C. The Mediation Session

The mediator will be committed to working as long as there is a possibility for resolution. The parties and counsel need to be just as committed to the process (e.g., any return travel plans should be flexible).

Before the mediation session, counsel should discuss with the mediator how the mediation session will be conducted and provide any input that may help towards having a productive and meaningful session. Depending on the program and individual practices of the mediators, mediations often start with a short joint session in which the mediator briefly discusses the purpose and possible benefits of mediation and explains the logistics of the mediation session and the rules of absolute confidentiality. Thereafter, the mediator may present the facts and issues of the appeal, as the mediator understands them, seeking correction and clarification from the parties. Finally, in some cases, the parties may agree in advance to give a brief presentation as part of the initial joint session, *focusing more on their business, rather than on their respective versions of the merits of the case.* This presentation, together with the mediation statements, should give the mediator a clear idea of what each side wants and expects from a successful settlement, as well as the reasons behind those wants and expectations. The mediator, alone with each party, will flesh out in greater detail these interests (versus positions) in private caucuses. In addition to informing the mediator, the joint session may be informative to recently engaged appellate counsel or party representatives who often have not had much settlement-related contact with the opposing side. And parties and counsel may have questions of their counterparts regarding the IP or products in the case, or more general business events, the responses to which may influence possible settlement options.[24]

In many cases, the parties will dispense with presentations during the joint session at the beginning of the mediation, but it is not uncommon for the mediator to bring the parties together at various times during the day to discuss targeted issues. These joint sessions typically include the mediator and may be between counsel only, parties only, or with everyone present. As noted before, mediation is a process that needs to be flexible enough to facilitate the greatest opportunity for the parties to reach a settlement.

At some point in the process, the mediator will review materials relevant to the mediation process to understand the issues and posture of the case as well as possible. Mediators often do more than serve as strict neutrals in a mere facilitative role. To mediate complex cases at the appellate level, a thorough review of relevant documents, such as rulings on appeal, motions papers filed in the trial court, any briefs filed on appeal, and, sometimes, selected documents from the joint appendix, are often an absolute necessity. Such review ensures that the parties, counsel, and the mediator are all on the

24. Notwithstanding all of the various opportunities to communicate during the litigation over the years, as well as the exchange of volumes of information (e.g., briefs, depositions, discovery), often the most beneficial communication for settling a case comes from straightforward questions and answers between party representatives in a "safe space."

same page regarding the case and builds the credibility of the mediator. It shows an understanding and dedication to the merits of the case and builds a basis for reality testing and evaluative feedback where appropriate.

As noted earlier in this chapter (see Section II.A), the courts' rules generally require each party to be represented at the mediation by its lead appellate counsel and/or by a party representative with actual settlement authority. Specifically, *actual settlement authority* does not mean sending a person allowed to accept or offer a minimum or maximum dollar amount. Rather, the party representative should be a person who can make independent decisions and has the knowledge necessary to generate, consider, and approve creative solutions. In-house counsel are also welcome to accompany the businessperson. If a party is a business entity, the general rule is that a businessperson with settlement authority must attend. Exceptions to this rule generally should be approved in advance.

Case in point: Before the scheduled mediation, one of the parties made a request to the mediator that "settlement counsel" replace its lead appellate attorney at the session. The party making the request believed that the settlement counsel would have sufficient familiarity with the case to participate fully at the session and with respect to any proposed settlement agreement. Based upon those representations, the mediator was amenable to the change and, as prescribed under the court's rules, provided notice to the other party. The other party was familiar with the identity of the settlement counsel, whom it respected, and readily agreed to the replacement.

Depending on the program rules, a party representative may be able to participate by telephone.[25] Bringing the right person(s) to the settlement table greatly improves the chances that a resolution will be reached. Because executive time may be at a premium, consider agreeing to a venue that makes it easier for the business representatives to attend and fully participate, even if it involves more travel for counsel; alternatively, if the court's program allows it, consider holding the session remotely. Although having all representatives participate in person is highly desirable, occasionally, there will be a situation where that may not be possible in order to maintain a reasonable time schedule for the mediation and have everyone participate.

25. *See, e.g.*, *Mediation (CAMP) FAQ*, *supra* note 6, Q-9 ("If a client is not within commuting distance, counsel may request permission for their client to participate by phone."); 7TH CIR. FAQS, *supra* note 5, at 1 ("If clients or insurance representatives are not directed to attend the initial mediation session, they must be available—with full settlement authority—to be consulted by phone for the duration of the mediation session.").

Case in point: There were multiple defendants involved in an appeal that included both U.S. and non-U.S. residents. The parties agreed to a time and location that permitted all of the representatives to participate in person or at least by telephone or videoconference. The mediation started in the evening in California to allow non-U.S. parties from Asia to participate by telephone.

The mediation session is an opportunity for the parties to think "outside of the box" and for creative brainstorming. Parties may arrive with clear interests and positions from which they do not intend to deviate. The mediator will hold in strict confidence anything that the parties say in caucus if that is a party's preference. Settlement may take an unexpected direction. To get the most out of the mediation session, *allow for the possibility that the mediation may work*. The parties may obtain a better result through mediation than the court can offer. This is the point of ADR—*alternative*, and sometimes better, resolutions.

D. Subsequent Sessions

A single mediated session frequently does not result in a settlement. Mediation is a process. At least half of the cases that are mediated settle at some point beyond the initial session, with some settling as late as after oral argument. After oral argument, one or both sides may feel less bullish about their positions. The risk may feel more real having been through the gauntlet of having certain parts of their arguments challenged by a panel of judges charged with deciding their case.

Sometimes, the participants need to check with others at the home or a foreign office or do further research into questions raised by the mediator or the other side in the course of pursuing unique resolutions. Questions may have been raised and parties may discover that they need additional information not readily available at the initial session for a creative or unanticipated resolution. As new possibilities arise to expand the proverbial pie, the parties may need additional time to consider and discuss new ways forward. Subject to the specific rules of the court, the appeal may be kept within the mediation program while this further exploration takes place to protect the confidentiality of further discussions between the parties and to maintain access to the mediator. As noted before, additional sessions (telephonic, remote, or in-person) may also be scheduled.

If the parties reach an agreement at the mediation session, they will often prepare and sign a term sheet or other memorialization of the material terms and conditions. To avoid disputes later when drafting the formal documents, in the term sheet, parties should strive to (1) set forth the agreed-upon terms and conditions in clear language that could be easily understood and followed and (2) address all key terms and conditions of their agreement (templates may help determine what those terms and conditions are). Consider keeping the mediator involved during the process of drafting the formal documents (e.g., settlement agreement, license) to help the parties settle any disputes that may arise during the drafting process.

It is advisable for parties to bring templates of the formal documents loaded on laptop computers that can be filled in or modified. This serves various purposes including (1) the documents remind counsel of the details that need to be covered to formally memorialize the parties' deal (i.e., a checklist); (2) at least some of the drafting is already done; and (3) if the parties can formalize their agreement at the session while they are together, it can save further time and money.

Even if the appeal does not settle at the first mediation session, the mediation has opened the lines of communication between opponents in what may be the first time in days, months, or even years. The parties are likely to leave the mediation feeling, at the very least, that they better understand the strengths and weaknesses of their and their opponent's case. To make what may seem like an unsuccessful mediation into a valuable exercise, both sides must put their very best proposals on the table before the session is over. With some frequency, when the true spread is known, and the parties and mediator remain engaged, appeals settle days after the mediation session appeared to be at a possible dead end.

E. Dismissal or Panel Decision

The purpose of the mediation program is to help parties achieve settlement. Once the parties reach a binding settlement agreement, there is no longer a case or controversy before the court, and the parties should jointly file a motion of voluntary dismissal or other appropriate motion (e.g., remand). If the case is not settled, then it remains on the docket and proceeds as if mediation had not occurred.[26] Even in the situation where a resolution is not

26. *See, e.g.*, *Mediation (CAMP) FAQ*, *supra* note 6, Q-35 ("To protect confidentiality, CAMP policy is that if a settlement is reached, any agreement must be reduced to writing and fully executed by all before it is binding on the parties. CAMP does not participate in the drafting of any settlement agreement. Counsel are expected to file a stipulation of dismissal of the appeal pursuant to [Federal Rule of Appellate Procedure] 42(b) once the settlement has been executed."); 7TH CIR. FAQS, *supra* note 5, at 2 ("By the conclusion of the Rule 33 process, the parties will either have reached an agreement to settle or learned how far apart they are and what the remaining obstacles to settlement are."); *The Mediation Process*, *supra* note 9 ("If the parties settle the case, the Circuit Mediator will work with them to ensure that the proper

achieved, the parties and their counsel have usually gleaned something useful from having participated in the process, such as a better understanding of the strengths and weaknesses of the case and the appeal (which can translate into more focused appellate briefs and arguments) and a better appreciation of the obstacles to settlement (which can be helpful for subsequent attempts at arriving at a resolution).

F. Do Not Try to Predict Settlement

Often, there is no rhyme or reason why cases chosen for the mediation program have settled. Presented here are some observations, not predictors, of challenges and surprises in settlements. The lesson to derive from this section is to keep an open mind going into the mediation.

1. Contingency Fee Cases

Contingency fee cases can be tough to settle, especially where the attorney puts his or her financial interests ahead of his or her client's interests. A good settlement may fail because the contingency fee lawyer would have to write off some portion of the fees to make a settlement worthwhile for the client. These cases can become more complex because the mediator may be forced to mediate with two different parties on the same side—the client and the lawyer. Ultimately, the client and the lawyer must work through the contingency issues.

2. Trial Counsel Is Also Appellate Counsel

Counsel may feel that they were treated unfairly by the trial court and need to save face in front of their client with a positive ruling from the appellate court. And counsel may be as unwilling to take responsibility for a settlement as the client—they both want a positive outcome from the court. Absent an appellate victory, counsel may encourage their clients to just "blame it on the court" as an unfair anomaly that went against counsel's best advice in taking and trying the case. Counsel who can step back from the emotions and ego of litigation provide the best service to their clients in mediation regardless of whether the case settles.

---

documentation dismissing the appeal is filed with the court. If the parties are unable to resolve their appeal, the matter will be released from the Mediation Program."); FED. CIR. APPELLATE MEDIATION PROGRAM GUIDELINES, *supra* note 5, ¶ 8 ("If settlement is reached, then the agreement must be in writing and binding on all parties. The appellant or the parties jointly must file a motion or stipulation of voluntary dismissal or other appropriate motion. If the case is not settled, then it remains on the docket and proceeds as if mediation had not been initiated.").

3. ANDA Cases Do Settle

Counsel who are well-heeled in the relevant antitrust law, have anticipated possible settlement options before the mediation session, and have investigated how design options that do not run afoul of antitrust laws increase their clients' ability to settle. These cases have also settled on terms involving payment "in-kind," distribution or manufacturing agreements, and the like, as advised by competent antitrust counsel.

4. The Passion of Sole Inventors

Sole inventors have a strong sense of value about the patent regardless of what a court has said thus far or the mediator's evaluation of infringement and validity. They may feel like "David" going up against a corporate "Goliath" and feel grievously wronged by a large company (perhaps a former employer) who they feel stole their IP. Corporations are generally hesitant to apologize or otherwise sooth an inventor's emotions or ego. Successful approaches have included nonmonetary ways to value the inventors (e.g., fellowships, consultant agreements, donations to charity).

5. NPE Cases Do Settle

The NPE is a business and will look to maximize its return relative to the effort expended. NPEs may have needs that can be addressed at mediation, and their business model may be based more on negotiated settlements than on a litigated result. A confidential, negotiated settlement with a minimal payment that is far less than the exposure and cost to litigate may be a win for both sides.

6. Cases Involving "Just" Money Can Be Easy to Settle

IP/Technology cases, which are essentially business disputes, have many reasons to settle, such as avoiding future litigation costs and the risk of an injunction or the expiration of the IP.

7. Summary Judgment Cases

These cases may leave the "winner" feeling less certain of the outcome on appeal and, in fact, may settle more easily than those that have made it through a full-blown jury trial and post-trial motions.

8. At a Minimum, Narrow the Issues

To the extent that the parties agree to narrow the issues on appeal as a result of going through a mediation process, that outcome may be reflected in their briefs and may be of tangential benefit to the court. Also, mediation may eliminate some, but not all, parties—a situation that may reduce briefing and the overall complexity of the case, thereby freeing up the court's time.

Case in point: In a case with multiple defendants, each had at least one unique issue on appeal in addition to numerous common issues. One group of defendants agreed to settle the case at the mediation. This removed their unique issues from the appeal, thereby simplifying the overall appeal.

III. Practice Tips for Effective Appellate Mediation

A. Effective Practices

- **Follow the directions for drafting the mediation statement**. A document that does not answer the questions asked by the program is likely to be rejected and is of little value to the process no matter how experienced the appellate advocate who authored it.
- **Get the most out of preliminary conversations with the Circuit Mediation Office**. Be candid. Counsel should not tell the mediator what they think the mediator wants to hear. Ask candid questions about the process and what is offered and expected.
- **Get the most out of the mediation session**. Keep an open mind, listen to and trust the mediator, trust the absolute confidentiality that the court has provided the parties, and take seriously that mediation at the appellate level is a unique opportunity to problem-solve creatively and obtain a better alternative result than the typical judicial remedies.
- **Carpe diem**. Counsel should impress upon their clients that this is the time and the place to honestly express exactly what they need to resolve the pending appeal and any broader disputes with their opponent so that the mediator can best assist the parties in reaching the desired solution.
- **Identify and bring participants with actual settlement authority**. Keep in mind that, under all of the courts' rules, each party must be represented at the mediation by participants with actual settlement authority.
- **Bring the most effective business advocates who are objective and business-focused**. The person who initiated the litigation or had principal responsibility for defending it may be *too close* to step back and see the need to take responsibility for a settlement rather than just throwing the potential results to the court and maintaining that he or she was right and the court was wrong if the ruling(s) goes against his or her company.

- **Prepare the client**. A separate chapter in this book (Chapter 6) covers in detail how to prepare clients for mediation, but it bears repeating that one of the most important functions counsel can serve as appellate advocates is to prepare themselves and their clients for the mediation session. They should review not only the strengths *and* weaknesses of their case (and be candid about them in the mediation statement), but other issues including possible creative solutions. Mediation is an interactive process unlike litigation or arbitration. Clients need to be prepared to be a part of the process. For example, counsel should encourage their clients to be armed with possible relevant information regarding sales, strategic planning, settlement options, and their opponent's business.
- **Have realistic expectations for the mediation**. Counsel should know what to expect at the mediation and ensure that their clients know what to expect, including timing, joint sessions, caucusing, and documenting any agreements made by the end of the day.
- **Be open to the unexpected**. Some disputes resolve themselves in ways that surprise one or more parties . . . and the mediator! Keep an open mind.
- **Think beyond the case(s) on appeal**. Is there a way to forge a lasting peace? Think globally!
- **Respect and understand the culture of others**. Although the parties have been fighting with each other in court, mediation is a time to step back and understand how and why they came to be in their present situation. Understanding the culture of others may uncover why the case has not settled thus far and it may enhance the chances of settling at the mediation.
- **Be honest if the mediator asks, in confidence, for the bottom line**. Hiding the ball from the mediator does not advance it; rather, doing so may hinder the mediator's ability to get the parties an acceptable resolution.

B. Ineffective Practices

- **Counsel convincing themselves, and maybe their clients, that their case is special, and, thus, it will not settle**. The case may have special or novel facts or legal issues (many do), but that should not be confused with a case's business potential to settle. Oftentimes, the special nature of the facts and circumstances of a case portend the most potential for settlement. Remember that clients normally are more interested in advancing their business than advancing the law.
- **Underestimating the importance of the mediation statement to the mediator**. It helps the mediator learn the history between

the parties, identify the strong and weak issues for each side, and understand the desired outcomes. Be honest and concise. There is no room in the statement for puffery and salesmanship.

- **Rehashing and arguing the merits as counsel would in appellate briefing**. Mediation is a decidedly different process from litigation or arbitration, in that legal positions take a back seat to the parties' business needs. The mediator will carefully read the prior rulings and pleadings. Counsel should keep in mind that the confidentiality protection afforded to the mediation statement is ironclad so they should take the opportunity to discuss candidly the disputed issues including the scope of any settlement beyond the matter(s) on appeal.
- **Manifesting a bad attitude**. This is the time to shed the scorched earth, take-no-prisoners attitude that some litigators exhibit. To best serve a client's interests in the mediation context, counsel must be willing to engage with their clients, the mediator, and with opposing counsel, and recognize that this is not a weakness.
- **Expecting an opponent(s) to bargain a particular way**. While some parties start off with their bottom line, others work in increments. Be patient and let the process unfold.
- **Saying, "I'm not going to bid against myself."** Someone must start the bidding. There is much research going both ways on who gets the advantage by going first. Parties will never be forced to pay a dime more than they offer or accept a penny less than they want. Offers are frequently only good for the duration of the mediation. Situations change (e.g., rulings are handed down, reexaminations may be filed, additional litigation is filed, remands), so no party should expect an offer at mediation to be the same offer on any other day unless so specified.
- **Letting emotion get in the way of sound business judgment**.
- **Failing to take the mediation program seriously**. Insofar as the mediation program is mandatory, the court takes it seriously. Failing to cooperate with the court staff or a volunteer mediator is sanctionable.

C. Why Mediation Skills Matter

Like the broader purpose of this book, an important purpose of this chapter is to impress upon appellate advocates in IP/Technology cases that representing parties in appellate mediation requires the practice of certain skills, strategies, and approaches that significantly differ from those practiced as an appellate advocate. Good appellate advocacy skills are not enough in mediation. Without acknowledging the differences between appellate and mediation advocacy and exercising those separate skills, strategies, and approaches, the parties are not likely the get the most out of the mediation process.

As mentioned previously in this chapter, often, parties who have been litigating against one another for some time, regardless of whether they are competitors, know only one way to relate to and communicate with one another—adversely and aggressively. Animosity between opposing counsel never helps achieve resolution. Settlement becomes even more challenging when counsel adopt or even fuel the emotions of their clients. Counsel should be willing to talk candidly with their clients (e.g., about the weaknesses in their case, future risks and costs) and constructively with opposing counsel, and recognize that, in both cases, candid and constructive talk is not a weakness. Although there may have been meritorious, well-thought-out reasons to proceed through trial, on appeal it may be time to reassess that strategy, and there should be no stigma attached to a genuine desire to seek a pragmatic, tailored, certain result to end the dispute.

An effective advocate in a court's mediation program begins by understanding the particulars of that program, including reviewing the court's rules, policies, and procedures, as well as the web page on the mediation program. Insofar as mediation is a flexible process, a good mediation advocate understands what the mediator expects from counsel and the parties in the mediation and provides input to the mediator about the mediation process both before and during the mediation session so as to maximize success. As discussed in detail in Chapter 6, good advocates take the time to prepare themselves and their client for participation in the mediation session (i.e., a business negotiation, not an argument on the merits).

If the stakes are high for the parties to the appeal, they are no less significant in the mediation, which can dispose of the case favorably. Thus, not preparing or preparing casually is a risky proposition. One of the critical differences between the appellate argument and the appellate mediation is that the parties will not actively participate as advocates at oral argument before the panel who will decide their case, while they will (and should) actively participate and advocate in the negotiations and decisions made during the mediation session(s). Even if counsel have prepared themselves and their clients previously in the same case for settlement discussions or a mediation, they must update the assessment of their case (see Chapter 3), reevaluate business options for settlement (companies are dynamic), and rethink their mediation team (e.g., business executives change, maybe the case did not settle earlier because of the parties' settlement teams).

Conclusion

Mediation can be a positive strategic approach for parties on appeal, provided that they have a skilled appellate mediation advocate representing them. An appellate advocate who is skilled in mediation practice can help his or her client understand all the potential benefits of mediation—from immediate monetary savings to future relationships, and a peaceful future (at least with this adversary). To help parties prepare for and optimally participate in the mediation, counsel must do their homework. Also, they must put thought into any mediation statement they submit to the program after consulting with their clients—it is not simply another form to complete perfunctorily. Draft meaningful, well-thought-out responses to the information requested in any pre-mediation statement. Bring the right decision maker(s), let the process unfold, and be prepared to work hard!

CHAPTER 8

Mediating Section 337 Disputes Regarding Infringing Imports at the International Trade Commission

Mark J. Abate and Molly R. Grammel[1]

A man who does not plan long ahead will find trouble at his door.

—Confucius

Introduction[2]

The U.S. International Trade Commission (the Commission or ITC) is a federal agency providing an alternative forum to U.S. federal district courts for owners of U.S. intellectual property (IP) rights that are being infringed.[3] Unlike infringement actions filed in federal district courts for damages and relief where the infringement is occurring within the United States, Section 337 of the Tariff Act of 1930[4] gives the ITC authority to adjudicate disputes between private parties to prevent importation of products that would infringe U.S. IP rights. The ITC has authority to exclude from importation products subject to a Section 337 investigation.

While the discussion of the mediation process and mediation advocacy elsewhere in this book applies equally to Section 337 investigations at the ITC, this chapter highlights special considerations and rules that apply in the context of mediating such disputes.

1. This chapter is a derivative work based upon Chapter 9 in the First and Second Editions of this book co-authored by the Hon. Theodore R. Essex (Ret.) and James R. Holbein, Esq., and the Hon. Theodore R. Essex (Ret.), Lisa R. Barton, Esq., and James R. Holbein, Esq., respectively.

2. See Glossary for definition of frequently used terms.

3. The ITC also has jurisdiction more broadly over issues relating to international trade, such as unfair competition disputes involving imported products.

4. Section 337 of the Tariff Act of 1930 is codified at 19 U.S.C. § 1337. Proceedings before the ITC under this statute are commonly referred to as "Section 337 investigations." This chapter will use that nomenclature or "Section 337 proceedings."

To appreciate the Commission's relevance today in the IP arena, and the special considerations that arise in mediating cases before the Commission, the chapter begins with an overview of Section 337 investigations. Then it outlines the Commission's mediation program and discusses factors to consider in mediating Section 337 investigations.

I. Overview of the Commission and Section 337 Investigations

A. The ITC

The ITC is an independent, quasi-judicial federal agency with broad investigative responsibilities on matters of trade. Pursuant to its responsibility for administering U.S. trade remedy laws, the Commission investigates matters involving imports of products that are allegedly unfairly competing in the marketplace. Although akin to litigation, and, for the most part conducted as such, Section 337 disputes are technically "investigations."[5] Under Section 337, parties may request that the Commission investigate infringement of U.S. utility and design patents, U.S. registered and common-law trademarks, and U.S. registered copyrights.[6] Parties may also assert other forms of unfair competition involving imported products, such as misappropriation of trade secrets or trade dress, passing off, and false advertising.[7]

For instance, the Commission has statutory authority to investigate an alleged violation of Section 337 where a complaint alleges that the named respondents have imported, sold for importation, or sold after importation articles that infringe a valid and enforceable U.S. patent.[8] Upon the finding

5. *See* 19 U.S.C. § 1337(b); 19 C.F.R. § 210.10.

6. *See* 19 U.S.C. § 1337(a).

7. *Id.*

8. *See* Commission Opinion at 2, Certain Compact Wallets & Components Thereof, Inv. No. 337-TA-1355 (USITC Aug. 13, 2024) ("[T]he Commission vacates the ID's use of the term 'subject matter jurisdiction' and clarifies that this term, along with 'personal jurisdiction' and 'in rem jurisdiction,' are merely shorthand for the Commission's statutory authority over the present investigation.") (All ITC decisions cited in this chapter are publicly available on the following website: https://edis.usitc.gov/external/?denied=true. The decisions can be accessed by creating a free account.); *see* Commission Determination to Review in Part a Final Initial Determination Finding No Violation of Section 337 and, on Review, to Affirm the Finding of No Violation; Termination of the Investigation at 2–3, Certain Video Processing Devices & Components Thereof, Inv. No. 337-TA-1343 (USITC Aug. 30, 2024) ("[T]he Commission clarifies that the terms 'subject matter jurisdiction,' 'personal jurisdiction,' and 'in rem jurisdiction' are not necessarily applicable to the Commission's investigative authority under section 337. The Commission is a 'creature of statute.'").

of a Section 337 violation, the Commission is required to issue an order excluding the products from entry into the United States—after considering the effect of such exclusion upon the public health and welfare, competitive conditions in the U.S. economy, the production of like or directly competitive products in the United States, and U.S. consumers.[9] The ITC can only grant prospective relief: an exclusion order barring future importation and a cease and desist order barring future conduct.[10] The Commission does not order monetary damages as a remedy.[11]

The ITC includes a panel of six commissioners (the Commissioner(s)). Each Commissioner is nominated by the president and confirmed by the U.S. Senate.[12] Relevant to Section 337 investigations, the ITC also includes (1) the Office of the General Counsel, (2) the Office of Administrative Law Judges, and (3) the Office of Unfair Import Investigations (OUII or OUII staff). The Office of the General Counsel provides assistance and advice to the Commissioners.[13] After a determination is made to institute an investigation, the Commission directs that an administrative law judge (ALJ) conduct an investigation, which includes developing an evidentiary record.[14] The Commission may also direct the OUII to investigate on behalf of the Commission as a party to the investigation.[15] The OUII acts as an independent party representing the public interest and participates in the investigation conducted by the ALJ.[16] Because the vast majority of investigations at the Commission involve patent infringement,[17] the Commission and its ALJs, officers, and staff members have significant patent litigation experience.

---

9. *See* Spansion, Inc. v. U.S. Int'l Trade Comm'n, 629 F.3d 1331, 1358 (Fed. Cir. 2010); 19 U.S.C. § 1337(d).

10. *See* Tex. Instruments, Inc. v. U.S. Int'l Trade Comm'n, 851 F.2d 342, 344 (Fed. Cir. 1988).

11. *See* Suprema, Inc. v. U.S. Int'l Trade Comm'n, 796 F.3d 1338, 1345 (Fed. Cir. 2015) (en banc).

12. *See* 19 U.S.C. § 1330(a).

13. *See Office of the General Counsel (GC)*, ITC, https://www.usitc.gov/offices/gc (last visited Mar. 23, 2025).

14. *See* 19 C.F.R. § 210.10.

15. *See* ITC, OIG-MR-17-12, Management Report—Description of OUII's Participation Selection Process 2–3 (2017), https://www.oversight.gov/sites/default/files/documents/reports/2017-08/OUII's%20Selection%20Process.pdf.

16. *See id.*; *see* 19 C.F.R. §§ 207.101–.102; *see Office of Unfair Import Investigations (OUII)*, ITC, https://www.usitc.gov/offices/ouii (last visited Mar. 23, 2025).

17. *See Section 337 Statistics: Types of Unfair Acts Alleged in Active Investigations by Fiscal Year*, ITC, https://www.usitc.gov/intellectual_property/337_statistics_types_unfair_acts_alleged_active.htm (last visited Mar. 23, 2025) (noting 87 percent of the unfair acts alleged in active investigations in 2024 were solely patent infringement).

B. Section 337 Investigations

Section 337 proceedings at the ITC generally involve three stages: (1) pre-institution, (2) ALJ trial proceeding, and (3) Commission review and final determination.

In the pre-institution phase, and even before a complainant files a complaint at the Commission, a complainant may submit a draft of its complaint to the OUII for an informal and confidential review.[18] Then, in a meeting with attorneys from the OUII, the OUII will provide oral feedback concerning whether the draft complaint complies with the Commission's pleadings standards and rules.[19]

A complaint requesting commencement of a Section 337 investigation requires more information than a federal district court infringement complaint. In addition to pleading the elements of infringement of an IP right, a Section 337 complainant must also allege the importation of an infringing article and the existence of a "domestic industry."[20] Generally speaking, a domestic industry requires proof that the complainant has made or is making significant investments in the U.S. economy that are related to the dispute at hand.[21] For example, in a patent infringement dispute, the complainant must plead that it is making significant/substantial domestic (i.e., U.S.) investments in products embodying its patent rights. Another reason for the fulsomeness of a Section 337 complaint is because the Commission has specific rules concerning background materials that must be filed in support of a Section 337 complaint (including copies of license agreements relied upon to establish standing or domestic industry, certified file histories of any asserted patents or trademarks, etc.).[22] In patent cases, claim charts must be provided with the complaint showing alleged infringement of each asserted independent patent claim.[23] And, because the Commission considers how the remedy requested will impact the public interest, the complainant is required to file a "statement of public interest" along with the complaint.[24]

Once the complaint is filed, the ITC has 30 days to review the complaint and determine whether to institute an investigation.[25] During this time, OUII staff may consult with the complainant, and sometimes with the proposed

18. *Id.*

19. *See* ITC, OIG-ER-11-13, Evaluation of Pre-Filing and Pre-Institution of Section 337 Investigations 8 (2011), https://www.oversight.gov/sites/default/files/documents/reports/2019-12/oig-er-11-13.pdf.

20. *See* 19 U.S.C. § 1337(a)(1)–(2).

21. *See* 19 C.F.R. § 210.12(a)(6).

22. *See, e.g.*, *id.* §§ 210.4, 210.8, 210.12, 210.52–.56.

23. *See id.* § 210.12(a)(9)(vii)–(ix).

24. *See id.* § 210.8(b).

25. *See id.* § 210.10(a).

respondents, to obtain additional information to make a decision on institution.[26] In some instances, OUII staff may request that changes be made to the complaint to make it more likely that the investigation will be instituted. The complaint can be amended at any time as of right before an investigation is instituted,[27] so compliance with the OUII's suggested changes can greatly increase the likelihood that an investigation is instituted. In certain circumstances, the Commission may decline to institute an investigation, for example, where the complaint contains insufficient factual allegations to support a cognizable claim under Section 337.[28]

If the Commissioners vote to institute an investigation, the next stage is the ALJ trial proceeding.[29] The trial proceeding before one of the ALJs is governed by the Administrative Procedure Act (APA).[30] The presiding ALJ oversees discovery and conducts the evidentiary hearing. Discovery in Section 337 actions is expedited, relative to district court actions, and is governed by the ITC's Rules of Practice and Procedure[31] and by detailed *ground rules* specific to each ALJ.[32] Although the ITC's rules roughly track the Federal Rules of Civil Procedure, the accelerated discovery pace has important strategic implications because discovery is usually concluded in five to seven months.

As in district court, parties in the ITC may seek discovery through a variety of methods: requests for admission, interrogatories, subpoenas, document

---

26. *See id.* § 210.56(a).

27. *See id.* § 210.14(a).

28. *See, e.g.*, Amarin Pharma, Inc. v. U.S. Int'l Trade Comm'n, 923 F.3d 959, 964–65 (Fed. Cir. 2019) (concluding that a complaint fails to state a cognizable claim for relief where the claims allege violations of the Federal Food, Drug, and Cosmetic Act (FDCA) that "are precluded by the FDCA, at least where the FDA [U.S. Food and Drug Administration] has not yet provided guidance as to whether violations of the FDCA have occurred").

29. *See* 19 U.S.C. § 1330(d)(5) ("Whenever, in any case in which the Commission is authorized to make an investigation upon its own motion, upon complaint, or upon application of any interested party, one-half of the number of commissioners voting agree that the investigation should be made, such investigation shall thereupon be carried out in accordance with the statutory authority covering the matter in question.").

30. *See* 19 C.F.R. § 210.36.

31. *See id.* §§ 207, 210.

32. *See* Commission Opinion at 26, Certain Flash Memory Controllers, Drives, Memory Cards & Media Players & Prods. Containing Same, Inv. No. 337-TA-619 (USITC Nov. 24, 2009) (citing the APA, 5 U.S.C. § 556(c), the Commission noted that "an ALJ has discretion to establish and enforce ground rules for the proper administration of an investigation"); *see, e.g.*, Notice of Ground Rules, Certain Pre-Stretched Synthetic Braiding Hair & Packaging Therefor, Inv. No. 337-TA-1415 (USITC Sept. 10, 2024).

requests, and depositions.[33] However, the timeline is much more compressed and most discovery responses are due within ten days of service. Third-party discovery is common in Section 337 investigations and is obtained through subpoenas.[34] The ITC's subpoena power is nationwide.[35] Discovery from foreign third parties, however, is difficult and time-consuming.

Once fact and expert discovery are completed, the investigation proceeds to the prehearing and hearing phases. All parties, including the OUII, file prehearing briefs. The prehearing brief provides the ALJ, opposing parties, and the OUII with notice of the arguments and evidence that a party expects to present at the hearing. The brief is also the final opportunity to raise issues to be considered in the investigation. Following post-hearing briefing, the ALJ issues a final initial determination (FID) on whether or not there is a violation of Section 337.[36] The FID is certified to the Commission along with the evidentiary record.[37] The ALJ also issues a recommended determination (RD) recommending an appropriate remedy in the event that the Commission finds a violation of Section 337.[38]

After the ALJ's FID is issued, the case then proceeds to the next stage—the Commission's review of the ALJ's FID and issuance of the Commission's final determination. The ALJ's FID becomes the Commission's final determination 45 days after the date of service of the FID in permanent relief proceedings, unless the Commission reviews the FID or extends its deadline.[39] Parties typically seek Commission review of FIDs by filing a petition for review.[40] The standard for granting review is a clear error of material fact, an error of law, or that there is a policy matter warranting consideration by the Commission.[41] The Commission may also review a FID on its own motion.[42]

If the ITC determines that there is a violation of Section 337, it then determines the appropriate remedy. The ITC's remedial orders are then submitted to the president for review before going into effect. This period is referred to as the 60-day presidential review period.[43] During this 60-day period, the subject imported articles are permitted entry into the United States or can be sold from inventory, provided a bond is posted.[44] At the

33. *See* 19 C.F.R. § 210.27(a).
34. *See id.* § 210.32(b).
35. *See* 19 U.S.C. § 1333(b).
36. *See* 19 C.F.R. § 210.42(a)(1)(i).
37. *Id.*
38. *See id.* § 210.42(a)(1)(ii).
39. *See id.* §§ 210.42(h), 210.66(b)
40. *See id.* § 210.43.
41. *See id.* §§ 210.43(b), 210.66(c).
42. *See id.* § 210.44.
43. *See* 19 U.S.C. § 1337(j).
44. *See id.* § 1337(j)(3).

conclusion of the 60-day presidential review period, the orders go into effect. The U.S. Customs and Border Protection (Customs) is tasked with enforcing ITC exclusion orders. Upon receipt of an exclusion order from the ITC, Customs will issue a memorandum to the ports providing details on enforcement of the exclusion order. Customs often consults with the ITC on the scope of the orders. The Commission's final determination is appealable to the U.S. Court of Appeals for the Federal Circuit.[45]

C. Section 337 Investigations as Distinguished from IP Infringement Court Cases

There are features of Section 337 investigations that differ from IP infringement cases brought in federal district court. For example, related to the jurisdiction of the ITC, the primary remedy in Section 337 investigations is an exclusion order that directs Customs to prevent infringing imports from entering the United States. In addition, the Commission may issue cease and desist orders against named importers and other persons engaged in unfair acts that violate Section 337. As mentioned previously, monetary damages are unavailable at the ITC. Thus, ITC litigants will typically file a parallel federal district court action to recover damages. The district court action will be stayed at the request of the accused infringer until the Section 337 investigation has concluded.[46] However, the decision of the ITC will not be preclusive in the federal district court action. Thus, litigants typically have to spend the time and money pursuing relief in tandem proceedings, first in the ITC and then in federal district court, if the parties to the underlying dispute do not settle during the ITC proceeding.

Furthermore, in patent infringement cases, while federal district court judges can exercise discretion to limit the number of patent claims that they hear on the ground of judicial efficiency, Article I ALJs are constrained by the terms of the APA to hear all asserted claims. In investigations involving patents, while ITC complainants arguably have the right to take more claims to the hearing, ALJs have urged complainants to reduce the number of asserted patent claims and urged respondents to reduce the number of prior art references relied upon. Indeed, nearly all ITC hearings are initially set for five days, and a party needs to show good cause for additional hearing time.

45. *See* 28 U.S.C. § 1295(a)(6).
46. *See id.* § 1659.

Another distinction from federal district court practice is that counterclaims are not allowed in a Section 337 investigation.[47] The preclusion of counterclaims prevents the respondent from asserting its own IP rights within the same investigation. A respondent can, however, file its own Section 337 investigation if the requirements for doing so are met. And respondents may also challenge the validity of asserted patents at the Patent Trial and Appeal Board (PTAB) of the U.S. Patent and Trademark Office (PTO). The ITC will not stay an investigation pending a PTAB ruling,[48] and the ITC will likely reach a decision before the PTAB.

An additional distinction from district court practice is the number of parties who may be named as respondents in a Section 337 investigation. Because the Commission's jurisdiction in Section 337 investigations is over imported products, a complainant can identify any products that are allegedly subject to the investigation, and then name as many relevant respondents as the complainant deems appropriate under the rules. There is no need to demonstrate personal jurisdiction, or that the ITC is an appropriate venue with respect to any of the respondents. As a result, a Section 337 investigation can include numerous unrelated respondents.

Finally, Section 337 investigations occur on a shorter timeline than infringement cases brought in federal district court. Section 337 investigations must be completed "at the earliest practicable time."[49] Thus, the ALJ's FID will, on average, issue within 12 months of when a complaint is filed.[50] As a result, discovery and interim merits determinations (such as a summary determination or construction of patent claims) are typically conducted on a compressed timeline relative to federal district court litigation. In patent investigations, most ALJs conduct claim construction hearings, although there is no guarantee that a claim construction order will issue in advance of expert discovery or even prior to the hearing.

47. *See* 19 C.F.R. § 210.14(e) ("[A] respondent may file a counterclaim at the Commission . . . in a separate document. A respondent who files such a counterclaim shall immediately file a notice of removal with a United States district court in which venue for any of the counterclaims raised would exist under 28 U.S.C. 1391."); *see also* Striking Apple's Fourth and Sixth Affirmative Defenses at 4, Certain Wireless Standard Compliant Elec. Devices, Including Commc'n Devices & Tablet Computs., Inv. No. 337-TA-953 (USITC Aug. 7, 2015) (finding respondents' sixth affirmative defense "constituted a counterclaim that must be pursued in district court pursuant to Commission Rule 210.14(e) rather than an affirmative defense").

48. *See, e.g.*, Denying Respondents' Motion to Stay the Investigation and Setting the Evidentiary Hearing Date, Certain Memory Modules & Components Thereof, Inv. No. 337-TA-1089 (USITC Apr. 11, 2019).

49. 19 U.S.C. § 1337(b)(1).

50. The Commission will set a target date for completing the investigation within 45 days after institution. *Id.*

II. The ITC Mediation Program for Section 337 Investigations

On October 28, 2008, the Commission began a pilot mediation program for Section 337 investigations, which led to the establishment of a permanent agency mediation program (the Program) on August 30, 2010. The Program is aimed at facilitating the settlement of disputes and enhancing the efficiency of Section 337 investigations, for example, by reducing the number of issues, patent claims, and/or respondents, and otherwise assisting the Commission to manage its growing caseload.[51] Brochures and manuals are available on the Commission's website as a resource to the public in using its mediation program.[52] The secretary to the Commission manages the Program and provides administrative support to the mediators and parties.[53]

All Section 337 investigations are eligible for participation in the Program.[54] Usually, the presiding ALJ issues a scheduling order with mandated mediation deadlines.[55] The litigating parties may also individually or jointly pursue mediation.[56] That is, formally, a party can make a request for mediation by filing a Confidential Request to Enter Mediation with the Commission secretary and serve copies on all other private parties to the investigation.[57] However, mediation is often initiated (either by the litigating parties or in compliance with the scheduling order) outside the Program and through standard practices, such as jointly agreeing to a mediator and making scheduling arrangements.

As with the mediation of cases pending before other tribunals, the Program provides a confidential, risk-free opportunity for parties to resolve their disputes expeditiously, at a lower cost, and in a manner that can provide

---

51. ITC, Pub. No. 4990, Section 337 Mediation Program Tenth Update 5 (2019), https://www.usitc.gov/publications/337/pub4990.pdf.

52. *See Mediation Program*, ITC, https://www.usitc.gov/intellectual_property/mediation.htm (last visited Mar. 23, 2025).

53. *See* ITC, *supra* note 51, at 5.

54. *Id.* at 9.

55. The deadlines for mediation will differ between ALJs and depend upon a case's unique features. The schedule is negotiated by the parties and then submitted to the ALJ for entry as an order. In negotiating the schedule, the parties work within the confines of the ITC rules and review recent scheduling orders of the ALJ to see what the ALJ has approved previously. The ALJs typically accept the parties' proposal, with the exception of the trial date, which the ALJ will determine depending on his or her schedule and courtroom availability.

56. *See* ITC, *supra* note 51, at 5.

57. *Id.* at 9. "Private" parties are parties to a Section 337 investigation other than the OUII.

more business certainty.[58] The Program is flexible, so the parties remain in control of the proceeding (e.g., the date and time of the proceeding).[59] Participating in the Program will not add time to the litigation process (i.e., the presiding ALJ will not stay the proceeding so that the parties can mediate), so the investigation will not be delayed.[60]

The parties have various options for engaging a mediator.[61] The parties may seek assistance from the Commission secretary in selecting an appropriate mediator.[62] The roster of mediators (which is often the first list parties consult in selecting a mediator) is composed of experienced IP and/or commercial mediators or former judges.[63] These mediators have agreed to participate in the Program and are prescreened by the Commission.[64] Mediators are prohibited from "active practice," meaning that the mediator is not appearing, and will not appear while serving as a member of the Commission's mediation roster, as a counsel for a party or amicus in any matter before the Commission or in any appeals from the Commission.[65] Mediators must not represent either party or any amicus for any purpose, and must disclose all past relationships with counsel, the counsel's firms, and the parties. Mediators also must follow strict conflict of interest standards by recusing himself or herself should (1) there be a conflict of interest, (2) they perceive a conflict of interest, or (3) a reasonable person would perceive a conflict of interest.[66]

Once assigned, the mediator will generally conduct the mediation process as any other type of commercial mediation. This includes contacting the parties to obtain background information on the dispute and to discuss the parties' positions regarding whether the Section 337 investigation is amenable to settlement, whether there are any impediments to a resolution, whether there are any nonnegotiable issues, and whether there are any jurisdictional issues such as a lack of importation of the accused product.[67] Before the mediation, the mediator may also review public pleadings and documents available on the ITC's docketing system (called the Electronic Document Information System, or EDIS) for the investigation at issue and/

58. *Id.* at 3.
59. *Id.* at 5.
60. *Id.* at 5, 9.
61. *Id.* at 17.
62. *Id.*
63. *See id.* at 5, 17–36 (providing the current roster of the ITC's approved mediators and their biographies).
64. *See id.* at 17.
65. *Id.* at 10.
66. *Id.* at 10–11 ("Mediators must err in favor of recusal when in doubt" regarding a potential conflict of interest).
67. *Id.*

or any related investigations.[68] The mediator may also request brief written submissions to help evaluate areas of agreement and dispute, to understand possible impediments, to learn of any prior settlement discussions, and to obtain current settlement proposals.[69]

Mediations are intended to last one day and, if conducted under the Program, are normally conducted at no expense to the litigants.[70] Under the Program, the Commission may provide physical space for the mediation, if available and if requested by the parties.[71] If longer mediation sessions are required, "it is expected the parties will compensate the mediator as a professional service provider."[72] In accordance with the Program, the mediator will require a party representative with actual settlement authority to attend the mediation.[73] *Actual settlement authority* does not simply mean sending a person authorized to accept a proposal or offer a minimum or maximum dollar amount.[74] Rather, the party representative should be a person who can make independent decisions and has the knowledge necessary to generate and consider creative solutions—generally a business principal.[75] The participation of decision makers is intended to increase the likelihood of obtaining a written agreement at the conclusion of the mediation that spells out the terms of settlement.[76]

As is typical in mediations, mediation under the Program is confidential, and the ITC has strong rules for protection of confidential business information.[77] Unless the parties agree otherwise, they and the mediator are prohibited from disclosing the substance of the mediation, subject only to certain enumerated exceptions—for example, in litigation regarding enforcement of an agreement reached through the mediation.[78] Each party's written submissions, if any, are for the eyes of the mediator only.[79] They are not shared with the other parties, the OUII staff (unless invited by the parties to participate in the mediation), the ALJ, or other ITC personnel, and they do not become part of the investigation record.[80] The mediator may communicate about the

68. *Id.*
69. *Id.*
70. *Id.* at 5.
71. *Id.* at 11.
72. *Id.* at 5–6.
73. *Id.* at 6.
74. *Id.*
75. *Id.*
76. *Id.*
77. *Id.* at 7–9.
78. *Id.* at 8.
79. *Id.*
80. *Id.*

mediation at a high level only with the Commission secretary.[81] Otherwise, mediators must protect the confidentiality of the substance of the mediation, including not complying with subpoenas or other demands for documents and information, while advising the general counsel of the ITC regarding the same.[82]

As with any form of mediation, the Program offers a confidential, quick, relatively inexpensive, and flexible alternative for resolving Section 337 proceedings with no risk to the parties for attempting to find a solution.[83] Even when the case itself does not fully settle, a mediation session can lead to a partial settlement or otherwise help the parties to narrow the issues before the ALJ.[84]

III. Considerations in Mediating Section 337 Investigations

This section addresses special considerations concerning the mediation of Section 337 investigations as a result of the unique nature of ITC proceedings.

A. Timing of Mediation and the Use of Inflection Points

The timing of mediation is an important factor in any litigated matter. Section 337 investigations present a unique circumstance in that they move on an intensely rapid schedule as required by statute. If too little time is devoted to mediation at the right time, then the pace and weight of the work in the investigation (e.g., full discovery including fact and expert depositions, claim interpretation briefing/hearing, summary judgment motions) can overwhelm the participants' ability to identify and act on real settlement opportunities. Mediation should be scheduled far enough along in the timeline of a Section 337 investigation such that the parties have a realistic opportunity to assess the merits of their case, but not so late in the case that insufficient time remains before a final decision is rendered.

There are a number of inflection points during the progress of a Section 337 investigation that may facilitate settlement because they inform case assessment (i.e., provide a reality check on the merits), uncover potential

81. *Id.*

82. *Id.* at 7–8; ITC, Nondisclosure Confidentiality Agreement for Mediators 1–2 (2015), https://www.usitc.gov/intellectual_property/documents/nondisclosure_agreement-mediator.pdf.

83. ITC, *supra* note 51, at 7–8.

84. *Id.* at 11.

business risks, or indicate that significant work is required in the case, which may implicate substantial expenses and company time. Thus, preplanning and time is required to conduct a mediation, including choosing the mediator and planning and scheduling the mediation with the mediator and the opposing party or parties.

The procedural orders defining the schedule for a Section 337 investigation typically include a deadline for mediation. To meet that deadline, the parties should consider inflection points from the inception of the investigation. For example, the filing of the Section 337 complaint itself provides an early opportunity to assess the merits of the claims as a result of the heightened pleading requirements mentioned earlier. Further, the OUII's pre-filing review and the Commission's review before institution—having the tendency of dissuading the filing of weaker claims—suggest the benefit of seriously considering early settlement discussions before making a significant investment in the investigation.

After a Section 337 investigation is instituted, the views of the OUII staff on merits issues, such as patent claim construction, can provide insight into the strengths and weaknesses of each party's position to inform settlement. And, as in federal district court, the ALJ's claim construction decision can motivate settlement. Because investigations are typically on a nine-month track from institution to hearing, claim construction occurs about six months after institution of the investigation, and that decision is handed down just before expert discovery commences. If the parties wish to consider mediation in conjunction with the ALJ's claim construction, then ample planning is required insofar as there is a tremendous amount of work associated with the claim construction proceeding and expert discovery stages of the investigation.

Additional events that may impact settlement considerations and pursuing mediation include the parties' summary determination motions, pretrial motions *in limine*, and high-priority objections, all of which are both filed shortly before the hearing and can be informative as to the strength of each party's trial presentations. The OUII staff's prehearing brief, in which the OUII takes a position on the merits of the investigation, can also have a salutary effect on settlement. As with the claim construction and expert discovery phases of the investigation, the parties will be intensely busy getting ready for the evidentiary hearing, so ample preplanning is required to schedule and conduct a mediation in that timeframe.

The parties' presentations and witnesses at the hearing may also inform settlement discussions. After the hearing, the ALJ has a specified amount of time set forth in the procedural order to issue his or her FID. Having a date certain for the FID may further influence settlement activity. Per the procedural order, mediation will have occurred previously, but the parties can use this opportunity to negotiate directly or through the mediator with follow-up communications. As mentioned earlier in this chapter, the FID may be appealed to the Commission. The pendency of this appeal within the Commission provides yet another opportunity to settle with or without facilitation by a mediator. Finally, the Commission decision can be appealed to the Federal Circuit, and the pendency of that appeal may provide a final opportunity to settle. In this regard, the prevailing party may wish to consider the effect of the Commission's participation in the Federal Circuit appeal as its own potential area of risk, inasmuch as the Commission's attorney may make concessions or stipulations that are unhelpful to the prevailing party.

Lastly, the expense and burden of the highly expedited proceedings in the ITC can act as strong leverage in mediation proceedings for Section 337 investigations. In addition, to a certain extent, deadlines in other parallel matters or countersuits may be relevant in the mediation of a Section 337 investigation. However, because parallel federal district court actions are typically stayed by request of the respondent, and because Section 337 investigations proceed more rapidly than parallel PTO proceedings, deadlines and inflection points in the Section 337 investigation are usually more impactful on settlement negotiations. For example, at the PTAB, petitions for post-grant review are frequently denied on discretionary grounds based on the co-pendency of a more rapid Section 337 investigation.

The following case in point illustrates in a Section 337 investigation the impact of timing considerations and parallel proceedings on settlement.

Case in point: A Section 337 investigation resulted in an ALJ's FID recommending exclusion of the accused products. However, on appeal to the Commission, the ALJ's decision was reversed such that the accused products were not excluded from importation. Then, while the Commission decision was on appeal to the Federal Circuit, the countersuit filed in federal district court (by the respondent in the investigation) proceeded. In the countersuit, the respondent asserted its own patents against the complainant in the investigation and was awarded treble damages. In hindsight, the complainant's settlement posture was the strongest after the issuance of the FID but *before* the Commission decision. The damages awarded in the countersuit flipped the settlement postures of the parties, resulting in settlement of the Section 337 investigation and the district court countersuit, as well as a related parallel litigation in Europe.

In sum, the unique features of a Section 337 investigation provide parties with many opportunities to plan for and participate in a mediation. From the inception of the investigation or prior to full-fledged fact discovery, they may consider mediation to curtail the significant costs of a Section 337 investigation. Substantive case milestones like decisions on discovery disputes, ALJ feedback at claim construction hearings and ALJ rulings on the same, and summary determination on key claims and defenses can serve as inflection points, providing feedback or a reality check on the merits and informing the settlement calculus. Furthermore, compelling opportunities exist in a Section 337 investigation to pursue mediation pre-evidentiary hearing, post-evidentiary hearing, pre-initial determination, and after the ALJ issues his or her initial determination. At each of these stages, the issues may be sufficiently crystallized and immediate for the parties to appreciate their litigation risk and to reach a business resolution. The parties may also take advantage of the fully developed record and Commission decision to negotiate resolution during the pendency of an appeal within the Commission and even to the Federal Circuit.

B. Selection of Mediator

As in any mediation, it is important that the parties select a mediator with relevant experience. Mediators listed in the ITC's brochure describing the Section 337 mediation program are selected based upon their mediation experience, including in Section 337 investigations. Because the result of a Section 337 investigation is the issuance or denial of an exclusion order, the mediator should have some exposure to ITC remedial orders and their enforcement through Customs so that they are able to discuss the risks and benefits of litigation in the ITC with the parties.

In any particular case, it may be important for the mediator to have some background in the IP issues being litigated, as well as the relevant IP, technology, and products at issue, and the product market and related economic issues. In addition, if the filing of a Section 337 investigation has spawned the filing of counter investigations, cases in federal district courts, the PTO, or forums around the world, or if other litigation has spawned the Section 337 investigation subject to mediation, then a mediator with experience resolving global disputes may be appropriate.

ITC cases typically involve multiple respondents. In that case, a mediator with experience in multiparty litigation may be appropriate. In many investigations, there is a primary respondent (e.g., the manufacturer of the product accused of infringement) and secondary respondents (e.g., distributors or importers of the manufacturer's accused product). In such investigations, it may be sufficient to mediate with the lead respondent alone. However, in other investigations, there may be multiple manufacturers of products accused of infringement each having its own importers and distributors calling for a mediator with experience with multiparty litigation.

To the extent that some of the respondents are foreign entities or have foreign principals attending the mediation, the mediator may need to be sensitive to and have experience with identifying and addressing cultural issues. The mediator may want to encourage foreign parties to bring to the mediation participants familiar with mediation and the settlement of litigation in the United States. Where a party requests the services of an interpreter at the mediation, the mediator should be willing to accommodate that request and be comfortable conducting the mediation with the participation of an interpreter.

Case in point: A mediator with wide-ranging experience skillfully navigated a mediation in a Section 337 investigation with foreign principals. While there were cultural and language issues to be addressed at the mediation, towards the end of the mediation session, the mediator brought the principals together for direct negotiations. The case did not settle at the mediation session but bringing the principals together facilitated further direct negotiations by them closer to the hearing date, which resulted in a settlement.

C. Selection of Party Representatives

Mediation sessions must include a company official with full settlement authority. To make a good-faith effort to settle the case during mediation, the ITC mediation program requires officials from the parties to attend who can bind their companies to the agreements that may be negotiated at such sessions (e.g., settlement, license). It is understood that such agreements will be subject to review by, for example, boards of directors, but it is critical in mediation to get settlement agreements negotiated in good faith by persons who can truly resolve the investigation.

It is also helpful to have as the party representative attending the mediation a person who has sufficient background in the dispute and Section 337 investigations generally. This is so the party representative can understand the parties' arguments during the course of the mediation (e.g., in mediation submissions, at the mediation session), the expedited nature of the proceedings, and the consequences of the Section 337 investigation. While the party representatives will be represented at the mediation by their outside counsel and can be advised on the merits of the arguments being made, having the requisite background allows the party representatives to bring their own independent judgment to the table at the mediation. For example, the party representative should have an understanding of the

- legal claims, IP, and the respondents' products giving rise to liability;
- parties' products and the market for those products so as to understand the impact that ITC exclusion orders and cease and desist orders will have on the parties' businesses; and
- Section 337 investigations including enforcement of ITC remedial orders.

Case in point: In the mediation of a Section 337 investigation, the respondent argued that it had the ability to design around the asserted patents and that it had already implemented the design-around. Indeed, the respondent represented that it would provide discovery on the design-around in the investigation. This put the complainant in the difficult position of either accusing the design-around of infringement in the investigation and risking a finding of noninfringement, or not accusing the design-around, which could be viewed as an admission that it was outside the scope of the investigation. The respondent maintained that any ITC remedial order would not exclude the design-around from the market such that, even if the ITC found a violation as to the original design, the complainant would not achieve its goal of excluding the respondent from the market.

To fully understand the impact that the alleged design-around would have on the investigation, the party representatives needed to understand the patent infringement claim, the accused product, the product category (i.e., whether consumers would accept the design-around as an alternative to the patented product), the ITC's practice regarding considering design-arounds, and Customs' enforcement of ITC remedial orders. In this matter, because the claimant's party representative was steeped in the dispute from its earliest stages, he could immediately appreciate the significance of the alleged design-around, took the respondent's arguments seriously, and understood counsel's advice at the mediation as to how to best respond.

D. Cultural Issues

Given that ITC jurisdiction is over imported products, respondents are oftentimes headquartered outside the United States, such that cross-cultural issues can become important in mediating disputes underlying Section 337 investigations. The parties, counsel, and the mediator should be attuned to differences in language,[85] culture, business practices, and legal regimes that may present issues so they can be addressed early. This can help in settlement discussions to ensure better communication and more focused and respectful negotiations, with greater likelihood of a successful outcome.

85. The parties may request that an interpreter participate at the mediation, for example, because a party does not speak the language of the other party or because a foreign principal with modest English language skills may want an interpreter to insure a full understanding of the discussion. Using an interpreter may prolong the mediation and create a different dynamic both in caucus and in a joint session that needs to be considered. It may also make it more challenging to agree on the precise language used in the settlement terms.

Case in point: During the mediation of a Section 337 investigation involving patent infringement claims, a foreign respondent's representative expressed the view that settlement would be dishonorable and, therefore, "heads would have to roll" for the respondent to settle for any significant amount of money. The respondent's representatives viewed settlement as an admission of wrongdoing such that someone would have to take blame for the alleged infringing conduct. While that misunderstanding scuttled the mediation, the parties later settled because the respondent apparently came to understand settlement as a business strategy to avoid risk as opposed to an admission of wrongdoing.

E. Scope of Mediation

The scope of the mediation in terms of the number and nature of the claims and parties that need to be addressed is also an important consideration in mediating the dispute underlying a Section 337 investigation. As mentioned, an investigation may involve multiple unrelated accused products and multiple unrelated parties, and there may be parallel proceedings in federal district courts and the PTO. In addition, there may be countersuits in federal district courts or in various international forums, each with its own timelines, potential benefits, and risks.

There are a number of ways to deal with mediations of investigations with multiple respondents. Nothing prevents settlement discussions between the complainant and each respondent individually. In fact, the complainant may be able to simplify the investigation by settling with some respondents while litigating against others. However, in some investigations, engaging each of the respondents in settlement discussions can be inefficient. In investigations where there are multiple accused products and multiple manufacturers, importers, and distributors of those products, the complainant will likely have no choice but to engage in mediation with each respondent group.

Case in point: In a Section 337 investigation that named the product manufacturer as a respondent and the importers and distributors as separate respondents, the complainant settled with the importer and distributor respondents while the investigation was ongoing. The importers and distributors agreed to immediately cease and desist from the alleged infringing conduct (e.g., importing, selling, or offering for sale the accused infringing products) and to abide by the final decision of the ITC with respect to the manufacturer respondent. By removing the respondents who settled, the scope of the investigation and the related mediation were more focused.

In addition, as mentioned, the parties to a Section 337 investigation are frequently also involved in related pending litigation in other venues. For example, because the remedies available from the Commission in a Section 337 investigation are limited to injunctive-style relief and do not include monetary damages, parallel federal district court suits are typically filed (and then oftentimes stayed at the request of the respondent). Furthermore, where the investigation involves patents, respondents frequently challenge the patents by petitioning the PTAB to initiate an inter partes review (IPR) post-grant patentability review. To the extent that the parties are able to resolve or narrow a Section 337 investigation through mediation, the resulting agreement will typically take into account related proceedings.

Ordinarily, parties to a mediation will address and attempt to resolve all disputes between the parties in a "global settlement." If a Section 337 investigation has prompted an IPR post-grant proceeding to invalidate the asserted patents, then parties will typically want to resolve both the Section 337 investigation and the IPR proceeding. If the respondent has filed a countersuit, resolution of the investigation will not necessarily resolve the countersuit. However, the ITC complainant would likely not unilaterally disarm by settling the investigation unless the countersuit is also resolved.

Parties sometimes address broader portfolios of products or IP than what is squarely at issue in the investigation, for example, the complainant may raise the possibility of infringement of a broader IP portfolio to provide additional leverage in settlement negotiations. Relatedly, the respondent may want assurances that, presuming a settlement, the complainant will not bring additional IP claims in the foreseeable future. And there are some situations where settlement of an investigation alone or in favor of proceeding in a different forum makes sense, for example, when the respondent ceases importation.

Case in point: A Section 337 investigation was initiated based upon the respondent manufacturing its alleged infringing products overseas and importing them into the United States. However, independent of the investigation, the respondent had planned to bring its manufacturing into the United States, which it did during the course of the investigation. Because ITC exclusion orders do not prevent distribution of products manufactured in the United States, once the manufacturing was brought here, the parties settled the Section 337 investigation. A parallel federal district court action, which would address manufacturing and sale of the alleged infringing products in the United States, continued.

IV. Procedural Considerations in Resolving Section 337 Investigations

The Commission rules provide specific procedures for resolution or narrowing of Section 337 investigations before the ALJ's FID. A party may move to terminate an investigation with respect to one or more of the respondents on the basis of a licensing or other settlement agreement.[86] In addition, an investigation may be terminated as to one or more respondents on the basis of a consent order.[87]

The rules require that agreements to settle investigations be provided to the ITC for review by the OUII staff, the ALJ presiding over the investigation, and the Commission for consistency with the public interest.[88] The settlement agreement must be submitted in unredacted form. However, the rules do permit submission of a redacted settlement agreement—redacting information the parties deem confidential such as any payment terms—for inclusion in the public record.[89] Consistent with the confidentiality provisions discussed earlier, the substance and contents of the mediation itself are not disclosed or reviewed as part of this process.

A consent order is an agreement by the respondent to refrain from importation of the allegedly infringing products. The respondent essentially consents to the entry of an exclusion order. While neither an admission of liability nor a determination on the merits, a consent order reflects the respondent's agreement not to sell for importation, not to import, or not to sell after importation the allegedly infringing products in exchange for termination of the investigation. A consent order can be submitted at any point in an investigation and does not require agreement by the complainant. Consent orders become null and void upon expiration of a relevant IP right or a finding that a relevant IP right is invalid or unenforceable in a final determination not subject to appeal.[90]

However, respondents should exercise caution before deciding to submit a consent order, either unilaterally or as a result of a negotiated resolution

86. *See* 19 C.F.R. § 210.21(a)(2), (b).

87. *See id.* § 210.21(c).

88. *Id.* § 210.21(b).

89. *See id.* §§ 210.21(b)(1), 201.6(a); *see also, e.g.*, Initial Determination Terminating the Investigation as to Certain Respondents and Limiting Service at 3–4, Certain Semiconductor Devices Having Layered Dummy Fill, Elec. Devices & Components Thereof, Inv. No. 337-TA-1342 (USITC Mar. 14, 2023) (finding that redacted public versions of a settlement agreement complied with 19 C.F.R. § 210.21(b)(1) since "they contain redactions of only information that qualifies as confidential business information under Commission Rule 201.6(a)").

90. 19 C.F.R. § 210.21(c)(3)(ii)(A).

with the complainant. A consent order carries substantial "civil penalties" (i.e., monetary penalties) for its violation and does not prevent a complainant from pursuing damages for the infringement in federal district court.

The risk of civil penalties can be substantial in view of the necessary breadth of a consent order. The rules require that all consent orders include specific statements, including that the respondent will not sell for importation, import, or sell after importation the subject articles except by consent, license, or settlement agreement with the complainant; and that the respondent will not seek judicial review or otherwise challenge or contest the validity of the consent order.[91]

A respondent will therefore be unable to challenge or revoke the consent order even if other respondents in the same investigation become free to import the accused products because, for example, the complainant failed to satisfy the domestic industry requirement.[92] In addition, the Commission has historically imposed hefty fines for violating consent orders, and the Federal Circuit accords to the Commission broad discretion on review. For example, the Federal Circuit found no abuse of discretion where, on remand from an appellate decision directing the Commission to consider whether to modify its assessment of $6 million in civil penalties in view of the invalidation of the subject patents after the consent order was violated, the Commission declined to do so.[93] The law relating to civil penalties is underdeveloped—there are very few published decisions imposing penalties—making it difficult to provide insight on the potential risk associated with violating a consent order.

Conclusion

Section 337 investigations at the ITC are a powerful tool for U.S. IP owners to prevent or stop infringement. But, as with any adversarial proceeding involving IP rights, enforcing such rights and defending against such enforcement can be complex and expensive, and can result in diversion of critical resources (e.g., people and money) away from a party's business. Fortunately, the ITC's mediation program is an equally powerful tool or "off ramp" for parties involved in Section 337 investigations to resolve that dispute and, often, other pending actions in which they are involved regarding

91. *See id.* § 210.21(c).

92. *See, e.g.*, Notice of Commission Determination to Deny a Petition to Rescind a Consent Order at 2, Certain Carburetors & Prods. Containing Such Carburetors, Inv. No. 337-TA-1123 (USITC Feb. 26, 2020).

93. DBN Holding, Inc. v. U.S. Int'l Trade Comm'n, 26 F.4th 1363, 1372 (Fed. Cir. 2022).

the same IP and products. While many features of the ITC's mediation program are similar to mediating other commercial (and international) cases, there are some unique features of Section 337 investigations that may influence advocacy and strategies in negotiating and resolving such disputes. Understanding those unique features is the first step to successfully mediating Section 337 investigations before the ITC.

PART IV

Adjudicative Proceedings for Deciding IP/Technology Disputes

CHAPTER 9

Arbitrating IP/Technology Cases: Considerations for Businesspeople and Advocates

Michael H. Diamant, Stephen P. Gilbert, Laura A. Kaster, and Harrie Samaras

Spectacular achievement is always preceded by unspectacular preparation.

—Robert H. Schuller

Introduction[1]

With limited exceptions, in intellectual property (IP) and technology disputes, arbitration is well suited to provide an efficient process and principled result. While there are numerous reasons why, key are (1) the ability to select a trier of fact with a background in, and understanding of, technology issues generally or even the specific technology at issue, and (2) the ability to craft an efficient and cost-effective process best suited for the particular dispute. Unlike court litigation, which is formally structured by the Federal Rules of Civil Procedure (Federal Rules), state rules, local rules, and/or judges' individual courtroom rules, arbitration is more flexible, providing the parties with far more control. Understanding the differences to maximize that flexibility is the mark of a good arbitration advocate.

Insofar as arbitration is a creature of contract, the parties are in the driver's seat in designing and, largely, in implementing the process. Clients can play an important role in both. Working with their outside counsel, and at times engaging with their counterpart, they can better use the flexibility of arbitration to meet time, cost, confidentiality, and other important business needs and concerns.

This chapter is not designed to teach all that is necessary to know about arbitration or arbitration advocacy; it assumes a basic knowledge of both. Rather, the chapter focuses on those aspects of arbitrating IP/Technology cases that can influence how parties adapt and manage the arbitration

1. See Glossary for definition of frequently used terms.

process to achieve an effective process and winning presentation.[2] The more that parties are prepared to make the most of arbitration's flexibility, the more likely they will feel well served by the process.

I. Considerations When Using Arbitration in IP/Technology Cases

Arbitration is used in a wide variety of IP/Technology disputes. IP disputes include those related to creation and ownership of IP rights, validity and enforceability of IP, scope of rights, infringement/misappropriation of rights including trade secrets, third-party rights, and transactions and breaches of contract involving IP/Technology rights. Technology disputes include a broad range of cases involving science and/or engineering issues. These can include design disputes, causation of failure, compliance with specifications, and determining whether a product or potential product falls within a contractual provision. These disputes may involve principles of physics, chemistry, biology, or software, or two or more of them. To understand fully the legal issues of a case, an understanding of the underlying science and/or engineering is not only helpful but necessary.

In addition to the factors normally involved when arbitrating commercial cases, IP/Technology disputes often involve specialized substantive areas of the law (e.g., patent, trade secret, trademark, copyright, U.S. Food and Drug Administration (FDA)) and areas of science and/or engineering. These cases also characteristically require some discovery. They have a variety of supporting documents (e.g., engineering diagrams, test results, lab notebooks, regulatory and prosecution documents, contracts, software code), there may be a need for emergency relief,[3] there is likely to be expert testimony, and there is a

2. The issues covered are those that this panel of arbitrator-authors deemed most worthy of discussing, and the ideas for handling them are from that panel's perspective.

3. For example, in a case involving the breach of a confidentiality provision where the owner of the confidential information is concerned that the other party will use or disseminate such information, emergency relief may be necessary. Major arbitral institutions have procedures for granting emergency relief. *See, e.g.*, American Arbitration Association, Commercial Arbitration Rules and Mediation Procedures R-39 (2022) [hereinafter AAA Commercial Rules], https://www.adr.org/sites/default/files/Commercial-Rules_Web.pdf; *2019 Administered Arbitration Rules*, Int'l Inst. for Conflict Prevention & Resol. [hereinafter *CPR Administered Rules*], https://drs.cpradr.org/rules/arbitration/administered-arbitration-rules-2019 (last visited Mar. 23, 2025) (Rule 14); *2018 CPR Non-Administered Arbitration Rules*, Int'l Inst. for Conflict Prevention & Resol. [hereinafter *CPR Non-Administered Rules*], https://drs.cpradr.org/rules/arbitration/non-administered/2018-cpr-non-administered-arbitration-rules (last visited Mar. 23, 2025) (Rule 14);

need for counsel to have a clear command of the IP/technical and legal issues (which are often intertwined) so that counsel can clearly and persuasively guide the arbitration panel through the technical evidence that is important to deciding the issues in dispute. Furthermore, in patent cases, parties should consider the possible impact of the requirements in 35 U.S.C. § 294(d) and (e) on confidentiality obligations and the enforceability of the award.

The potential benefits of arbitration in IP/Technology cases are numerous. Consider a dispute between the two parties to a royalty-bearing patent license regarding whether a licensed patent covers a new product or process made or used by and marketed by the licensee. A lawsuit to resolve the dispute may injure what each party hopes will be an ongoing and profitable relationship, take years to resolve, become known to others in the industry, endanger the confidentiality of trade secrets, disrupt each side's business operations with potentially broad discovery demands, and likely impose costs that extend beyond the litigation. Furthermore, businesspeople often simply want answers sooner rather than later so that they can avoid long-term uncertainty.

The licensor and licensee could agree to arbitrate with an expedited timetable (e.g., four months from appointment of the panel to award); voluntary focused discovery (i.e., no requests for admission, no interrogatories, and one time-limited deposition per side); a limit on the number of hearing witnesses; the hearing time limited to just a few days; a panel having the requisite subject matter expertise (e.g., patent, licensing, relevant technology or product area); an award stating simply *yes* or *no* to an agreed-upon question (i.e., the product is or is not royalty-bearing); a stipulation for past damages (i.e., the amount of royalty) if the product is found to be royalty-bearing (i.e., a *yes*); and an agreement that each side will bear the cost of its attorneys, witnesses, and expert(s), with the other costs of the arbitration split 50-50. This kind of proceeding *does, in fact,* occur in IP/Technology disputes. Such a proceeding would potentially have numerous benefits, including quick and certain resolution; confidentiality regarding the dispute and underlying proprietary information; minimal business disruption; preservation of the relationship (particularly important when the parties have an ongoing relationship); and reduced cost.

It is difficult to define the average length of IP/Technology arbitrations. However, experience indicates that many U.S. commercial arbitrations generally require no more than about a year from panel appointment to issuance

---

JAMS, JAMS Comprehensive Arbitration Rules & Procedures Rule 2 (2021) [hereinafter JAMS Rules & Procedures], https://www.jamsadr.com/files/Uploads/Documents/JAMS-Rules/JAMS_Comprehensive_Arbitration_Rules-2021.pdf. Under those rules, an emergency arbitration panel can be appointed, a hearing held, and relief granted within just a few days.

of the award, and there are cases requiring far less time. Furthermore, in considering the length of an arbitration proceeding, it is estimated that the percentage of awards that parties challenge is small, with reported opinions indicating that challenges succeed only a small percentage of the time (variously estimated as up to 20 percent).[4] Indeed, there are limited bases for a court to set aside an award.[5] For example, 9 U.S.C. § 10(a) enumerates the grounds for vacatur in an arbitration governed by the Federal Arbitration Act (FAA) (state arbitration laws are similar):[6]

> (1) where the award was procured by corruption, fraud, or undue means;
>
> (2) where there was evident partiality or corruption in the arbitrators, or either of them;
>
> (3) where the arbitrators were guilty of misconduct in refusing to postpone the hearing, upon sufficient cause shown, or in refusing to hear evidence pertinent and material to the controversy; or of any other misbehavior by which the rights of any party have been prejudiced; or
>
> (4) where the arbitrators exceeded their powers, or so imperfectly executed them that a mutual, final, and definite award upon the subject matter submitted was not made.[7]

Under the FAA, court proceedings to confirm an award must be brought within one year after the award is made,[8] but notice of a motion to vacate,

---

4. *See, e.g.*, Lawrence R. Mills et al., *Vacating Arbitration Awards*, DISP. RESOL. MAG., Summer 2005, at 23–27 (roughly 20 percent of awards vacated); LAWRENCE R. MILLS ET AL., AAA, VACATUR OF ARBITRATION AWARDS: A REAL-WORLD REVIEW OF THE CASE LAW (2023), https://go.adr.org/rs/294-SFS-516/images/Why_Courts_Vacate_Awards-2023_AAA_Panel_Con-Brewer-Vacatur_of_Arbitration_Awards_11.7.22.pdf (similar).

5. *See* Ramos-Santiago v. United Parcel Serv., 524 F.3d 120, 123 (1st Cir. 2008) ("A federal court's review of an arbitrator's decision . . . is 'extremely narrow and exceedingly deferential.'" (internal footnotes omitted)).

6. Many IP/Technology agreements fall within the ambit of the FAA because, broadly speaking, it applies (among other things) to arbitration agreements concerning "commerce" (e.g., interstate commerce), although the parties can agree that a state arbitration statute applies. Arbitration, 9 U.S.C. § 1 *et seq.* (current through Jan. 1, 2024).

7. There is an ongoing debate after *Hall Street Associates, L.L.C. v. Mattel, Inc.*, 552 U.S. 576 (2008), as to whether an award could still be vacated for "manifest disregard of law."

8. Some entities have a standing policy of moving to confirm each favorable arbitration award. One reason is that, in some states, an award does not have issue or claim preclusion effect unless and until a court confirms it so that it *becomes* a judgment (and once it is a judgment, the court's enforcement powers are available).

modify, or correct an award must be served within three months after the award is filed or delivered.[9] Courts often deal quickly with proceedings to vacate or confirm arbitration awards, particularly unchallenged requests to confirm. That said, arbitration awards in commercial matters will not be in court, either to vacate or confirm, because the parties will generally honor and carry out the award. The majority of requests to vacate will be resolved quickly and will not succeed. Therefore, the expeditious final decision that is important to so many businesses is achievable.

II. Selecting a Panel[10]

The ability to choose an arbitral panel is often a major reason parties choose arbitration over litigation. Although the parties may be amenable to discussing panel selection issues after a dispute arises, the existence of the dispute may adversely affect the cooperation of the parties and their ability to agree on, for example, the number of panel members, panelist criteria, the method of panel selection,[11] or an interview process. Thus, as discussed in Chapter 2, the parties may want to address such issues in their arbitration agreement based upon the kind of disputes they anticipate.

Many of the well-known administering arbitral institutions have specialty panels (i.e., technology and/or IP) from which parties can select candidates. Furthermore, their experienced staff play an important role in helping the parties identify candidates who meet criteria they have identified (e.g., in the arbitration clause, since the arbitration commenced) and in helping the parties select criteria (and then candidates) where none exist.[12] Also, parties can search for candidates on the internet insofar as arbitrators often publicly

9. *See* 9 U.S.C. §§ 9, 12 (2016).

10. The term "panel" refers to the arbitration panel constituted for a particular case, typically composed of one or three arbitrators.

11. There are many processes for selecting a panel. The parties, for example, can set forth such a process in their pre-dispute or submission agreement or rely on the process in the arbitral rules they adopt. The International Institute for Conflict Prevention & Resolution (CPR) in Rule 5.4 of both its administered and non-administered rules provides a unique mechanism for constituting a tri-partite panel whereby parties select their party-appointed panelists without the candidates knowing which party designated them. *See CPR Administered Rules* and *CPR Non-Administered Rules, supra* note 3, Rule 5.4.

12. If an arbitral institution does not have panelists with education or experience in the particular, likely narrow, area of technology at issue, parties should consider a broader but relevant area of technology for searching. Panelists with that background can then be educated through the briefs and witnesses about the specific science and technology relevant to the case.

disclose their areas of specialization along with their credentials and biographical information.[13] There are other organizations, such as the Silicon Valley Arbitration & Mediation Center (SVAMC),[14] that do not administer arbitrations but carefully vet individuals to qualify for their specialized lists of technology-knowledgeable neutrals (e.g., the SVAMC's Tech List), and many of those neutrals also appear on the rosters of well-known arbitral institutions. In addition, there are professional and honorary organizations like the College of Commercial Arbitrators (CCA)[15] and the Chartered Institute of Arbitrators (CIArb)[16] that also vet individuals before acceptance, thereby providing additional strong credentials.

Once candidates are identified, the parties have various options for investigating their background and experience. In addition to information provided by an administering arbitral institution, as mentioned earlier in this chapter, parties can obtain online information about a candidate's education, experience, credentials, publications, and presentations from, for example, the candidate's website, the website of certain arbitral institutions,[17] and professional and honorary associations of which the candidate is a member. Furthermore, counsel may request references directly from candidates (e.g., advocates who have appeared before the candidate or arbitrators with whom they have served) whom they can then call for further due diligence (assuming those references are not prohibited under existing confidentiality obligations from disclosing information about their past experiences with the candidate).

Another means for winnowing down a list of candidates is for the parties to request more specific information about the background and experience of a candidate related to the dispute (e.g., by sending questions to candidates

13. Before selecting an arbitral institution to administer future disputes, counsel should consider searching its list of available panelists and their backgrounds to see if they have individuals who have a technology background that fits within the technology of anticipated disputes. If that information is not publicly available, the organization upon request may share the technology backgrounds of its panelists. They are not likely to share the names without charge if they also separately charge for assisting in the selection process itself. The parties can also agree in their arbitration provision to have the option of using panelists not on the administering institution's list but still use that institution to administer the arbitration.

14. *See generally* SVAMC, https://www.svamc.org (last visited Mar. 23, 2025).

15. *See generally* CCA, http://www.ccarbitrators.org (last visited Mar. 23, 2025).

16. *See generally* CIArb, http://www.ciarb.org (last visited Mar. 23, 2025).

17. *See generally Search Neutral Directory*, JAMS, https://www.jamsadr.com/neutrals/search (last visited Mar. 23, 2025); *Find a CPR Neutral*, CPR, https://drs.cpradr.org/neutrals/find-a-neutral (last visited Mar. 23, 2025); *WIPO Domain Name Panelists*, World Intell. Prop. Org., https://www.wipo.int/amc/en/domains/panel/panelists.html (last visited Mar. 23, 2025).

through the case manager of the arbitral institution helping the parties to select their panel). The kinds of requests and questions that parties may find relevant to a particular case are:

- Please describe your experience with the technology or industry involved in the dispute.
- Please describe your experience as an arbitrator or, alternatively, in arbitration proceedings generally and in the area of the subject technology or industry.
- What is your familiarity with [state] law?
- What is your experience, either as advocate or neutral, regarding the subject technology or industry?
- Summarize your experience, either as advocate or neutral, in disputes concerning patents and indicate whether you have a background in the relevant science or technology.
- Summarize your experience, either as advocate or neutral, regarding issues arising in development agreements concerning the subject technology or industry.

Counsel may also interview candidates, although there is a difference of opinion as to the value of interviews. Interviewing a short list of five or more candidates takes time and expense that may not be justified. In some cases, interviewing the final two candidates may be sufficient. The American Arbitration Association (AAA) offers an enhanced neutral selection process that enables the parties to interview candidates or pose agreed-upon written questions to ascertain, for example, the candidate's relative experience in similar disputes.[18]

The rules of the road for the interview, timing, participants, and scope of inquiry should be clearly established in writing before the interview occurs. The CIArb has developed guidelines that provide practical guidance for interviewing arbitral candidates.[19]

Under Canon III.B.(1) of the Code of Ethics for Arbitrators in Commercial Disputes, when candidates are being considered for appointment, they

> (b) may respond to inquiries from a party or its counsel designed to determine . . . [their] suitability and availability for the appointment. In any such dialogue, the prospective arbitrator[s] may receive

---

18. *See* AAA, Fact Sheet: Enhanced Arbitrator Selection Process for Large Complex Cases (2017), https://go.adr.org/rs/294-SFS-516/images/Enhanced_Arbitrator_Selection_Process_LargeCase.pdf.

19. *See* CIArb, International Arbitration Practice Guideline: Interviews for Prospective Arbitrators (2015), https://www.ciarb.org/media/0v4pnwao/1-interviews-for-prospective-arbitrators-2015.pdf.

information from a party or its counsel disclosing the general nature of the dispute but should not permit them to discuss the merits of the case.

Candidates usually welcome joint interviews that do not address the specific issues in dispute. Important topics to cover in an interview include availability for hearing dates and for promptly rendering an award. Also, counsel may inquire about the interviewee's technical background, expertise, understanding of legal matters, licensing or other industry experience, and management style and preferences.[20] While technical or scientific knowledge may be relevant in selecting an arbitrator, seeking an arbitrator with very specific narrow knowledge may not be possible or even necessary.

Case in point: Counsel contacted arbitrators seeking expertise in the manufacture of artificial rubies. Knowledge of physical chemistry or the use of the type of specialized equipment involved was deemed insufficient. Finding an experienced technology arbitrator with that specific narrow experience would likely be impossible and probably unnecessary.

There is no prescribed method by which interviews must be conducted. They may be held by phone, in person, or by audioconference or videoconference. Some candidates will undertake individual party interviews, but may want to set the limits on the questioning and even record the interview and possibly disclose it to the other party. Some refuse individual interviews.

Case in point: In a detailed arbitration clause, the parties specified interviews with potential panelists for selecting a tri-partite panel from a list of candidates identified in the clause by name. The interviews were in person with both counsel present. Counsel focused on the candidates' patent law experience and discussed the arbitration process tailored by the parties, which the arbitral panel would have to follow.

20. For tri-partite panels, the parties may want one or more of the panelists to be an industry professional rather than a lawyer. In highly specialized industries, this can be helpful. Some non-lawyer professionals, however, do not believe a fair outcome can result if the law mandates the outcome. If the parties want the technical expertise of such professionals, but they want to satisfy their expectations that their legal rights will be fully recognized and legal issues decided according to the applicable law, they may want to interview such candidates, as well as lawyer candidates with whom such a professional would be serving, to gain comfort that their expectations will be respected.

Casting the net widely may enhance the kind of diversity that can improve decision-making. In addition, where time is of the essence, consider the schedules of the candidates and their ability to meet the needs of the parties. Having to reschedule hearing dates can undermine the efficiency of the process and add to costs.

III. What Can the Panel Do? Sources of Arbitral Authority

A good starting point for any commercial arbitration is to consider the sources of arbitral authority because, simply put, they determine the metes and bounds of what a panel can do. If a panel acts outside the scope of its authority, it may well result in partial or complete vacatur of an award. In any given case, the sources of authority may include the parties' arbitration agreements,[21] the set of arbitration rules, treaties,[22] federal and state statutes, federal and state court decisions,[23] guidelines of arbitral institutions, and guidelines from other organizations (e.g., bar associations).

Perhaps the most important source of the panel's authority is the parties' arbitration agreement. As discussed in Chapter 2, the agreement often addresses a variety of issues relating to the arbitration, including the authority of the panel in the proceeding: Which set of rules will be used? What type of relief can the panel award? For example, an arbitration agreement may expressly permit the panel to award any type of relief it deems appropriate, even if a court hearing the same dispute could not award that relief.

---

21. The parties' agreements include not just the original arbitration agreement (whether pre- or post-dispute) providing the authority to commence the arbitration, but also all the other agreements the parties make during the course of the arbitration proceeding (e.g., to withdraw the panel's authority to award attorneys' fees even if the original agreement provided that authority).

22. Treaty sources of authority include the 1958 Convention on the Recognition and Enforcement of Foreign Arbitral Awards (New York Convention) and the 1975 Inter-American Convention on International Commercial Arbitration (Panama Convention). For example, the New York Convention allows a party to bring an arbitral award from any first country that adheres to the New York Convention (e.g., the United States) to the courts of any second country that also adheres to the New York Convention (e.g., France) and have it enforced by those courts; approximately 172 countries are signatories.

23. Numerous federal and state cases may affect a panel's authority. *See, e.g.*, Reliastar Life Ins. Co. v. EMC Nat'l Life Co., 564 F.3d 81 (2d Cir. 2009) (finding that arbitrators can award attorneys' fees as sanctions even though arbitration agreement specified each party would bear expenses of its attorneys and of arbitrator it appointed).

Likewise, the parties may have authorized the panel to award attorneys' fees.[24] Alternatively, an agreement may expressly bar the panel from awarding relief such as punitive or consequential damages.

Arbitral institutions have at least one set of rules (usually their commercial rules or a specially drafted subset of their commercial rules) for conducting IP/Technology disputes and may have a specific set of rules for patent cases.[25] Sometimes the arbitration agreement names the set of rules to use; if not, the arbitral institution usually has a procedure/rule specifying which of its sets of rules to use in a given situation.[26] Although, at a high level, the sets of rules of the various institutions are similar from set to set, the rules may differ on significant issues (e.g., the scope of information exchange, the type of relief that can be awarded, appointment of an emergency panel, the power to impose sanctions, and time limits for holding the evidentiary hearing and rendering the award).

Federal statutory sources of authority include 9 U.S.C. Chapter 1 (general provisions of the FAA), 9 U.S.C. Chapter 2 (which provides for enforcement of the New York Convention), and 9 U.S.C. Chapter 3 (which provides for enforcement of the Panama Convention).[27] In the IP area, several sections of the federal patent and copyright statutes expressly sanction arbitration: 35 U.S.C. § 135 (Derivation proceedings),[28] 35 U.S.C. § 294 (Voluntary arbitration),[29] and 17 U.S.C. § 907 (Limitation on exclusive rights: innocent infringement).[30]

State statutory sources of authority include the state arbitration statutes, most of which are based on the 1955 Uniform Arbitration Act (amended in

---

24. The rules of arbitral organizations differ on this issue. For example, Rule R-49(d)(ii) of the AAA Commercial Rules provides that an award may include attorneys' fees if all parties have requested them (e.g., both parties requesting attorneys' fees in their pleadings) or it is authorized by law or their arbitration agreement. *See* AAA Commercial Rules, *supra* note 3, Rule R-49(d)(ii).

25. *See, e.g.*, AAA Commercial Rules, *supra* note 3; *CPR Non-Administered Rules*, *supra* note 3; JAMS Rules & Procedures, *supra* note 3. See Chapter 2 for a discussion of arbitral institutional rules specifically related to patent cases.

26. *See, e.g.*, AAA Commercial Rules, *supra* note 3, Rule R-1(a).

27. *See* Arbitration, 9 U.S.C. § 1 *et seq.* (current through Jan. 1, 2024).

28. *See* 35 U.S.C. § 135, Derivation Proceedings (2016), http://uscode.house.gov/view.xhtml?req=granuleid:USC-prelim-title35-section135&num=0&edition=prelim (last visited Mar. 23, 2025).

29. *See* 35 U.S.C. § 294, Voluntary Arbitration (2016), http://uscode.house.gov/view.xhtml?req=granuleid:USC-prelim-title35-section294&num=0&edition=prelim (last visited Mar. 23, 2025).

30. *See* 17 U.S.C. § 907, Limitation on Exclusive Rights: Innocent Infringement (2016), http://uscode.house.gov/view.xhtml?req=granuleid:USC-prelim-title17-section907&num=0&edition=prelim (last visited Mar. 23, 2025).

1956) or the 2000 Revised Uniform Arbitration Act, promulgated by the National Conference of Commissioners on Uniform State Laws.[31] The structure of the FAA is relatively bare and provides little in the way of details regarding arbitral procedure.[32] State arbitration statutes often address additional matters (e.g., authority to order provisional remedies, to control discovery, to award certain relief). The U.S. Supreme Court has decided that the FAA preempts state statutes to the extent the state statute conflicts with the FAA (i.e., there is conflict rather than field preemption).[33]

Although typically not binding on a panel (unless the parties have agreed otherwise), parties, panels, and courts often consult and rely on the guidelines of various provider and non-provider institutions for guidance concerning important issues that arise in an arbitration proceeding. These include the following:

a. The International Centre for Dispute Resolution (ICDR) in 1999 promulgated its "Guidelines for Arbitrators Concerning Exchanges of Information" (updated in 2021), much of which has now been incorporated into the latest ICDR arbitration rules.[34]
b. The International Bar Association (IBA) has promulgated guidelines concerning the taking of evidence, drafting arbitration clauses, and conflicts of interest in international arbitrations.[35]
c. The CIArb has promulgated various arbitration guidelines/protocols concerning provisional/interim relief, interim measures of protection,

---

31. *See Arbitration Act*, UNIF. L. COMM'N, https://www.uniformlaws.org/committees/community-home?CommunityKey=a0ad71d6-085f-4648-857a e9c893ac2736 (last visited Mar. 23, 2025).

32. The FAA provides generally for enforcement of contracts requiring arbitration; court appointment of arbitrators or umpires; compelling attendance of witnesses at arbitration hearings; and confirmation, vacatur, and modification/correction of arbitration awards.

33. *See* Volt Info. Scis., Inc. v. Bd. of Trs. of Leland Stanford Junior Univ., 489 U.S. 468, 477 (1989) ("[E]ven when Congress has not completely displaced state regulation in an area, state law may nonetheless be pre-empted to the extent that it actually conflicts with federal law.").

34. *See* ICDR, https://www.icdr.org/ (last visited Mar. 23, 2025) (search for "guidelines"); *see also* ICDR, INTERNATIONAL DISPUTE RESOLUTION PROCEDURES (INCLUDING MEDIATION AND ARBITRATION RULES) Rule 21 (2021) [hereinafter ICDR ARBITRATION RULES], https://www.icdr.org/sites/default/files/document_repository/ICDR_Rules_1.pdf.

35. These guidelines may, for example, be adopted for use with institutional or ad hoc rules governing international arbitrations. They reflect procedures in use in many different legal systems, and they may be particularly useful when the parties come from different legal cultures. *See generally IBA Guides and Reports*, IBA, https://www.ibanet.org/resources (last visited Mar. 23, 2025).

challenges to arbitrator jurisdiction, panel-appointed experts, multiparty arbitrations, orders relating to costs, drafting an award, and e-disclosure.[36]

d. The New York State Bar Association has published guidelines about conducting the prehearing phases of domestic and international arbitrations (e.g., discovery (including e-discovery), dispositive motions, and adjournments).[37]

IV. Privacy and Confidentiality: A Distinction with a Difference

A. Introduction

Some prime motivations for using arbitration are to protect the dispute from public exposure and, in IP/Technology cases, to maximize the chance of protecting privileged and confidential information.[38]

Almost all definitions of arbitration include the word *private* or *privacy*, so counsel often assume that everything about an arbitration proceeding is both private and confidential. That assumption is, in fact, incorrect, as privacy is not necessarily protected outside the proceeding, and privacy does not itself protect the confidentiality of materials or testimony submitted in the proceeding. Thus, it is important that counsel understand the boundaries and differences between arbitration privacy and confidentiality. In this regard, counsel should consider three practical questions: (1) How can the parties maximize the duties of all participants (e.g., counsel, parties, and witnesses) to maintain confidentiality about the proceeding outside of the arbitration? (2) What can advocates and arbitral panels do to protect the information exchanged during the proceeding, including the documents, testimony, and the reasoning and results set forth in the award? and (3) What

36. *See generally Professional Practice Guidelines—International Arbitration*, CIArb, https://www.ciarb.org/resources/professional-practice-guidelines/international-arbitration/ (last visited Mar. 23, 2025).

37. *See* New York State Bar Association, Guidelines for the Arbitrator's Conduct of the Pre-Hearing Phase of Domestic Commercial Arbitrations and Guidelines for the Arbitrator's Conduct of the Pre-Hearing Phase of International Arbitrations [hereinafter NYSBA Guidelines], https://www.adr.org/sites/default/files/document_repository/NYSBA%20Guidelines%20for%20the%20Arbitrator%27s%20Conduct.pdf (last visited Mar. 23, 2025).

38. The term "privileged information" is used in this chapter to refer to both attorney-client privilege and work-product protection as used in Rule 502 of the Federal Rules of Evidence. "Confidential information" is used in this chapter as a shorthand for information, including trade secrets, competitive and sensitive business information and communications, and scientific development work.

special steps do the parties need to take to ensure that the use of privileged and confidential information in the arbitration does not waive or otherwise jeopardize its protected status?

B. Maintaining Privacy and Confidentiality in Arbitration

The scope of privacy protection available varies by the country or state where the arbitration proceeding is held; the location of the seat in international arbitrations; the choice of arbitration rules; the location of enforcement; and the location where a third party seeks materials from an arbitration proceeding. The times to focus on the confidentiality of an arbitration proceeding are at the clause-drafting stage and again at the commencement of the arbitration (e.g., in the terms of reference, the preliminary scheduling and procedural order, or an order addressing confidentiality).

Parties also need to protect their privileged and confidential information within the arbitration proceeding by seeking a protective order and then appropriately marking and maintaining such information in accordance with the order. They should remain attuned to different obligations imposed on parties, counsel, and witnesses, and ensure coverage of participants not governed by applicable organizational rules. Finally, corporate parties also need to consider the obligations for regulatory reporting or other mandated disclosures to be sure the imposed or agreed-upon strictures do not prohibit them from complying with the required reporting.

1. Privacy of the Hearing

Although in some cases the parties may agree to the presence at the evidentiary hearing of corporate representatives other than the designated representatives and testifying witnesses, some rules permit the panel to exclude nonrepresentatives or to require panel approval.[39] Additionally, with remote hearings commonplace, representatives and lawyers from corporations and law firms who would not necessarily attend an in-person hearing might want

39. *See, e.g.*, AAA Commercial Rules, *supra* note 3, Rule R-26 (giving the panel discretion to admit any person other than parties and representatives); *CIETAC Current Arbitration Rules*, China Int'l Econ. & Trade Arb. Comm'n [hereinafter *CIETAC Arbitration Rules*], http://www.cietac.org/index.php?m=Page&a=index&id=531&l=en (last visited Mar. 23, 2025) (Article 38) (providing that hearings shall be held *in camera*); *2021 Arbitration Rules*, Int'l Chamber Com. [hereinafter *ICC Arbitration Rules*], https://iccwbo.org/dispute-resolution/dispute-resolution-services/arbitration/rules-procedure/2021-arbitration-rules/ (last visited Mar. 23, 2025) (Article 26(3)) ("Save with the approval of the arbitral tribunal and the parties, persons not involved in the proceedings shall not be admitted.").

to attend a remote hearing. Assuming counsel and the panel permit such additional individuals to attend the evidentiary hearing, efforts should be made to ensure that they abide by whatever rules or procedures are in place for protecting the privacy (and confidentiality) of the proceeding. To ensure that only permitted individuals are in the hearing room, a panel may begin the hearing by listing the counsel, party representatives, and witnesses who were expected to attend the hearing, or it may have each of the presiding counsel introduce their side and compare attendees to a list provided to the panel by counsel before the hearing.

It also may be helpful, where appropriate, to have more than one waiting area for witnesses, so that witnesses from each party who have yet to testify are not forced to sit with witnesses from the opposing party(ies).

2. Confidentiality Obligations of Participants

Most arbitral institutions treat the privacy of an arbitration proceeding as a completely separate issue from the obligations of the participants to protect disclosure of the fact of a dispute and the confidentiality of the information contained in the proceeding, documents, testimony, and award. Importantly, the obligations of the various participants differ. Typically, the panel and the arbitral institution's administrative personnel are obligated to protect information about the proceeding itself and documents and testimony submitted to the panel or institution, as well as the award.[40] However, the obligations of the parties, their counsel, and witnesses vary. In the absence of requirements in the terms of reference, orders of the panel, agreement of the parties and witnesses, or applicable law or rules, parties, counsel, and witnesses may not have an obligation to maintain the confidentiality of either procedural or substantive information.[41]

a) Obligations Under the Rules of U.S.-Based Arbitral Institutions

The Canons of Ethics for Arbitrators in Commercial Disputes govern the obligations of arbitral panels on commercial disputes to maintain the confidentiality of such proceedings. However, the AAA specifies in its Statement

---

40. *See, e.g.*, AAA Commercial Rules, *supra* note 3, Rule R-45(a) ("Unless otherwise required by applicable law, court order, or the parties' agreement, the AAA and the arbitrator shall keep confidential all matters relating to the arbitration or the award.").

41. *See, e.g., id.* Rule R-45(b) ("Upon the agreement of the parties or the request of any party, the arbitrator may make orders concerning the confidentiality of the arbitration proceedings or of any other matters in connection with the arbitration and may take measures for protecting trade secrets and confidential information.").

of Ethical Principles that, while arbitrators and AAA staff have a duty of confidentiality, it "takes no position" as to whether the parties should enter into a confidentiality agreement or agreed-upon (stipulated) order pertaining to the confidentiality of the proceeding or the award:

> An arbitration proceeding is a private process. In addition, AAA staff and AAA neutrals have an ethical obligation to keep information confidential. However, the AAA takes no position on whether parties should or should not agree to keep the proceeding and award confidential between themselves. The parties always have a right to disclose details of the proceeding, unless they have a separate confidentiality agreement. Where public agencies are involved in disputes, these public agencies routinely make the award public.[42]

JAMS rules permit arbitral panels to enter confidentiality or protective orders for trade secrets and other sensitive information but impose confidentiality only upon the panel and JAMS.[43] Thus, neither parties nor witnesses are covered. International Institute for Conflict Prevention & Resolution (CPR) rules provide for confidentiality obligations of parties, the panel, and CPR, but not witnesses.[44]

In considering issues of confidentiality when drafting an arbitration clause, a prudent drafter will select rules and applicable procedural and substantive law carefully to maximize the protection of privileged and confidential information. Moreover, once a dispute arises, counsel should revisit the issue and consider whether the arbitration clause should be supplemented by, for example, provisions in the terms of reference or a protective order.

b) Obligations Under the Rules of International-Based Arbitral Institutions

The most protective organizational rules may be found in China, Hong Kong, London, and Singapore. Article 33 of the China International Economic and Trade Arbitration Commission (CIETAC) rules, for example, imposes an obligation of confidentiality on all parties likely to become aware of the process, including witnesses. It creates a presumption that the hearings will be *in camera* and specifies that all attendees at the hearings and administrators be precluded from publicly discussing both substantive and procedural matters relating to the arbitration.[45] In Hong Kong, Rule 45 of the Hong Kong

42. *See AAA Statement of Ethical Principles*, AAA, https://www.adr.org/StatementofEthicalPrinciples (last visited Mar. 23, 2025).

43. *See* JAMS Rules & Procedures, *supra* note 3, Rule 26.

44. *See CPR Non-Administered Rules*, *supra* note 3, Rule 18 (Confidentiality); *CPR Administered Rules*, *supra* note 2, Rule 20 (Confidentiality).

45. *See CIETAC Arbitration Rules*, *supra* note 39, art. 33.

International Arbitration Centre (HKIAC) rules provides a presumption of confidentiality and addresses the parties, the arbitral panel, and the arbitral institution's administrators, as well as experts and witnesses.[46] In London, the London Court of International Arbitration (LCIA) rules cover the arbitration award itself—a distinction that is significant—making it confidential except to the extent required for legal enforcement. The rules also provide a technique that could be voluntarily accepted by the parties in any other arbitral setting: "The parties shall seek the same undertaking of confidentiality from all those that it involves in the arbitration, including but not limited to any authorised representative, witness of fact, expert or service provider."[47] The revised rules of the Singapore International Arbitration Centre (SIAC) provide that the parties, arbitrators, and panel-appointed experts—witnesses are not mentioned—must keep arbitration matters and the existence of the arbitration confidential except for legal enforcement.[48]

The rules of the World Intellectual Property Organization (WIPO) cover the panel, parties, and witnesses, and protect the confidentiality of the fact of the dispute and the award, like the LCIA, as well as any evidence or information provided to the panel.[49] WIPO imposes confidentiality about the existence of the proceeding but provides an exception for legal obligations or a "good faith duty of candor" to a third party. WIPO rules also specifically address witnesses and make their duty to maintain confidentiality a duty of the party presenting the witness.[50] The key exception to the WIPO confidentiality obligations is for enforcement or a court challenge to the arbitration award. In that circumstance, notice to the affected party is required, and disclosures must be limited to what is legally required.

When an international arbitration is possible in a future dispute, practitioners drafting arbitration clauses should consider as a factor in deciding what rules to choose both rules and law that address confidentiality. Although most nations that have addressed the issue treat the confidentiality issue as a substantive question governed by the law the parties selected to govern the underlying contract, Switzerland and France appear to treat

46. *See 2018 Administered Arbitration Rules*, HKIAC, http://www.hkiac.org/arbitration/rules-practice-notes/administered-arbitration-rules (last visited Mar. 23, 2025) (Article 45).

47. *See LCIA Arbitration Rules 2020*, LCIA [hereinafter *LCIA Rules*], https://www.lcia.org/Dispute_Resolution_Services/lcia-arbitration-rules-2020.aspx (last visited Mar. 23, 2025) (Articles 30.1 and 30.3).

48. *See* SIAC, SIAC Rules Rules 39.1–39.4 (2016), https://siac.org.sg/wp-content/uploads/2022/06/SIAC-Rules-2016-English_28-Feb-2017.pdf.

49. *See WIPO Arbitration Rules*, WIPO, https://www.wipo.int/amc/en/arbitration/rules/index.html (last visited Mar. 23, 2025) (Articles 75–78).

50. *See id.* art. 76(b).

confidentiality as part of the *lex arbitri* (i.e., governed by the seat of the arbitration).[51] In addition, the law of the country in which the document or information was created may afford certain confidentiality expectations or requirements that should be considered (e.g., personal and/or business information may be treated differently in different countries). If an arbitral dispute eventually arises, the parties should take note of whether there are any changes in the rules or law to decide whether additional measures are needed to adequately protect the confidentiality of the proceeding.

3. Preserving Confidentiality in a Scheduling Order, Confidentiality Order, or Terms of Reference

As discussed, although the scope of confidentiality in an arbitration proceeding embraces what the parties, panel, administrators, and witnesses may disclose about the matter, even when such confidentiality is recognized, it does not necessarily protect privileged and confidential information that one party discloses to another party during an arbitration proceeding. Parties should avoid disclosing such information to opposing parties, the panel, experts, or any other third parties without first establishing confidentiality protections either by supplementing their arbitration provision (if necessary),[52] including such provisions in the terms of reference, or, as parties commonly do in IP/Technology cases, agreeing to a protective order (see Section V.C.7 of this chapter on protective orders).

Situations may arise in which a party responding to a request to produce documents, for example, objects because of the documents' confidential nature. In exceptional circumstances, if the propriety of an objection can be determined only by reviewing the document, the panel may, at the request of a party or on its own volition, and after consultation with the parties, either conduct an *in camera* review of the document or designate an independent and impartial expert or confidentiality advisor to determine whether the information is to be so classified, and, if so, decide under what conditions and to whom it may, in part or in whole, be disclosed.[53] If the parties adopt,

51. *See* Jean-François Poudret & Sébastien Besson, Comparative Law of International Arbitration 376 (2d ed. 2007).

52. Even where the parties mention something about confidentiality in their arbitration provision, they should consider having a clear, more detailed agreement, for example, about what they consider to be confidential information, who has access to it, and how it should be marked and treated during and after the arbitration proceeding.

53. There is significant disagreement regarding the propriety of the panel or a panel member conducting an *in camera* review even though judges in some jurisdictions are not disqualified from hearing the rest of a case after they have conducted such a review; practices may vary with the jurisdiction. At the same time, having an

for example, WIPO's Arbitration Rules[54] or the IBA Rules on the Taking of Evidence in International Arbitration[55] (e.g., in their arbitration agreement or in the terms of reference), those rules will provide procedures for addressing such situations.

C. The Problem of Potential Disclosure in the United States

Risks to the confidentiality of the materials and information submitted in an arbitration proceeding may arise after the proceeding when a nonparty seeks discovery of such materials or information in unrelated proceedings—third parties who were never a party to the proceeding are not covered at all by rules or orders of the arbitral panel. If a nonparty to an arbitration seeks discovery relating to that proceeding, U.S. courts have held that the private parties to that arbitration cannot bind that nonparty to their confidentiality agreement, and the courts have ordered production of arbitration documents. For example, in rejecting a plea to protect arbitral information from disclosure, Judge Easterbrook reasoned in *Gotham Holdings LP v. Health Grades, Inc.*:

> Contracts bind only the parties. No one can "agree" with someone else that a stranger's resort to discovery under the Federal Rules of Civil Procedure will be cut off. . . . Indeed, we have stated more broadly that a person's desire for confidentiality is not honored in litigation. Trade secrets, privileges, and statutes or rules requiring confidentiality must be respected, *see* Fed. R. Civ. P. 45(c)(3)(A)(iii), but litigants' preference for secrecy does not create a legal bar to disclosure. . . . Health Grades and Hewitt Associates were entitled to agree that they would not voluntarily disclose any information related to the arbitration. . . . Disclosure would be authorized only when a third party had a legal right of access.[56]

---

independent third party conduct the *in camera* review requires time and money to select the third party and for that person to become familiar enough with the matter to put the privilege claims in context. Panels sometimes include in an early procedural order that, if the panel conducts an *in camera* review, it will not be grounds for thereafter challenging the panel or attacking the award.

54. *See WIPO Arbitration Rules*, *supra* note 49, art. 54(b)–(e).

55. *See, e.g.*, IBA, IBA Rules on the Taking of Evidence in International Arbitration art. 3, ¶ 8 (2020), https://www.ibanet.org/MediaHandler?id=def0807b-9fec-43ef-b624-f2cb2af7cf7b.

56. Gotham Holdings LP v. Health Grades, Inc., 580 F.3d 664, 665–66 (7th Cir. 2009) (citations omitted). The confidentiality agreement between Health Grades and Hewitt Associates in the arbitration provided that materials from the arbitration may be disclosed in response to a subpoena. *Id.*

The confidentiality issue in the *Gotham Holdings* case arose in litigation pending in the Southern District of New York between Gotham Holdings (plaintiff) and Health Grades (defendant, party in an earlier arbitration) when Health Grades sought to rely on an earlier-issued arbitration award (and related documents) that it posited supported its view of the merits in the litigation. When Gotham Holdings asked to see documents related to the arbitration, Health Grades refused, relying on a confidentiality agreement between it and Hewitt Associates (the other party in the earlier arbitration). In response, Gotham Holdings argued that, by relying on the award, Health Grades had waived confidentiality, and it served a subpoena on Hewitt Associates and moved to enforce it in the Northern District of Illinois, where Hewitt Associates' principal offices were located. The district court and then the Seventh Circuit required compliance with the subpoena.

Another exposure risk may arise if a party decides to enforce an arbitration award in court. In *Global Reinsurance Corp.-U.S. Branch v. Argonaut Insurance Co.*,[57] Global filed a petition to confirm arbitration awards entered in its favor against Argonaut. In conjunction with its petition, Global filed a motion to seal those awards. The court initially granted Global's motion to seal, finding that Global overcame the presumption in favor of the public's access to judicial documents. Argonaut moved the court to reconsider its ruling and to unseal the arbitration awards. Upon reconsideration, the court reversed its prior decision and found that Global had not made a showing of harm sufficient to justify impinging the presumption of access to judicial materials.[58]

Veleron Holding, BV v. Morgan Stanley[59] is one of the few cases to address the interplay of international arbitration confidentiality rules and

57. Nos. 07 Civ. 8196(PKC), 07 Civ. 8350(PKC), 2008 WL 1805459 (S.D.N.Y. Apr. 24, 2008).

58. *See also* Baxter Int'l Inc. v. Abbott Lab'ys, 297 F.3d 544 (7th Cir. 2002). Baxter and Abbott were involved in an arbitration proceeding related to a patent license. Baxter was unsuccessful in the arbitration, so it filed an action in federal district court seeking to set aside the award (the district court opinion not only referenced the license, but it also included extended quotations from it). *Id.* at 547. Unsuccessful again, Baxter appealed to the Seventh Circuit. Baxter and Abbott filed a joint motion to file certain documents (including the license) under seal. In denying the motion, the Seventh Circuit noted that trade secrets, privileged information, and information required by statute to be maintained in confidence are all entitled to secrecy on appeal (*id.* at 546), but reasoned that the parties had never argued that the license (or other documents they had sought to protect) fell into such categories; rather, they had only contended that confidentiality for the documents served their business interests. *Id.* The Seventh Circuit further reasoned that, without being in a protected class, "dispositive documents in any litigation enter the public record notwithstanding any earlier agreement. How else are observers to know what the suit is about or assess the judges' disposition of it?" *Id.*

59. No. 12 Civ. 5966(CM), 2014 WL 1569610, at *1 (S.D.N.Y. Apr. 16, 2014).

U.S. judicial proceedings. Veleron claimed that Morgan Stanley had violated U.S. securities law by shorting the stock of a company that was subject to a notice of acceleration of a margin call (loan). It also claimed that Morgan Stanley (as the disposal agent obligated to sell that stock) had improperly informed certain select customers of the identity of the security before making a public announcement of the sale. An arbitration held under the auspices of the LCIA had been brought against OJSC Russian Machines (RM) to collect on the guarantee for the underlying loan. RM disclosed the arbitration file to Veleron (one of its wholly owned subsidiaries), and the LCIA held that RM had violated its rules in doing so.

The district court held that the sanctions for that conduct would be up to the London panel but that, in the United States, it would not conduct an insider trading securities action according to the "utmost secrecy" imposed by the LCIA.[60] The court held that there is both a constitutional and common-law right of access to judicial documents relevant to the performance of the judicial function.[61] Moreover, the district court found that Morgan Stanley itself was not party to any private arbitration agreement, nor was it permitted to cloak itself with secrecy in the United States. The court also unsealed the entire arbitration file, subject to proof that individual documents might meet traditional confidentiality requirements.[62]

D. State Law Variances Regarding Confidentiality

State law also varies and may affect arbitration confidentiality in cases brought in U.S. courts. Under *Volt Information Sciences, Inc. v. Board of Trustees of Leland Stanford Junior University*,[63] the parties may clearly specify that the arbitration law and process of a specified state will govern. There are at least four states that have general (although varied) statutory protections for arbitration communications: Arkansas,[64] California,[65]

60. The district court also noted that it believed the LCIA Rules did not entirely immunize evidence from disclosure outside of the arbitration proceeding (e.g., if there is a legal duty to disclose materials and documents, or if disclosure is "reasonably necessary" so that a party can "protect or pursue a legal right" in some other forum). The court further noted that, from reading one of the LCIA's awards, English law accepts disclosure of otherwise confidential arbitration material where the "interests of justice" so allow. Veleron Holding, BV v. Morgan Stanley, No. 12 Civ. 5966 (CM), 2014 WL 1569610, at *4 (S.D.N.Y. Apr. 16, 2014).

61. *See id.* at *6.

62. *See id.* at *2.

63. 489 U.S. 468, 476 (1989).

64. Ark. Code Ann. § 16-7-206 (West 2010) (current through May 3, 2024).

65. Cal. Evid. Code § 703.5 (West 1994) (current through 2024 Reg. Sess. Ch. 11).

Missouri,[66] and Texas.[67] Several states apply a settlement privilege to an arbitration proceeding (e.g., hearing and deposition transcripts, the award) and may be more sympathetic to claims of confidentiality.

In *Group Health Plan, Inc. v. BJC Health Systems, Inc.*,[68] Group Health Plan sought an injunction (as a party in a pending arbitration) to prevent BJC from obtaining arbitration materials. The materials sought related to an earlier arbitration to which Group Health Plan was not a party. The trial court took testimony on the confidential nature of the documents—some documents contained patient information. The trial court imposed the injunction (reversing the arbitrator's ruling, denying the injunction), and the appellate court affirmed, relying heavily on Missouri's arbitration statute (a provision relating specifically to the confidentiality of arbitration proceedings) and the fact that the parties had entered into a stipulated protective order also signed by the arbitration panel in the earlier arbitration, providing for the confidentiality of materials designated by the parties as confidential.[69]

E. The Patent Act Requirements Under Section 294

Under the Patent Act and, specifically, 35 U.S.C. § 294, patent disputes, including invalidity and infringement, are arbitrable. Under § 294(d), any award must be reported to the U.S. Patent and Trademark Office (PTO) and becomes part of the patent prosecution file of the patent at issue. The award is not enforceable until such a report is made.[70] Thus, full confidentiality is not

---

66. Mo. Ann. Stat. § 435.014 (West 1986) (current through end of first session of 102d Gen. Assemb.).

67. Tex. Civ. Prac. & Rem. Code Ann. § 154.073 (West 2001) (current through the fourth session of the 88th Leg.).

68. 30 S.W.3d 198 (Mo. Ct. App. 2000).

69. In *Soligenix v. Emergent Product Development*, the Delaware Court of Chancery denied Emergent's request to maintain the confidentiality of portions of its verified petition to vacate arbitration award (Petition) and certain attached exhibits (including the award). *See* Soligenix, Inc. v. Emergent Prod. Dev., No. 2022-0880-PAF, 47 Del. J. Corp. L. 831 (2023). The court's ruling relied heavily on the Court of Chancery's Rule 5.1, embodying the fundamental principle that "proceedings in a civil action are a matter of public record." *Id.* at 840–41 (quoting Ct. Ch. R. 5.1(a)). The chancery court found that, under Rule 5.1(b), Emergent failed to carry its burden of establishing good cause, that is, producing evidence that disclosure of the Petition, award, and other exhibits would cause it the requisite harm. *Id.* at 841. "'[G]ood cause' for Confidential Treatment shall exist only if the public interest in access to Court proceedings is outweighed by the harm that public disclosure of sensitive, non-public information would cause." Ct. Ch. R. 5.1(b)(2).

70. *See* 35 U.S.C. § 294(e) (2016).

possible with respect to arbitrating patent disputes in the United States, including where issues of invalidity and infringement are raised and addressed.

F. Considerations for Practitioners

When the parties deem confidentiality important in an arbitration proceeding, consider doing the follow:

- Include a provision in the arbitration agreement that expresses the parties' intent that the fact of arbitration and the information submitted to the panel in the arbitration (e.g., briefs, witness statements, testimony, the reasoning and outcome expressed in the award) be maintained as confidential by all participants (e.g., the panel, witnesses, experts, and arbitral institution administrative personnel), except as required by law or for financial reporting requirements.
- Include governing law in an arbitration agreement that is sympathetic to protecting confidentiality rights.
- Choose rules that maximize the confidentiality obligations of the panel, the administrative personnel of the administering arbitral institution, and the parties, when selecting an administering institution or arbitration rules. Ensure that testifying witnesses and third parties related to the arbitration (e.g., those who provide documents and/or testimony) are covered by having them sign an undertaking.
- Provide for enforcement of the award in a country that permits the court to maintain confidentiality of the parties' identity and privacy for the enforcement proceeding.
- Include in the arbitration agreement, or request that the panel enter in the terms of reference or a scheduling or protective order, how documents and information consisting of privileged and confidential information will be treated to avoid forfeiting their status.
- Provide a provision in the terms of reference or a protective order for the post-hearing treatment of privileged and confidential materials.
- Provide (e.g., in a protective order) that notice and consent must be provided by the other party if privileged or confidential information is requested by a third party after the arbitration is concluded, unless disclosure is required by law or in connection with enforcement or challenge to the award.
- Have, or at least consider the need to have, in the terms of reference or a protective order, an arbitral expert review privileged and/or confidential documents (without including WIPO or IBA rules) in the event that there is a dispute about disclosing them to the panel or opposing party.

- Explore whether the panel should issue an award with or without reasons. There are countervailing considerations, but enforcement of or challenge to the award and disputes related to patents are circumstances where there is serious potential for disclosure or publication of the award and confidential information.
- Ask the panel to avoid including confidential information in a reasoned award.

V. Process Considerations and Strategies

A. Early Attention to Problem Issues Related to Arbitration Provisions

1. Unworkable Provisions

Most IP/Technology arbitrations occur because parties insert into contracts (e.g., a settlement agreement resolving a patent infringement suit or a license) a pre-dispute clause providing for arbitration if particular disputes arise.[71] In doing so, they are agreeing to a process at a time when they do not know what disputes may arise, what the surrounding circumstances will be, or what the parties' business needs will be. Once the dispute arises, it is often counsel who had nothing to do with negotiating the contract or the arbitration clause that are responsible for arbitrating the case.

For example, it is not uncommon in technology-based collaboration agreements for parties to include ambitious deadlines for various aspects of the arbitration process to ensure an expeditious resolution of future disputes. Although that is understandable, the provisions may include time frames for important events that bear no relation to the realities of achieving those objectives—actually choosing a panel, conducting discovery, holding the evidentiary hearing, and preparing the reasoned award. In other cases, a pre-dispute arbitration provision may include ambiguous limitations. The result in either case is an unworkable provision.

Insofar as arbitration is contractual, the parties may, and should, address the impractical limitations early. This discussion can occur prior to filing a demand for arbitration or after one is filed. This may be easy, challenging, or

71. In IP/Technology disputes, parties may also initiate an arbitration proceeding using a submission agreement when they cannot resolve their dispute by other means. This may occur, for example, where there is no contractual relationship between the disputants or, if there is one, the parties did not provide in the contract(s) for arbitration. Or, the parties may have provided for arbitration but not of the kind of dispute that has now arisen.

impossible, depending upon the relationships between counsel, the relationships between the parties, and the number of parties involved.

The benefits to be gained by the parties addressing the effectiveness of the arbitration provision up front include (1) *party self-determination*—although the arbitration panel will do its best to resolve the issue, the panel's decision may not meet the parties' wants or needs; (2) *cost and time efficiencies*—whatever issues the parties cannot resolve themselves will cost them time and money for the panel to decide; and (3) *receiving the most from the process*—clients do not benefit from a process that is unsuitable for them. Conversely, parties benefit from a fair process that meets their respective needs.

If the arbitration is administered, and the parties have not been able to fix an unworkable provision on their own, they may enlist the help of their case manager to devise a solution. They could raise the issue ex parte with the case manager or jointly with the other party (e.g., in correspondence or at an "administrative conference" held before the panel is appointed). If the parties cannot agree on improved terms before the panel is appointed, they should raise such issues early in the proceeding (e.g., at the preliminary hearing or initial case management conference) so that the panel can resolve them and provide the parties with an improved, clear process to follow. If the parties do not raise the issues, the panel will often raise them and attempt to get the parties to agree on a modified and more practical provision.

2. Ineffective Provisions

A significant issue in IP/Technology cases that is often overlooked is whether there are other agreements relating to the transaction or the project with other parties who would likely be involved should a dispute arise. The complicating situation is where agreements with some parties have arbitration provisions and others do not and/or have clauses with different procedures or different administering institutions. One consequence may be having some issues tried in one or more courts in different jurisdictions and others before one or more arbitral panels, with potentially inconsistent results. Ideally, each agreement among the parties involved in a project should not only provide for arbitration with the same rules and administered by the same institution, but they should also empower the panel to join related arbitrations into one proceeding. Not all organizational rules empower panels with the default authority to combine separately filed arbitrations without the agreement of all parties. For example, JAMS rules[72] permit the combination of related proceedings, as do the AAA Commercial Rules (Rule R-8). Pursuant to AAA Commercial Rule R-8, arbitrations may be consolidated

72. *See* JAMS Rules & Procedures, *supra* note 3, Rule 6.

if all parties agree, or if there is not full agreement of all parties, the party or parties seeking consolidation may submit a written request to the AAA, and the AAA will either designate the arbitrator assigned in the first-filed case or appoint a consolidation arbitrator solely to decide the request. If such a second arbitrator is appointed, that arbitrator will have no jurisdiction to decide any other issues in the case unless the parties agree otherwise. If the organizational rules under which one or more possible arbitrations will be conducted do not empower the panel to combine related proceedings, the parties should consider empowering each panel to combine its arbitration with other arbitrations needed for a fair and complete adjudication of the dispute. All parties would need to agree to such powers, ideally, in their arbitration agreements, or later, after the disputes arise.

Case in point: A large manufacturing company with numerous facilities throughout the United States and abroad experienced a failed implementation of an enterprise software system. The transaction for acquiring the system resulted in three main agreements, each having its own arbitration clause providing for a different arbitration process (among other differences). All of the clauses provided for the AAA as the administering institution, but the case took place before the AAA amended its rules to provide for consolidation. Fortunately, the panel was ultimately able to help the parties reach agreement on one set of procedural rules and on a compromise location for the hearing. Were the case to be filed under the AAA's current Commercial Rules, if there was no agreement to consolidate, the party or parties seeking consolidation or joinder would have a mechanism under Rule R-8.

B. Setting the Stage and Establishing Credibility Early

1. Just the Facts . . .

Virtually no formal pleadings are required to commence an arbitration proceeding.[73] What is in the notice or demand required in arbitration, and any response, is often the only statement of the case the panel will have until prehearing briefs—assuming the parties submit them. These initial filings set the factual, legal, and technical stage in an IP/Technology case, but they also help the panel understand the early requests of the parties (e.g., concerning proposed schedules, protective order, and discovery disputes).

In addition to telling one's side of the story, in IP/Technology cases, it is often instructive for the panel to know (1) the relationship of the parties to one another, their respective businesses (particularly as they relate to the dispute), and, where relevant, their predecessors (e.g., the original parties

73. *See, e.g.*, AAA COMMERCIAL RULES, *supra* note 3, Rules R-4, R-5.

to a license agreement); (2) an overview of the IP/Technology in dispute or implicated in the dispute; (3) the identification of key individuals involved in the dispute (e.g., inventor, creator of copyrighted subject matter); (4) the agreements at issue, including any disputed or key language or terms; (5) a timeline of key events (e.g., creation of copyrighted material, sale in commerce of trademarked product, development of the patented invention, license negotiations, testing for FDA approval); (6) an overview or reference to relevant testing that may be important to the legal claims for relief; (7) an identification of the legal claims and general factual support; and (8) the relief requested for each legal claim. For many cases, addressing some subset of these issues will likely be appropriate and more than adequate.

Lest the message here seem to advocate *fact* rather than *notice* pleading, there are some important caveats. Counsel should avoid getting lost in the weeds or providing unnecessary and distracting facts. Each side should tell its story in clear and concise prose organized in numbered paragraphs. Successive unnumbered paragraphs containing rambling rants, complaints, or pejoratives *are not helpful*. Furthermore, avoid *ad hominem* attacks and adverbs that inflame—just the facts! In presenting a case to one or three experienced and tech-savvy panel members, if it comes across as weak, unsupported, or deconstructed, the panel may not trust what it is reading. Conversely, if a pleading is direct and straightforward, stating a clear and logical story, a party is more likely to establish at least initial credibility with the panel. Furthermore, any discovery permitted is likely to be keyed to the dispute as described in the pleadings.

Each pleading provides an opportunity for a side to tell its story and start (or continue) the process of persuasion.

2. Avoid Proliferating Claims and Defenses

All too often, arbitration demands, responses, and counterclaims reflect the pleading requirements of the Federal Rules or local rules of a federal district court, in that they are seemingly drafted to avoid waiving any claims or defenses as they would in federal court. That ignores an important aspect of arbitration and jeopardizes one of its many benefits (i.e., reaching a fair result in an efficient, cost-effective way). The reality is that a party's success or failure in arbitration *will not* be based on how many claims or defenses a party can list based on a set of facts.

Case in point: A response to an arbitration demand in a complex breach of contract case listed 38 affirmative defenses, more than double the number (18) listed in Federal Rule 8, thereby obscuring the defenses most likely to succeed.

No allegation or claim of the demand is deemed admitted unless specifically admitted by the respondent. If the respondent does not file a response, under AAA Commercial Rule R-5(a) and CPR Administered Arbitration Rule 3.6, for example, all allegations and claims are deemed denied. However, failing to file a response leaves the panel with just the other side's story. Thus, it may be a lost opportunity not to file any response.

Because arbitration is not about technical rules of pleading, the pleadings should focus on providing the other party and the panel with an understanding of the dispute by sufficiently and clearly setting forth and explaining the key claims, defenses, and relief requested and the applicable legal basis for each. Restating the claims in counts, with either repeating the factual allegations or incorporating them in successive counts, each resting on another legal theory should be avoided. Similarly, referring to each paragraph in the demand and then either admitting, denying, or making a speaking defense, is not worthwhile. Consider simply denying the claims generally, and stating in summary terms any applicable defense and any additional operative facts relevant to the defenses.

C. The Preliminary Hearing and Beyond—Fit the Form to the Function for a Sensible Arbitration

Familiarity with the litigation process is not adequate. If counsel conduct the arbitration process as if it were litigation, the case is destined to be costly in terms of both time and money. Knowledge of the rules and processes available in arbitration is key, especially an understanding that any discovery must be much more focused. Most of the issues addressed at the preliminary hearing are not covered by the parties' arbitration provision, and many may not even be covered by the applicable arbitration rules.

As mentioned earlier, because arbitration is a creature of agreement, the parties may impose various limits to expedite the proceeding. It takes forethought, however, to fashion an arbitration process that meets the specific needs of a given dispute, provides the cost and time efficiencies parties usually desire, and maintains a fundamentally fair process. The parties will be best served if they carefully consider the details of the arbitration process they need before the preliminary hearing so that the resulting initial scheduling order reflects a fair and workable process that meets their objectives.

There is a growing, though not universal, trend for panels to ask parties, in addition to counsel, to attend the preliminary hearing, at least by videoconference or phone. The AAA now encourages party attendance.[74] The thought is that having party representatives attending these preliminary

---

74. *See id.* Rule R-21.

conferences will promote their buy-in to the process and help ensure that they understand what counsel are requesting and the costs that would be incurred, for example, if extensive discovery or other expensive procedures are sought. Where there is the opportunity to attend the preliminary hearing counsel should consult with their clients. Some clients want to participate or at least observe. If that is the case, they should attend.

1. Preparation, Conduct, Strategy

a) Preparing for the Preliminary Hearing

The period between the commencement of the arbitration proceeding and the preliminary hearing is *not* downtime. Where an arbitral institution administers the case, the case manager usually sends counsel a list of issues (e.g., like the list attached as the Appendix to this chapter or P-2 in AAA Commercial Rules) that they should be prepared to discuss at the preliminary hearing. If the case is self-administered, the panel may provide directly to counsel such a list. Alternatively, some panels may send counsel a draft proposed scheduling order containing blanks for specific dates, times, and numbers and ask counsel to fill in the blanks for its consideration. Regardless of what means the panel uses to communicate with counsel about the key scheduling and procedural issues, what is most important is that counsel for both sides meet and confer before the preliminary hearing to discuss whichever items on the list relate to their case and are important to their clients and perhaps reach agreements on many of them. In fact, some panels (directly or through the case manager) may alert counsel that they expect them to meet and confer on each issue before the preliminary hearing and provide to the panel a joint document before the hearing indicating the items on which the parties can agree and any items in dispute, with short explanations of their respective positions on any items about which they disagree. Going through this process in advance can reduce the time spent during the preliminary hearing and, in any case, encourages counsel and parties to earlier identify (and, hopefully, address) issues that may cause inefficiencies or delays if they are not identified until later in the arbitration.

Every issue that counsel anticipate may arise should be raised with the panel at the preliminary hearing to ensure it is not overlooked in the scheduling order and to try to avoid delays and surprises later because it was not considered early in the process.[75] In IP/Technology cases, possible issues to discuss at the preliminary hearing include the joinder of parties to related

75. *See, e.g.*, *CPR Administered Rules* and *CPR Non-Administered Rules*, *supra* note 3, Rule 9.3; JAMS Rules & Procedures, *supra* note 3, Rule 16; AAA Commercial Rules, *supra* note 3, Rule R-22.

licenses or other contracts; further pleadings;[76] threshold issues (e.g., arbitrability, jurisdiction); interim issues (e.g., issuing injunctive relief, establishing an escrow); need for a protective order; information exchange (e.g., site visits, identifying experts, scheduling expert reports, presenting experts, technology tutorials, claim construction (in patent cases), summonses/subpoenas, and the summons/subpoena process); number of hearing days;[77] and dispositive motions.

Counsel should review and be prepared at the preliminary hearing to discuss implementing the arbitration process set forth in the governing alternative dispute resolution (ADR) provision and rules. They should have a well-thought-out schedule and process and be reasonable in scheduling and procedural requests. Counsel should have the parties' and witnesses' schedules at hand so the hearing may be efficiently scheduled and delays avoided.

b) Make a Good First Impression

The preliminary hearing is the first chance counsel have to speak with the panel. In IP/Technology cases, with one or more arbitrators who likely were selected because they understand the technology issues, it is particularly important that counsel present themselves in a manner that shows they understand the technology and that their arguments and positions are based on good science and/or engineering.

The preliminary hearing also can be an opportunity to provide a short and reasonable summary of each side's view of the case, if the panel either requests or will permit it. It is never helpful for counsel to overstate their case or assert something they will not, in all likelihood, be able to prove. The panel, just as a jury, will remember what counsel promised to prove and did not. However, having read the pleadings, the panel may tell counsel that it only wants a procedural discussion and not anything about the merits of the case. If so, respect that request and only discuss procedural issues. However, if the procedural issues require some understanding of the

76. If there is a need for further pleadings to understand a side's claims or defenses, to amend claims or defenses, or to quantify claims, the panel will generally establish dates. In IP/Technology cases, the parties may be required to specify particular issues (e.g., in a patent case, something akin to a claim construction chart).

77. The panel and/or the parties may want to establish a special method of presenting witnesses, or they may decide to limit the time each side will be permitted (e.g., through the use of a chess clock, a testimonial road map, or other means). IP/Technology cases may present issues in witness presentation because explaining the technology at issue and how it relates to legal issues can require significant time, and panelists will likely want to ask questions to gain a clear understanding of those issues.

background, counsel should inquire whether they may be permitted to provide some context.

c) Exercise Civility

Counsel should be civil throughout the arbitration proceeding, and the parties and counsel should try to accommodate each other to the extent possible. Differences will arise, but it is to the clients' advantage that counsel be perceived as reasonable and cooperative. If opposing counsel is difficult, no matter how tempting or how much your client encourages responding tit for tat, doing so only raises the level of tension and draws more inappropriate conduct. It is best always to be the adult in the room. *Ad hominem* attacks diminish the credibility of the attacker and will be unfavorably remembered by the panel.

d) Teaching and Reinforcing Key Points Throughout the Case

Even with a technologically savvy panel, it is advantageous to clearly and persuasively present technical evidence and background information that is unique and integral to a particular dispute. The technical evidence can be useful to the panel to understand and rule on preliminary issues (e.g., concerning discovery) and to understand and rule on determinative issues of patent infringement, trade secret misappropriation, and a myriad of contract disputes. Thus, counsel should have a concrete idea at the preliminary hearing of how to effectively use the flexibility of the arbitration process to introduce, reinforce, and ultimately connect the key technical evidence to the legal claims (e.g., by tutorials, prehearing briefs, witness presentation, post-hearing briefs, and argument).

e) Meet Your Burden(s) of Proof and Present Your Case Clearly and Efficiently

There are no style points in arbitration. Drama is counterproductive. It is best to present the relevant facts in a clear, concise, and organized manner. Then provide the relevant law and explain directly how the law applies to the facts, so as to not just authorize but also *require* the relief requested. Experienced arbitrators try their best to make their rulings consistent with the proven facts and the applicable law. Each party, whether as claimant or respondent, needs to keep in mind its burdens of proof on the various claims and defenses. If claimant does not meet its burden of proof on a claim, that claim will be dismissed. Similarly, if respondent does not meet its burden on its defense(s), and claimant has met its burden on the claim, the claim will prevail. Drama and theatrics that may work with a jury generally will not work and may be counterproductive with arbitrators, who generally have seen it all before. Just prove the operative facts, cite the governing law, and explain why the facts and law mandate the finding(s) and award requested.

2. Know the Governing Rules

Unlike the single set of Federal Rules, there are many sets of arbitration rules promulgated by various arbitral institutions. The differences in rules may reflect their use for (1) U.S. or international proceedings; (2) administered or non-administered proceedings; and (3) specific kinds of cases (e.g., patent cases). Where the parties have drafted their own ad hoc rules, there may be both big-picture and detailed aspects of the rules that have a particular significance to them. A party's case could be adversely affected by its counsel's lack of familiarity with the applicable rules. For example: Do the rules permit information exchange—what evidence will counsel have to prove its side's claims, counterclaims, defenses, and for rebuttal? Do the rules provide for the use of experts—how will counsel prove trademark, copyright, or patent infringement, trade secret misappropriation, and damages? Do the rules permit procedural motions—how will counsel obtain documents from an uncooperative opposing counsel? Thus, counsel should know what the governing rules permit (or do not permit) in case he or she needs to negotiate rule changes or refinements with opposing counsel or to request them from the panel at the preliminary hearing.

Unlike the detailed Federal Rules, which lay out precise pre-trial, trial, and post-trial procedures, arbitration rules are comparatively general and provide for a relatively flexible process. The generality of the rules can be beguiling or misleading, because what arbitration rules lack in detail, they make up for in opportunity—giving advocates the ability to craft a process that works best for any particular case. Thus, although the applicable set of arbitration rules may seem like a quick read, read them again (and again).

3. Bifurcation

Panels often lean toward hearing the entire case in one tranche. In the right case, however, bifurcation can save considerable time and money. Factors arguing against bifurcation include (1) substantial overlap of the evidence to be presented between the parts of a case considered for bifurcation; (2) crowded calendars, which may delay scheduling a hearing on the severed, later part of the case within a reasonable time after the hearing on the earlier part; (3) potential unavailability of key participants if the matter continues beyond a certain date; (4) the parties' need for complete resolution of the matter by a certain date; and (5) the time and expense of multiple hearings. Conversely, for example, an expeditious determination of a key liability issue can lead to the narrowing of a hearing on the remaining issues or the settling of the case, and, if the panel finds no liability on any issue, the parties can avoid the entire damages portion of the case (e.g., damages discovery, expert reports, trial). In some cases, including patent cases, it may be efficient to hear the matter in phases, with the first phase used to determine exactly what the patent claims mean or the meaning of technical or scientific terms, akin to a *Markman* hearing.[78] A similar approach may apply to some trade secret and restrictive covenant cases, for example, where days of testimony and reams of exhibits can be eliminated if issues are limited by a determination of what claims can legally be pursued.

In cases where attorneys' fees and/or costs are claimed, the panel may bifurcate the hearing, issue an award addressing liability and damages, and instruct the prevailing party, as determined by the panel, to submit evidence of its fees and expenses. Another practice is to designate the prevailing party in an interim or procedural order, and make a later finding as to the amount of damages. In either case, the prevailing party will submit attorneys' fees and expense claims, and the non-prevailing party will typically be allowed to respond. The panel may or may not hold an oral evidentiary hearing as to fees and costs. Yet another approach is to accept evidence as to fees during the hearing from both sides, receive post-hearing briefs, possibly conduct oral argument, and incorporate an award of fees into the final award with no interim awards. That, of course, creates a problem if post-briefing legal fees will be incurred that could not have been part of the earlier submissions. In that case, a supplemental submission is made to cover such fees.

Bifurcating the case into phases may have another benefit. After key issues such as scope of claims, limits of liability, or definition or existence of trade secrets are resolved in a preliminary order, parties often are motivated to settle the dispute, resulting in a significant cost and time savings to the parties.

4. *Is This a Case for a Tutorial?*

A panel may benefit from a technology tutorial, especially where technology is integral to the issues it needs to decide. Further, a tutorial may help the parties procedurally by focusing and shortening prehearing submissions,

78. The Supreme Court in *Markman v. Westview Instruments, Inc.*, 517 U.S. 370 (1996), held that the court, and not the jury, should decide construction issues defining the meaning (and, thereby, the scope) of patent claims. As a result, courts in patent jury cases hear the case in two phases. The first phase is the "*Markman* hearing" or "claim construction hearing." Once the court issues the order construing the claims, the case proceeds to a merits trial.

possibly reducing the number of witnesses at the evidentiary hearing, and potentially shortening the length of their testimony.

Generally, unless the panel decides to make it a part of the evidentiary record, a technology tutorial is a non-evidentiary, neutral presentation prepared to educate the panel. There is no particular structure for a tutorial. The parties could present one solely on the papers (e.g., included as part of the prehearing submission), as a stand-alone presentation (e.g., with slides and handouts), at the evidentiary hearing through witnesses (expert and/or fact), or as a combination of them. There are no hard and fast rules regarding who should present a tutorial, but the panel may express some preference. The parties could cooperate and present a joint tutorial, but, more often, they each present their own using a member of their hearing team (e.g., an attorney with a Ph.D. in the area of the subject technology), an outside expert (often a party's testifying expert), or an in-house employee having the requisite technical education and experience. Unless the panel orders otherwise, the parties need not mirror each other with regard to who presents the tutorial—one party could use an in-house expert and the other an outside expert.

The tutorial should not constitute an opening statement or focus on a party's legal positions, but counsel may seek guidance or permission from the panel about linking the technical points made to the disputed legal claims to ensure the panel understands the significance of the topics explained in the tutorial with the issues in dispute. The tutorial is the time to ensure that the panel grasps the underlying technology—both big-picture and relevant details—so that when counsel present the evidence, the panel will absorb it the way each party intends.

An effective technology tutorial takes thought, time, and money, so the parties should consider:

- Would the panel benefit from a stand-alone technology tutorial?
- When is the optimal time to present it?
- What would it cover (e.g., high-level background, scientific principles, chemical mechanisms, manufacturing processes, technical data, testing procedures)?
- How would the parties present it?
- Who would present it (e.g., fact witness, outside counsel, technical expert)?
- Do available materials exist that could constitute or augment a tutorial (e.g., TED Talks)?

In IP/Technology cases, the panel may or may not raise the issue of a tutorial before the preliminary hearing. If, however, counsel believe the panel would benefit from one or, for strategic reasons, they want to present one, counsel should raise that topic at the preliminary hearing so that the panel can consider and possibly schedule it. Before the preliminary hearing, counsel should discuss with one another the considerations set forth in the previous list to see if they concur on having a tutorial and the details related to it or to identify any areas of disagreement to discuss with the panel. Counsel should consider discussing with the panel what background issues would be helpful and what would be unnecessary.

It is important to understand the background and expertise of the arbitrators. Some basic science tutorials are unnecessary for arbitrators with significant scientific education and experience, while it may be key for arbitrators without that background. Generally, the most helpful tutorial for technically experienced arbitrators is a presentation as to the specific science or technology that is necessary to understand and decide issues in the case. The panel may defer deciding if and when to schedule a tutorial until after the case has progressed to a point at which it can determine whether the cost of and time for a tutorial are justified.

5. Can This Case Be Arbitrated "Site" Unseen?

The topic of a site visit may arise in a variety of contexts. For example, suppose one party commences an arbitration proceeding against a former manufacturing partner for breach of a confidentiality provision and trade secret misappropriation after the former partner begins selling equipment that allegedly was made using (or that practices) the complainant's proprietary process. The parties may suggest that the arbitration panel visit the site where the equipment in question was made or is operating. Or, in a patent infringement case involving machinery that allegedly practices the patented process and is too large or difficult to transport to the hearing, the parties may invite the panel to a site where the machinery is operated.

The most time-consuming aspect of a site visit, regardless of whether the panel attends or possibly only the experts attend, often is the parties' negotiation of ground rules for the visit (e.g., who can attend, what the attendees are permitted to see and ask, whether photos or video can be taken). Furthermore, the time and travel cost of counsel, possibly also of experts and the panel, can be considerable. Thus, the time and expense of a site visit should be balanced against whether still photographs, videography, an animated presentation, or the like can be an effective means for educating and communicating necessary information to the panel.

In preparation for the preliminary hearing, counsel should discuss with one another whether a site visit is necessary, including who should attend, when the visit may be scheduled, what it would entail, and what ground rules will govern so that they can informatively discuss the issue with the panel and the panel can make an informed decision and possibly schedule it.[79] In lieu of a site visit, when it is beneficial for the panel to see firsthand the devices or products at issue and for witnesses to be able to physically point out specific properties or components of the devices or products, it may potentially be more cost and time efficient to transport the devices or products to the site of the hearing if that is practical. This possibility should also be explored at the preliminary hearing.

6. Information Exchange (aka Discovery)?

In IP/Technology cases, the amount of information exchange that the parties may need to prove their claims and defenses can vary. Such cases have the potential to encompass high volumes of documents (e.g., regulatory approval, prosecution, product development information), third-party discovery (e.g., prior IP owners, inventors, developers, creators), and multiple experts (e.g., damages, technical, marketing, industry). Some arbitration provisions impose discovery limits, ranging from limiting discovery to document production only (with perhaps a deposition) to, in rare cases, providing full discovery under the Federal Rules.[80] An obvious dilemma with putting discovery limits in a pre-dispute arbitration provision is that, without knowing the particulars of future disputes, the limits imposed may later impair effective presentation of a claim or a defense or, alternatively, may sanction full-blown litigation-style discovery that is far out of proportion to what is being arbitrated. Accordingly, more often than not, the arbitration provision is silent on discovery, the parties having decided that, if a dispute arises, they will rely on the rules governing the arbitration and on the panel's discretion.

a) The Authority to Pursue Information Exchange

To determine the authority to pursue discovery and any limitations to it, counsel should begin by looking at the parties' arbitration provision, the

79. If the site visit involves viewing the operation of machinery on the premises of a third party, the parties may need to obtain permission to access the premises and the equipment, to take photos or video, to ask questions of the machine operator, to operate the machinery without interfering with the third party's use of the equipment for its business, and to obtain dates for the visit.

80. The Federal Rules of Civil Procedure are not the rules parties usually adopt in an arbitration provision. On rare occasions, however, a provision provides that those rules will govern discovery. Even if the panel does not *sua sponte* raise the wisdom or practicality of following the Federal Rules, the parties can voluntarily agree to limit discovery or, without agreement, one of the parties can move the panel to limit discovery to the needs of the case, and, in particular, point to the proportionality requirements in the Federal Rules and to any limitations on discovery in the applicable arbitration rules.

governing arbitration rules, and controlling law. Counsel may want to consult—or even formally adopt—well-known guidelines from various arbitral institutions and other organizations for practical options in pursuing discovery in arbitration.[81] Counsel should be prepared to discuss at the preliminary hearing the underpinnings mentioned here to support their request for information or to rebut their opponent's request for the same.

b) Controlling Litigation-Style Discovery

The arbitration rules of the major arbitral institutions empower panels to control discovery to achieve a time- and cost-efficient resolution of the dispute while giving the parties equal treatment and safeguarding their opportunity to fairly present their claims and defenses.[82] And because the singular driver of costs and delay in arbitration is discovery, the CCA *Protocols for Expeditious, Cost-Effective Commercial Arbitration* encourages participation of the parties in the preliminary hearing so that, if counsel are leaning toward unnecessary discovery, the parties can rein them in (hearing what the panel has to say may cause the parties to avoid pursuing expensive discovery or to suggest alternatives to the scope of discovery counsel are seeking).[83] Similarly, the New York State Bar Association's Dispute Resolution Section has issued a pamphlet encouraging the parties and arbitrators to use a focused approach to discovery, limiting it to matters relevant to the filed claims, defenses, and counterclaims.[84]

Counsel should try to tailor their requests for information to what they need to prove their case. A party's desire to go on a fishing expedition may suggest (at best) that counsel does not yet know its case or (at worst) that it recognizes its case is not strong and/or that it wishes to burden the other

81. *See supra* Section III.

82. *See, e.g.*, AAA Commercial Rules, *supra* note 3, Rule R-23 (regarding document production generally and electronically stored information); *CPR Non-Administered Rules*, *supra* note 3, Rule 11 (Discovery); JAMS Rules & Procedures, *supra* note 3, Rule 17(b) (allowing each party to take one deposition and giving the panel the discretion to permit additional depositions guided by certain enumerated factors); *JAMS Recommended Arbitration Discovery Protocols for Domestic, Commercial Cases*, JAMS (Jan. 6, 2010), http://www.jamsadr.com/arbitration-discovery-protocols.

83. *See* CCA, Protocols for Expeditious, Cost-Effective Commercial Arbitration 26–29 (Thomas J. Stipanowich et al. eds., 2010), https://www.ccarbitrators.org/wp-content/uploads/2021/05/CCA_Protocols.pdf ("In-house counsel should attend the first case management conference as well as all important subsequent conferences and hearings during the arbitration process in person or by telephone, should require periodic status reports from outside counsel, and should actively partner in the management of the arbitration rather than relinquishing such control to outside counsel.").

84. *See* NYSBA Guidelines, *supra* note 37.

side. Furthermore, unless there is a good reason (e.g., significantly different degrees of difficulty for the two sides to prove their respective cases or limited access to information by one side), the discovery burden on both sides will usually be equivalent. Experienced panels do not want either side unfairly burdened, and a request by one side for the panel to intervene to curtail discovery it regards as burdensome will not be well received if that same party is unduly burdening the other side.

Panels often discourage requests for admission, interrogatories (except perhaps for information such as the location and custodians of relevant documents),[85] and numerous depositions. If, however, both sides agree to discovery beyond just document production, and the additional discovery they desire is supportable (e.g., given the arbitration provision, governing rules/guidelines, nature of the dispute, what is at stake, and the reasons articulated), a panel will usually accede to the parties' agreement. Counsel who go into a preliminary hearing with a well-thought-out and appropriately limited discovery plan, and who know what a panel is likely to do, have a much greater likelihood of getting the desired discovery. In cases where conducting a few depositions objectively seems reasonable, counsel sometimes say they still want (or have already agreed to) more depositions. The panel may suggest that each side consider who are the two or three most important deponents, promptly take just their depositions, and renew their request for additional depositions only if counsel can articulate a persuasive argument for them; often, the initial depositions are more than sufficient.[86]

c) Expert Discovery

A scheduling order may provide for the disclosure of experts followed by the disclosure of rebuttal experts, the submission of expert reports possibly followed by rebuttal expert reports and depositions, and the subsequent close of discovery (because expert reports and depositions commonly occur after document production and fact witness depositions). Typically, the disclosed

---

85. Requests for admission are generally not cost-effective and generally are not permitted. Counsel usually will forgo interrogatories if both sides agree or the panel orders the parties to disclose the sort of information required to be disclosed under Federal Rule of Civil Procedure 26(a)(1)(A), with which counsel are presumably familiar and comfortable from litigation. While setting the schedule for the arbitration at the preliminary hearing, a panel may want to secure an agreement to make such voluntary disclosures within a week or so following the preliminary hearing and memorialize this in the scheduling and procedural order that ensues. Thus, each side will receive the information much sooner (and less expensively) than if it had to propound interrogatories, wait until the deadline for a response, possibly argue with the other side about objections, and wait for the panel to rule.

86. In international arbitrations, depositions are typically not permitted.

experts who submitted reports will testify at the hearing.[87] In determining whether to order rebuttal reports, a panel may consider the following: whether the case is U.S. domestic or international, whether the panel has permitted expert depositions, whether the expert is being used to help a party carry its burden on an issue, whether parties have requested rebuttal reports, and whether ordering rebuttal reports will impact the length of the overall schedule.

Many panels do not permit expert depositions if the experts are already submitting reports. The parties and the panel may also agree that the expert's report will serve as that expert's direct testimony at the hearing, and that cross- and redirect examinations will be handled with live testimony. Some parties opt not to take any expert depositions even if permitted, while others take depositions hoping that it will save them time at the evidentiary hearing. If the report is used as the expert's direct testimony, at the hearing, the proponent of the expert may offer abbreviated direct testimony to "warm up" the expert, authenticate the report, and offer rebuttal to what was in the opposing expert report, after which cross-examination starts.[88]

Submission of expert reports before the hearing serves several purposes: (1) it is a form of discovery that enables the parties and their respective experts to be better prepared at the hearing and possibly eliminates the need for expert depositions or allows each party to prepare its experts for any depositions; (2) it helps to educate the panel and prepare it for the hearing; and (3) it can alert the panel that it needs additional information and/or a tutorial, if not already scheduled. As discussed in Section V.C.4 of this chapter, a good use of experts is in presenting a tutorial for the panel that more broadly introduces the technical subject matter, industry practices, prior art and infringement issues in a patent-related matter, and damages theories and calculations.

d) Electronic Discovery

The preliminary hearing is also when counsel should discuss with the panel electronically stored documents and the scope, necessity, reasonableness, and cost of production. Parties often agree on an electronically stored information (ESI) protocol that will govern electronic discovery. The panel and

87. There are many IP/Technology cases in which one or more parties identify multiple experts who will testify at the evidentiary hearing and who submit reports. However, before or at the hearing, a party may determine that one or more experts will not testify.

88. In international arbitrations, and now often in domestic U.S. arbitrations, witness statements are used instead of direct testimony of witnesses, with live cross-examination, saving hearing time and expense.

well-prepared advocates should work to develop such a protocol that is cost-effective, and yet does not deprive a party of necessary information. When disputes arise, panels often require the parties to try in the first instance to resolve any discovery disputes on their own. When the dispute involves electronic discovery and counsel are unable to resolve it, an experienced panel can help the parties find a practical way forward.

Case in point: Consider a request by one party for all emails in the possession of the other party on a particular topic met by an objection that the request is burdensome. The panel tested the soundness of the objection by asking both sides to name the few individuals most likely to have sent or received an email on the named topic and to identify a few key words any email on that topic would almost certainly contain. The panel then asked the objecting side to run a simple search to determine how many emails were either sent or received by each of the few named individuals containing the key words. The total number (even without accounting for duplication) was far lower than the number objecting counsel asserted. The objection subsequently disappeared.

e) Summonses/Subpoenas

Third-party summonses/subpoenas for discovery and trial are not uncommon in IP/Technology cases. For example, documents and testimony may be sought from third parties who negotiated the agreement at issue, worked on the product or IP at issue, or were involved in the conduct at issue (e.g., misrepresentation, breach, tortious interference). Typically, the panel will raise the issue of whether the parties will be seeking third-party discovery at the preliminary hearing so that the issue can be included in the scheduling order by setting sufficient time to handle logistics and any delays. How a panel handles objections to and implementation of summonses and subpoenas depends upon various factors including the parties' and the panel's preferences and the governing law.[89]

Even if the panel permits third-party discovery depositions, they still may not occur unless the witnesses agree to voluntarily appear. For example,

89. For a helpful resource on summons practice under the FAA, see "A Model Federal Arbitration Summons to Testify and Present Documentary Evidence at an Arbitration Hearing" by the International Commercial Disputes Committee and the Arbitration Committee of the New York City Bar Association, https://www2.nycbar.org/pdf/report/uploads/20072911-ABCNYModelArbitralSubpoena.pdf (last visited Mar. 23, 2025).

many federal circuit courts and some federal district courts have held that the FAA does not permit a panel to issue deposition summonses to nonparties (state arbitration law may be more permissive). One possible solution where panels do not have the power to summon/subpoena a nonparty to a deposition is for the panel to schedule a hearing day in the jurisdiction of the witness and issue a hearing summons/subpoena. That day of hearing can be set well in advance of the rest of the evidentiary hearing. Of course, as a hearing day, whatever the witness says is now evidence in the hearing. Unlike a discovery deposition, where some or all of the testimony will never be presented to the panel, as a day of hearing, the panel will hear it all. To save costs, with the agreement of the parties, where there is a panel of three arbitrators, one arbitrator can be selected to preside over the hearing day for that witness. The transcript is then provided to the entire panel.

Where summonses/subpoenas are requested, panels have various approaches for considering them. Some sign any that are submitted to them. Others sign them only if they were previously submitted to opposing counsel and opposing counsel does not object. If there is an objection, the panel may hold a short hearing or accept written submissions regarding whether to issue the summons/subpoena as submitted or to order its revision. Still other panels carefully review any submitted summons/subpoena as to form and scope, whether or not there is an objection, and, if they deem necessary, require that the scope be modified before they will sign it.

7. Protective Orders

As previously discussed, although arbitration rules usually provide for the privacy of the arbitration proceeding, such rules may not address the issue of protecting privileged and confidential information involved in the proceeding (e.g., documents, testimony). One way the parties typically address the practical details of handling such information during and after the arbitration process is through the entry of a protective order.

If the panel or arbitration institution does not raise the issue of a protective order in the list of topics the panel will cover at the preliminary hearing, counsel should raise the issue.[90] Counsel should consider exchanging drafts of the protective order even before the preliminary hearing so that they can report at the hearing that they have agreed on an order, that discussions are under way, or that there are disputes they want the panel to resolve.

---

90. *See CPR Non-Administered Rules*, *supra* note 3, Rule 11 ("The Tribunal may issue orders to protect the confidentiality of proprietary information, trade secrets and other sensitive information disclosed in discovery.").

The form, general content, and procedures of a protective order in arbitration are much like they are in litigation. Because the information sought to be discovered in IP/Technology cases may be the true *crown jewels* (e.g., formulas, techniques) of the parties, a one-level protective order may not be enough. In many cases, the protective order may need two levels of confidentiality, where the first level allows the parties access and requires confidentiality and non-use of the information produced, and the second level allows only outside counsel and precleared independent experts access, but not the parties themselves.

The panel may sign the order if counsel request that it do so; some panels prefer to approve and sign such orders. Parties typically provide in their draft order for the protection of privileged and confidential information throughout the arbitration proceeding and following completion of the proceeding. A common mistake, however, is that parties provide that the arbitration panel will enforce any violations of the order not only during the arbitration proceeding but also thereafter. After the panel has issued its award, it is *functus officio* and, thus, has no authority to enforce protective order violations. However, if the protective order is in the form of an agreement between the parties, they can enforce it in a court, or if the protective order contains an arbitration clause, the parties can agree to reappoint the original panel or a new panel can be created to enforce the confidentiality agreement.

Relatedly, in negotiating the return or destruction of confidential information, the parties should generally exempt the panel and any arbitral institution (leaving it to their respective document destruction practices) because the time for such return or destruction will likely be well after the panel has become *functus officio*. Finally, for a panel to enforce the terms of any protective order against a nonparty who signs an undertaking to the order, that nonparty should also affirm its consent to submit to the jurisdiction of the panel during the arbitration proceeding. The nonparty should also consent in the undertaking to the jurisdiction of applicable courts for enforcement of the protective order after the panel has become *functus officio.*

8. Motions in Arbitration

Although motion practice in commercial arbitration is not as prevalent as in commercial litigation, it is not uncommon for parties to bring motions in IP/Technology cases on a variety of issues, including whether an arbitration panel has jurisdiction over the disputed claims; all or part of a case should be dismissed; pleadings should be amended;[91] a party should be dismissed

91. Because formal pleadings are not required in arbitration, dismissals based on formalistic pleading requirements are uncommon and may be frowned upon. The lack

from, or can intervene in, an arbitration;[92] a party must produce certain information; particular individuals should be permitted to see confidential documents; certain evidence should be excluded at the evidentiary hearing; and a party should prevail on an issue as a matter of law. Other issues that can be determined by motion may include governing law, governing arbitration rules, limitations of damages, limitations of remedies, whether some or all of the claims set forth a legally cognizable cause of action, and whether some of the defenses are, in fact, valid legal or equitable defenses. Before determining whether to accept and consider such a motion, the panel will often request a brief explanation of why the motion will expedite the arbitration before permitting the motion to be scheduled or filed. If the panel determines that accepting and ruling on the motion would not significantly reduce the time and cost of the ultimate hearing on the merits, it can decide not to permit the motion.

In preparation for the preliminary hearing, counsel should confer regarding motions they anticipate bringing to determine if they can resolve the underlying issue(s) or at least establish a briefing and hearing schedule to propose to the panel. If the parties do not have any particular motions in mind at the time of the preliminary hearing, they may at least want to discuss procedural options to propose to the panel to expedite motion practice should a dispute arise later (e.g., how and when to alert the panel about a dispute, how to prepare the panel to decide the dispute, i.e., short letter briefs, oral briefing, etc.) and/or to set a deadline for filing dispositive motions. Some of the more common motions encountered in IP/Technology cases are discussed in the following sections.

a) Motion to Dismiss for Arbitrability/Jurisdiction Challenges

At the preliminary hearing, counsel should alert the panel if there is a dispute about the arbitrability of any of the claims or defenses and the jurisdiction of the panel over the parties. In IP/Technology cases, such issues may arise, for example, (1) in a license dispute where the parties have tried to limit

---

or level of specificity, however, may become relevant to a party when considering how to prepare its case and what it should propose for the case schedule (e.g., need for experts, scope of discovery) and to the panel in determining the schedule. If there is a question as to what claims and defenses the parties are pursuing and what should be included in the schedule (e.g., discovery, technology tutorial, subpoenas, site visit, length of hearing), then the parties should consider requesting a more definite statement of the claims or defenses at the preliminary hearing. The panel may order this by making a simple request rather than having the parties engage in motion practice.

92. Issues related to intervention should be raised early so that, if the panel permits another party to intervene, the scheduling order can take that into account and avoid delay.

the panel's determination to breaches of contract and carve out infringement issues for court determination; (2) in a settlement agreement dispute related to a prior infringement case where the parties have tried to limit the panel's determination to new infringement claims and carve out patent invalidity issues for court determination; and (3) in a license dispute where individuals beyond the signatories on the license have been named as parties to the arbitration.

If such threshold issues exist, then briefing, possible argument, and a decision are often scheduled as a preliminary matter even before the remainder of the schedule is established. The parties, however, may want to consider other options to address these issues that take into account their need to obtain a decision in a cost-effective and timely manner.

Case in point: In a contract dispute involving the alleged breach of a settlement agreement that concluded an earlier patent infringement case between the parties, the parties set forth in their arbitration pleadings numerous claims, defenses, and counterclaims. There was a provision in the settlement agreement purporting to carve out from any future arbitration certain issues, but the parties disputed what issues were arbitrable. They agreed that the panel would decide the arbitrability issue.

The parties could have spent time and money briefing and arguing the arbitrability issue, but at the preliminary hearing, the panel indicated there was a significant probability that a decision on that issue could result in certain issues being decided by the panel and others by a court. Besides the significantly different time frames for obtaining a final decision from each forum, it was highly likely that the parties would duplicate their efforts in both fora, which would double costs and possibly result in inconsistent rulings on some of the issues. Based on a suggestion from the panel, the parties agreed to arbitrate the infringement issue first, because a determination on that issue was likely to moot at least some of the other issues in the case and expedite the resolution of others.

b) Discovery Motions

If discovery is permitted in an arbitration proceeding and there are any discovery disputes, formal motions to compel or to seek a protective order to prevent discovery are generally not permitted. Rather, panels often provide in a scheduling order that the parties must meet and confer to try to resolve discovery disputes before requesting relief. If the attorneys designated by each party to discuss and resolve discovery issues are unsuccessful, it is worth having other team members for each party take a fresh look at the issues and talk with their clients to determine whether a solution has been overlooked or if a motion is worth the time and resources.

There are various ways to handle efficiently discovery disputes. For example, a scheduling order may set deadlines for bringing discovery disputes to the panel's attention in accordance with scheduled events (e.g., submission of a protective order, objections to document requests, or document production). Alternatively, the scheduling order may permit the parties on a rolling basis to bring discovery disputes to the panel but set a deadline beyond which the parties may not raise them. Where counsel cannot reach an agreement and seek the panel's assistance, panels employ various options to decide disputes depending, for example, on the nature and complexity of the disputed issues. To control costs and time while not compromising its ability to resolve the dispute, a panel may request (1) short simultaneous or staggered opening submissions, leaving open the possibility for reply briefs or oral argument; (2) joint submissions, leaving open the possibility for reply briefs or oral argument; or (3) oral argument on the disputed issues on a videoconference or phone conference with counsel and the panel, with the decision rendered in real time or shortly after panel deliberation.[93] This last option is often used when a dispute arises during a deposition, but it can be used at other times. Often, before any formal submissions of briefs, a short telephonic or videoconference among counsel and the arbitrator(s) can resolve the dispute and the parties can move on.

With tri-partite panels, it is not uncommon for the chairperson to ask counsel (with agreement of the other panel members) at the preliminary hearing whether they would agree to have the chairperson alone decide discovery disputes (and other non-substantive, procedural matters), perhaps with the understanding that any party, a panel member, or the chairperson has the right to require that the full panel review any specific matter. This saves time and cost. Even where the parties agree to this, the chairperson may choose to consult with the other panel members to decide all or selected discovery disputes. For example, in IP/Technology cases it is not uncommon for a dispute over requests for production to implicate a consideration of merits-based issues. Although a panel will not be deciding such issues to resolve the discovery dispute, the chairperson may want the other arbitrators involved in deciding it.

93. In some cases, it may be enough for the panel to have a general understanding of the technology, but in other situations, the panel may need more detailed information to understand the relationship of the technology to the legal claims and scope of the disputed discovery. Because preparing the panel to decide discovery disputes often proceeds with minimal briefing and argument, the parties may want to refer to the factual and technical foundation in their initial pleading documents while using the limited briefing and argument time to explain to the panel the specifics of the discovery dispute.

c) Dispositive Motions

Rule R-34 of the AAA Commercial Rules[94] expressly authorizes the panel to "allow the filing of and make rulings upon" a dispositive motion. Under Rule R-34, a panel may allow for and rule on a dispositive motion only "if the arbitrator determines the moving party has shown that the motion is likely to succeed and to dispose of or narrow the issues in the case." Further, Rule R-34 states that "the arbitrator shall consider the time and cost associated with the briefing of a dispositive motion in deciding whether to allow any such motion." Thus, under Rule R-34, it is likely that an arbitration panel would order the parties to first submit a short request asking for permission to file a dispositive motion before permitting them to file the motion itself.[95]

A panel may deny a request to file a dispositive motion out of concern that a refusal to hear relevant and material evidence would be a ground for vacatur of the award. In IP/Technology cases, the facts necessary to decide a dispositive motion are often disputed and difficult to isolate from the facts that will be heard on other issues at the evidentiary hearing, in which case it is usually more efficient to hear all the evidence together. Furthermore, a panel may deny a dispositive motion where the evidentiary hearing is imminent and the time required to render an award after the hearing is not significantly more than the time to decide a dispositive motion (with briefing and a hearing). Some questions that arbitral panels consider before permitting parties to file dispositive motions include: How sound is the motion and what is its likelihood of success? Are there issues of material fact that would

94. *See* AAA Commercial Rules, *supra* note 3, Rule R-34. In the international arena, the arbitration rules of many of the major international arbitration providers do not directly address the issue of dispositive motions, but they include general provisions that give arbitrators the latitude to conduct the proceeding, including the authority to consider dispositive motions. *See, e.g.*, ICDR Arbitration Rules, *supra* note 34, art. 23; *ICC Arbitration Rules*, *supra* note 39, art. 25; *LCIA Rules*, *supra* note 47, art. 14; *UNCITRAL Arbitration Rules*, U.N. Comm'n on Int'l Trade L., https://uncitral.un.org/en/texts/arbitration/contractualtexts/arbitration (last visited Mar. 23, 2025) (Articles 27–28).

95. To promote efficiency and avoid the submission of dispositive motions that are unlikely to be granted, it is common for arbitrators to require that a party desiring to file a dispositive motion first send a short letter to the arbitrator(s), with a copy to opposing counsel, summarizing the basis for the proposed motion. If the arbitrators determine that it would be efficient to consider and rule on such a motion because it would likely remove issues from the evidentiary hearing, they will grant the leave to file it. However, if it appears that the issues(s) are sufficiently fact-based that they should be decided through the evidentiary hearing, and, thus, there is little likelihood that the motion would be granted, or that there would be no significant cost savings or time efficiencies by deciding the issues through motion, then leave likely would be denied.

preclude ruling in favor of the movant(s)? Will the motion, if granted, really reduce costs and expedite the arbitration or will it have the opposite result?[96]

Parties may bring motions for partial disposition aimed at eliminating issues or claims that could lengthen the hearing, and that will permit the parties to focus their hearing time on the material issues in dispute. If the case is large enough to justify the additional expense of a motion for partial disposition, it may reduce the overall cost and time of the proceeding. Examples of issues for which arbitration panels have granted, and courts have confirmed, a partial disposition include res judicata and collateral estoppel; the plain meaning of a contract; statute of limitations;[97] standing; preemption; waiver and estoppel; failure to comply with a contractual claim or notice procedure; whether the evidence is sufficient to permit a rational inference by a trier of fact; and failure to state a claim because no duty was owing.[98] Panels have also granted dispositive motions on arbitrability and jurisdictional issues. Panels have denied dispositive motions in IP/Technology cases where key license provisions were ambiguous because of multiple amendments to the license; issues of fact existed regarding patent infringement; a legal issue was intertwined or dependent upon material fact issues in dispute; and a fact issue existed regarding which contract in a series of contracts controlled.

If one or both parties want to file a dispositive motion, they should raise this with the panel at the preliminary hearing so that the panel can consider it in planning the schedule for the proceeding, including setting a deadline for filing dispositive motions. The panel may issue a relatively short scheduling order focused primarily on the motion briefing (or request to file a dispositive motion) and delay or condition the remainder of scheduling on the outcome of a decision on the motion.

9. Pre-Hearing Briefs

At the preliminary hearing, the panel will discuss with the parties whether to have prehearing briefs, their type and form, and when to submit them. Whether such briefing is scheduled may depend upon the number and complexity of the issues in dispute; how much is at stake (cost/benefit); whether the parties have covered or will cover the key issues in their pleadings, subsequent submissions on either discovery disputes or dispositive motions, a technology tutorial, or opening statements; whether there will be

96. *See* Edna Sussman & Solomon Ebere, *Reflections on the Use of Dispositive Motions in Arbitration*, 4 NYSBA N.Y. Disp. Resol. Law., Spring 2011, at 28.

97. Whether statutes of limitations apply in commercial arbitration matters may be an open question in some jurisdictions.

98. *See* Sussman & Ebere, *supra* note 96, at 29.

post-hearing briefing; and the preferences of the panel and counsel. Prehearing briefs can also obviate the need to do formal opening statements at the evidentiary hearing (or at least shorten openings so that they may be directed at responding to the other party's prehearing brief), thereby saving time and money at the hearing.

Prehearing briefing need not be an all-or-nothing event (i.e., long briefs or none). They may be short and focused on select issues providing a framework or laying a foundation for the evidence the panel will hear at the evidentiary hearing. For example, if the time frame within which certain acts occurred is a focus, the briefing may present a detailed timeline and discuss how the evidence will show who did what and when.

Assuming the parties submit prehearing briefs, counsel may use them to "prime the pump" or attune the panel to technical evidence it will hear at the hearing. This can be done in various ways, including:

- Paint a backstory or present a theme that includes key points and their relevance to the legal claims and defenses.
- Define key technical, regulatory, or industry terms, concepts, and tests; this may be done in the form of a self-contained list or glossary, or definitions may be peppered throughout the brief when each term is first used.
- Provide a road map to key evidence and tie this, if relevant, to a chronology (e.g., dates when a trademark was used in commerce; dates when testing was done to obtain FDA approval; dates when confidential information was disclosed and subsequent dates when a competing product was sold; dates when a series of licenses were signed and relevant intervening activities occurred).
- Provide an overview of the evidence the parties will present (e.g., explain key tests, experiments, and their results; discuss measurements and metrics and their significance).
- Cross-reference definitions, discussions, and explanations with expert reports; the brief can provide the legal context for the reports and reinforce what is in the reports in a more abbreviated form.

Panels often ask the parties to include in their prehearing briefs an agreed list of the issues they want the panel to decide. Having such a list will avoid problems later (e.g., a disagreement or misunderstanding as to what issues are to be covered by the evidentiary hearing; concerns about what issues the panel should decide in the award; and assertions by a disappointed party that the panel exceeded its authority and awarded relief as to issues not submitted).

Prehearing and post-hearing briefs should clearly set forth the monetary and injunctive relief requested. If there are any changes along the way (e.g., from when the pleadings or prehearing briefs are filed), let the panel know as soon as possible but certainly before the close of the evidence, in case the panel wants further information or argument. Some panels may request that, after the conclusion of the evidence, the parties submit either an agreed listing of issues to be decided or, if they cannot agree, separate listings.

To expedite the evidentiary hearing, counsel may want to include in the prehearing brief, or submit at the same time, written stipulations of undisputed facts. This obviates the need to present undisputed background facts or to identify undisputed operative documents through testimony at the hearing unless doing so is necessary for telling a cohesive story. In an IP/Technology case, such stipulations (e.g., when a trademark registration, copyright registration, or patent issued; when a product was first sold; how a product is used) can also save time and money in preparing the award. If the panel does not raise the parties' submission of stipulated facts before the preliminary hearing, then counsel should discuss this issue in advance and raise the issue before or at the preliminary hearing.

10. Witness Disclosures

Counsel may agree to the date for filing witness lists, or the panel's preference may dictate timing. Parties may file the lists late in the case, just before the evidentiary hearing (e.g., along with a prehearing submission), earlier in the case, or some combination (i.e., an initial version, followed by one or more updates). Witness lists serve many purposes. For example, early-filed, *may call* witness lists provide the panel with the opportunity to update their conflicts check, make necessary disclosures, and timely address any issues. Early witness lists also provide the parties with additional disclosures that can assist with planning discovery. Later-filed, *will call* witness lists help counsel plan their hearing presentation and the panel to manage the hearing. More generally, witness lists may inform the panel about upcoming evidence and the backgrounds and connections of the witnesses to the disputed issues in the case. For example, a witness description on a witness list may set forth:

> Dr. X has been the head of research and development for Research Company for 25 years. She led the development efforts with regard to [the product at issue] under the "Development and Licensing Agreement" that Research Company entered into with Licensing Company. Dr. X will testify about the research and monetary investment that Research Company made, and the challenges it had, in developing and testing the product.

Even if expert reports may not be due for some time, the early disclosure of experts (e.g., names, affiliations, and curricula vitae (CVs)), as with fact witnesses, is important to avoid a late disruption due to possible conflicts. If counsel insist on not disclosing expert identification information to each other early, they can disclose such information exclusively to the panel pending submission of expert reports provided they agree that such disclosures just to the panel will not constitute improper ex parte communications.

VI. The Evidentiary Hearing

A. Exhibits[99]

In some cases, there is a modest number of exhibits (e.g., the contract in dispute, earlier drafts, related emails), while, in other cases, there are numerous exhibits (e.g., patent prosecution correspondence, voluminous batch-production records, scanning electron micrographs, test results, schematics, FDA submission documents). Even with numerous exhibits, there are typically only a handful of key exhibits—cases are not usually decided on thousands of documents. Those few are the exhibits the panel will be referring to again and again while deciding the matter.[100] Every panel and counsel will have their own preferences regarding how to organize, assemble, and present exhibits; this is often discussed at the preliminary hearing. What follows are considerations for handling exhibits.

1. Format of Exhibits

Exhibits may be submitted in many forms. Where the numbers are limited, a binder of written documents may be the most efficient. However, many arbitrators prefer the exhibits to be submitted in searchable electronic format accessible for downloading, whether through a secure document repository, thumb drive, or other electronic device, or a secure download, which allows for markup. This should be discussed among counsel and the panel at

99. This section deals mainly with exhibit logistics before, during, and after the hearing. Using exhibits effectively is important. For example, if counsel shows a witness a contract that the witness has never seen before, counsel should reconsider the wisdom of nonetheless examining the witness about the meaning of a particular paragraph in the contract. Alternatively, even if a witness has seen a document before, counsel should reconsider the temptation to read into the record paragraph after paragraph of the document while asking the witness if counsel has read it accurately. If counsel is seeking to emphasize certain language from an exhibit in evidence, counsel could do so by directly referencing that language during an opening statement or closing argument.

100. A timeline-demonstrative exhibit is often helpful, especially when there are more than just a few important dates in the story each side is trying to tell.

the preliminary hearing and then incorporated in the scheduling order. The AAA, other arbitration administrators, and many private companies provide secure document repositories that may be implemented by agreement.

2. Legible and Clearly Marked

All exhibits should be clean, legible, and clearly marked with unique exhibit numbers (preferably on each page). Also, each page of an exhibit should be clearly marked with a number (e.g., Bates number) that allows each page of each exhibit to be independently identified and referenced (e.g., by hearing witnesses, in memoranda, and in the award). Ideally, whether denominated joint exhibits or otherwise, there should not be duplication in different sets of exhibits, and all references in submissions should be consistent.

3. Easily Located and Separate

Whether electronic or hard copy, each exhibit should be easily located and readily separable from all the other exhibits. Where the documents are provided in electronic form, they should be indexed by document number for easy electronic access. If exhibits are provided in paper form, they should be organized in a clear, simple manner, for example, by placing the numbered exhibits in loose-leaf binders behind tabbed dividers with corresponding numbers. Each binder should have, just inside the front cover, an index listing all of the exhibits in the case, not just those in the particular binder (this allows anyone to open any of the binders and determine in which binder each exhibit is located). The cover and spine of the binder should each bear a label with the case name, name of the panelist, binder number, and range of exhibit numbers within that binder. Where exhibits are voluminous, they are often submitted in electronic form. Often, however, hard copies of the key exhibits or key documents in the exhibits are provided to the panel in a binder.

4. Summary of Record for Voluminous Exhibits

In some cases, the exhibits are so voluminous (e.g., development/licensing of an FDA-approved pharmaceutical product, large stacks of prior art, U.S. and foreign prosecution histories, sales and cost records for damages presentations) that they cannot conveniently be presented to the panel (in total) as printed records or as summary charts (as permitted in federal courts under Federal Rule of Evidence 1006) and must be presented in a more practical form (e.g., electronically, if they all are going to be made of record). It is advisable to have as an exhibit (in paper form) a summary of the records.

Counsel may agree that voluminous exhibits will be provided in electronic format except for those items and pages about which witnesses will be testifying. Or, for example, counsel could agree that only the U.S. prosecution history needs to be in hard copy, and that all corresponding foreign prosecution histories will be furnished only in electronic form unless a hard copy is needed by a witness or requested by the panel.[101]

5. Cooperation of Counsel

It is advisable that opposing counsel work together to assemble a joint set of exhibits containing only one copy of each document (e.g., labeled "J-1" to "J-__"). It is inefficient and potentially confusing if each side introduces a copy of the same document (e.g., executed contract, patent, or trademark registration) as its own exhibit. To the extent counsel cannot agree that a document should be in the joint set of exhibits, each side could also submit its own presumably small set of exhibits (claimant's exhibits should be labeled "C-1" to "C-__" and respondent's "R-1" to "R-__"). Preferably, all admissibility objections to exhibits (e.g., on grounds of authenticity and the like) are handled by counsel and, if necessary, by the panel, before the hearing begins so that there are few exhibits that are just claimant's or respondent's, and time is not wasted during the hearing to address admissibility issues.[102] Arbitral panels tend to admit into evidence all exhibits reasonably related to the claims and defenses and to take exhibits *for what they're worth*, since they decide the admissibility, relevance, and materiality (i.e., the weight) to be accorded each piece of evidence,[103] and they want to avoid (e.g., in a motion to vacate the award) an allegation that they refused to hear evidence pertinent and material to the controversy. Thus, objections to proposed exhibits based, for example, upon an alleged lack of relevance, are not

101. Another expedient for presenting information contained in numerous exhibits is illustrated in proving damages. Rather than presenting large numbers of documents showing costs incurred or sales, after allowing the other side to review the raw documents or data, the relevant numbers can be summarized in a chart by category and then that chart submitted as the exhibit. *See, e.g.*, FED. R. EVID. 1006. Such a process should be discussed and adopted at the preliminary hearing and included in the initial scheduling order.

102. For example, the two sides could be ordered to exchange proposed exhibits before the hearing and to agree (to the extent possible) upon the joint set of exhibits before the hearing. A video or telephonic hearing just after that could then be held to discuss and rule on any objections to proposed exhibits that are not joint exhibits (if it is a joint exhibit, there is no admissibility objection) in time to refer to joint exhibits in the parties' prehearing briefs.

103. *See, e.g.*, AAA COMMERCIAL RULES, *supra* note 3, Rule R-35(b).

likely to succeed. However, the procedures regarding admission of evidence should be clear—are all joint exhibits "in" evidence or must they be referred to in briefing or at the hearing, or must they be offered into evidence? An efficient and effective practice is to have the composition of the evidentiary record set forth clearly in advance so as to manage the parties' expectations regarding what will comprise the record and assist counsel in smoothly and efficiently preparing the case for presentation at the evidentiary hearing. In addition, if there are prehearing briefs that cite to the exhibits, the arbitrators can confidently review the exhibits as part of the record.

6. Ensure Easy Access to the Panel

Some panel members prefer to have copies of all of the admissible exhibits sent to them before the evidentiary hearing only in searchable electronic form, particularly in cases having voluminous documents. Having the exhibits in searchable electronic form allows the panel to review those of interest in connection with its review of the prehearing briefs.[104] Along with the electronic copies of the exhibits, some panels may request a spreadsheet (in electronic and searchable format) listing all of the exhibits by number, name, date, author(s), and recipient(s), particularly if there are many exhibits. Having such a spreadsheet allows the panel to sort the exhibits, for example, by sender, recipient, or date. Thus, for instance, being able to sort exhibits by date allows the panel to identify (and then review) all documents dated just before and just after an event of interest. The exhibit list may also include a column showing whether there is a stipulation concerning each exhibit and, if not, other columns allowing the panel to keep track of whether an exhibit has been admitted.

During the hearing, it is likely that additional exhibits will be admitted into evidence (e.g., exhibits used to answer a question the panel poses or to impeach a witness). Copies of those should be numbered, placed in the binders (if their size permits), and also sent to the panel after the hearing. If counsel previously provided the panel with electronic copies of the exhibits, counsel may be asked to provide the panel with an updated set of the exhibits in electronic form along with a revised spreadsheet of the exhibits.

After the hearing, panel members typically ask that their respective set of exhibits used at the hearing be sent to them (along with any hearing transcripts, post-hearing briefs, and cited authorities) to prepare the award. Some panel members prefer to have counsel omit sending any exhibits that have not been cited in the prehearing briefs or admitted during the hearing and

104. Before the evidentiary hearing, counsel may instead provide the panel with just those exhibits cited in their prehearing briefs.

that counsel will not be referencing in their closing arguments or in post-hearing briefs.

A process should also be established for each side to disclose each proposed demonstrative exhibit to the other side a reasonable amount of time before the exhibit is to be used. If counsel cannot agree on that, the panel will likely establish a schedule. Such a process obviously does not apply to demonstratives created by witnesses while testifying at the hearing.

B. Opening Statements

A side's opening statement should be used to create a road map of the key evidence that side will present to the panel, including which witness(es) will present that evidence (this information should dovetail with the witness list). In an IP/Technology case, openings may also be an opportune time for counsel to explain linkages between the relevant or technical evidence and the legal claims (e.g., product development, creation of a copyrighted work, use in commerce of a trademarked or patented product). Choosing to do so here and in what detail may depend upon whether closing arguments and post-hearing briefs have been scheduled. Accordingly, if counsel foreshadowed the presentation of technical evidence (e.g., tests, experimental results) or discussed scientific definitions, concepts, or theories in a prehearing brief, they can use the opening statement to reinforce or build on what was introduced there. For example:

> You will hear testimony from Dr. Y, a dedicated employee of Giant Computer Company for ten years, who will explain the procedures the company used to design, refine, and test the widely used router that embodies the technology at the heart of this trade secret misappropriation case.

If counsel believe that anything they intend to promise in an opening statement relating to proof at the hearing relies on a demonstration at the hearing that may be objectionable, counsel should seek permission and a favorable admissibility ruling in advance (e.g., at the final prehearing conference). If counsel promise what they cannot ultimately deliver, they may be left with proof and credibility problems.

C. Testimony

1. General Guidance

Counsel should not present irrelevant evidence. They should focus on the key issues for which they bear the burden of proof and direct their evidence and arguments to them. For example, after obtaining testimony from a credible witness, calling more witnesses just to confirm that earlier testimony can waste valuable time, frustrate the panel, and lead to unintended consequences, including diminishing the effect of a strong witness by calling a second witness on the same issue who turns out to be a weak witness.

Procedures for taking and presenting testimony in arbitration can be flexible. For example, witnesses in other parts of the world may be available remotely to testify by way of a videoconference platform or simply a telephone connection. If considering eliciting testimony from remote witnesses, counsel should investigate the applicable jurisdictions' rules regarding the administration of the oath to the witness (i.e., swearing-in of the witness). Where a witness's schedule or location (time zone) creates availability issues, panels often permit witnesses to be taken out of order. The order of witnesses and an accompanying brief paragraph describing the expected testimony is a useful tool to help the panel and counsel manage the hearing, particularly in IP/Technology cases where there can be multiple experts and fact witnesses testifying about, for example, various aspects of the IP, technology, and regulatory issues.

Use expert and fact witnesses with knowledge and experience in the relevant areas (technology, industry practices, damages) to teach and reinforce whatever information is important in deciding the disputed issues. If, for example, the prehearing briefs and/or opening statements introduced scientific concepts and terminology, reinforce and expand on those during direct examination. For example:

> Mr. Smith, I would like to ask you some questions about how Druglera was formulated. Can you explain to the panel what it means to formulate a drug? [Answer]
>
> Did you test the safety and efficacy of the drug to obtain FDA approval? [Yes.]
>
> Can you explain to the panel what it means for a drug to be safe? [Answer]
>
> Can you explain to the panel what it means for a drug to be efficacious? [Answer]

In a technology case, counsel should consider the use of charts, graphs, schematics, videos of tests, data tables, and even formulas and analyses, depending on the case, to assist the panel in fully understanding the substance of the dispute and the claim of the parties as to what happened and why. Other considerations for presenting testimonial evidence to an arbitral panel in IP/Technology cases include the following.

2. Fact Witness Statements

Domestic arbitrations have begun to adopt the practice that is the norm in international arbitration of using written statements of witnesses for their direct testimony (in lieu of a direct examination) and permitting live cross- and redirect examinations. Often, even though witness statements are used, counsel are permitted to do a short, live direct, to introduce the witness and give a very short summary of the testimony ("warm up" the witness). The use of witness statements can shorten the time needed for the evidentiary hearing and give the panel before the hearing a better understanding of the case that they will hear. However, counsel should be careful that the witness statements actually state the testimony of the witnesses in their own words and are not simply counsel writing what he or she would want the witness to say (counsel sometimes forget that, which in turn can lead to unfortunate testimony during cross-examination). The witness statements *are not* additional briefs, but rather a clear, efficient statement of testimony.

Although there can be disagreement between the parties and the panel regarding whether witness statements should be used in a particular case, experience has shown that they can be very helpful to the panel in certain instances. For example, where key disputed issues rely on a detailed account of what occurred, setting forth that information in a witness statement can help the panel prepare for the hearing and more easily follow cross-examination at the hearing.

3. Expert Testimony

a) Whether to Call an Expert

Carefully consider whether each planned expert is needed. Counsel sometimes believe that to establish credibility, they need to have one or more independent expert witnesses. Unless the expert can add something significant to the case, such testimony may be unnecessary. Using in-house "experts" to provide necessary background, for example, in the relevant technology or industry, can add credibility to a party's case, as well as save time and money. Here are examples where experts were *not* helpful to the panel.

Case in point: In a multi-week software dispute, the claimant called a certified public accountant (CPA) to testify regarding damages. His report took all of the damages numbers to which a fact witness was going to testify and summarized and totaled them. He did the same thing live at the hearing. In essence, the CPA testified to simple arithmetic, providing nothing that helped the panel determine damages.

Case in point: An expert spent an entire day explaining the structure and operation of a complex software system. However, the issue in the case was whether a particular function of that system, the operation of which was not in dispute, infringed a patent. The expert's testimony had nothing to do with the relevant patent's claims or how the software related to those particular claims.

Case in point: One expert testified in detail as to why a machine failed, and a second testified as to why a contractor had overcharged, but both had to change their testimony when confronted on cross-examination with additional undisputed facts already in evidence that counsel had never previously shared with them.

Notwithstanding these examples, testimony from experts can be valuable to the panel (e.g., to prove substantial similarity or likelihood of confusion, to explain whether a product falls within a defined contractual term). In a technology case, for example, a properly qualified technical expert can, among other things, educate panelists about special knowledge and experience in the relevant field, industry standards, or particular technologies; explain how particular devices or systems operate and/or what caused them to malfunction; describe the various tests and analyses they employed to reach their conclusions; or describe generally accepted designs that might have avoided the problems experienced. IP/Technology cases also typically benefit from damages experts, particularly when a party is relying on damages theories or complex damages projections. Good experts can win a case. Unqualified experts, experts testifying outside of their area of expertise, experts relying on erroneous or incomplete facts or assumptions, or unprepared experts waste time and money and can lose a case.[105]

b) Taking Expert Testimony

Taking expert testimony in arbitration can be more creative and flexible than in court (i.e., live witness testimony followed by cross and redirect). On the simplest level, after both counsel have questioned an expert, the panelists

105. Depending on the applicable rules, or by agreement if necessary, the panel may consider hiring a neutral expert to advise on particular technology issues. This is common in international arbitrations, but far less so in U.S. arbitrations. The parties split the cost and will likely participate in the neutral expert selection process. The expert issues a report that is provided to the panel and the parties, with the parties having the opportunity to respond and possibly to examine the neutral expert. This technique does create issues relating to how the panel selects the neutral expert and how much authority the expert believes he or she has.

may have a dialogue with the expert. Where appropriate, rather than have claimant's expert testify during claimant's case and respondent's expert testify during respondent's case, the experts could each testify issue by issue. Thus, claimant's expert would testify as to issue No. 1 and would be cross-examined, and then respondent's expert would testify as to issue No. 1 and would be cross-examined, and so on.

Another method, called "hot-tubbing," "witness conferencing," "concurrent testimony," or "tandem examination," has all of the experts on a specific topic sworn and in the hearing room together, each listening and commenting on the other's testimony, asking each other questions, and responding to the panel's questions. Tandem examination of experts is reported to have originated in the Australian court system.[106] If the panel believes tandem examination would be useful, it can circulate a suggested protocol (there are many possible variations) and allow the parties to propose modifications. Sample guidelines follow.

1. The witnesses (e.g., two experts) are accepted by stipulation of the parties as experts.
2. Both experts are sworn in at the same time and take the stand at the same time.
3. The opinions and CVs of the experts are previously submitted to the panel in their reports.
4. Claimant's counsel may ask the initial questions, which are answered first by the claimant's witness and then by the respondent's witness. Each question is the same to each expert witness to allow the experts to answer each other's arguments at the same time and to allow counsel and the panel to hear both sides of the issue virtually simultaneously.
5. At the conclusion of questions by claimant's counsel, respondent's counsel may ask questions that have not been asked or that are otherwise relevant to its case.
6. The panel may ask questions of both witnesses at any point and must permit each witness to answer.
7. When claimant's and respondent's counsel have completed their round of questions, there is a break to permit each side to consult with its own expert, and there is then an additional round of questions in the format of paragraphs 4 to 6. At the option of counsel, this second round of questions may be asked by the experts of each

106. *See* Frances P. Kao et al., *Into the Hot Tub . . . a Practical Guide to Alternative Expert Witness Procedures in International Arbitration*, 44 INT'L L. 1035, 1037 (2010).

other or counsel may continue the questioning, having had input from their respective experts.

8. The experts should be informed that the flexibility of the arbitration process encourages them to comment on each other's testimony and even engage in direct dialogue with each other, if appropriate and if agreed to in advance by counsel.

c) Expert Credibility

The credibility of experts, particularly where testing or surveys are involved, often depends on their designing and supervising the test or survey so that they can adequately support the results. Experts should avoid providing testimony on the ultimate issues the panel must decide or simply acting as additional counsel with a relevant degree. Although the panel is unlikely to strictly enforce *Daubert* standards,[107] shaky qualifications or testimony will impair the reliability and usefulness of the expert opinion. The experts are there to assist the panel, to teach, and to assess the opposing expert's report or evaluation.

An expert's credibility may also be affected by how the expert responds to panel questions. Counsel should ensure that expert witnesses are prepared to answer questions not only from counsel but also from the panel. Expert witnesses may be comfortable talking with peers within their workplace, others in their field, or students (if they teach), but they may not be comfortable when the panel asks questions that appear to challenge their testimony (e.g., questions to clarify, hypotheticals). Furthermore, experts should be aware of their role in the case and at the evidentiary hearing. For example, technical experts should understand the difference between explaining technical concepts in the context of their jobs and positions (e.g., in a company, as a consultant, or for academic purposes), on the one hand, and providing evidence to support legal claims and remedies, on the other.

Furthermore, in the context of answering questions, it is sometimes the case that an expert will not respond "yes" or "no" to a yes or no question and instead reply with a "maybe" followed by a lengthy explanation or just the lengthy explanation. Such a response may be dismissed by the panel as non-responsive or it may affect the expert's credibility particularly if the expert answered yes or no to the same question in a deposition, or the question is taken from the expert's report and a yes or no would be expected. That said, a simple "yes" or "no" may not be appropriate or possible, as issues may be more complex or require additional conditions or facts before they can be answered "yes" or "no." In such circumstances, counsel or the expert should explain why he or she cannot answer simply as requested.

---

107. Daubert v. Merrell Dow Pharms., Inc., 509 U.S. 579 (1993).

The expert's credibility depends in part on his or her ability and manner to respond genuinely and spontaneously to questions asked by the panel, and not simply to repeat what is in the report. Moreover, an expert should truly be an expert and know when to say "I don't know." The expert should be an expert in the subject matter at issue, not merely highly educated and/or experienced in a certain or many areas of technology but not in the specific subject matter that is at issue in the case. Needless to say, arrogance and the like do not play well in front of an arbitration panel. The expert's testimony is part of the evidentiary support for the claims or defenses at issue, and experts need to perform the important role of providing such support.

D. Using Depositions

An opportune time to raise the issue of using depositions at the hearing is often at the final prehearing conference. If the parties want to submit testimony by written or video deposition, the depositions (i.e., transcript and/or video recording) should be submitted either before or during the hearing, depending on the panel's preference. Reading a transcribed deposition to the panel is a waste of time and rarely permitted. Furthermore, reading depositions can change the meaning and intent of the testimony dramatically, depending on the reader's inflections. Transcribed depositions ideally should be either edited or the relevant testimony delineated and marked, so the panel can quickly read only the portions of interest. Parties seeking to use the videorecorded deposition of a witness may do so by incorporating the showing of the relevant deposition portions as part of their case at the evidentiary hearing so that it may be transcribed by the court reporter.

Using depositions for impeachment is often of little benefit except in rare cases and can waste valuable time. The most beneficial use is when a witness directly contradicts prior deposition testimony that is both relevant and material to an issue in the case, particularly when that issue is material to deciding the case.

E. Decorum, Rhetoric, and Drama at the Hearing

Arbitration typically takes place in a conference room, a relatively small space in comparison to most courtrooms, in which the parties, counsel, witnesses, and the panel spend many hours, sometimes over many days. Dramatic or suggestive gestures or facial expressions by anyone are inappropriate.[108] Similarly, impolite or aggressive questioning of witnesses can

108. Counsel should instruct corporate representatives and witnesses not to make facial expressions to, or eye contact with, any panel member during the hearing to

come across as harsh. Any maltreatment of administrative personnel is noticeable. The parties will be best served when their counsel observe professional social graces and display a calm, methodical approach that is and appears to be calculated to assist the panel in reaching a fair result.

The techniques that counsel often use before a jury to make or emphasize points are unnecessary in arbitration and do not play well to experienced panelists. The hearing room is often smaller than a court room, and counsel and the witnesses generally speak from a position much closer to the arbitrator(s) than they would in a courtroom. There simply is an intimacy in an arbitration hearing that does not occur in a court proceeding. Counsel should recognize the difference. Counsel should make their points clearly and support them with oral testimony, documents, and/or physical exhibits.

F. Post-Hearing Briefs

Various factors determine whether the parties will file post-hearing briefs, including the panel's preference; whether the parties agree; cost considerations; and the complexity of the facts, technology, IP, and contractual and legal issues. A post-hearing brief gives the parties an opportunity to integrate the testimony, documentary evidence, and the applicable law in a single document to provide the panel with a clean framework for analyzing the disputed issues and writing the award. Such briefs also give counsel the opportunity to address (e.g., clarify, explain, emphasize) evidence or arguments that could be perceived as emerging weaker or stronger after the evidentiary hearing. For example, if evidence adduced at the hearing seemingly weakens a legal claim or defense set forth in the prehearing brief, that party in its post-hearing brief may want to explain why that is not the case and emphasize other evidence supporting the claim or defense.

Some panels schedule the filing of post-hearing briefs as part of their initial pre-trial scheduling order, while others decide later in the proceeding whether to have the parties submit them (e.g., at the final prehearing conference or at the end of the evidentiary hearing). Thus, if the panel does not schedule post-hearing briefs early in the proceeding, and there is any chance that the other party may not agree to them or a panel may not permit them, counsel will want to ensure that they have already adequately and persuasively taught the panel what it needs to know about the relevant facts and legal issues to make the ultimate factual and legal determinations in their client's favor.

---

communicate information or a reaction (e.g., about another witness testifying or an argument by opposing counsel). Similarly, witnesses should refrain from making eye contact with others on their side for approval of what they are saying while testifying.

It is not uncommon in IP/Technology cases for the panel to send to counsel a short list of questions that they want counsel to address in their post-hearing briefs. This should occur shortly after the end of the evidentiary hearing and well before the post-hearing briefs are due. Some panels may request that the questions be answered separately in the briefs while other panels will permit counsel to address the questions as part of their briefing incorporated into a discussion of other issues. The intent of such questions will vary. For example, they may simply seek clarification of points made in earlier briefing or argument, they may be giving counsel the opportunity to persuade the panel with a stronger argument or by marshalling the best evidence presented at the hearing, or they may be wanting counsel to leave the comfort of legal advocacy and replace it with a more candid discussion of a party's position and the underlying reasons. The panel may also schedule post-hearing questions from the panel to be addressed orally.

If a road map of the evidence (including a chronology with important dates) might be helpful or persuasive for panel deliberations or for preparing a reasoned award, counsel should present one in the post-hearing submission (e.g., concerning development and testing of a device, the FDA approval process, when respondent was exposed to confidential information). Events and dates should be tied to relevant supporting evidence (i.e., with focused citations to the transcript and exhibits).

In IP/Technology cases seeking monetary relief, panels often require specificity in damages requests, and the post-hearing brief is one place to provide this—if it has not already been sufficiently provided elsewhere (e.g., in a prehearing brief or in an expert's report).[109] For example, it is helpful for the panel to have (1) the legal support for all damages, including citation to relevant statutes, rules, and cases; (2) arithmetic calculations and a statement of any assumptions made; and (3) damages calculations, including any interest claimed, based upon the various ways a panel may decide the case in view of the parties' positions and comments from the panel. Counsel may want to avoid providing the panel with only one damages calculation for their favored number because the panel may not agree with all of their assumptions or positions. Interest calculations (when applicable) may be particularly thorny but should not be ignored—both sides should provide assistance to the panel and can do so without making concessions. Some panels will ask each party to prepare an award setting forth the monetary relief it is requesting with the particularity required for the case.

109. The evidentiary hearing may have been bifurcated, with a preliminary order addressing liability, and a separate proceeding, by live hearing and/or written submissions, on damages.

G. Post-Hearing Closing Arguments

Often in IP/Technology cases, the panel or the parties will request closing arguments. This is helpful to the panel before its deliberations and writing the award. In some cases, the decision of whether or when to schedule closing arguments will occur early in the case, perhaps at the time of the preliminary hearing. In other cases, that decision will not be made until the later part of a case, for example, at the final prehearing conference or a few days before the end of the evidentiary hearing. Closing arguments may be held at the conclusion of the parties' presentation of evidence, regardless of whether the parties will submit post-hearing briefs. In other cases, closing arguments may be held in person or remotely after the parties submit their post-hearing briefs. Those arguments may simply constitute the traditional style of closing arguments, and, depending upon the preference of the panel, counsel may be permitted to argue for a period of time without interruption or they may be interrupted by panel questions. It is often the case in IP/Technology cases, however, that the panel will permit counsel to proceed with their closing arguments uninterrupted for a period of time followed by a session (it could last an hour or more) of panel questions—a "hot panel."[110] As a courtesy to counsel, a panel will let counsel know the procedure it will follow before oral argument is scheduled so counsel may prepare accordingly.

Parties may vary their strategy regarding what evidence and issues to focus on in their closing arguments depending on when closing arguments are held (e.g., at the close of the case or after post-hearing briefing). The panel may ask counsel to exchange materials they intend to use at the oral arguments in advance. Here are some things to consider in preparing for closings:

- Slide presentations can summarize and compress key evidence and points on which the panel should focus in its deliberations. Panel members may want to take notes on the slides during closing arguments and refer to them during deliberations and when writing the award. Thus, counsel should provide the panel with a copy of their presentation slides and any other handouts before beginning their closing argument.
- In a handout or in slides, summarize the key evidence. Consider putting photos of the witnesses next to the summaries as a memory aid. For documents, provide the exhibit number of those documents admitted into evidence, and, for testimony, provide citations to the hearing transcripts.

110. A session of only panel questions can be intimidating or welcomed. It can be intimidating because it may take counsel "off script." In other cases, it may be welcomed because it gives counsel the opportunity to know what issues are of concern to the panel, and it permits counsel the opportunity to clarify and persuade the panel on those issues.

- Provide a road map or timeline of key events (e.g., product development and/or testing) with reference to supporting documents and testimony.
- Link the material factual evidence to proof of the elements of the disputed legal claims.
- Be fully prepared to answer the panel's questions, particularly when the panel requests closing arguments after the parties have submitted post-hearing briefs. The panel will then have had time to think about the case and pinpoint those issues that will help decide the case.

H. Awards

The parties may agree to a reasoned award in the arbitration agreement, or either party may request one in the demand/response. If the agreement and pleadings are silent on the issue, the default rule for whether the award is to be simple or reasoned may depend on the governing set of rules. For example, for commercial domestic cases governed by the AAA Commercial Rules, the default type of award is *standard* (or bare) but, in practice, in IP/Technology cases, the type of award typically issued is a *reasoned* award (by request of the parties) and for international cases, it is *reasoned*.[111] If the type of award is not specified in the arbitration agreement, pleadings, or otherwise mandated (e.g., by the rules), during the preliminary hearing, the panel will usually ask counsel what type of award the parties want. If both parties agree, the panel will most likely follow their wishes. If the parties disagree, the panel may ask the parties to submit short letters explaining their views. The panel may decide then on the type of award or postpone the decision until closer to the evidentiary hearing and then revisit the issue with the parties.

It is up to the parties as to whether a stenographer will be engaged to record the evidentiary hearing and create a transcript. If the award is to be a reasoned award, panels will often request an official transcript of the

---

111. *See* AAA Commercial Rules, *supra* note 3, Rule R-48(b) ("The arbitrator need not render a reasoned award unless the parties request such an award in writing prior to appointment of the arbitrator or unless the arbitrator determines that a reasoned award is appropriate."); *see also* ICDR Arbitration Rules, *supra* note 33, art. 34(1) (reading in part: "The tribunal shall state the reasons upon which an award is based, unless the parties have agreed that no reasons need be given."). The difference is attributable in large measure to the likely antipathy a foreign court will have for an award that sets forth no reasons for the outcome when the award is presented for enforcement. International awards also have specific requirements if they are to meet the New York Convention and the applicable procedural rules (e.g., UNCITRAL Arbitration Rules). A discussion of required formats and content for international awards is beyond the scope of this chapter, which addresses only domestic awards.

hearing, but it is still the parties' choice (however, without an official transcript, the parties may disagree about what a witness testified to, thereby making the panel's job more difficult, and open a door to a challenge of the award). As mentioned earlier in the chapter, stipulations of uncontested background facts can be useful to the panel and save it time in combing the record for that information (e.g., names of inventors, patent numbers, dates of filing, registration numbers, an inventor's employment history, dates of incorporation).

As stated previously, there are standard awards and there are reasoned awards. A standard award states only who won, who lost, and the relief (including any damages) awarded (e.g., "Party B breached the contract, and Party B must pay Party A $x within y days of the date of this award") with no reasons given. A reasoned award is an award in which the panel gives reasons for its conclusions, typically including an explanation of the decisional principles (e.g., procedural and substantive principles), an analysis of the evidence bearing on the alleged facts, and an application of the decisional rules to the facts. Sometimes an award contains so-called findings of fact and conclusions of law, but that is in essence a more stylized and much more expensive form of a reasoned award.[112] In appropriate situations in IP/Technology cases, parties may request a form of award that gives them an efficient closure on key issues in dispute, rather than the traditional standard or reasoned award. For example, parties may set forth specific questions analogous to a special verdict for the panel to answer that address liability and damages issues.[113] Experience has also shown that parties may choose "baseball arbitration" as a process to decide damages to be paid.[114]

---

112. Findings of fact and conclusions of law entail the panel listing each fact it found necessary to support the award and providing the legal authority for how such facts resulted in the award. Some panels ask both sides to submit proposed findings of fact and conclusions of law in lieu of or in addition to post-hearing briefs. Others may ask the prevailing party to submit its proposal; sometimes the panel does all the drafting itself. Under the AAA Commercial Rules and other rule sets, unless extended by agreement of the parties, the award must be issued within 30 days after the close of the hearing. Preparing findings of fact and conclusions of law after a lengthy hearing can be time-consuming. Without an agreed extension of time, it may be unlikely for even a sole panelist, let alone a tri-partite panel, to complete and submit findings of fact and conclusions of law in a one-month period. Due to the costs and time involved, this form of award is not common in commercial domestic (U.S.) arbitrations.

113. For example, in a contract dispute over who pays for certain testing, one question may be: "Is Company A liable for the amounts Company B has invoiced it that Company B alleges are 'Testing Costs?'"

114. The term "baseball arbitration" derives from major league player-salary arbitration and refers to the process where each side selects a number that it requests in

Several factors may prompt parties to request standard rather than reasoned awards including the ones that are discussed in the following sections.

1. Collateral Estoppel in Later Actions

Collateral estoppel regarding an issue in a later action requires that the issue in question must have been actually decided in an earlier action, that its determination must have been essential to the earlier judgment, and that the party in the later action against whom collateral estoppel is asserted must have had a full and fair opportunity to litigate the issue in the earlier action.[115] Factors such as the relative informality of an arbitration proceeding, the relative incompleteness of the record (e.g., not having full discovery), the absence of a reasoned opinion (in some cases) that fully reflects the basis for and scope of the panel's decision, and the governing law have caused courts to exercise considerable discretion in deciding whether to apply estoppel to arbitration awards. A standard award is less likely than a reasoned award to be held by a later panel as a sufficient basis for collateral estoppel.

2. Confidentiality

If the losing party asks a court to vacate the award, the award itself will be an exhibit in that proceeding, and the court likely will not allow the entire award to be filed under seal (the court may allow portions of the award disclosing highly sensitive information, for example, trade secrets, to be filed under seal). In patent cases, the patentee, assignee, or licensee has an obligation under 35 U.S.C. § 294 when an award is made by an arbitration panel to give notice of it in writing to the director of the PTO, which includes a copy of the award. Thus, parties who are concerned about maintaining the confidentiality of what is in the award in a patent case may consider opting for a standard award. In IP/Technology cases, it may be the case that a reasoned award will contain trade secret or confidential information, whether technological, business, or both. In some cases, the parties and the panel have agreed that the award itself will be a standard award and that the panel will provide the parties with a separate, non-award document containing the reasons for its award. Another option is for the panel to ask the parties (e.g., at the end of the evidentiary hearing) what they consider to be trade secret or confidential information that should not be mentioned in the award.

---

the award, and the panel can only pick one of the two numbers and no other. The award must be either for either A or B and not a compromise.

115. Dean Witter Reynolds Inc. v. Byrd, 470 U.S. 213 (1985); Postlewaite v. McGraw-Hill, Inc., 333 F.3d 42, 48 (2d Cir. 2003); City of New York v. Welsbach Elec. Corp., 878 N.E.2d 966, 968 (N.Y. 2007).

3. Cost

A reasoned award in a complex case (e.g., an IP/Technology case) may run 50 to 100 pages or more, but a standard award in the same case might be only two or three pages. There is obviously a substantial incremental cost associated with preparing a reasoned award.

4. Risk Versus Reward

A party may be concerned that, if a reasoned award is disclosed to the public (e.g., because it is an exhibit in an award confirmation proceeding), third parties may be spurred to make similar claims, parroting the panel's reasoning, whether or not collateral estoppel attaches.

Notwithstanding such possible downsides to a reasoned award, parties in IP/Technology cases typically want one for a variety of reasons, including giving the parties assurance that there has been full consideration of their positions and evidence and, when parties continue to work together, providing them reasoning that might help guide their ongoing relationship. In addition, if there is an ongoing relationship—for example, in a rate-setting or patent royalty-setting case—the parties may want to understand the panel's reasoning as a guide to their dealing with those and similar issues in the future.

Conclusion

Arbitration can provide an efficient and reliable means of adjudicating IP/Technology disputes when counsel effectively use the unique procedures and flexibility allowed by arbitration. If arbitration is approached as merely another venue for federal court litigation with privately selected judges, many of arbitration's benefits will be lost. With counsel working cooperatively with each other and the panel, a process can be tailored to the specific needs and unique issues of the case that will instill confidence in the parties that the panel gave them a full and fair hearing and understood their evidence and arguments. If the parties are fully comfortable that they have had a fair hearing, they will be more likely to accept the arbitration process and the resulting award.

APPENDIX

Preliminary Hearing Topics

The panel requests that, before the preliminary hearing, the parties confer and, to the extent possible, agree about the following, which the panel will discuss at the hearing. Please prepare a writing noting the agreements and any issues that remain open to share with the panel on the day before the preliminary hearing. The parties should also review the [Administrative Organization's] Sample Preliminary Hearing Order/List and suggest any topics that may have been omitted from it but are significant to the parties.

1. Confirm the panel.
2. Are any jurisdictional questions raised?
3. Include the governing law under the contract and the governing law and rules applicable to the arbitration.
4. Are all necessary or appropriate parties included in the arbitration?
5. Do the parties anticipate any amendments to claims, counterclaims, or defenses?
6. Are there other related proceedings pending (e.g., court, arbitrations, PTO, U.S. International Trade Commission), and, if so, can they be combined/consolidated with this arbitration or should this arbitration be stayed pending resolution of some other proceeding?
7. Do the parties agree to accelerated or direct exchange (email exchange simultaneously copying the parties, arbitrators, and administrative organization if available under its rules)?
8. Is there a need for expedition?
9. Is there a need for a protective/confidentiality order? If so, designate a deadline to provide the panel with a draft order.
10. Are there any threshold or dispositive issues whose resolution might expedite resolution of the case, including any preconditions to the arbitration? If so, when will such motions be filed?
11. Will some form of bifurcation create an efficiency and cost saving (e.g., in an infringement case, should the issue of infringement be decided after an initial hearing, and damages, if there is infringement, be decided after a second hearing?)?
12. Do the parties anticipate motion practice that might expedite the process, and, if so, at what stage, and what deadlines do the parties suggest?

13. Information exchange—Do the parties have the relevant and material evidence required for the arbitration or is document exchange required, and, if so, how can the panel assist the parties in managing document or e-discovery issues? Should the parties agree to a "so ordered" ESI protocol and/or an artificial intelligence (AI) protocol?
14. Document exchange:
    a. When are document requests to be served?
    b. When are objections to be lodged?
    c. When are the parties to meet and confer to try to resolve the objections?
    d. When are unresolved objections to be brought to the panel's attention?
    e. When will a hearing be held to resolve those objections?
    f. When will document exchange (including, if the parties agree, production of a document log for which privilege is claimed) occur?
15. If there is to be e-discovery, how are the costs to be allocated?
16. Will depositions be necessary, and, if so, how many?
17. Summonses/subpoenas:
    a. Will summonses/subpoenas be required?
    b. If discovery summonses/subpoenas are required, does the panel have authority to issue them in/for the relevant jurisdiction(s)? If not, is there a work-around, such as setting a day of hearing in the witness's jurisdiction?
    c. Include the deadline for requesting summonses/subpoenas and for objecting to their issuance.
18. Are there specific tests that need to be performed by one or both parties, or by an independent, mutually approved or panel-selected expert?
19. Are expert witnesses anticipated? If so, when will experts be identified? Do the parties require a hot-tubbing protocol?
20. Will expert reports be exchanged? If so, when?
21. Will a technical tutorial be helpful to the panel? At what stage and how will it be presented and by whom? Will it be on or off the record?
22. When will the parties provide the panel with stipulated and contested issues of law and fact?
23. When will the parties identify witnesses ("may call" and "will call" witness lists) and will they testify live at the hearing or by other means?
24. The parties should suggest a method for identifying, numbering, and pre-marking exhibits and a date for their exchange at least ten

days prior to the hearing. Exhibits should be joint exhibits to the extent possible.

25. Is there a protocol for pre-marking and designating exhibits?
26. When and how will counsel provide exhibits to the panel?
27. Will counsel stipulate to the admissibility of exhibits before the hearing? Set a date for hearing on admissibility issues. Will exhibits be considered admitted when submitted prehearing or will they have to be referred to at the hearing?
28. Include dates for status conferences, including a final prehearing status conference.
29. Suggest dates for prehearing briefs if they are to be filed.
30. Hearing:
    a. What will be the format for the hearing (e.g., in person, remote, hybrid)? If remote or hybrid, when will the parties provide the panel with a protocol for the hearing?
    b. Where will the hearing be held?
    c. Will the parties want opening statements, closing arguments, and/or post-hearing briefs? When will any briefs be filed?
    d. Do the parties wish to submit direct testimony in writing?
    e. Do the parties want to control the timing of the hearing (e.g., by a chess-clock process)?
    f. How much time do the parties anticipate they will need for the hearing?
    g. Will videoconferencing be needed for any witnesses? If so, is a videoconference hearing protocol needed?
    h. Will there be a stenographic transcript or other record of the proceeding, and, if so, who will arrange for that and how will the costs be handled?
    i. What is the order of the witnesses?
    j. How will expert testimony be presented (e.g., by written witness statements with cross-examination, or through hot-tubbing (e.g., having all experts in the room at the same time, with each expert having the opportunity to respond to and ask questions of the other expert))?
    k. What are the specific issues that the parties are submitting in the arbitration to be ultimately decided and addressed in the award?
    l. What type of award is requested (i.e., a standard award, a reasoned award (what kind of reasons—findings of fact and conclusions of law))?
    m. Is the proceeding to be deemed an international arbitration, requiring that the award comply with the New York Convention? If so, what is the seat of the arbitration?

n. Do the parties agree on a method for allocating costs?
o. Will any interpreters be needed? If so, when and how will they be identified?
p. Is an award of attorneys' fees required or allowed by the arbitration agreement or applicable rules or law? If so, on what basis are they to be awarded (e.g., to the party that prevails on all or the majority of its claims/defenses)?

31. Be prepared with an agreement as to several sets of consecutive dates sufficient for the hearing for consideration by the panel.
32. The parties should acknowledge their obligation to promptly inform the panel of any newly discovered potential conflicts or waive them.
33. Do the parties have additional issues not included in this list? If so, what are they?

CHAPTER 10

UDRP Proceedings: How Advocates Can Put Their Best Foot Forward

Steven M. Levy and Harrie Samaras[1]

Introduction[2]

The Uniform Domain Name Dispute Resolution Policy (UDRP or Policy)[3] was adopted by the Internet Corporation for Assigned Names and Numbers (ICANN), as recommended by the World Intellectual Property Organization (WIPO). It provides an administrative forum for adjudicating trademark disputes relating to the abusive registration and use of internet domain names. UDRP proceedings are international in scope and provide a single forum for resolving internet domain name disputes regardless of where the registrar, the domain name holder, or the trademark owner filing the complaint are located. The panelists deciding the cases are experts from around the world in various fields including trademark law, domain name issues, electronic commerce, the internet, and dispute resolution.

UDRP proceedings also provide a more expeditious, inexpensive, and informal option for resolving internet domain name disputes than going to court. For example, hearings are nonexistent,[4] the issues decided are limited in scope, and the extent of written submissions and proofs are comparatively less than in litigation. That said, complainants and respondents

1. This chapter is a derivative work of Chapter 11 from the First and Second Editions of this book previously co-authored by Dina Leytes, Deputy General Counsel, Comcast Cable, and Harrie Samaras.

2. See Glossary for definition of frequently used terms.

3. *See Uniform Domain Name Dispute Resolution Policy*, Internet Corp. for Assigned Names & Nos. (Aug. 26, 1999), https://www.icann.org/resources/pages/policy-2012-02-25-en [hereinafter *Policy*].

4. *See generally Rules for Uniform Domain Name Dispute Resolution Policy*, ICANN (July 31, 2015), https://www.icann.org/resources/pages/udrp-rules-2015-03-11-en [hereinafter *Rules*]. Pursuant to Rule 13 of the Rules, there shall be no in-person hearings (including hearings by teleconference, videoconference, and web conference) unless the panel determines, only as an exceptional matter, that a hearing is necessary in order for it to make its decision.

alike should take seriously the evidence and arguments they submit for a panel's consideration, asking: Do the arguments effectively and persuasively address each element of the Policy? Are the assertions credible? Is there sufficient supporting evidence? Indeed, many UDRP decisions demonstrate that otherwise experienced litigation advocates sometimes underestimate the UDRP, yielding negative outcomes that can adversely affect client relationships and a firm's reputation. Expert pre-complaint assessment will go a long way towards building client confidence by saving the unnecessary expenditure of time and money on a case with little likelihood of success.

This chapter will focus on issues that frequently arise in UDRP proceedings and will offer advocates[5] ideas on how best to present their case in a UDRP proceeding.

I. History and Purpose of the UDRP

A. The Internet and Trademarks

Each website and computer on the internet can be identified by a unique string of numbers known as an Internet Protocol (IP) address. These are also used in email addresses. Because IP addresses are not particularly easy for internet users to remember, user-friendly names that are easy to recall—domain names—were created. Often domain names incorporate well-known trademarks.

Once a domain name is registered, it cannot be registered or used at the same time by another.[6] There are some cases where someone who registers a domain name incorporating a trademark owned by another may have a valid, good-faith basis for registering the domain name. For example, the domain name may correspond to the registrant's own business or product name. Other times, someone may have acted in bad faith in registering the domain name—perhaps with an intention to benefit by reselling the domain name to the trademark owner at a significant profit or by redirecting internet

5. The word "advocates" is used here in its broadest sense. Parties may utilize internal or external legal counsel, but are not required to do so. A party may proceed without legal counsel as a *pro se* complainant or respondent.

6. *See, e.g.*, Bankwell Fin. Grp., Inc. v. Whois Priv. Prot. Serv., Inc., Case No. D2015-1664 (WIPO Nov. 13, 2015) (noting that the system of domain name registration is generally a "first-come, first-served system," and that "[a]bsent pre-existing rights which may be used to revoke a registration, the first person in time to register a domain name would normally be entitled to use the domain name for any legitimate purpose it wishes"). The WIPO cases and panel decisions cited in this chapter are accessible at *Search WIPO Cases and WIPO Panel Decisions*, WIPO, https://www.wipo.int/amc/en/domains/search/ (last visited Mar. 23, 2025).

traffic away from the owner. In cases where a domain name registrant has acted in bad faith, a policy was needed to resolve disputes and minimize harm to the trademark owner in a more expedient and less expensive manner than traditional litigation.

B. What Is a Top-Level Domain and What Purpose Does It Serve?

The Domain Name System (DNS) organizes domain names based on hierarchies and contains multiple levels so that internet traffic can be directed efficiently. Reading from right to left, each level in a domain name is separated by a dot. For example, in the domain name www.americanbar.org, *.org* is the top-level domain (TLD), *.americanbar* is the second-level domain, and *www* (or other text to the left of the second dot) is the third-level domain. All that is typically required for a domain name is the TLD and the second-level domain. Third-level domains are usually not required, technically speaking, but are commonly used nonetheless to organize domain names. Third and subsequent levels are also not subject to the UDRP as the Policy only covers the domain name itself, which is made up of the first and second levels.

Currently, there are nearly 1,600 TLDs. For example, there are more than 250 country-code top-level domain names (ccTLDs), such as *.ar* for Argentina and *.ph* for the Philippines. There are also generic top-level domains (gTLDs), such as the familiar *.com* and *.org*. Some gTLDs, .com and .org among them, are unsponsored, which means that they are open for registration by the general public. Other gTLDs are sponsored, which means that they are intended for use by specific user communities (e.g., *.museum* and *.edu*). In recent years, there has been an expansion of the domain name landscape. Beginning in 2013, more than 1,000 "new" gTLDs[7] have been introduced—often with mixed levels of success. A few examples of new brand gTLDs that have been launched and are in use by trademark owners include store.abbott (resolves to a shopping site for an American pharmaceuticals and health care products company), news.bloomberg (resolves to the news site for the American financial software, data, and media company), and markets.saxo (resolves to the home page for the institutional division of a Danish bank). Generic words have also been used as gTLDs, such as *.site*, *.store*, *.football*, and *.online*, and these are available for anyone to register.

---

7. A full list of "new" gTLDs may be found at https://newgtlds.icann.org/en/program-status/delegated-strings (last visited Mar. 23, 2025).

Notably, the UDRP is applicable to all gTLDs, but only to those ccTLDs that have adopted the UDRP (or variations thereof) voluntarily.[8] When considering instituting an enforcement action against a ccTLD domain name, it is critical to examine the appropriate policy as there may be minor differences from the UDRP. Practitioners have been chastised for using a UDRP complaint template in a ccTLD case and inadvertently missing an important element of argument and proof.[9]

Coexisting with UDRP proceedings is the Uniform Rapid Suspension (URS) policy.[10] The ideas in this chapter are in principle applicable to the URS, which employs the same substantive elements as the UDRP and was designed to be faster and cheaper than the UDRP.[11] Nonetheless, it is the less popular of the two options among trademark owners. One reason is that the standard of proof that complainants must overcome under the URS policy is more stringent than under the UDRP. That standard is *clear and convincing evidence*, while the UDRP standard is a *preponderance of the evidence*. This higher standard underscores that the URS policy is intended only for the most straightforward cases of abusive registration. Another, more significant drawback for many trademark owners is that the URS policy, unlike the UDRP, does not allow a winning complainant to obtain transfer of a domain name, but only a limited suspension of it. After the suspension period has concluded, any party, including the same registrant, is able to register the disputed domain name.

C. Creation of ICANN and the Policy

ICANN was formed in 1998 with the mission to coordinate, at the overall level, the global internet's systems of unique identifiers, and in particular to ensure the stable and secure operation of the internet's unique identifier

---

8. *See ccTLD Database*, WIPO, https://www.wipo.int/amc/en/domains/cctld_db/index.html (last visited Mar. 23, 2025) (listing many ccTLD dispute policies).

9. *See, e.g.*, Belting Bronco Merch. Inc. v. Waqas Anwar, Case No. FA2403002088060 (FORUM Apr. 8, 2024). The FORUM cases and panel decisions cited in this chapter are available at *Search Domain Name Dispute Proceedings & Decisions*, FORUM, https://www.adrforum.com/domain-dispute/search-decisions (last visited Mar. 23, 2025).

10. *See* ICANN, Uniform Rapid Suspension System (2024) [hereinafter URS Policy], https://newgtlds.icann.org/sites/default/files/procedure-21feb24-en.pdf.

11. Note that the URS Policy is only applicable to "new" gTLDs and may not currently be used for enforcement against legacy TLDs like .com, .net, .org, and so on. *See* ICANN, Uniform Rapid Suspension System Rules Rule 3(f) (2024), https://newgtlds.icann.org/sites/default/files/rules-21feb24-en.pdf.

systems.[12] Early on, ICANN commissioned a report from WIPO to address the conflict between domain names and trademarks. Published on April 30, 1999, The Management of Internet Names and Addresses: Intellectual Property Issues: Final Report of the WIPO Internet Domain Name Process (WIPO's Final Report) recommended the establishment of a mandatory administrative procedure concerning abusive registrations that would allow for a neutral decision maker to address international disputes.[13] Each domain name registrant would be required to submit to the procedure should such a proceeding be initiated against them. The report expressed the hope that, "with experience and time, confidence will be built up in the credibility and consistency of decisions made under the procedure, so that the parties would resort less and less to litigation."[14] To promote consistency, decisions would be made publicly available. All of the guiding principles set forth in WIPO's Final Report were incorporated into the UDRP and adopted by ICANN. This includes a definition of abusive registration that later became the three elements that a complainant must prove in order to prevail. The UDRP became effective on December 1, 1999.

D. The Limited Scope of the Policy

As mentioned previously, some of the benefits of UDRP proceedings are that they provide an expeditious and cost-effective resolution to internet domain name disputes. An important key to having a streamlined proceeding is that the Policy is limited to a narrow category of cases. More specifically, the Policy was designed to prevent clear-cut cases of abusive registration and use commonly known as *cybersquatting*.[15] Thus, not every dispute involving a domain name comes within the ambit of the Policy. And the Policy does not

12. *See Bylaws for Internet Corporation for Assigned Names and Numbers*, ICANN (Jan. 9, 2025), http://www.icann.org/resources/pages/governance/bylaws-en.

13. *See* WIPO, THE MANAGEMENT OF INTERNET NAMES AND ADDRESSES: INTELLECTUAL PROPERTY ISSUES: FINAL REPORT OF THE WIPO INTERNET DOMAIN NAME PROCESS (1999), https://www.wipo.int/export/sites/www/amc/en/docs/report-final1.pdf.

14. *Id.*

15. *See, e.g.*, ICANN, SECOND STAFF REPORT ON IMPLEMENTATION DOCUMENTS FOR THE UNIFORM DISPUTE RESOLUTION POLICY (1999), http:www.icann.org/udrp/udrp-second-staff-report-24oct99.htm ("Except in cases involving 'abusive registrations' made with bad faith intent to profit commercially from others' trademarks (e.g., cybersquatting and cyberpiracy) the adopted policy leaves the resolution of disputes to the courts and calls for registrars not to disturb a registration until those courts decide."). "The adopted policy establishes a streamlined, inexpensive administrative dispute-resolution procedure intended only for the relatively narrow class of cases of 'abusive registrations.'" *Id.*

contemplate that panels will serve as tribunals of general jurisdiction over any and all disputes that are somehow related to domain names.[16] The Policy is notably also a pan-national framework with its own set of jurisprudence, so the domestic laws of individual countries typically are not applied.

The following are examples of cases in which panels concluded that a clear-cut case of cybersquatting did not exist, that the disputed issues fell outside the scope of the Policy, and/or that courts should decide the case:

- *Airpromote Ltd. v. Nick Sunnar*, Case No. D2021-1544 (WIPO July 13, 2021) (denying the complaint because the panel found that the issues raised by the parties in the UDRP proceeding were just a small part of the complex shareholder/director dispute that were inappropriate for determination under the Policy)
- *Kostel, LLC & Constantin Calugher v. Mohamed Atef*, Case No. FA2405002100428 (FORUM July 12, 2024) (denying a case where "control of the domain name is central to the other remedies sought in the court cases, as it is the only means by which the parties' customers can gain access to the parties' retail outlets. More importantly, resolving the domain name issue in this case necessarily involves sorting through the same competing factual allegations that will determine the other issues in those cases.")
- *Yellow Lark International, Inc. v. Bernacchi*, Case No. D2015-1406 (WIPO Sept. 22, 2015) (denying the complaint because the panel deemed the UDRP proceeding an inadequate forum for generating sufficient evidence (i.e., no discovery), and the panel deemed the dispute (a terminated business relationship implicating various legal, monetary, and equitable issues) one that a court should decide)
- *Fluke Corp. v. Erwin Bryson/fixmyfluke/Nelson Bryson*, Case No. FA2203001988399 (FORUM July 6, 2022) (denying the complaint because, even though respondent raised a legitimate argument of nominative fair use of complainant's trademark, the majority of the panel held that the case involved sufficient issues of fact and law such that it seemed ill-suited to a definitive resolution through the Policy and would benefit from the full range of evidentiary tools

---

16. Paragraph 5 of the Policy states:

> All other disputes between you [respondent] and any party other than us [ICANN] regarding your [respondent] domain name registration that are not brought pursuant to the mandatory administrative proceeding provisions of Paragraph 4 shall be resolved between you [respondent] and such other party through any court, arbitration or other proceeding that may be available.

Policy, *supra* note 3.

available in a courtroom such as discovery, witness testimony, and cross-examination)

- *Mriya Aid Org Inc. v. Russell Wynings/Dru Wynings*, Case No. 20450-UDRP (CIIDRC May 1, 2023) (denying the complaint because much of the substance of the dispute between the parties turned on issues of trademark ownership, validity, and licensing)
- *EvoPlay LLC v. Ziganshin*, Case No. D2015-0222 (WIPO Apr. 16, 2012) (denying the complaint, citing potential issues of complainant's standing, the validity of the underlying trademark rights, trademark abandonment issues, acquiescence of the purported licensors in respondent's conduct, and unclean hands)

As shown in these cases, complainants have the burden of demonstrating to a panel that the dispute falls within the limited scope of the Policy or else they risk a dismissal of their case or denial of the requested relief in the UDRP proceeding.

E. How the Policy Is Enforced

The Policy is addressed to domain name registrants in relevant TLDs and all ICANN-accredited registrars follow it. It is implemented in accordance with ICANN's Rules for Uniform Domain Name Dispute Resolution Policy (the Rules) and the supplemental rules of each dispute resolution provider (e.g., WIPO, FORUM, the Czech Arbitration Court (CAC), the Canadian International Internet Dispute Resolution Centre (CIIDRC), the Asian Domain Name Dispute Resolution Centre (ADNDRC)). Supplemental rules may address issues such as applicable fees and word limits. Where supplemental rules conflict with the Rules, the latter supersede. The Rules include defined terms and set out procedures and requirements for the various stages of a UDRP proceeding, including:

1. How to initiate a UDRP proceeding
2. What information must be included in the complaint and the response
3. Appointment of the panel and its powers
4. The language of the proceeding
5. The basis of the panel's decision and its timing

The Rules were last updated on July 31, 2015. The updates impact complaint-filing practices, WIPO model pleadings, registrar "lock" practices, and party settlement practices.

One of the many advantages of the Policy is that there is no need to obtain jurisdiction over the domain name or its registrant. As all ICANN-accredited registrars adhere to the Policy, it is applied through contractual consent when registrants click "I Agree" at the point of domain name registration. This makes it quite convenient and efficient to pursue domain names owned by people in far-flung parts of the world that would be expensive and difficult, if not impossible, to access through the court system.

II. Prosecuting and Defending a UDRP Case

A. What Does the Trademark Owner Need to Prove Under the Policy?

Pursuant to the UDRP, any person or company in the world can file a domain name complaint concerning a gTLD. According to paragraph 4(a) of the Policy, the administrative procedure described in the UDRP is only available for disputes concerning an alleged abusive registration of a domain name that meet all of the following criteria:

(i) The domain name registered by the domain name registrant is identical or confusingly similar to a trademark or service mark in which the complainant (the person or entity bringing the complaint) has rights.

(ii) The domain name registrant has no rights or legitimate interests in respect of the domain name in question.

(iii) The domain name has been registered and is being used in bad faith.[17]

---

17. Paragraph 4(b) of the Policy sets out the following examples of circumstances that a panel will consider to be evidence of the bad-faith registration and use of a domain name:

> (i) Circumstances indicating that the domain name was registered or acquired primarily for the purpose of selling, renting, or otherwise transferring the domain name registration to the Complainant who is the owner of the trademark or service mark or to a competitor of that Complainant, for valuable consideration in excess of the domain name registrant's out-of-pocket costs directly related to the domain name; or
>
> (ii) The domain name was registered in order to prevent the owner of the trademark or service mark from reflecting the mark in a corresponding domain name, provided that the domain name registrant has engaged in a pattern of such conduct; or
>
> (iii) The domain name was registered primarily for the purpose of disrupting the business of a competitor; or
>
> (iv) By using the domain name, the domain name registrant intentionally attempted to attract for financial gain, Internet users to the registrant's website or other on-line location, by creating a likelihood of confusion with the

To prevail on its complaint, a complainant must prove that elements (i) through (iii) are present. The general standard of proof under the Policy is *on balance*—often expressed as the *balance of probabilities* or *preponderance of the evidence* standard.[18] Under this standard, the complainant would typically need to establish that it is more likely than not that the claimed fact is true.[19] As discussed in more detail later, conclusory statements unsupported by evidence that merely repeat or paraphrase the criteria or scenarios under paragraphs 4(a)(i) through 4(a)(iii) of the Policy will be insufficient to carry a complainant's burden.[20] And considering the limits of UDRP proceedings, and the high rate of respondent defaults, complainants still need to fully present their case and be prepared for respondents who (even while representing themselves) raise sufficient facts to rebut the allegations set forth in the complaint.

When a respondent defaults, the Rules direct the panel to "proceed to a decision on the complaint."[21] The panel is charged with rendering its decision "on the basis of the statements and documents submitted."[22] In default cases, the panel draws such inferences from the respondent's failure to comply with the Rules "as it considers appropriate."[23] Even where a respondent defaults, however, a complainant must carry its burden of proof on the three aforementioned elements or risk having its complaint denied. That is, the complainant's allegations are not *deemed admitted*. Panelists regularly reject complaints that are not supported by evidence, even where there is a default.[24] This point bears emphasizing as so many practitioners, even

---

> Complainant's mark as to the source, sponsorship, affiliation, or endorsement of the registrant's website or location or of a product or service on the registrant's website or location.

These examples, however, are not exclusive. The panel may be presented with evidence of other circumstances that demonstrate that the respondent registered and used a domain name in bad faith.

Id.

18. For a discussion on the general standard of proof under the Policy, see WIPO, Overview of WIPO Panel Views on Selected UDRP Questions ¶ 4.2 (3d ed. 2017) [hereinafter WIPO Overview 3.0], https://www.wipo.int/amc/en/domains/search/overview3.0/.

19. *See id.*

20. *See id.*; *see also* KEEN, Inc. v. Mureza, Case No. D2015-1892 (WIPO Dec. 7, 2015); Koninklijke Philips Elecs. N.V. v. Relson Ltd., Case No. DWS2001-0003 (WIPO Nov. 15, 2001).

21. *Rules*, *supra* note 4, Rule 14(a); *see also id.* Rule 5(f).

22. *Id.* Rule 15(a).

23. *Id.* Rule 14(b).

24. *See, e.g.*, Hyzon Motors USA Inc. v. Undeveloped Escrow, Undeveloped Escrow, Case No. D2024-0536 (WIPO Apr. 8, 2024); Roper v. Chretien, Case No.

though highly experienced in litigation, underestimate UDRP proceedings and receive denials based on a failure to present critical evidence or assert a relevant argument.[25]

With regard to the second element of the Policy (rights or legitimate interests), the question arises whether a complainant is required to prove a negative—that the respondent lacks rights or legitimate interests in the domain name—requiring information that is often primarily within the knowledge of the respondent. The consensus or clear majority view of panelists is that the complainant must present a prima facie case that the respondent lacks rights or legitimate interests.[26] If that is done, the burden of production shifts to the respondent to come forward with appropriate allegations or evidence demonstrating rights or legitimate interests in the domain name.[27] If the respondent fails to do so, a complainant is generally deemed to have satisfied paragraph 4(a)(ii) of the Policy. If, however, the respondent comes forward with some allegations or evidence of relevant rights or legitimate interests, the panel then weighs all the evidence, with the overall burden of proof always remaining on the complainant.[28]

With regard to the third element of the Policy (bad faith), panels require both bad-faith registration *and* use. This conjunctive requirement can be critical and will be discussed more fully later in this chapter.

B. How May the Respondent Respond Under the Policy?

Under Rule 5(c), among other things, the respondent is directed to "[r]espond specifically to the statements and allegations contained in the complaint and include any and all bases for the respondent (domain name holder) to retain registration and use of the disputed domain name." If the domain name owner fails to respond substantively to a complaint, the panel may accept as true all of the allegations of the complaint.[29] Furthermore, Rule 14(b)

D2014-0843 (WIPO July 7, 2014); Coffee Bean Direct Corp. v. Pope, Case No. D2010-0162 (WIPO Apr. 5, 2010); Sapa Extrusions Inc. v. Sapa Info. Mgmt., Case No. D2009-1785 (WIPO Feb. 20, 2010); EAuto, L.L.C. v. EAuto Parts, Case No. D2000-0096 (WIPO Apr. 9, 2000).

25. *See, e.g.*, Tassel Ridge Winery, LLC v. Rome Uata, Case No. FA2401002080417 (FORUM Feb. 18, 2024) (deciding that although complainant demonstrated its trademark rights, that alone did not provide evidence of the scope and reputation of its mark to support a claim that the mark was well known and was targeted by respondent).

26. *See* WIPO Overview 3.0, *supra* note 18, ¶ 2.1 (This standard has been adopted by panelists at other dispute providers.).

27. *See id.*

28. *See id.*

29. *See, e.g.*, Talk City, Inc. v. Robertson, Case No. D2000-0009 (WIPO Feb. 29, 2000).

provides that the panel "shall draw such inferences" from the respondent's failure to comply with the Rules "as it considers appropriate." Like complainants, respondents should not rely merely on conclusory statements that parrot the Policy elements and must also support their defense with appropriate arguments and evidence.

In addressing the element embodied in paragraph 4(a)(ii), the Policy provides respondents with nonexclusive examples of how to demonstrate their rights to and legitimate interests in the disputed domain name. Specifically, paragraph 4(c) of the Policy provides as follows:

> Any of the following circumstances, in particular but without limitation, if found by the Panel to be proved based on its evaluation of all evidence presented, shall demonstrate your rights or legitimate interests to the domain name for purposes of Paragraph 4(a)(ii):
>
> (i) before any notice to you of the dispute, your use of, or demonstrable preparations to use, the domain name or a name corresponding to the domain name in connection with a bona fide offering of goods or services; or[30]
>
> (ii) you (as an individual, business, or other organization) have been commonly known by the domain name, even if you have acquired no trademark or service mark rights; or
>
> (iii) you are making a legitimate noncommercial or fair use of the domain name, without intent for commercial gain to misleadingly divert consumers or to tarnish the trademark or service mark at issue.

In addition to showing rights or legitimate interests in the disputed domain name, respondents can defeat a complaint by focusing their attack on facts and evidence that will refute one of the other two elements of the Policy, or a component of one of the elements,[31] and/or raise defenses, such

30. *See, e.g.*, Accenture Glob. Servs. Ltd. v. Binuraj, Case No. D2014-1328 (WIPO Sept. 22, 2014).

31. *See, e.g.*, Spokane Hoopfest Ass'n v. Glenn Smith, Hoopfest Basketball, Case No. D2024-0797 (WIPO May 14, 2024) (denying the complaint because complainant did not show respondent's prior use was not bona fide in view of evidence complainant adduced showing respondent's prior 15-year use of "Hoopfest" and complainant failed to show bad-faith (targeted) registration); *see also* Int'l Lighting Corp. v. Beat Brunner, Case No. D2015-2029 (WIPO Dec. 28, 2015) (denying the complaint, finding both that respondent's evidence clearly established it had carried out a genuine and bona fide business long before it became aware of complainant and it was known by the name that in substance is identical to the domain name, and noting complainant failed to provide any evidence to support its use of the mark at issue); CSS Polymers Inc. v. Beirne, Case No. D2009-1179 (WIPO June 26, 2009) (denying the complaint, noting that respondent made a record of documents such as invoices, purchase orders, sales

as protected free speech, acquiescence, commonly used marks, generic or descriptive marks, legitimate rights as a surname, or legitimate rights from prior use.[32]

Where a complainant has delayed in taking action against a respondent after the time the respondent registered an infringing domain name, respondents have raised the defense of laches or argued for something similar to it. The consensus view of panels is that the doctrine or defense of laches does not generally apply in UDRP proceedings. In this regard, panels have noted that the remedies under the Policy are injunctive rather than compensatory in nature, and that a principal concern is to avoid ongoing or future confusion as to the source of communications, goods, or services.[33] Thus, if a complainant has otherwise carried its burden of proof on the three elements under the Policy, delay in bringing a complaint does not, in itself, prevent a complainant from filing or otherwise succeeding under the Policy.[34] Panels have noted, however, that a delay in bringing a complaint under the Policy may make it more difficult for a complainant to establish its case on the merits, particularly in relation to the second and third elements of the Policy (i.e., rights and legitimate interests and bad faith).[35]

Another possible defense is "reverse domain name hijacking" (RDNH), which may also be found by a panel on its own accord even in default cases.[36]

---

orders, and picking sheets showing that complainant was doing business under a name that was different from the trade name in which complainant was claiming rights).

32. *See, e.g.*, Digicel Caribbean Ltd. v. Domains by Proxy, LLC, Case No. D2015-1854 (WIPO Nov. 26, 2015) (finding that First Amendment rights by unhappy customer supported rights/legitimate interests); Vanguard Trademark Holdings USA LLC v. Adm'r, Domain/Vertical Axis, Inc., Case No. FA1104001383694 (FORUM May 31, 2011); Maharashtra Tourism Dev. Corp. Ltd. v. Bestway Tours & Safaris PVT Ltd., Case No. D2015-0595 (WIPO June 24, 2015); Lost Dogs Home Ltd. v. Bailey, Case No. D2013-0408 (WIPO Apr. 25, 2013); Boehringer Ingelheim Pharma GmbH & Co.KG v. Ilgam Nurtdinov, Case No. UDRP-105197 (CAC Feb. 2, 2015); Shabby Chic Brands, LLC v. Belle Escape, Case No. D2012-0828 (WIPO June 5, 2012); Shakespeare Co. LLC v. Pflueger, Case No. D2010-1126 (WIPO Aug. 19, 2010); Fox News Network, LLC v. Domains by Proxy, Inc., Case No. D2007-1782 (WIPO Feb. 26, 2008); NCsoft Corp. v. Johnson, Case No. D2007-0342 (WIPO June 8, 2007).

33. *See* WIPO Overview 3.0, *supra* note 18, ¶ 4.17 and the cases cited therein.

34. *See id.*

35. *See id.*; *see also* Coachella Music Festival, LLC v. Tim Householder, Case No. FA2402002086077 (FORUM Mar. 28, 2024); Restored Church of God v. Alexa Props., LLC, Case No. D2013-0320 (WIPO Mar. 21, 2013); Harvard Lampoon, Inc. v. Reflex Publ'g Inc., Case No. D2011-0716 (WIPO July 26, 2011); Sapa Extrusions Inc. v. Sapa Info. Mgmt., Case No. D2009-1785 (WIPO Feb. 20, 2010).

36. *See, e.g.*, Aromatech, Ltd. v. Carlos Paredes, Case No. D2024-0911 (WIPO May 3, 2024) (denying the complaint after finding sua sponte that complainant

Rule 1 defines RDNH as "using the Policy in bad faith to attempt to deprive a registered domain name holder of a domain name." Generally, where a respondent can prove that a complainant brought its complaint under the Policy knowing the respondent had superior rights or that the complaint was objectively unsupportable, an RDNH defense may be asserted.[37] A finding of RDNH depends heavily on the factual circumstances surrounding each case.

Due to the increased use of the Policy and regardless of the underlying reasons or motivations of complainants (e.g., failure to investigate, a flawed complaint, bullying respondent), respondents are raising RDNH as a defense more often and panels have been finding in their favor. However, RDNH has been described as a "toothless tiger"[38] without any real consequence to the complainant (e.g., penalties, using a past finding of RDNH against a complainant for future similar RDNH conduct). That said, it would be imprudent to conclude that a determination of RDNH does not have a practical effect. Rule 15(e) provides that, if,

> after considering the submissions the Panel finds that the complaint was brought in bad faith, for example in an attempt at Reverse Domain Name Hijacking or was brought primarily to harass the domain name holder, the Panel shall declare in its decision that the complaint was brought in bad faith and constitutes an abuse of the administrative proceeding.

Insofar as all UDRP decisions are made public, such a finding can have an adverse impact on the reputation of a trademark owner and its counsel.

C. Remedies Under the Policy

Under paragraph 4(i) of the Policy, the remedies available to a successful complainant are limited to cancellation of the domain name registration

---

committed RDNH, noting "the Complainant and its legal representatives ought to have recognised it would not be possible to establish bad faith registration" in view of facts of record in complainant's possession); *see also* Music Together, LLC v. Justine Chadly, In Harmony Music, Case No. D2023-5355 (WIPO Mar. 28, 2024); New Forests Asset Mgmt. Pty Ltd. v. Schorsch, Case No. D2015-1415 (WIPO Nov. 13, 2015); E-Renter USA Ltd. v. Domain Hostmaster, No. D2015-0784 (WIPO July 10, 2015); Webpass, Inc. v. Breitenbach, No. D2010-1796 (WIPO Dec. 2, 2010); Collective Media, Inc. v. CKV, No. D2008-0641 (WIPO July 31, 2008).

37. *See, e.g.*, SK Lubricants Ams. v. Sabatini, Case No. D2015-1566 (WIPO Nov. 23, 2015); Vantage Sols., LLC v. zhu yan, Case No. FA2312002076392 (FORUM Jan. 23, 2024).

38. Alistair Payne, *Reverse Domain Name Hijacking: Toothless Tiger or Flag of Disingenuity?*, WTR Daily (Sept. 29, 2011), https://www.lexology.com/library/detail.aspx?g=7060c75c-914d-4a09-88bd-cefe49f1a397.

or, more commonly, transferring it to the complainant. These remedies are directly enforced through the registrar—without having to go to court. A panel cannot award equitable or monetary relief, such as injunctions, costs, or damages. If the complainant cannot meet the requirements of the Policy, the panel dismisses the case. The approximate rate of transfer overall under the UDRP is 91 percent, with an 8 percent complaint denial rate, and a 1 percent domain name cancellation rate.[39]

The limited remedies are certainly a consideration in deciding whether to bring an action against a respondent under the Policy. Most complainants request transfer rather than cancellation of a domain name. Although a complainant may be satisfied with simply having the domain name canceled, a decision canceling the domain name will put it back on the market, available for purchase possibly by new infringers.

D. Availability of Court Proceedings

When someone registers a domain name in a gTLD and in a number of ccTLDs, the Policy[40] is incorporated by reference into the registration agreement between the domain name registrant and the registrar. The incorporation of the Policy subjects the registrant to the administrative UDRP proceedings if a dispute arises between the registrant and a trademark owner over the registration and use of the registered domain name.[41] This contractual obligation eliminates the need to obtain jurisdiction over the domain name or its registrant and allows the Policy to seamlessly function on a global basis. However, while having the option of UDRP proceedings, trademark owners who prefer a court proceeding are not precluded from filing a lawsuit (e.g., trademark infringement and related claims) in a court of competent jurisdiction. This latter approach may be preferred where relief, beyond transfer or cancellation of the disputed domain name, is desired (e.g., monetary damages, an injunction, or other equitable relief).

39. Statistics are based on data obtained at UDRP Tools, https://udrp.tools (last visited Mar. 23, 2025).

40. The Policy is applicable to second-level domain name registrations in the following gTLDs: .aero, .asia, .biz, .cat, .com, .coop, .info, .jobs, .mobi, .museum, .name, .net, .org, .pro, .tel, and .travel. The Policy also applies to all "new" gTLDs. *See also supra* note 8 for further information on ccTLDs that have adopted the Policy or variations thereon.

41. Paragraph 4(a) of the Policy advises all registrants for domain names that, in accordance with the terms of their registration agreement, they will be "required to submit to a mandatory administrative proceeding in the event that a third party (a 'complainant') asserts to the applicable Provider, in compliance with the Rules of Procedure, that" the three elements of the Policy are present. *Policy*, *supra* note 3.

Similarly, under paragraph 4(k) of the Policy, the UDRP proceeding requirement does not prevent the domain name registrant (respondent) or the third party (trademark owner/complainant) from commencing an action in a court of competent jurisdiction for independent resolution. This is typically the jurisdiction where either the respondent or domain name registrar is located. Thus, either party can file a lawsuit after the administrative proceeding is concluded if it is unsatisfied with the outcome. An unsuccessful respondent can block implementation of a transfer or cancellation by filing a lawsuit within ten business days after a panel decision. Likewise, an unsuccessful complainant may commence a lawsuit against the respondent (e.g., in the United States under the Anticybersquatting Consumer Protection Act, 15 U.S.C. § 1125(d)), seeking a court order to transfer the domain name to them and monetary damages for trademark infringement.

Under the Policy, court and UDRP proceedings may occur at the same time.[42] Thus, either party can initiate court litigation during a UDRP proceeding. Rule 18(a) gives the panel discretion to suspend, terminate, or continue a UDRP proceeding where the disputed domain name is the subject of other pending legal proceedings. However, if the legal proceeding is only tangentially related to the domain name (e.g., a distinct contractual or monetary dispute between the parties), the panel will typically continue the UDRP proceeding.[43]

If a panel decides that the domain name registration should be canceled or transferred, the domain name registrar ordinarily will implement that order after ten business days have passed.[44] The respondent may stay that action by commencing a lawsuit against the complainant in the "Mutual Jurisdiction" previously specified by the complainant in its complaint.[45] The panel decision will be implemented unless, during that ten-day period, the domain name registrar has received from the respondent official documentation (e.g., a copy of a complaint, file-stamped by the clerk of the court) that it has commenced a lawsuit against the complainant in a jurisdiction to which the complainant had submitted in accordance with the Rules.[46] If the

42. See *Rules*, *supra* note 4, Rule 18(a), which contemplates the concurrence of UDRP and court proceedings: "In the event of any legal proceedings initiated prior to or during an administrative proceeding in respect of a domain-name dispute that is the subject of the complaint, the Panel shall have the discretion to decide whether to suspend or terminate the administrative proceeding, or to proceed to a decision."

43. *See, e.g.*, Kibar Holding A.Ş. & Kibar Diş Ticaret A.Ş. v. Dr. Mehmet Kahveci, Case No. D2012-1417 (WIPO Sept. 6, 2012).

44. *See Policy*, *supra* note 3, ¶ 4(k).

45. *See id.*

46. *See id.* As part of their complaint, complainants must agree to submit to the jurisdiction of the courts in a "Mutual Jurisdiction" with regard to a challenge to the

domain name registrar receives documentation that the respondent has commenced a lawsuit within the ten-day period, it will not implement the panel's decision and it will not take any further action until receiving (1) evidence satisfactory of a resolution between the parties; (2) evidence satisfactory that the lawsuit has been dismissed or withdrawn; or (3) a copy of an order from such court dismissing the lawsuit or ordering that the respondent does not have the right to continue to use the disputed domain name.[47] Apart from the option for external judicial consideration described here, there is currently no appeal mechanism within the Policy, though one has been proposed for consideration.[48]

Courts are not bound by UDRP panel determinations.[49] Where a domain name subject to a UDRP panel decision is involved in a court proceeding, the court case is generally acknowledged to represent a de novo hearing of the case under its applicable national law.

III. Mechanics of Bringing and Defending a UDRP Proceeding

A. Overview of Five Basic Stages of a UDRP Proceeding

A UDRP proceeding can be broken down into five basic stages. These are:

1. The filing of a complaint with an ICANN-accredited dispute resolution provider of the complainant's choice
2. The filing of a response by the person or entity against whom the complaint was made
3. The appointment by the chosen dispute resolution provider of an administrative panel comprising one or three panelists who will decide the dispute
4. The issuance of the administrative panel's decision and notification of the decision to all relevant parties
5. If the complainant prevails, the implementation of the administrative panel's decision by the domain name registrar to transfer the domain name registration from the respondent to the complainant or, in very rare cases, cancel the registration

---

proceeding canceling or transferring the domain name at issue. *See Rules*, *supra* note 4, Rule 1 (defining "Mutual Jurisdiction"); *see also id.* Rule 3(b)(xii).

47. *See Policy*, *supra* note 3, ¶ 4(k).

48. *See* UDRP.Group, https://udrp.group (last visited Mar. 23, 2025), for a range of UDRP proposals that are drafted in the hopes of achieving a high level of consensus amongst participants in the UDRP ecosystem.

49. *See* WIPO OVERVIEW 3.0, *supra* note 18, ¶ 4.14 and the cases cited therein.

Under the Rules, and barring extenuating circumstances, a UDRP proceeding filed with WIPO is normally concluded within 60 days of when the dispute resolution provider receives the complaint.

B. Model Complaints

The information a complainant needs to include in a UDRP complaint is set out in Rule 3. While there is specific information that must be included in every complaint, there is no standard form of complaint prescribed by ICANN. As mentioned earlier, some dispute resolution providers have prepared model complaints with filing guidelines that a party may use if it chooses.[50] Using the model complaint does not preclude the possibility that the complaint as filed may be found deficient, nor does it guarantee a complainant's success on the merits. Under the supplemental rules of most providers, a complaint must be submitted in electronic form. A complainant may file by downloading and completing the model complaint as an electronic document to submit via email to the provider or by completing and submitting the electronic form of the model complaint directly online at the provider's website.

After the complaint is filed, it undergoes a compliance review by the provider to ensure that it meets all the formal requirements set out in the Policy, the Rules, and supplemental rules. Examples of items that the provider will check include whether the complaint includes the coversheet used by some providers and all of the items listed in Rule 3(b), whether it complies with the maximum word limit (excluding annexes), and whether the complainant has paid the correct filing fees.

C. Model Responses

The required information for a response is set out in Rule 5. As with the complaint, some dispute providers also have prepared an optional model response to assist respondents in meeting the requirements of the Policy and the Rules.[51] The proceeding officially commences once the dispute

50. *See UDRP Model Complaint and Filing Guidelines*, WIPO, http://www.wipo.int/amc/en/domains/complainant/ (last visited Mar. 23, 2025); *Uniform Domain Name Dispute Resolution Policy (UDRP)*, FORUM [hereinafter FORUM UDRP], https://www.adrforum.com/domain-dispute/udrp (last visited Mar. 23, 2025); *File a UDRP Complaint*, CIIDRC [hereinafter CIIDRC UDRP], https://ciidrc.org/how-it-works/file-a-udrp-complaint/ (last visited Mar. 23, 2025).

51. *See UDRP Model Response and Filing Guidelines*, WIPO, http://www.wipo.int/amc/en/domains/respondent/ (last visited Mar. 23, 2025); FORUM UDRP, *supra* note 50; CIIDRC UDRP, *supra* note 50.

resolution provider has formally notified the respondent in accordance with Rule 2(a) and Rule 4. According to Rule 5(a), a respondent must submit its response within 20 days of the commencement of the UDRP proceeding.

The updated Rules, in effect as of July 31, 2015, provide that a respondent may obtain at no cost, upon request, a four-day extension of time to submit a response.[52] A respondent that does not file its response within the deadline will be considered in default. As discussed earlier, a default by the respondent does not automatically result in a decision in the complainant's favor. The dispute resolution provider will appoint a panel that will decide the dispute based on the information and evidence provided by the complainant and applicable law, and the panel may draw such inferences as it deems appropriate from the respondent's default. If a response is filed within a few days after the deadline, the panel will decide, in its discretion, whether to admit and consider the late-filed response (it often does, especially if the respondent appears *pro se*).

D. Supplemental Pleadings

A panel may, in its sole discretion, request additional statements or documents from the parties.[53] In addition, panels have the discretion to decide whether to accept an unsolicited supplemental filing from either party. The party submitting such a filing would typically need to demonstrate its relevance and why it was unable to provide that information in its complaint or response. The consensus view of panels is that such an unsolicited filing may be accepted under "exceptional" circumstances. Bearing in mind the need for procedural efficiency and the obligation to treat each party fairly, panels are unlikely to find "exceptional" circumstances unless new facts or evidence have arisen that were not available or that the party submitting the supplemental filing could not reasonably have known at the time of its initial filing.[54] Panels are concerned that "the admission of a further submission from one party may lead the other party to submit a further document in reply, which may lead to a further submission by the first party, and so on, thereby compromising the procedural economy sought to be established by the Policy and the Rules."[55] Panels that do request an additional filing or accept an unsolicited filing from either party commonly allow the other party the opportunity to file a reply to such supplemental filing. The panel

---

52. *See Rules*, *supra* note 4, Rule 5(b).

53. *See id.* Rule 12.

54. *See, e.g.*, New Forests Asset Mgmt. Pty Ltd. v. Schorsch, Case No. D2015-1415 (WIPO Nov. 13, 2015).

55. E.W. Scripps Co. v. Sinologic Indus., Case No. D2003-0447 (WIPO July 1, 2003).

would usually address the admissibility of supplemental filings in an order or in its final decision.

E. Procedural Considerations

1. Language of Proceeding

Pursuant to Rule 11, the language of the proceeding will normally be the language of the registrar's relevant domain name registration agreement unless the parties to the proceeding mutually agree otherwise. Under Rules 10(b) and (c) the panel does, however, have the discretion to designate a different language, taking into consideration the circumstances of the proceeding (e.g., the nationality of the parties, the language of past correspondence between the parties, the language of the content for the corresponding website, the degree of burden on the parties in translating documents). If the complainant unilaterally requests that the language of the proceeding be other than the language of the registration agreement, the dispute provider may make a preliminary determination to accept the complaint as it was filed, accept a response in either language, and/or appoint a panel familiar with both languages if possible.[56] The final decision regarding the language of the proceeding is then left to the panel.[57] Once appointed, the panel also has the authority to order parties to translate documents that are not in the language of the proceeding.[58]

2. Consolidation

Panels are empowered under Rule 10(e) to consolidate domain name disputes, and they have determined that consolidation of proceedings involving multiple complainants and multiple respondents is permitted under the

56. *See, e.g.*, Pentair, Inc. v. Xu, Case No. D2015-2330 (WIPO Feb. 11, 2015); *see also* Universal City Studios LLC v. Gao Hong Mei, Case No. FA2205001998325 (FORUM July 7, 2022) (deciding although the registration agreement was written in Chinese, thereby making the language of the proceedings in Chinese, the proceeding would be conducted in English because the language requirement was satisfied through the Chinese language complaint and commencement notification).

57. *See* Watercraft Superstore, Inc. v. Mei Zhen Huang, Case No. FA24 06002102351 (FORUM July 11, 2024) (determining that although the registration agreement was in Chinese (as was the notice and commencement notification), thereby making the language of the proceedings in Chinese, the proceedings would be conducted in English, noting that the disputed domain name resolved to an English language website and wanting to ensure efficiency and fairness for both parties).

58. *See Rules*, *supra* note 4, Rule 11(b).

Policy and the Rules.[59] The consensus of panels is that consolidation by multiple complainants is permitted when "(i) the complainants either have a specific common grievance against the respondent, or the respondent has engaged in common conduct that has affected the complainants' individual rights in a similar fashion; and (ii) it would be equitable and procedurally efficient to permit the consolidation."[60] In the case of a complaint brought against more than one respondent, the consensus of WIPO panels is that consolidation is appropriate where "(i) the domain names or the websites to which they resolve are subject to common control, and (ii) the consolidation would be fair and equitable to all parties."[61] The burden to demonstrate that consolidation is appropriate falls on the filing party or parties. Consolidation of proceedings typically requires a request for consolidation that establishes that the relevant criteria have been met.

3. Refiling

A refiled case is where a complainant submits a second complaint involving the same domain name(s) and the same respondent(s) as an earlier-filed complaint that was denied. The Policy, the Rules, and the dispute provider's supplemental rules do not address the admissibility of a refiled complaint, nor do they provide for an administrative rehearing or appeal before a new panel. The Rules do state that a panel may consider "any rules and principles of law that it deems applicable."[62] Accordingly, panels have refused to rule in a complainant's favor in a refiled case on certain widely accepted legal principles found in both common-law and civil-law jurisdictions, such as res judicata (preclusion of identical claims), judicial efficiency, and the fundamental fairness of not burdening a respondent with repetitious complaints.[63] The consensus of panels is to accept a refiled case only on the basis of newly available evidence that did not exist or was reasonably unavailable to the complainant during the original case showing that relevant new actions have occurred since the original decision, breach of natural justice or due process, or other serious misconduct (e.g., perjured evidence) in the original case.[64]

---

59. *See, e.g.*, Universal Music Grp. N.V. & Universal City Studios LLC v. JT U Animation/U Animation, Case No. FA2402002085375 (FORUM May 20, 2024); Speedo Holdings B.V. v. Smitt, Case No. D2010-0281 (WIPO May 18, 2010).

60. *See* WIPO OVERVIEW 3.0, *supra* note 18, ¶ 4.11.1 and the cases cited therein.

61. Toronto-Dominion Bank v. Lopz232 morriss/LaQuinta Inn/Rashid Mustafa/ David Kallusky, Case No. FA2310002066467 (FORUM Nov. 14, 2023).

62. *See Rules*, *supra* note 4, Rule 15(a).

63. *See, e.g.*, Sensis Pty Ltd. v. Yellow Page Mktg. B.V., Case No. D2011-0057 (WIPO Mar. 15, 2011).

64. *See* WIPO OVERVIEW 3.0, *supra* note 18, ¶ 4.18.

A complainant must clearly state that it is refiling an earlier-filed UDRP complaint, as it is not within the practice of dispute providers to investigate this during their preliminary review of filed cases. Failure to make such a disclosure may constitute a material omission for the purpose of a panel determination of RDNH.

A refiled complaint must include one or more of the aforementioned grounds that justify a refiling. The dispute resolution provider, or a panel, will then assess whether the refiled complaint has pled the grounds that may justify its consideration.[65] The only exception is where the prior case was denied "without prejudice," thus indicating a panel's consent to the refiling of a complaint if certain deficiencies are corrected.[66]

4. Settlement During Proceeding

WIPO panels have a long-standing practice of permitting parties to suspend proceedings when mutually requested to enable settlement prior to panel appointment.[67] The July 31, 2015, update to the Rules and subsequent updates to the supplemental rules of some providers codify this practice.[68] The Rules now provide a sequence of steps that parties must follow to suspend a proceeding to pursue a possible settlement.[69] First, the parties must notify the dispute resolution provider of their mutual interest in suspending the proceeding to discuss settlement. The provider then notifies the registrar that the proceeding is suspended, and the disputed domain name remains locked during the

65. *See, e.g.*, Art4Now, Inc. v. Gerald Waggoner/The Waggoner Law Firm, Case No. FA2312002074746 (FORUM Mar. 15, 2011).

66. *See, e.g.*, Pioneer Nat. Res. USA, Inc. v. FU, LEI, Case No. FA2303002034572 (FORUM Apr. 12, 2023).

67. *See* WIPO Overview 3.0, *supra* note 18, ¶ 4.9 and the cases cited therein.

68. *See Rules*, *supra* note 4, Rule 17; *see also World Intellectual Property Organization Supplemental Rules for Uniform Domain Name Dispute Resolution Policy*, WIPO (July 31, 2015) [hereinafter *WIPO Supplemental Rules*], http://www.wipo.int/amc/en/domains/supplemental/eudrp/newrules.html (Rule 13); FORUM, The FORUM's Supplemental Rules to ICANN'S Uniform Domain Name Dispute Resolution Policy Rule 6(b) (2019), https://view.officeapps.live.com/op/view.aspx?src=https%3A%2F%2Fwww.adrforum.com%2Fassets%2Fresources%2Fdomain%2Fudrp%2FFinalUDRPSupplementalRules_Eff2019.docx&wd; CAC, Supplemental ADR Rules of the Arbitration Court Attached to the Czech Chamber of Commerce and the Agricultural Chamber of the Czech Republic Rule 11, https://eu.adr.eu/data/2024-gdpr-rules/en-2022-adr-supplemental-rules-cac.pdf (last visited Mar. 23, 2025); *CIIDRC Supplemental Rules*, CIIDRC, https://ciidrc.org/domain-name-disputes/ciidrc-supplemental-rules/ (last visited Mar. 23, 2025) (Rule 11).

69. *See Rules*, *supra* note 4, Rule 17(a)(i)–(vii).

suspension. If the parties agree to settle, they must complete a settlement form, sometimes provided by the dispute provider, that summarizes the essential terms of the agreement.[70] While a standard settlement form is not intended to be a settlement agreement itself, it is a confidential document, and the dispute resolution provider may not disclose the completed standard settlement form to any third party. In accordance with Rule 17(a)(vii), settlement is without prejudice unless otherwise stipulated to by the parties in the standard settlement form. If settlement is reached, the provider instructs the registrar to unlock the domain name to implement the agreement.

IV. The Key Elements of a Successful UDRP Proceeding—Preparation and Advocacy

A. Resources

There is a cornucopia of easily accessible resources to help advocates with both the substantive and procedural aspects of their cases. Some of those resources have already been mentioned but will be discussed briefly here for completeness.

1. The Policy

Although the Policy is formally a contractual relationship between the registrar (or other registration authority in the case of a ccTLD) and its customer (the domain name holder/registrant/respondent), it sets out the nuts and bolts of the UDRP administrative proceeding for both the trademark owner (complainant) and the respondent. Indeed, the analytical framework of panel decisions is based on the Policy, and panels generously cite to the Policy in their decisions—most often paragraph 4, as this sets out the required elements of proof for a successful claim. Thus, it should be the starting point for advocates who are new to UDRP proceedings, as well as a mainstay for veteran advocates.

2. The (Governing) Rules

The Rules complement the Policy and help effectuate it. They set forth the steps of a UDRP proceeding and provide guidance about what the parties need to do throughout. Each of the dispute resolution providers have

70. WIPO's standard settlement form is set forth in Annex F to the WIPO Supplemental Rules. Other dispute providers maintain their own settlement forms. *See, e.g.*, FORUM UDRP, *supra* note 50.

promulgated their own rules—supplemental rules—to administer the proceedings. As of July 31, 2015, updated UDRP rules went into effect and both parties and advocates are advised to consult the most current supplemental rules of their chosen dispute provider as these are updated from time to time. As with the Policy, advocates should have a thorough understanding of the Rules (and the supplemental rules).

3. WIPO Overview 3.0

Decision-making authority on substantive and procedural issues under the Policy and the Rules lies exclusively with the appointed panels. The Third Edition of the Overview of WIPO Panel Views on Selected UDRP Questions (WIPO Overview 3.0 or the Overview) is a rich summary of the consensus or clear majority views of panels from thousands of WIPO cases on about 50 commonly occurring substantive and procedural questions in UDRP proceedings.[71] It also provides citations to exemplary cases on each issue addressed. The original and current Overview were created, updated, and expanded to maximize the consistency of the UDRP system. However, insofar as UDRP decisions cover a multitude of facts and arguments, and the panelists and parties represent a broad array of jurisdictions, there cannot be a consensus on all issues. Further, the Overview is cited in decisions from other dispute providers as panels often seek to create consensus on frequently encountered issues across all dispute providers.

Panelists are not bound by the Overview or prior panel decisions. If, however, counsel cite to prior cases where the holdings support their argument and where the facts and circumstances are similar with their case, those cases may provide a foundation for, and add to the persuasiveness of, their arguments.

4. UDRP Case Databases

While there is no official centralized database of UDRP decisions, each dispute provider maintains searchable copies of their own decisions and there are some pan-provider searchable databases that are usable by participants in these proceedings.[72]

71. *See* WIPO Overview 3.0, *supra* note 18.

72. See, e.g., free searchable databases hosted by WIPO, FORUM, CAC, CIIDRC, and ADNDRC at *Search WIPO Cases and WIPO Panel Decisions*, *supra* note 6; *Search Domain Name Dispute Proceedings & Decisions*, *supra* note 9; *Decisions*, Arb. Ctr. for Internet Disps., https://udrp.adr.eu/decisions/list (last visited Mar. 23, 2025); *Domain Name Disputes—CIIDRC Decisions*, CIIDRC, https://ciidrc.org/domain-name-disputes/ciidrc-decisions/ (last visited Mar. 23, 2025); and *UDRP*

5. Dispute Provider Legal Indices of UDRP Cases[73]

Some dispute resolution providers offer an index on their individual websites for performing research on substantive and procedural issues. The index typically covers all UDRP decisions from that provider and is continually updated with newly decided cases. Decisions may be searched (1) based upon "domain name" category (e.g., associations and institutions, geographical identifiers, individuals, industry and commerce) or (2) by frequently occurring issues (e.g., confusing similarity, bad-faith "phishing," multiple complainants).

6. Policy Guides[74]

Policy guides are akin to *frequently asked questions* and are helpful resources for beginners and veterans alike, addressing a variety of practical procedural questions, including guidance on preparing and filing a complaint and response; the roles of the panel, the registrar, and the dispute provider; and fees. These guides are also a good resource for clients, answering important questions about the proceedings in a clear and concise manner.

7. Pleading Templates[75]

Some dispute providers' websites offer detailed templates and guidance for preparing and filing the complaint and response. That said, even with these resources, parties too often fall short in the quality of their submissions. As discussed more fully later in this chapter, the substance that goes into the pleadings is critical to a party's success.

Decisions—Uniform Domain Name Dispute Resolution Policy, ADNDRC, https://www.adndrc.org/decisions/udrp (last visited Mar. 23, 2025), respectively, and UDRP Tools, *supra* note 39, a commercially available compendium of decisions from multiple dispute resolution providers.

73. *See, e.g., Legal Index of WIPO UDRP Panel Decisions*, WIPO, http://www.wipo.int/amc/en/domains/search/legalindex.jsp (last visited Mar. 23, 2025); *Search Domain Name Dispute Proceedings & Decisions*, *supra* note 9.

74. *See WIPO Guide to the Uniform Domain Name Dispute Resolution Policy (UDRP)*, WIPO [hereinafter *WIPO Guide to UDRP*], http://www.wipo.int/amc/en/domains/guide/index.html (last visited Mar. 23, 2025); *UDRP FAQ*, FORUM, https://www.adrforum.com/domain-dispute/udrp#faq (last visited Mar. 23, 2025); *Frequently Asked Questions*, CIIDRC, https://ciidrc.org/frequently-asked-questions/ (last visited Mar. 23, 2025).

75. *See WIPO Guide to UDRP*, *supra* note 74, ¶ C; *see also id.* ¶ D.

8. Whois Records

Every domain name has an associated ownership file which is known as the "Whois" record (i.e., who is the owner). In years past, these records were a useful tool in identifying the owner of a domain name, listing the personal and organization names, postal addresses, and phone and email information. However, in 2018, the European Union (EU) implemented the General Data Protection Regulation (GDPR), which prohibited the unauthorized disclosure of identifying information for EU individuals (though business entities are not covered by this regulation). Unfortunately, most domain name registrars took this opportunity to hide most of the information contained in Whois records for *all* domain names, even those owned by non-EU individuals or business entities. At present, most Whois records simply say "Redacted for Privacy" and only provide very limited information about the domain name such as the creation date, the renewal date, the name of the registrar, and the listed IP server addresses. This has created an impediment to UDRP participants in a number of ways. For example, pre-complaint contact is nearly impossible, thus reducing the ability to negotiate a settlement of the dispute before incurring the cost of a UDRP proceeding. Also, complainants are often unable to identify other domain names that are owned by the same respondent, thus limiting their ability to include multiple domain names in a single complaint, as well as the possibility of showing a pattern of bad-faith conduct under paragraph 4(b)(ii) of the Policy.[76] Efforts are currently underway at ICANN to address this problem, but it is unclear when or how it will be addressed.

B. Marshaling Evidence: Building a Case Foundation

Complainants and respondents alike have been unsuccessful in UDRP proceedings when key evidence is nonexistent or has proved insufficient to support asserted claims and defenses. As mentioned earlier, although UDRP proceedings are streamlined and inexpensive, they should not be underestimated. Marshaling probative evidence to support one's written assertions is a critical step that deserves sufficient time and resources.

In some cases, the lack of evidence may not be remedied if, for example, the evidence no longer exists or it never existed. Necessary evidence can be unwittingly lost when a business periodically purges documents and electronically stored information, when it moves to a new location and does not

76. *See, e.g.*, Moncler S.p.A. v. Yao Tom, Lee Fei, Geryi Wang, Case No. D2015-2244 (WIPO Jan. 18, 2018) ("[T]he Panel f[ound] that, by its registration of the 50 Disputed Domain Names, Respondent has engaged in a 'pattern' of conduct that also constitutes bad faith, pursuant to paragraph 4(b)(ii) of the Policy.").

move all existing hard-copy documents and examples of trademark usage (e.g., packaging, signage) or does not want to pay to have such documents and information stored, or when a business does not appreciate the importance of maintaining certain documents (e.g., to prove common-law rights, to prove legitimate interests in a domain name). In other cases, documents simply may never have existed to support representations and arguments that advocates may advance.

What may be the case, more often than not, is that the lack or insufficiency of evidence could have been remedied with additional effort on the part of both counsel and client. Simply because the proceedings are expedited and relatively informal should not signal to clients or counsel that it is satisfactory to participate in UDRP proceedings without expending sufficient efforts and resources (e.g., to locate evidence, identify relevant cases, articulate arguments). In fact, as discussed earlier, panels do not hesitate to deny complaints (even those that are unchallenged) where complainants have given short shrift to what is required to prove their case. The necessary effort is well worth the time and money considering that (1) UDRP proceedings are decided on the briefs, so they should reflect all the available evidence to support each element; (2) decisions are often the final determination for the parties—de novo court proceedings are not common; (3) a panel decision can have a significant impact on the business of both parties (particularly where the respondent has legitimate rights or interests in the domain name); (4) the submissions and accompanying exhibits may themselves provide leverage for a negotiated settlement; and (5) an adverse decision based on poorly crafted pleadings can have a negative impact on the reputation of the parties and their advocates.

Resourcefulness and thoroughness in collecting documents and information can pay off.

Case in point: The panel denied the complaint because the complainant failed to prove that the respondent lacked a right or legitimate interest in the domain name, and that respondent registered the domain name in bad faith. To successfully defeat the complaint, the respondent marshaled information from the Whois database, a bank statement, email messages, a control panel screenshot, letters, IP address history information, an archive.org screenshot, an invoice, a check that had been paid, a sworn declaration from a key player, and a business plan.[77]

77. *See* Nintendo of Am. Inc. v. Domain Priv. Grp., Case No. D2013-0322 (WIPO June 19, 2013).

Case in point: The panel denied the complaint because the complainant failed to prove rights in the mark, noting that the evidence of record—undated business cards; a promotional letter, promotional materials, and data sheets all dated after the domain name was registered; a late-dated invoice providing evidence of use for a limited time period; and two advertisements (one undated and the other having a late date also showing use for a limited period)—did not support the time period of use represented by the chief executive officer (CEO) in his sworn statement.[78]

It may be challenging for a complainant to meet the requisite burden of proof, particularly where a respondent files a response and has a plausible good-faith explanation for registering the domain name at issue.

Case in point: The respondent had registered the domain name familypolicyfoundation.org. The complainant claimed trademark rights in the phrase FAMILY POLICY FOUNDATION, citing a U.S. registration on the U.S. patent and Trademark Office's Supplemental Register with a disclaimer of "foundation" as a generic term. The panel denied the case, finding that the complainant had failed to prove its ownership of trademark rights under paragraph 4(a)(i) of the Policy. Specifically, it stated that "although Complainant has adduced evidence, much of it involves internal or outward communications made by Complainant, and there is very little evidence of any degree of third-party or public recognition concerning Complainant's mark (such as proof of consumer recognition, or unsolicited media coverage or third-party publications) as a distinctive identifier of Complainant's services." Worse yet, "some of the evidence introduced by Complainant would appear to undermine its arguments that its mark has become a distinctive identifier or that Complainant has otherwise acquired common-law rights. In particular, this evidence indicates that Complainant has been inconsistent in the use of its mark . . . ."[79]

---

78. *See* CSS Polymers Inc. v. Beirne, Case No. D2009-1179 (WIPO Sept. 11, 2009).

79. *See* Fam. Pol'y Found. v. John Skinner, Case No. D2024-0098 (WIPO Mar. 27, 2024). In a similar fact pattern, the first complaint to be denied under the URS pertained to the domain name branson.guru. The complainant, Virgin Enterprises Limited, claimed that there was no reason for the respondent to have registered the domain name other than to cause confusion with the founder of Virgin, Richard Branson. The domain name was used in connection with a monetized page of pay-per-click links that did not reference Richard Branson and no response was submitted. The complaint failed because the complainant provided scant evidence of trademark rights in BRANSON and no evidence that the respondent's use targeted the complainant's BRANSON mark. *See* Virgin Enters. Ltd. v. lawrence fain, Case No. FA1402001545807 (FORUM Mar. 20, 2014).

As in court proceedings, collecting evidence can be as simple as gathering it from publicly available online sources. However, it often involves outside counsel and/or in-house counsel collaborating with other individuals within their business (e.g., marketing, sales, finance, administrative) to consider how a particular Policy element may be proven or refuted and where such evidence may be found. Counsel must be clear on what needs to be proven and by what standard of proof and make sure that the individuals helping to gather supporting evidence are equally clear. For example, if a party is trying to establish unregistered or common-law rights through continuous use of a mark for eight years, evidence of using the mark once within the eight-year window or only within the week before the complaint is filed will not be enough. Or, if counsel are trying to establish trademark use, evidence only of trade name use will not suffice.[80] If counsel are not clear on the amount and kind of evidence to collect, they should speak with other practitioners experienced in UDRP proceedings and use the resources set forth earlier in this chapter to find cases where the lack of sufficient evidence was determinative in the panel's ruling.[81] Such decisions often discuss the nature and amount of evidence and why it was or was not probative.[82]

Advocates must carefully investigate where supporting evidence may be located.[83] Does it exist at a business site in hard-copy or electronic files? How many possible sites need to be searched if a business has multiple facilities? May evidence be found with third parties (e.g., marketing agency, media monitoring services, vendors)? Is it in storage? Does it exist in publicly available locations (e.g., in public libraries, on the internet, from governmental agencies)? The following are commonly used sources of evidence in UDRP proceedings:

---

80. *See, e.g.*, ABBT Neth. B.V. v. Miessler, Case No. D2015-2378 (WIPO Feb. 25, 2016).

81. *See* WIPO Overview 3.0, *supra* note 18, ¶ 1.13.

82. *See* Alex Mill Co., LLC v. Registration Priv., Case No. FA2402002082246 (FORUM Mar. 1, 2024) ("While trademark registrations and images of a complainant's website may be used to help support claimed ownership of trademark rights, they do not speak to the reputation that such mark has achieved with consumers, the industry, or the general public. For this, additional evidence of marketing, advertising, and how the mark is perceived by those outside of Complainant's organization should be submitted.").

83. *See* KEEN, Inc. v. Mureza, Case No. D2015-1892 (WIPO July 12, 2015) (finding no rights or legitimate interests, noting that the respondent provided no evidence to support the assertion that it had begun its outdoor clothing business before the complainant had commenced its business, and specifically noting that materials such as original invoices, affidavits from suppliers, or extracts from dated paperwork that businesses typically generate may have been probative).

- Whois searches, both current and archived (e.g., for current and past owners of a disputed domain name, for relevant dates and contact information related to the domain name, for the registrar's identity)
- Relevant government offices (e.g., U.S. Patent and Trademark Office and other trademark offices) for records relating to trademark rights, trademark use, relevant dates, and ownership
- Business correspondence (emails, letters, etc.) (e.g., related to ownership of the relevant trademark, use of the mark as a trademark, use for the relevant time period, offer to sell the domain name for profit, rights, or legitimate use of the disputed domain name)
- Internal business documents, including agreements (e.g., assignments, licenses, asset purchase agreements) that could impact a complainant's right to bring a UDRP proceeding (i.e., standing) or a respondent's rights and legitimate interests to use a disputed domain namc[84]
- Sales information (e.g., units and/or dollars, relevant time periods, places sold—number and location of mortar-and-brick stores, internet presence, catalog sales) related to the mark at issue (e.g., sworn statement from chief financial officer explaining with particularity the financial information)
- Advertising, marketing, or promotional information (e.g., advertising dollars spent, relevant time periods, places advertised (e.g., print, radio, television, movies, internet (websites, ads, social media), trade shows, sponsored events)), and circulation information (e.g., number of subscribers, print/internet circulation) related to the mark at issue, with an accompanying sworn statement from a company executive or knowledgeable employee explaining with particularity the information; including clear and probative documentary evidence as to the actual use of the mark in advertising (e.g., pictures of the mark in conjunction with products/services advertised, signage, event sponsorship)
- Internet information (e.g., gleaned from searches and websites, electronic documents, and articles) that may establish, for example, the popularity, recognition (or lack thereof),[85] and the time frame of

84. *See, e.g.*, Germanwings GmbH v. Hin und Weg Flugreisenzentrale GmbH, Case No. D2011-1218 (WIPO Sept. 22, 2011) (denying the complaint because the complainant's submission was inconsistent with regard to its alleged affiliation with the trademark's owner and the complainant failed to provide evidence of a chain of licenses linking it to the trademark owner and enabling it to enforce trademark rights); *see also* Sigorta v. Sancak, Case No. D2011-0111 (WIPO Apr. 5, 2011).

85. In *Secret Flying Ltd. v. Linghost*, Case No. D2015-1164 (WIPO Aug. 24, 2015), the panel considered (without deciding) whether the complainant had proved

use of a trademark (e.g., to establish rights in a mark, or to prove or defend bad-faith registration or legitimate rights)

- Dispute provider websites and other UDRP decision databases[86]—to search for information relating to the domain name in dispute and prior cases involving the complainant and the respondent
- Third-party references (e.g., articles, advertisements) and compilations (a summary of publicity or media coverage about the mark, including specific press clippings, copies of internet and print news articles for the relevant years) about the mark at issue to prove, for example, common-law rights and the renown of a mark

Complainants should monitor the website associated with the disputed domain name over time. If multiple pages of a website are necessary to demonstrate or reinforce a point, include the multiple pages in the pleadings.[87] And, if a party is providing copies of web pages for any purpose (e.g., to demonstrate the use of a mark for a particular period of time), then the pages should indicate in some self-authenticating way the relevant dates. Counsel should be aware of what they are saving or copying to ensure that (1) all of the probative information from the web page is included (e.g., dates and domain information sufficient to authenticate the web page and the address bar showing the URL and domain name of the web page) and

---

common-law rights in the expression *Secret Flying*, which it noted is composed of dictionary terms that may be descriptive or suggestive of the complainant's flight-related services. It examined the complainant's evidence of (1) 700,000 visitors to the complainant's website, www.secretflying.com, since 2014, with some 1.8 million user sessions and more than four million page views; (2) Google Analytics reports for the period September 14, 2014, through July 2, 2015; (3) more than 75,000 *likes* of the complainant's Facebook page; and (4) a copy of an invoice issued in January 2015 for the cost of printing 10,000 flyers advertising the *website www.secretflying.com* and using the name *Secret Flying* that were purportedly distributed in London over the period January to June 2015. In assessing this proof, the panel noted that the figures were not provided in any particular comparative context (e.g., the occurrence of the same or similar numbers for other brands in the complainant's area of trade) and commented that the figures alone did not demonstrate the extent of any reputation in the name *Secret Flying*.

86. *E.g.*, UDRP Tools, *supra* note 39; *see also* UDRP Search, https://udrpsearch.com (last visited Mar. 23, 2025).

87. For example, when asserting that the disputed domain name resolves to monetized pay-per-click links or advertisements, it is a good practice to submit not just a screenshot of the website's home page, but also images of the subsequent pages reached by clicking on some of the monetized links or ads up to and including examples of third-party sites that may ultimately be reached through the page. Similarly, if a phishing email refers to attached bank wire instructions, submit a copy of the attachment as well.

(2) all information is readable, including the small print. The pages copied or otherwise saved should appear to the panel as they appeared to the public on the internet. The placement and size of information may be relevant to a panel, and arrows, highlighting, or other callouts on complex pages may help to focus the panel's attention on important content. Often, website pages produced *as is* when the complaint is filed cannot be accessed online after the fact because respondents take them down or change them. If important information has been truncated or is not readable, a panel may not be able to give it the expected weight.

In addition, complainants may choose to send correspondence to the contact information listed in the Whois database. If a complainant is able to provide evidence to demonstrate to the panel that the contact information provided by a respondent is invalid or that a respondent made a demand for payment that exceeds the respondent's out-of-pocket costs in connection with the disputed domain name, such evidence will help to establish a respondent's bad-faith registration and use.

In addition to marshaling one's own evidence, it is becoming increasingly important to verify evidence submitted by one's opponent. While forged and misleading evidence has always been an occasional part of the UDRP landscape, with the advent of artificial intelligence (AI) it has become easier for unscrupulous actors to create fake evidence that may support their case (e.g., create the impression of a legitimate interest in a domain name). In one reported decision, the panel rejected a number of the respondent's claims based on what the panel found was a false U.S. trademark registration certificate and a forged agreement granting it an equity stake in the complainant's company.[88] Whether the forged documents were the result of AI is unknown, but the point is that advocates must have a heightened sense of awareness that AI makes producing fake documents easier if a party is so inclined to use them.

C. Thorough Case Advocacy

To be persuasive, parties must invest the necessary time to present sufficient evidence and advocate their case based on that evidence and applicable cases. In a UDRP proceeding, parties typically have one opportunity to advocate their position, so they should avoid boilerplate submissions. Rather, parties should treat their submissions with the level of attention they would give to summary judgment motions. Here are some specific tips to consider.

---

88. *See* Universal Music Grp. N.V. & Universal City Studios LLC v. JT U Animation/U Animation, Case No. FA2402002085375 (FORUM May 20, 2024).

1. *Bald Assertions of Fact Are Not Enough*

To carry one's burden of proof, a party must demonstrate with sufficient evidence what it is trying to prove, not simply make bald, unsubstantiated allegations.[89] "Mere 'assertions' are nothing more than argument and must in each case be based on facts proved through evidence."[90] Trademark owners must get it right the first time, as panels are not inclined to provide complainants with the opportunity to do over what they should have done the first time—support their claims with sufficient evidence.[91] And when given the opportunity to explain the unexplainable, comply—otherwise, the panel is left to draw conclusions and inferences that are likely to be unfavorable.[92]

As discussed previously in this chapter, adequate proof may include documentary evidence, exhibits, affidavits, and legal citations to national law, as well as other UDRP decisions. National law can provide a framework for arguments and support for a position counsel is espousing. It is particularly applicable when both the complainant and the respondent reside in the same jurisdiction and would reasonably expect to be subject to the same laws. For example, First Amendment protections may confer rights and legitimate interests to a respondent using a domain name as part of a criticism site where the use is fair and noncommercial and both parties reside in the United States, but not elsewhere in the world.[93]

---

89. *See, e.g.*, Iowa Fam. Pol'y Ctr. v. Basic Rts. Or., Case No. D2011-1846 (WIPO Dec. 20, 2011) (denying the complaint, noting that, to meet the burden of showing bad-faith registration, "[c]omplainant must ordinarily demonstrate (not simply allege) that respondent had actual knowledge of complainant's mark and selected the disputed domain name to take advantage of it"); *see also* TerraCycle, Inc. v. Natasha Nowakowski, Case No. D2011-1569 (WIPO Oct. 31, 2011) (denying the complaint for unsubstantiated claims of trademark use); Yellow Pages Media, Inc. v. Yellow Pages Media, Inc., Case No. D2005-0718 (WIPO Sept. 3, 2005) (denying the complaint, finding that "complainant failed to present any evidence that respondent intentionally committed the acts set forth" in paragraph 4(b)(iv) of the Policy).

90. Koninklijke Philips Elecs. N.V. v. Relson Ltd., Case No. DWS2001-0003 (WIPO Nov. 15, 2001).

91. *See, e.g.*, Williams v. Bbhinds Pty Ltd., Case No. DAU2013-0010 (WIPO May 21, 2013) (denying the complaint, noting with regard to the lack of evidence of trademark rights: "The Panel has considered but is not in the circumstances minded to grant the complainant another bite at the cherry by way of a Panel Order requesting that evidence of either the date of registration of the Australian trade mark, or of preceding trade mark rights be provided.").

92. *See, e.g.*, Digicel Caribbean Ltd. v. Domains by Proxy, LLC, Case No. D2015-1855 (WIPO Nov. 18, 2015).

93. *See* WIPO Overview 3.0, *supra* note 18, ¶ 2.6.

2. Presentation Is Important

Counsel should submit legal arguments and evidence in a logical manner that clearly addresses each of the elements under the Policy. In addition, parties should proofread pleadings and minimize typographical errors. Pleadings that are sloppy, illogical, inconsistent, or omit key facts or relevant UDRP elements will likely be viewed with a critical eye by the panel and undermine a party's credibility.

3. Pleadings Should Tell a Credible Story

Insofar as UDRP proceedings lack evidentiary hearings and discovery (including document exchanges and cross-examination of witnesses), through which decision makers ordinarily can assess the credibility of witnesses in person and the authenticity of documents, advocates need to ensure that their evidence and arguments tell a credible and persuasive story.[94]

Case in point: In a case involving the well-known GOT MILK? mark,[95] the respondent real estate business registered the disputed domain name gotmilko.com, asserting that it had the right to use the company's owners' names (J. and D. Milko) in advertising. In holding for the complainant, the panel rejected that argument because there was no evidence in the record that respondent, or its vice president, was ever commonly known by "gotmilko.com."[96] The respondent also claimed rights or legitimate interests in gotmilko.com because it maintained that it was common for realtors to use a marketing campaign highlighting their availability to customers and clients—that is, the respondent argued that the alleged intent of the campaign was to convince people to reach or "get" Milko to sell or buy their next property. The panel also rejected that argument because there was nothing in the record, including on the respondent's website, evidencing a "marketing campaign" to highlight the respondent's availability either generally to customers and clients or, more specifically, in terms of the public reaching ("get or got") the Milkos.

Overstatements about facts for which there is no proof can risk credibility and lose cases. To carry one's burden of proof, there must be adequate

94. *See, e.g.*, Coolmath.com LLC v. Delvin Dragon, Case No. D2015-2232 (WIPO Jan. 17, 2016); Carrefour v. Ling, Case No. D2015-2019 (WIPO Jan. 8, 2016); Tradax IP Licensing Ltd. v. Tim, Case No. D2015-2246 (WIPO Jan. 19, 2015).

95. *See* Ca. Milk Processor Bd. v. Domains by Proxy Inc., Case No. D2011-1870 (WIPO Dec. 8, 2011).

96. *See also* FNAC SA v. Laticinios Itaruma Ind. e Com. Ltda, Case No. D2015-2038 (WIPO Dec. 30, 2015); Facebook Inc. v. West, Case No. D2015-1766 (WIPO Nov. 25, 2015).

proof of the facts asserted. As the panel in *Iowa Family Policy Center v. Basic Rights Oregon* stated in an attempt to give the complainant the benefit of the doubt:

> For example, Complainant states generally that it has "spent millions of dollars over the last decade building the reputation of [its mark] and that Respondent has attempted to leverage off the "recognition, reputation and legitimacy of the [M]ark". . . . [T]here is no support in the record for such declarations . . . . The Panel must weigh this lack of evidence against Respondent's clear representation that it had neither heard of Complainant's organization, nor did it have knowledge of Complainant's registered trademark before registering the Domain Names.[97]

Furthermore, in rejecting a respondent's attempt to establish rights or legitimate interests, the panel in *Cerulean Studios, LLC v. Cai* stated:

> The Respondent has claimed to have used the mark Trillian on his company's local specialty products, such as lotus seeds, edible lilies, wolfberries, fruits and soyabean "long before" the Complainant started these proceedings and that "over the years" its brand "Trillian" has achieved excellent reputation. However, the Respondent has not provided any reliable or convincing evidence that he or his company used the mark Trillian or that it has achieved recognition and enjoyed a strong reputation. He has not given evidence of the volume of sales or details of his company's marketing efforts or the period of those sales.[98]

4. Panels Will Not Assume Facts That Are Not in Evidence

This point can be exemplified in the obligation a complainant has to set forth evidence of its rights in a mark under paragraph 4(a)(i) of the Policy. Normally, this element of standing is met by providing a copy of a trademark registration issued by any national or multinational governing body.[99]

---

97. Iowa Fam. Pol'y Ctr. v. Basic Rts. Or., Case No. D2011-1846 (WIPO Dec. 20, 2011).

98. Cerulean Studios, LLC v. Cai, Case No. D2013-0902 (WIPO Oct. 7, 2013). *See also* Walker Hamill Ltd. v. Doyle, No. D2015-2049 (WIPO Dec. 23, 2015) (finding no rights or legitimate interests because the panel deemed the four invoices submitted insufficient to show that the respondent was commonly known by the disputed domain name).

99. Even where a complainant produces a trademark registration, it is important for the claimant to demonstrate that the registration evinces rights in a mark with which the domain name at issue is identical or confusingly similar. *See, e.g.*, Jones

Panels have typically found that trademark registrations that are automatic or unexamined (such as U.S. state registrations as opposed to U.S. federal registrations) are not owed the same deference under the UDRP as examined registrations.[100] And complainants relying on trademark registrations listed solely on the U.S. patent and Trademark Office's Supplemental Register are expected to show secondary meaning[101] to establish trademark rights under the policy. Although similar in nature to proof of common-law rights or the scope of a mark's reputation, evidence of secondary meaning for descriptive marks is even more critical to establishing rights in order to satisfy the threshold nature of paragraph 4(a)(i). Even where such standing is established, panels may scrutinize the degree of deference owed such marks in evaluating the second and third elements.[102]

A common error made by complainants is to provide a copy of a trademark registration certificate naming a predecessor as the owner but fail to provide evidence of a subsequent assignment or owner name change. This may result in unnecessary delay if a panel issues a procedural order

---

Apparel Grp., Inc. v. jonesapparelgroup.com, Case No. D2001-0719 (WIPO July 19, 2001) (denying the complaint because, although complainant pled that it "owns all right, title and interest in and to, inter alia, the marks JONES APPAREL GROUP, JONES NEW YORK and JONES WEAR," it did not, in fact, have a trademark registration for JONESAPPARELGROUP, and the domain name at issue was jonesapparelgroup.com).

100. *See* WIPO Overview 3.0, *supra* note 18, ¶ 1.1; *see also* Spicher v. Frogi Design, Case No. D2015-0606 (WIPO June 3, 2015); S. Fork Hardware, Inc. v. Vulcan Sales, Inc., Case No. D2013-0199 (WIPO Mar. 14, 2015). Similarly, an intent to use (ITU) application, without evidence of common-law rights, has been considered a lack of proof of trademark rights. *See* Kemosabe Ent., LLC v. Nazzaro, Case No. D2012-1893 (WIPO Nov. 19, 2012).

101. *See* U.S. Patent and Trademark Office, Trademark Manual of Examining Procedure § 1212 (2024) ("A term which is descriptive . . . may, through usage by one producer with reference to his product, acquire a special significance so that to the consuming public the word has come to mean that the product is produced by that particular manufacturer. . . . This is what is known as secondary meaning."). Further, "[t]he crux of the secondary meaning doctrine is that the mark comes to identify not only the goods but the source of those goods. To establish secondary meaning, it must be shown that the primary significance of the term in the minds of the consuming public is not the product but the producer." *Id.*

102. *See* WIPO Overview 3.0, *supra* note 18, ¶ 1.2.

requesting clarification[103] or, in a worst-case scenario, an outright denial of the claim based on a failure to name the proper complaining party.[104]

Cases under the Policy may be maintained based upon unregistered or common-law trademark or service mark rights. If a complainant is relying on common-law rights to show rights in a mark, under paragraph 1.1 of WIPO Overview 3.0, it must show that the name has become a distinctive identifier associated with the complainant or its goods or services. Relevant evidence of this includes the length and amount of sales under the trademark, the nature and extent of advertising, consumer surveys, and media recognition.[105] As is often the case, where a party represents (e.g., in a declaration or by attorney argument) use for a particular period of time and in a particular manner, the evidence should support the scope and nature of the representation. In cases involving alleged common-law rights that comprise descriptive or dictionary words (and, therefore, not inherently distinctive), there may be a greater onus on the complainant to present compelling evidence of secondary meaning or distinctiveness.[106]

Support for common-law rights, even when undisputed (e.g., the respondent has defaulted), that consists of an attorney statement alone, a conclusory declaration, documents that are not coextensive with the alleged dates of usc, undated documents, or documents that do not demonstrate use of

---

103. *See, e.g.*, Bankers Tr. Co., BTC Fin. Corp. & BTC Cap. Mgmt. v. Jerlene McElroy, Case No. FA1910001868981 (FORUM Dec. 2, 2019) (ordering complainant to submit additional evidence to supplement what was in the record regarding the assignment of ownership rights in the subject trademark).

104. *See, e.g.*, Eddie Whiteley (Amnack LTD (T/A) Doncaster Cables) v. ang ka si te guang dong dian lan ke ji you xian gong si, Case No. UDRP-105593 (CAC Oct. 22, 2022).

105. *See, e.g.*, Mo. Lottery Comm'n v. SED Domain Servs., Case No. D2014-0118 (WIPO Mar. 7, 2014) (finding common-law rights in the asserted mark where the evidence showed that the complainant began using the mark in January 1986 and, since that date, had cumulative sales under the mark of more than 15 billion USD; it had incurred advertising expenditures in support of the mark in excess of 125 million USD; the then-current annual sales exceeded 1 billion USD; and its then-current annual advertising expenditure exceeded 12 million USD).

106. *See* WIPO OVERVIEW 3.0, *supra* note 18, ¶ 1.13; *see also* Mascot Media Circle, LLC v. WhoIsGuard, Inc., Case No. D2015-1209 (WIPO Sept. 14, 2015) (denying unopposed complaint because the complainant failed to show that its unregistered mark ONLINEMBA is inherently distinctive or acquired distinctiveness used on a website for a business that provides comprehensive resources and up-to-date information on how to choose the best online masters of business administration (MBA) program); Secret Flying Ltd. v. Linghost, Case No. D2015-1164 (WIPO Aug. 24, 2015); Roper v. Chretien, Case No. D2014-0843 (WIPO July 7, 2014).

the claimed mark may not suffice to support the asserted rights.[107] As indicated, some businesses may not appreciate the need to maintain records to support their trademark rights, and, in some cases, because of business acquisitions, relocations, fires, or floods, company records may simply no longer exist. That said, the internet, government agencies, and even newspapers, magazines, and social media sites have archives that complainants and their representatives can search for supporting evidence. And often, finding the requisite documents may simply require creativity and resourcefulness regarding where to look in the company's files. Furthermore, third parties who are or have been associated with the company (e.g., current employees, consultants, retired employees) can be very helpful in piecing together the historical use of the mark, along with documentary evidence. In addition to helping locate evidence, their declarations, along with supporting documents, can be probative evidence to establish standing.

It is also critical to understand that trademark rights do not automatically equal brand reputation. Where a complainant's evidence falls short of showing the renown of its mark, particularly when the mark is a common descriptive phrase or is in use by multiple unrelated businesses, the complainant may have problems proving or having the panel infer that the respondent knew about the complainant and specifically targeted its rights in the mark when it registered the disputed domain name.[108] Additionally, lack of evidence showing that a mark is famous or well known when it is simply a dictionary word(s) can result in a finding that the respondent has rights or legitimate interests in the domain name.[109] Similarly, if a complainant

107. *See, e.g.*, CSS Polymers Inc. v. Beirne, Case No. D2009-1179 (WIPO Nov. 9, 2009) (denying the complaint for lacking evidence of trademark rights because the documents failed to show continuous use of the alleged mark since the date alleged by the complainant's CEO in a sworn statement of record and use of the mark for a sufficient length of time or sufficient sales to support secondary meaning; also, the evidence of advertising did not support use—one advertisement was not dated and the other was dated long after the respondent registered the domain name); Restored Church of God v. Alexa Props., LLC, Case No. D2013-0320 (WIPO Mar. 21, 2013) (denying the complaint for lacking evidence of trademark rights because the complainant's only evidence related to use of *The Real Truth Magazine*, not the alleged *RT* mark).

108. *See, e.g.*, Teaching Co., LLC v. Brendhan Hight, Case No. D2014-0448 (WIPO June 4, 2014); Yellow Pages Media, Inc. v. Yellow Pages Media, Inc., Case No. D2005-0718 (WIPO Sept. 3, 2005).

109. *See, e.g.*, Iowa Fam. Pol'y Ctr. v. Basic Rts. Or., Case No. D2011-1846 (WIPO Dec. 20, 2011).

cannot prove trademark rights before a domain name was registered, it may impact a finding of bad-faith registration.[110]

5. Construct a Solid Foundation of Circumstantial Evidence

The criticality of the pleadings cannot be overemphasized in UDRP proceedings where there is no opportunity for discovery, in-person testimony, or other traditional forms of advocacy. Collecting and presenting evidence of bad-faith registration and use, which typically consists of circumstantial evidence, provides a good example of how advocates should be diligent in building their case. The possible difficulties of showing bad-faith use and registration under the UDRP and examples of how parties may win or lose a case on this element are discussed in Section IV.D.3.

6. Do Not Assume That Panels Will Conduct Independent Investigations

Under Rule 10(a), a panel is empowered to "conduct the administrative proceeding in such manner as it considers appropriate." This has been interpreted to allow for panels to conduct some limited, independent research of publicly available resources such as internet search engines, trademark office databases, Whois records, and the like.[111] However, even assuming a panelist was inclined to access a publicly available resource for some reason, not only would such conduct be unpredictable, but also the intent of a panelist to access such a resource might not be for investigative purposes. The panelists are not there to do the work of the parties, who must undertake the requisite investigation before presenting any pleading to the panel for consideration. Common examples include evidence of trademark reputation (do not expect a panel to know the mark or research it), current trademark ownership (panels may not search trademark office assignment databases), and the ownership history of a disputed domain name (archived Whois records are not always available to panels). Practitioners are also advised to submit actual screenshots of a referenced website rather than only provide a URL and similarly to provide images of trademark certificates rather than only registration numbers.

110. *See, e.g.*, QIQ Commc'ns Pty Ltd. v. Netico, Inc., Case No. D2014-1024 (WIPO July 30, 2014).

111. *See* WIPO Overview 3.0, *supra* note 18, ¶ 4.8.

7. The Most Common Errors in Complaints

It is worth noting that the Rules require both complainants and respondents (or their representatives) to sign a certification that the pleading is "complete and accurate," and that it is "not being presented for any improper purpose, such as to harass." While *pro se* parties who file pleadings themselves may get some leeway from panels, professional representatives, such as lawyers, are expected to understand the ins and outs of the Policy, its precedents, and its procedures and to present carefully constructed and well-supported pleadings. Some of the most common mistakes that lead to poor outcomes are as follows:

- The disputed domain name predates the asserted trademark, resulting in a finding of no bad-faith registration.
- The complaint is filed primarily to pressure the respondent into selling the domain name (a "Plan B" case).
- Insufficient evidence of trademark reputation is provided.
- An incorrect complainant is named (e.g., not the owner of the submitted trademark registration).
- The disputed domain name is not confusingly similar to the asserted trademark.
- Critical evidence is missing or misrepresented.
- The respondent is commonly known by the disputed domain name (e.g., a surname or legitimate business name).
- The respondent's use is legitimate or otherwise fair (e.g., a genuine fan or criticism site).
- One of the three Policy elements is not addressed at all.
- There is another pending legal action that directly impacts the disputed domain name.
- New facts come to light in the response that are not anticipated by the complainant.[112]

D. Frequently Arising Issues

The jurisprudence of the UDRP is quite broad and dates back to 1999. It is often underestimated by those new to the field, and this is done at great peril. While it is beyond the scope of this chapter to explore the full depth of the substantive and procedural issues under the UDRP,[113] the following touches

---

112. *See* Steven M. Levy, *How to Lose a UDRP Case*, UDRP.Grp., https://udrp.group/how-to-lose-a-udrp-case/ (last visited Mar. 23, 2025).

113. For a detailed desktop reference work on the many nuanced issues arising under UDRP practice, see Gerald M. Levine, The Clash of Trademarks and Domain Names on the Internet (2024).

on the three required elements of the Policy and some highlights that are frequently encountered by practitioners.

1. Trademark Rights and Confusing Similarity

Paragraph 4(a)(i) of the UDRP requires two components: evidence of a complainant's trademark rights and an assertion that the disputed domain name is confusingly similar to that mark. This has often been described as a "standing" or "threshold" requirement, as it is the first and most basic element of asserting a claim under the Policy.[114] Proof of trademark rights is often made by submitting images of a few and most relevant trademark registration certificates (e.g., most similar to and predating the registration date of the disputed domain name). Certificates originating from a national or transnational trademark office are accepted, though U.S. state trademark registrations typically are not, due to the lack of substantive examination by such agencies. However, a registration is not required, and trademark rights may also be proven through actual use in commerce (i.e., at common law), though this requires the submission of substantial evidence demonstrating that the claimed mark has gained secondary meaning through use.[115]

The second component of paragraph 4(a)(i) is to assert that the disputed domain name is identical or confusingly similar to the asserted trademark. This is not the same as proving a likelihood of confusion under the multifactor tests applied by various U.S. courts, but, rather, is a simpler examination of whether the mark is recognizable in the domain name under an appearance, sound, and meaning test. Further, this test typically discounts the TLD that is appended to the disputed domain name, as this is a technically required element for the domain name to perform its function. Examples include:

The second level of the domain name is identical to the asserted mark. The term "identical" in paragraph 4(a)(i) usually refers to the second level of the domain name (i.e., to the left of the dot). For example, where the complainant owns the trademark AMARO GIULIANI, the panel found that the amarogiuliani.com domain name is identical to the mark, discounting the lack of a space between the two words and the use of the ".com" gTLD, both of which are due to technical requirements of domain names.[116]

Is the mark recognizable within the domain name? The addition of other words to a mark often does not alleviate confusing similarity if the mark is still recognizable within the disputed domain name. Thus, for

---

114. *See* WIPO Overview 3.0, *supra* note 18, ¶ 1.2.

115. *See id.* ¶ 1.3.

116. *See* Giuliani S.p.A. v. Giuliani S.p.A., Case No. UDRP-106581 (CAC July 24, 2024).

example, freeclickbankprofits.com was held to be confusingly similar to the trademark CLICKBANK.[117] By contrast, despite it resolving to arguably bad-faith website content, a case against the domain name peopleincasinos.com was denied where it was held that "there is no visual or aural confusion at all in the present case between the PLEIN trademark and the disputed domain name. It is not sufficient that the trademark is only visible when the viewer is told it is definitely there."[118]

Generic or descriptive words may still be confusingly similar to a mark. A domain name comprising a generic or descriptive word may satisfy the standing requirement under the very focused analysis of paragraph 4(a)(i), yet not satisfy another element of the Policy (i.e., paragraphs 4(a)(ii) or (iii)). For example, a panel held that the domain name young.com was confusingly similar to the complainant's registered YOUNG trademark under paragraph 4(a)(i). Nevertheless, the claim against young.com was denied on the ground that it is composed of a generic or descriptive word, and, thus, the respondent had not registered it in bad faith.[119]

2. *Rights or Legitimate Interests*

This second element of the Policy gives respondents an opportunity to demonstrate why they are entitled to register and use a disputed domain name. However, as so many UDRP cases are decided on default, panels have recognized that this could result in the often impossible task of proving a negative, requiring information that is primarily if not exclusively within the knowledge of the respondent. The most common means of showing rights or legitimate interests are set out in paragraph 4(c) of the Policy, and these should each be addressed when drafting a complaint in anticipation of possible claims that may be made should a response be filed. Examples of each 4(c) scenario include the following:

What is and is not a bona fide offering of goods or services under paragraph 4(c)(i)? It is well accepted that typical cybersquatting activities such as phishing and other scams, selling competing or counterfeit products, and redirection to porn or gambling sites do not constitute the bona fide offering of goods or services. However, the legitimate operation of a business

117. *See* Click Sales, Inc. v. Suspended Domain, Case No. FA2406002103414 (FORUM July 26, 2024) (deciding that adding generic or descriptive terms such as "free" and "profits" did not differentiate the disputed domain name from the mark at issue).

118. *See* Philipp Plein v. Kimberly Webb, Case No. D2014-0778 (WIPO July 30, 2014).

119. *See* Young Pharms., Inc. v. Xiaopeng Zhou, Case No. D2024-1699 (WIPO July 11, 2014).

in a field that is different from that in which the complainant has trademark rights may qualify as such. For example, the owner of revued.com defeated a claim brought by a software/technology retailer in the United States who owns the REVUED mark for certain software applications. The respondent asserted that it operates a U.K.-based business-to-business review site and submitted into evidence a copy of a Scotland certificate of incorporation and evidence of its YouTube channel, LinkedIn page, and posted blogs. The panel found that the respondent had demonstrated that it is making a bona fide offering of services under the domain name, or, at a minimum, that it is making demonstrable preparations for such an offering under Policy paragraph 4(c)(i).[120] Similarly, pay-per-click links on the website of a disputed domain name may be bona fide if they are unrelated to a complainant's business and the asserted mark is not well known.[121]

When is a respondent commonly known by a disputed domain name under paragraph 4(c)(ii)? The term "commonly known" can refer to a business entity name, but this defense is often asserted based on personal names. For example, the majority of a three-member panel rejected a respondent's assertion that he is known by the nickname "Lambo" based on limited evidence and awarded a transfer of the lambo.com domain name to the maker of Lamborghini automobiles.[122] A different result was obtained in a claim brought by a local supermarket chain against the domain name dagostino.com where the respondent provided evidence that her family name is "D'Agostino," and that she inherited a computer services business from her father that is operated under that name.[123]

A legitimate noncommercial or fair use can defeat a claim under paragraph 4(c)(iii). This section of the Policy mainly concerns itself with fan, criticism, and other websites that implicate principles of free speech. It can also cover nominative fair use of a trademark. Perhaps the most well-known case in this last category is a decision setting out a four-part test for nominative fair use. The claim against okidataparts.com was rejected where (1) the respondent was actually selling genuine trademarked parts; (2) it was using the domain name to *only* sell such trademarked goods, and not those of other brands or companies; (3) the site accurately disclosed its relationship (or lack thereof) with the trademark owner; and (4) the respondent was

120. *See* Revued, LLC v. Andrew Jack, Case No. FA2309002061242 (FORUM Oct. 9, 2023).

121. *See, e.g.*, Tassel Ridge Winery, LLC v. Rome Uata, Case No. FA240 1002080417 (FORUM Feb. 18, 2024).

122. *See* Automobili Lamborghini S.p.A. v. Domain Adm'r, See PrivacyGuardian.org/Richard Blair, Case No. D2022-1570 (WIPO Aug. 2, 2022).

123. *See* D'Agostinos Mkts., Inc. d/b/a D'Agostino Supermarkets v. Louise Murphy/WebSiteText, Case No. FA2003001889900 (FORUM Apr. 29, 2020).

not trying to corner the market in all domain names related to the asserted mark.[124] With respect to fan sites, a claim against stevierayvaughan.com was denied where the site offered a biography of the famous musician, along with a discussion of his band and the Los Angeles music scene, including mention of other musicians who were contemporaries of Stevie Ray Vaughan.[125] Further, although the resolving website displayed some commercial offerings, these were deemed nominal and intended only to offset the costs of operating the site. Similar outcomes have been seen for legitimate criticism and protest sites.[126]

3. Bad-Faith Registration and Use

In UDRP proceedings, a showing of bad-faith registration and use is essential. In court proceedings, a complainant may, through documents, depositions, and admissions, discover evidence of a respondent's bad faith. Because there is no discovery in UDRP proceedings, a potential complainant is normally going to need the respondent's bad faith to be apparent (e.g., evidence of an intentional targeting of the asserted mark on the respondent's website, the lack of any credible good-faith explanation for incorporating a well-known mark into the domain name). Panels often base their finding of bad-faith registration and use on a combination of facts and circumstances. What follows are some examples of where bad-faith registration and use was found.

Searches would have identified a preexisting mark. The respondent registered the domain names serviziclienti-intesasanpaolo.com and servizi-intesasanpaolo.com (1) eight years after the oldest registration of the trademarks at issue; (2) consisting of the term "Intesasanpaolo" that the complainant had used since 2002 and for which it had obtained trademark registrations; (3) using a term that a domain name registrant would not accidentally think of; and (4) while a simple search of a trademark register or the internet would have informed the respondent about the complainant and its INTESA-SANPAOLO marks.[127] This approach works for well-known marks but may be less successful if the mark is widely used by others and is thus not unique to the complainant. A panel may determine that a respondent did not act in bad faith even if a prior trademark search had revealed

124. *See* Oki Data Ams., Inc. v. ASD, Inc., Case No. D2001-0903 (WIPO Nov. 6, 2001).

125. *See* Est. of Stevie Ray Vaughan v. Maxory LLC, Case No. FA2402002081987 (FORUM Feb. 29, 2024).

126. *See, e.g.*, Homer TLC, Inc. v. GreenPeople, Case No. FA0508000550345 (FORUM Oct. 25, 2005).

127. *See* Intesa Sanpaolo S.p.A. v. Marcus, Case No. D2016-0305 (WIPO Apr. 12, 2016).

adoption of similar marks by multiple businesses. In this scenario, additional evidence may be needed to show that the respondent was specifically targeting the complainant's mark rather than a diluted group of mark owners.[128]

Registration of a domain name with actual knowledge of the complainant. The respondent registered the domain name miramax-films.com (1) more than 30 years after the complainant first started using the MIRAMAX mark (the key brand of the complainant and its name); (2) in view of the complainant's extensive presence on the internet and worldwide reputation; (3) adding a word to the MIRAMAX mark that describes the complainant's core business (films); and (4) making the disputed domain name resolve to the complainant's own website as part of a phishing operation that involved sending emails to internet users pretending to be the complainant in an attempt to solicit sensitive personal and financial information.[129]

Registration to perpetuate scams. The respondent registered a series of domain names using the entirety of the complainant's well-known PENSKE mark and used at least one of them, penske-hr.com (1) to suggest employment/human relations with Penske; (2) in relation to a website that mimicked the complainant's website; and (3) to perpetrate a scam by sending emails and correspondence to job seekers. Furthermore, the respondent used a privacy shield, as well as the stolen identities and contact information of others, to register some or all of the disputed domain names.[130]

A similar finding was reached where the smoothiekingdecals.org domain name was used in a phishing scheme. After a victim registered for a supposed car wrap advertising program, the scammer would send the victim a fake check in an amount that exceeded the promised compensation with the instruction that the victim deposit the check into his or her bank account and then wire the excess funds (from that account) to another company that would wrap their vehicle. In reality, the funds from the victim's own account were being wired to the scammer, the fraudulent check would be rejected by the victim's bank, and the victim would be debited for the amount wired to the scammer.[131]

---

128. *See, e.g.*, Sonata Software Ltd. v. Narendra Ghimire, Deep Vision Architects, Case No. DAI2023-0051 (WIPO Mar. 11, 2024); *see also* WIPO Overview 3.0, *supra* note 18, ¶ 3.2.3.

129. *See* Miramax Film NY, LLC v. Nicolas, Case No. D2016-0299 (WIPO Apr. 5, 2016).

130. *See* Penske Truck Leasing Co., L.P. v. DelCorso, Case No. D2016-0521 (WIPO May 2, 2016); *see also* Hike Ltd. v. Abdullah, Case No. D2016-0459 (WIPO Apr. 25, 2016); Société anonyme des eaux minérales d'Evian (SAEME) v. Alex Gledson/Whoisguard, Inc., Case No. D2016-0433 (WIPO May 6, 2016).

131. *See* Smoothie King Franchises, Inc. v. gbwagent gbw, Case No. FA221 1002020248 (FORUM Dec. 22, 2022).

Complainant enjoys an international reputation. The respondents registered the domain names facebooksz.com and facebookwatches.com in view of the fact that the complainant and its trademark FACEBOOK enjoy a worldwide reputation and, although access to the Facebook website was blocked in China, there was wide media coverage and publicity by the international and Chinese press.[132]

Where a domain name is used only in connection with its prospective sale. The respondent, among other things, used the domain name solely in connection with a website offering it for sale, even though the content of the corresponding website did not specifically target the complainant. Despite the asserted mark not being well known, the panel determined that the respondent was, in fact, targeting the complainant, as the disputed domain name was registered one day after the filing of the complainant's trademark application.[133]

Respondents engaging in a pattern of bad conduct. The respondent registered the domain name nhl.net (1) incorporating the complainant's famous NHL mark (National Hockey League); (2) redirecting the public to a non-active page; (3) having had at least ten UDRP decisions under the Policy decided against it in the past five years (four occurring in the past year); and (4) owning hundreds of domain names that are identical to, or incorporate, the well-known marks of other companies (e.g., Abercrombie & Fitch, Armani, Amazon.com).[134]

Domain name redirects to salacious content. The respondent registered the domain radiomariahispana.org (1) directing the public to salacious content on how to enter the prostitution industry in Japan, and (2) likely tarnished the complainant, a Christian radio service, with a false association.[135]

Where a monetary demand is in excess of the respondent's documented out-of-pocket expenses. The respondent registered b.mw with knowledge of the complainant's mark and offered the domain name for sale

132. *See* Facebook, Inc. v. Allien, Case No. D2016-0255 (WIPO Apr. 10, 2016); *see also* Missoni S.p.A. v. Brave Leng, Case No. D2016-0237 (WIPO Apr. 7, 2016); Zapata Holding v. Gross, Case No. D2016-0441 (WIPO Apr. 21, 2016); HusmanHagberg AB v. Jung, Case No. D2015-2275 (WIPO Feb. 18, 2016).

133. *See* Hashkey Digit. Asset Grp. Ltd. v. a12222222, Case No. FA2109001965048 (FORUM Nov. 1, 2021).

134. *See* Nat'l Hockey League v. Jean Lucas, Case No. D2016-0315 (WIPO Mar. 29, 2016); *see also* Nvidia Corp. v. Domain Manager, Case No. D2016-0462 (WIPO May 2, 2016) (finding bad faith where (1) the respondent owned more than 4,000 domain names out of which more than 300 began with *www* followed by a registered trademark; (2) the mark at issue, NVIDIA, was a coined term exclusively connected to the complainant; and (3) the domain name wwwnvidia.com was confusingly similar to the complainant's mark, and the respondent had no relationship with complainant).

135. *See* Associazione Radio Maria v. Yamamoto, Case No. D2015-0386 (WIPO Apr. 26, 2015).

for an amount well in excess of any out-of-pocket registration costs.[136] Of course, asking a high price does not, in isolation, signal bad faith. Where a domain name is generic or descriptive, was registered prior to the existence of a complainant's trademark rights, or is used for a respondent's own business, a legitimate sales offer may be found, and, thus, will likely not support a finding of bad faith.[137]

While bad-faith *use* is typically easy to demonstrate in the aforementioned examples of cybersquatting, there are situations where bad-faith *registration* presents some challenging issues. Under the conjunctive requirement of paragraph 4(a)(iii), a complainant must show both in order to succeed. It may be impossible to prove bad-faith registration if the respondent registered the disputed domain name at a time before the complainant's trademark rights came into effect. After all, how can a domain name have been registered to target a trademark that does not yet exist? The rare exception to this may occur where the complainant can prove that the respondent knew of and anticipated the complainant's trademark rights (e.g., it learned of an upcoming brand and registered the disputed domain name to target the mark in the hopes of selling it to the complainant).[138] If the domain name is currently being used in bad faith but predates the trademark, the UDRP is likely not the right vehicle for enforcement, and the trademark owner should consider another venue such as litigation in an appropriate court.

A closely related issue is the date on which the domain name was acquired by the respondent, as this is often looked to as the date of "registration" under UDRP jurisprudence.[139] While the domain name may have originally been created on an earlier date (often a separate entry in the Whois record), if it was later acquired by the respondent, that later date acts as the date of registration for purposes of the paragraph 4(a)(iii) analysis. An exception to this may arise where the respondent acquired the domain name from a related entity, such as a predecessor corporation over which it has

---

136. *See* Bayerische Motoren Werke AG v. Masakazu/Living by Blue Co., Ltd., Case No. DMW2015-0001 (WIPO Sept. 22, 2015); *see also* Rainbow Play Sys., Inc. v. Freeplay Pty Ltd., Case No. DAU2015-0035 (WIPO Nov. 27, 2015) (finding bad-faith registration and use where the respondent, a former distributor for the complainant, was seeking payment from the complainant in the amount of 20,000 AUD, an amount "in excess of documented out-of-pocket expenses associated with the disputed domain name").

137. *See, e.g.*, Sage Glob. Servs. Ltd. v. Narendra Ghimire, Deep Vision Architects, Case No. DAI2023-0010 (WIPO Sept. 1, 2023).

138. *See* WIPO Overview 3.0, *supra* note 18, ¶ 3.8.2; *see also* Kendall Jenner, Kendall Jenner, Inc. & Whalerock Celebrity Subscription LLC v. Jorly James, Cooknames, Case Nos. D2015-1189 and D2015-1190 (WIPO Aug. 21, 2015) (consolidated, decision granting transfer of the disputed domain names).

139. *See* WIPO Overview 3.0, *supra* note 18, ¶ 3.8.1.

common control, and it can be said that there is a continuity of ownership of the domain name from a date prior to the most recent acquisition.[140]

Regardless of whether bad-faith use is presently occurring, complainants and their representatives would be wise to research the ownership history of a disputed domain name and refrain from using the UDRP where there is a possibility that trademark rights may have arisen *after* the respondent acquired the domain name. Failing to heed this warning has routinely resulted in findings of RDNH.[141]

E. One- or Three-Member Panel: Strategic Considerations

The panel is appointed after the filing of a response or after the due date on which the response was to have been filed (including any permitted extension) in the case of a respondent's default. A panel may be a single-member panel or a three-member panel. A panel will comprise a single member if both parties indicate that they would like a single member panel (or, in the event of the respondent's default, if the complainant designates a single-member panel). A panel will comprise three members if either the complainant or the respondent requests a three-member panel. In the case of a single-member panel, the dispute provider appoints the panel. For a three-member panel, the provider will generally try to appoint one panel member requested by each of the parties where possible. The third or presiding panelist is appointed on the basis of preferences indicated by the parties from a list of five candidates sent to the parties by the provider. Prior to appointment, all panelists must confirm that they are independent of the parties, the dispute resolution provider, and ICANN, and that serving on the panel does not constitute a conflict of interest. In addition, the dispute provider may take into account factors such as nationality, location, language skills, qualifications, experience, and citations in the pleadings.

Absent exceptional circumstances, the panel is required to notify its decision to the dispute resolution provider within 14 days after its appointment.[142] Within three days after receiving the decision, the provider must communicate the full text of the decision to each party, the concerned

---

140. *See, e.g.*, Bankwell Fin. Grp., Inc. v. Whois Priv. Prot. Serv., Inc./Domain Manager, Affordable Webhosting, Inc., Advert., Case No. D2015-1664 (WIPO Nov. 13, 2015) (deciding that "[w]here an unbroken chain of underlying ownership by a single person is established, a change in the recorded WhoIs details will not be considered a new registration for the purposes of the UDRP.").

141. *See, e.g.*, Playhouse Int'l Pty Ltd. v. Stephen Marshall, Stephen Marshall, Case No. D2023-3884 (WIPO Oct. 17, 2023).

142. *See Rules*, *supra* note 4, Rule 15.

registrar for implementation, and ICANN.[143] Decisions are published in full unless, as an exceptional case, the panel decides to redact portions of its decision.[144] As discussed earlier in this chapter, paragraph 4(k) of the Policy allows a domain name registrant who loses in a proceeding to challenge the result of the panel's decision by filing a lawsuit in the appropriate court (typically the mutual jurisdiction selected by the complainant in its initial complaint). If no lawsuit is filed prior to the expiration of the ten-day period, the decision will be implemented.

One-member panels decide the vast majority of cases under the Policy. However, there are strategic reasons that may motivate either party to elect a three-member panel, particularly in difficult cases. Where a three-member panel is appointed, a two-member majority will decide the outcome of the proceeding. If a party believes that reasonable minds may differ about the application of the Policy to the facts at hand, it may decide to request a three-member panel to have the opportunity to nominate a panelist that it believes will be sympathetic to its position and able to persuade at least one other panelist of the same. Perhaps for this reason, three-member panels have a significantly lower rate of transferring domain names than single-member panels. The rate of granted claims for single-member panels, across all providers, is 93 percent, with a 7 percent complaint denial rate.[145] The rate of granted claims for three-member panels is 45 percent, with a 55 percent complaint denial rate.[146]

F. Use of Legal Counsel

Attorneys who are knowledgeable about intellectual property rights and experienced with the Policy and UDRP proceedings can help a party locate probative evidence, document and present the evidence, and address the elements of the Policy. However, a party's submission does not need to be prepared or submitted by legal counsel, nor is there any requirement that a complaint or response be certified or notarized. Indeed, the Policy was intentionally designed to be utilized without legal assistance, and complainants and respondents are both able to proceed *pro se*. According to the records of the major dispute providers, 89 percent of overall complainants and 10 percent of overall respondents obtained external representation.[147] Out of 89 percent of complainants that are represented and where a decision

143. *See id.* Rule 16(a).

144. *See Policy*, *supra* note 3, ¶ 4(j); *see also Rules*, *supra* note 4, Rule 16(b).

145. Statistics are based on information obtained from UDRP Tools, *supra* note 39, as of May 18, 2024.

146. *See id.*

147. *See id.*

was rendered, 87 percent of the cases resulted in a domain name transfer, 11 percent resulted in a denial of the complaint, and 2 percent resulted in a domain name cancellation.[148] Out of 10 percent of respondents that are represented and where a decision was rendered, 51 percent of the cases result in a domain name transfer, and 49 percent result in a denial of the complaint.[149] The rate of transfer where a respondent is represented by counsel is significantly lower (51 percent transfer) than where a respondent is not represented by counsel (95 percent transfer). In a case where reasonable minds may disagree about how to interpret the facts, engaging counsel may help a respondent obtain a favorable outcome.

Conclusion

The Policy is intended to offer an administrative forum for expeditiously and inexpensively adjudicating trademark disputes relating to clear cases of abusive registration and use of internet domain names. The expeditious nature of the proceeding, however, comes at a cost because at least some degree of credibility assessment is sacrificed. Accordingly, parties should not undercut the resources necessary to make their one shot successful. Thus, to get the most from UDRP proceedings, advocates and clients should ensure that they are providing the panel with the best and most complete evidence and arguments to address the key aspects of the Policy and support their representations. Consider the following advice:

- Avoid a bare-bones complaint or response. The submission generally is the only chance parties or their counsel have to explain facts with supported evidence and to cite to relevant prior decisions.
- All plausible and supported assertions in a complaint are generally taken as true where a respondent does not answer.
- Provide relevant, ample, and complete documentary evidence, certainly coextensive with any representations.
- Do not make assumptions. Even a trademark that is famous or an abuse that is obvious to counsel must be proven by evidence.
- Panels are effectively serving "pro bono." Counsel cannot expect them to fill holes in the parties' arguments or evidence.

148. *See id.*
149. *See id.*

CHAPTER 11

Resolving Small-Value Copyright Claims Through the Copyright Claims Board

Theo Cheng[1]

> *The judicial system is the most expensive machine ever invented for finding out what happened and what to do about it.*
>
> —Irving R. Kaufman

Introduction[2]

In the United States, it is the responsibility of the copyright owner (or the owner's exclusive licensee) to enforce its rights in the copyrighted works it owns against alleged infringers. Under the U.S. copyright system, legal enforcement of copyrights falls within the exclusive jurisdiction of the federal courts.[3] Copyright holders already have the initial burden of ensuring that they have registered their work to properly prosecute a lawsuit in federal court.[4] But they also have to pay an accompanying initial filing fee to commence that action,[5] propound and respond to broad discovery under the

---

1. For their assistance in preparing this chapter, the author gratefully acknowledges David Carson, Esq., former Copyright Claims Officer for the Copyright Claims Board, and Melissa M. Eckhause, Esq., Co-Director, Arts & Entertainment Law Clinic, and Assistant Professor of Law at University of Detroit Mercy.

2. See Glossary for definition of frequently used terms.

3. *See* 28 U.S.C. § 1338(a) ("The district courts shall have original jurisdiction of any civil action arising under any Act of Congress relating to patents, plant variety protection, copyrights and trademarks. No State court shall have jurisdiction over any claim for relief arising under any Act of Congress relating to patents, plant variety protection, or copyrights.").

4. *See* Fourth Est. Pub. Benefit Corp. v. Wallstreet.com, LLC, 139 S. Ct. 881 (2019) (holding that, except in specific limited circumstances, a copyright infringement suit may only be commenced after the U.S. Copyright Office registers the copyright in the work at issue).

5. Currently, the filing fee to commence a federal court action is $350. *See* 28 U.S.C. § 1914(a) ("The clerk of each district court shall require the parties

Federal Rules of Civil Procedure (Rules), comply with other procedures set forth in those Rules, and await a lengthy turn for a court or jury to decide their case. In 2020, civil cases in the federal trial courts experienced a median length of 27 months from filing to trial, with close to 10 percent of cases pending for more than three years.[6] Moreover, in 2022, the median cost of litigating a copyright infringement case with less than $1 million at risk in federal court from pretrial through the appeals process was $193,000.[7] Additionally, the investment of emotional capital in a protracted litigation are yet further costs with which to contend.

The Copyright Act of 1976 permits a prevailing party to recover its reasonable attorneys' fees and costs from the losing party. However, unlike other statutory fee-shifting provisions, the recovery is not guaranteed and lies within the sound discretion of the court.[8] The burden to prosecute and/or defend a copyright claim in court thus falls particularly hard on individuals and small businesses who typically lack sufficient resources, both in terms of time and money. That burden is exacerbated—and the benefits of federal court litigation outweighed—especially when the dollar value of the claim is small. In particular, visual artists, songwriters, authors, and other smaller creators are severely impacted by the high cost of federal litigation because the individual value of their works or transactions is frequently too low to warrant the expense of litigation, and most attorneys will not even consider representing clients in these small-value cases.

---

instituting any civil action, suit or proceeding in such court, whether by original process, removal or otherwise, to pay a filing fee of $350, except that on application for a writ of habeas corpus the filing fee shall be $5."). Some courts may also impose an administrative fee of up to $52, bringing the total to $402. *See District Court Miscellaneous Fee Schedule*, U.S. CTS,. https://www.uscourts.gov/court-programs/fees/district-court-miscellaneous-fee-schedule (last visited Mar. 23, 2025).

6. *See The Need for Additional Judgeships: Litigants Suffer When Cases Linger*, U.S. CTS. (Nov. 18, 2024), https://www.uscourts.gov/data-news/judiciary-news/2024/11/18/need-additional-judgeships-litigants-suffer-when-cases-linger ("Nationally, the average time between filing a civil case and trial is a little over two years. In many of these overworked courts, the average time between filing and trial is much longer, often three to four years."); CONGRESSIONAL RESEARCH SERVICE, IF11349, LAWSUITS AGAINST THE FEDERAL GOVERNMENT: BASIC FEDERAL COURT PROCEDURE AND TIMELINES 1 (2020), https://crsreports.congress.gov/product/pdf/IF/IF11349.

7. AMERICAN INTELLECTUAL PROPERTY LAW ASSOCIATION, 2023 REPORT OF THE ECONOMIC SURVEY 65, 76 (2023).

8. *See* 17 U.S.C. § 505 ("In any civil action under this title, the court in its discretion may allow the recovery of full costs by or against any party other than the United States or an officer thereof. Except as otherwise provided by this title, the court may also award a reasonable attorney's fee to the prevailing party as part of the costs.").

Until recently, copyright owners having small-value copyright claims did not have a viable court forum where they can litigate such claims, leading many of them to feel disenfranchised.

I. The Copyright Claims Board

After many failed attempts, the U.S. Congress addressed this problem, and a new law was enacted. On December 27, 2020, the Copyright Alternative in Small Claims Enforcement (CASE) Act of 2019 was signed into law. The statute, codified in Chapter 15 of Title 17 of the U.S. Code, established a new three-member tribunal called the Copyright Claims Board (CCB or the Board) within the U.S. Copyright Office to handle small dollar-value copyright claims.[9]

The CCB is a voluntary, alternative forum to federal court for resolving copyright disputes up to $30,000. Parties who are sued in the CCB also have the right to opt out of the proceeding. Copyright holders with claims under $30,000 can still choose to file an action in federal court. They may also pursue negotiation, mediation, arbitration, or any other form of dispute resolution. They can even decide to take no action at all and let the alleged transgression remain unchallenged.

The CCB began accepting claims on June 16, 2022.[10]

A. The Structure of the CCB

The full-time members of the CCB—referred to as "Copyright Claims Officers" (CCOs)—are appointed by the Librarian of Congress after consulting with the Register of Copyrights.[11] Each CCO must be an attorney with at least seven years of legal experience.[12] Two of them must have "substantial experience in the evaluation, litigation, or adjudication of copyright infringement claims," and, as between them, they must "have represented or presided over a diversity of copyright interests, including those of both owners and users of copyrighted works."[13] The third CCO must "have substantial familiarity with copyright law and experience in the field of alternative dispute resolution, including the resolution of litigation matters through that

9. *See id.* § 1502.

10. *See* U.S. Copyright Office, *Copyright Claims Board to Begin Accepting Claims Later This Month*, NewsNet (June 2, 2022), https://www.copyright.gov/newsnet/2022/966.html.

11. *See* 17 U.S.C. § 1502(b)(1).

12. *See id.* § 1502(b)(3)(A)(i).

13. *Id.* § 1502(b)(3)(A)(ii).

method of resolution."[14] The CASE Act also provides for the hiring of Copyright Claims Attorneys to assist the members of the tribunal.[15] On July 20, 2021, the Copyright Office announced the appointment of the three inaugural CCOs: David Carson, Monica P. McCabe, and Brad R. Newberg.[16]

B. Litigating a CCB Proceeding

The CCB is essentially a "virtual courthouse," in that the entire proceeding is generally conducted online, and there is no requirement to appear in person at a physical location. To that end, CCB proceedings are intended to be streamlined and function akin to an arbitration proceeding, and the CASE Act generally affords the CCB flexibility in ensuring that the parties receive due process in this forum. The Board holds case management conferences with the parties, affords an opportunity for limited discovery (typically, only the production of relevant information and documents and written interrogatories), and receives evidence through written submissions (at times also holding live hearings). The CCB has promulgated regulations governing practice before the tribunal[17] and published an online handbook to assist litigants with various procedural aspects of filing, prosecuting, and defending a case in this forum.[18]

---

14. *Id.* § 1502(b)(3)(A)(iii).

15. *See id.* § 1502(b)(2).

16. *See* U.S. Copyright Office, *Copyright Office Announces Appointments of Copyright Claims Board Officers*, NewsNet (July 20, 2021), https://www.copyright.gov/newsnet/2021/906.html. Mr. Carson most recently served as director of the Copyright Policy Team in the Office of Policy and International Affairs at the U.S. Patent and Trademark Office and previously held positions with the International Federation of the Phonographic Industry and the Copyright Office. Ms. McCabe was a partner in, and chair of, the Intellectual Property Practice at Phillips Nizer LLP, specializing in copyrights, trademarks, and entertainment law; she also served as a mediator on, among others, the International Trademark Association's Panel of Neutrals, the U.S. District Court for the Southern District of New York, and the New York Supreme Court's Commercial Division in Manhattan and Suffolk Counties. Mr. Newberg was a partner at McGuireWoods LLP where he led the firm's copyright and trademark litigation practice, with a special emphasis on copyrights, trademarks, domain names, trade secrets, dilution, and unfair competition. For more information on the current CCOs, see *About the Copyright Claims Board*, CCB, https://ccb.gov/about/ (last visited Mar. 23, 2025). Under the CASE Act, the first CCO appointed shall serve a term of four years, with subsequently appointed CCOs serving for, respectively, five and six years. *See* 17 U.S.C. § 1502(b)(5)(B). Mr. Carson's appointment became effective on July 6, 2021, and, thus, he will step down as a CCO on July 6, 2025.

17. *See generally* 37 C.F.R. pts. 201–212, 220–235.

18. *See generally* U.S. Copyright Office, Copyright Claims Board Handbook (2024) [hereinafter CCB Handbook], https://ccb.gov/handbook/.

1. CCB Jurisdiction

The CCB has jurisdiction to hear three main types of claims, along with defenses and associated counterclaims.[19] The three types are (1) a claim for copyright infringement brought by the owner of a copyrighted work; (2) a claim for a declaration of noninfringement of a copyrighted work; and (3) a claim challenging a Digital Millennium Copyright Act (DMCA)[20] takedown notice (or counternotice) on the ground that it contains some misrepresentation. Thus, the jurisdiction of the CCB not only includes affirmative claims brought by owners of copyrighted works, but also defenses to allegations of infringement and claims brought by users of copyrighted works.[21]

2. Commencing a Proceeding in the CCB

The CCB has created a free, electronic filing and case management system called eCCB. Parties and their representatives can create accounts within the eCCB system enabling them to file and receive documents. Absent special permission, all CCB proceedings must use the eCCB system because—like the electronic case filing systems in court—it allows all parties and the CCB to receive and confirm filings immediately.[22]

There is a modest filing fee associated with commencing a proceeding before the CCB.[23] And as a small claims tribunal, the CCB was also designed to permit litigants the option to represent themselves or to obtain representation by an attorney or a qualified law student. Moreover, unlike

19. *See* 17 U.S.C. § 1504(c).

20. The Digital Millennium Copyright Act of 1998 (DMCA) is codified in section 512 of Title 17 of the U.S. Code. Generally, the "notice and takedown" process under that statute affords copyright holders the ability to request that an online platform remove content that they believe infringes on their copyright by sending a formal "takedown notice" to the platform, which then has the obligation to remove the content upon receiving the notice, so long as the notice meets certain statutorily required criteria.

21. For more information on how to commence one of these claims before the CCB, see CCB Handbook, *supra* note 18, ch. 3. For more information on interposing counterclaims in a CCB proceeding, see *id.* ch. 12. The CCB also offers a more streamlined "smaller claims" track for cases where only $5,000 or less is at stake. *See id.* ch. 4; 37 C.F.R. § 226.

22. For more information on the eCCB system, see CCB Handbook, *supra* note 17, ch. 2.

23. Currently, claimants must pay a first fee of $40, followed by a second fee of $60 if the respondent does not opt out. *See* 37 C.F.R. § 201.3(g).

in federal court, businesses and organizations do not need an attorney to represent them before the CCB.[24]

Once a claim or counterclaim has been filed with the CCB, the Board undertakes a Compliance Review stage, through which it reviews the filing to ensure that the claimant (the party filing the claim) has provided sufficient information to enable a respondent (the party named as the defendant in the proceeding) or a counterclaim respondent to answer it, as well as compliance with both the Copyright Act and the CCB's regulations.[25] If everything is in compliance, the claimant will be notified and will then be able to serve the claim on the party entitled to respond. In the case of noncompliance, the claimant will be afforded two opportunities to rectify the situation. If the problem is remedied, the compliance review process starts over; if the problem is not remedied, the CCB will dismiss the filing without prejudice.[26]

Additionally, the CCB may also dismiss as "unsuitable" any claims that it is not permitted to handle. A claim or counterclaim may be dismissed as unsuitable if:

1. A "necessary party" is not included as a participant in the proceeding.
2. An essential witness, evidence, or expert testimony will be missing given that the CCB does not have the power to compel third parties to testify or produce documents.
3. The CCB has issued a temporary stay on new filings.
4. It would require the determination of an issue of law or fact that exceeds the CCB's competence to determine.
5. The CCB concludes for some other reason that the claim is not suitable for determination by the CCB.

A respondent or counterclaim respondent who believes that the claim or counterclaim is unsuitable can affirmatively request that the CCB dismiss the claim or counterclaim. The CCB may also determine on its own

24. For example, a business or organization may be represented by a law student or an in-house attorney. They may also be represented by an owner, partner, officer, or member of the business or organization, or even an authorized employee of the business or organization, so long as they certify that they are an authorized agent of the business or organization and they have the authority to bind the business or the organization. For more information on representation before the CCB, see CCB Handbook, *supra* note 18, ch. 5. *See also* 17 U.S.C. § 1506(d). A listing of pro bono assistance resources is also available on the CCB's website at *Pro Bono Assistance*, CCB, https://ccb.gov/pro-bono-assistance/ (last visited Mar. 23, 2025).

25. *See* 37 C.F.R. § 224.1.

26. For more information on the Compliance Review stage, see CCB Handbook, *supra* note 18, ch. 6. *See also* 17 U.S.C. § 1506(f). For more information on service of the claim after the Compliance Review process, see CCB Handbook, *supra* note 18, ch. 8.

initiative that a claim or counterclaim is unsuitable without a party's request. If the CCB dismisses a claim or counterclaim for being unsuitable, it will provide a preliminary ruling on unsuitability, to which a party can request reconsideration by the Board.[27]

3. Opting Out of the CCB

Consistent with a voluntary arbitration process, one of the hallmarks of the CCB system is the ability of respondents to opt out of it.[28] Respondents are afforded 60 days after service of a claim in which to decide whether to participate in or to opt out of the proceeding.[29] Opting out results in a dismissal of the proceeding without prejudice and terminates the jurisdiction of the CCB.[30] If the parties decide to go forward before the CCB, however, they will forgo the right to be heard before a federal court, the right to a jury trial, the right to an injunction, and the possibility of more damages.[31]

Although the opt-out right might seem to render the CASE Act superfluous, the statute also contains several provisions designed to incentivize and encourage respondents to participate in a CCB proceeding. For example, in federal court, a successful plaintiff may be awarded up to $150,000 in statutory damages per work infringed.[32] The CASE Act, however, limits that amount to a maximum of $15,000 if the work was timely registered.[33] The statute also limits the total amount of damages that can be awarded in each case to no more than $30,000,[34] as compared to federal court, where there is no limit under the Copyright Act. By providing for a cap on damages, a CCB proceeding affords respondents with a measure of predictability, as compared to the amount of exposure it might face in a court litigation.

Moreover, participating in a CCB proceeding will undoubtedly be less costly than a federal court case, principally because the process itself is akin to an arbitration proceeding. As noted previously, it is so streamlined that there may even be no need to retain an attorney. Thus, for example, unlike in federal court, in-person appearances would not be necessary and discovery

27. For more information on the CCB's unsuitability determinations, see CCB Handbook, *supra* note 18, ch. 7. *See also* 17 U.S.C. § 1506(f)(3); 37 C.F.R. § 224.2.

28. *See* 17 U.S.C. § 1506(i).

29. *See id.*; 37 C.F.R. § 223.1(e).

30. *See* 17 U.S.C. § 1506(i); 37 C.F.R. § 223.1(a).

31. *See* 17 U.S.C. §§ 1506(i), 1507(a).

32. *See id.* § 504(c)(2).

33. *See id.* § 1504(e)(1)(A)(ii)(I). If the work was not timely registered, statutory damages are limited to $7,500. *See id.* § 1504(e)(1)(A)(ii)(II).

34. *See id.* § 1504(e)(1)(D).

is more limited. The formal rules of evidence also do not typically apply.[35] The cap on damages again also helps make that phase of the dispute much more manageable.[36]

Table 11.1 summarizes some of the salient differences between a CCB proceeding and a federal court litigation, which might be relevant to a claimant in deciding whether to commence a CCB proceeding in the first instance or a respondent in considering whether to opt out.

Table 11.1: Notable Differences Between the CCB and Federal District Court

CCB	Federal District Court
Federal registration of the copyrighted work is not necessary in order to file a claim with the CCB.	Federal registration of the copyrighted work is a prerequisite to commencing a court action.
The CCB comprises decision makers having copyright subject matter background and experience.	A plaintiff would be assigned a generalist judge who may or may not have any prior exposure to copyright disputes. The matter may also ultimately be decided by a lay jury.
The CCB only hears claims related to copyright, and a claimant who seeks the adjudication of other, non-copyrighted claims would have to bring those claims in another forum.	A plaintiff would be able to adjudicate copyright and related non-copyright claims in a single proceeding.
CCB proceedings are streamlined, which means that they typically take less time and cost considerably less.	Federal courts adhere to both civil procedure and evidence rules, which tend to lengthen both the time and cost to a final judgment.
Discovery is limited, principally to the exchange of key documents and information between the parties.	Discovery under the Rules is significantly broader than before the CCB for both parties and non-parties. A court case may be more appropriate for complex disputes, particularly those involving many third-party witnesses or the necessity of expert witnesses.

35. *See id.* § 1506(o).

36. *See* CCB, Key Statistics (June 2022–September 2024) 2 (2024) [hereinafter Key Statistics], https://ccb.gov/CCB-Statistics-and-FAQs-Oct-2024.pdf.

CCB	**Federal District Court**
A claimant cannot seek a total award of more than $30,000, no matter how many claims it asserts.	There is no limit to the damages a plaintiff can seek.
For a timely registered work, a claimant is limited to statutory damages of $15,000.	For a timely registered work, a plaintiff is limited to statutory damages of $150,000.
For an untimely registered work, a claimant can recover up to $7,500 in statutory damages.	For an untimely registered work, a plaintiff cannot recover statutory damages at all (or its attorneys' fees).
The CCB has no authority to issue injunctive relief absent the consent of the respondent.	A court may issue injunctive relief on the consent of the parties or, in the absence of consent, so long as the legal requirements have been satisfied by the plaintiff.
Attorneys' fees are capped at $5,000 and only available in cases of bad faith.	A prevailing party may be able to recover its reasonable attorneys' fees and costs (but not its fees if the work was untimely registered).

The CASE Act also includes several safeguards to prevent against frivolous lawsuits and trolling. The CCB not only has the authority to dismiss frivolous claims, but also to award attorneys' fees of up to $5,000 when it has found bad-faith conduct (or more in extraordinary circumstances); prohibit the bad-faith actor from filing a case for one year; and dismiss all pending cases filed by the bad-faith actor.[37] In addition, if the Board finds that, on more than one occasion within a 12-month period, a party pursued a claim, counterclaim, or defense before the CCB for a harassing or other improper purpose, or without a reasonable basis in law or fact, the CCB will bar that party from initiating a claim before the CCB for a period of 12 months[38]—a restriction that does not nominally exist in the Rules but could theoretically be imposed by a federal court judge.

Furthermore, because the CCB process is optional, each time a respondent opts out, the owner loses the nonrefundable first filing fee, thereby providing respondents with some leverage against a litigious plaintiff or attorney. The damages caps under the statute also serve as a disincentive to litigants who might consider making threats of large, unpredictable copyright damages awards in an effort to drive disputes towards a settlement.

37. *See* 17 U.S.C. § 1506(y)(2).

38. *See id.* § 1506(y)(3); *see also* 37 C.F.R. § 232.4.

4. Information and Document Exchange

Assuming the respondent does not opt out and files a response and any counterclaims, and the claimant has responded to those counterclaims,[39] the parties will then engage in a discovery process where information and documents are exchanged.[40] Initially, a pre-discovery conference between the parties and a CCO will take place to make sure that everyone understands what they must do in discovery.

By statute, discovery in a CCB proceeding is "limited to the production of relevant information and documents, written interrogatories, and written requests for admission."[41] However, in contrast to court litigation, the discovery afforded in a CCB proceeding is actually quite limited. The CCB has established a standard process and forms that the parties must use so that discovery can be completed as efficiently as possible. A party that seeks more must persuade the Board that such additional information or documents are needed. Moreover, while some of the typical written discovery devices are utilized, there are no depositions in CCB proceedings. After discovery ends, there will be another conference to discuss any updates the parties have for the CCB, how discovery information will be used, the possibility of settlement, and the next steps toward the CCB issuing a final determination.[42]

5. Presenting the Case Before the CCB

Cases are presented before the CCB only through written submissions. Specifically, after the post-discovery conference, the parties will be afforded time under a scheduling order to use the information they have collected to prepare their respective written testimony. This testimony is intended to allow the parties an opportunity to explain to the CCB why they believe they should prevail and will typically include a party statement, evidence, and any witness statements.

The parties submit their written testimony to the CCB in phases:

- First, the party making a claim or counterclaim will file its opening testimony by the date designated in a scheduling order.

---

39. For more information on filing a response to a claim in a CCB proceeding, see CCB Handbook, *supra* note 18, ch. 11.

40. The CCB labels this the beginning of the Active Phase of the proceeding, which ends when the parties complete the discovery process. For more information about the Active Phase, see *id.* ch. 10.

41. 17 U.S.C. § 1506(n).

42. For more information on the nature and scope of the discovery process in a CCB proceeding, see CCB Handbook, *supra* note 18, ch. 14.

- Then, the party responding to the claim or counterclaim will file its response to the testimony.
- Finally, the party making the claim or counterclaim will have the option to file its reply testimony.

Once the reply testimony is filed, no further testimony or evidence is permitted to be submitted unless the CCB specifically requests it or grants permission to file it.[43]

After all the testimony has been filed, the CCB will review the parties' submissions and decide whether to hold a virtual hearing to further discuss the issues and evidence with the parties. Parties may also request that the CCB hold a hearing by including the request in the party statement or submitting a request through a separate, fillable form on eCCB no later than seven days after the deadline for reply party statements. It is up to the CCB to decide whether a hearing would, in fact, be helpful to the process. If the CCB decides to schedule a hearing, it will issue a revised scheduling order with the date of the hearing.

At such a hearing,[44] all parties will have an opportunity to present their positions to the CCOs, ask questions of the other parties and any witnesses attending the hearing, and refer to evidence. The CCB will use the hearing to discuss the case with the parties and hear the oral testimony of optional witnesses brought by the parties. The parties and any witnesses will answer questions from the CCOs and the other parties about the issues in the proceeding.

The CCB may also schedule a prehearing conference to discuss with the parties how the hearing will be conducted, as well as any other relevant issues. The scheduling order may also include deadlines for submitting any additional evidence that the CCB has requested.[45]

6. Final Determination

After the hearing (or if, as is more often the case, the CCB has determined that no hearing is necessary), the CCOs will then use the materials submitted by the parties to arrive at and issue a final determination in the proceeding,[46] identifying the party who prevailed in the case and the damages awarded, if

---

43. For more information on presenting the case through written testimony before the CCB, see *id.* ch. 17.

44. *See* 17 U.S.C. § 1506(p).

45. For more information on the hearing in a CCB proceeding, see CCB HANDBOOK, *supra* note 18, ch. 18.

46. For more information on the CCB's final determination, see *id.* ch. 21.

any, in a writing that explains the factual and legal bases for its decision.[47] Although the CCB does not issue injunctive relief, it will order a respondent to cease infringement if the respondent agrees to do so.[48]

The final determination will contain factual findings based upon a preponderance of the evidence[49] standard and circumscribed and bound by judicial precedent. When there is conflicting judicial precedent, the CCB must follow the law of the jurisdiction where the action could have been brought if filed in a federal district court.[50] Alternatively, if the action could have been filed in more than one jurisdiction, the CCB would follow the law of the jurisdiction that it "determines has the most significant ties to the parties and conduct at issue."[51]

After the CCB issues its final determination, a party has 30 days in which to request reconsideration by the Board if it can identify "a clear error of law or fact material to the outcome, or a technical mistake."[52] The CCB can then either deny the request or issue an amended final determination.[53] If the CCB denies the reconsideration request, the aggrieved party may, within another 30 days, seek a review of the final determination by the Register of Copyrights, limited to whether the CCB abused its discretion in denying reconsideration of the determination.[54] The Register can either deny the request for review or remand the proceeding to the CCB for reconsideration of the issues specified in the remand and for the issuance of an amended final determination.[55] With the exception of a procedure thereafter for confirming, vacating, or modifying the CCB's determination in federal district court[56] (similar to an arbitration award under the Federal Arbitration Act[57]), there are no further merits-based appeals or reviews of the CCB's determination.

II. Present Experience Under the CCB

The cumulative experience of the CCB over the first two years and three months of its operations suggests that it has had a positive impact on the resolution of small-value copyright claims. During the period June 2022 through

47. *See* 17 U.S.C. § 1506(t)(1)(B).
48. *See id.* § 1506(t)(1)(C).
49. *See id.* § 1506(s).
50. *See id.* § 1506(a)(2).
51. *Id.*
52. *Id.* §1506(w).
53. *See id.*; *see also* 37 C.F.R. § 230.
54. *See* 17 U.S.C. § 1506(x).
55. *See id.*; *see also* 37 C.F.R. § 231.
56. *See* 17 U.S.C. § 1508.
57. *See* 9 U.S.C. §§ 9–11.

September 2024, a total of 989 cases were filed with the CCB, with 54 percent of them being placed on a standard track with a damages cap of $30,000, and the other 46 percent of them comprising smaller claims with a damages cap of $5,000.[58] Moreover, 63 percent of those cases involved self-represented individuals and 16 percent involved an in-house or authorized company representative. Only 21 percent were represented by outside counsel.[59]

The CCB dismissed 391 of these cases in this time period during the Compliance Review stage.[60] But it also issued 23 final determinations, the first of which was on February 28, 2023.[61] That case, which had been referred to the CCB by the U.S. District Court for the Northern District of California two months before the Board officially began accepting cases,[62] was resolved by the CCB in just eight months—a far cry from the median length of 27 months from filing to trial in federal court (although there was no compliance review or opt-out period in that case, and the parties had already engaged in discovery). The very next final determination issued by the CCB took just over one year to resolve—again, a time period much shorter than the median time for a federal court action.[63]

Although parties to a CCB proceeding are not required to report any settlement of a pending dispute, settlements were reported to the CCB during this same time period in 79 of the cases, and another 82 were voluntarily withdrawn, without any indication of settlement status.[64]

Conclusion

Essentially, a CCB proceeding is a small claims arbitration process for lower dollar-value copyright claims. As a form of alternative dispute resolution, it utilizes decision makers with subject matter expertise, and embraces the

58. *See* Key Statistics, *supra* note 36, at 1. The CCB also offers a more streamlined "smaller claims" track for cases with somewhat different rules where only $5,000 or less is at stake. *See* CCB Handbook, *supra* note 18, ch. 4.

59. *See* Key Statistics, *supra* note 36, at 1.

60. *See id.* at 2.

61. *See id.* All of the CCB's final determinations are available on its website at https://dockets.ccb.gov/search/documents?search=&docTypeGroup=type%3A19&partyName=&startDate=&endDate=&columns=docket&columns=id&columns=documentTitle&columns=documentType&columns=parties&columns=submittedDate (last visited Mar. 23, 2025).

62. *See generally* Oppenheimer v. Prutton, No. 22-CCB-0045 (C.C.B. Feb. 28, 2023), https://dockets.ccb.gov/document/download/2220 (last visited Mar. 23, 2025).

63. *See generally* Hursey v. Lavaca LLC, No. 22-CCB-0056 (C.C.B. Aug. 24, 2023), https://dockets.ccb.gov/document/download/4770 (last visited Mar. 23, 2025).

64. *See* Key Statistics, *supra* note 36, at 2.

expeditious and cost-effective hallmarks of arbitration, while ensuring a measure of fairness and due process. Although it remains to be seen how the CCB will fare in the years to come, the experience to date has been encouraging, and copyright owners should generally welcome the advent of this new forum for resolving small-value copyright claims in the face of the delays and expense currently being experienced through the federal court system.

CHAPTER 12

Mastering the Use of a Special Master[1] in Intellectual Property Litigation

Gale R. ("Pete") Peterson[2]

When a patent infringement case is of monstrous scale, able parties gear up to meet the challenge. District judges should consider doing the same. One option is a patent special master: an experienced litigator who can supplement the regular court staff for a particularly demanding case. The parties fund this attorney, who ideally should have the savvy and work ethic to help a beleaguered district judge pacify an unruly beast. The rubric of "special master" is a means to this end. Judges have an undoubted power to seek consent for such special master proposals, and parties commonly go along with bench suggestions about special masters. The patent special master idea thus is promising and practical. In the right case, it is worth a try.

—Judge John Shepard Wiley, Jr.[3]

The same can be said about complex copyright, trade secret, and trademark cases.

1. There have been recent efforts, principally by the Academy of Court Appointed Masters (renamed Academy of Court-Appointed Neutrals (ACAN)) to replace the term "special master" (or "master") with "court-appointed neutral" to reflect the potentially broad and varying scope of duties that may be delegated to that position. The term "special master" or "master" will continue to be used here because that term currently remains the more widely used term.

2. This chapter was originally authored by Don W. Martens, one of the named partners of Knobbe Martens Olson and Bear, for the First Edition of this book. The current chapter is a derivative work of that chapter and the subsequent chapter from the Second Edition of this book, authored by Don Martens and Pete Peterson.

3. John Shepard Wiley, Jr., *Taming Patent: Six Steps for Surviving Scary Patent Cases*, 50 UCLA L. Rev. 1413, 1473 (2003) (footnote omitted).

Introduction[4]

A special master is a private person appointed by the court to assist in handling some aspect of a lawsuit. The master is a surrogate of the court. Unlike other forms of alternative dispute resolution (ADR), using a master is not an alternative to the judicial process, but provides an alternative *within* the judicial process that is calculated to gain an expedited determination with the help of an expert in the applicable issues. A special master differs from a court-appointed expert under Federal Rule of Evidence 706. A Rule 706 expert advises the court, often privately in chambers, on facts within his or her expertise and may be deposed and called to testify before a jury by the court or the parties.

Rule 53 of the Federal Rules of Civil Procedure[5] provides for the appointment of a master.[6] That rule refers to a special master simply as a "master" so the same term is used here. Also, sometimes, various labels have been used to describe a master in terms of his or her specific duties (e.g., *trial master, discovery master, pretrial master,* and *post-trial master*).[7] The term "master" will be used in this chapter to generally cover an individual appointed pursuant to Rule 53 regardless of the tasks referred to the master by the appointing court.

The court's order appointing a master must, inter alia, state the master's duties, including "any investigation or enforcement duties, and any limits on the master's authority."[8] Generally a master reviews briefs and evidence, holds hearings (which may include evidentiary hearings), and submits a written report to the court.[9] In essence, that *report* is the master's response to the court on the matters assigned in the court's order.

The master's report may or may not also include a *recommendation*, namely, the master's recommendation for how the court should rule on the matters assigned to the master in the appointing order. In intellectual property (IP) cases, especially patent infringement cases, although there is no general rule, courts typically request both a report and a recommendation, thus entitled "Report and Recommendation Regarding [matter(s) referred by the court]" (Report and Recommendation).

Usually, the master in an IP case is an experienced IP attorney who is quite familiar with the referenced issues. Because IP litigation often is quite

---

4. See Glossary for definition of frequently used terms.

5. References to the various sections of Rule 53 of the Federal Rules of Civil Procedure in this chapter will be "Rule 53 _."

6. Although "masters" may also be appointed under various state court rules or statutes, those are beyond the scope of this chapter.

7. *See* FED. R. CIV. P. 53, Advisory Comm. Notes (2003 amendment).

8. FED. R. CIV. P. 53(b)(2)(A).

9. *See id.* 53(e).

complex in substance and form and court dockets are full, courts, at least in some jurisdictions, have been increasingly inclined to appoint masters in IP cases, especially patent infringement cases.[10]

Masters are used in all types of IP litigation for complex and time-consuming pretrial or post-trial issues. A study by the Federal Judicial Center concluded that masters are used much more often in patent cases than in criminal and civil cases generally.[11] Although masters are used in patent infringement cases for many purposes, as discussed in more detail later, their most common use in those cases is for *Markman*[12] claim construction rulings and related summary judgment motions on the infringement issues.

Following the U.S. Supreme Court's decision in *Markman*, the U.S. Court of Appeals for the Federal Circuit decided *Cybor Corp. v. FAS Technologies, Inc.*, holding that, as a purely legal issue, patent claim construction is subject to de novo review on appeal (despite that such construction may involve factual evidentiary findings).[13] That generally continues to be the rule (but see discussion of *Teva Pharmaceuticals USA Inc. v. Sandoz, Inc.* later in this chapter). Thus, district courts may spend countless hours reviewing briefs and in hearings, including evidentiary hearings and technology tutorials, en route to issuing a claim construction order only to have it overturned by the Federal Circuit.

Also, the Federal Circuit has historically refused to grant interlocutory appeals of a district court's claim construction orders. Thus, cases typically proceeded through trial (which may include a jury trial) and final judgment. Because claim construction is frequently decisive on the issue

---

10. *See generally* Neil A. Smith, *Complex Patent Suits: The Use of Special Masters for Claim Construction*, LANDSLIDE, Sept./Oct. 2009, at 36, https://www.sheppardmullin.com/media/publication/831_Neil%20Smith%20-%20The%20Use%20of%20Special%20Masters%20for%20Claim%20Construction.pdf.

11. *See* JAY P. KESAN & GWENDOLYN G. BALL, FEDERAL JUDICIAL CENTER, A STUDY OF THE ROLE AND IMPACT OF SPECIAL MASTERS IN PATENT CASES 2–3 (2009), https://papers.ssrn.com/sol3/papers.cfm?abstract_id=1372366 (last visited Mar. 23, 2025); *see also* David G. Oberdick, *Special Masters in Western District of Pennsylvania Help Expedite Patent Cases*, MERITAS IP NEWSL. (Apr. 2014), https://docs.meritas.org/EmailFiles/global_ip/april-2014-david-oberdick.htm ("To help accelerate the judicial process, many courts in the Western District of Pennsylvania are using special masters to help judges understand and address technical or scientific complexities in each case. This process, and the examples discussed below, can have application to other courts as well."); George C. Hanks, Jr., *Searching from Within: The Role of Magistrate Judges in Federal Multi-District Litigation*, 99 JUDICATURE 46 (2015) (discussing results of a study on the use of federal magistrate judges versus special masters in multidistrict litigation cases).

12. *See* Markman v. Westview Instruments, Inc., 517 U.S. 370 (1996) and the Glossary definition.

13. *See* 138 F.3d 1448 (Fed. Cir. 1998) (en banc).

of infringement (and sometimes on the issue of validity), when the Federal Circuit reviews claim construction de novo on appeal, with no deference to the trial court, the result is a high reversal rate on appeal—and necessitates further demands on a district court's time after remand, which could include a new trial—with the associated additional expense for the parties and the additional time commitment by the district court.

That de novo review and high reversal rate led former Chief District Judge James F. Holderman to write:

> Something has to change when your boss, upon reviewing your work, continues to tell you year after year that you are doing your job incorrectly about one-third to one-half the time, and your customers continue to tell you their costs are too high. That is the predicament in which we United States district court judges have collectively found ourselves over the past decade when presiding over patent litigation.[14]

Judge Holderman recommended the increased use of masters:

> To benefit fully from the guidance the Federal Circuit will be providing us in its precedential opinions as to the patent law and procedure, I believe we district judges should increase our use of specialized advisors, such as special masters, to assist us in better understanding the technology involved in the specific patent cases before us. A special master is generally a court-appointed attorney or professor authorized under our Federal Rule of Civil Procedure 53 to assist judges in various pretrial proceedings, such as discovery, settlement, recommendations for findings of law and fact, the formulation of remedies, or the calculation of damages.[15]

Judge Holderman continued:

> The premise behind a district judge's designation of a special master to assist the judge with claim construction or other tasks in patent litigation is to delegate to an individual with a better technical background an otherwise judicial task and obtain a recommendation from that person that can be evaluated by the parties and the judge before the judge decides to accept or reject the special master's recommendation. The special masters selected for such tasks would have technical expertise that would assist us district judges, who

---

14. James F. Holderman & Halley Guren, *The Patent Litigation Predicament in the Unites States*, 2007 J. L. Tech. & Pol'y 1 (2007), https://illinoisjltp.com/file/101/02-24-08_Holderman_AHW_FINAL.pdf.

15. *Id.* at 117.

> typically do not have the extensive background that is necessary to address a particular patent. Employing the expertise of special masters more than we district judges do at the present time would help us to be better informed when making our claim language determinations and, hopefully, to lower the reversal rate. For example, Judge John T. Ward [sic T. John Ward] in the United States District Court of the Eastern District of Texas, who has helped to make the Eastern District of Texas one of the busiest federal districts for patent litigation filings, in part due to the enactment of the Eastern District of Texas's local patent rules, appoints technical advisors to provide recommendations as to claim construction. More of us district judges could follow Judge Ward's lead and appoint special masters or technical advisors to assist us in evaluating the issues raised by the technological advances of patents-in-suit before us.[16]

In 2015, the Supreme Court decided *Teva Pharmaceuticals USA Inc. v. Sandoz, Inc.*, in which the Court reversed the Federal Circuit's across-the-board de novo review standard for claim construction.[17] The Supreme Court held that, when a district court decides claim construction solely on the *intrinsic record*, namely, the written record associated with the prosecution and issuance of a patent, the review standard is de novo. However, if the district court relies on *extrinsic evidence*, for example expert testimony introduced via declarations or evidentiary hearings, the Federal Circuit must review the district court's factual findings under the clear error standard of Rule 52.

Although the foregoing illustrates the use of masters for claim construction in patent infringement litigation, the use of masters in IP cases generally can be for such varied purposes as resolving discovery disputes, determining damages, enforcing orders, and occasionally conducting nonjury trials in patent, copyright, trademark, and trade secret cases. For example, in *JCW Investments, Inc. v. Novelty, Inc.*, a case involving alleged copyright infringement, trademark infringement, and unfair competition claims, the district court appointed a master to resolve a dispute regarding an award of attorneys' fees.[18] Masters may also be used to assist the court in ruling on admissibility of expert testimony under *Daubert*.[19] Masters may further be used in resolving electronic discovery, or e-discovery, disputes. For example, the Western District of Pennsylvania maintains a list of approved *electronic*

16. *Id.* at 117–18. See discussion in Section I.B contrasting technical advisors and special masters.
17. 135 S. Ct. 831 (2015).
18. *See* 482 F.3d 910 (7th Cir. 2007).
19. *See* Daubert v. Merrell Dow Pharms., Inc., 509 U.S. 579 (1993).

discovery special masters who may be appointed to resolve disputes regarding *electronically stored information*.[20] Any complex or time-consuming issue may be a candidate for a master.

This chapter describes strategies and practice pointers in using masters in IP cases. It not only discusses the nuts and bolts of this practice but also points out advantages and disadvantages of using a master. Section I discusses the appointment and use of a master in general, and Section II discusses the use of discovery masters. Both are applicable to all types of IP cases, as well as other cases. Section III.A discusses the use of a master in patent cases for claim construction. The remainder of Section III discusses the use of masters for other patent issues. Section IV is specific to copyright cases; Section V addresses trademark cases; and Section VI focuses on trade secret cases.

The reader with a particular case in mind for the use of a master should read Section I and then turn to the following applicable sections.

I. Appointing and Using a Master in IP Cases

Rule 53, Masters, provides, in part:

> (a) Appointment
>
> (1) *Scope*. Unless a statute provides otherwise, a court may appoint a master only to:
>
> (A) perform duties consented to by the parties;
>
> (B) hold trial proceedings and make or recommend findings of fact on issues to be decided without a jury if appointment is warranted by:
>
> (i) some exceptional condition; or
>
> (ii) the need to perform an accounting or resolve a difficult computation of damages; or
>
> (C) address pretrial and posttrial matters that cannot be effectively and timely addressed by an available district judge or magistrate judge of the district.
>
> (2) *Disqualification*. A master must not have a relationship to the parties, attorneys, action, or court that would require disqualification of a judge under 28 U.S.C. § 455, unless the parties, with the court's approval, consent to the appointment after the master discloses any potential grounds for disqualification.

---

20. *See Electronic Discovery Information*, U.S. Dist. Ct. W. Dist. Pa., https://www.pawd.uscourts.gov/electronic-discovery-information (last visited Mar. 23, 2025); *Special Masters*, U.S. Dist. Ct. W. Dist. Pa., https://www.pawd.uscourts.gov/special-masters (last visited Mar. 23, 2025); *see also* Craig Ball, E-Discovery: A Special Master's Perspective (2010), http://www.craigball.com/EDD_SM_PERSP.pdf.

(3) *Possible Expense or Delay*. In appointing a master, the court must consider the fairness of imposing the likely expenses on the parties and must protect against unreasonable expense or delay.[21]

In addition to Rule 53, the website for the Academy of Court-Appointed Neutrals (ACAN) includes, among other resources, a "benchbook" entitled *Appointing Special Masters and Other Judicial Adjuncts: A Benchbook for Judges and Lawyers*.[22] That benchbook includes examples of various roles masters/judicial adjuncts can serve, requirements for appointment orders, ethical and other concerns, a discussion of Rule 53, a list of state court rules governing appointment of masters, a sampling of cases in both federal and state courts in which masters were appointed, and extensive appendices, including a checklist of items to include in appointment orders, sample appointment orders, and a list of literature discussing the use of masters.

A. Deciding to Appoint a Master

Sometimes the judge may raise the subject of appointing a master; sometimes the parties suggest it. However, even when the parties all agree that a master would be useful, the court retains unfettered discretion to decide whether a master should be appointed.

Before appointing a master, the court must give the parties notice and an opportunity to be heard.[23] Appointment of a master for pretrial or post-trial matters requires consent of the parties, unless the court finds that a master is required to address matters "that cannot be effectively and timely addressed by an available district judge or magistrate judge of the district."[24] The Advisory Committee Notes to Rule 53 (2003 Amendment) comment that a pretrial master should be appointed "only when the need is clear." However, the committee notes also advise that "[t]he court's responsibility to interpret patent claims as a matter of law, for example, may be greatly assisted by appointing a master who has expert knowledge of the field in which the patent operates."[25]

Many judges understandably are reluctant to appoint a master without consent of all parties. Thus, the parties usually, but not always, have the

---

21. Fed. R. Civ. P. 53(a).
22. *See* ACAN, Appointing Neutrals Handbook (2024), https://www.courtappointedneutrals.org/benchbook/appointing-neutrals-handbook/ (last visited Mar. 23, 2025).
23. *See* Fed. R. Civ. P. 53(b)(1).
24. *Id.* 53(a)(1)(A), (C).
25. *Id.*

ability to control the decision as to whether a master will be appointed. There are many reasons parties may want to request or consent to the appointment of a master, including the following:

- The master usually is more experienced in the relevant issues than the judge, particularly in IP cases.
- The parties usually are involved in selecting the master, while selecting the judge is beyond their control.
- The parties have much greater influence over when hearings will be held by a master, how long they will last, and what procedures will govern the hearings, including whether live testimony will be permitted.
- The appointing order can specify the date by which a decision must be made, which is often faster than the time a judge would render a decision.
- A master is able to devote more time to analyzing complex and heavily contested issues than the court with its busy calendar.
- A master usually is better able to handle ongoing discovery disputes on an expedited basis than the court or magistrate judge.
- If the issue involves technology, an experienced IP lawyer may be more likely to reach a correct decision and be upheld on appeal.

The advantages of using a master in complex litigation have been recognized as follows:

> Masters can devote blocks of time to an event which judges do not have available. They can meet and confer with lawyers and parties regarding issues in ways judges cannot. They may be the only available judicial specialist to help an overloaded and unavailable court staff. They can add a balanced perspective for judges from the world of practice and business and filter in an unbiased way what lawyers submit and parties allege. They can, in short, assist judges in achieving civil justice.[26]

A report to the Federal Judicial Center concluded that masters were almost uniformly found to be effective by those using them:

> Almost all of the judges and attorneys told us that the special masters were effective. Moreover, all judges and almost all attorneys thought that the benefits of appointing the masters outweighed any

26. Mark A. Fellows & Roger S. Haydock, *Federal Court Special Masters: A Vital Resource in the Era of Complex Litigation*, 31 Wm. Mitchell L. Rev. 1269, 1271 (2005); *but see* Hanks, *supra* note 10 (advocating use of federal magistrate judges in complex litigation).

> drawbacks and said they would, with the benefit of hindsight, still support the appointments. Attorneys said this regardless of how the special masters' appointments initially came about, and even regardless of whether the masters' involvement benefited their clients. Likewise, almost all special masters we interviewed thought that their appointments were warranted and would not change any terms of their appointments.[27]

Another frequently overlooked benefit to using a master, especially for claim construction and summary judgment proceedings in patent infringement cases, is the ability to have two bites, and possibly three bites, at the apple. Under Rule 53(e), the master prepares a report for the court pursuant to the appointing order. As noted earlier in this chapter, that report may or may not include a recommendation from the master regarding how the court should rule on the assigned matters. However, particularly in patent infringement litigation, a master is typically required by an appointment order to prepare a Report and Recommendation for the court. The parties then have 21 days (which may be shortened by the court) in which to file objections to it.[28] The district court then reviews the master's Report and Recommendation along with the parties' objections. Thus, when a master is used, parties have at least two bites—a first bite in proceedings before the master, which may include a multiday evidentiary hearing,[29] and a second bite in filing objections to the master's Report and Recommendation. Objections to the master's legal conclusions are reviewed de novo.[30] Objections to findings of

---

27. Thomas E. Willging et al., Federal Judicial Center, Special Masters' Incidence and Activity: Report to the Judicial Conference's Advisory Committee on Civil Rules and Its Subcommittee on Special Masters (2000) [hereinafter Willging Report], http://www.uscourts.gov/sites/dcfault/files/specmast.pdf.

28. *See* Fed. R. Civ. P. 53(f)(2).

29. As noted earlier, the resolution of disputes relating to the meaning of terms and phrases in patent claims may be decisive on the issue of infringement and possibly on validity. Under *Markman*, claim construction is a question for the court, rather than a jury. Further, as noted earlier in this chapter, after the Supreme Court's decision in *Teva Pharmaceuticals USA Inc. v. Sandoz, Inc.*, there may be some incentive for district courts to hold evidentiary hearings or otherwise consider evidence beyond the text of the patent and its prosecution history. District court dockets frequently limit a court's ability to schedule more than one-half or a full day to a claim construction hearing whereas a master may have the ability to schedule one to three (or more) days for an evidentiary hearing. That may be coupled with a technology tutorial. Although the master typically presides at the evidentiary hearing, it is not unusual for the judge of the appointing court and/or the judge's law clerk to attend all or part of the hearing.

30. *See* Fed. R. Civ. P. 53(f)(4).

fact are also reviewed de novo, unless the parties otherwise stipulate and the court agrees.[31] Procedural matters are reviewed for an abuse of discretion.[32]

There is also a potential for three bites if the master issues a draft Report and Recommendation. Rule 53 does not expressly include a provision for a draft Report and Recommendation. However, neither Rule 53 nor most court appointment orders precludes issuance of such a draft. Also, the Advisory Committee Notes to Rule 53 (2003 Amendment) advise that, "[b]efore formally making an order, report, or recommendations, a master may find it helpful to circulate a draft to the parties for review and comment. The usefulness of this practice depends on the nature of the master's proposed action."[33] Before issuing such a draft, some masters believe it to be better practice to ask the parties at the conclusion of the claim construction hearing whether they would like to receive such a draft. If the parties agree, the master may issue a draft Report and Recommendation for the parties' comments. After considering the parties' comments, the master will then issue a final Report and Recommendation.[34]

To the extent that some may view the district court's subsequent review of a master's Report and Recommendation on claim construction to be a rubber stamp, from experience, that has not been the result. Rule 53, as noted, provides for de novo review of the master's Report and Recommendation, and experience shows that the reviewing court routinely conducts such a de novo review. Accordingly, the parties' arguments vis-à-vis claim construction may be fully vetted before the district court, not only once, but at least twice, and possible three or four times. If the master and court do not accept a party's claim construction arguments after such thorough vetting, and if that construction is decisive on infringement and/or validity, substantial expenses associated with trial (and possibly retrial) can be avoided by consenting to entry of judgment and taking an appeal.

Thus, a qualified master is likely to provide many advantages for both the parties and the court. However, a master certainly is not appropriate for all IP cases. Some of the reasons parties may not want to request or consent to the appointment of a master include:

- There is the added cost of the master's fees, which typically are at the hourly rate of an experienced attorney (in comparison with the legal fees in a complex IP case, the costs of a master are frequently minor).

---

31. *See id.* 53(f)(3).
32. *See id.* 53(f)(5).
33. Fed. R. Civ. P. 53(b), Advisory Comm. Notes (2003 amendment).
34. Even a fourth bite is theoretically possible through a motion for reconsideration.

- The issues in the case are not too complex or time-consuming for the court or a magistrate judge to handle well.
- The particular generalist judge assigned to the case is more likely to be favorable to one party's side of the case than a specialized master.
- The parties may want to use pretrial proceedings to educate the judge about their case, rather than passing a portion off to a master who will not be trying the case (this can backfire if the judge simply becomes frustrated with the complexities of the portion that could have been referred to a master).
- Depending upon the judge's docket and reputation for timeliness, there may be time lost by the process of selecting a master, getting him or her up to speed, preparation of a thorough master's report, and the court hearing objections to the report.

However, the study of the use of masters conducted for the Federal Judicial Center found that the benefits uniformly outweighed the disadvantages:

> The drawback to appointing a master cited most often by judges, masters, and attorneys was the additional cost to the parties. In addition, several attorneys thought the appointment slowed the case down or, contrary to their expectations, did not speed up resolution. Yet, none of our interviewees found that these drawbacks outweighed the benefits in a given case.[35]

The parties may raise the option of a master, but often the court raises it sua sponte during a status conference or a hearing on another subject. Although the court may wish for expeditious, even on-the-spot, consideration by counsel, requesting time to consider the appointment with the parties, as well as to identify candidates, usually is prudent.

If the court says "I need help" and the parties prefer not to use a master, they may be able to convince the court that, in this case, a magistrate judge would be more appropriate for any of the reasons listed previously.

In complex IP cases, using a well-qualified master provides the opportunity for expert evaluation of complex issues while still leaving for the judge or jury the ultimate decision in the case. Unlike other ADR procedures, the right to appeal is preserved. Thus, using a master can be an excellent and efficient option.

---

35. Willging Report, *supra* note 27, at 9.

B. Variations on Rule 53 Masters

The Eastern District of Texas has historically used a variation on the practice of appointing a Rule 53 master. The U.S. Court of Customs and Patent Appeals (CCPA), one of the two predecessor courts to the Federal Circuit (the other being the U.S. Court of Claims) employed individuals having both technical and legal backgrounds as "technical advisors" to the judges. The role entailed providing the employing judge with the services of a traditional law clerk, as well as one having a technical background—thus the title "technical advisor," as opposed to law clerk.

The Eastern District of Texas began hearing a large number of patent cases in the 1990s for reasons beyond the scope of this chapter. As a consequence, some judges began appointing experienced IP practitioners as technical advisors to the court to function in much the same manner as technical advisors had functioned before the CCPA. Those appointments have been made within the inherent discretion of the court.

Typically, the appointment of a technical advisor has been subject to the advice and consent of the parties. The duties assigned to that person vary by the case, and the appointing chambers. However, unlike an appointment of a master under Rule 53, a technical advisor in the Eastern District of Texas does not issue a Report and Recommendation, but, rather, consults with the court on whatever matters and duties are assigned by the court.

C. Selecting the Master

Rule 53(b)(1) specifically provides that the parties may suggest candidates for appointment as the master. The Advisory Committee Notes to Rule 53 (2003 Amendment) confirm that "[o]ften it will be useful to engage the parties in the process of identifying the master, inviting nominations, and reviewing potential candidates."[36] Sometimes the parties are able to agree on a single candidate to submit to the court for approval. Other times each side provides one or more names to the court, and the court then selects a master from the list. And sometimes, to the chagrin of the parties, the court selects a master not recommended by either party, but known to the court. Involvement by counsel in one way or the other can be important, as the judge may have limited knowledge of qualified available candidates and may appoint a favorite local attorney with no expertise on the issues.

Judge Wiley correctly notes in his article that the pool of candidates to serve as a special master is national. "E-mailed messages and documents

36. FED. R. CIV. P. 53(b), Advisory Comm. Notes (2003 amendment).

can reduce the need for travel, and the cost and inconvenience of travel may be slight anyway compared to the scale of a truly large patent fight."[37]

In addition, the COVID-19 pandemic of 2020–2023 significantly increased the use of remote hearings by courts through the use of various commercially available remote meeting platform technologies. Remote hearings may also be provided by various court reporting and other companies. Although telephonic hearings have been used by courts for years, remote hearings (with the ability for both video and audio communication, the presentation of exhibits and documents "on-screen," and "breakout rooms" for private conversations), in conjunction with email communications, have expanded the ability of courts to hold not only "argument hearings" on motions and the like, but also to conduct evidentiary hearings with witnesses and exhibits (including demonstrative exhibits). As a result, appointment of a master far from the forum of the dispute should not be a decisive impediment.

The names of eligible candidates can be obtained by searching for cases where a master has been used. The name of the master may not appear in the published decision, but it may be obtained from the court file using an available database. Assuming the master's previous report is not under seal, the report, objections, and the court's action can all be reviewed. Counsel involved in the prior case may be consulted about the master. Another source of masters may be attorneys who have served as arbitrators in IP cases. Parties may find such individuals by searching publicly available rosters, on the internet, and by word of mouth, for example, from colleagues in professional organizations.

Further sources of potential candidates are (1) recommendations from local counsel in the forum venue based on prior cases (which frequently provide a primary source of potential candidates, as well as information regarding how potential masters have performed in prior cases, including whether any have exhibited leanings for the plaintiff or defendant); (2) a search of LexisNexis or Westlaw (or alternative sources such as Fastcase or Google Scholar) for published Reports and Recommendations by the prospective master or cases in which the master is identified by name (which may also give some insight to a particular prospective master's *view* on various issues); (3) the website for the ACAN (https://www.courtappointedneutrals.org/); and (4) websites for organizations providing neutral services, such as the American Arbitration Association, the International Institute for Conflict Prevention & Resolution (CPR), and FedArb, or providing a vetted list of neutrals (e.g., Silicon Valley Arbitration & Mediation Center).

37. Wiley, *supra* note 3, at 1463.

If the parties wish to avoid the master knowing which party nominated him or her, they may jointly contact prospective masters to obtain information about their background and availability, with counsel for all parties on the telephone or by email from one counsel on behalf of everyone.

Rule 53(a)(2), entitled "Disqualification," provides that "[a] master must not have a relationship to the parties, attorneys, action, or court that would require disqualification of a judge under 28 U.S.C. § 455, unless the parties, with the court's approval, consent to the appointment after the master discloses any potential grounds for disqualification." Thus, before the parties select a candidate, or the court appoints a candidate, as the master, the candidate must conduct a conflict check and determine whether any grounds for disqualification under 28 U.S.C. § 455 exist. If any potential grounds for disqualification exist, the potential master is obligated to inform the parties and the court. Depending on the potential candidate's disclosure, the grounds for disqualification may—or may not—be waived by the parties.

Assuming that the potential master candidate has not disclosed any disqualifying events, or, to the extent permitted, the parties have waived the same, and the master files a Rule 53 affidavit to that effect, the court may issue an order pursuant to Rule 53(b) appointing the master.

Note that, if a court makes an appointment of an adjunct (neutral) under the court's inherent authority, rather than pursuant to Rule 53 (for example, the Eastern District of Texas's appointment of "technical advisors"), a formal affidavit under 28 U.S.C. § 455 may not be strictly required (although the court may require one). Nevertheless, it is considered "best practice" that any potential "neutral" observe all applicable ethical rules and requirements, including, but not necessarily limited to, those of § 455.

Generally, in selecting a proposed master, the parties should seek relevant experience as an IP attorney, knowledge of, or aptitude for, the specific subject matter, experience as a special master or arbitrator, a judicial temperament, a reputation for integrity, and knowledge of the relevant area of IP law.

D. What Belongs in the Order of Appointment?

Rule 53(b)(2) specifies in detail the required contents of the order appointing a master. Generally, the court will be receptive to the parties preparing a proposed order. A sample order is found in the appendix to this chapter. The Federal Rules of Civil Procedure do not specify the effect of an inadequacy in the appointing order. If the order does not satisfy all of the requirements of Rule 53(b)(2), or is otherwise ambiguous or incomplete, either party, or both, may object or seek clarification. Discussed here are some key elements of Rule 53(b)(2), but the rule should be reviewed carefully each time counsel drafts or receives an order.

1. Statement of Reasonable Diligence

The appointing order must direct the master to proceed with all reasonable diligence.[38] This normally is done by a simple statement to that effect. It is also preferable for the order to set a date by which the master's Report and Recommendation must be filed. See Appendix at 2.

2. Master's Duties

The order must specify the master's duties.[39] The Advisory Committee Notes to Rule 53 (2003 Amendment) contemplate a "precise designation of the master's duties." Ideally the court's order strikes a balance between useful generality and detail. On the one hand, a very general statement of the duties provides the master with the flexibility to adjust as the matter evolves. This can result in efficiencies and expedite the proceeding. On the other hand, tightly defining the master's duties could avoid a runaway master.

How the order articulates the master's duties should depend upon the nature of the project and counsel's confidence in the master. If the master has a known history of efficiently handling prior master assignments, the flexibility of the general statement of duties makes sense. Otherwise, a more detailed statement may be in order. The order in the appendix to this chapter exemplifies a balanced approach to the amount of detail by

- specifically directing the master to construe specified claims in an identified patent;[40]
- giving the master discretion to hold an oral *Markman* hearing (which could include an evidentiary hearing, if the parties request one, and the court does not preclude it[41]; alternatively, claim construction can be decided on the briefs alone or through a telephone conference (or remote) hearing);
- directing the master to confer jointly with the parties within seven days for setting the process and schedule for claim construction and arranging such other steps as necessary;[42] and
- specifically limiting filings to those already made unless the master and the parties agree otherwise.[43]

---

38. *See* Fed. R. Civ. P. 53(b)(2).
39. *See id.* 53(b)(2)(A).
40. *See* app. at 1.
41. *Id.* at 2.
42. *Id.*
43. *Id.*

The order also must specify any special limits on the master's authority.[44] Absent any contrary direction in the order, pursuant to Rule 53(c)(1), the master may

- regulate all proceedings;
- take all appropriate measures to perform the assigned duties fairly and efficiently; and
- if conducting an evidentiary hearing, exercise the appointing court's power to compel, take, and record evidence.

Those authorizations generally are appropriate in IP cases and seldom need to be altered. The sample order appended to this chapter is silent on this, so it does not establish any alterations.

3. Sanctions

Rule 53(c)(2) grants the master authority to impose on a party any non-contempt sanction provided by Rule 37 or 45. Additionally, a master may recommend to the court a contempt sanction against a party and sanctions against a nonparty. Often the parties prefer to leave sanctioning to the judge and, in the order, propose to limit the master to recommending sanctions. However, if the master's duties include resolving discovery disputes, granting the master authority to impose sanctions may expedite the discovery process.

4. Ex Parte Communications

The order of appointment must specify whether ex parte communications between the master and the court or a party will be permitted.[45] Substantive ex parte communications between the master and a party are generally inappropriate both before and after appointment. Experience shows that the order nearly always states this.

Some judges may prefer to use the master as a consultant, discussing various aspects of the case with the master ex parte. Such ex parte communications can detract from the quasi-judicial nature of the appointment. Such communications sometimes raise anxieties among counsel about what is going on behind closed doors. Requiring the master to act independently of the judge and submit a written report removes much of the mystery and concern, which can otherwise arise.

As noted previously in this chapter, the Eastern District of Texas has historically appointed technical advisors instead of Rule 53 masters. Because

44. Fed. R. Civ. P. 53(b)(2)(A).
45. *See id.* 53(b)(2)(B); *see also* app. at 2.

the technical advisor is functioning in a capacity similar to that of a law clerk, there is typically frequent ex parte contact between that person and the court.

5. Master's Record

The order must specify the nature of the materials (e.g., briefs and exhibits) to be preserved from the master assignment and filed with the court.[46] Normally, this can be broadly stated to require the making and filing of a complete record of all evidence considered by the master in making findings or recommendations.[47] Of course, any evidence containing confidential information should be filed under seal if a protective order requiring that is in place. As a result, sometimes the master's Report and Recommendation must likewise be filed under seal. However, many courts require the parties to identify what portion or portions of the Report and Recommendation contain confidential information, which may be thereafter redacted. A redacted version of the Report and Recommendation may then be publicly filed with the court.

6. Master's Report

Although Rule 53(b)(2) does not specifically mention the master's report among the items that must be included in the appointing order, as noted, the report may, or may not, include recommendations. The Advisory Committee Notes to Rule 53 (2003 Amendment) explain that, "[i]n some circumstances a master may be appointed under Rule 53(a)(1)(A) or (C) to take evidence and report without recommendations."[48] Accordingly, it is preferable if the appointing order specifies whether the master should include recommendations in addition to a report.

7. Standard of Review

Rule 53(b)(2)(D) provides that the appointing order must specify the standard of review of the master's orders, findings, and recommendations. Rule 53(f)(3) governs review of a master's factual findings. Rule 53(f)(4) governs review of a master's legal conclusions.

---

46. *See* Fed. R. Civ. P. 53(b)(2)(C).
47. *See* app. at 2.
48. Fed. R. Civ. P. 53(b), Advisory Comm. Notes (2003 amendment).

8. Deadline for Master's Report

It is very important that the order set a deadline for the master's report.[49] One of the advantages of using a master is the ability to control the schedule. Usually, if the parties propose reasonable time limits, the court will agree, so long as the court does not perceive the time limit as unduly slowing the progress of the case. Experience shows that it is fairly typical for the court to specify that a master's Report and Recommendation is due within 30 days following the conclusion of a claim construction hearing or other event. That time period may, of course, be lengthened at the request of the master or the parties.

9. Master's Compensation

Pursuant to Rules 53(b)(2)(E) and 53(g)(1), the court must fix the basis and terms for the master's compensation and state them in the order of appointment. However, the court may change the terms and basis for a master's compensation "after giving notice and an opportunity to be heard."[50]

Some appointment orders specify that a master's statement be paid within a set amount of time (e.g., within 30 days from receipt). Other appointment orders do not impose a time limit.

The compensation can be calculated in a variety of ways. For example, it may be at an hourly or daily billing rate, a fixed fee for the entire project, or a combination of an hourly rate with a maximum for the project. During the master selection process—assuming the parties are involved—the parties typically request a potential master's billing rate—whether hourly, daily, or by project. At this stage, the master likely has little information on the actual case or what duties the master will be asked to undertake. Thus, the master's compensation, at this stage, is necessarily somewhat generic.

However, following the appointment and an identification of the master's assigned duties, depending on the stage of the case, it is preferable if the master advises the parties of the estimated fees and expenses for fulfilling the court's appointment order. Some courts have included doing so within the appointment order. Even if the court does not do so, experience indicates that it is a preferable practice for the master to give the parties an estimate of the fees and expenses for complying with the court's appointment order. Although such an estimate may include a range—even perhaps a broad range to account for unforeseen circumstances—the parties should receive at least an estimate insofar as the appointment as a master should not be viewed as a carte blanche for billing. If the estimate exceeds the parties'

49. *See* Fed. R. Civ. P. 53(b)(2)(D); *see also* app. at 2.
50. *See* Fed. R. Civ. P. 53(g)(1).

expectations, then the parties should be free to recommend appointment of a different master.

Frequently, the parties split the cost.[51] However, when there are multiple parties on either side of the "v.," the court has the discretion to allocate the master's fee in a manner other than 50 percent for the plaintiff(s) and 50 percent for the defendant(s). Rule 53(g)(3) provides:

> The court must allocate payment among the parties after considering the nature and amount of the controversy, the parties' means, and the extent to which any party is more responsible than other parties for the reference to a master. An interim allocation may be amended to reflect a decision on the merits.[52]

Although it is common to bill the parties monthly and directly, without involvement of the court, that practice varies, not only among courts, but also among individual judges in the same court. The court's appointment order preferably specifies the master's billing practice. Some appointment orders permit periodic (e.g., monthly) billing to the parties directly. Other appointment orders require that bills be submitted to the court first for review and subsequent transmittal to the parties. In some instances, courts review and then send the actual statement to the parties. In other instances, courts review the bills and then issue an order to the parties to pay a certain amount to the master or technical advisor without an identification of specific services and/or expenses. Some appointment orders specify that a master delay billing until the conclusion of the appointment.

Some master's appointments may be for relatively short specific projects like claim construction, while other appointments may extend over discovery, claim construction, summary judgment motions, and other pretrial and post-trial matters. Thus, a master's appointment may extend over the course of months or even years. The underlying intent of Rule 53 is for the court to retain ultimate control over the fees and expenses incurred by a master that the parties are required to pay. No party, however, wants to be hit by a potentially huge unanticipated bill at the conclusion of the appointment. Thus, it may be prudent to keep both the court and the parties periodically informed of the amount of fees and expenses that a master has billed to a matter.[53]

---

51. *See* app. at 2.
52. Fed. R. Civ. P. 53(g)(3).
53. It may be that, if a court insists on delaying a master's billing to the end of the appointment—particularly a long one—even over the objection of the master and/or parties, a prospective master may either (1) decline to serve or (2) insist that the master's monthly statements be served on both the court and the parties so that both have a current appreciation for the fees and costs being incurred.

In sum, appointment orders should preferably require (1) the master to provide an estimate to the parties and the court of the fees and charges for performing the duties assigned by the court in the appointment order; (2) periodic (e.g., monthly) statements sent directly to the parties, with copies to the court, detailing the master's services and expenses; and (3) an order requiring payment within a set amount of time (e.g., 30–60 days), unless a party files an objection with the court. The court would retain discretion in allocating fees for responding to such an objection.

E. Preliminary Conference

If the master does not set an early preliminary conference, counsel should request one. A telephone (or remote) conference usually is adequate. Some of the topics counsel will likely want to address with the master at this preliminary conference are:

1. What is the status of the case? Are there motions pending? Have they been briefed? Are more motions anticipated?
2. Is there a schedule and procedure for briefing, including page limits and reply briefs?
3. What is the length and procedure for hearings? Will there be live testimony?
4. Will the hearing be by telephone conference or remote or face-to-face?
5. If the hearing is face-to-face, where will it take place? Frequently the appointing judge will permit use of a courtroom for major hearings. Not only is the courtroom arranged and equipped for the hearing, but it is also convenient for the judge and clerks to listen in if they choose—and they often do. A hotel or office conference room also is common and either is acceptable.
6. Will there be a transcript (no matter whether the hearing is held at the court, outside the court, or remotely)? A transcript reduces the need for the master to be distracted by taking notes and provides a record for supporting any objections to the master's report, but it is an added cost. Often, judges prefer that the parties hire the judge's regular reporter if the hearing is in the courthouse. This is something the parties need to discuss with the appointing court.
7. If the hearing is remote, the considerations change, and there are several options available:
   a. Remote hearings may be arranged—
      (1) By the court and/or appointed master—this is generally atypical but depends on the court and the appointed master.

(2) By one of the law firms involved in the case (with or without a cost-sharing arrangement with the opposing party), and with or without a court reporter (depending on whether the parties want a transcript).

(3) By an independent court reporting firm that handles all details of the remote hearing, including transcription of the same (generally, the most expensive option).

b. Remote hearings may be recorded (provided all participants agree).

(1) In general, federal courts discourage live or recorded videotaping of court proceedings (except for depositions).

(2) If the parties request a recorded remote hearing, it seems preferrable to obtain the court's approval.

F. Hearing

For face-to-face hearings, counsel jointly should make all the logistical and physical arrangements well in advance of the hearing. The needs will vary considerably from case to case and location to location. When the parties hold the hearing in a law firm or hotel conference room, the surroundings may seem informal compared with a hearing held in a courtroom. That should not fool counsel. They should be every bit as prepared as for the judge. The hearing may or may not be as formal, but it should be conducted as if it were before the judge.

Counsel should tailor their argument to the background of the master. They should not waste their time explaining well-known principles of law or practice to a master who is experienced in such matters and almost assuredly will have studied the briefs. In preparation for the hearing:

- Confirm the location.
- Confirm the physical setup, including a lectern and a witness chair if required.
- Plan to use visual aids, but ensure that the images are easily visible to the master, witnesses, if any, and opposing counsel. Test all of the equipment in the hearing room well before the hearing starts.
- Arrange for a court reporter, if appropriate.
- Prepare a physical or electronic hearing notebook for the master (depending on his or her preference), including exhibits to which counsel will refer and copies of their visual aids.
- Discuss all the procedural aspects and logistics with opposing counsel and seek approval of the master, preferably jointly, as needed well in advance of the hearing.

- Plan ahead for remote and hybrid hearings because courts have issued rules/guidelines/orders for them that are too numerous to address here, but with which must be complied. In addition, some organizations, such as the American Arbitration Association-International Centre for Dispute Resolution (AAA-ICDR) have published various suggested orders and procedures for remote hearings (AAA-ICDR Model Order and Procedures for a Virtual Hearing via Teleconference).[54]

G. Master's Report

The master must file a written report with the court and serve the report on the parties.[55] In IP litigation, it is typical that the report will include recommendations. However, as previously mentioned, that depends on the court's appointment order.

H. Preparing Objections to the Master's Report

Under Rule 53(f)(2), after the master serves his or her report, the parties have 21 days (or longer or shorter with leave of the court) in which to file objections or a motion to adopt or modify.[56] Frequently, the parties thoroughly brief their objections and the court conducts an oral hearing, but, many times, the parties' objections are heard on the briefs, without an oral hearing. This process of carefully considering objections, as the court is required to undertake under Rule 53(f), avoids the judge merely *rubber-stamping* the master and goes a long way to committing the judge to the resulting decision.[57]

In briefing objections to the court, counsel should treat the objections like an appellate brief. The briefing should clearly identify the nature of the

---

54. *See* AAA-ICDR, AAA-ICDR® Model Order and Procedures for a Virtual Hearing via Videoconference (2021), https://go.adr.org/rs/294-SFS-516/images/AAA270_AAA-ICDR%20Model%20Order%20and%20Procedures%20for%20a%20Virtual%20Hearing%20via%20Videoconference.pdf. These protocols may be revised and adopted by the parties and the master.

55. *See* Fed. R. Civ. P. 53(e).

56. For example, the district court has the power to change the 21 days to some lesser, reasonable time period, thereby addressing the frequently voiced concern about the "delay" created by the objection period along with the time period to respond and reply.

57. *See* Burlington N. R.R. Co. v. Dep't of Revenue, 934 F.2d 1064, 1072 (9th Cir. 1991) ("[T]he district court's 'rubber stamp' of the master's order is an inexcusable abdication of judicial responsibility and a violation of article III of the Constitution.").

issue being considered (e.g., factual, legal, procedural) and the standard of review as specified in Rule 53 or as modified by the appointing order. Objections should not simply make broad complaints about what the master did or did not do, but should be very specific as to the alleged error. The parties normally should brief the background and issues to the judge taking into account his or her lesser familiarity with the disputed issues and the subject matter than the master who is familiar with both. Counsel will need to provide the relevant factual background (e.g., technology, timeline, support for legal claims) so that the court can review the master's recommendation in accordance with the proper standard of review.

If the court delays unduly in acting on the master's report, the parties may want to inquire with the courtroom clerk as to the status or ask the master to follow up. The parties might also leverage the decision and reasoning embodied in the master's report to mediate the case or even to arbitrate the case.

I. Using a Trial Master

A master may be appointed, by consent of the parties, to conduct the entire trial or some portion of the trial, in either nonjury cases or in cases tried to a jury.[58]

For example, in *Eastman Kodak Co. v. AGFA-Gevaert N.V.*,[59] the master held a bench trial that resolved all the patent issues in the case, including infringement and noninfringement, patent validity, whether patent claims were enforceable, whether infringement was willful, and patent marking under 35 U.S.C. § 287. The master provided a Report and Recommendation "to the court as to how the issues of liability in this case should be resolved."[60] The district court adopted the Report and Recommendation in its entirety, explaining that the master's "analysis of the facts is so comprehensive and so complete, additional discussion of the factual issues would serve no fruitful purpose."[61]

In a sense, a master hearing the entire case is like an arbitration but with the right to appeal, first by objections to the district court judge and then to the court of appeals.

Without consent of the parties, a master cannot conduct a jury trial, but may be appointed to conduct a trial in a nonjury case if there is "some exceptional condition" or it involves an accounting or resolving a difficult computation of

58. *See* FED. R. CIV. P. 53(a)(1)(A), Advisory Comm. Notes (2003 amendment).
59. 560 F. Supp. 2d 227 (W.D.N.Y. 2008).
60. *Id.* at 234–35.
61. *Id.*

damages.[62] Complexity of the case alone is insufficient to support a referral to a trial master. In *La Buy v. Howes Leather Co.*,[63] the district court referred the trial of a nonjury antitrust action involving 87 plaintiffs to a trial master without the consent of the parties. The court's decision was based on the complexity of the case, the length of trial time expected, the congestion of the court's calendar, and "voluminous accounting which would be necessary in the event plaintiffs prevailed."[64] In affirming the Seventh Circuit's grant of a writ of mandamus to vacate the referral to a master, the U.S. Supreme Court held that the referral of the trial duties to a master "amounted to little less than an abdication of the judicial function," and, when ordered without consent of the parties, it should be the exception not the rule. The Court commented that the complexity of the case was not a viable ground for referral to a master and instead "is an impelling reason for trial before a regular, experienced trial judge."[65] Also, the Court noted that the accounting might justify a referral, but only after the court determined liability.[66]

Under the current post-2003 version of Rule 53(a)(1), "[u]nless a statute provides otherwise, a court may appoint a master only to: . . . (B) hold trial proceedings and make or recommend findings of fact on issues to be decided without a jury if appointment is warranted by: (i) some exceptional condition."[67] The Advisory Committee Notes to Rule 53 (2003 Amendment) explain:

> These limits are reflected in the provisions of subparagraph (a)(1)(B) that restrict appointments to exercise trial functions. The Supreme Court gave clear direction to this trend in *La Buy v. Howes Leather Co.*, 352 U.S. 249 (1957); earlier roots are sketched in *Los Angeles Brush Mfg. Corp. v. James*, 272 U.S. 701 (1927). As to nonjury trials, this trend has developed through elaboration of the "exceptional condition" requirement in present Rule 53(b). This phrase is retained, and will continue to have the same force as it has developed. Although the provision that a reference "shall be the exception and not the rule" is deleted, its meaning is embraced for this setting by the exceptional condition requirement.[68]

The Supreme Court's reference in *La Buy* to an "accounting" is addressed in Rule 53(a)(1)(B)(ii), namely, "the need to perform an accounting or resolve

62. *See* FED. R. CIV. P. 53(a)(1)(B).
63. 352 U.S. 249 (1957).
64. *Id.* at 259.
65. *Id.*
66. *See id.* at 256–59; *see also* Fellows & Haydock, *supra* note 26, at 1285–87.
67. FED. R. CIV. P. 53(a)(1).
68. *Id.* 53, Advisory Comm. Notes (2003 amendment).

a difficult computation of damages." The Advisory Committee Notes to Rule 53 (2003 Amendment) explain:

> Subparagraph (a)(1)(B)(ii) carries forward the approach of present Rule 53(b), which exempts from the "exceptional condition" requirement "matters of account and of difficult computation of damages." This approach is justified only as to essentially ministerial determinations that require mastery of much detailed information but that do not require extensive determinations of credibility. Evaluations of witness credibility should only be assigned to a trial master when justified by an exceptional condition.[69]

II. Using a Discovery Master

"With the emergence of ever more complex civil litigation and even more congested dockets, the need for discovery masters has simply become accepted . . . ."[70]

A. Why Use a Discovery Master?

Masters frequently oversee discovery in IP cases.[71] No matter what kind of IP is involved, courts often turn to masters where a case has complexities and there is the potential for ongoing discovery issues that need resolution. *Religious Technology Center v. Scott* involved a claim of infringement of more than 31 trademarks and other IP claims.[72] The circuit court noted that the trial judge had appointed a master for discovery and motion practice because of the complexity of the litigation, the number of parties to the litigation, the large number of motions and motions for reconsideration already characteristic of the litigation, and the need to reduce to manageable proportions what was estimated to be three months' trial time. The trial court expressed satisfaction, noting "[t]he appointment of the Special Master 4 years ago has considerably relieved the burden to this Court."[73]

---

69. *Id.*

70. Fellows & Haydock, *supra* note 26, at 1272.

71. *See* Kesan & Ball, *supra* note 11, at 17 (reporting that discovery issues were addressed by masters in 27 patent cases terminating in 2005–2006 as compared to 34 cases addressing claim construction issues and ten addressing infringement issues).

72. *See* No. 94-55781, 1996 WL 171443, at *3 (9th Cir. Apr. 11, 1996) (unpublished opinion).

73. *Id.*; *see also In re* Napster, Inc. Copyright Litig., 191 F. Supp. 2d 1087 (N.D. Cal. 2008) (referring oversight of discovery on ownership of copyright to numerous musical works).

Discovery is a very expensive part of civil litigation generally and complex IP litigation in particular. Electronic discovery issues have exacerbated the problem. Discovery disputes abound and they are often very contentious. IP discovery disputes are fact-intensive, frequently require an understanding of substantive IP law, are typically document heavy, and oftentimes include privilege and work product issues. It can be challenging for judges to evaluate in the early stages of a case the need for the disputed discovery and the burden of providing it. Judges also are sometimes frustrated by the bulk of material involved and the time it takes.

Courts often refer discovery disputes and management to magistrate judges. A magistrate judge has the advantage of no cost to the parties and usually is experienced in discovery disputes. However, a master trained in the applicable IP and having an ability to deal with complex IP facts and documents may provide an alternative with a substantial advantage in efficiency and result.

The parties often are frustrated by the time delay in resolving discovery disputes before the judge. They want a fast decision so the discovery can keep moving. A master is more likely than the judge to be able to block out, on short notice, the time required for thorough consideration of the dispute on an expedited basis, with limited briefing by the parties.

B. Using a Master to Expedite Resolution of Discovery Disputes

The practice in many district courts of requiring full briefing and a full hearing by the court for discovery disputes often results in extended delays and added expense. In contrast, often, a one- or two-page electronically filed letter brief from each side and a telephone conference hearing are sufficient for a discovery master. The whole process can be completed in a few days, if necessary. In fact, it is not uncommon for the master to permit a telephonic (or remote) hearing during a deposition to resolve disputes efficiently before the deposition ends. The master's order can be rendered orally, but the master should confirm it in some written form (e.g., email or facsimile) to the parties during the deposition or promptly thereafter.

Whatever procedures the discovery master and the parties adopt in a given case should be specified in a standing order that the master or the court enters. Furthermore, that order should be filed with the court. The details of the order should be varied to fit the case or the dispute and the desires of the master and the parties. A master provides the opportunity for flexibility and procedures more expedited and less costly to the parties than resolving a dispute before the judge.

Of course, there can be some risk in using abbreviated discovery resolution procedures. Sometimes the full significance and merits of the issue are not developed or appreciated with such an expedited procedure. More detail and further briefing may change the master's outlook.[74] Whether to employ expedited procedures for a particular dispute requires judgment and balance on the part of counsel and the master. Often the need for a prompt resolution of a discovery dispute outweighs the need for extensive briefing and hearings.

Rule 53(d) requires that all orders issued by the master must be in writing and filed with the court clerk. As mentioned earlier, either party then has 21 days to object to the order, and the court must decide the disputed issue(s) based on the objections.[75] That requires full briefing and oral argument (if permitted) on the court's regular hearing calendar. The Rule 53 procedure means that a master's discovery order cannot be effective for at least 21 days awaiting the possibility of a party objecting, unless the parties agree or the court orders otherwise. Further, if an objection is filed, the order may not be effective for months while the objection is briefed, heard, and decided. Thus, although the 21-day time period for objections works well for substantive matters (e.g., summary judgment motions), it is not practical for most discovery disputes requiring a prompt decision to keep the case moving.

Fortunately, Rule 53 provides for the court to shorten the 21-day period for objections. With a helpful judge, those 21 days can be reduced to a few days, with an opposition filed a few days later and a hearing within a few days thereafter. The parties should consider proposing to the master such an expedited schedule at the preliminary conference, before the first discovery dispute arises.

Case in point: In an IP case where a discovery master was appointed, the court ordered that any *appeals* from the master's discovery orders be filed via fax within 48 hours after the decision issued. The court then promptly resolved the dispute. That proved effective in keeping discovery in a huge multiparty case, consolidated by the panel on multidistrict litigation, on track and timely.

Many district courts require that counsel meet and confer on discovery disputes before filing a motion. One would think that should be a productive process. Unfortunately, the meet-and-confer process often is given only lip

74. *See* Wayne D. Brazil, *Special Masters in Complex Cases: Extending the Judiciary or Reshaping Adjudication?*, 53 U. Chi. L. Rev. 394, 420 (1986).

75. *See* Fed. R. Civ. P. 53(f)(2), (3).

service by counsel, without any serious attempt to discuss and find a practical resolution. Often, the meet and confer works better if lead trial counsel participate. They usually have the broader picture of what is really needed and the difficulties involved and have more authority to compromise. If local rules permit, the master may issue a standing order that, in all discovery disputes, lead counsel must meet and confer by telephone or in person (not just in writing) before the motion is filed. The parties may want to suggest that to the master at the preliminary conference.

Rule 53(c) empowers the master to impose non-contempt sanctions under Rule 37 or Rule 45. The Ninth Circuit has noted that a master cannot issue a case-dispositive sanction.[76]

C. Using a Master to Manage Discovery

A discovery master may also provide hands-on management of discovery including working with the parties on generating and adhering to a discovery schedule and helping the parties avoid disputes over discovery-related issues. More specifically, the master may work with the parties to schedule periodic status conferences, resolve in advance minor disputes over deposition dates and locations, anticipate other possible disputes, and help the parties avoid them. Also, the master may require that the parties develop a detailed outline for discovery, including dates and locations for depositions, a specific schedule for written discovery, and guidelines for producing electronic discovery. If the parties or the court want the master to serve in this capacity, it may be prudent for the court to include this duty in the order appointing the master.

III. Using a Master in Patent Cases

The Federal Circuit has recognized that, "[w]here complicated issues of patent law are involved, the appointment of an experienced patent attorney [as a master] is quite appropriate."[77] Similarly, many district courts have recognized the benefits of masters in patent cases.[78] A judge confronted with a

76. *See Religious Tech. Center*, 1996 WL 171443, at *3 (the master did not have the authority to dismiss the plaintiff's claims, but the district court treated the master's dismissal order as a recommendation that the court properly adopted).

77. Constant v. Advanced Micro-Devices, Inc., 848 F.2d 1560, 1567 (Fed. Cir. 1988).

78. Holderman & Guren, *supra* note 14.

patent case of any complexity is often appreciative of the assistance that the master provides.[79]

A. Using a *Markman* Master[80]

"[T]o decide what the claims mean is nearly always to decide the case."[81] Patent claim construction is the most common use of masters in patent cases.

1. Deciding Whether to Use a Markman *Master*

Under *Markman*, claim construction is a question of law exclusively for the judge.[82] The job of construing patent claims has been frustrating for many district court judges who believe they are not well equipped to handle the complex technical and patent issues presented. Moreover, ongoing case law developments have made the law applicable to claim construction complex.[83]

---

79. *See* Chrimar Sys., Inc. v. Cisco Sys., Inc., 318 F. Supp. 2d 476, 490 nn.14, 15 (E.D. Mich. 2004) (noting that, "as evidenced by the extensive papers produced by the parties explaining the technology, the detailed questions posed by the Special Master to the experts, and the Report and Recommendations itself, the Special Master clearly understood the technology involved and issued a well-reasoned and thorough report" and concluding that the "Special Master's Report and Recommendations has been helpful to the Court"); Eaton Corp. v. Meritor, LLC, 504 F. Supp. 2d 217, 227 (E.D. Mich. 2007) (noting that, where a master made recommendations on issues of infringement and invalidity, "[t]he Special Master's Report effectively served to clarify the issues, and the parties' responses to the Report fleshed out and provided perspective on the state of the evidence in this case. . . . The Court appreciates the important role played by [the] Special Master . . . . Although the Court has not adopted the Report in its entirety, the process using input from [the] Special Master . . . has undoubtedly resulted in a better informed decision."); Wolf Designs, Inc. v. DHR & Co., Inc., 231 F.R.D. 430, 440 (N.D. Ga. 2005) (reasoning that appointing a master would be helpful in a design patent case: "[M]any judges in this Court and in other district courts have begun to routinely appoint special masters to handle all pretrial matters in patent cases . . . . Beyond improving the efficiency of the proceeding and permitting a quicker resolution, the Court can also perceive a value from utilizing a special master in terms of the quality of the analysis. For example, in a design patent case, the Court is uncertain how to implement the boiler plate standards to be used in determining whether a design is obvious, and hence not suitable for patent protection, or instead whether a design is novel.").

80. *See* Kesan & Ball, *supra* note 11; Smith, *supra* note 10.

81. Markman v. Westview Instruments, Inc., 52 F.3d 967, 989 (Fed. Cir. 1995) (en banc) (Mayer, J., concurring).

82. *See id.* at 970–71.

83. The Federal Circuit reviews the claim construction ruling de novo (*see* Cybor Corp. v. FAS Tech., Inc., 138 F.3d 1448, 1451 (Fed. Cir. 1998)); however, as noted

District court judges are well aware that the reversal rate at the Federal Circuit on claim construction issues is high. As the Federal Circuit has consistently declined to accept interlocutory appeals on claim construction rulings under 28 U.S.C. § 1292(b), the district court is forced to construe the claims as best it can—either grant summary judgment of noninfringement or conduct a trial based on that claim construction—and then try it again if the Federal Circuit reverses the claim construction ruling.

The high rate of reversal and the inefficiency of trying a complex patent case twice has caused much frustration among district court judges. In an attempt to avoid this, some judges and litigants are looking to experienced patent lawyers to serve as masters. A 2009 study commissioned by the Federal Judicial Center found that, in complex patent cases, only half as many cases were appealed if a master were involved.[84] In fact, the benefit of using a master for claim interpretation in patent cases is specifically noted in the Advisory Committee Notes to Rule 53 (2003 Amendments):

> The court's responsibility to interpret patent claims as a matter of law, for example, may be greatly assisted by appointing a master who has expert knowledge of the field in which the patent operates. Review of the master's findings will be de novo . . . , but the advantages of initial determination by a master may make the process more effective and timely than disposition by the judge acting alone.[85]

Some counsel prefer to use the *Markman* hearing to educate the judge regarding the technology and issues in the case. However, it takes far less of the judge's time to be educated from the master's report and the parties' objections than to start from ground zero. The judge is likely to appreciate the time saved.

That the pool of master candidates is national in scope is particularly true of the appointment of a master for claim construction. Preliminary conferences can be held by telephone, remotely, and by email. Only the *Markman* hearing requires the presence of the parties and the master in one location—and that has been modified by the widespread use of remote hearings.

---

earlier in this chapter, the Supreme Court in *Teva* at least partially overruled *Cybor*, setting forth different standards of review for different categories of evidence. Meanwhile, subsequent Federal Circuit cases interpreting and applying *Cybo*r and *Teva* have provided district courts with novel analyses that are not easily applied as precedent. *See, e.g.*, Shire Dev., LLC v. Watson Pharms., Inc., 787 F.3d 1359, 1368 (Fed. Cir. 2015); Enzo Biochem Inc. v. Applera Corp., 780 F.3d 1149, 1156 (Fed. Cir. 2015); CardSoft v. VeriFone, Inc., 807 F.3d 1346, 1350 (Fed. Cir. 2015).

84. *See* Kesan & Ball, *supra* note 11, at 11.

85. Fed. R. Civ. P. 53, Advisory Comm. Notes (2003 amendment).

A court may appoint a master to construe claims either in the context of a pure *Markman* determination or in the context of motions for summary judgment of infringement or noninfringement. Depending upon the case, it may be helpful to hear live testimony from technical experts for both sides (but, again, the use of remote hearings permits the use of "live testimony" in a "remote hearing," along with the use of exhibits, slide presentations, etc.). Usually, a tutorial by the experts is a better solution, but it depends on the case.

The flexibility of procedures available at the joint request of the parties using a master is shown as follows: (1) in one case involving a claim construction and summary judgment motion, the parties jointly requested that the master hear several days of technical expert testimony; and (2) in another case, the parties requested construction of more than 100 claim terms in 16 high technology patents. When asked to reduce the number to fewer representative claim terms, the parties jointly pointed out that one of the important reasons they recommended retaining a master was that they wanted all 100+ claim terms construed.

Of course, masters are an added expense, while the judge is not. Thus, a master may not be right in a low-budget case. However, frequently, not many patent cases that reach the claim construction stage are low budget. If the use of a master substantially reduces the risk of trying the case twice, it certainly is worth considering as a cost-saving measure in the long run.

2. Deciding When to Appoint a Markman Master

There is much debate over when claim construction should be performed. Defendants usually want it early, while plaintiffs often want it delayed until they have sufficient discovery to determine the infringement issue. Many courts refuse to entertain claim construction until discovery is complete. Some courts, such as the Northern District of California, have local rules setting forth the claim construction procedure and schedule.

Sometimes the claim construction and/or summary judgment issues have been fully briefed before a master is appointed. That briefing informs the court about the scope and complexity of the issues and may cause the court to recognize it needs help. It expedites the overall litigation process if counsel consider earlier whether to use a master for claim construction or summary judgment so that the selection and appointment process can be complete before the briefing. Otherwise, choosing the master (e.g., identifying candidates, performing conflict checks, determining availability within the confines of the extant scheduling order) may cause delay. Early appointment also enables the parties to brief the issues customized to the master's expertise on the legal issues and understanding of the technology.

3. Deciding What to Cover at the Preliminary Conference

Preliminary conferences in general are discussed at Section I.E. Some additional topics to be resolved at a *Markman* preliminary conference are:

- **The status of claim construction**. Has claim construction been briefed? If not, what is the briefing schedule? How many patents and claims are involved? How many claim terms are disputed? Can the number of disputed claim terms be reduced?
- **Length of the claim construction hearing**. Hearings can be as short as a few hours and as long as several days. A half-day or full-day hearing is more typical. Ask for as much time as the parties need or as little as they can afford. That is one of the advantages of using a master.
- **Will there be live testimony (in person, through a remote hearing, or both)**? It would be unusual for the master, an experienced patent lawyer, to want patent expert testimony. However, counsel should not assume that masters generally exclude it. Live technical expert testimony is sometimes used. In complex technology cases, masters may prefer a tutorial at which counsel or opposing experts describe the technology. Even if the master is generally familiar with the technology, he or she is unlikely to have familiarity at the detailed level specific to the *Markman* issues.
- **What will be the order of oral argument**? Will the master hear arguments from each side on all of the disputed claim terms one claim term at a time or groupings related to claim terms? The latter, which could make the hearing more focused, is sometimes referred to as a *ping-pong*—a term coined by former Chief Judge Leonard Davis of the Eastern District of Texas. Whether the parties choose to present their claim construction arguments in ping-pong fashion or otherwise is a decision for the parties—and at the discretion of the master.[86]
- **Where will the hearing be held**? Occasionally, the hearing is held telephonically, but, more commonly, *Markman* hearings are held in a hearing room with the master and all counsel present. The courtroom works well, if the appointing judge is willing to make it available. The physical arrangement in courtrooms is usually optimal for the hearing. More importantly, use of the courtroom provides the judge and his or her clerks a readily available opportunity to listen

---

86. Some masters prefer a ping-pong presentation because (1) the parties' arguments vis-à-vis a specific disputed term or phrase can be considered together and (2) in the printed transcript, the parties' arguments vis-à-vis a specific term or phrase appear in the same portion of the transcript, which expedites review.

to all or part of the hearing. Hotel and office conference rooms appropriately arranged and technologically outfitted are also common places to conduct hearings.

- **Will the master issue a tentative ruling**? If so, when will that occur in advance of the hearing? See Section III.A.6. Some masters issue tentative rulings or questions on disputed claim terms in advance of a hearing via email to the parties, giving them advance notice of such tentative rulings and questions, along with the underlying rationale. The parties then may choose to address them directly during the subsequent hearing. From the master's perspective, however, the emphasis must remain on *tentative*. From the parties' perspective, an advance email with the master's tentative thoughts gives the parties an opportunity to focus their arguments at a subsequent hearing. And this points out another benefit to the use of masters. Unlike the formality associated with communications with the court, masters have some flexibility in their communications with the parties. Overall, of course, the objective of claim construction—or any other issue referred to a master for a Report and Recommendation, including discovery issues—is to fully vet whatever issues are at stake. Frequently, informal email communications, provided that the communications are directed to *all* parties, allow an opportunity to go beyond the formality of briefs and to focus on the actual issues at stake.
- **Will the hearing be transcribed**? It is best to have the *Markman* hearing transcribed in order to preserve the record for the court's use in considering objections to the master's report. There also may be disputes over concessions or waivers made at the hearing. If the hearing is conducted remotely, the considerations regarding recording a remote hearing will apply.
- **Will there be post-hearing briefs**? See Section III.A.7.

4. Deciding What to Include in the Briefing

Markman briefs before a master are similar to those before the court. However, the briefs should be directed to the level of expertise of the master. The master will need to prepare a report and typically will want to include an explanation to the judge of basic legal principles involved in claim construction. Thus, the master may appreciate a single section on the law of claim construction, written with the judge in mind. In fact, if well done and balanced, counsel may find it essentially copied in the report.

In most cases, however, the master will be well acquainted with the law of claim construction. There may, however, be a unique issue of claim construction at issue. Despite that claims have been required since the Patent Act of 1836, there potentially remain issues of first impression. If so, the briefing should clearly identify the same. Similarly, when briefing other issues to a master, the briefing should identify whether the issue is one subject to Federal Circuit law or whether the issue must be resolved as a matter of applicable regional circuit law.

The keyword for briefing is *candor*. If there are cases both supporting and not supporting a proposition, both should be disclosed and discussed. Cases not supporting the proposition should be distinguished on grounds pertinent to the current question or issue. In general, a master performing his or her task diligently will actually review the cited cases. If a pattern is detected of citing cases for the wrong proposition, or if there is a pattern of clipping quotes, typically, a diligent master will detect that and may be inclined to question the veracity of the brief as a whole. It is better to confront adverse authority directly.

5. Making the Most of a Technology Tutorial

A technology tutorial can be presented immediately before the in-person oral (or remote oral) hearing on claim construction or summary judgment, but sometimes it is an entirely separate hearing a week or two before the *Markman* hearing. It can be helpful to the master to have the tutorial in advance of the hearing date as an early preparation step. The tutorial sometimes eliminates the need for expert testimony at the *Markman* hearing and can decrease the time for the hearing.

Just as a tutorial for the judge or the jury, the tutorial for the master should make extensive use of visual aids such as slides and charts.[87] Copies of these should be placed in a notebook so the master can make notes on them and review them later, or at least be provided in electronic form. Also, it is important to make of record all of the parties' submissions under Rule 53(b)(2)(C), namely, "the nature of the materials to be preserved and filed as the record of the master's activities."

Experience shows that the tutorial presentation works best in a lecture format, not by way of examination—questions by counsel and answers by the expert. Masters have differing views on whether cross-examination is helpful so counsel should raise this issue before the hearing so that they

87. If applicable, the parties should ask the master if he or she wants to be shown samples of the patented and accused products. Some parties may want the master to see the accused products and others will not. Similarly, some masters will want to see the accused products and others will not.

can prepare accordingly.[88] Overall, the tutorial is a teaching exercise not a trial. The master can question the experts where the parties indicate disagreement or the master seeks clarification or more detail. Nevertheless, frequently, tutorials are fashioned to advocate a particular claim construction, as opposed to being strictly neutral. If the parties insist on this format, cross-examination may make sense.

Masters may disagree on whether there should be a transcript of the tutorial. Some believe that a transcript is required, especially in view of the Supreme Court's decision in *Teva*,[89] which, as discussed earlier in this chapter, set forth different standards of review for different categories of evidence. Although the Court did not address technology tutorials per se, to the extent that the district court and/or the master may rely on the tutorial, that comprises extrinsic material for which a court may apply the clear error standard of review. Without a transcript, separating the two may be difficult or impossible and may result in a reversal.

Because the parties will be familiar with the master's education and experience in the technology, they should gear the discussion of the technology to that background. They should also present the technology in a way that is consistent with their theory of the case, but not cross the line between teaching the technology and arguing their claim construction. It is helpful to specifically refer to key parts of the patent specification and drawings and generally focus on the claimed portions. However, an obviously slanted and argumentative tutorial will generally not be appreciated or helpful.

As mentioned earlier in this chapter, consider inviting the judge and his or her law clerks to attend the tutorial. It is an opportunity to educate them as well for later review of the master's Report and Recommendation.

6. Consider the Benefits of a Tentative Ruling

While the practice varies among masters and from case to case, it sometimes is helpful if the master issues a tentative ruling after the parties submit their briefs and about a week before the *Markman* hearing. The parties may want

88. A variation of a traditional evidentiary hearing (i.e., direct examination followed by cross-examination) is for the parties to use witness statements for direct examination that the parties exchange before the evidentiary hearing, along with the witness's curriculum vitae (CV). At the hearing, any *Daubert* challenges to the witnesses can be resolved based on the pre-submitted witness statement and the CV. If the witness survives that challenge, then the witness would be cross-examined on the basis of the direct examination in the witness statement, followed by any redirect and, possibly, any recross. Subjecting an expert to the rigors of cross-examination on his or her expert report/witness statement can be useful.

89. Teva Pharms. USA Inc. v. Sandoz, Inc., 135 S. Ct. 831 (2015).

to suggest that the master issue a tentative ruling, particularly if there are many claim terms in dispute. Sometimes a major reduction in the number of disputed claim terms results from a comprehensive tentative ruling that gives not only tentative constructions of each disputed claim term but also the reasons. While a district court judge may have an established practice of providing (or not providing) tentative rulings on motions, a master may well be more flexible. Counsel should use the tentative ruling to revise their visual aids and oral arguments to focus on the key points and any questions the master has raised.

Notwithstanding the benefits of a tentative ruling (e.g., narrowing the number of claims and focusing the hearing), a downside is that the ruling may turn a party's attention away from arguing the merits to arguing why the tentative ruling is wrong. Thus, issuing a tentative ruling before the *Markman* hearing may be helpful in a particular case but not in *all* cases. An alternative is for the master to provide his or her tentative thoughts on particular issues by email before the hearing and then, after the hearing, issue, or supplement the email with, a draft Report and Recommendation, followed by party briefing, before issuing a final Report and Recommendation on claim construction.[90] This can be helpful in fully vetting the claim construction arguments. However, the parties should be consulted about what procedures they prefer.

7. Preparing for the Hearing

The hearing before a master may or may not be as formal as if it were conducted before the judge, but it is just as important to clients. The importance of preparation and organization is amplified in a *Markman* hearing where numerous claim terms are in dispute. Be prepared to react to compromise constructions the master may propose. Tailor arguments to the background of the master. Do not waste time explaining well-known principles of claim construction to a master who is experienced in such matters and almost assuredly will have studied the briefs.

In an exceptionally complex case, or one with many disputed claim terms, consider proposing that the parties file a short post-hearing brief. Of course, cost and time issues need to be considered. Any request for post-hearing briefs

90. As noted earlier in this chapter, the pre-2003 version of Rule 53 specifically allowed for such a draft. Rule 53 after the 2003 amendment does not contain an express provision for a draft, but the Advisory Committee Notes to Rule 53 (2003 Amendment) provide that, "[b]efore formally making an order, report, or recommendations, a master may find it helpful to circulate a draft to the parties for review and comment. The usefulness of this practice depends on the nature of the master's proposed action."

preferably is made at the preliminary conference with the master so that the briefing can be built into the time schedule and the budget. However, if the parties conclude at the hearing that such briefs may be helpful, propose it then and suggest an adjustment of the schedule if necessary.

8. Filing Objections to the Markman Master's Report

The objections to a master's report discussed at Section I.H apply also to claim construction reports. In filing objections on claim construction rulings, the parties should pick their battles carefully and not lose the judge by a shotgun approach. Often the judge referred claim construction to a master to avoid the large number of complex issues. The judge may give considerable deference to the master, so the parties should reserve objections to the few most critical constructions to reduce the risk of a wholesale denial.

B. Using a Master for Patent Summary Judgment Motions, Discovery, Case Management, and Other Issues

The same master commonly hears motions for summary judgment of infringement or noninfringement concurrently with claim construction. Likewise, that same master often hears *Daubert* motions to exclude expert testimony at trial or for claim construction or summary judgment motions. Using the same master for multiple motions results in obvious efficiencies for the parties.

For the same reasons that referral to a master is appropriate for summary judgment of infringement or noninfringement, referral to a master is also appropriate for summary judgment on defenses (e.g., anticipation, obviousness, laches, estoppel). In fact, a master can be useful in nearly any aspect of a patent infringement case as the following examples illustrate:

1. *Medline Industries, LP v. C.R. Bard, Inc.*, No. 1:20-cv-03981-JPB, 2024 U.S. Dist. LEXIS 173111 (N.D. Ga. Sept. 5, 2024) (*Master role*: conduct claim construction proceedings.)
2. *Daedalus Blue, LLC v. Microstrategy Inc.*, No. 2:20CV551 (RCY), 2023 U.S. Dist. LEXIS 152932 (E.D. Va. Aug. 29, 2023) (*Master role*: *Daubert* motion.)
3. *Midwest Athletics & Sports Alliance LLC v. Xerox Corp.*, 545 F. Supp. 3d 16 (W.D.N.Y. 2021) (*Master role*: motion to stay district court proceedings in pending inter partes review.)
4. *First Quality Tissue, LLC v. Irving Consumer Products Ltd.*, No. 19-428-RGA, 2021 U.S. Dist. LEXIS 142701 (D. Del. July 29, 2021) (*Master role*: attorney-client privilege disputes.)

5. *California Expanded Metal Products v. James A. Klein*, No. C18-0659JLR, 2021 U.S. Dist. LEXIS 206116 (W.D. Wash. Oct. 22, 2021) (*Master role*: oversee contempt proceedings and discovery issues related to violation of permanent injunction.)
6. *Horizon Global Americas Inc. v. Curt Manufacturing, LLC*, No. 17-11879, 2020 U.S. Dist. LEXIS 46576 (E.D. Mich. Mar. 18, 2020) (*Master role*: case management in patent infringement case.)
7. *Ravin Crossbows, LLC v. Hunter's Manufacturing Co., Inc.*, No. 5:18-cv-1729, 2020 U.S. Dist. LEXIS 243599 (N.D. Ohio Dec. 29, 2020) (*Master role*: document review pursuant to scheduled mediation.)
8. *Genesis Attachments, LLC v. Detroit Edge Tool Co.*, No. 19-cv-1126616-v-402-wmc, 2019 U.S. Dist. LEXIS 72411 (E.D. Mich. July 29, 2019) (*Master role*: conduct claim construction proceedings, address discovery disputes, and scheduling matters.)
9. *Magna Electronics, Inc. v. Valeo, Inc.*, No. 13-11376, 2018 U.S. Dist. LEXIS 69908 (E.D. Mich. Apr. 26, 2018) (*Master role*: summary judgment of noninfringement, invalidity.)
10. *Intellectual Ventures I LLC v. Capital One Financial Corp.*, 280 F. Supp. 3d 691 (D. Md. 2017) (*Master role*: discovery and patent infringement and invalidity issues.)
11. *Nuance Communications v. Abbyy USA Software House*, 813 F.3d 1368 (Fed. Cir. 2016) (*Master role*: case management to establish schedule (e.g., claim construction hearing, discovery, mediation, trial).)
12. *High Point Sarl v. Sprint Nextel Corp.*, 817 F.3d 1325 (Fed. Cir. 2016) (*Master role*: summary judgment on laches and estoppel defenses.)
13. *Veritas Operating Corp. v. Microsoft Corp.*, No. C06-0703-JCC, 2008 WL 657936 (W.D. Wash. Feb. 20, 2008) (*Master role*: summary judgment motions of invalidity and noninfringement.)
14. *Invitrogen Corp. v. Clontech Laboratories, Inc.*, 429 F.3d 1052 (Fed. Cir. 2005); *North American Container, Inc. v. Plastipak Packaging, Inc.*, 415 F.3d 1335 (Fed. Cir. 2005) (*Master role*: determine invalidity challenges involving the recapture rule in § 251 reissues.)
15. *CA, Inc. v. Simple.com, Inc.*, 621 F. Supp. 2d 45 (E.D.N.Y. 2009); *In re '639 Patent Litigation*, No. CIV.A.97-12416-RCL, 2000 WL 33706441 (D. Mass. Aug. 16, 2000); *Lannette Co. v. KV Pharms.*, No. 8-338 JJF, 2008 WL 4974579 (D. Del. Nov. 21, 2008) (*Master role*: determine issues involving the doctrine of inequitable conduct.)
16. *Smart Parts, Inc. v. WPD Ltd.*, No. 02-1557-KI, 2005 WL 45834 (D. Or. Jan. 7, 2005) (*Master role*: determine cross-motions for summary judgment on inventorship issues.)

C. Using a Master for Patent Damages and Attorneys' Fees

Masters are engaged to resolve a variety of issues related to patent damages. For example, in *Transco Products, Inc. v. Performance Contracting, Inc.*,[91] the court referred to a master the issue of whether price erosion damages are warranted as part of lost profits. Masters have decided whether lost profits should be awarded on a theory of convoyed sales and whether a reasonable royalty should be awarded instead of lost profits.[92] Where a reasonable royalty is the appropriate measure of damages, a court has referred to a master the calculation of the rate.[93] In *Veritas Operating Corp.*,[94] the master determined that the patentee failed to adequately prove damages. And in *Transweb, LLC v. 3M Innovative Properties Co.*,[95] a special master reviewed a jury's award of attorneys' fees before the district court issued its determination.

IV. Using a Master in Copyright Cases

Copyright cases can present a host of complexities that are well suited for a master's attention. For example, those complexities may relate to the technicalities involved in determining infringement of copyrighted works (such as software, music, or books), defenses, and damages. And, as in other IP cases, masters may be used to address discovery disputes.[96]

---

91. 131 F. Supp. 2d. 976 (N.D. Ill. 2001).

92. *Id.* at 980–81.

93. Code-Alarm, Inc. v. Electromotive Tech. Corp., No. 96-1368, 1997 WL 311542, at *2–3 (Fed. Cir. June 4, 1997) (unpublished opinion).

94. Veritas Operating Corp. v. Microsoft Corp., No. C06-0703-JCC, 2008 WL 657936, at *2 (W.D. Wash. Feb. 20, 2008).

95. *See* 812 F.3d 1295, 1309 (Fed. Cir. 2016); *see also* Finjan, Inc. v. Juniper Networks, Inc., No. C 17-05659 WHA, 2021 U.S. Dist. LEXIS 138945 (N.D. Cal. July 26, 2021) (adopting a special master's Report and Recommendation for attorneys' fees); Straight Path IP Grp., Inc. v. Cisco Sys., Inc., 11 F. Supp. 3d 1026 (N.D. Cal. 2019) (appointing a special master for attorneys' fee determination in patent case).

96. *See, e.g.*, Pearson Educ., Inc. v. Chegg, Inc., No. 21-16866, 2023 U.S. Dist. LEXIS 96179 (D.N.J. June 2, 2023); Warner Records Inc. v. Charter Commc'ns, Inc., 454 F. Supp. 3d 1069 (D. Colo. Apr. 15, 2020); Ford Motor Co. v. Versata Software, Inc. f/k/a Trilogy Software, Inc., No. 15-10628-MFL-EAS, consolidated with No. 15-cv-11624, 2017 U.S. Dist. LEXIS 178004 (E.D. Mich. Aug. 15, 2017).

A. Determining Software Copyright Infringement

Just as courts often use a master to assist with patent claim construction, a master with expert knowledge in reading software code can be invaluable to a court in determining infringement of a software copyright.[97] In this regard, the court in *RGIS, LLC v. A.S.T., Inc.*, commented: "Because the judicial officers involved in this case lack [competence in reading computer source codes], it is necessary to have the assistance of a competent computer expert capable of a factual analysis interpreting and comparing computer source codes."[98]

Here are other examples of cases in which courts have enlisted masters to assist them in analyzing technical issues of copyright infringement in software cases:

1. *Ecimos, LLC v. Carrier Corp.*, 971 F.3d 616 (6th Cir. 2020) (*Master role*: supervise development of new, noninfringing database during stay of permanent injunction.)
2. *Engineering Dynamics, Inc. v. Structural Software, Inc.*, 26 F.3d 1335 (5th Cir. 1994) (*Master role*: determine copyright infringement of user manual describing input/output formats for structural analysis of building construction.)
3. *Micro Consulting, Inc. v. Zubeldia*, 959 F.2d 245 (10th Cir. 1992) (*Master role*: district court properly referred to a nonlawyer master the factual issues regarding infringement of copyrighted software, reserving for the court the legal conclusions.)
4. *NetTech Solutions, LLC v. Zippark.com*, No. 01 Civ. A. 2683 (SAS), 2001 WL 1111966 (S.D.N.Y. Sept. 20, 2001) (*Master role*: court referred software copyright infringement issue to master because of its highly technical nature)
5. *Professional Market Research, Inc. v. AC Nielsen Corp.*, No. 03-2314 (GAG), 2009 WL 1259956 (D.P.R. May 4, 2009) (*Master role*: nonlawyer master determined accused source code was not substantially similar to copyrighted code.)
6. *Johnson Controls Inc. v. Phoenix Control Systems, Inc.*, 886 F.2d 1173 (9th Cir. 1989) (*Master role*: in granting a motion for preliminary injunction against infringement of a computer program, the court referred the infringement issue to a master.)

97. *See* Charles A. Wright et al., Wright & Miller, Federal Practice and Procedure (Civil) § 2601 (2d).

98. RGIS, LLC v. A.S.T., Inc., No. 2:07-CV-10975, 2008 WL 186349, at *2 (E.D. Mich. Jan. 22, 2008).

B. Determining Copyright Infringement in Non-Software Cases

In *Latin American Music Co. v. Archdiocese of San Juan*,[99] the court referred to a master a consolidation of complicated and extremely fact-intensive copyright cases, involving rights to nearly 500 musical compositions, including the issues of

- authorship, ownership, and compliance with statutory requirements;
- infringement; and
- missed royalty payments.

The court gave the master broad powers to require production of evidence at his request and to call and examine witnesses.

Other examples of copyright cases assigning issues to a master include *Museum Boutique Intercontinental, Ltd. v. Picasso*[100] (enforcement of a continuing court order involving ownership of copyrights of 234 Picasso works) and *Subafilms, Ltd. v. MGM-Pathe Communications Co.*[101] (allegations that videocassette distribution of the animated Beatles motion picture *Yellow Submarine* constituted copyright infringement and breach of a film distribution agreement).

C. Determining Copyright Damages

When using masters for copyright damages, courts often use them only to conduct an accounting. If no legal issues need to be resolved, an accountant may be the best choice. However, if legal issues such as damages theories or adequacy of proof are involved, a practicing copyright lawyer may be the better choice. Examples of cases where masters were used to determine damages are:

1. *Peter Pan Fabrics, Inc. v. Jobela Fabrics, Inc.*, 329 F.2d 194 (2d Cir. 1964). The master adopted the cumulative theory of damages, awarding both defendant's profits and plaintiff's lost profits. The district court rejected the lost profits portion of the master's recommendation for insufficient evidence of the damages. The Second Circuit affirmed.
2. *Nolan v. Sam Fox Publishing Co.*, 499 F.2d 1394 (2d Cir. 1974). An accounting for royalty payments was referred to a master after the

99. *See* No. 96-2312 (PG), 2005 WL 1847013 (D.P.R. Aug. 2, 2005).
100. 880 F. Supp. 153 (S.D.N.Y. 1995).
101. 24 F.3d 1088 (9th Cir. 1994).

district court denied plaintiff's request for rescission of the royalty agreement.

3. *Allen-Myland, Inc. v. IBM Corp.*, No. 85-6166, 1992 WL 41644 (E.D. Pa. Feb. 28, 1992). The court referred to a master the issues of damages and the determination of which (accused) tapes should be destroyed as infringing IBM's copyright.
4. *Rosette v. Rainbo Record Manufacturing Corp.*, 546 F.2d 461 (2d Cir. 1976). The court referred an accounting to a master.

V. Using a Master in Trademark Cases

Courts use masters in trademark cases to assist with many different issues, including reviewing survey evidence, enforcing consent decrees, determining damages, handling discovery matters,[102] and negotiating agreements.[103]

A. Determining Exclusion of Survey Evidence

In *Louis Vuitton Malletier v. Dooney & Bourke, Inc.*,[104] the court used two special masters to determine which of the parties' surveys and corresponding testimony of six experts should be excluded. The masters recommended exclusion of the majority of the expert testimony because, "while methodological flaws in a survey generally raise 'questions of weight rather than admissibility, questions of weight, when sufficiently accumulated, become so serious as to require exclusion.'"[105] The court praised the special masters' work and largely adopted their findings:

> Upon review of the [Report and Recommendation], it is beyond cavil that the Special Masters discharged their duty with careful consideration and thoughtful analysis of the parties' opposing positions, the factual details of the expert reports and testimony at issue, the relevant evidentiary rules, and the case law. The Special

102. *See, e.g.*, Crocs, Inc. v. Joybees, Inc., Lead Consolidated Case No. 1:21-cv-02859-GPG-SBP, Member Case No. 1:23-cv-01719-GPG-SBP, 2024 U.S. Dist. LEXIS 50672 (D. Colo. Mar. 21, 2024); Engage Healthcare Commc'ns, LLC v. Intellisphere, LLC, No. 12-cv-00787(FLW)(LHG), 2017 U.S. Dist. LEXIS 135101 (D.N.J. Apr. 26, 2017).

103. *See, e.g.*, Patsy's Italian Rest., Inc. v. Anthony Banas d/b/a Patsy's, Patsy's Pizzeria, Nos. 06-CV-0729 (RER), 06-CV-5857 (RER), 2016 U.S. Dist. LEXIS 4314 (E.D.N.Y. Jan. 12, 2016) (offering the assistance of a special master for negotiating a concurrent use agreement for the service marks at issue).

104. 525 F. Supp. 2d 558 (S.D.N.Y. 2007).

105. *Id.* at 563 (quoting the special masters' Report and Recommendation).

> Masters considered each expert's survey on its own terms and while the number of exclusions may seem large, that is more properly attributed to the number of experts proffered by the parties than to over-exclusion by the Special Masters.[106]

B. Determining Likelihood of Confusion

In *Calvin Klein Cosmetics v. Parfums de Coeur, Ltd.*,[107] the court appointed a master to determine whether an accused trademark infringer's disclaimer sticker negated confusion. The district court adopted the master's recommendation that the disclaimer sticker was adequate to avoid confusion. The Eighth Circuit affirmed.

Although referral of the likelihood of confusion issue is appropriate, cases should not be routinely referred to a master without consent.[108]

C. Enforcing Consent Decrees

In *Manhattan Industries, Inc. v. Sweater Bee by Banff, Ltd.*, the court appointed a master to determine compliance with a trademark consent decree permitting each party to use the KIMBERLY mark on all advertising material, brochures, labels, envelopes, business cards, and the like in connection with the sale, distribution, and advertising of women's apparel, but only when accompanied by a source reference in close proximity to the mark (e.g., "Kimberly by Sweater Bee" and "Kimberly by Bayard").[109]

After the consent decree, Sweater Bee sued, claiming "that Manhattan repeatedly had failed to use an appropriate source reference in conjunction with the Kimberly name, in violation of the consent judgment."[110] The court referred the matter to a master, who was to conduct discovery and an evidentiary hearing, report to the district court whether there had been a civil contempt of the consent judgment, and, if so, determine the amount of damages suffered by Sweater Bee.[111] The Eighth Circuit summarized the master's findings:

> In reaching his decision, the special master reviewed various violations of the terms of the consent judgment, finding repeated omissions of the required source references in clothing labels and hang

106. *Id.* at 564.
107. 824 F.2d 665 (8th Cir. 1987).
108. *See* Fed. R. Civ. P. 53(a)(1).
109. *See* 885 F.2d 1, 2 (2d Cir. 1989).
110. *Id.* at 3.
111. *See id.*

> tags, sales invoices, dealings with salesmen . . . stationary, advertising . . . and New York lobby listings, building directories, and telephone listings. . . .
>
> Despite finding widespread contemptuous conduct, the special master concluded that Manhattan's conduct was not willful. . . .
>
> Additionally, the master determined that there was no evidence that any actual or potential customers of Sweater Bee were or would be confused or deceived by [Manhattan's] misconduct, particularly because of the sophistication of the customers.
>
> Consequently, the special master concluded that Sweater Bee had not shown any loss of sales or profits or, for that matter, any other type of pecuniary harm.[112]

D. Determining Trademark Damages

As in all IP cases, an accounting or difficult computation of damages in a trademark case is properly referred to a master with or without consent, and without the need for showing "some exceptional conditions."[113]

However, in *Textron, Inc. v. Spi-Dell Watch & Jewelry Co.*,[114] the appellate court warned that damages should not be referred to a master when they appear to be very small:

> In view of the minuscule amount of profit proved in the accounting so far, allegedly $3,000 in one year and $5,000 in another, it is questionable whether the trial court was warranted in referring the matter to a master, thus incurring additional fees. It might have been preferable for the court itself to proceed with the accounting at least in the early stages.[115]

E. Calculating Attorneys' Fees and Costs

JWC Investments, Inc. v. Novelty, Inc.[116] was a suit for copyright infringement, trademark infringement, and unfair competition. The plaintiff won on all the claims. The district court awarded $116,000 based on lost profits resulting from the copyright infringement, $125,000 in lost profits attributable

112. *Id.* at 4.

113. Fed. R. Civ. P. 53(a)(1)(B)(ii); *see also* Feathercombs v. Solo Prods. Corp., 306 F.2d 251 (2d Cir. 1962); Grotrian v. Steinway & Sons, 523 F.2d 1331 (2d Cir. 1975); Novell, Inc. v. Network Trade Ctr., Inc., 187 F.R.D. 657 (D. Utah 1999).

114. 406 F.2d 544 (2d Cir. 1968).

115. *Id.* at 546 n.1.

116. 482 F.3d 910 (7th Cir. 2007).

to trademark infringement, and $50,000 in punitive damages based on state unfair competition law. The plaintiff also sought attorneys' fees.

Because the fee petition was hotly disputed, the district court appointed a special master to resolve these ancillary disputes. The master issued a 54-page report recommending a total award of $596,399.82. The court commented that "the case took on a life of its own unnecessarily and litigiously," observing that Novelty unnecessarily increased the fees sought by "contesting practically every issue."[117] In addition, the court noted that, "without proof that plaintiff's attorneys fabricated time records or padded them in an inappropriate matter, there is simply no reason to reduce the fees generated by time that was so obviously well-spent from plaintiff's perspective."[118]

VI. Using a Master in Trade Secret Cases

Trade secret cases, like patent cases, often involve technology and voluminous technical documents. Thus, they are candidates for referral to a master for many of the same reasons as patent cases. For example, *Litton Systems, Inc. v. Ssangyong Cement Industrial Co.*[119] involved claims of misappropriation of trade secrets and documents relating to radar and microwave technology. The district court appointed a master to determine whether any parties destroyed relevant documents with knowledge that such destruction constituted spoliation of evidence. The master found that one party had destroyed documents, and the district court adopted the master's factual findings.[120]

In *Utstarcom, Inc. v. Starent Networks Corp.*,[121] a master was appointed to determine the plaintiff's motion for a return of specific documents allegedly containing the plaintiff's trade secrets relating to wireless cellular technology. The master reviewed in detail the documents in question and accompanying expert testimony as to whether they included trade secret information. He recommended denial of the motion because the showing that the documents contained trade secrets was inadequate.[122]

---

117. *Id.* at 920.

118. *Id.*

119. No. 96-1034, 1997 WL 59360 (Fed. Cir. Feb. 13, 1997) (unpublished opinion).

120. *Id.*

121. 675 F. Supp. 2d 854 (N.D. Ill. 2009).

122. *See also* Shumway v. Wright, No. 4:19-cv-00058-DN-PK, 2019 U.S. Dist. LEXIS 228716 (D. Utah Sept. 4, 2019) (appointing special master to locate and isolate misappropriated trade secret information and to facilitate the return of unrelated property and data and for other matters, including privilege claims and disputes under the protective order relating to the seizure of trade secrets).

Conclusion

While masters are most commonly used in patent cases for claim construction and discovery, a master is appropriate and helpful in many IP cases for a host of issues, as this chapter illustrates. With the crowded dockets in our courts, the parties should consider recommending the use of a master to assist the court in any complex IP case. Hopefully, this chapter will guide counsel through that decision-making process and the best practices to follow if the court appoints a master.

APPENDIX

Order for Special Master

APPENDIX A

IN THE UNITED STATES DISTRICT COURT

FOR THE CENTRAL DISTRICT OF CALIFORNIA

ABC, INC. Plaintiff, v. XYZ, INC. Defendant.	Civil Action No. ____________

ORDER OF APPOINTMENT OF SPECIAL MASTER AND REFERENCE OF MOTION

On ________, with the consent of the parties, the Court directed the parties to file a notice regarding the appointment of a special master in which the parties would agree on or submit nominations for the appointment of a special master. On________, the parties filed a notice informing the Court that they agreed upon Don W. Martens as a special master in this case. An affidavit pursuant to Federal Rule of Civil Procedure 53(b)(3) was included along with the parties' notice. The Court, having reviewed the parties' notice, agrees with them regarding Martens' suitability to serve as a special master in this case.

Consequently, Don W. Martens is hereby appointed as SPECIAL MASTER in this cause to construe Claims _______ of United States Patent No. _________. *See* Fed. R. Civ. P. 53. The clerk of Court shall place Martens on this cause's docket, including his contact information:

(Contact Information)

The clerk of Court shall mail or fax to Martens a copy of this order.

Further, Defendant's Motion for Claim Construction is hereby REFERRED to Martens. Martens must proceed with all reasonable diligence in reviewing such motion and,

-1-

no later than (date), file with the Court either a report and recommendation on such motion or a status update regarding such motion's review.

Martens shall have the discretion to hold a *Markman* hearing on claim construction pursuant to Federal Rule of Civil Procedure 53(c) & (d), should he choose to do so.

Martens may not engage in any *ex parte* communication with the Court or either party until the Court has entered an order adopting, affirming, modifying, or reversing Martens' report and recommendation pursuant to Federal Rule of Civil Procedure 53(g). This qualification includes rulings on any Federal Rule of Civil Procedure 59(e) motion to reconsider the Court's adoption, affirmance, modification, or reversal of Martens' report and recommendation.

Martens shall maintain a record of any and all materials and evidence considered by him during the process of claim construction. Martens must file such record with the Court at the same time he files his report and recommendation regarding claim construction.

No later than seven (7) days after the date of this order's issuance Martens must confer jointly with the parties to this cause for purposes of setting the process and schedule for claim construction and arranging for such other steps as Martens may deem appropriate to carry out his responsibilities as special master consistent with the terms of this order of appointment. Martens' review of Defendant's claim construction motion shall be limited to the filing already made in this Court unless Martens and the parties agree otherwise.

Pursuant to the parties' agreement, Martens' compensation pursuant to Federal Rule of Civil Procedure 53(h) shall be at the hourly rate already agreed between the parties and Martens and shall be equally divided between the parties. Upon the completion of Martens' duties as special master the parties shall jointly move for the fixation of Martens' compensation pursuant to Federal Rule of Civil Procedure 53(h). If Martens and the parties agree, Martens may make interim billings for time and costs incurred and such billings can be paid subject to adjustment upon the court fixing the total compensation.

Finally, the parties shall immediately remit to Martens copies of all relevant filings (i.e. the claim-construction motion, response, reply, appendices, and proposed electronic orders), unless the parties and Martens deem such copies unnecessary in their conference.

Signed (date)_______________

____
United States District Judge

Glossary

ADR is an acronym for "alternative dispute resolution," which refers to processes for resolving disputes other than by litigation, including mediation and arbitration. See Chapter 1 for the definitions of commonly employed forms of ADR used in intellectual property (IP)/Technology cases.

Ex Parte Communications mean communications made, for example, to a judge or arbitrator outside the presence of all the parties or their lawyers—a one-sided communication. Such communications are generally not permitted so as to avoid undermining the fairness of a proceeding by introducing new information to the decision maker (e.g., the judge or arbitration panel) without giving the other party an opportunity to explain or respond. The concept is also used in the context of mediation, for example, when the parties agree that they want to provide submissions solely to the mediator—not exchanged.

Intellectual Property refers to the rights associated with intangible assets (non-physical property) owned by a person or company and protected against use without consent. Examples of IP rights include patents, trademarks, copyrights, and trade secrets.

IP/Technology Agreements may encompass one or more types of IP and/or technology and include various types of agreements, such as license agreements, joint development agreements, consulting agreements, know-how and trade secret agreements, as well as settlement agreements and coexistence agreements arising from litigations or contract disputes.

IP/Technology Disputes may concern disputes about the existence (e.g., creation, duration) of certain IP and/or technology; who created it (e.g., inventorship, derivation, authorship); who owns it; the validity and enforceability of the rights; the scope of the rights (e.g., common law, statutory, treaty/convention); whether rights have been infringed or misappropriated; whether unfair competition has occurred; whether a third party has rights in, under, or to the IP/Technology (e.g., by license); encumbrances or limitations on the rights or on the holders of those rights; and transactions involving IP/Technology (e.g., sale, grant of security interest, license, joint development, consulting, settlement agreements, coexistence) and issues related to such agreements (e.g., breach of warranty, failure to timely conduct research and development, failure to commercialize, failure to halt third-party infringement, failure to indemnify).

Moreover, in our modern technology-driven economy, IP/Technology disputes increasingly arise between parties who are not traditionally seen solely as

IP or technology companies. For example, disputes in the energy, construction, aviation, and health care industries, where different forms of IP and technology increasingly play a role in both the supply chain and daily operations, are often disputes about IP and/or technology.

***Markman* (or Claim Construction) Hearings/Rulings** follow from the U.S. Supreme Court case of *Markman v. Westview Instruments, Inc.*, 517 U.S. 370 (1996), in which the Court held that the trial court, and not the jury, should decide issues construing the meaning (and, thereby, the scope) of patent claims.

Mediation generally refers to the entire mediation process (e.g., both ex parte and inter partes communications), and not just the scheduled session attended by all of the parties (in-person or remote).

Step or Escalation Clause is a contractual provision requiring parties to escalate a dispute through varying levels of review or management (e.g., open-door, peer-review, senior corporate management) or other processes such as mediation before an adjudicative process like arbitration or litigation may proceed.

Technology broadly relates to science and/or engineering. Those disciplines include scientific principles and/or engineering applications (e.g., compliance with technical specifications, failure of complex mechanical or electrical equipment, software development and performance, chemistry, development of biomedical devices and pharmaceutical products, clinical trials).

Technology Tutorial is a means of explaining the background of the technology at issue or implicated in a dispute, for example, to a decision maker such as a judge, special master, or arbitration panel. It may be an oral or written presentation (or a combination of the two), using no presentation media or multiple forms of media. It may be presented by counsel, a party, or an expert.

Index

J

L

M

About the ABA Section of Intellectual Property Law

From its strength within the American Bar Association, the ABA Section of Intellectual Property Law (ABA-IPL) advances the development and improvement of intellectual property laws and their fair and just administration. The Section furthers the goals of its members by sharing knowledge and balanced insight on the full spectrum of intellectual property law and practice, including patents, trademarks, copyright, design, and trade secrets. Providing a forum for rich perspectives and reasoned commentary, ABA-IPL serves as the ABA voice of intellectual property law within the profession, before policy makers, and with the public.

Books from the ABA Section of Intellectual Property Law (ABA-IPL)

AMERICAN BAR ASSOCIATION
Intellectual Property Law Section

Title	Regular Price	ABA-IPL Member Price
ADR Advocacy, Strategies, and Practices for Intellectual Property and Technology Cases, 3rd Ed. (5370273)	$179.95	**$144.95**
ANDA Litigation, 4th Ed. (5370274)	$395.00	**$355.00**
Antitrust Issues in Intellectual Property Law, 2nd Ed. (5370263)	$149.95	**$119.95**
Arbitrating Patent Disputes (5370229)	$89.95	**$74.95**
Biosimilars Litigation and Client Counseling (5370267)	$169.95	**$139.95**
Careers in IP Law (5370204) (The ebook is complimentary with ABA-IPL Section membership)	$24.95	**$16.95**
Commercialization of IP Rights in China (5370241)	$119.95	**$95.95**
A Comprehensive Patent Practice Form Book (5370260)	$139.95	**$109.95**
Computer Games and Immersive Entertainment, 2nd Ed. (5370239)	$89.95	**$69.95**
Copyright Litigation Strategies (5370228)	$369.00	**$285.00**
Copyright Remedies (5370208)	$89.95	**$74.95**
Crash Course on U.S. Patent Law (5370221)	$39.95	**$34.95**
The DMCA Handbook, 2nd Ed. (5370234)	$79.95	**$64.95**
The Essential Case Law Guide to PTAB Trials (5370233)	$249.95	**$199.95**
The Essentials of Japanese Patent Prosecution (5370245)	$149.95	**$119.95**
Intellectual Property and Technology Due Diligence (5370236)	$219.95	**$179.95**
The Intellectual Property Law Handbook, 2nd Ed. (5620154)	$139.95	**$109.95**
IP Protection in China, 2nd Ed. (5370270)	$149.95	**$119.95**
IP Strategies for Medical Device Technologies (5370238)	$149.95	**$119.95**
IP Valuation for the Future (5370237)	$89.95	**$59.95**
The Law of Trade Secret Litigation Under the Uniform Trade Secrets Act, 2nd Ed. (5370242)	$369.95	**$295.95**
A Lawyer's Guide to Section 337 Investigations before the U.S. International Trade Commission, 5th Ed. (5370266)	$139.95	**$109.95**
Legal Guide to Video Game Development, 2nd Ed. (5370227)	$74.95	**$59.95**
A Legal Strategist's Guide to Trademark Trial and Appeal Board Practice, 5th Ed. (5370275)	$179.95	**$144.95**
Marketing Your Invention, Product, or Journey, 4th Ed. (5370271)	$59.95	**$47.95**
New Practitioner's Guide to Intellectual Property (5370198)	$89.95	**$69.95**
Patent Claim Drafting Practice (5370259)	$179.95	**$144.95**
Patent Freedom to Operate Searches, Opinions, Techniques, and Studies (5370230)	$139.95	**$109.95**

Title	Regular Price	ABA-IPL Member Price
Patent Litigation Strategies Handbook, 5th Ed. (5370269)	$395.00	**$355.00**
Patent Trial Advocacy Casebook, 3rd Ed. (5370124)	$149.95	**$119.95**
Patently Persuasive, 2nd Ed. (5370272)	$139.95	**$119.95**
The Practitioner's Guide to the PCT, 2nd Ed. (5370261)	$139.95	**$109.95**
The Practitioner's Guide to Trials Before the Patent Trial and Appeal Board, 3rd Ed. (5370258)	$169.95	**$139.95**
Pre-ANDA Litigation, 3rd Ed. (5370256)	$349.00	**$259.00**
Preliminary Relief in Patent Infringement Disputes (5370194)	$119.95	**$94.95**
Principles of Patent Claim Drafting and Patent Claim Analysis (5370268)	$159.95	**$127.95**
Right of Publicity (5370215)	$89.95	**$74.95**
Settlement of Patent Litigation and Disputes (5370192)	$179.95	**$144.95**
Starting an IP Law Practice (5370202)	$54.95	**$34.95**
Summary of Covenants Not to Compete (5370244)	$179.95	**$144.95**
The Tech Contracts Handbook, 3rd Ed. (5370248)	$42.95	**$33.95**
Trademark and Deceptive Advertising Surveys, 2nd Ed. (5370255)	$189.95	**$151.95**
What Is a Copyright, 4th Ed. (5370257)	$19.95	**$16.95**
What Is a Patent, 4th Ed. (5370262)	$19.95	**$16.95**
What Is a Trademark, 5th Ed. (5370254)	$19.95	**$16.95**
What Is a Trade Secret (5370265)	$19.95	**$16.95**

Jeff Salyards
Executive Editor
ABA Publishing
jeff.salyards@americanbar.org